PHILIP'S

ESSENTIAL WORLD ATLAS

CONTENTS

WORLD

8-9 World: Northern part
10-11 World: Southern part
12-13 Arctic
14-15 Antarctic

EUROPE

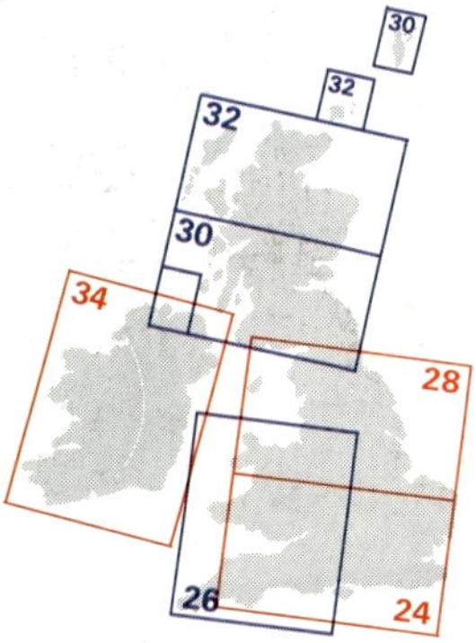

16-17 Europe: Physical
18-19 Europe: Political

20-21 British Isles: South
22-23 British Isles: North
24-25 Southern England
26-27 Wales and South West England
28-29 Northern England
30-31 Southern Scotland
32-33 Northern Scotland
34-35 Ireland

Published in Great Britain in 1996
by George Philip Limited,
an imprint of Reed Books,
Michelin House, 81 Fulham Road, London SW3 6RB

Cartography by Philip's

ISBN 0-540-06379-7

A CIP catalogue record for this book is available from the British Library

Printed in Hong Kong

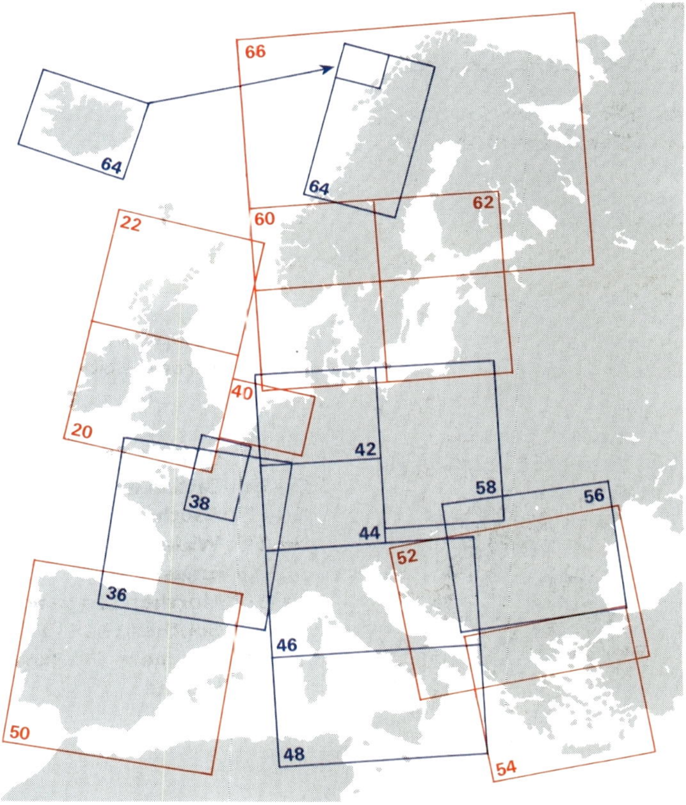
66
64
64
62
60
22
20
40
42
38
58
56
44
52
36
46
50
48
54

36-37 France
38-39 Northern France
40-41 Netherlands
42-43 Germany and the Low Countries
44-45 Alpine Lands
46-47 Northern Italy and Corsica
48-49 Southern Italy and Sardinia
50-51 Spain and Portugal
52-53 Danube Lands
54-55 Greece and Albania
56-57 Romania
58-59 Central Europe
60-61 Southern Scandinavia
62-63 Baltic Lands
64-65 North West Scandinavia and Iceland
66-67 Northern Scandinavia

ASIA

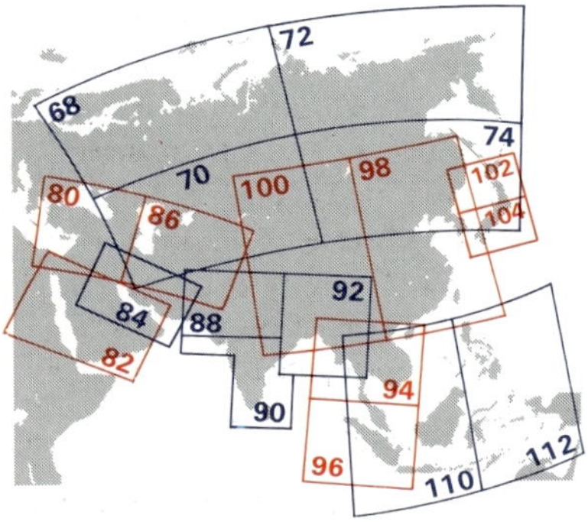
68
72
74
70
80
86
100
98
102
104
84
88
92
82
90
94
96
110
112

68-69 Eastern Europe
70-71 Kazakstan and Central Asia
72-73 North East Russia
74-75 South East Russia and Mongolia

76-77 Asia: Physical
78-79 Asia: Political

80-81 Turkey and the Middle East
82-83 Arabian Peninsula
84-85 The Gulf
86-87 Central Asia and Afghanistan
88-89 Pakistan and North West India
90-91 Central and Southern India, Sri Lanka
92-93 Eastern India, Bangladesh and Burma
94-95 Mainland South East Asia
96-97 The Malay Peninsula
98-99 China: East
100-101 China: West

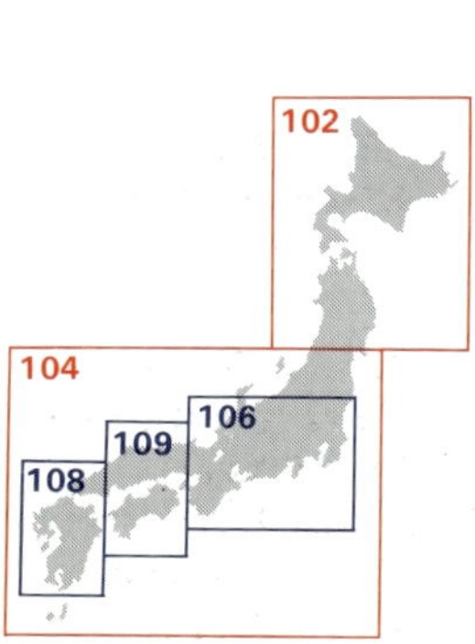
102
104
106
109
108

102-103 Japan: North
104-105 Japan: South
106-107 Japan: Tokyo, Kyoto, Osaka
108-109 Japan: Kyushu, West Honshu and Shikoku

110-111 Indonesia: West
112-113 Indonesia: East

AUSTRALASIA

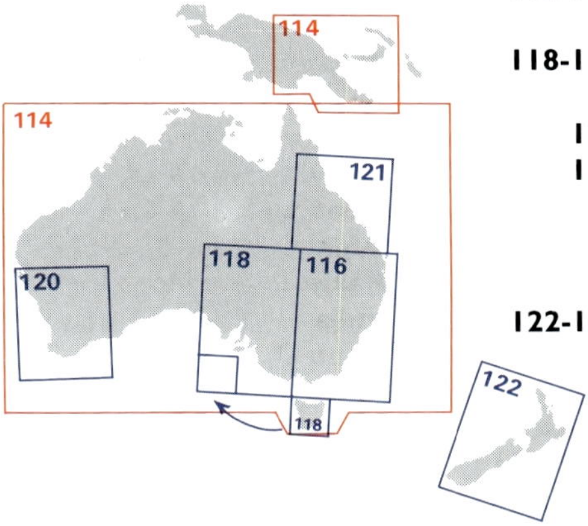

114-115	Australia, New Zealand and Papua New Guinea
116-117	Australia: Brisbane, Sydney and Melbourne
118-119	Australia: Adelaide, Melbourne and Tasmania
120	Australia: Perth
121	Australia: North East Queensland
122-123	New Zealand, Central and South West Pacific

AFRICA

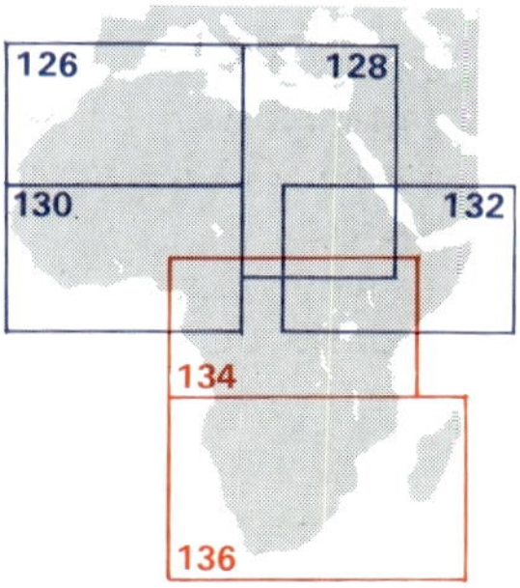

124	Africa: Physical
125	Africa: Political
126-127	Africa: North West
128-129	Africa: North East
130-131	Africa: West
132-133	Africa: East
134-135	Africa: Central
136-137	Africa: South

NORTH AMERICA

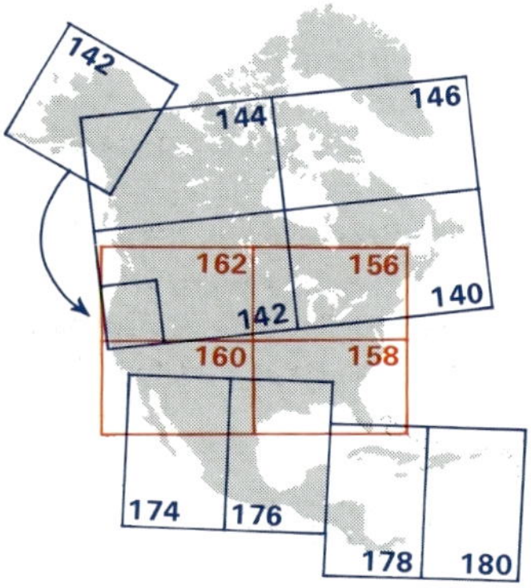

138 North America: Physical
139 North America: Political

140-141 Canada: South East
142-143 Canada: South West and Alaska
144-145 Canada: North West
146-147 Canada: North East
148-149 Canada: Saint Lawrence Estuary
150-151 Canada: The Great Lakes
152-153 Canada: Southern Saskatchewan and Manitoba
154-155 Canada: Southern British Columbia and Alberta

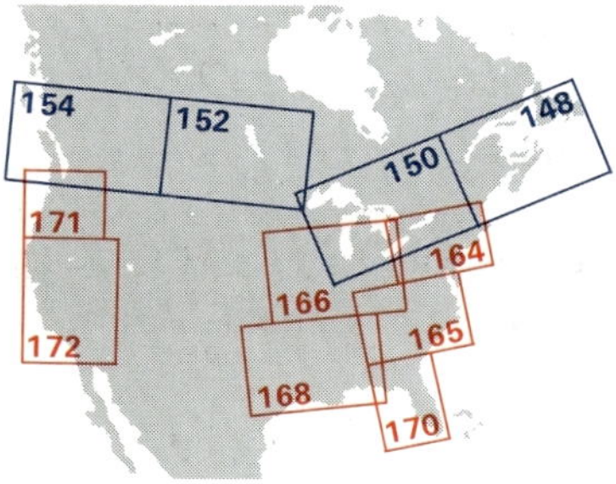

156-157 USA: North East
158-159 USA: South East
160-161 USA: South West
162-163 USA: North West
164 USA: Boston, New York, Washington
165 USA: Washington, Atlanta
166-167 USA: Upper Mississippi
168-169 USA: Lower Mississippi and Gulf Coast
170 USA: Florida
171 USA: Columbia Basin
172-173 USA: California

174-175 Mexico: West
176-177 Mexico: East
178-179 Caribbean: West
180-181 Caribbean: East

South America

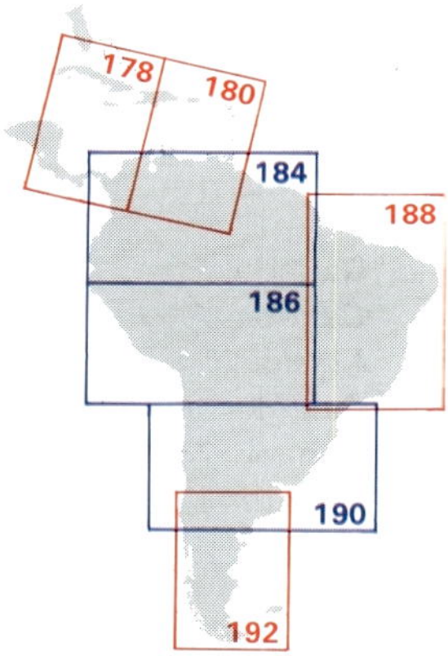

182	**South America: Physical**
183	**South America: Political**
184-185	**South America: North West**
186-187	**South America: West**
188-189	**South America: East**
190-191	**South America: Central**
192	**South America: South**

INDEX

MAP SYMBOLS

Settlement symbols in order of size

International boundary

Internal boundary

Principal railway

Principal road

Canal

Principal airport

Tunnel

Permanent river

Intermittent river

Permanent lake

Intermittent lake

Marsh

▲ 8848 Altitude above sea level

▼ 10497 Depth below sea level

263 Level of lake

18 Indicates the adjoining map

As far as possible the de facto situation of international boundaries is shown

Scale note
To the right of each map title there is a number representing the scale of the map for example, 1 : 2 000 000. This means that one centimetre on the map represents 2 million centimetres or 20 kilometres on the ground. Or, if the number is 1 : 40 000 000, one centimetre represents 40 million centimetres or 400 kilometres.

Height and depth colours

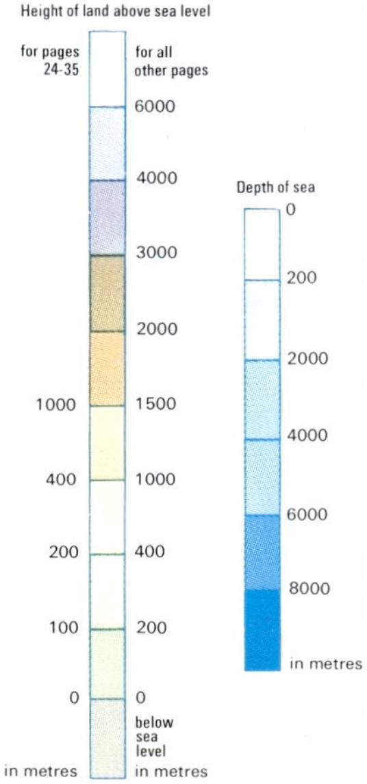

WORLD : NORTHERN PART

ARCTIC OCEAN
North Pole
Magnetic Pole
Arctic Circle
Tropic of Cancer
International Dateline
PROJECTION CENTRED ON LONDON
RUSSIA
CHINA
INDIA
MONGOLIA
KAZAKSTAN
UZBEKISTAN
TURKMENISTAN
AFGHANISTAN
PAKISTAN
NEPAL
BANGLADESH
BURMA
THAILAND
CAMBODIA
VIETNAM
TAIWAN
KOREA
JAPAN
SRI LANKA
MALDIVES
Laccadives
IRAN
IRAQ
KUWAIT
SAUDI ARABIA
OMAN
YEMEN
SYRIA
JORDAN
ISRAEL
TURKEY
GEORGIA
EGYPT
GREECE
ITALY
FRANCE
SPAIN
TUNISIA
MOROCCO
FINLAND
SWEDEN
NORWAY
GERMANY
UNITED KINGDOM
IRELAND
ICELAND
GREENLAND
CANADA
UNITED STATES
MEXICO
BAHAMAS
CUBA
JAMAICA
GUATEMALA
EL SALVADOR
HONDURAS
NICARAGUA
COSTA RICA
PANAMA
COLOMBIA
VENEZUELA
ECUADOR
PERU
TRINIDAD & TOBAGO
Tokyo
Seoul
Pyongyang
Peking
Shanghai
Hongkong
Hanoi
Bangkok
Rangoon
Dacca
Calcutta
Colombo
Bombay
Karachi
Delhi
Katmandu
Islamabad
Kabul
Alma Ata
Ulan Bator
Ashkhabad
Tehran
Bagdad
Riyadh
Muscat
Beirut
Jerusalem
Cairo
Ankara
Athens
Moscow
Helsinki
Stockholm
Oslo
Copenhagen
Warsaw
Budapest
Berlin
Bonn
Amsterdam
London
Paris
Rome
Tunis
Tripoli
Algiers
Rabat
Madrid
Lisbon
Gibraltar
Madeira
Canary Is.
Azores
Reykjavik
Godthåb
Anchorage
Vancouver
San Francisco
Los Angeles
Toronto
Ottawa
New York
Washington
Bermuda
Havana
Kingston
Mexico City
Caracas
Port of Spain
Bogotá
Quito
180
160
140
120
100
80

1 : 120 000 000

PROJECTION CENTRED ON SAN FRANCISCO
PROJECTION CENTRED ON CAPETOWN
Capital Cities
TIME ZONES
9.00 6.00
Time Zone in hours fast (+) or slow (−) of Greenwich Mean Time
Standard Time not the Zone hour
No Official Time
All distances measured through the centre
of the map are correct for scale
West from Greenwich
East from Greenwich
Equator
Tropic of Capricorn
ALGERIA
LIBYA
W. SAHARA
MAURITANIA
MALI
NIGER
CHAD
SUDAN
ETHIOPIA
SOMALIA
NIGERIA
ZAÏRE
ANGOLA
ZAMBIA
TANZANIA
KENYA
MOZAMBIQUE
NAMIBIA
BOTSWANA
SOUTH AFRICA
MADAGASCAR
B R A Z I L
BOLIVIA
FRENCH GUIANA
CAPE VERDE IS.
Ascension
St. Helena
SEYCHELLES
MAURITIUS
Chagos Arch.
ATLANTIC OCEAN
PACIFIC OCEAN
INDIAN OCEAN
North Pole
South Pole
Arctic Circle
Antarctic Circle
International Dateline

PROJECTION CENTRED ON THE ANTIPODES OF LONDON
East from Greenwich
West from Greenwich
International Dateline
Equator
Tropic of Cancer
Tropic of Capricorn
Antarctic Circle
PACIFIC OCEAN
PACIFIC OCEAN
INDIAN OCEAN
Galapagos Is.
Easter I.
Pitcairn I.
Tuamotu Arch.
Marquesas Is.
Tahiti
FRENCH POLYNESIA
Kiritimati
Hawaiian Is.
Midway I.
Cook Is.
SAMOA
TONGA
FIJI
TUVALU
KIRIBATI
Marshall Is.
Wake I.
Bonin I.
Northern Marianas
Guam
Caroline Is.
SOLOMON IS.
VANUATU
New Caledonia
PAPUA NEW GUINEA
Port Moresby
NEW ZEALAND
Auckland
Wellington
Antipodes I.
Macquarie I.
Auckland I.
Victoria Land
Adélie Land
AUSTRALIA
Sydney
Canberra
Perth
INDONESIA
Jakarta
PHILIPPINES
Manila
BRUNEI
MALAYSIA
Kuala Lumpur
Singapore
VIETNAM
Ho Chi Minh City
80
100
120
140
160
180

1 : 120 000 000

• Capital Cities

TIME ZONES

9.00	6.00	Time zone in hours fast (+) or slow (−) of Greenwich Mean Time
		Standard Time not the Zone hour

ARCTIC REGIONS
EUREKA
TEMPERATURE
Range 51.7°C
PRESSURE
M.S.L.
ANNUAL
PRECIPITATION
Total 58.2mm.
J F M A M J J A S O N D
Eureka
80°00'N
85°56'W
PACIFIC OCEAN
Bering Sea
Sea of Okhotsk
ARCTIC OCEAN
Beaufort Sea
Laptev Sea
SIBERIA
ALASKA
CANADA
NORTH AMERICA
Aleutian Islands
Kurilskiye Ostrova
Sakhalin
Poluostrov Kamchatka
Bering Str.
Proliv Longa
Ostrova Vrangelya
Novosibirskiye O-va
Severnaya Zemlya
Poluostrov Taymyr
Verkhoyanskiy Khrebet
Plato Putorana
Mt. McKinley 6194
Mt. Logan 6050
Mt. St. Elias 5489
Great Bear Lake
Gt. Slave Lake
Banks I.
Victoria Island
Parry Is.
Sverdrup Is.
Axel Heiberg I.
Rocky Mountains
Mackenzie
Yukon
Lena
Kolyma
Amundsen "Norge" (1926)

1 : 42 000 000

Arctic Explorers
Cook 1778
Franklin 1826–47
McClure 1850–53
Nordenskiöld ("Vega") 1878–79
De Long 1881
Nansen ("Fram") 1893–96
Abruzzi & Cagni 1899–1900
Sverdrup 1902
Peary 1892–1906
Amundsen 1903–6 & 1926
Peary 1908–9
Knud Rasmussen 1912
Koch 1913
Stefánsson 1914–15
Byrd 1926 (by air)
Wilkins 1928 (by air)
Lindsay 1934
Papanin (Drift of Soviet Expedition) 1937–38
"Sedov" 1937–40
Knuth (Danish Pearyland Expedition) 1948–49
Seas open all year
Extreme limits of drift-ice
Seas covered by pack-ice in Spring
Seas permanently covered by pack-ice
Ice-caps and permanent ice shelf
Progress of Exploration
Coasts explored before 1800
" " between 1800 & 1850
" " between 1850 & 1900
" " since 1900
Byrd 1926 Highest latitudes reached by explorers with date
GREENLAND (To Denmark)
Baffin Bay
Davis Str.
Denmark Strait
Greenland Sea
Norwegian Sea
Barents Sea
Kara Sea
Lincoln Sea
McKinley Sea
ATLANTIC OCEAN
North Sea
Baltic Sea
Gulf of Bothnia
G. of Finland
Skagerrak
Foxe Basin
Foxe Channel
Hudson Str.
Ellesmere I.
Devon I.
Melville Pen.
Southampton I.
Pr. Charles I.
Bylot I.
C. Columbia
Peary Ld.
Rasmussen Land
Knud Rasmussen Land
Kong Frederik VIII.s. Land
Kong Christian X.s. Land
Kong Christian IX.s. Land
Kong Frederik IX.s. Land
Kong Frederik VI.s. Kyst
Gunnbjørn Fjeld 3700
Mont Forel 3360
K. Farvel
Svalbard
Vestspitsbergen
Nordaustlandet
Edgeøya
Sørkapp
Bjørnøya
Jan Mayen
ICELAND
Hekla 1491
Reykjavík
Faroe Is.
Shetland Is.
Orkney Is.
Hebrides
Rockall
BRITISH ISLES
SCOTLAND
IRELAND
ENGLAND
WALES
London
Edinburgh
Glasgow
Dublin
Belfast
Liverpool
Cork
C. Clear
Zemlya Frantsa Iosifa
Alexandra Ld.
Ostrov Graham Bell
Z. Vilcheka
O. Ushakova
O. Uedineniya
O. Vise
Novaya Zemlya
O. Vaygach
Ostrov Belyy
Poluostrov Yamal
Ostrov Kolguyev
Kolskiy Poluostrov
Beloye More
NORWAY
SWEDEN
FINLAND
DENMARK
GERMANY
POLAND
EST.
LATVIA
LITH.
NETH.
BELG.
EUROPE
ASIA
Nordkapp
Hammerfest
Tromsø
Lofoten
Trondheim
Bergen
Oslo
Stockholm
København
Helsinki
St. Peterburg
Moskva
Arkhangelsk
Murmansk
Ladozhskoye Ozero
Onezhskoye Ozero
Chudskoye Ozero
Hamburg
Berlin
Warszawa
Praha
Amsterdam
Arctic Circle
POLE
Peary 1909
Byrd 1926
Amundsen 1926
Herbert 1969
Cagni 1900

ANTARCTIC

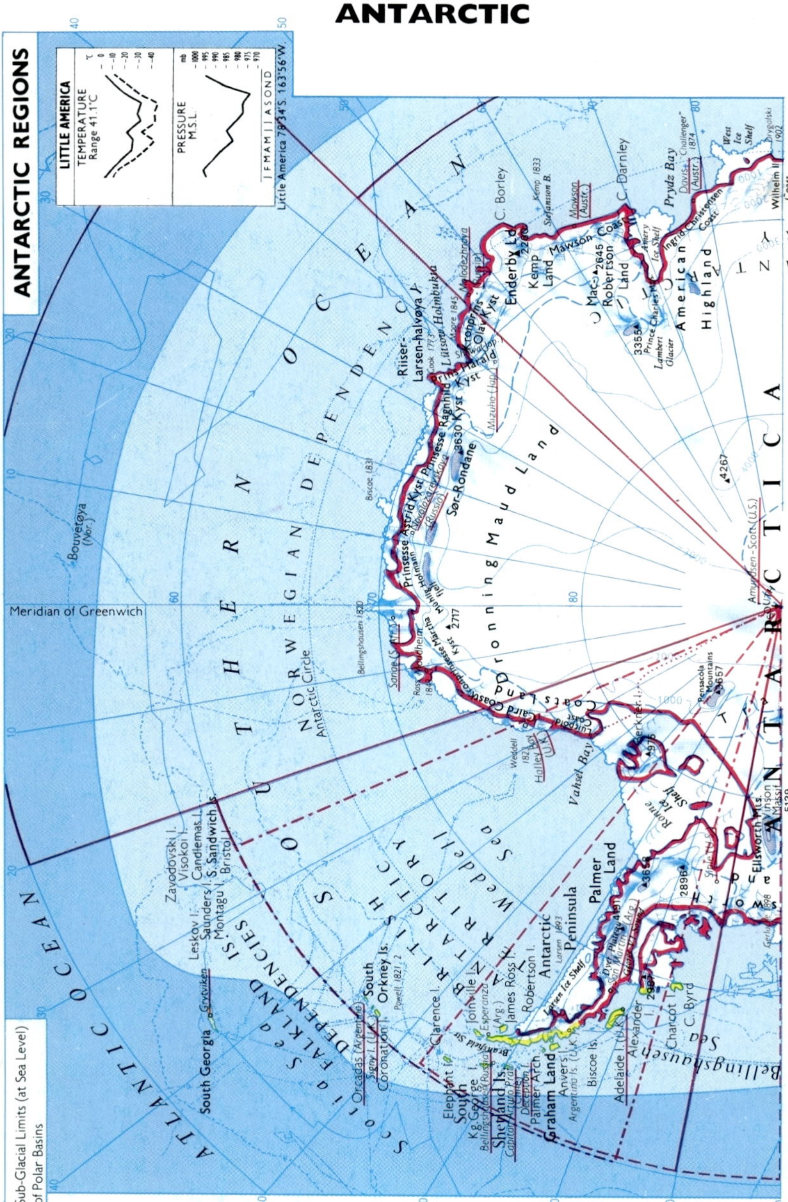
ANTARCTIC REGIONS
LITTLE AMERICA
TEMPERATURE
Range 41.1°C
PRESSURE
M.S.L.
J F M A M J J A S O N D
Little America 78°34'S. 163°56'W.
ATLANTIC OCEAN
SOUTHERN OCEAN
NORWEGIAN DEPENDENCY
BRITISH ANTARCTIC TERRITORY
FALKLAND IS. DEPENDENCIES
ANTARCTICA
Scotia Sea
Weddell Sea
Bellingshausen Sea
Meridian of Greenwich
Antarctic Circle
Bouvetøya (Nor.)
South Georgia
Grytviken
Zavodovski I.
Visokoi I.
Leskov I.
Candlemas I.
Saunders I.
S. Sandwich Is.
Montagu I.
Bristol I.
South Orkney Is.
Coronation I.
Signy I. (U.K.)
Orcadas (Argentina)
Elephant I.
Clarence I.
South Shetland Is.
Kg. George I.
Deception I.
Graham Land
Palmer Arch.
Anvers I.
Biscoe Is.
Adelaide I. (U.K.)
Alexander I.
Charcot I.
C. Byrd
Antarctic Peninsula
Palmer Land
James Ross I.
Joinville I.
Robertson I.
Larsen Ice Shelf
Vahsel Bay
Halley Bay (U.K.)
Coats Land
Ronne Ice Shelf
Berkner I.
Ellsworth Mts.
Vinson Massif
5139
Pensacola Mountains
Amundsen-Scott (U.S.)
Dronning Maud Land
Sør-Rondane
Prinsesse Astrid Kyst
Prinsesse Ragnhild Kyst
Prins Harald Kyst
Kronprins Olav Kyst
Riiser-Larsen-halvøya
Lützow-Holmbukta
Enderby Ld.
Kemp Land
Mawson Coast
Mawson (Austr.)
Robertson Land
Lambert Glacier
Prince Charles Mts.
Amery Ice Shelf
Prydz Bay
C. Darnley
C. Borley
American Highland
Ingrid Christensen Coast
Wilhelm II Coast
West Ice Shelf
Davis (Austr.)
Molodezhnaya
Mizuho (Jap.)
Sanae (S. Afr.)
Bellingshausen 1820
Biscoe 1831
Weddell 1823
Cook 1773
Kemp 1833
4267
3630
3355
2645
2717
4191
2896
3658
2987
Sub-Glacial Limits (at Sea Level) of Polar Basins

1 : 42 000 000

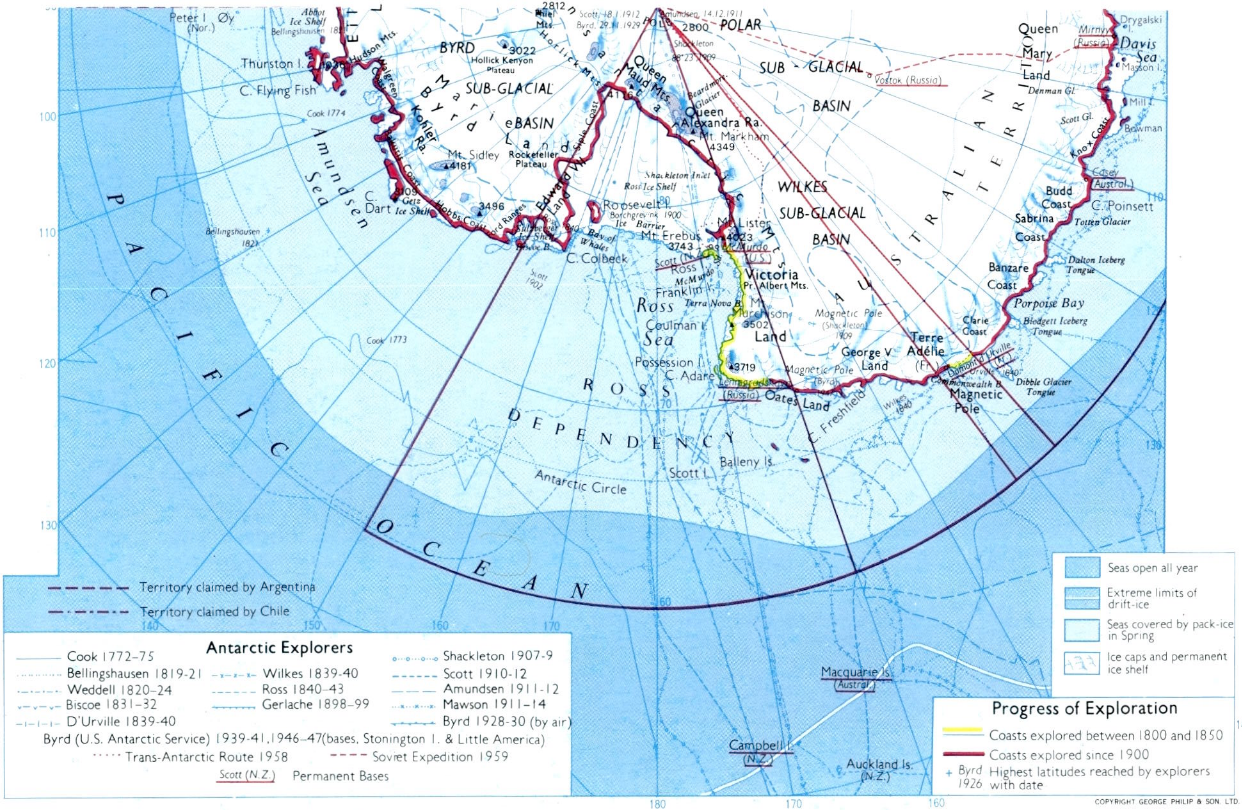
PACIFIC OCEAN
Amundsen Sea
Ross Sea
ROSS DEPENDENCY
AUSTRALIAN TERRITORY
POLAR SUB-GLACIAL BASIN
WILKES SUB-GLACIAL BASIN
BYRD SUB-GLACIAL BASIN
Marie Byrd Land
Edward VII Land
Victoria Land
George V Land
Terre Adélie (Fr.)
Queen Mary Land
Oates Land
Davis Sea
Antarctic Circle
Peter I Øy (Nor.)
Thurston I.
C. Flying Fish
C. Dart
C. Colbeck
C. Adare
C. Poinsett
C. Freshfield
Ross I.
Franklin I.
Coulman I.
Possession I.
Scott I.
Balleny Is.
Macquarie Is. (Austral.)
Campbell I. (N.Z.)
Auckland Is. (N.Z.)
Bay of Whales
Porpoise Bay
Roosevelt I.
Ross Ice Shelf
Shackleton Inlet
Queen Maud Mts.
Queen Alexandra Ra.
Mt. Markham 4349
Mt. Erebus 3743
Mt. Lister 4023
Mt. Sidley 4181
Kohler Ra.
Hollick Kenyon Plateau
Rockefeller Plateau
Pr. Albert Mts.
Magnetic Pole
Vostok (Russia)
Mirnyy (Russia)
Casey (Austral.)
Scott (N.Z.)
McMurdo (U.S.)
Budd Coast
Sabrina Coast
Banzare Coast
Clarie Coast
Knox Coast
Totten Glacier
Dalton Iceberg Tongue
Blodgett Iceberg Tongue
Dibble Glacier Tongue
Commonwealth B.
Denman Gl.
Scott Gl.
Amundsen 14.12.1911
Scott 18.1.1912
Byrd 29.11.1929
Shackleton 88°23' 1909
Cook 1773
Cook 1774
Bellingshausen 1821
Scott 1902
Territory claimed by Argentina
Territory claimed by Chile
Antarctic Explorers
Cook 1772–75
Bellingshausen 1819-21
Weddell 1820–24
Biscoe 1831–32
D'Urville 1839-40
Wilkes 1839-40
Ross 1840–43
Gerlache 1898–99
Shackleton 1907-9
Scott 1910-12
Amundsen 1911-12
Mawson 1911–14
Byrd 1928-30 (by air)
Byrd (U.S. Antarctic Service) 1939-41, 1946–47 (bases, Stonington I. & Little America)
Trans-Antarctic Route 1958
Soviet Expedition 1959
Scott (N.Z.) Permanent Bases
Seas open all year
Extreme limits of drift-ice
Seas covered by pack-ice in Spring
Ice caps and permanent ice shelf
Progress of Exploration
Coasts explored between 1800 and 1850
Coasts explored since 1900
Byrd 1926 Highest latitudes reached by explorers with date
COPYRIGHT GEORGE PHILIP & SON LTD.

EUROPE: PHYSICAL

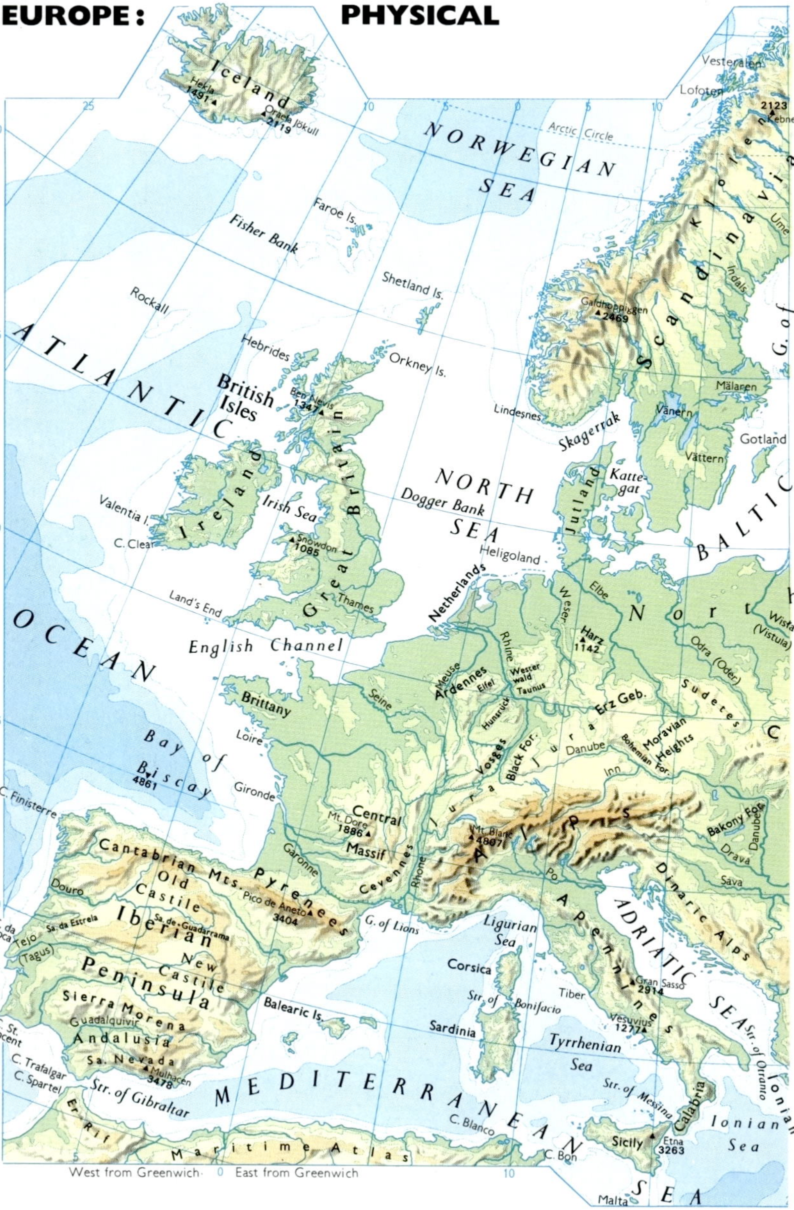
Iceland
Hekla 1491
Oraefa Jökull 2119
NORWEGIAN SEA
Arctic Circle
Vesterålen
Lofoten
2123 Kebnekaise
Faroe Is.
Fisher Bank
Shetland Is.
Rockall
Hebrides
Orkney Is.
ATLANTIC OCEAN
British Isles
Ben Nevis 1347
Great Britain
Ireland
Irish Sea
Valentia I.
C. Clear
Snowdon 1085
Land's End
Thames
English Channel
NORTH SEA
Dogger Bank
Heligoland
Netherlands
Lindesnes
Skagerrak
Kattegat
Jutland
Galdhøpiggen 2469
Scandinavia
Kjølen
Ume
Indals
G. of
Mälaren
Vänern
Vättern
Gotland
BALTIC
North
Elbe
Weser
Harz 1142
Wisła (Vistula)
Odra (Oder)
Sudetes
Rhine
Wester wald
Taunus
Meuse
Ardennes
Eifel
Hunsrück
Erz Geb.
Moravian Heights
Bohemian For.
Seine
Brittany
Loire
Bay of Biscay
4861
Gironde
C. Finisterre
Vosges
Black For.
Jura
Danube
Inn
Central Massif
Mt. Dore 1886
Mt. Blanc 4807
ALPS
Bakony For.
Drava
Sava
Garonne
Cevennes
Rhone
Po
Dinaric Alps
Cantabrian Mts.
Pyrenees
Pico de Aneto 3404
Old Castile
Douro
Iberian Peninsula
C. da Roca
Sa. da Estrela
Sa. de Guadarrama
Tejo (Tagus)
New Castile
Sierra Morena
Guadalquivir
Andalusia
Sa. Nevada
Mulhacen 3478
C. St. Vincent
C. Trafalgar
C. Spartel
Str. of Gibraltar
Er Rif
Maritime Atlas
G. of Lions
Ligurian Sea
Corsica
Str. of Bonifacio
Sardinia
Balearic Is.
Apennines
Gran Sasso 2914
Tiber
Vesuvius 1277
ADRIATIC SEA
Str. of Otranto
Tyrrhenian Sea
Str. of Messina
Calabria
Sicily
Etna 3263
Ionian Sea
C. Blanco
C. Bon
Malta
MEDITERRANEAN SEA
West from Greenwich
East from Greenwich

1 : 24 000 000

North Cape
Nordkinn
Mts.
L. Inari
Lapland
Kola Peninsula
Torne
White Sea
Mezen
Ural Mountains
Bothnia
Finland
Onega
N. Dvina
L. Onega
European Plain
L. Ladoga
Svir
Kama
G. of Finland
Neva
Rybinsk Res.
L. Chudskoye
SEA
Volga
G. of Riga
Central Russian Uplands
Volga Uplands
Obshchi Syrt
W. Dvina
Oka
Niemen
Don
Pripyat
Pripyat (Pripet)
Marshes
Ural
Volga
Tsimlyansk Res.
Ukraine
Dnepr (Dnieper)
CASPIAN SEA
−28
2655
Tatra
Carpathians
Dnestr (Dniester)
Bug
Don
Manych
Prut
Sea of Azov
Kuban
Plain of Hungary
Mures
Crimea
Terek
Tisza
Transylvanian Alps
Danube
Str. of Kerch
Caucasus
Elbrus 5633
Wallachia
BLACK SEA
Rion
Kura
Danube
Morava
2211
Balkans
Armenia
Araks
Rhodope
Bosporus
5166
Ararat
L. Van
L. Urmia
Balkan Peninsula
S. of Marmara
Pindus
Ida 1766
Kizil Irmak
Kurdistan
Aegean Sea
L. Tuz
Tigris
Anatolia
Erciyas 3770
Taurus
Euphrates
Morea
Is.
5121
C. Matapan
Cyprus
1951
Crete
30
35
40
45
50
55
60
65

EUROPE: POLITICAL

ICELAND
Reykjavik
Akureyri
Húsavík
ATLANTIC OCEAN
Arctic Circle
Føroyar (Den.)
Shetland Is.
Orkney Is.
Hebrides
UNITED KINGDOM
SCOTLAND
N.I.
WALES
ENGLAND
Inverness
Aberdeen
Dundee
Glasgow
Edinburgh
Londonderry
Belfast
I. of Man
Carlisle
Newcastle
Leeds
York
Hull
Manchester
Liverpool
Sheffield
Birmingham
Norwich
Swansea
Cardiff
Bristol
Southampton
Portsmouth
Plymouth
LONDON
Dover
Scilly Is.
IRELAND
Galway
Limerick
Dublin
Cork
C. Clear
NORTH SEA
Skagerrak
Kattegat
NORWAY
Tromsø
Narvik
Luleå
Kristiansund
Trondheim
Östersund
Indalsälven
Sundsvall
Bergen
Lillehammer
Oslo
Drammen
Stavanger
Gävle
Uppsala
STOCKHOLM
Vänern
Örebro
Eskilstuna
Göteborg
Vättern
Jönköping
Kalmar
Karlskrona
Malmö
SWEDEN
G. of
DENMARK
Ålborg
Århus
KØBENHAVN
Esbjerg
Flensburg
Kiel
BALTIC
Rostock
Gdynia
Gdańsk
Szczecin
Bydgoszcz
Wisła
Poznań
Łódź
POLAND
Wrocław
Częstochowa
Katowice
Ostrava
Groningen
NETHERLANDS
Amsterdam
's-Gravenhage
Rotterdam
Oostende
Antwerpen
BELGIUM
BRUSSEL
Lille
Calais
LUX.
Luxembourg
Hamburg
Bremen
Elbe
Hannover
Weser
BERLIN
Magdeburg
Oder
GERMANY
Dortmund
Essen
Köln
Bonn
Halle
Leipzig
Chemnitz
Dresden
Wiesbaden
Frankfurt
Würzburg
Nürnberg
Rhine
Stuttgart
München
Freiburg
Donau
PRAHA
Plzeň
CZECH REP.
Brno
SLOVAK
Bratislava
WIEN
Linz
Salzburg
AUSTRIA
Innsbruck
Graz
BUDAPEST
HUNGARY
Pécs
English Channel
Cherbourg
Le Havre
Rouen
Seine
Caen
Brest
Rennes
PARIS
Reims
Metz
Strasbourg
Le Mans
Loire
Orléans
Nantes
Tours
FRANCE
Dijon
Mulhouse
Limoges
Clermont-Ferrand
Périgueux
St-Étienne
Lyon
Saône
Grenoble
Rhône
Bordeaux
Garonne
Toulouse
Montpellier
Avignon
Perpignan
Sète
Marseille
Toulon
Nice
Monaco
BAY OF BISCAY
Basel
Bern
Zürich
SWITZERLAND
Genève
Trento
Milano
Brescia
Trieste
Venezia
Torino
Génova
La Spezia
Bologna
Ravenna
San Marino
Firenze
Livorno
ITALY
Ancona
ROMA
Tevere
Nápoli
Bari
Taranto
Brindisi
Messina
Reggio
Palermo
Sicilia
Catánia
Ljubljana
SLOVENIA
Zagreb
CROATIA
BOSNIA-HERZ.
Sarajevo
Split
Dubrovnik
YUGO
ADRIATIC SEA
Tirane
ALBANIA
Kérkira
Ionian Sea
Tyrrhenian Sea
Corse
Ajaccio
Sassari
Sardegna
Cagliari
Pantelleria (Ital.)
MALTA
MEDITERRANEAN SEA
La Coruña
C. Finisterre
Oviedo
Santander
Bilbao
San Sebastián
Bayonne
Vigo
Porto
Douro
Coimbra
PORTUGAL
LISBOA
Tajo
Lagos
Valladolid
Duero
Ebro
Andorra
Zaragoza
MADRID
SPAIN
Toledo
Guadiana
Badajoz
Barcelona
Valencia
Islas Baleares
Menorca
Mallorca
Palma
Ibiza
Córdoba
Guadalquivir
Sevilla
Murcia
Alicante
Cádiz
Málaga
Granada
Almería
Cartagena
Str. of Gibraltar
Gibraltar (Br.)
Tanger
Ceuta (Sp.)
MOROCCO
Rabat
Meknes
Fès
Melilla (Sp.)
Oran
Tlemcen
Alger
Blida
ALGERIA
Constantine
Skikda
Annaba
TUNISIA
Tunis
West from Greenwich
East from Greenwich

1 : 24 000 000

Hammerfest
Pechenga
Murmansk
Kiruna
Gällivare
Luleå
Bothnia
Vaasa
Kuopio
Tampere
FINLAND
Helsinki
Vyborg
Ladozhskoye Ozero
Kronshtadt
St. Peterburg
Beloye More
Arkhangelsk
Mezen
Onezhskoye Ozero
Sev. Dvina
Kotlas
Kirov
Perm
Nizhniy Tagil
Yekaterinburg
Izhevsk
Zlatoust
Chelyabinsk
Ufa
Magnitogorsk
Orsk
Orenburg
RUSSIA
Vologda
Kostroma
Rybinskoye Vdkhr
Yaroslavl
Volga
Ivanovo
Nizhniy Novgorod
Kazan
Samara
Syzran
Tallinn
ESTONIA
Chudskoye Ozero
Novgorod
Pskov
LATVIA
Liepaja
Riga
Daugava
Daugavpils
MOSKVA
Klaipeda
LITHUANIA
Kaunas
Vilnius
Kaliningrad
Zap. Dvina
Vitebsk
Smolensk
Tula
Penza
Mogilev
BELARUS
Minsk
Orel
Tambov
Saratov
Uralsk
Ural
KAZAKSTAN
Gomel
Kursk
Don
Voronezh
Bialystok
Pripyat
Brest
WARSZAWA
Chernigov
Lublin
Bug
Kiyev
Kharkov
Volgograd
Atyrau
Kraków
Zhitomir
Dnepr
Lugansk
Lvov
Berdichev
UKRAINE
Donetsk
Astrakhan
CASPIAN SEA
REP
Dnestr
Kirovograd
Dnepropetrovsk
Zaporozhye
Taganrog
Rostov
Chernovtsy
Krivoy Rog
Nikolayev
Miskolc
Debrecen
MOLDOVA
Kishinev
Odessa
Kherson
Azovskoye More
Stavropol
Makhachkala
RY
Cluj-Napoca
Iaşi
Szeged
ROMANIA
Galaţi
Timişoara
Braşov
Kerch
Krasnodar
Novorossiysk
Derbent
Sevastopol
Ploieşti
BUCUREŞTI
Constanţa
BLACK SEA
GEORGIA
Tbilisi
Baku
AZERBAIJAN
SERBIA
Dunărea
Ruse
Oryakhovo
Pleven
Varna
Batumi
ARMENIA
Niš
Sofiya
BULGARIA
Sliven
Burgas
Sinop
Samsun
Trabzon
Yerevan
Araks
Skopje
MACEDONIA
Plovdiv
Edirne
Kastamonu
Erzurum
Tabrīz
İSTANBUL
Üsküdar
Thessaloníki
TURKEY
Bursa
Ankara
Malatya
Balikesir
Kayseri
Diyarbakir
GREECE
IRAN
Al Mawşil
İzmir
Aydın
Konya
Adana
İskenderun
SYRIA
Halab
IRAQ
Tigris
Pátrai
Piraiévs
ATHÍNAI
Antalya
CYPRUS
Nicosia
Limassol
Iráklion
Kriti
COPYRIGHT, GEORGE PHILIP & SON LTD

22
C. Malin
I. Tory
Portrush
North Channel
Coleraine
Aran I.
Derryveagh Mts.
Londonderry
Antrim Mts.
Letterkenny
Lifford
Larne
Stranraer
Wigtown
Ballymena
Antrim
Donegal
NORTHERN IRELAND
Bangor
L. Neagh
Belfast
Mull of Galloway
Donegal Bay
Killala Bay
Bundoran
L. Erne
Omagh
Blackwater
Lisburn
Erris Hd.
Sligo
Enniskillen
Armagh
Downpatrick
Dundrum
Upper L. Erne
ISLE OF MAN
Ballina
Monaghan
Mourne Mts.
Clones
Newry
Douglas
L. Conn
Leitrim
Achill I.
Carrick-on-Shannon
Clare I.
Castlebar
Cavan
Greenore
Dundalk
Westport
Longford
Ceanannus Mór
Drogheda
IRISH S
L. Mask
Roscommon
An Uaimh
Connemara
Ree
Mullingar
Boyne
L. Corrib
Balbriggan
Athlone
IRELAND
Galway
Athenry
Dublin
Anglesey
Galway Bay
Tullamore
(Baile Atha Cliath)
Holyhead
Dun Laoghaire
Liffey
Bray
Birr
Kildare
Naas
Llangefni
Port Laoise
Caernarfon Bay
L. Derg
Athy
Wicklow Mts.
Wicklow
Ennis
Pwllheli
Nenagh
Carlow
Loop Hd.
Kilrush
Limerick
Arklow
Thurles
Kilkenny
Shannon
Golden Vale
Listowel
Cardigan Bay
Tipperary
Enniscorthy
Rath Luirc
Carrick-on-Suir
Clonmel
New Ross
Tralee
Wexford
Waterford
Rosslare
Mallow
Blackwater
Killarney
Fermoy
Macgillycuddy's Reeks
Dungarvan
Carnsore Pt.
St. George's Channel
Fishguard
Cardigan
Cahirciveen
1040
Youghal
Blarney
St. David's Hd.
Cork
Lee
Cobh
Haverfordwest
Tywi
Bandon
Bantry
Kinsale
Cork Harbour
Carmarthen
Castletown Bere
Pembroke
Llanelli
Milford Haven
C. Clear
Bristol C
Lundy I.
Hartland Point
Bude
St. Austell
Devonport
Truro
Camborne
Penzance
Falmouth
Land's End
Scilly Is.
Lizard
10
8
50

1 : 4 000 000

23

NORTH SEA
ENGLISH CHANNEL
ENGLAND
WALES
Dumfries
Newcastle
Tynemouth
South Shields
Gateshead
Sunderland
Carlisle
Solway Firth
Durham
Hartlepool
Whitehaven
Stockton
Middlesbrough
Whitby
St. Bee's Hd.
978
Scafell Pike
Cumbrian Mts.
Appleby
Darlington
N. York Moors
Pennine Range
Kendal
Windermere
Northallerton
Scarborough
Flamborough Hd.
Barrow
Ripon
York
Lancaster
Morecambe Bay
Keighley
Beverley
Blackpool
Burnley
Leeds
Hull
Preston
Halifax
Bradford
Blackburn
Huddersfield
Wakefield
Scunthorpe
Spurn Hd.
Bolton
Oldham
Barnsley
Grimsby
Liverpool Bay
St. Helens
Salford
Doncaster
Manchester
Rotherham
Birkenhead
Liverpool
Stockport
Sheffield
Beaumaris
Macclesfield
Chesterfield
Lincoln
Rhyl
Denbigh
Chester
Mansfield
Skegness
Caernarfon
Ruthin
1085
Snowdon
Crewe
Wrexham
Stoke-on-Trent
Derby
Nottingham
Grantham
Sleaford
Boston
The Wash
Kings Lynn
Norwich
Gt. Yarmouth
Lowestoft
Stafford
Burton-upon-Trent
The Fens
Shrewsbury
Telford
Wolverhampton
Dolgellau (Dolgelley)
Welshpool
Walsall
Leicester
Oakham
Peterborough
Birmingham
Kidderminster
Coventry
Corby
Ely
Aberystwyth
Rugby
Huntingdon
Cambrian Mts.
Rhayader
Presteigne
Llandrindod Wells
Worcester
Warwick
Leamington
Stratford-on-Avon
Wellingborough
Cambridge
Bury St. Edmunds
Northampton
Bedford
Ipswich
Hereford
Milton Keynes
Colchester
Harwich
The Naze
Brecon
Luton
Cheltenham
Gloucester
Monmouth
Cotswolds
Hertford
St. Albans
Chelmsford
Merthyr Tydfil
Oxford
Aylesbury
Chiltern Hills
Watford
Rhondda
Swansea
Newport
Swindon
Slough
LONDON
Southend
Thames
Port Talbot
Cardiff
Bristol
Windsor
Reading
Chatham
Gillingham
Margate
Canterbury
Bath
Trowbridge
Weston-super-Mare
Salisbury Plain
Aldershot
Guildford
Reigate
N. Downs
Maidstone
Dover
Folkestone
Ilfracombe
Exmoor
Barnstaple
Wells
Wilton
Salisbury
Winchester
The Weald
Ashford
Taunton
Yeovil
Southampton
Chichester
South Downs
Lewes
Hastings
Eastbourne
Axminster
Poole
Portsmouth
Worthing
Brighton
Newhaven
Dartmoor
Exeter
Dorchester
Newport
Isle of Wight
Weymouth
Needles
Bournemouth
Torquay
Plymouth
Dartmouth
Start Pt.
Dieppe
West from Greenwich
East from Greenwich
54
52
50
4
2
0

36

ATLANTIC OCEAN
Outer Hebrides
Lewis
Stornoway
Harris
North Uist
Benbecula
South Uist
Barra
St. Kilda
North Minch
Inner Hebrides
Portree
Skye
Kyle of Lochalsh
Rhum
Eigg
Coll
Tiree
Staffa
Iona
Mull
Firth of Lorn
Colonsay
Jura
Islay
Kintyre
Arran
North West Highlands
L. Shin
Lairg
Ullapool
Invergordon
Dingwall
L. Ness
Mallaig
Fort William
1343
Ben Nevis
Ballachulish
Oban
Grampian
Lochgilphead
L. Lomond
Helensburgh
Greenock
Dumbarton
Rothesay
Paisley
Glasgow
Kilmarnock
Saltcoats
Irvine
Prestwick
Ayr
Campbeltown
Firth of Clyde
North Channel
Stranraer
Wigtown
Mull of Galloway
ISLE OF MAN
Douglas
Malin Hd.
Tory I.
Portrush
Coleraine
Antrim Mts.
Aran I.
Derryveagh Mts.
Letterkenny
Lifford
Londonderry
Ballymena
Larne
Antrim
NORTHERN IRELAND
Bangor
Belfast
L. Neagh
Lisburn
Donegal
Donegal Bay
Killala Bay
Bundoran
Erris Hd.
L. Erne
Omagh
Blackwater
Sligo
Enniskillen
Armagh
Downpatrick
Dundrum
Upper L. Erne
Monaghan
Clones
Newry
Mourne Mts.
Ballina
L. Conn
Achill I.
Clare I.
Castlebar
Leitrim
Carrick-on-Shannon
Cavan
Greenore
Dundalk
IRELAND
Westport
Longford
Ceanannus Mor
An Uaimh
Drogheda
Connemara
L. Mask
Roscommon
IRISH S
West from Greenwich
10
8
6
58
56
20

1 : 4 000 000

Pentland Firth
Thurso
Wick
Golspie
Moray Firth
Lossiemouth
Elgin
Nairn
Fraserburgh
Banff
Peterhead
Inverness
Spey
Don
Kingussie
Ballater
Balmoral
Dee
Aberdeen
Stonehaven
Blair Atholl
Montrose
Forfar
Arbroath
L. Tay
Tay
Crieff
Dundee
Firth of Tay
Perth
Cupar
St. Andrews
Stirling
Kinross
Leven
Forth
Alloa
Kirkcaldy
Dunfermline
Firth of Forth
Dunbar
Falkirk
Edinburgh
Haddington
Leith
Berwick-on-Tweed
Duns
Hamilton
Motherwell
Clyde
Galashiels
Peebles
St. Boswells
Selkirk
Jedburgh
Cheviot Hills
Alnwick
Sanquhar
Moffat
Hawick
Nith
Dumfries
Newcastle
Tynemouth
South Shields
Tyne
Gateshead
Sunderland
Kirkcudbright
Solway Firth
Carlisle
Eden
Durham
Hartlepool
Pennine Range
Cumbrian Mts.
Whitehaven
978
Scafell Pike
St. Bee's Hd.
Appleby
Stockton
Middlesbrough
Whitby
Darlington
N. York Moors
Swale
Northallerton
Kendal
Windermere
Scarborough
ENGLAND
Flamborough Hd.
Barrow
Ripon
Lancaster
York
Morecambe Bay
Ribble
Keighley
Wharfe
Beverley
Blackpool
Burnley
Leeds
Hull
Preston
Halifax
Bradford
Aire
Humber
Blackburn
Huddersfield
Wakefield
Scunthorpe
Grimsby
Spurn Hd.
Bolton
Oldham
Barnsley
Doncaster
St. Helens
Salford
Manchester
Rotherham
Birkenhead
Liverpool
Mersey
Stockport
Sheffield
NORTH SEA
E A
Orkney Is.
Westray
N. Ronaldsay
Sanday
Stronsay
Mainland
Hoy
Kirkwall
South Ronaldsay
Pentland Firth
Shetland Is.
Unst
Yell
Mainland
Foula
Lerwick
Fair I.
4
2
3
0
59
60
56
54
21

COPYRIGHT GEORGE PHILIP & SON LTD

26 28 26 27

Towyn
Aberdovey
Dovey
Machynlleth
Borth
Plynlimon
Aberystwyth
CARDIGANSHIRE
Tregaron
Aberayron
Teifi
Lampeter
Llandovery
CARMARTHENSHIRE
Llandeilo
Carmarthen
Tywi
Ammanford
Llanelli
SWANSEA
Swansea
Gower
Port Talbot
Neath
Porthcawl
Bridgend
Maesteg
Black Mt.
Aberdare
Merthyr Tydfil
Rhondda
Pontypridd
Brecon
886
Brecon Beacons
Black Mts.
Ebbw Vale
Tredegar
Abergavenny
Cwmbran
Pontypool
Monmouth
Newport
Caerphilly
Cardiff
Barry
Usk
Rhymney
W A L E S
POWYS
Rhayader
Builth
Llandrindod Wells
Radnor Forest
New Radnor
Presteign
Knighton
Newtown
Llanidloes
Montgomery
Welshpool
Severn
Wye
Hay-on-Wye
Hereford
SHROPSHIRE
Ironbridge
Wolverhampton
Bridgnorth
Clee Hills
Ludlow
Kidderminster
Stourbridge
Dudley
Tipton
Walsall
West Bromwich
Warley
Birmingham
W. MIDLANDS
Tamworth
Nuneaton
Coventry
WARWICK
Redditch
Leamington
Warwick
Stratford-on-Avon
Edge Hill
Droitwich
HEREFORD & WORCESTER
Worcester
Leominster
Teme
Malvern Hills
Malvern
Ledbury
Tewkesbury
Evesham
Avon
Ross-on-Wye
Forest of Dean
Cleeve Hill
330
Cheltenham
Gloucester
GLOUCESTER
Stroud
Cirencester
Cotswold Hills
Windrush
Witney
OXF
Thames
Vale of White
Swindon
Berksh Dow
Chepstow
Avonmouth
Clevedon
Bristol
Chippenham
Marlborough Downs
Marlborough
Kennet
AVON
Bath
Trowbridge
Devizes
Ham
297
Walbury Hill
WILTS
Radstock
Frome
Salisbury Plain
Andover
Stonehenge
Test
Salisbury
Wilton
Mere
H
Bristol Channel
Weston-super-Mare
Mendip Hills
Wells
Glastonbury
Bruton
Brue
Polden Hills
Bridgwater
Quantock Hills
SOMERSET
Minehead
Lynton
Ilfracombe
Dunkery Beacon
520
Exmoor
Barnstaple
S. Molton
Bideford
Torridge
Taw
Taunton
Wellington
Parrett
Yeo
Yeovil
Sherborne
Shaftesbury
Tiverton
Exe
Chard
Blandford
Stour
New Forest
Lymington
Solent
DEVON
Honiton
DORSET
Axminster
Okehampton
Yes Tor
618
Exeter
Teign
Bridport
Dorchester
Poole
Bournemouth
Christchurch
Needles
Sidmouth
Lyme Regis
I. of Purbeck
Swanage
St. Alban's Hd.
Weymouth
Portland I.
Portland Bill
Exmouth
Teignmouth
Dartmoor
Tamar
Tavistock
Newton Abbot
Torquay (Torbay)
Paignton
Dart
Devonport
Totnes
Plymouth
Dartmouth
Kingsbridge
Salcombe
Start Pt.
Eddystone
E N G L I S H
52
51
4
3
2
1
2
3
4
5
6
7
8
9
10
11

1 : 2 000 000

29

LEICESTER
Leicester
Hinckley
Stamford
Peterborough
Fletton
March
Downham Market
Wymondham
Yare
Lowestoft
Breckland
Little Ouse
Beccles
Bungay
Market Harborough
Rockingham Forest
Corby
Rugby
Kettering
CAMBRIDGE
Ely
Thetford
Diss
Waveney
Southwold
NORTHAMPTON
Wellingborough
Huntingdon
Rushden
Lark
Mildenhall
Ouse
St. Ives
Newmarket
Saxmundham
Sizewell
Daventry
Northampton
St. Neots
Cam
Cambridge
Bury St. Edmunds
Stowmarket
SUFFOLK
Aldeburgh
Orford Ness
Bedford
Banbury
Milton Keynes
BEDFORD
Saffron Walden
Ipswich
Orwell
Sudbury
Stour
Felixstowe
Cherwell
Bletchley
Buckingham
Hitchin
Letchworth
Stevenage
Bishop's Stortford
Braintree
Colchester
Harwich
The Naze
Walton-on-the-Naze
Bicester
Dunstable
ORD
BUCKS
Woodstock
Luton
HERTFORD
ESSEX
Hertford
Clacton
Mersea
Aylesbury
Chiltern Hills
Oxford
Hemel Hempstead
St. Albans
Harlow
Chelmsford
Maldon
Abingdon
Thame
Watford
Epping
Lea
Horse
High Wycombe
Enfield
Brentwood
Barnet
Foulness
Harrow
Redbridge
Southend
Brent
Havering
Basildon
Shoeburyness
Hillingdon
Maidenhead
Slough
Newham
Grays
Thames
Ealing
LONDON
Tilbury
Sheerness
Whitstable
Herne Bay
Margate
North Foreland
BERKS
Windsor
Richmond
Greenwich
Gravesend
Sheppey
Thanet
Reading
Thames
Bromley
Rochester
Gillingham
Newbury
Staines
Kingston
Croydon
Chatham
Canterbury
Ramsgate
Farnborough
Woking
North Downs
Basingstoke
Aldershot
SURREY
Maidstone
Deal
Tonbridge
KENT
Stour
Guildford
294
Reigate
Medway
South Foreland
Leith Hill
E. Grinstead
Tunbridge Wells
Ashford
Dover
Alton
Haslemere
Crawley
Folkestone
Itchen
Winchester
The Weald
Haywards Heath
Romney Marsh
Hythe
HANTS
Horsham
Rother
New Romney
WEST SUSSEX
EAST SUSSEX
Rye
51
52
Eastleigh
South Downs
Battle
Dungeness
Southampton
Ouse
Lewes
Fareham
Chichester
Brighton
Hastings
Havant
Bexhill
Gosport
Hove
Cowes
Spithead
Portsmouth
Worthing
Eastbourne
Hayling I.
Littlehampton
Newhaven
Beachy Hd.
Newport
Ryde
Selsey Bill
Bognor Regis
ISLE OF WIGHT
Ventnor
St. Catherine's Point
CHANNEL
Welsh Unitary Authorities
(from April 1996)
1. Neath Port Talbot
2. Rhondda Cynon Taff
3. Bridgend
4. Merthyr Tydfil
5. Caerphilly
6. Vale of Glamorgan
7. Cardiff
8. Blaenau Gwent
9. Torfaen
10. Newport
11. Monmouthshire
1
West from Greenwich
0
East from Greenwich

28

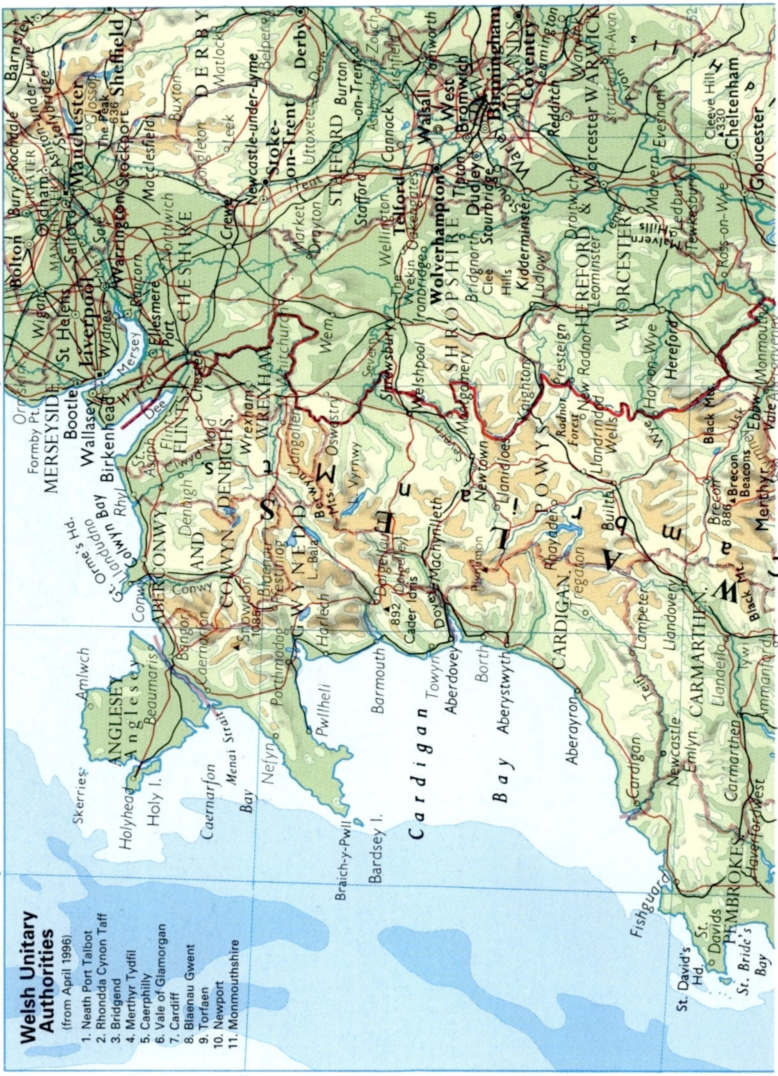
Welsh Unitary Authorities
(from April 1996)
1. Neath Port Talbot
2. Rhondda Cynon Taff
3. Bridgend
4. Merthyr Tydfil
5. Caerphilly
6. Vale of Glamorgan
7. Cardiff
8. Blaenau Gwent
9. Torfaen
10. Newport
11. Monmouthshire
Cardigan Bay
St. Bride's Bay
Caernarfon Bay
Colwyn Bay
Holyhead
Holy I.
Skerries
Anglesey
Amlwch
Beaumaris
Menai Strait
Bangor
Caernarfon
Conwy
Llandudno
Rhyl
Snowdon 1085
Harlech
Porthmadog
Pwllheli
Nefyn
Bardsey I.
Braich-y-Pwll
Barmouth
Dolgellau
Cader Idris 892
Towyn
Aberdovey
Machynlleth
Borth
Aberystwyth
Aberayron
Cardigan
Fishguard
St. Davids
St. David's Hd.
Newcastle Emlyn
Carmarthen
Haverfordwest
Lampeter
Llandovery
Ammanford
Brecon
Brecon Beacons 886
Merthyr
Black Mt.
Builth Wells
Llandrindod Wells
Rhayader
Llanidloes
Newtown
Montgomery
Welshpool
Shrewsbury
Knighton
Presteigne
New Radnor
Radnor Forest
Hay-on-Wye
Hereford
Monmouth
Abergavenny
Ross-on-Wye
Gloucester
Cheltenham
Cleeve Hill 330
Tewkesbury
Ledbury
Malvern Hills
Worcester
Evesham
Redditch
Leominster
Ludlow
Kidderminster
Stourbridge
Bridgnorth
Wolverhampton
Dudley
West Bromwich
Walsall
Birmingham
Coventry
Leamington
Warwick
Tamworth
Lichfield
Cannock
Telford
Stafford
Burton-on-Trent
Derby
Uttoxeter
Stoke-on-Trent
Newcastle-under-Lyme
Leek
Matlock
Buxton
Crewe
Congleton
Macclesfield
Stockport
Manchester
Sheffield
The Peak 636
Oldham
Bolton
Bury
Rochdale
Barnsley
Wigan
St Helens
Warrington
Runcorn
Widnes
Liverpool
Bootle
Birkenhead
Wallasey
Ellesmere Port
Chester
Wrexham
Llangollen
Oswestry
Whitchurch
Wem
Bala
Denbigh
Formby Pt.
MERSEYSIDE
CHESHIRE
SHROPSHIRE
STAFFORD
DERBY
HEREFORD & WORCESTER
WARWICK
POWYS
CARDIGAN
CARMARTHEN
PEMBROKE
GWYNEDD
WREXHAM
FLINTS
DENBIGHS
ABERCONWY AND COLWYN
WALES
53
52
2
3
4
5

35

1 : 2 000 000

24
36
Bristol Channel
Milford Haven
Pembroke
Tenby
Carmarthen Bay
Llanelli
SWANSEA
Swansea
Gower
Burry Port
Port Talbot
Porthcawl
Neath
Maesteg
Aberdare
Rhondda
Pontypridd
Bridgend
Barry
Cardiff
Cwmbran
Pontypool
Newport
Tredegar
Chepstow
Forest of Dean
GLOUCESTER
Stroud
Cirencester
Swindon
Thames
Marlborough Downs
Kennet
Avon
Chippenham
Bristol
Avonmouth
Clevedon
Weston-super-Mare
AVON
Bath
Trowbridge
Devizes
WILTS
Salisbury Plain
Stonehenge
Salisbury
Wilton
New Forest
Lymington
Christchurch
Bournemouth
Poole
Swanage
St. Alban's Hd.
I. of Purbeck
Weymouth
Portland I.
Portland Bill
Dorchester
DORSET
Blandford
Stour
Shaftesbury
Sherborne
Mere
Frome
Radstock
Mendip Hills
Wells
Glastonbury
Bruton
Polden Hills
Brue
Bridgwater
SOMERSET
Quantock Hills
Taunton
Wellington
Yeovil
Yeo
Parrett
Chard
Axminster
Bridport
Lyme Regis
Honiton
Sidmouth
Exmouth
Teignmouth
Torquay (Torbay)
Paignton
Dartmouth
Start Pt.
Kingsbridge
Salcombe
Eddystone
Minehead
Exmoor
Dunkery Beacon 520
Lynton
Barnstaple
S. Molton
Tiverton
Exe
Exeter
Teign
Newton Abbot
Dart
Totnes
DEVON
Taw
Okehampton
Yes Tor 618
Dartmoor
Tavistock
Plymouth
Devonport
Plymouth Sound
Tamar
Torridge
Ilfracombe
Braunton
Bideford
Holsworthy
Launceston
Hartland Point
Lundy
Bude
Boscastle
Bodmin Moor
Brown Willy 419
Bodmin
Looe
Fowey
CORNWALL
St. Austell
Padstow
Newquay
Truro
Falmouth
Redruth
Camborne
Helston
Lizard
St. Michael's Mount
Penzance
St. Ives
Land's End
5 West from Greenwich
4
3
2
51
50

NORTHERN ENGLAND

NORTHUMBERLAND
Ashington
Morpeth
Blyth
N. Tyne
Wallsend
Tynemouth
South Shields
Newcastle
Blaydon
Tyne
TYNE & WEAR
HADRIAN'S WALL
Hexham
Gateshead
Sunderland
Consett
Houghton-le-Spring
Durham
Dumfries
Annan
Gretna Green
Newton Stewart
Castle Douglas
Dalbeattie
Dee
Kirkcudbright
Wigtown
Wigtown Bay
Whithorn
Solway Firth
Silloth
Carlisle
Eden
S. Tyne
Alston
Cross Fell
893
Wear
DURHAM
Maryport
Workington
Derwent
Skiddaw
931
Penrith
Derwentwater
CUMBRIA
Keswick
Helvellyn
950
Ullswater
Appleby
Tees
Bishop Auckland
Barnard Castle
Whitehaven
St. Bee's Hd.
Shap
Cumbrian Mts.
Brough
Darlington
Sca Fell
978
Ambleside
Richmond
Seascale
Windermere
Kendal
Northallerton
Swale
Wensleydale
Whernside
737
Ure
Millom
Ulverston
Lune
Ingleborough
723
Pen-y-Ghent
693
704
Gt. Whernside
Nidd
NORTH
Ripon
Barrow-in-Furness
Furness
Walney I.
Morecambe
Morecambe Bay
Heysham
Lancaster
Settle
YORKSH
Knaresborough
Harrogate
Forest of Bowland
Pennines
Pt. of Ayre
Ramsey
Snaefell
620
Peel
ISLE OF MAN
Port Erin
Douglas
Castletown
IRISH
SEA
Fleetwood
Ribble
Skipton
Keighley
Cleveleys
Fylde
LANCASHIRE
Nelson
Colne
Blackpool
Bradford
Leeds
Burnley
W. YORKSHIRE
Preston
Accrington
Halifax
Wakefield
Lytham-St. Annes
Blackburn
Dewsbury
Southport
Chorley
Calder
Rochdale
Huddersfield
Ormskirk
Bolton
Bury
Formby Pt.
GREATER MANCHESTER
Oldham
Ashton-under-Lyne
Wigan
MERSEYSIDE
Stalybridge
Barnsley
SOUTH YORKS
St Helens
Salford
Bootle
Manchester
Liverpool
Glossop
Wallasey
Mersey
Sale
The Peak
636
Sheffield
Birkenhead
Widnes
Warrington
Stockport
Skerries
Amlwch
Gt. Orme's Hd.
Llandudno
Colwyn Bay
Rhyl
Holyhead
ANGLESEY
Anglesey
Conwy
Wirral
Runcorn
Holy I.
Beaumaris
St. Asaph
Dee
Ellesmere Port
Macclesfield
Chesterfield
ABERCONWY AND COLWYN
Flint
Northwich
Buxton
Bangor
Denbigh
Clwyd
FLINTS.
CHESHIRE
Caernarfon
Chester
Congleton
DERBY
Menai Strait
Caernarfon Bay
Mold
DENBIGHS.
Matlock
Snowdon
1085
Crewe
Leek
Wrexham
WREXHAM
Newcastle-under-Lyme
Derwent
Nefyn
Blaenau Ffestiniog
Stoke-on-Trent
Belper
Porthmadog
Whitchurch
Market Drayton
Trent
Uttoxeter
Llangollen
GWYNEDD
Derby
Pwllheli
Harlech
L. Bala
Berwyn Mts.
Dove
Oswestry
Wem
STAFFORD
Burton-on-Trent
Ashby-de-la-Zouch
L. Vyrnwy
Stafford
Bardsey I.
Barmouth
Severn
Dolgellau (Dolgelley)
WALES
Shrewsbury
Wellington
Cannock
Lichfield
892
Cader Idris
The Wrekin
(Telford)
Oakengates
Welshpool
Ironbridge
Walsall
Tamworth
Towyn
Dovey
Machynlleth
Wolverhampton
West Bromwich
Nuneaton
Aberdovey
SHROPSHIRE
Tipton
Montgomery
Newtown
Bridgnorth
Dudley
Stourbridge
Birmingham
Stour
Warley
W. MIDLANDS
Coventry
55
54
53
4
3
2
West from Greenwich
31
34
26
24

1 : 2 000 000

NORTH
SEA
55
54
53
1
0
1
East from Greenwich
25
Peterlee
Hartlepool
Stockton
Billingham
Tees Bay
CLEVELAND
Redcar
(Teeside)
Middlesbrough
Thornaby on Tees
Cleveland
Esk
Whitby
N. York Moors
Scarborough
Pickering
Thirsk
Filey
Rye
Malton
York Wolds
Flamborough Hd.
Bridlington
IRE
Driffield
York
Wharfe
Derwent
Hull
Hornsea
Beverley
Holderness
Selby
Ouse
HUMBERSIDE
Hull
Withernsea
Aire
Castleford
Pontefract
Goole
Barton-upon-Humber
Immingham
Humber
Spurn Hd.
Don
Scunthorpe
Greater Grimsby
Cleethorpes
Doncaster
Brigg
Lincoln Wolds
TH
SHIRE
Trent
Rotherham
Gainsborough
Market Rasen
Louth
Mablethorpe
Worksop
East Retford
Alford
Lincoln
Horncastle
NOTTS
Mansfield
LINCOLN
Skegness
Sherwood
Sutton -in-Ashfield
Newark
Witham
Alfreton
Heanor
Forest
Ilkeston
Sleaford
Boston
The Wash
Hunstanton
Wells
Cromer
Nottingham
Grantham
Beeston
The
Sandringham
North Walsham
Long Eaton
Fakenham
Bourne
Spalding
The Broads
Loughborough
Kings Lynn
Bure
Great Yarmouth
Fens
Nene
Gt. Ouse
Coalville
Melton Mowbray
Oakham
Welland
Wisbech
NORFOLK
Norwich
LEICESTER
Leicester
Downham Market
Yare
Stamford
Peterborough
Wymondham
Lowestoft
Hinckley
Fletton
March
Breckland
Beccles
Little Ouse
Corby
Rugby

32

Scottish Local Authorities
(from April 1996)
1. City of Aberdeen
2. City of Dundee
3. Dumbarton & Clydebank
4. East Dunbartonshire
5. City of Glasgow
6. Inverclyde
7. Renfrewshire
8. East Renfrewshire
9. North Lanarkshire
10. Falkirk
11. Clackmannan
12. West Lothian
13. City of Edinburgh
14. Midlothian
SHETLAND IS.
On same scale
ATLANTIC OCEAN
Barra
Barra Hd.
Rhum
Eigg
Muck
Pt. of Ardnamurchan
Coll
Tiree
Staffa
Iona
Colonsay
Rubh a' Mhail
Islay
Bowmore
Port Ellen
Gigha
Jura
Sound of Jura
Mallaig
L. Morar
Arisaig
L. Moidart
L. Shiel
L. Eil
L. Arkaig
Glen Garry
Lochaber
L. Lochy
L. Oich
Fort William
Ben Nevis 1343
Ardgour
Loch Sunart
Glen Coe
Ballachulish
Rannoch Moor
Tobermory
Morvern
L. Linnhe
Sound of Mull
Lismore
Loch Etive
Orchy
Ben Cruachan 1124
Mull
Ben More 966
Firth of Lorn
Oban
ARGYLL & BUTE
B. Vorlich 942
Inveraray
L. Awe
Crinan
Lochgilphead
Helensburgh
Dunoon
Greenock
Port Glasgow
Tarbert
Loch Fyne
Rothesay
Bute
Largs
NORTH
Ardrossan
Saltcoats
Goat Fell 874
Arran
Brodick
AYRSHIRE
Kintyre
Campbeltown
Firth of Clyde
Ailsa Craig
Girvan
SOUTH AYRSHIRE
Mull of Kintyre
Rathlin
Fair Hd.
Ballycastle
Trostan 554
North Channel
L. Ryan
Gal
NORTHERN IRELAND
Ballymena
Larne
Stranraer
Portpatrick
Luce Bay
Belfast Lough
Belfast
Bangor
Newtownards
Mull of Galloway
Unst
Yell Sound
Yell
Fetlar
SHETLAND
Whalsay
Mainland
Foula
Scalloway
Lerwick
Bressay
Sumburgh Hd.
57
56
60
7
6
5
2
West from Greenwich

33

34

1 : 2 000 000

33

Kingussie
Newtonmore
Cairn Toul
1292
Ben Macdhui
1311
Ballater
Aboyne
Banchory
Balmoral
Braemar
Stonehaven
Badenoch
Glen Spean
Grampian Highlands
Lochnagar
1154
N. Esk
Forest of Atholl
Tilt
Braes of Angus
Laurencekirk
Inverbervie
Garry
Blair Atholl
Pass of Killiecrankie
ANGUS
Brechin
Montrose
L. Rannoch
L. Tummel
Pitlochry
Kirriemuir
S. Esk
Strathmore
Isla
Tay
Alyth
Forfar
Aberfeldy
Blairgowrie
Sidlaw Hills
Arbroath
Ben Lawers
1214
L. Tay
Dunkeld
Breadalbane
PERTHSHIRE & KINROSS
Dundee
Broughty Ferry
NORTH SEA
Killin
Scone
Carse of Gowrie
Firth of Tay
Tayport
L. Earn
Crieff
Perth
Ben More
1174
B. Vorlich
983
Earn
Cupar
FIFE
St. Andrews
Fife Ness
L. Katrine
Callander
Ochil Hills
Kinross
L. Leven
Leven
Anstruther
974
Ben Lomond
Trossachs
STIRLING
Dunblane
Forth
Cowdenbeath
Glenrothes
Lochgelly
Buckhaven
11
Alloa
Kirkcaldy
Firth of Forth
Bass Rock
L. Lomond
Stirling
Bannockburn
Dunfermline
Prestonpans
Bo'ness
Rosyth
North Berwick
Dunbar
3
Cumbernauld
Grangemouth
10
Linlithgow
Leith
EAST LOTHIAN
Haddington
56
Dumbarton
4
Falkirk
Clydebank
Kirkintilloch
Edinburgh
13
Musselburgh
St. Abbs Hd.
Eyemouth
Renfrew
Glasgow
Airdrie
12
Livingston
Dalkeith
Lammermuir Hills
Paisley
5
9
Coatbridge
Bathgate
14
Penicuik
Pentland Hills
7
Johnstone
Rutherglen
Motherwell
Duns
Berwick-upon-Tweed
8
E. Kilbride
Wishaw
Holy I.
Hamilton
Carstairs
Moorfoot Hills
Clyde
Peebles
Coldstream
Irvine
Kilmarnock
SOUTH LANARKSHIRE
Lanark
Tweed
Galashiels
Flodden
Till
Biggar
EAST
Melrose
Kelso
Troon
Prestwick
Ayr
Broad Law
840
Ettrick
Selkirk
The Cheviot
816
Cumnock
BORDERS
Jedburgh
Ayr
AYRSHIRE
Hawick
Leadhills
Southern Uplands
Coquet
Doon
Sanquhar
Nith
Moffat
Teviot
Cheviot Hills
Dalmellington
Esk
DUMFRIES AND GALLOWAY
Langholm
N. Tyne
Merrick 843
Lockerbie
Annan
Gretna Green
Ken
Dumfries
ENGLAND
Hexham
55
Cree
Annan
HADRIAN'S WALL
Castle Douglas
Newton Stewart
Dalbeattie
Carlisle
Gatehouse of Fleet
Wigtown
S. Tyne
Alston
Kirkcudbright
Solway Firth
Wear
Wigtown Bay
Whithorn
Cross Fell
893
Derwent
Penrith
Tees
Barnard Castle
Workington
Skiddaw
931
Ullswater
Cumbrian Mts.
4
3
2
57

28

Scottish Local Authorities
(from April 1996)
1. City of Aberdeen
2. City of Dundee
C. Wrath
Durness
L. Eriboll
Butt of Lewis
L. Laxford
Reay Forest
Eddrachillis Bay
Flannan Is.
L. Roag
Broad Bay
Stornoway
Lewis
Eye Pen.
Lochinver
Enard Bay
L. Assynt
B. More Assynt
Outer Hebrides
North Minch
WESTERN ISLES
L. Seaforth
Tarbert
Harris
L. Broom
Ullapool
L. Ewe
B. Dearg
1081
Sound of Harris
Rubha Hunish
L. Gairloch
L. Maree
L. Fannich
North Uist
Lochmaddy
Little Minch
Snizort
Trotternish
L. Torridon
Rona
Sound of Raasay
Inner Sound
Raasay
Monach Is.
Benbecula
Portree
Skye
L. Carron
Stromeferry
Farrar
North West Highlands
HIGHL
Inner Hebrides
South Uist
Ben More
L. Bracadale
Scalpay
Kyle of Lochalsh
Dornie
Glen Affric
Lochboisdale
Cuillin Hills
L. Hourn
Glen Moriston
Fort Augustus
Sound of Barra
Cuillin Sound
Canna
Sound of Sleat
Glen Garry
L. Oich
Barra
Rhum
Mallaig
L. Morar
Lochaber
Lochy
L. Arkaig
Eigg
Arisdig
Muck
L. Moidart
L. Shiel
L. Eil
Fort William
Ben Nevis
1343
Barra Hd.
Ardgour
Pt. of Ardnamurchan
Loch Sunart
Rannoch Moor
Coll
Tobermory
Morvern
L. Linnhe
Glen Coe
Ballachulish
Sound of Mull
Lismore
Loch Etive
Orchy
Tiree
Ben Cruachan
1124
Staffa
Mull
Ben More
966
Firth of Lorn
Oban
Lorn
58
57
8
7
6
5
West from Greenwich

30

1 : 2 000 000

30

ORKNEY IS.
On same scale
For Shetland Is. see page 30
North Ronaldsay
Westray
Eday
Sanday
Rousay
Stronsay
Mainland
Shapinsay
ORKNEY
Stromness
Kirkwall
Scapa Flow
Hoy
South Ronaldsay
Pentland Firth
Dunnet Hd.
John O'Groats
59
Orkney Is.
Hoy
Scapa Flow
South Ronaldsay
Pentland Firth
Dunnet Hd.
Strathy Pt.
Thurso
Dounreay
John O'Groats
Noss Hd.
Wick
Tongue
Ben Hope 927
Naver
Halladale
Lybster
Helmsdale
Ord of Caithness
Helmsdale
Loch Shin
Brora
Lairg
Brora
Oykell
Golspie
Dornoch
Dornoch Firth
Tarbat Ness
Moray Firth
Tain
Invergordon
Ben Wyvis 1045
Cromarty
Strathpeffer
Conon
Dingwall
Fortrose
Beauly
Inverness
Culloden Moor
Nairn
Forres
Elgin
Lossiemouth
Cullen
Portsoy
Banff
Macduff
Kinnaird's Head
Fraserburgh
Rattray Head
Buckie
Buchan
Keith
Deveron
Turriff
Peterhead
Buchan Ness
Rothes
MORAY
Dufftown
Huntly
Ythan
Ellon
Findhorn
Spey
Grantown-on-Spey
ABERDEENSHIRE
Inverurie
Don
Loch Ness
Glen More
Strath Spey
Tomintoul
Alford
Aberdeen
Girdle Ness
Aviemore
Monadhliath Mts.
Cairn Gorm 1245
Cairngorm Mts.
Kingussie
Ben Macdhui 1311
Ballater
Aboyne
Dee
Banchory
Newtonmore
Cairn Toul 1292
Balmoral
Braemar
57
Stonehaven
Glen Spean
Badenoch
Grampian Highlands
Lochnagar 1154
N. Esk
Forest of Atholl
Tilt
Braes of Angus
Laurencekirk
Inverbervie
Garry
Blair Atholl
Brechin
Pass of Killiecrankie
ANGUS
Montrose
L. Rannoch
L. Tummel
Pitlochry
Kirriemuir
S. Esk
Tay
Isla
Strathmore
Forfar
Aberfeldy
Alyth
Blairgowrie
Ben Lawers 1214
L. Tay
Dunkeld
Tay
Sidlaw Hills
Arbroath
Breadalbane
PERTHSHIRE & KINROSS
Dundee
Broughty Ferry
Killin
Scone
Carse of Gowrie
Firth of Tay
L. Earn
Tayport
Ben More 1174
B. Vorlich 983
Crieff
Perth
Earn
Cupar
St. Andrews
NORTH SEA
4
3
2

31

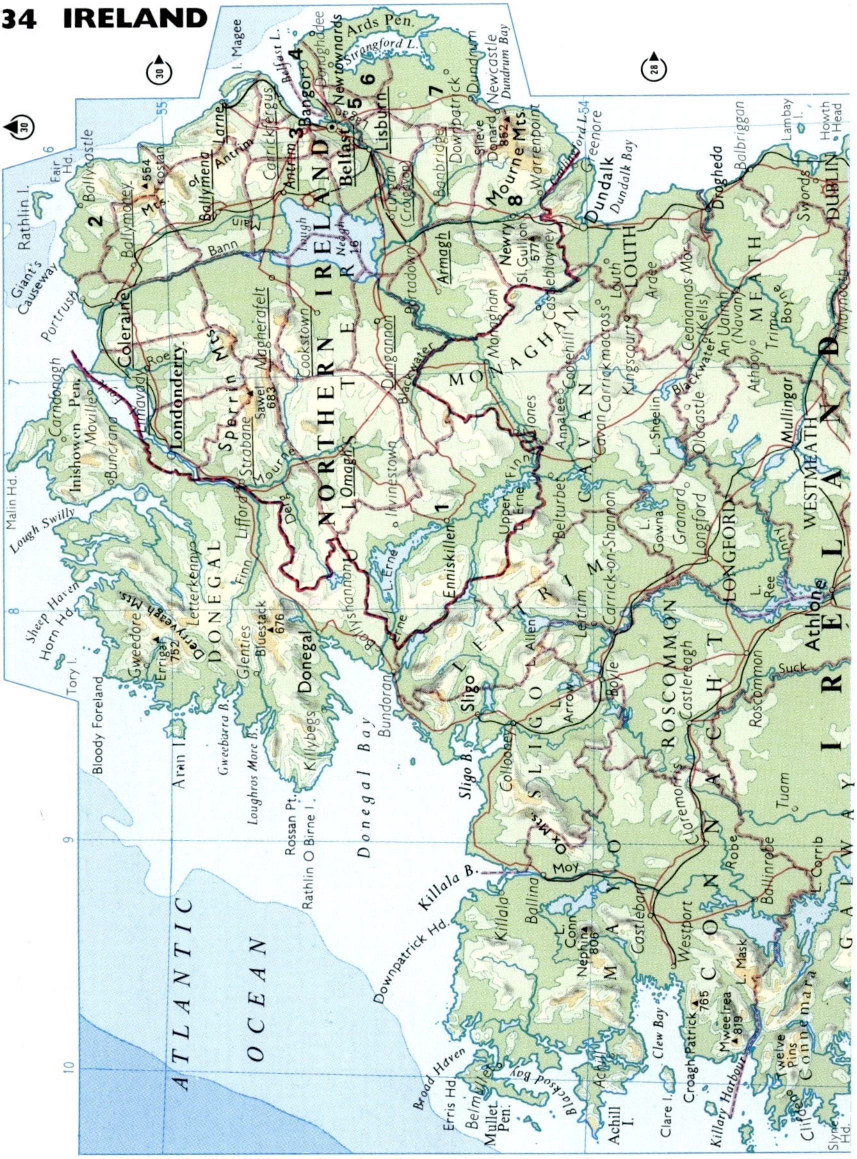
ATLANTIC
OCEAN
NORTHERN IRELAND
IRELAND
Donegal Bay
Rathlin I.
Giant's Causeway
Portrush
Coleraine
Ballymoney
Ballycastle
Fair Hd.
Ballymena
Larne
Antrim
Carrickfergus
Bangor
Newtownards
Ards Pen.
Strangford L.
Belfast
Lisburn
Lough Neagh
Armagh
Newry
Dundalk
Dundalk Bay
Mourne Mts.
Downpatrick
Newcastle
Dundrum Bay
Londonderry
Limavady
Sperrin Mts.
Strabane
Omagh
Cookstown
Dungannon
Magherafelt
Enniskillen
Lough Erne
Inishowen Pen.
Malin Hd.
Lough Swilly
Letterkenny
DONEGAL
Derryveagh Mts.
Errigal 752
Gweedore
Horn Hd.
Sheep Haven
Tory I.
Bloody Foreland
Aran I.
Gweebarra B.
Loughros More B.
Killybegs
Donegal
Bluestack 676
Glenties
Rossan Pt.
Rathlin O Birne I.
Bundoran
Ballyshannon
Sligo
Sligo B.
SLIGO
LEITRIM
Carrick-on-Shannon
Boyle
ROSCOMMON
Roscommon
Castlerea
CAVAN
Cavan
MONAGHAN
Monaghan
LOUTH
Drogheda
MEATH
DUBLIN
Mullingar
WESTMEATH
LONGFORD
Longford
Athlone
L. Ree
Killala B.
Killala
Ballina
Moy
Ox Mts.
MAYO
Castlebar
Westport
Clew Bay
Croagh Patrick 765
Mweelrea 819
Killary Harbour
L. Mask
L. Corrib
Tuam
Connemara
Twelve Pins
Clifden
Slyne Hd.
Achill I.
Clare I.
Blacksod Bay
Broad Haven
Belmullet
Erris Hd.
Mullet Pen.
Downpatrick Hd.
Nephin 806
L. Conn
CONNACHT
GALWAY
LEINSTER

1 : 2 000 000

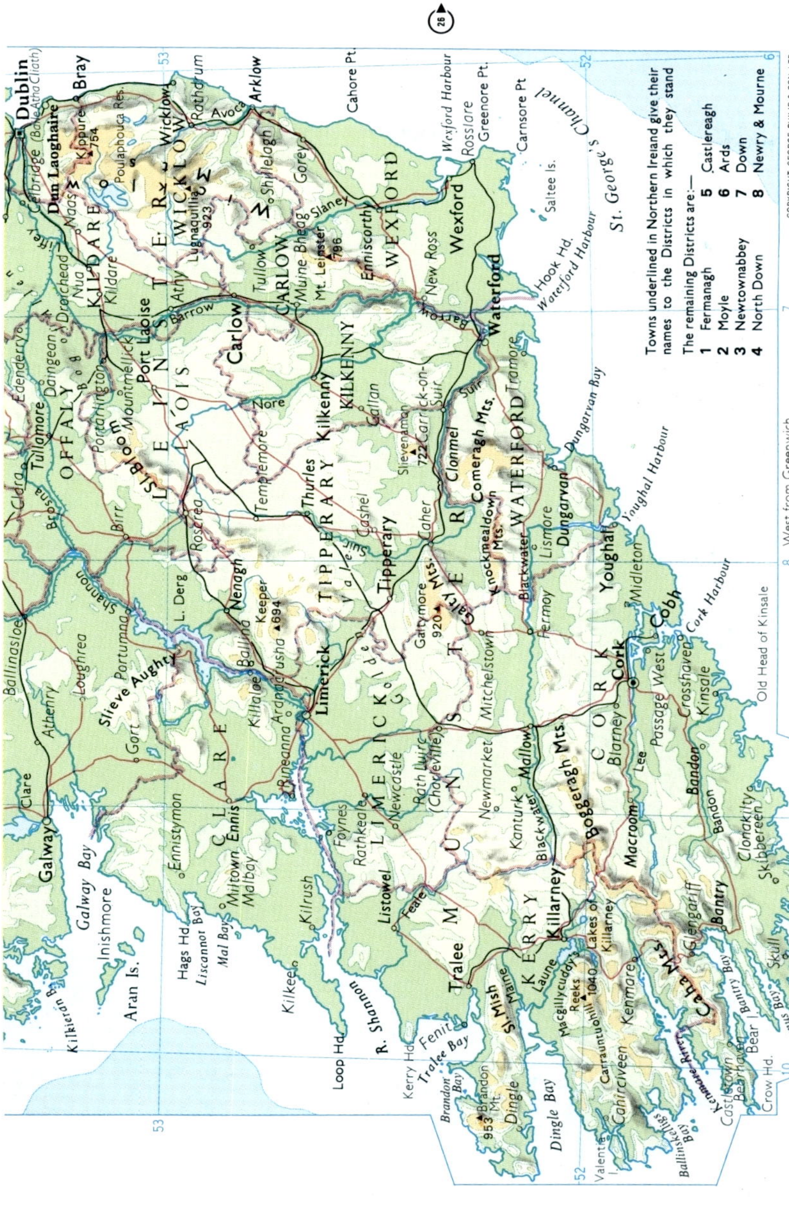
26
Dublin
Dun Laoghaire
Bray
Kippure 754
Poulaphouca Res.
Wicklow
Rathdrum
Avoca
Arklow
Cahore Pt.
Wexford Harbour
Rosslare
Greenore Pt.
Carnsore Pt
St. George's Channel
Saltee Is.
Hook Hd.
Waterford Harbour
Wexford
New Ross
Gorey
Shillelagh
Lugnaquilla 923
WICKLOW
KILDARE
Naas
Kildare
Droichead Nua
Liffey
Slaney
Enniscorthy
Mt. Leinster 796
WEXFORD
CARLOW
Muine Bheag
Tullow
Athy
Carlow
Barrow
Port Laoise
Portarlington
Mountmellick
LAOIS
L E I N S T E R
OFFALY
Tullamore
Daingean
Edenderry
Clara
Brosna
Birr
Sl. Bloom
Roscrea
Templemore
Thurles
Nore
Kilkenny
KILKENNY
Callan
Carrick-on-Suir
Slievenamon 722
Clonmel
Suir
Waterford
Tramore
Comeragh Mts.
WATERFORD
Dungarvan
Dungarvan Bay
Youghal Harbour
Youghal
Lismore
Knockmealdown Mts.
Blackwater
Fermoy
Midleton
Cobh
Cork Harbour
Cork
Passage West
Crosshaven
Kinsale
Old Head of Kinsale
Bandon
Clonakilty
Skibbereen
Baltimore
C. Clear
Skull
Mizen Hd.
Dunmanus Bay
Bantry Bay
Bantry
Glengarriff
Bear I.
Castletown Bearhaven
Crow Hd.
Caha Mts.
Kenmare
Kenmare River
Ballinskelligs Bay
Cahirciveen
Valentia I.
Carrauntuohill 1040
Macgillycuddy's Reeks
Lakes of Killarney
Killarney
Laune
Dingle Bay
Dingle
Brandon Mt. 953
Brandon Bay
Sl. Mish
Maine
Tralee
Tralee Bay
Fenit
Kerry Hd.
KERRY
Listowel
Feale
R. Shannon
Loop Hd.
Kilkee
Kilrush
Mal Bay
Miltown Malbay
Liscannor Bay
Hags Hd.
Ennistymon
Ennis
CLARE
Aran Is.
Inishmore
Kilkieran B.
Galway Bay
Galway
Clare
Athenry
Gort
Slieve Aughty
Loughrea
Ballinasloe
Portumna
Shannon
L. Derg
Killaloe
Ballina
Keeper 694
Arranacrusha
Limerick
Rineanna
Foynes
Rathkeale
Newcastle
LIMERICK
Golden Vale
Rath Luirc (Charleville)
Galtymore 920
Galty Mts.
Mitchelstown
Tipperary
TIPPERARY
Cashel
Caher
Nenagh
MUNSTER
Newmarket
Kanturk
Mallow
Boggeragh Mts.
Blarney
CORK
Lee
Macroom
53
52
6
7
8
9
10
West from Greenwich
Towns underlined in Northern Ireland give their names to the Districts in which they stand
The remaining Districts are:—
1 Fermanagh
2 Moyle
3 Newtownabbey
4 North Down
5 Castlereagh
6 Ards
7 Down
8 Newry & Mourne
COPYRIGHT. GEORGE PHILIP & SON. LTD

21
51
ENGLISH CHANNEL
Channel Is. (Br.)
Alderney
Guernsey
St. Peter Port
Jersey
St. Helier
Cap de la Hague
Pointe de Barfleur
Cherbourg
Valognes
Carentan
Bayeux
Caen
St-Lô
Cap Gris-Nez
Boulogne-sur-Mer
Outreau
Étaples
Berck-Plage
Le Tréport
50
Dieppe
Neufchâtel-en-Bray
Fécamp
Bolbec
Le Havre
Deauville
Trouville
Rouen
Elbeuf
Louviers
Seine
Vernon
Lisieux
Bernay
Evreux
Mantes-la-Jolie
Dreux
NORMANDIE
Granville
Vire
Falaise
Flers
Argentan
Avranches
St-Malo
St-Servan-sur-Mer
Lannion
Guingamp
Morlaix
St-Brieuc
Dinan
Ile d'Ouessant
Brest
Landerneau
BRETAGNE
391
Crozon
Châteaulin
Douarnenez
326
Pointe du Raz
48
Quimper
Loudéac
Pontivy
Rennes
Vitré
Laval
Fougères
MAINE
417
Alençon
PERCHE
Verneuil-sur-Avre
Chartres
Nogent-le-Rotrou
BEAUCE
Châteaudun
ORL
Le Mans
Concarneau
Pointe de Penmarch
Quimperlé
Hennebont
Ploërmel
Lorient
Auray
Vannes
Redon
Vilaine
Ile de Groix
Belle-Ile
St-Nazaire
La Baule
Châteaubriant
Sarthe
La Flèche
Vendôme
Château-Renault
Loire
Blois
Angers
ANJOU
TOURAINE
Amboise
Tours
Cher
Nantes
Saumur
Chinon
Vienne
Indre
Cholet
Ile de Noirmoutier
Ile d'Yeu
Les Herbiers
Bressuire
Creuse
Châtellerault
Château
FRA
POITOU
Chantonnay
Parthenay
La Roche-sur-Yon
Fontenay-le-Comte
Poitiers
Le Blanc
Argenton-sur-Creuse
Les-Sables d'Olonne
Ile de Ré
Niort
AUNIS
46
La Rochelle
MAR
Bellac
Confolens
Rochefort
Ile d'Oleron
Saintes
ANGOUMOIS
St-Junien
Limoges
Royan
Cognac
Angoulême
SAINTONGE
LIMOUSIN
Pointe de Grave
Le Verdon-sur-Mer
Gironde
St-Yrieix-la-Perche
Bay of Biscay
Dronne
Ribérac
Périgueux
Pauillac
Brive-la-Gaillar
Médoc
Coutras
Libourne
Dordogne
Bordeaux
Bergerac
Gourdon
Cap Ferret
Arcachon
La Teste
GUYENNE
Langon
Garonne
Marmande
Lot
Cahors
Tonneins
Villeneuve-sur-Lot
Landes
Mimizan
Agen
Moissac
Aveyron
Nérac
Morcenx
Mont-de-Marsan
Castelsarrasin
Montauban
Tarn
Castets
GASCOGNE
Adour
Dax
Auch
Toulous
Orthez
BEARN
Muret
Biarritz
Bayonne
St-Jean-de-Luz
Hendaye
Mourenx-Ville-Nouvelle
Pau
Tarbes
Lannemezan
Pamiers
Oloron Ste-Marie
Lourdes
Bagnères de Bigorre
St-Gaudens
Foix
FOIX
C. Corse
Bastia
Calvi
Mt. Cinto
2710
Haute-Corse
Mte. Rotondo
2625
Corse
42
Ajaccio
Corse du Sud
Porto Vecchio
Bonifacio
Bouches de Bonifacio
44
Santander
Santoña
Torrelavega
Guecho
Portugalete
Sestao
San Sebastián
Bilbao
Guernica
Eibar
Irún
Durango
Tolosa
Reinosa
SPAIN
PYRENEES
2504
3298
3355
Mt Perdido
Pic d'Aneto
3404
Maladeta
ANDORRA
Andorra la Vella
Jaca
West from Greenwich
1 : 5 000 000

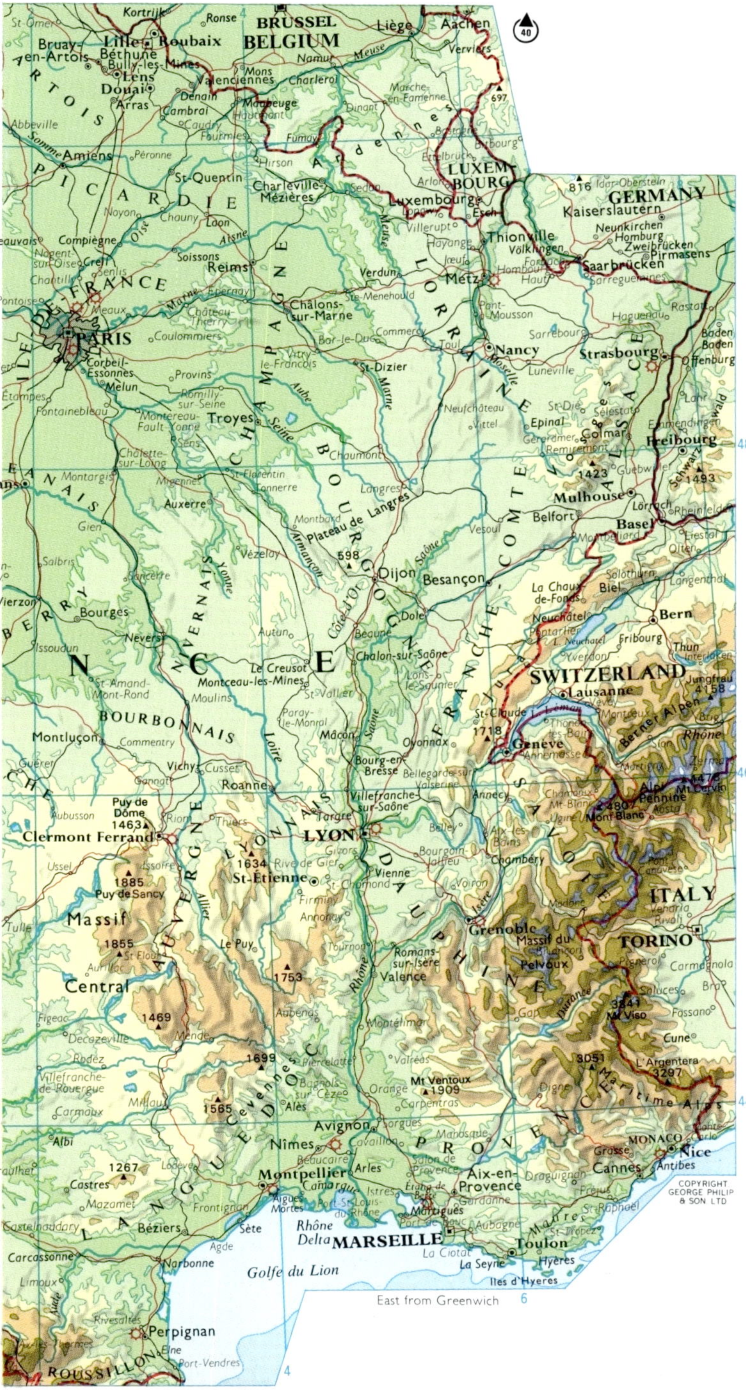
BRUSSEL
BELGIUM
Kortrijk
Ronse
Liège
Aachen
St-Omer
Lille
Roubaix
Bruay-en-Artois
Béthune
Bully-les-Mines
Lens
Douai
Arras
Namur
Meuse
Mons
Charleroi
Valenciennes
Denain
Cambrai
Maubeuge
Verviers
Marche-en-Famenne
Dinant
Ardennes
ARTOIS
Abbeville
Somme
Amiens
Péronne
St-Quentin
Hirson
Charleville-Mézières
Sedan
LUXEMBOURG
Luxembourg
Esch
Arlon
Bitburg
Idar-Oberstein
816
GERMANY
Kaiserslautern
Neunkirchen
Homburg
Zweibrücken
Pirmasens
Saarbrücken
Völklingen
Sarreguemines
Thionville
Villerupt
Hayange
Metz
PICARDIE
Noyon
Chauny
Laon
Aisne
Oise
Beauvais
Compiègne
Nogent-sur-Oise
Creil
Senlis
Chantilly
Soissons
Reims
Verdun
LORRAINE
Pont-à-Mousson
ILE DE FRANCE
Pontoise
Meaux
Marne
Epernay
Château-Thierry
Châlons-sur-Marne
Ste-Menehould
Commercy
Bar-le-Duc
Toul
Nancy
Haguenau
Rastatt
Sarrebourg
Strasbourg
Baden-Baden
Offenburg
PARIS
Corbeil-Essonnes
Melun
Coulommiers
Provins
Vitry-le-François
St-Dizier
Lunéville
Moselle
ALSACE
Étampes
Fontainebleau
Romilly-sur-Seine
Montereau-Fault-Yonne
Troyes
Sens
Aube
Seine
CHAMPAGNE
Neufchâteau
Vittel
Epinal
St-Dié
Sélestat
Colmar
Gérardmer
Remiremont
Emmendingen
Freiburg
Schwarzwald
1423
1493
48
Orléans
Montargis
Châlette-sur-Loing
Migennes
St-Florentin
Tonnerre
Chaumont
Langres
BOURGOGNE
Plateau de Langres
Auxerre
Gien
Montbard
Vesoul
Belfort
Mulhouse
Guebwiller
Lörrach
Rheinfelden
Basel
Montbéliard
Liestal
Olten
Solothurn
Langenthal
Biel
Salbris
Vézelay
598
Dijon
Besançon
Saône
Armançon
Yonne
NIVERNAIS
FRANCHE-COMTÉ
La Chaux-de-Fonds
Neuchâtel
Bern
Vierzon
BERRY
Bourges
Sancerre
Nevers
Autun
Côte d'Or
Dole
Beaune
Pontarlier
L. Neuchâtel
Yverdon
Fribourg
Thun
Interlaken
Issoudun
Chalon-sur-Saône
Le Creusot
Montceau-les-Mines
Lons-le-Saunier
FRANCE
SWITZERLAND
Lausanne
Jungfrau
4158
St-Amand-Mont-Rond
Moulins
Paray-le-Monial
St-Vallier
BOURBONNAIS
Mâcon
Oyonnax
Jura
St-Claude
1718
Genève
Léman
Vevey
Montreux
Thonon-les-Bains
Berner Alpen
Rhône
Montluçon
Commentry
Vichy
Cusset
Roanne
Loire
Bourg-en-Bresse
Bellegarde-sur-Valserine
Annecy
Annemasse
Sion
Zermatt
Alpi Pennine
Mt Cervin
4478
46
Guéret
Aubusson
Puy de Dôme
1463
Clermont Ferrand
Riom
Thiers
LYONNAIS
Tarare
Villefranche-sur-Saône
LYON
Givors
Rive de Gier
1634
St-Étienne
St-Chamond
Vienne
Bourgoin-Jallieu
Chambéry
Aix-les-Bains
Belley
Chamonix-Mt-Blanc
Ugine
Mont Blanc
4807
Aosta
SAVOIE
Ussel
Issoire
1885
Puy de Sancy
AUVERGNE
Allier
Firminy
Annonay
Voiron
Isère
Grenoble
DAUPHINÉ
ITALY
Venaria
Rivoli
TORINO
Tulle
Massif
Central
1855
Plomb du Cantal
Aurillac
Le Puy
Tournon
1753
Romans-sur-Isère
Valence
Rhône
Massif du Pelvoux
Briançon
Pinerolo
Carmagnola
Bra
Saluzzo
Figeac
Decazeville
1469
Mende
Aubenas
Montélimar
Gap
Durance
3841
Mt Viso
Fossano
Cuneo
Rodez
1699
Pierrelatte
Valréas
Mt Ventoux
1909
3051
L'Argentera
3297
Villefranche-de-Rouergue
Millau
Cévennes
1565
Bagnols-sur-Cèze
Alès
Orange
Carpentras
Digne
Maritime Alps
44
Carmaux
Albi
Avignon
Sorgues
Cavaillon
Manosque
PROVENCE
Nîmes
Beaucaire
Arles
Salon-de-Provence
MONACO
Monte Carlo
Nice
Antibes
Grasse
Cannes
Graulhet
1267
Castres
Lodève
LANGUEDOC
Montpellier
Camargue
Istres
Aix-en-Provence
Draguignan
Fréjus
St-Raphaël
Mazamet
Frontignan
Aigues-Mortes
Port-St-Louis-du-Rhône
Étang de Berre
Gardanne
Martigues
Aubagne
Maures
St-Tropez
Castelnaudary
Béziers
Sète
Agde
Rhône Delta
MARSEILLE
La Ciotat
Toulon
La Seyne
Hyères
Iles d'Hyeres
Carcassonne
Narbonne
Golfe du Lion
Limoux
Aude
Rivesaltes
Perpignan
Elne
Port-Vendres
ROUSSILLON
East from Greenwich
4
6
COPYRIGHT GEORGE PHILIP & SON LTD

40
42
44
46

NORTHERN FRANCE

40

25

ENGLAND
ENGLISH CHANNEL
Str. of Dover
BELGIUM
Flandre
Artois
Picardie
Pays de Caux
Pays de Bray
Vermandois
Soissonnais
Santerre
Vimeu
Marquenterre
Ponthieu
Cambrésis
Collines de l'Artois
Boulonnais
Roumois
Plaine de la Flandre
Flandre Maritime
Hastings
Eastbourne
Bexhill
Battle
Rye
Hythe
Folkestone
New Romney
Dungeness
Calais
Boulogne-sur-Mer
Dunkerque
Malo-les-Bains
Grande-Synthe
Gravelines
St.-Omer
Hazebrouck
Armentières
LILLE
ROUBAIX
Tourcoing
Mouscron
Courtrai
Tournai
Douai
Lens
Béthune
Arras
Cambrai
Valenciennes
Denain
Maubeuge
Mons
Charleroi
BRUSSEL
Malines
GAND
Alost
Renaix
Ath
St.-Quentin
AMIENS
Abbeville
Dieppe
Le Tréport
Fécamp
Yvetot
ROUEN
LE HAVRE
Beauvais
Compiègne
Noyon
Laon
Montdidier
Péronne
Albert
Doullens
Hesdin
Montreuil
Étaples
Berck-Plage
Le Touquet-Paris-Plage
St.-Valery-sur-Somme
Cayeux-sur-Mer
Baie de la Somme
Neufchâtel-en-Bray
Forges-les-Eaux
Gournay-en-Bray
Aumale
Bolbec
Lillebonne
Honfleur
Trouville
Sotteville-lès-Rouen
Seine
Somme
Oise

1 : 2 000 000

42

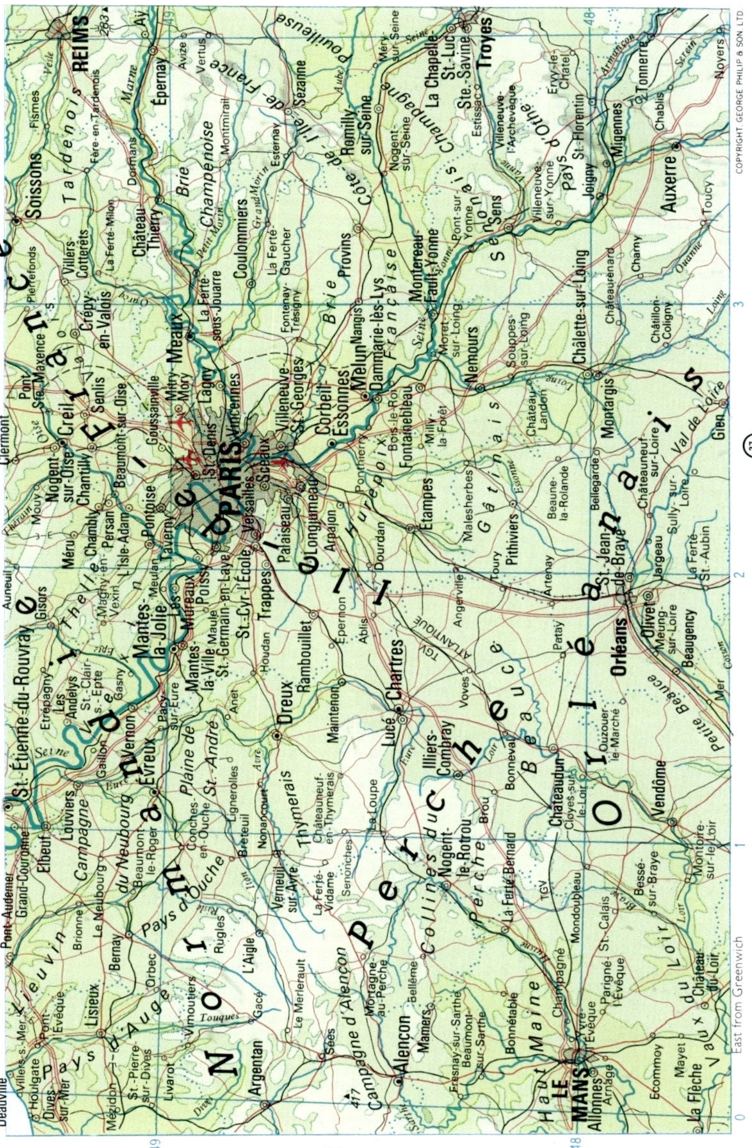
Normandie
Île-de-France
Perche
Orléanais
Champagne
PARIS
REIMS
Troyes
Le Mans
Orléans
Chartres
Alençon
Évreux
Soissons
Épernay
Meaux
Melun
Fontainebleau
Étampes
Dreux
Versailles
St.-Denis
Vincennes
Pontoise
Senlis
Creil
Chantilly
Beauvais
Provins
Coulommiers
Château-Thierry
Sézanne
Romilly-sur-Seine
Nogent-sur-Seine
Sens
Auxerre
Joigny
Montargis
Gien
Pithiviers
Nemours
Montereau-Fault-Yonne
Rambouillet
Mantes-la-Jolie
Vernon
Lisieux
Argentan
L'Aigle
Bernay
Elbeuf
Louviers
Vendôme
Châteaudun
Nogent-le-Rotrou
La Ferté-Bernard
Beaugency
Deauville
Beauce
Gâtinais
Hurepoix
Brie
Vexin
Pays d'Auge
Pays d'Ouche
Campagne d'Alençon
Seine
Marne
Loire
Yonne
Loir
Eure
East from Greenwich
COPYRIGHT GEORGE PHILIP & SON LTD.

36

37

WESTFRIESCHE
Terschelling
Vlieland
Texel
Den Burgo
Wadden
Den Helder
Den Oever
Staveren
Middenmeer
IJssel
NOORD HOLLAND
NORTH SEA
Bergen-Binnen
Enkhuizen
Alkmaar
Hoorn
Heiloo
Castricum
Wormerveer
Purmerend
Edam
Volendam
Beverwijk
IJmuiden
Velsen
Zaanstad
Marken
Haarlem
AMSTERDAM
Zandvoort
Heemstede
Amstelveen
Weesp
Huizen
Hillegom
Aalsmeer
Bussum
Laren
Noordwijk-aan-Zee
Lisse
Hilversum
Baarn
Katwijk-aan-Zee
Wassenaar
Leiden
Soest
Oude
Scheveningen
Alphen
UTRECHT
s'GRAVENHAGE
(The Hague)
Voorburg
Rijn
Utrecht
Zeist
Waddinxveen
Delft
Rijswijk
Gouda
IJsselstein
Hoek van Holland
Europoort
Naaldwijk
Lek
Maassluis
ROTTERDAM
Vlaardingen
Schiedam
Leerdam
Tiel
Hellevoetsluis
Sliedrecht
Geldermalsen
Goeree
ZUID HOLLAND
Gorinchem
Ouddorp
Overflakkee
Dordrecht
Hardinxveld
Brouwershaven
Middelharnis
Waalwijk
Schouwen
Made
Zierikzee
NE
Noord Beveland
's Hertogenbosch
Oosterschelde
NOORD BRABANT
Dongen
Vught
Walcheren
Oosterhout
Oudenbosch
Breda
Boxtel
Middelburg
Goes
Bergen-op Zoom
Roosendaal
Tilburg
Oisterwijk
Vlissingen
(Flushing)
ZEELAND
Goirle
Westerschelde
Essen
Baarle Nassau
Blankenberge
Zeebrugge
Heist
Knokke
Oostende
(Ostend)
Kalmthout
Rijkevorsel
Terneuzen
Kapellen
Brasschaat
Turnhout
Brugge
(Bruges)
Hulst
ANTWERPEN
Arendonk
Maldegem
Merksem
Schoten
Eeklo
Beveren
Antwerpen
Lommel
Zelzate
Deurne
Mol
Nieuwpoort
Eernegem
OOST-
St-Niklaas
Hoboken
Geel
Leopoldsburg
Veurne
Torhout
Schelde
Lier
Herentals
Lokeren
Berlaar
Diksmuide
WEST
St-Amandsberg
Boom
Duffel
Nethe
(Nete)
Tessenderlo
Ruiselede
Gent (Gand)
Ledeberg
Willebroek
Lo
Hoogledge
Tielt
B
E
Mechelen
L
G
I
Poperinge
Roeselare
Deinze
Wetteren
Lebbeke
Aarschot
Diest
VLAANDEREN
Aalst
Demer
Passendale
Ingelmunster
Asse
Vilvoorde
Hasselt
Izegem
Evere
Kessel-Lo
Ieper
Harelbeke
Zottegem
Jette
Diepenbeek
Menen
Kortrijk
Oudenaarde
Ninove
BRUSSEL
(Bruxelles)
Leuven
53
52
51
3
4
5
East from Greenwich
38

1 : 2 000 000

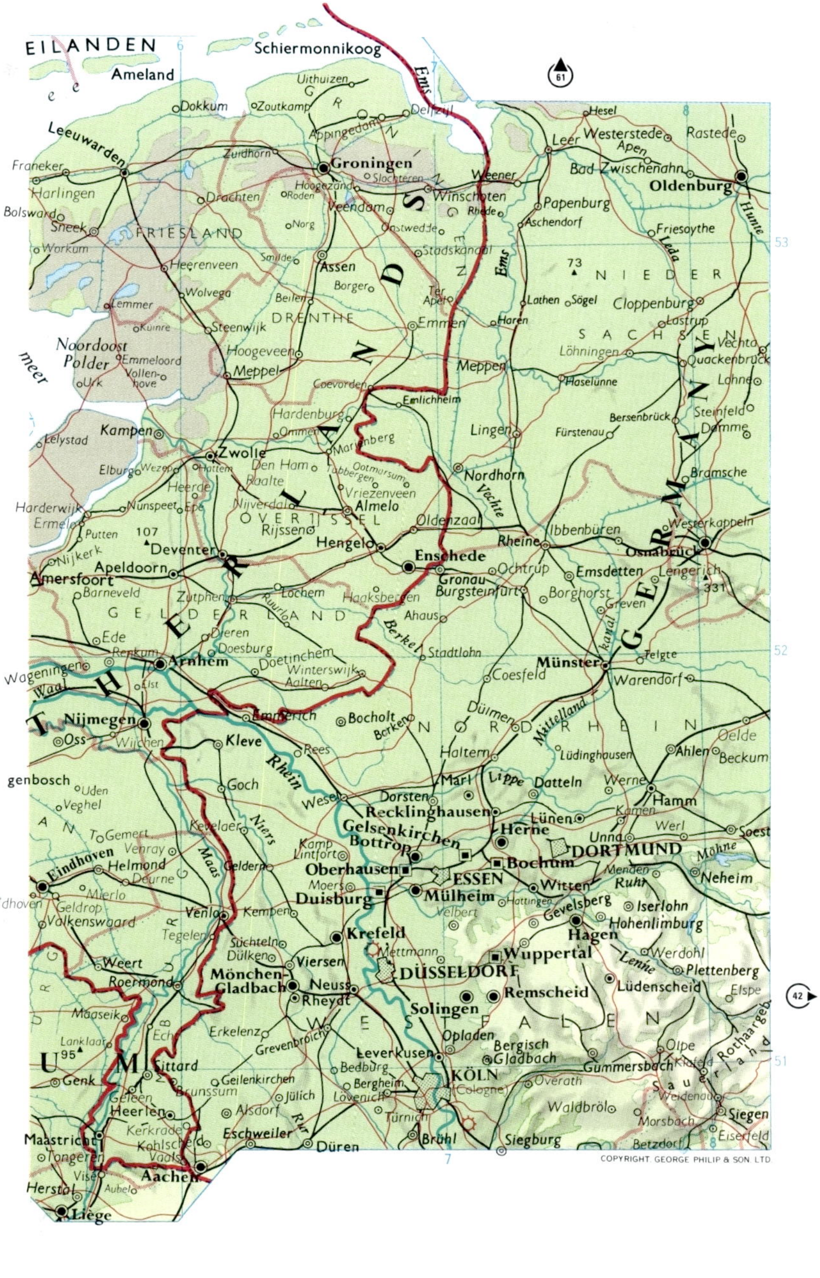
EILANDEN
Schiermonnikoog
Ameland
Ems
61
Uithuizen
Dokkum
Zoutkamp
Delfzijl
Leeuwarden
Appingedam
Hesel
Leer
Westerstede
Rastede
Apen
Zuidhorn
Groningen
Franeker
Weener
Bad Zwischenahn
Oldenburg
Harlingen
Hoogezand
Slochteren
Winschoten
Drachten
Roden
Veendam
Papenburg
Bolsward
Rhede
Aschendorf
Hunte
Sneek
FRIESLAND
Norg
Onstwedde
Friesoythe
Workum
Stadskanaal
53
Leda
Smilde
Heerenveen
Assen
Ems
73
NIEDER
Borger
Wolvega
Ter Apel
Beilen
Lathen
Sögel
Cloppenburg
Lemmer
DRENTHE
Emmen
Haren
Lastrup
Kuinre
Steenwijk
SACHSEN
Noordoost Polder
Emmeloord
Hoogeveen
Löhningen
Vechta
meer
Vollenhove
Meppel
Meppen
Quackenbrück
Urk
Coevorden
Haselünne
Lohne
Emlichheim
Hardenburg
Bersenbrück
Steinfeld
Lelystad
Kampen
Ommen
Lingen
Fürstenau
Damme
Mariënberg
Zwolle
Elburg
Wezep
Hattem
Den Ham
Ootmarsum
Tubbergen
Nordhorn
Bramsche
Heerde
Raalte
Vriezenveen
Vechte
Harderwijk
Nunspeet
Epe
Nijverdal
Almelo
Ermelo
OVERIJSSEL
Oldenzaal
Westerkappeln
Putten
107
Rijssen
Ibbenbüren
Hengelo
Rheine
Osnabrück
Nijkerk
Deventer
Enschede
Apeldoorn
Ochtrup
Emsdetten
Lengerich
Amersfoort
Gronau
Burgsteinfurt
331
Barneveld
Zutphen
Lochem
Haaksbergen
Borghorst
Greven
GELDERLAND
Ruurlo
Ahaus
Berkel
Dieren
Ede
Doesburg
Stadtlohn
Renkum
Doetinchem
Telgte
Arnhem
Münster
52
Wageningen
Winterswijk
Coesfeld
Waal
Elst
Aalten
Warendorf
Dülmen
Nijmegen
Emmerich
Bocholt
Oss
Borken
NORDRHEIN
Mittelland
Oelde
Wijchen
Kleve
Rees
Haltern
Lüdinghausen
Ahlen
Beckum
Rhein
Goch
Marl
Lippe
Datteln
Werne
genbosch
Uden
Veghel
Wesel
Dorsten
Hamm
Recklinghausen
Lünen
Kamen
Gelsenkirchen
Herne
Werl
Gemert
Kevelaer
Kamp Lintfort
Bottrop
Unna
Soest
Venray
Niers
DORTMUND
Möhne
Eindhoven
Helmond
Oberhausen
ESSEN
Bochum
Menden
Deurne
Maas
Geldern
Moers
Witten
Ruhr
Neheim
Mierlo
Duisburg
Mülheim
Hattingen
Geldrop
Velbert
Gevelsberg
Iserlohn
Valkenswaard
Venlo
Kempen
Hagen
Hohenlimburg
Tegelen
Krefeld
Süchteln
Dülken
Mettmann
Wuppertal
Werdohl
Weert
Viersen
Lenne
Plettenberg
Mönchen-Gladbach
DÜSSELDORF
Roermond
Neuss
Lüdenscheid
Elspe
42
Rheydt
Remscheid
Maaseik
Solingen
Echt
WESTFALEN
Erkelenz
Opladen
Lanklaar
95
Grevenbroich
Bergisch Gladbach
Olpe
Sittard
Leverkusen
51
Genk
Bedburg
KÖLN
Gummersbach
Kirchen
Geilenkirchen
(Cologne)
Overath
Sauerland
Brunssum
Jülich
Bergheim
Rothaargeb
Geleen
Lövenich
Weidenau
Heerlen
Alsdorf
Waldbröl
Kerkrade
Rur
Tüirnich
Morsbach
Siegen
Maastricht
Kohlscheid
Eschweiler
Brühl
Betzdorf
Eiserfeld
Tongeren
Vaals
Düren
Siegburg
7
8
Visé
Aachen
Herstal
Aubel
Liège

NORTH SEA
NETHERLANDS
BELGIUM
LUX.
FRANCE
Helgoland
Ost-friesische Inseln
Deutsche Bucht
Terschelling
Ameland
Schiermonnikoog
Borkum
Norderney
Wangerooge
Texel
Den Helder
Leeuwarden
Groningen
Wilhelmshaven
Emden
Cuxhaven
Bremerhaven
Oldenburg
Bremen
Alkmaar
Haarlem
Amsterdam
IJsselmeer
's-Gravenhage
(The Hague)
Hoek van Holland
Leiden
Hilversum
Utrecht
Rotterdam
Dordrecht
Schiedam
Gouda
Apeldoorn
Arnhem
Nijmegen
Enschede
Deventer
Zwolle
Kampen
Meppel
Assen
Sneek
Hoorn
Zaandam
Almelo
Breda
Tilburg
Eindhoven
's-Hertogenbosch
Vlissingen
Zeebrugge
Oostende
Brugge
Antwerpen
Gent (Gand)
Schelde
Kortrijk
Leie
Aalst
Mechelen
Brussel
(Bruxelles)
Leuven
Maastricht
Liège
Tourcoing
Roubaix
Lille
Tournai
Mons
Namur
Charleroi
Meuse
Verviers
Eupen
Malmedy
Aachen
Heerlen
Turnhout
Mönchengladbach
Krefeld
Düsseldorf
Oberhausen
Duisburg
Mülheim
Gelsenkirchen
Essen
Bochum
Dortmund
Hamm
Hagen
Wuppertal
Remscheid
Köln
(Cologne)
Bonn
Bocholt
Lippe
Münster
NORDRHEIN-WESTFALEN
Teutoburger Wald
Osnabrück
Rheine
Lingen
Ems
NIEDERSACHSEN
Verden
Aller
Nienburg
Weser
Minden
Hannover
Leine
Herford
Bielefeld
Hameln
Detmold
Paderborn
Göttingen
Kassel
Münden
Fulda
Ruhr
Rothaargeb.
840
Eder
Siegen
Sieg
Marburg
Westerwald
Wetzlar
Giessen
Lahn
Limburg
Vogelsberg
772
950
Rhön
Koblenz
RHEINLAND
Eifel
Ardennes
Taunus
Frankfurt
Hanau
Wiesbaden
Mainz
Offenbach
Aschaffenburg
Spessart
Main
Würzburg
Darmstadt
Hunsrück
Mosel
Trier
PFALZ
Worms
Kaiserslautern
Ludwigshafen
Mannheim
SAARLAND
Neunkirchen
Saar
Saarbrücken
Speyer
Heidelberg
Neckar
Karlsruhe
Heilbronn
Pforzheim
BADEN-WÜRTTEMBERG
Ludwigsburg
Stuttgart
Esslingen
Baden-Baden
Hagueneau
Tübingen
Reutlingen
Ulm
Schwäbische Alb
Rottweil
Biberach
Iller
Schwarzwald
Strasbourg
Rhein (Rhine)
Freiburg
Colmar
ALSACE
Vosges
1424
(Danube)
Donau
Tuttlingen
Mulhouse
Belfort
Schaffhausen
Memmingen
Ravensburg
Friedrichshafen
Kempten
Konstanz
Bodensee
Basel
Winterthur
St. Gallen
Bregenz
VORARLBERG
Zürich
Aarau
Biel
Aare
Solothurn
Douai
Valenciennes
Cambrai
St. Quentin
Hirson
Charleville-Mézières
Sedan
Luxembourg
Longwy
Thionville
Laon
Aisne
Soissons
Reims
Château Thierry
Épernay
Châlons-sur-Marne
Vitry-le-François
Verdun
Metz
LORRAINE
CHAMPAGNE
Aube
St. Dizier
Bar-le-Duc
Toul
Nancy
Lunéville
Troyes
Seine
Marne
Chaumont
St. Dié
Épinal
Langres
Plateau de Langres
Avallon
Elbe
Brunsbüttelkoog
Glückstadt
SCHLES
Nord
GE
HESSEN
4
6
8
10
52
50
48
East from Greenwich
38
44

1 : 5 000 000

BALTIC SEA
POLAND
GERMANY
CZECH REPUBLIC
AUSTRIA
Flensburg
Schleswig
Kiel
Fehmarn
Puttgarden
Mecklenburger Bucht
Warnemünde
Neumünster
HOLSTEIN
Ostsee-Kanal
Lübeck
Altona
Hamburg
Harburg
Wismar
Rostock
Güstrow
Stralsund
Greifswald
Sassnitz
Rügen
Usedom
Świnoujście
Wolin
Oder Haff
Kołobrzeg
Koszalin
Darłowo
Słupsk
Szczecinek
Schwerin
Parchim
Lauenburg
Lüneburg
Lüneburger Heide
Elbe
Elde
Uelzen
Müritz See
Neu Brandenburg
Neustrelitz
Prenzlau
Szczecin (Stettin)
Goleniów
Dąbie
Stargard
Choszczno
Piła
Wittenberge
Havel
Neuruppin
Oranienburg
Eberswalde
Odra (Oder)
Celle
Stendal
Rathenow
Spandau
Charlottenburg
BERLIN
Potsdam
Brandenburg
Kostrzyn
Gorzów
Noteć (Netze)
Skwierzyna
Międzychód
Warta (Warthe)
Poznań
Hildesheim
Braunschweig
Salzgitter
Magdeburg
Luckenwalde
Spree
Frankfurt
Nowy Tomyśl
Świebodzin
Grodzisk
Kościan
Goslar
Halberstadt
Brocken
1142
Harz
Zerbst
Wittenberg
Dessau
Gubin
Zielona Góra
Cottbus
Forst
Bóbr
Leszno
Bernburg
Nordhausen
Halle
Mulde
Torgau
Spremberg
Żary
Żagań
Głogów
Lauchhammer
Nysa (Neisse)
Mühlhausen
Merseburg
Saale
Leipzig
Grossenhain
Naumburg
Bolesławiec
Silesia
Werra
Eisenach
Erfurt
Jena
Zeitz
Gotha
Weimar
Meissen
Bautzen
Görlitz
Legnica
Wrocław
Gera
Dresden
Chemnitz
(Karl-Marx-Stadt)
Glauchau
Zwickau
Liberec
Jelenia Góra
Świdnica
Thüringer Wald
Reichenbach
Usti nad Labem
Riesengebirge
1602
Śnieżka
Wałbrzych
Plauen
Teplice
Jablonec
Erzgebirge
Most
Litoměřice
Trutnov
Sudety
Coburg
Hof
Ohre
Chomutov
Mladá Boleslav
Kłodzko
Schweinfurt
Fichtelgebirge
Karlovy Vary
Hradec Králové
Cheb
Kladno
1051
Bayreuth
Praha (Prague)
Bamberg
Rhein-Donau
Beroun
Kolín
Labe (Elbe)
Pardubice
1492
Šumperk
Erlangen
Naab
Plzeň (Pilsen)
Příbram
Sázava
Vrchovina
Fürth
Nürnberg
Amberg
Ansbach
Fränkische Alb
Böhmerwald
Vltava
Havlíčkův Brod
Olomouc
Prostějov
BAYERN
Klatovy
Písek
Tábor
Českomoravská
Jihlava
Třebíč
Brno (Brünn)
1457
Regensburg
České Budějovice
Třeboň
Slavkov (Austerlitz)
Donauwörth
Deggendorf
Znojmo
Hodonín
Ingolstadt
1378
Gmünd
Isar
Morava
Augsburg
Landshut
Passau
Zwettl
Horn
Freising
Amper
Inn
Freistadt
Malé Karpaty
Lech
München (Munich)
OBER-
ÖSTERREICH
Ried
Wels
Linz
Urfahr
NIEDER-
ÖSTERREICH
Stockerau
Rosenheim
Steyr
Salzburg
Gmunden
Bad Ischl
Kufstein
12
14
16
54
52
50
48
61
58
59
45

42

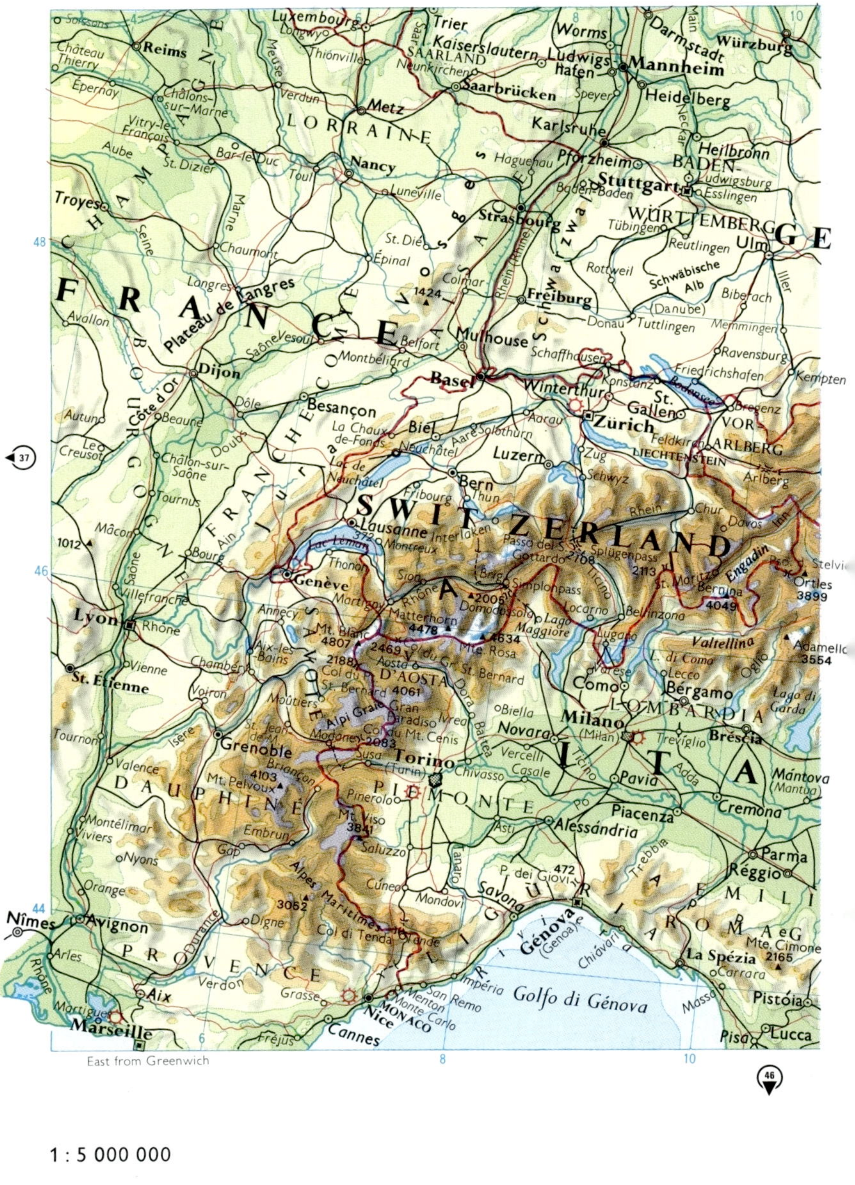

Luxembourg
Longwy
Trier
Worms
Darmstadt
Würzburg
Main
Reims
Château Thierry
Soissons
Thionville
Saar
SAARLAND
Kaiserslautern
Ludwigshafen
Mannheim
Neunkirchen
Épernay
Châlons-sur-Marne
Verdun
Meuse
Saarbrücken
Speyer
Heidelberg
Metz
LORRAINE
Karlsruhe
Neckar
Heilbronn
Vitry-le-François
Aube
St. Dizier
Bar-le-Duc
Toul
Nancy
Haguenau
Pforzheim
BADEN-
Stuttgart
Ludwigsburg
Esslingen
Baden-Baden
Troyes
CHAMPAGNE
Marne
Lunéville
Strasbourg
WÜRTTEMBERG
Tübingen
Seine
Chaumont
St. Dié
Épinal
Vosges
ALSACE
Schwarzwald
Reutlingen
Ulm
GE
Rottweil
Schwäbische Alb
Iller
Langres
Colmar
Rhein (Rhine)
1424
Freiburg
Biberach
FRANCE
Plateau de Langres
(Danube)
Donau
Tuttlingen
Memmingen
Avallon
Saône
Vesoul
Belfort
Mulhouse
Schaffhausen
Ravensburg
Montbéliard
Dijon
BOURGOGNE
Basel
Konstanz
Friedrichshafen
Bodensee
Kempten
Winterthur
St. Gallen
Bregenz
Côte d'Or
Dôle
Besançon
Aarau
Zürich
Autun
Beaune
La Chaux-de-Fonds
Biel
Solothurn
Aare
VORARLBERG
Feldkirch
LIECHTENSTEIN
Le Creusot
Doubs
Neuchâtel
Luzern
Zug
Chalon-sur-Saône
Lac de Neuchâtel
Jura
FRANCHE COMTÉ
Bern
Schwyz
Arlberg
Tournus
Fribourg
Thun
SWITZERLAND
Rhein
Chur
Davos
Inn
Mâcon
1012
Lausanne
Montreux
372
Lac Léman
Interlaken
Passo del S. Gottardo
2108
Splügenpass
2113
Engadin
Stelvio
Ain
Bourg
Thonon
Sion
St. Moritz
Ortles
3899
Genève
Rhône
Brig
2005
Simplonpass
Bernina
4049
Villefranche
Martigny
Ticino
Locarno
Bellinzona
Lyon
Rhône
Annecy
Matterhorn
4478
Domodossola
Lago Maggiore
Lugano
SAVOIE
Mt. Blanc
4807
Mte. Rosa
4634
Valtellina
Adamello
3554
Aix-les-Bains
2469
Col du Gr. St. Bernard
Vienne
Chambéry
2188
Col du Pt. St. Bernard
Aosta
Dora
L. di Como
Lecco
Oglio
St. Étienne
V. D'AOSTA
4061
Varese
Como
Bergamo
Voiron
Moûtiers
Alpi Graie
Gran Paradiso
Biella
LOMBARDIA
Lago di Garda
Ivrea
Baltea
Milano
(Milan)
St. Jean de M.
Tournon
Isère
Grenoble
Modane
Col du Mt. Cenis
2083
Novara
Vercelli
Treviglio
Brescia
Valence
Susa
Torino
(Turin)
Chivasso
Casale
Ticino
Adda
Pavia
Mántova
(Mantua)
DAUPHINÉ
Briançon
4103
Mt. Pelvoux
ITALIA
PIEMONTE
Pinerolo
Po
Piacenza
Cremona
Montélimar
Viviers
Mt. Viso
3841
Asti
Alessándria
Embrun
Saluzzo
Trebbia
Parma
Nyons
Gap
Tanaro
472
P. dei Giovi
Réggio
Orange
Cúneo
Mondovì
Savona
LIGURIA
EMILIA ROMAGNA
3052
Alpes Maritimes
Nîmes
Avignon
Durance
Digne
Col di Tenda
Génova
(Genoa)
Mte. Cimone
2165
Arles
PROVENCE
Chiávari
La Spézia
Carrara
Verdon
Riviera
Rhône
Aix
Grasse
Nice
Menton
San Remo
Impéria
Golfo di Génova
Massa
Pistóia
Martigues
MONACO
Monte Carlo
Marseille
Cannes
Fréjus
Pisa
Lucca
4
6
8
10
48
46
44
East from Greenwich

37

46

1 : 5 000 000

43

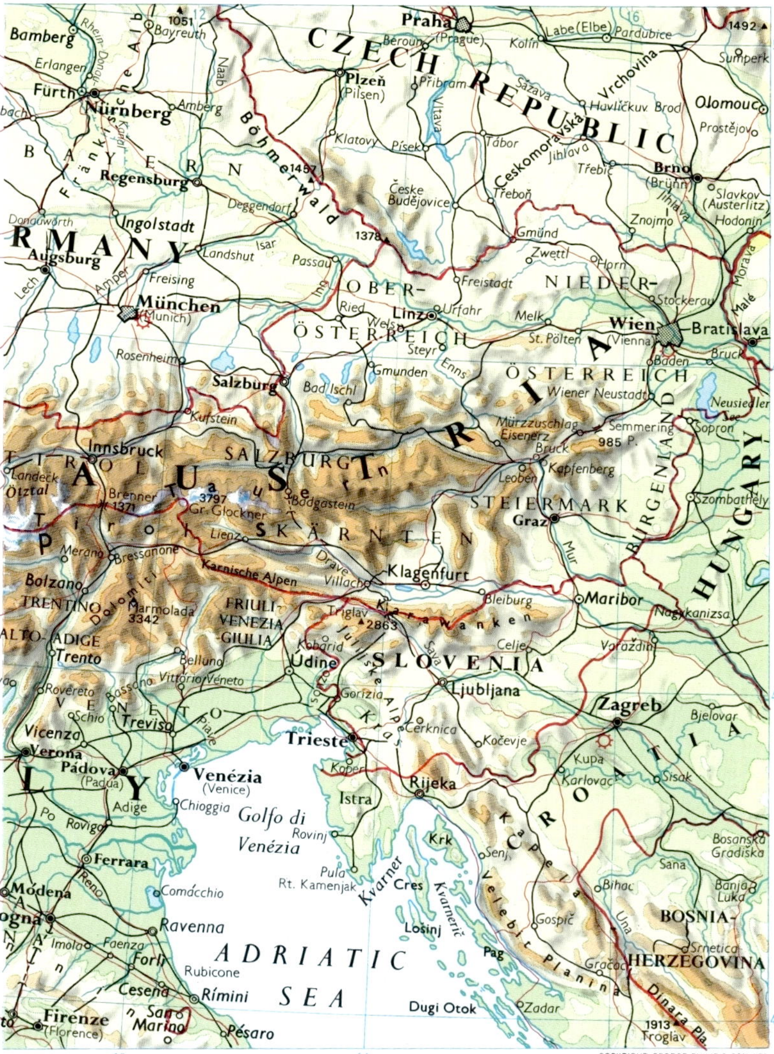
CZECH REPUBLIC
Praha
(Prague)
Beroun
Kolín
Labe (Elbe)
Pardubice
1492
Šumperk
Plzeň
(Pilsen)
Příbram
Sázava
Vrchovina
Havlíčkův Brod
Olomouc
Prostějov
Klatovy
Písek
Vltava
Tábor
Českomoravská
Jihlava
Třebíč
Brno
(Brünn)
Jihlava
Slavkov
(Austerlitz)
Hodonín
České Budějovice
Třeboň
Znojmo
Böhmerwald
1457
1378
Bamberg
1051
Bayreuth
Erlangen
Fürth
Nürnberg
Amberg
Ansbach
Naab
Fränkische Alb
BAYERN
Regensburg
Deggendorf
Donauwörth
Ingolstadt
GERMANY
Augsburg
Landshut
Isar
Passau
Lech
Amper
Freising
München
(Munich)
Inn
Rosenheim
Salzburg
Kufstein
Innsbruck
TIROL
Landeck
Ötztal
Brenner
1371
3797
Gr. Glockner
Badgastein
Lienz
Tauern
AUSTRIA
OBER-ÖSTERREICH
Ried
Wels
Linz
Urfahr
Steyr
Enns
Gmunden
Bad Ischl
Freistadt
Gmünd
Zwettl
Horn
NIEDER-ÖSTERREICH
Melk
St. Pölten
Stockerau
Wien
(Vienna)
Bratislava
Malé
Morava
Baden
Bruck
Wiener Neustadt
Neusiedler See
Sopron
Mürzzuschlag
Semmering
985 P.
Eisenerz
Bruck
Kapfenberg
Leoben
SALZBURG
STEIERMARK
Graz
Mur
KÄRNTEN
BURGENLAND
Szombathely
HUNGARY
Drave
Villach
Klagenfurt
Bleiburg
Karnische Alpen
Karawanken
Maribor
Nagykanizsa
Varaždin
Merano
Bressanone
Bolzano
Dolomiti
TRENTINO-ALTO-ADIGE
Marmolada
3342
FRIULI-VENEZIA-GIULIA
Trento
Belluno
Riva
Rovereto
Bassano
Vittorio Veneto
VENETO
Schio
Treviso
Piave
Vicenza
Verona
Pádova
(Padua)
Venézia
(Venice)
Chioggia
Adige
Po
Rovigo
Ferrara
Reno
Módena
Comácchio
Bologna
Ravenna
Imola
Faenza
Forlì
Cesena
Rubicone
Rímini
San Marino
Pésaro
Firenze
(Florence)
Prato
ITALY
Triglav
2863
Julijske Alpe
Kobarid
Údine
SLOVENIA
Sava
Celje
Ljubljana
Isonzo
Gorizia
Kras
Cerknica
Kočevje
Trieste
Koper
Istra
Rijeka
Zagreb
Bjelovar
Kupa
Karlovac
Sisak
CROATIA
Golfo di Venézia
Rovinj
Pula
Rt. Kamenjak
Kvarner
Krk
Cres
Kvarnerić
Lošinj
Senj
Kapela
Velebit Planina
Bihać
Gospić
Una
Sana
Bosanska Gradiška
Banja Luka
BOSNIA-HERZEGOVINA
Srnetica
Gračac
Pag
ADRIATIC SEA
Dugi Otok
Zadar
Dinara Pla.
1913
Troglav
50
48
46
44
12
14
16

59

52

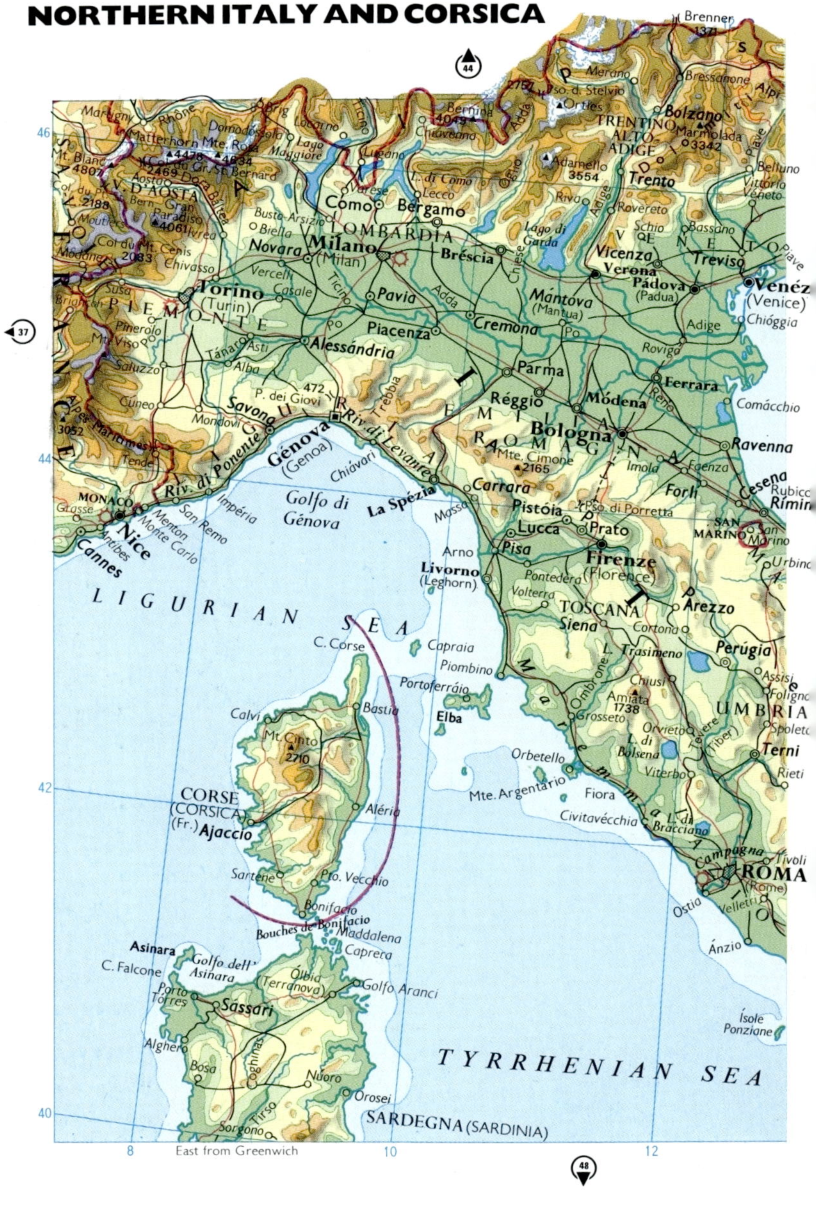
Brenner
1371
Merano
Bressanone
Bolzano
Pso. d. Stelvio
Ortles
Bernina
4049
Chiavenna
Adda
TRENTINO ALTO ADIGE
Marmolada
3342
Belluno
Vittorio Veneto
Adamello
3554
Trento
Riva
Rovereto
Schio
Bassano
Treviso
Piave
VENETO
Vicenza
Verona
Pádova
(Padua)
Venézia
(Venice)
Chióggia
Adige
Rovigo
Ferrara
Comácchio
Ravenna
Cesena
Rímini
SAN MARINO
Urbino
Martigny
Rhône
Domodóssola
Locarno
Lago Maggiore
Lugano
L. di Como
Lecco
Como
Bergamo
Varese
Busto Arsizio
Biella
LOMBARDIA
Lago di Garda
Brescia
Chiese
Novara
Milano
(Milan)
Matterhorn
Mte. Rosa
4478
4634
Mt. Blanc
4807
Col du Gr. St. Bernard
2469
Aosta
V. D'AOSTA
Dora Baltea
Gran Paradiso
4061
Ivrea
Col du Mt. Cenis
2083
Chivasso
Modane
Susa
Briançon
Vercelli
Casale
Ticino
Torino
(Turin)
PIEMONTE
Pavia
Mántova
(Mantua)
Cremona
Piacenza
Po
Pinerolo
Mt. Viso
Saluzzo
Tánaro
Asti
Alba
Alessándria
Parma
Réggio
Módena
Bologna
EMILIA ROMAGNA
Imola
Faenza
Forlì
Cuneo
Mondovì
P. dei Giovi
472
Trebbia
Savona
LIGURIA
Génova
(Genoa)
Riv. di Levante
Chiávari
Alpes Maritimes
3052
Tende
Riv. di Ponente
Mte. Cimone
2165
Carrara
Massa
La Spézia
Pistóia
Pso. di Porretta
MONACO
Grasse
Nice
Cannes
Antibes
Menton
Monte Carlo
San Remo
Impéria
Golfo di Génova
Lucca
Prato
Firenze
(Florence)
Arno
Pisa
Livorno
(Leghorn)
Pontedera
Volterra
TOSCANA
Siena
Arezzo
Cortona
L. Trasimeno
Perúgia
Assisi
Foligno
UMBRIA
Spoleto
Terni
Rieti
LIGURIAN SEA
C. Corse
Capraia
Piombino
Portoferráio
Elba
Bastia
Calvi
Mt. Cinto
2710
Chiusi
Amiata
1738
Ombrone
Grosseto
Maremma
Orvieto
Tevere
(Tiber)
L. di Bolsena
Viterbo
Orbetello
Mte. Argentario
Fiora
Civitavécchia
L. di Bracciano
CORSE
(CORSICA)
(Fr.)
Ajaccio
Aléria
Sartène
Pto. Vecchio
Bonifacio
Bouches de Bonifacio
Campagna
Tívoli
ROMA
(Rome)
LAZIO
Ostia
Velletri
Ánzio
Maddalena
Caprera
Asinara
Golfo dell' Asinara
C. Falcone
Porto Tórres
Ólbia
(Terranova)
Golfo Aranci
Sassari
Alghero
Coghinas
Bosa
Nuoro
Orosei
Tirso
Sorgono
SARDEGNA (SARDINIA)
Ísole Ponziane
TYRRHENIAN SEA
46
44
42
40
8
10
12
East from Greenwich
44
37
48

1 : 5 000 000

AUSTRIA
45
Drave
Villach
Carniche
Triglav
2863
FRIULI
VENEZIA
GIULIA
Kobarid
(Caporetto)
Klagenfurt
Bleiburg
Karawanken
Maribor
Nagykanizsa
Kaposvár
Kapos
Szekszárd
Drava
Varaždin
Celje
HUNGARY
Údine
Tagliamento
Ljubljana
Sava
Pécs
Mohács
Gorizia
Isonzo
SLOVENIA
Zagreb
46
Bjelovar
Drava
Cerknica
Kras
Trieste
Postojna
Kočevje
Kupa
Koper
CROATIA
Sisak
Osijek
Karlovac
Istra
Rijeka
(Fiume)
Sava
Novska
Golfo di
Venézia
Brod
Vinkovci
Rovinj
Krk
Kapela
Una
Bosanska
Gradiška
52
Pula
(Pola)
Rt. Kamenjak
Kvarner
Cres
Kvarnerić
Senj
Bihać
Banja Luka
Odžak
Bosna
Brčko
Lošinj
Gospič
Kremen
1591
Unac
Sana
Vrbas
&
Tešanj
Tuzla
ADRIATIC
Pag
Velebit Planina
Gračac
Srnetica
BOSNIA-
Travnik
Dugi Otok
Zadar
Dinara Planina
HERZEGOVINA
Pésaro
Fano
1913
Troglav
44
Sarajevo
Senigállia
Ancona
Šibenik
Dalmacija
Konjic
Loreto
Split
Macerata
Fabriano
Civitanova
MARCHE
Brač
Neretva
Mostar
Hvar
Monti
Vettore
2478
San Benedetto
Vis
Stolac
Ascoli Piceno
Korčula
Lastovo
Teramo
Gran Sasso
2914
Pescara
Dubrovnik
Trebinje
Chieti
L'Aquila
Salto
Palagruža
(Croatia)
Hercegnovi
ABRUZZI
Ortona
Lanciano
Mt. Amaro
2795
Vasto
SEA
Térmoli
1224
42
Sannicandro
MOLISE
S. Severo
Monte Gargano
1056
Monte S. Ángelo
Frosinone
Campobasso
G. di Manfredónia
Fóggia
Fondi
Cerignola
Barletta
Trani
Terracina
Gaeta
Benevento
Ofanto
Molfetta
Garigliano
Caserta
Andria
Corato
Bari
Volturno
Aversa
PUGLIA
Vesuvio
Avellino
Monopoli
1277
Spinazzola
Putignano
Íschia
Nocera
CAMPANIA
Matera
(Naples) Napoli
Torre Annunziata
Éboli
Potenza
Capri
Sorrento
Castellammare
Salerno
Sele
BASILICATA
Taranto
Brindisi
Francavilla
Lecce
14
16
49

46

CORSE (CORSICA)
Sartene
Pto. Vecchio
Bonifacio
Bouches de Bonifacio
Maddalena
Caprera
Asinara
C. Falcone
Golfo dell' Asinara
Porto Tórres
Sássari
Ólbia (Terranova)
Golfo Aranci
Alghero
Coghinas
Bosa
Nuoro
Orosei
Tirso
Sorgono
SARDEGNA (SARDINIA)
C. Mte. Santo
Mt. Gennargentu
1834
Arbatax
Golfo di Oristano
Oristano
Terralba
Ierzu
Samassi
Iglesias
Cágliari
Portoscuso
Carbonia
G. di Palmas
Golfo di Cágliari
C. Carbonara
C. Spartivento
3719
TYRRHENIAN SEA
Campagna
Tivoli
ROMA (Rome)
Velletri
Ostia
Ánzio
Latina
Sabáudia
Terracina
Ísole Ponziane
Ustica (It.)
MEDITERRANEAN
Isole Égadi
Trápani
Érice
Castellammare
Paler
Segesta
Alcamo
Favignana
Marsala
Castelvetrano
Menfi
Selinunte
Sciacca
Platani
Pto. Empédocle
Agrigento
La Galite
Binzert (Bizerte)
C. Bon
G. de Tunis
Béja
Tunis
Pantelleria (Ital.)
Nabeul
TUNISIA
1730
G. de Hammamet
Sousse
Kairouan
Tebessa
Lampedusa (Ital.)
8
10
12
40
38
36
East from Greenwich

127

1 : 5 000 000

47
52
54
ADRIATIC
SEA
IONIAN
SEA
I A N
N E A N S E A
MOLISE
CAMPANIA
PUGLIA
BASILICATA
CALABRIA
Appennini
2795
Mt. Amaro
Vasto
Térmoli
Sannicandro
Monte Gargano
Monte S. Ángelo
1056
1224
S. Severo
Campobasso
Frosinone
Fondi
Fóggia
G. di Manfredónia
Cerignola
Barletta
Trani
Molfetta
Benevento
Ofanto
Andria
Corato
Bari
Gaeta
Garigliano
Volturno
Caserta
Aversa
Vesuvio
1277
Avellino
Spinazzola
Monopoli
Putignano
Íschia
Nápoli
(Naples)
Torre Annunziata
Nocera
Potenza
Matera
Brindisi
Capri
Sorrento
Castellammare
Salerno
Eboli
Taranto
Francavilla
Sele
Agri
Lecce
Str. of Otranto
Sazan
Ulcinj
Bojana
Nardo
Galatina
Otranto
C. d'Otranto
Gallípoli
Pisciotta
Sinni
Golfo di Táranto
2271
Capo Sta. Maria di Leuca
Corigliano
Cosenza
1929
Crotone
Sambiase
Nicastro
Catanzaro
C. Rizzuto
Squillace
Strómboli
Isole Eólie o Lípari
Salina
Lípari
Vulcano
Palmi
Pizzo
C. Peloro
Scilla
Taurianova
Términi
Cefalù
Milazzo
Patti
Messina
Réggio
Mistretta
Monti Nebrodi
Str. di Messina
C. Spartivento
Etna
3340
Adrano
Giarre
Caltanissetta
Enna
Paternò
Catánia
Piazza
Favara
Lentini
Caltagirone
Augusta
Ferla
Licata
Salso
Gela
Siracusa
(Syracuse)
Ragusa
Vittória
Modica
Noto
Ispica
C. Passero
Gozo
Comino
Valletta
Mdina
MALTA
42
40
38
36
14
16
18

Bay of Biscay
ATLANTIC OCEAN
C. Ortegal
Ortigueira
Vivero
Ribadeo
Luarca
C. de Peñas
Avilés
Gijón
Villaviciosa
Llanes
S. Vicente de la Barquera
Torrelavega
Santander
Santoña
Guecho
Guernica
Bilbao
Durango
La Coruña
El Ferrol
1056
Villalba
Pravia
Grado
Oviedo
Mieres
Langreo
Picos de Europa
2648
CANTABRIA
ASTURIAS
Cordillera Cantábrica
Carballo
Corcubión
C. Finisterre
Lugo
Fonsagrada
Cangas
Puerto de Pajares
Sa. de Alba
Reinosa
Sestao
Vitoria
PAIS V
Santiago de Compostela
GALICIA
Villagarcía
La Estrada
Lalín
Chantada
Monforte
Ponferrada
La Robla
León
Saldaña
Pisuerga
Paso Pancorbo
Miranda de Ebro
Ebro
Pontevedra
Marín
Redondela
Vigo
Tuy
Orense
Sil
Mts. de León
Astorga
2188
Esla
Sahagún
Burgos
LA RIOJA
Sierra de la Demanda
2262
2926
Minho
Caminha
Viana do Castelo
MINHO
Braga
Chaves
Bragança
Sa. de la Culebra
Palencia
Arlanzón
CASTILLA Y LEÓN
Ofir
Póvoa de Varzim
Matozinhos
Porto
DOURO
TRAS OS MONTES
ALTO DOURO
Miranda
Vila Real
Tâmega
Zamora
Tordesillas
Valladolid
Duero
Torre de Moncorvo
Douro
Lamego
Tormes
Medina
Eresma
Adaja
Ovar
LITORAL
BEIRA-ALTA
Ledesma
Salamanca
Arévalo
Segovia
Sierra de Guadarrama
Peñalara
2430
Sigüenza
Henares
Vouga
Viseu
Pinhel
Aveiro
Mondego
Guarda
Ciudad Rodrigo
Fuentes de Oñoro
Peña de Francia
Avila
MADRID
El Escorial
Jarama
Guadalajara
Alcalá de Henares
Coimbra
1991
Covilhã
Sa. de Gata
Sierra de Gredos
2592
Pico de Almanzor
Navalcarnero
Vallecas
Figueira da Foz
BEIRA LITORAL
Serra da Estrela
Fundão
BEIRA-BAIXA
Plasencia
Tiétar
Alberche
Chinchón
Aranjuez
Pombal
Zêzere
Castelo Branco
Talavera de la Reina
Toledo
Ocaña
Leiria
Batalha
Alcobaça
Tomar
Alcántara
Tajo
CASTILLA-LA MANCHA
Peniche
ESTREMADURA
RIBATEJO
Abrantes
Valencia de Alcántara
Cáceres
Trujillo
Sa. de Guadalupe
1443
Montes de Toledo
Quintanar
Torres Vedras
Santarém
Vila Franca
Portalegre
Alburquerque
ALTO ALENTEJO
Alcázar de San Juan
Mafra
Sintra
C. da Roca
Estoril
Lisboa
(Lisbon)
Tejo
Montijo
Barreiro
Almada
Herrera
Guadiana
Tomelloso
Mérida
Badajoz
Elvas
Villanueva de la Serena
Manzanares
Setúbal
Redondo
Évora
Almendralejo
Don Benito
Almadén
Ciudad Real
Valdepeñas
C. Espichel
Baía de Setúbal
Viana
Olivenza
Zafra
Puertollano
Hinojosa
Despeñaperros
Jerez
Pueblonuevo
Pozoblanco
Sierra Morena
BAIXO
Beja
Azuaga
Belmez
Fuente Ovejuna
La Carolina
Linares
Ubeda
Baeza
Aljustrel
Barrancos
Andújar
Montoro
Sines
ALENTEJO
Guadiana
Aracena
Constantina
Córdoba
Castro del Río
Jaén
Minas de Riotinto
Mértola
Nerva
Guadalquivir
Montilla
Martos
Alcaudete
Alcalá
Monchique
Sa. do Malhão
Valverde
Sanlúcar la Mayor
Carmona
Écija
Lucena
Baza
Sa. de Monchique
902
ALGARVE
Huelva
La Palma
Sevilla
Marchena
Utrera
Puente Genil
Genil
Granada
Guadix
C. de S. Vicente
Tavira
Loulé
Faro
Osuna
Loja
Sa. Nevada
3478
Mulhacén
Sagres
Lagos
Portimão
Vila Real de S. António
Ayamonte
Morón
Bobadilla
Antequera
Golfo de Cádiz
Lebrija
Guadalete
Ronda
Sanlúcar de Barrameda
Jerez
Arcos
Málaga
Coín
Torremolinos
Vélez Málaga
Guadalhorce
Motril
Adra
Berja
Puerto de Sta. María
Cádiz
S. Fernando
Chiclana
Medina-Sidonia
Vejer
Marbella
C. Trafalgar
Algeciras
Tarifa
La Línea de la Concepción
Gibraltar (Br.)
Pt. Europa
Strait of Gibraltar
C. Spartel
Tanger
Ceuta (Sp.)
MOROCCO
Alborán (Sp.)
SPAIN
PORTUGAL
ANDALUCIA
EXTREMADURA
Sierra de Guadarrama
West from Greenwich
10
8
6
42
40
38

126

1 : 6 000 000

36

F R A N C E
Toulouse
Montpellier
Béziers
Narbonne
Golfe du Lion
Carcassonne
Perpignan
Port-Vendres
Port-Bou
C. Creus
Golfo de Rosas
Rosas
Bayonne
Biarritz
San Sebastián
Pau
Tarbes
Lourdes
Orthez
Dax
Mont-de-Marsan
Condom
Auch
Castres
Sète
Agde
Foix
Can. du Midi
Pamplona
NAVARRA
Roncevaux
Tolosa
Alsasua
Logroño
Tafalla
Tudela
Calahorra
Huesca
ANDORRA
Andorra
Col de la Perche
Seo de Urgel
Tremp
Maladeta
Somport 1640
Puerto de
Gerona
Palamós
S. Feliu de Guíxols
Lloret
Calella
Mataró
Granollers
Tarrasa
Sabadell
Badalona
Hospitalet
Barcelona
Llobregat
Sitges
Vich
Manresa
Cardona
Igualada
Cervera
Lérida
Monzón
Balaguer
Zaragoza
ARAGON
Moncayo
Sa. de Moncayo
2316
Soria
Almazán
Calatayud
Jalón
Ebro
Caspe
Alcañiz
Reus
Valls
Tarragona
Costa Dorada
Costa Brava
Golfo de San Jorge
Tortosa
C. de Tortosa
Calamocha
Montalbán
Mts. del Maestrazgo
2019
Morella
Vinaroz
Teruel
Sa. de Albarracín
Serranía de Cuenca
Cuenca
Castellón de la Plana
Onda
Villarreal
Islas Columbretes
Sagunto
Liria
Requena
Valencia
Albufera de Valencia
Golfo de Valencia
Sueca
Cullera
Algemesí
Alcira
Játiva
Denia
C. Nao
Alcoy
Villena
Almansa
Yecla
Albacete
La Roda
Villarroblero
Cabriel
Júcar
Altea
Benidorm
Costa Blanca
Alicante
Elche
Jumilla
Cieza
Hellín
MURCIA
Murcia
Orihuela
Cehegín
Caravaca
La Sagra 2381
Vélez Rubio
Sangonera
Alhama
Lorca
Aguilas
Mazarrón
Cartagena
Mar Menor
C. de Palos
Torrevieja
Segura
Cuevas de Almanzora
Almanzora
Vera
Almería
C. de Gata
Sa. de Alcaraz 1790
ISLAS BALEARES
Menorca
Mahón
Mallorca
Palma
Sóller
1445
Inca
Manacor
Cala Millor
Magaluf
Arenal
Bahía de Palma
Cabrera
Ibiza
S. Antonio
Formentera
2224
2850
MEDITERRANEAN SEA
ALGERIA
Alger (Algiers)
Thenia
Boufarik
Koléa
Blida
Ténès
42
40
38
2
0
2
East from Greenwich

127

59

HUNGARY
Villach
Triglav
2863
Kobarid
(Caporetto)
Klagenfurt
Bleiburg
Karawanken
Maribor
Nagykanizsa
Kaposvár
Kapos
Szekszárd
Kiskőrös
Szentes
Békéscsaba
Kalocsa
Kiskunhalas
Hódmezővásárhely
Makó
Arad
Celje
Drava
Varaždin
Baja
Szeged
Ljubljana
Sava
SLOVENIA
Gorizia
Pécs
Mohács
Subotica
Senta
Kikinda
Zagreb
Bjelovar
Cerknica
Kočevje
Postojna
Trieste
Koper
Kupa
CROATIA
Sombor
Timişoara
Bečej
Osijek
Istra
Rijeka
(Fiume)
Karlovac
Sisak
Novska
Novi Sad
Zrenjanin
Petrovaradin
Vinkovci
Brod
Rovinj
Pula
(Pola)
Rt. Kamenjak
Krk
Cres
Lošinj
Kvarner
Kvarnerić
Senj
Kapela
Velebit Planina
Una
Bosanska Gradiška
Unac
Bihać
Banja Luka
Odžak
Bosna
Brčko
Sremska Mitrovica
Zemun
Beograd
(Belgrade)
Pančevo
Vršac
Bela Crkva
Bijeljina
Smederevo
Požarevac
Gospić
Kremen
1591
Gračac
Pag
Sana
Srnetica
Vrbas
Tešanj
Tuzla
Drina
BOSNIA-HERZEGOVINA
Travnik
Valjevo
Morava
Dugi Otok
Zadar
Dinara Planina
1913
Troglav
Han Pijesak
Sarajevo
Višegrad
Titovo Užice
Kragujevac
Čačak
Kraljevo
Kruševac
Šibenik
Split
Dalmacija
Konjic
Neretva
YUGOSLAVIA
Brač
Hvar
Mostar
Pljevlja
Novi Pazar
Kopaonik
Ibar Pl.
Kuršumlija
Vis
Stolac
2522
Durmitor
Tara
Kosovska Mitrovica
Korčula
Lastovo
Nikšić
MONTENEGRO
Priština
Dubrovnik
Trebinje
Peć
Beli Drim
Palagruža
(Croatia)
Hercegnovi
Kotor
Cetinje
Podgorica
(Titograd)
Đakovica
Prizren
Ortona
Lanciano
Skadarsko Jezero
Drini
Šar Pl.
2496
Crna Gora
Skopje
Vasto
Termoli
Bar
Shkodra
Tetovo
1224
MOLISE
Sannicandro
S. Severo
Monte Gargano
1056
Monte S. Ángelo
Ulcinj
Bojana
Korab
2764
Solunska
2540
Campobasso
Fóggia
G. di Manfredónia
Kep-i-Rodonit
Debar
MACE
ADRIATIC SEA
ITALY
Cerignola
Barletta
Trani
Molfetta
Kep-i-Palit
Durrësi
Tirana
2259
Jablanica
Benevento
Ofanto
Andria
Corato
Bari
Ohrid
Bitola
(Monastir)
Caserta
Aversa
Vesuvio
1277
Avellino
Spinazzola
Monopoli
Putignano
Shkumbini
Elbasani
Ohridsko Jezero
Prespansko Jezero
Flórina
Ischia
Napoli
(Naples)
Nocera
Éboli
CAMPANIA
Potenza
Matera
Brindisi
Str. of Otranto
Semani
Tomorrit
2480
Berati
Capri
Sorrento
Castellammare
Salerno
Sele
BASILICATA
Taranto
Francavilla
Sazan
Vlóra
Korça
Kastoría
Lecce
PUGLIA
Agri
Nardo
Galatina
Otranto
C. d'Otranto
Vjosa
ALBANIA
Smólikas
2637
Pisciotta
Sinni
Golfo di Táranto
Gallípoli
Gjirokastra
2271
Capo Sta. Maria di Leuca
Pindos
Ioánnina
Kérkira
(Corfu)
ÍPIROS
Corigliano
IONIAN SEA
Cosenza
1929
Árta
47
49
44
42
40
14
16
18
20
East from Greenwich

1 : 6 000 000

57

ROMANIA
BULGARIA
TURKEY
GREECE
MACEDONIA
BLACK SEA
ÆGEAN SEA
Marmara denizi
Transilvania
Carpathians
Carpaţii Meridionali
Valahia
Dobruja
Stara Planina
Rhodopi Planina
Makedhonia
Thráki
Thessalia
Bucureşti
(Bucharest)
Sofiya
(Sofia)
Istanbul
Üsküdar
Thessaloníki
Edirne
Plovdiv
Varna
Burgas
Constanţa
Galaţi
Brăila
Ploieşti
Braşov
Sibiu
Alba-Iulia
Craiova
Ruse (Ruschuk)
Pleven
Stara Zagora
Dimitrovgrad
Khaskovo
Kŭrdzhali
Smolyan
Zlatograd
Xánthi
Komotini
Alexandroúpolis
Kavalla
Dráma
Sérrai
Kolarovgrad
(Sjumen)
Tŭrgovishte
Tŭrnovo
Gabrovo
Kazanlŭk
Sliven
Yambol
Elkhovo
Aytos
Poljanovgrad
Dobrich
Balchik
Nos Kaliakra
Mangalia
Mamaia
Cernavodă
Călăraşi
Silistra
Tutrakan
Olteniţa
Giurgiu
Zimnicea
Turnu Măgurele
Corabia
Caracal
Slatina
Piteşti
Tîrgovişte
Cîmpina
Cîmpulung
Rîmnicu Vîlcea
Tîrgu-Jiu
Turnu-Severin
Orşova
Mehadia
Caransebeş
Reşiţa
Lugoj
Deva
Simeria
Brad
Alb
Abrud
Mţii Bihor
1848
Mediaş
Sighişoara
Odorhei
Sfîntu-Gheorghe
Bretcu
Făgăraş
Olt
Petroşeni
Paringul Mare
2518
Peleaga
2509
2535
350 Vf. Omul
Vf. Negoiu
2507
P. Turnu Roşu
Porţile de Fier
Bîrlad
Tecuci
Focşani
Rîmnicu Sărat
Buzău
Siret
(Sereth)
Prut
Kagul
Bolgrad
Ozero Sasyk
Kiliya
Ismail
Reni
Tulcea
Sulina
Gura Portiţei
Dunărea (Danube)
Ialomiţa
Prahova
Dâmboviţa
Argeş
Vedea
Jiu
Dunărea (Danube)
Negotin
Bor
Vidin
Calafát
Lom
Oryakhovo
Somovit
Svishtov
Razgrad
Gorna Oryakhovitsa
Zaječar
Timok
Niš
2168
Vratsa
Teteven
Vezhen
2198
Shiptjenski P.
Shipka
Tundza
Pirot
Suva Pl.
Južna Morava
Leskovac
P. Dragoman
Pernik
Radomir
Vranje
Trajanova Vrata
Maritsa
Pazardzhik
Stanke Dimitrov
(Marek)
Musala
2925
Kyustendil
Kumanovo
Kocani
Štip
Titov Veles
Vardar
Prilep
Crna
Strumica
Petrich
Struma
Pirin Planina
Mesta
Arda
Dhidhimótikhon
Ergene
Kırklareli
Istranca Dağları
1018
Karadeniz Boğazi
Beykoz
Tekirdağ
Marmara
Imralı
Bandırma
Bursa
Simav
Enez
Saros Körfezi
Gelibolu
(Gallipoli)
Çanakkale
Çanakkale Boğazı
Troy (Ilium)
Ida
1766
Edremit
Balıkesir
Edremit Körfezi
Ayvalık
Bergama
(Pergamum)
Kırkağaç
Akhisar
Baba Burun
Lésvos
Mitilíni
968
Bozcaada
Moúdhros
Límnos
Ákra Pláka
Gökçeada
Samothráki
1600
Thásos
1127
Philippi
Dojran
Edhessa
Yiannitsa
Véroia
Kozáni
Aliákmon
Oros Ólimbos
2917
(Olympus)
Ossa
1978
Piniós
Kalabáka
Tríkkala
Lárisa
Kardhítsa
Fársala
Vólos
Pagastikós Kólpos
Thermaikós Kólpos
Políyiros
Ákra Platí
Toronaíos Kólpos
Singitikós Kólpos
Áthos
2033
Ákra Ámbelos
Áyios Evstrátios
Voríai Sporádhes
Iliodhrómia
1575
Oros
22
24
26
28
46
44
42
40

80

54

52
Podgorica
(Titograd)
Cetinje
Pec
Beli Drim
Đakovica
Prizren
Skadarsko Jezero
Drini
Bar
Shkodra
Ulcinj
Bojana
Kep-i-Rodonit
Kep-i-Palit
Durrësi
Tirana
Shkumbini
Elbasani
Semani
Berati
Tomorit
2480
Sazan
Vlóra
Vjosa
Gjirokastra
ALBANIA
Korab
2764
Debar
2259
Jablanica
Ohrid
Ohridsko Jezero
Prepansko Jezero
Korça
Skopje
Tetovo
Solunska
2540
Veles
Kocani
Štip
MACEDONIA
Vardar
Strumica
Petrich
Prilep
Crna
Bitola
(Monastir)
Dojran
Struma
Pirin Planina
Flórina
Edhessa
Yiannitsa
Thessaloníki
Políyros
Thermaikós Kólpos
Kastoría
Véroia
Kozáni
Aliákmon
Óros Ólimbos
2917
(Olympus)
Smólikas
2637
Pindos
Píndhos Óros
Piniós
Óssa
1978
Kalabáka
Tríkkala
Lárisa
Ioánnina
ÍPIROS
THESSALIA
Vólos
Pagastikós Kólpos
Kardhítsa
Fársala
Árta
Préveza
Lamía
Akhelóos
Thermopílai
Gióna
2510
Agrínion
STEREA ELLAS
Parnassós
2457
Návpaktos
Mesolóngion
Patraikós Kólpos
Korinthiakós Kólpos
Pátrai
Aíyon
Erímanthos
2224
Killíni
2376
Kórinthos
Mycenæ
Mikínai
Árgos
Návplion
PELOPÓNNISOS
Pírgos
Olympia
Trípolis
Argolikós Kólpos
Kiparissiakós Kólpos
Kiparissía
Filiatrá
Messíni
Kalamáta
Spárti
Pílos
Taíyetos Óros
Yíthion
Lakonikós Kólpos
Messiniakós Kólpos
Ákra Taínaron
Kíthira
GREECE
Kérkira
(Corfu)
Levkás
(Sta. Maura)
Itháki
Kefallinía
Argostólion
Zákinthos
IÓNIOI NÍSOI
Str. of Otranto
Bríndisi
Francavilla
ITALY
Lecce
Nardo
Galatina
Otranto
C. d'Otranto
Gallípoli
Capo Sta. Maria di Leuca
1224
5121
49
IONIAN SEA
MEDITERRANEAN
42
40
38
36
18
20
22
East from Greenwich

1 : 5 000 000

53

BULGARIA
TURKEY
Rhodopi Planina
Khaskovo
Kŭrdzhali
Arda
Smolyan
Zlatograd
Mesta
Edirne
Kirklareli
Dhidhimótikhon
Karadeniz Boğazi
Beykoz
İstanbul
Üsküdar
Ergene
MAKEDHONIA
Xánthi
THRÁKI
Komotiní
Dráma
Philippi
Kavalla
Sérrai
Tekirdağ
Marmara denizi
Marmara
İmralı
Alexandroúpolis
Enez
Thásos
1127
Saros Körfezi
Gelibolu
(Gallipoli)
Bandırma
Bursa
2543
Samothráki
1600
Ákra Platí
Gökçeada
Çanakkale
Simav
Kirmasti
Áthos
2033
Singitikós Kólpos
Toronaíos Kólpos
Ákra Pláka
Çanakkale Boğazi
Troy (Ilium)
Límnos
Moúdhros
Bozcaada
Ida
1766
Edremit
Balıkesir
2181
Ákra Ámbelos
Áyios Evstrátios
Baba Burun
Edremit Körfezi
Ayvalık
TURKEY
1575
Iliodhrómia
Lésvos
Mitilíni
Bergama
(Pergamum)
Kirkağaç
Anadolu
968
Akhisar
Voríai Sporádhes
AEGEAN SEA
Skíros
Izmir Körfezi
Aliağa
Manisa
Gediz
Menemen
Turgutlu
2157
Alaşehir
1297
İzmir
(Smyrna)
Sarigöl
Dhírfis
1743
Évvoia
Khíos
Khalkís
Çeşme
Ephesus
Kuşadası
Aydın
Büyük Menderes
2308
Thívai
Marathón
Ákra Kafirévs
1398
Mégara
Athínai
(Athens)
Pireévs
(Piraeus)
Salamís
Ándros
Samos
Ikaría
Saronikós Kólpos
Aíyina
Lávrion
Kéa
Tínos
Míkonos
Foúrnoi
Mandalya Körfezi
Muğla
2294
DHODHEKÁNISOS
Ermoúpolis
Síros
Kíthnos
Ídhra
Rinía
Pátmos
KIKLÁDHES
Páros
Sérifos
1001
Náxos
Kálimnos
Kos
Kerme Körfezi
Sífnos
Amorgós
Íos
Astipálaia
Síkinos
Mílos
Ródhos
Tílos
Thíra
Ródhos
4486
Ákra Maléa
Kíthira
Antikíthira
Ákra Spátha
Kólpos Khanion
KRITI
Kárpathos
1215
Kólpos Soudhas
Réthimnon
Ákra Stavros
Iráklion
Kólpos Merabéllou
Kásos
Khaniá
Lévka Óri
2452
Kóra Sfakíon
Ídhi Óros
2456
Knossos
Díkti
2148
Ierápetra
Ákra Líthinon
24
26
28
40
38
36

80

58

59

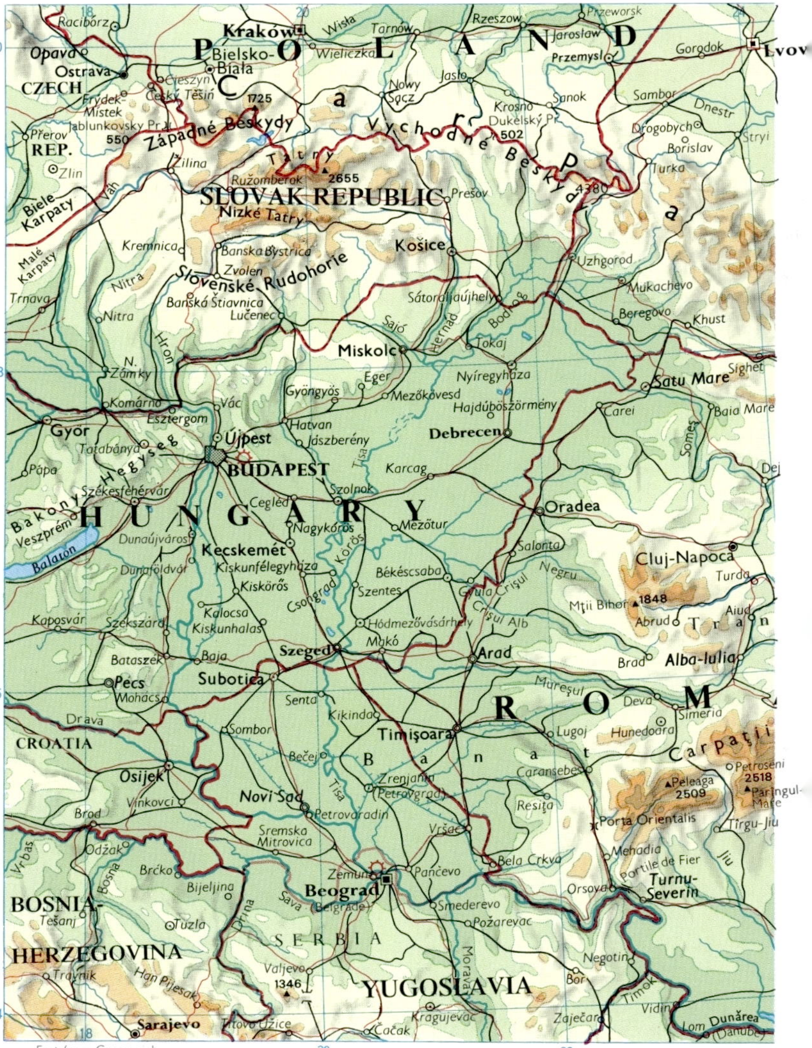
POLAND
Kraków
Wisła
Tarnów
Rzeszow
Przeworsk
Jarosław
Racibórz
Opava
Ostrava
CZECH REP.
Bielsko-Biała
Wieliczka
Cieszyn
Český Těšín
Frýdek-Místek
Jablunkovský Pr.
550
1725
Západné Beskydy
Nowy Sącz
Jasło
Krosno
Dukelský Pr.
502
Sanok
Przemysl
Gorodok
Lvov
Sambor
Dnestr
Drogobych
Borislav
Stryi
Turka
Přerov
Zlín
Žilina
Tatry
Ružomberok
2655
Vychodné Beskydy
Karpaty
1380
SLOVAK REPUBLIC
Prešov
Nízké Tatry
Biele Karpaty
Váh
Malé Karpaty
Kremnica
Banská Bystrica
Zvolen
Slovenské Rudohorie
Košice
Uzhgorod
Mukachevo
Trnava
Nitra
Banská Štiavnica
Lučenec
Sátoraljaújhely
Bodrog
Beregovo
Khust
Hron
Sajó
Hernád
Tokaj
Miskolc
N. Zámky
Eger
Gyöngyös
Mezőkövesd
Nyíregyháza
Satu Mare
Sighet
Komárno
Esztergom
Vác
Hajdúböszörmény
Carei
Baia Mare
Gyor
Hatvan
Újpest
Tatabánya
Jászberény
Debrecen
Someş
Pápa
BUDAPEST
Tisza
Karcag
Dej
Székesfehérvár
Szolnok
Bakony
Veszprém
Cegléd
HUNGARY
Oradea
Nagykőrös
Mezőtúr
Dunaújváros
Kecskemét
Salonta
Cluj-Napoca
Balaton
Dunaföldvár
Kiskunfélegyháza
Körös
Békéscsaba
Negru
Turda
Kiskőrös
Csongrád
Szentes
Gyula
Crişul
Kalocsa
Mţii Bihor
1848
Kaposvár
Szekszárd
Kiskunhalas
Hódmezővásárhely
Crişul Alb
Abrud
Aiud
Makó
Bataszek
Baja
Szeged
Arad
Brad
Alba-Iulia
Pecs
Subotica
Mohacs
Mureşul
Senta
ROMANIA
Deva
Simeria
Drava
Kikinda
Timişoara
Lugoj
Hunedoara
CROATIA
Sombor
Carpaţii
Banat
Bečej
Petroşeni
Osijek
Caransebeş
2518
Zrenjanin
(Petrovgrad)
Peleaga
2509
Parîngul-Mare
Tisa
Novi Sad
Vinkovci
Reşiţa
Brod
Petrovaradin
Porta Orientalis
Tîrgu-Jiu
Sremska Mitrovica
Vršac
Mehadia
Jiu
Vrbas
Odžak
Portile de Fier
Bela Crkva
Bosna
Brčko
Zemun
Pančevo
Bijeljina
Beograd
Orsova
Turnu-Severin
BOSNIA-HERZEGOVINA
Sava
(Belgrade)
Drina
Smederevo
Tešanj
Tuzla
Požarevac
SERBIA
Morava
Negotin
Travnik
Han Pijesak
Valjevo
1346
Bor
YUGOSLAVIA
Timok
Kragujevac
Zaječar
Vidin
Sarajevo
Titovo Užice
Čačak
Lom
Dunărea
(Danube)
50
48
46
44
18
20
22
East from Greenwich

52

1 : 5 000 000

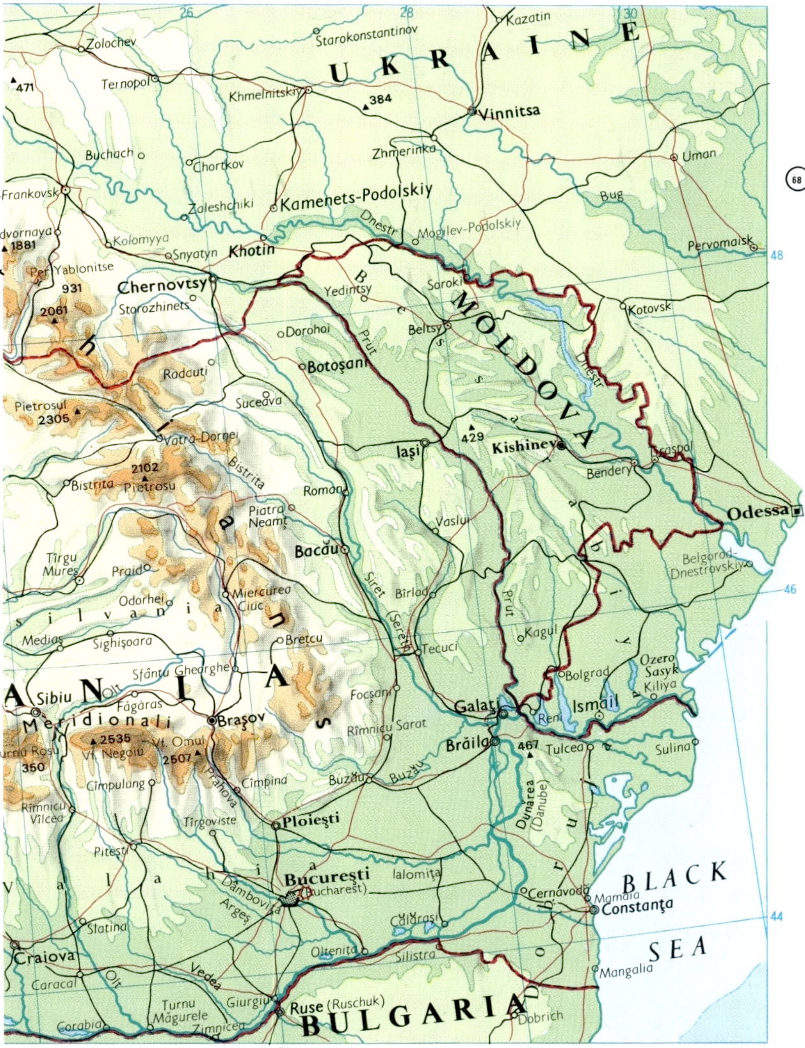
UKRAINE
MOLDOVA
BULGARIA
BLACK SEA
Kazatin
Starokonstantinov
Zolochev
Ternopol
471
Khmelnitskiy
384
Vinnitsa
Zhmerinka
Uman
Buchach
Chortkov
ano-Frankovsk
Zaleshchiki
Kamenets-Podolskiy
Bug
Dnestr
Mogilev-Podolskiy
Pervomaisk
Nadvornaya
1881
Kolomyya
Snyatyn
Khotin
Per. Yablonitse
931
Chernovtsy
Yedintsy
Soroki
Kotovsk
2061
Storozhinets
Dorohoi
Beltsy
Prut
Botoşani
Radauti
Pietrosul
2305
Suceava
Vatra-Dornei
Iaşi
429
Kishinev
Tiraspol
Bendery
2102
Pietrosu
Bistrita
Roman
Piatra Neamţ
Odessa
Vaslui
Bacău
Tîrgu Mureş
Praid
Belgorod-Dnestrovskiy
Miercurea Ciuc
Odorhei
Bîrlad
Siret (Seret)
Mediaş
Sighişoara
Breţcu
Kagul
Tecuci
Ozero Sasyk
Kiliya
Bolgrad
Sfântu Gheorghe
Sibiu
Olt
Făgăras
Focşani
Galaţi
Ismail
Reni
Meridionali
Braşov
Rîmnicu Sarat
Brăila
467
Tulcea
Sulina
Turnu Roşu
350
2535
Vf. Negoiu
Vf. Omul
2507
Cîmpina
Buzău
Cîmpulung
Prahova
Dunărea (Danube)
Rîmnicu Vîlcea
Tîrgoviste
Ploieşti
Piteşti
Bucureşti
(Bucharest)
Ialomiţa
Cernavodă
Mamaia
Constanţa
Dâmboviţa
Argeş
Călăraşi
Slatina
Olteniţa
Silistra
Craiova
Mangalia
Caracal
Olt
Vedea
Turnu Măgurele
Giurgiu
Ruse (Ruschuk)
Dobrich
Corabia
Zimnicea
26
28
30
48
46
44
24

COPYRIGHT. GEORGE PHILIP & SON. LTD.

68

53

68

63

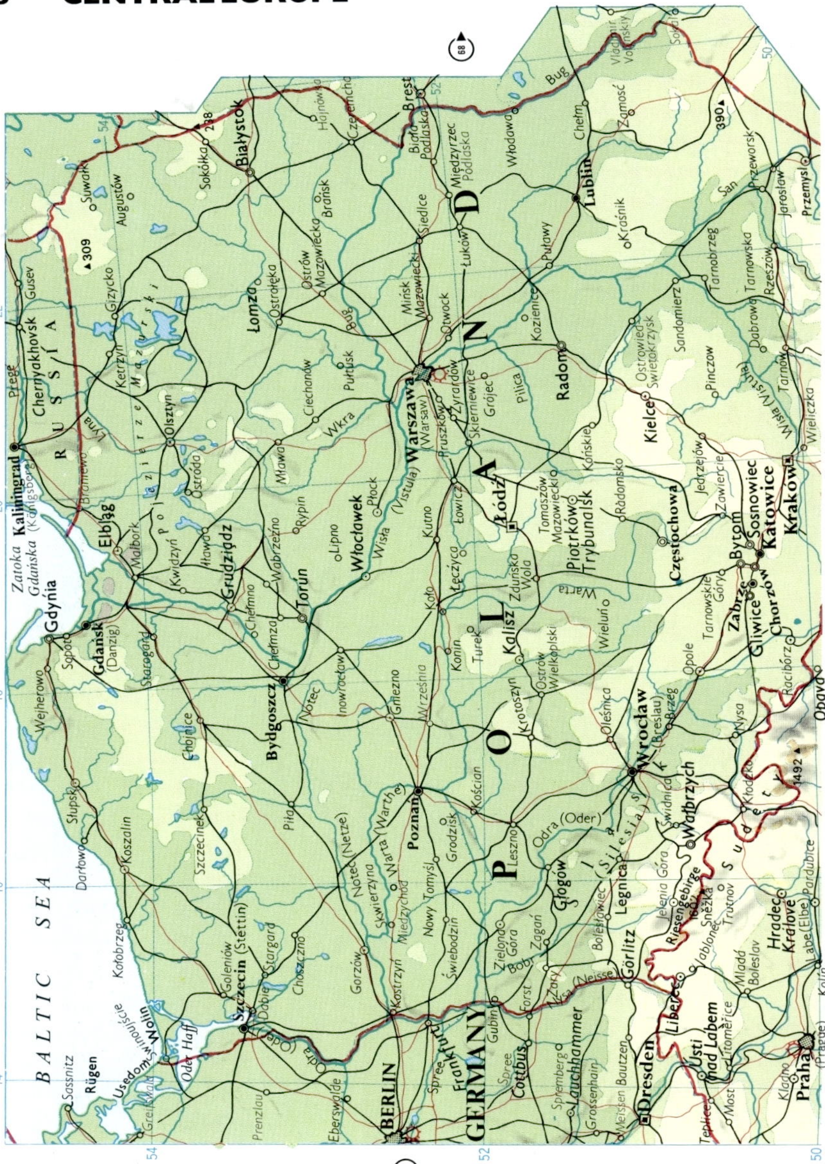
BALTIC SEA
RUSSIA
POLAND
GERMANY
BERLIN
Warszawa
(Warsaw)
Kaliningrad
(Königsberg)
Gdańsk
(Danzig)
Gdynia
Szczecin (Stettin)
Poznań
Wrocław
(Breslau)
Łódź
Kraków
Katowice
Lublin
Białystok
Bydgoszcz
Toruń
Olsztyn
Radom
Kielce
Częstochowa
Dresden
Praha
(Prague)
Zatoka Gdańska
Oder Haff
Sudety
Śląsk
Wisła
(Vistula)
Odra (Oder)
Warta
Bug
Pilica
Notec
Spree
Nysa (Neisse)
Labe (Elbe)
Pojezierze Mazurskie
1492
309
390
238

43

1 : 5 000 000

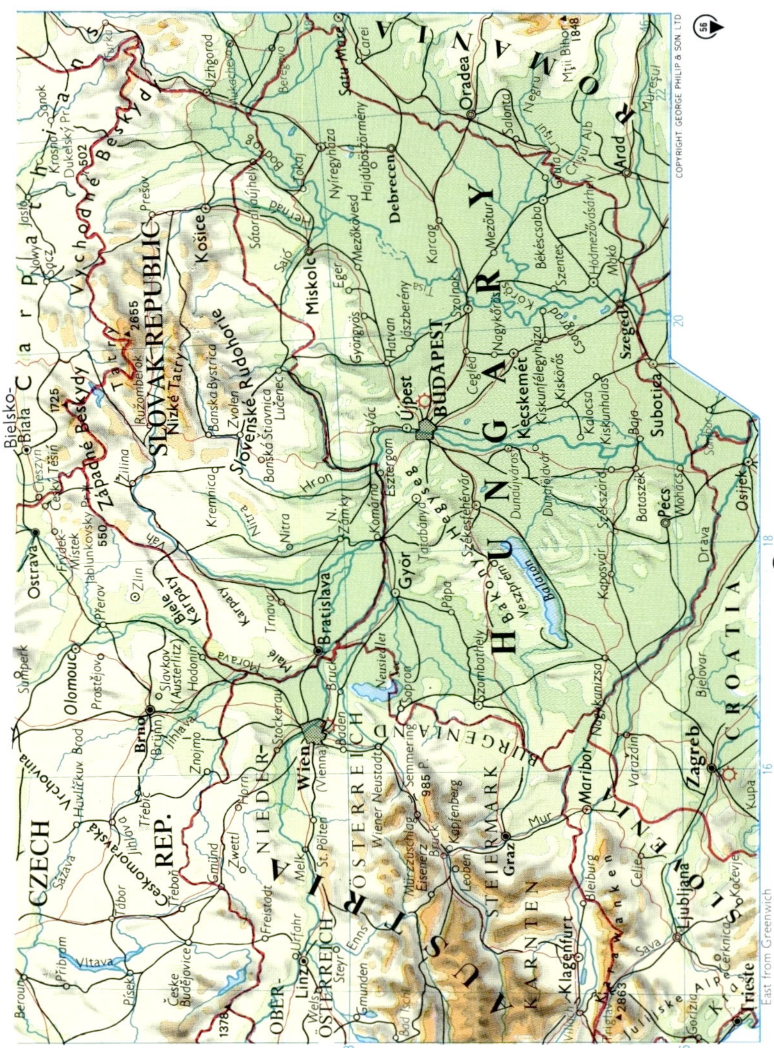
CZECH REP.
SLOVAK REPUBLIC
HUNGARY
AUSTRIA
ROMANIA
CROATIA
SLOVENIA
NIEDER-ÖSTERREICH
OBER-ÖSTERREICH
STEIERMARK
KÄRNTEN
BURGENLAND
Carpathians
Východné Beskydy
Západné Beskydy
Tatry
Nizké Tatry
Slovenské Rudohorie
Biele Karpaty
Malé Karpaty
Bakony
Českomoravská Vrchovina
Karawanken
Julijske Alpe
Praha
Wien (Vienna)
Bratislava
Budapest
Brno (Brünn)
Ostrava
Olomouc
Košice
Miskolc
Debrecen
Szeged
Pécs
Győr
Kecskemét
Zagreb
Ljubljana
Graz
Linz
Klagenfurt
Maribor
Trieste
Oradea
Arad
Subotica
Osijek
Uzhgorod
Bielsko-Biała
Balaton
Neusiedler See
Dunaj
Tisa
Vltava
Drava
Mur
Sava
2655
1725
1848
2863
1378
985
East from Greenwich
COPYRIGHT GEORGE PHILIP & SON LTD
16
18
20
22
46
48
45
52
56

SOUTHERN SCANDINAVIA

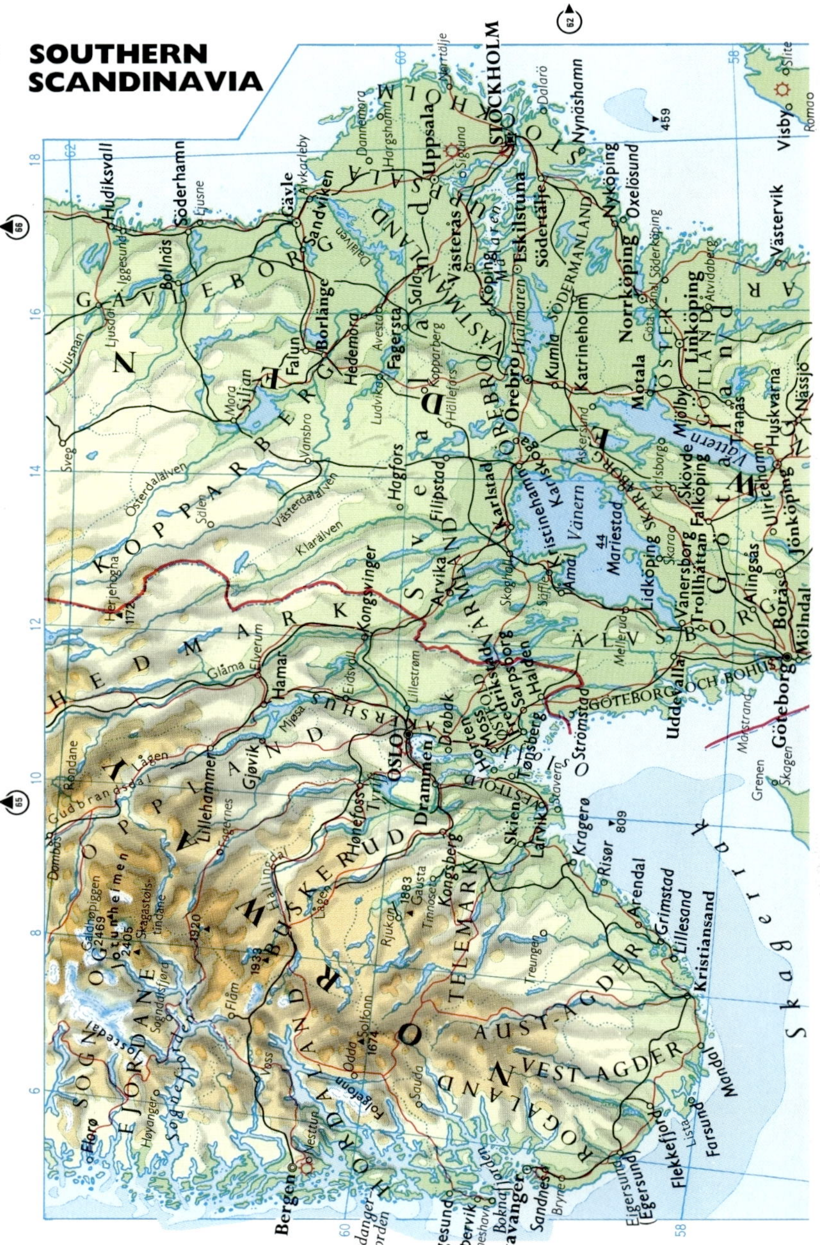

STOCKHOLM
OSLO
Uppsala
Gävle
Hudiksvall
Söderhamn
Bollnäs
Sandviken
Borlänge
Falun
Hedemora
Fagersta
Västerås
Köping
Eskilstuna
Södertälje
Nyköping
Norrköping
Linköping
Motala
Örebro
Karlstad
Kristinehamn
Karlskoga
Filipstad
Hagfors
Arvika
Kongsvinger
Hamar
Lillehammer
Gjøvik
Hønefoss
Drammen
Kongsberg
Skien
Larvik
Tønsberg
Horten
Moss
Fredrikstad
Sarpsborg
Halden
Strömstad
Uddevalla
Vänersborg
Trollhättan
Göteborg
Mölndal
Borås
Alingsås
Jönköping
Huskvarna
Skövde
Mariestad
Lidköping
Åmål
Vänern
Vättern
Västervik
Visby
Kragerø
Risør
Arendal
Grimstad
Lillesand
Kristiansand
Mandal
Farsund
Flekkefjord
Egersund
Sandnes
Stavanger
Haugesund
Kopervik
Bergen
Florø
Voss
Odda
Hardangerfjorden
Sognefjorden
Jotunheimen
Galdhøpiggen 2469
Skagastølstindane 2405
Gausta 1883
Skagerrak
HEDMARK
OPPLAND
BUSKERUD
TELEMARK
AUST-AGDER
VEST-AGDER
ROGALAND
HORDALAND
SOGN OG FJORDANE
KOPPARBERG
GÄVLEBORG
VÄRMLAND
VÄSTMANLAND
UPPSALA
STOCKHOLM
ÖREBRO
SÖDERMANLAND
ÖSTERGÖTLAND
SKARABORG
ÄLVSBORG
GÖTEBORG OCH BOHUS
NORWAY
SWEDEN

1 : 5 000 000

DENMARK
GERMANY
POLAND
NETH
BALTIC SEA
Kattegat
The Sound
Gotland
Öland
Bornholm
Hjørring
Frederikshavn
Brønderslev
Læsø
Thisted
Nørresundby
Hals
Ålborg
Limfjorden
Limfjorden
Skive
Hobro
Lemvig
Struer
Viborg
Randers
Holstebro
Ringkøbing
Herning
Silkeborg
Ebeltoft
Anholt
Yding Skovhøj
173
Århus
Horsens
Vejle
Fredericia
Blåvands Huk
Esbjerg
Ribe
Kolding
Odense
Fyn
Lille Bælt
Store Bælt
Kalundborg
Roskilde
Sjælland
Korsør
Svendborg
Nordfriesische Inseln
Sylt
Åbenrå
Flensburg
Sønderborg
Lolland
Nakskov
Nykøbing
Falster
Møn
Rødby Havn
Gedser
Fehmarn
Puttgarden
Kieler Bucht
Schleswig
Rendsburg
Tönning
Helgoland
Deutsche Bucht
Brunsbüttelkoog
Nord-Ostsee kanal
Kiel
Grossenbrode
Warnemünde
Eutin
Travemünde
Lübeck
Wismar
Rostock
Güstrow
Schwerin
Hamburg
Lauenburg
Lüneburg
171
Elbe
Itzehoe
Glückstadt
Stade
Cuxhaven
Weser
Bremerhaven
Bremen
Verden
Oldenburg
Wilhelmshaven
Norderney
Ostfriesische Inseln
Emden
Leer
Ems
Groningen
Assen
Wittenberge
Stralsund
Greifswald
Peene
Anklam
Neustrelitz
Prenzlau
179
Rügen
Sassnitz
Kap Arkona
Usedom
Świnoujście
Wolin
Szczecin (Stettin)
Dąbie
Stargard Szczeciński
Pyrzyce
Oder
Kołobrzeg
Koszalin
Darłowo
Słupsk
Wałcz
Piła
Helsingør
Helsingborg
Ängelholm
Landskrona
KØBENHAVN (Copenhagen)
Malmö
Lund
Falsterbo
Trelleborg
Ystad
MALMÖHUS
KRISTIANSTAD
Kristianstad
Sölvesborg
Karlshamn
Karlskrona
BLEKINGE
Rønne
Neksø
HALLAND
Kungsbacka
Varberg
Falkenberg
Halmstad
Laholm
JÖNKÖPING
Värnamo
377
Vetlanda
KRONOBERG
Ljungby
Alvesta
Växjö
Nybro
Kalmar
KALMAR
Oskarshamn
Borgholm
Hemse
Burgsvik
Hoburgen
56
54
10
12
14
16
East from Greenwich
63

42
43

67 66 60

GULF OF BOTHNIA
GULF OF FINLAND
BALTIC SEA
FINLAND
ESTONIA
HELSINKI (Helsingfors)
STOCKHOLM
Tallinn
Tampere
Turku (Åbo)
Pori
Rauma
Uusikaupunki
Naantali
Hangö (Hanko)
Ekenäs (Tammisaari)
Porkkala
Lahti
Kotka
Loviisa (Lovisa)
Heinola
Mikkeli
Hämeenlinna
Riihimäki
Hyvinkää
Porvoo
Salo
Loimaa
Kokemäenjoki
Päijänne
Kymi
Åland (Ahvenanmaa)
Mariehamn (Maarianhamina)
Ålands hav
Hiiumaa (Dagö)
Kärdla
Saaremaa (Ösel)
Haapsalu
Paldiski
Rakvere
Kunda
Pärnu
Viljandi
Valga
Valmiera
Cesis
Mõisaküla
Ainaži
Ruhnu
Rigas Jūras Licis (Gulf of Riga)
Gotska Sandön
Fårö
Gotland
Visby
Slite
Hudiksvall
Söderhamn
Ljusne
Bollnäs
Iggesund
Ljusdal
Ljusnan
Gävle
Älvkarleby
Sandviken
Dalälven
Falun
Borlänge
Hedemora
Avesta
Fagersta
Sala
Ludvika
Kopparberg
Hällefors
Mora
Siljan
Sveg
Västerås
Köping
Uppsala
Sigtuna
Dannemora
Hargshamn
Norrtälje
Dalarö
Nynäshamn
Södertälje
Eskilstuna
Mälaren
Hjälmaren
Örebro
Kumla
Karlskoga
Katrineholm
Nyköping
Oxelösund
Norrköping
Söderköping
Linköping
Åtvidaberg
Motala
Mjölby
Askersund
Karlsborg
Vättern
Tranås
Huskvarna
Nässjö
Västervik
Göta Kanal
KOPPARBERG
ÖREBRO
SÖDERMANLAND
VÄSTMANLAND
GÄVLEBORG
UPPSALA
STOCKHOLM
ÖSTERGÖTLAND
TURUN JA PORI
HÄME
UUDENMAA
Svealand
Götaland
459
285

1 : 5 000 000

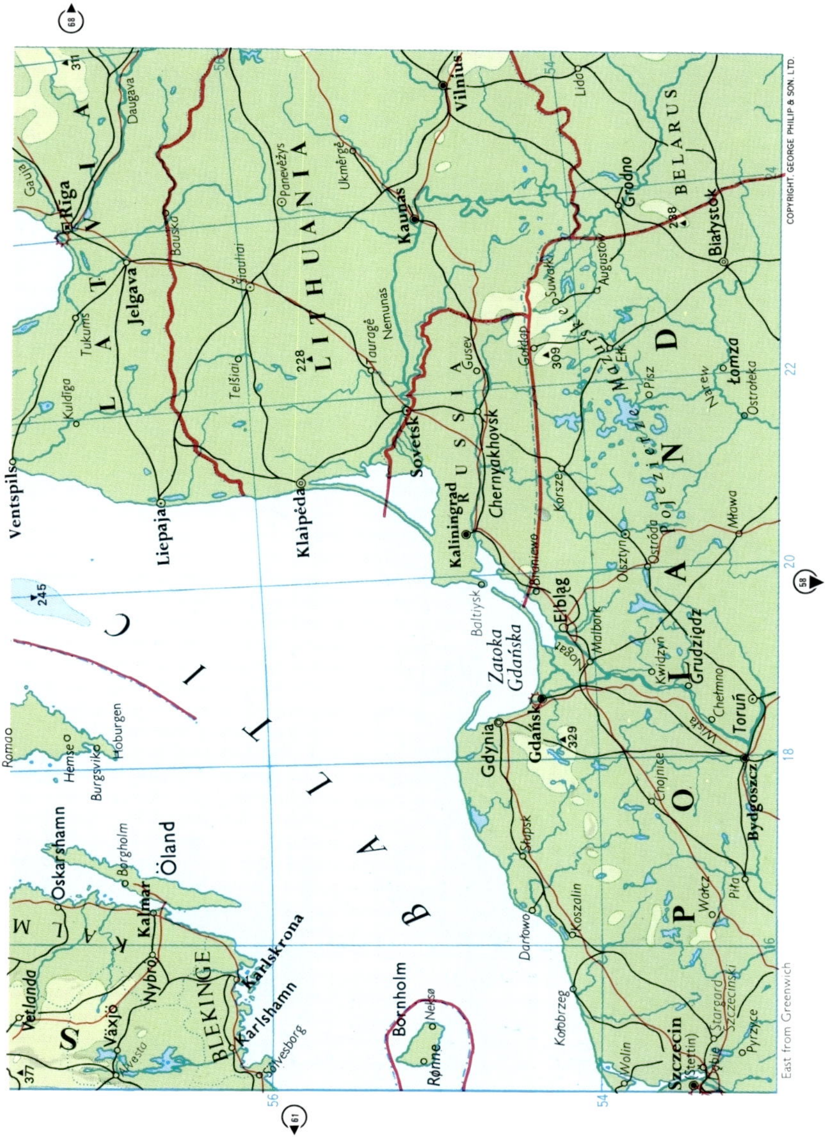
Riga
Gauja
Daugava
Jelgava
Tukums
Kuldīga
Ventspils
Liepaja
Bauska
Šiauliai
Panevėžys
Ukmergė
Kaunas
Vilnius
Telšiai
Tauragė
Nemunas
Klaipėda
Sovetsk
Gusev
Chernyakhovsk
Kaliningrad
Baltiysk
Zatoka Gdańska
Gdynia
Gdańsk
Elbląg
Malbork
Nogat
Braniewo
Olsztyn
Ostróda
Kwidzyn
Grudziądz
Chełmno
Toruń
Wisła
Bydgoszcz
Chojnice
Słupsk
Koszalin
Darłowo
Kołobrzeg
Wolin
Szczecin
(Stettin)
Stargard Szczeciński
Pyrzyce
Wałcz
Piła
Mława
Narew
Łomża
Ostrołęka
Pisz
Ełk
Gołdap
Suwałki
Augustów
Białystok
Grodno
Lida
Korsze
LATVIA
LITHUANIA
RUSSIA
POLAND
BELARUS
Pojezierze Mazurskie
BALTIC
Bornholm
Rønne
Nexø
Sölvesborg
Karlshamn
Karlskrona
BLEKINGE
Växjö
Vetlanda
Nybro
Kalmar
Oskarshamn
Öland
Borgholm
Burgsvik
Hemse
Romao
Hoburgen
Åsnen
SMÅLAND
377
245
311
228
238
309
329
56
54
16
18
20
22
24
East from Greenwich
68
58
61
COPYRIGHT, GEORGE PHILIP & SON, LTD.

ICELAND
on the same scale
as general map
West from 18 Greenwich
Arctic Circle
Vatnajökull
Ódáðahraun
Hofsjökull
Langjökull
Mýrdalsjökull
Snæfellsjökull
Drangajökull
Eiríksjökull
Öræfajökull
Reykjavík
Keflavík
Hafnarfjörður
Akranes
Akureyri
Húsavík
Sauðárkrókur
Siglufjörður
Ísafjörður
Seyðisfjörður
Faxaflói
Breiðafjörður
Húnaflói
Skagafjörður
Eyjafjörður
Skjálfandi
Axarfjörður
Vopnafjörður
Vopnafjörður
Héraðsflói
Grímsey
Flatey
Vestmannaeyjar
Surtsey
Hekla
Torfajökull
Askja
Herðubreið
Snæfell
Mývatn
Dettifoss
Geysir
Þórisvatn
Hvítá
Þjórsá
Jökulsá á Fjöllum
Skjálfandafljót
Lagarfljót
Blanda
Héraðsvötn
Kirkjubæjarklaustur
Ingólfshöfði
Reykjanes
Horn
Straumnes
Glettinganes
Fontur
Digranes
Rifstangi
Raufarhöfn
Þórshöfn
Bakkafjörður
Egilsstaðir
Eskifjörður
Neskaupstaður
Djúpivogur
Höfn
Stokksnes
Laki
Grænalón
Eyrarbakki
Stokkseyri
Þorlákshöfn
Kópavogur
Borgarnes
Blönduós
Hólmavík
Stykkishólmur
Ólafsvík
Gláma
1:5 000 000
Senja
Andfjorden
Hinnøy
Harstad
Narvik
Ofotfjorden
Tysfjorden
Vesterålen
Langøy
Lofoten
Austvågøy
Vestvågøy
Moskenesøya
Moskenstraumen
Værøy
Vestfjorden
Svolvær
Hamarøy
Bodø
Fauske
Saltfjorden
Folda
Sulitjelma
Sarektjåkkå
Frostisen
2090
1913
1744
2119
1833
1682
1460
1538
1675
1491
1446
1251
925
920

1 : 5 000 000

66

NORWEGIAN SEA
Arctic Circle
East from Greenwich
Stadlandet
Ålesund
Volda
Molde
Kristiansund
Smøla
Hitra
Frøya
Frohavet
Åndalsnes
Romsdalen
Dovrefjell
2286
Snøhetta
Orkla
Løkken
Orkanger
Trondheim
Trondheimsfjorden
Støren
Gaula
Røros
Femund
1604
Levanger
Verdalsøra
Steinkjer
Namsos
Folda
Vikna
Vega
Vegafj.
Alsten
Dønna
Grong
Namsen
Tunnsjøen
1390
Børgefjell
1703
Vefsna
Mosjøen
Mo
1915
Svartisen
1599
Røssvatnet
Nasa
1214
Lønsdal
Storuman
Uddjaur
Sorsele
Stensele
1589
VÄSTERBOTTEN
Malgomaj
Vojmsjön
Vilhelmina
Ångermanälven
Hoting
Tåsjön
Flåsjön
Ströms vattudal
Strömsund
Hotagen
Kallsjön
Östersund
Storsjön
Sylarna
1766
Hede
Ljungan
Bräcke
Ånge
Bispfors
Indalsälven
Kramfors
Sollefteå
Sundsvall
N.-TRØNDELAG
SØR-TRØNDELAG
MØRE OG ROMSDAL
JÄMTLAND
VÄSTERNORRLAND
COPYRIGHT GEORGE PHILIP & SON LTD
66
64
62
8
10
12
14
16

60

NORWEGIAN SEA
Arctic Circle
Vesterålen
Senja
Tromsø
Lofoten
Vestfjorden
Narvik
Torneträsk
2117
Kebnekaise
Kiruna
Stora Lulevatten
Gällivare
Bodø
Sulitjelma 1913
Lule älv
Hornavan
Storavan
Mosjøen
Vega
Vikna
Foldafj.
Storuman
Skellefteå
Vilhelmina
Norrland
Trondheimfj.
Steinkjer
Levanger
Vännäs
Umeå
Ume älv
Kristiansund
Molde
Trondheim
Ångermanälven
Örnsköldsvik
Ålesund
Östersund
Stadlandet
Dovrefjell
Storsjön
Snøhetta 2286
Bräcke
Ånge
Indals
Härnösand
Florø
Jotunheimen
Galdhøpiggen 2469
Ljusnan
Sundsvall
Höyanger
Gulf of
Sognefj.
Lillehammer
Glåma
Österdalälven
Hudiksvall
Bergen
Hamar
Mora
Söderhamn
Hardangerfj.
Mjøsa
Västerdalälven
Klarälven
Falun
Gävle
Oslo
Dal
Dannemora
Ahvenanmaa
Haugesund
Drammen
Svealand
Sala
Skien
Oslofj.
Karlstad
Västerås
Mälaren
Uppsala
Åland
Stavanger
Larvik
Fredrikstad
Hjalmaren
Egersund
Halden
Örebro
Arendal
Vänern
Eskilstuna
Stockholm
Kristiansand
East from Greenwich
Lindesnes
Mandal
NORWAY
SWEDEN
60
70
65
0
5
10
15
20

1 : 10 000 000

13
BARENTS SEA
Nordkapp
Nordkinn
Hammerfest
Sørøya
Vardø
Vardsø
Varangerfj.
Tana
Pechenga
Murmansk
Inari
Inari
Porttipahta
Lokka
Lappland
Kirovsk
Kolskiy Poluostrov
Torneträsk
Kemijoki
Kandalaksha
Rovaniemi
Beloye More
Tornio
Kemi
Boden
Haparanda
Luleå
Piteå
Kem
Arkhangelsk
Oulu
Belomorsk
Oulu
Skellefteå
Raahe
Onega
Oulu-järvi
Kajaani
Onega
Bothnia
Iisalmi
Karelia
RUSSIA
Vaasa
Kuopio
FINLAND
Joensuu
Onezhskoye Ozero
Jyväskylä
Petrozavodsk
Tampere
Saimaa
Pori
Imatra
Uusikaupunki
Ladozhskoye Ozero
Hämeenlinna
Oz. Beloye
Lahti
Vyborg
Turku
Helsinki
Kotka
Kronshtadt
St. Peterburg
Tikhvin
Gulf of Finland
Hangö
Porkkala
Cherepovets
Kohtla-Järve
Tallinn
Narva
Malaya Vishera
25
30
35
40
45
70
65
60
68
62
68

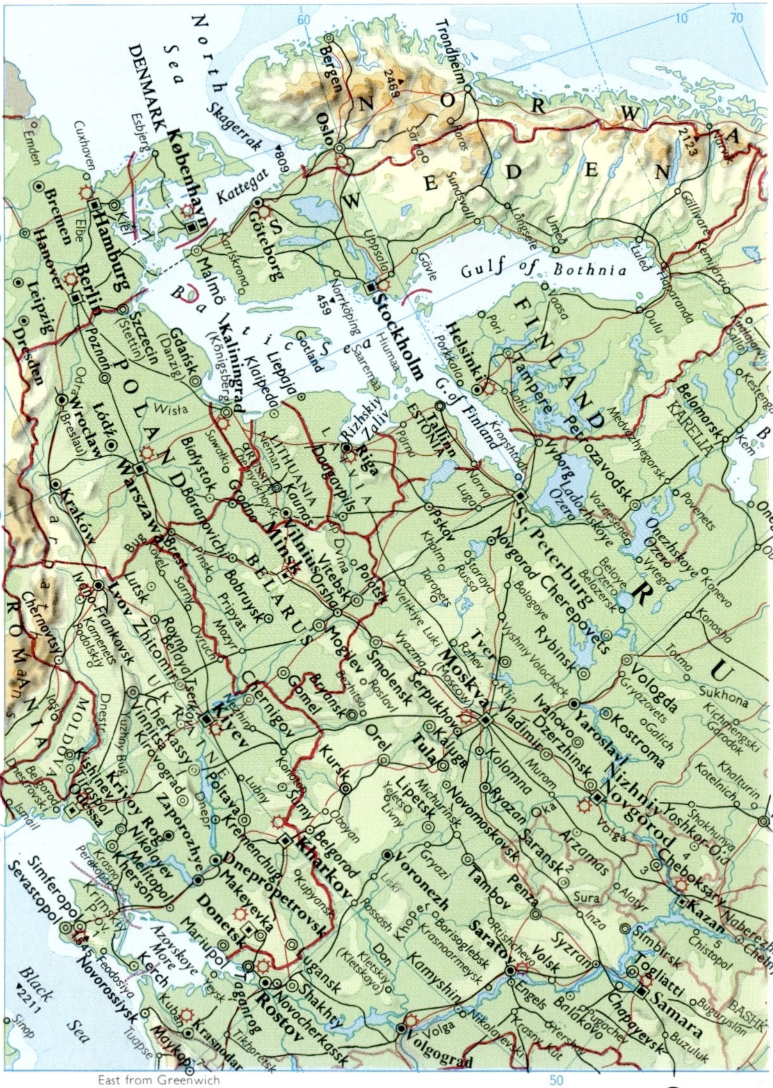
North Sea
Skagerrak
Kattegat
DENMARK
København
Esbjerg
Cuxhaven
Emden
Bremen
Hamburg
Kiel
Elbe
Hanover
Berlin
Leipzig
Dresden
Bergen
Oslo
Trondheim
2469
2123
NORWAY
SWEDEN
Göteborg
Malmö
Karlskrona
Uppsala
Stockholm
Norrköping
459
Gävle
Sundsvall
Umeå
Luleå
Gällivare
Narvik
Gulf of Bothnia
FINLAND
Vaasa
Pori
Oulu
Tornio
Haparanda
Helsinki
Tampere
Lahti
Porkkala
G. of Finland
Baltic Sea
Gotland
Saaremaa
Hiiumaa
Rizhskiy Zaliv
Szczecin
(Stettin)
Gdańsk
(Danzig)
Kaliningrad
(Königsberg)
Klaipeda
Liepaja
Poznań
Wrocław
(Breslau)
Łódź
Warszawa
Kraków
Wisła
POLAND
Białystok
Suwałki
LITHUANIA
Kaunas
Vilnius
Neman
Riga
LATVIA
Daugavpils
ESTONIA
Tallinn
Pärnu
Narva
Pskov
Luga
St. Peterburg
Vyborg
Kronshtadt
Ladozhskoye Ozero
Petrozavodsk
Onezhskoye Ozero
Medvezhyegorsk
Belomorsk
KARELIA
Kem
Kestenga
Povenets
Onega
Vytegra
Konosha
Beloye Ozero
Belozersk
Cherepovets
Rybinsk
Vologda
Totma
Sukhona
Gryazovets
Galich
Kostroma
Yaroslavl
Ivanovo
Dzerzhinsk
Nizhniy Novgorod
Kotelnich
Kirov
Yoshkar-Ola
Cheboksary
Kazan
Naberezhnyye Chelny
Chistopol
Simbirsk
Togliatti
Samara
Buguruslan
Buzuluk
Novgorod
Kholm
Staraya Russa
Toropets
Bologoye
Vyshniy Volochek
Velikiye Luki
Rzhev
Tver
Klin
Moskva
(Moscow)
Vladimir
Vyazma
Smolensk
Serpukhov
Kaluga
Tula
Kolomna
Murom
Ryazan
Arzamas
Saransk
Penza
Alatyr
Inza
Syzran
Sura
Volga
Volsk
Saratov
Engels
Balakovo
Pugachev
Chapayevsk
Kamyshin
Volgograd
Nikolayevsk
Tambov
Michurinsk
Lipetsk
Novomoskovsk
Yelets
Livny
Orel
Bryansk
Roslavl
Kursk
Oboyan
Belgorod
Kharkov
Kupyansk
Voronezh
Gryazi
Liski
Rossosh
Borisoglebsk
Khoper
Don
Krasnoarmeysk
Rtishchevo
BELARUS
Grodno
Baranovichi
Brest
Pinsk
Minsk
Bobruysk
Vitebsk
Orsha
Polotsk
Mogilev
Gomel
Mozyr
Pripyat
UKRAINE
Lutsk
Rovno
Lvov
Ivano-Frankovsk
Chernovtsy
Kamenets Podolskiy
Zhitomir
Berdichev
Vinnitsa
Kiyev
Chernigov
Cherkassy
Kirovograd
Nezhin
Konotop
Sumy
Poltava
Lubny
Kremenchug
Dnepr
Dnepropetrovsk
Zaporozhye
Krivoy Rog
Nikolayev
Kherson
Odessa
Melitopol
Makeyevka
Donetsk
Mariupol
Lugansk
Shakhty
Taganrog
Rostov
Novocherkassk
Krasnodar
Maykop
Tikhoretsk
Novorossiysk
Tuapse
Kerch
Feodosiya
Simferopol
Sevastopol
Krimskiy P-ov.
Azovskoye More
Yeysk
Kuban
MOLDOVA
Kishinev
Tiraspol
Belgorod Dnestrovskiy
Izmail
Dnestr
ROMANIA
Black Sea
2211
Sinop
East from Greenwich
10
20
30
50
60
70

58

57

70

1 : 20 000 000

13

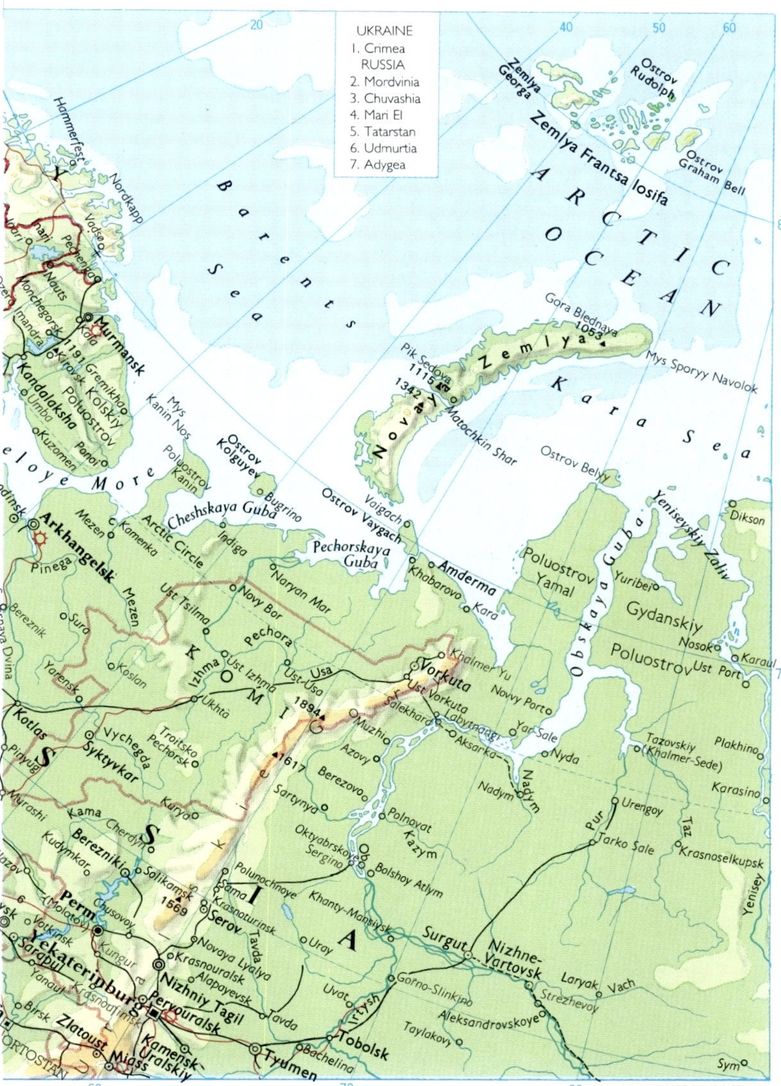
UKRAINE
1. Crimea
RUSSIA
2. Mordvinia
3. Chuvashia
4. Mari El
5. Tatarstan
6. Udmurtia
7. Adygea
ARCTIC OCEAN
Barents Sea
Kara Sea
Zemlya Georga
Ostrov Rudolph
Zemlya Frantsa Iosifa
Ostrov Graham Bell
Novaya Zemlya
Gora Blednaya
1053
Pik Sedova
1115
1342
Mys Sporyy Navolok
Matochkin Shar
Ostrov Belyy
Ostrov Kolguyev
Mys Kanin Nos
Poluostrov Kanin
Bugrino
Vaigach
Ostrov Vaygach
Cheshskaya Guba
Pechorskaya Guba
Arctic Circle
Indiga
Amderma
Khabarovo
Kara
Poluostrov Yamal
Obskaya Guba
Yeniseyskiy Zaliv
Dikson
Yuribei
Gydanskiy Poluostrov
Nosok
Karaul
Ust Port
Hammerfest
Nordkapp
Vadsø
Pechenga
Nauts
Monchegorsk
Ozero Imandra
Murmansk
Kola
1191
Kirovsk
Gremikha
Kolskiy Poluostrov
Kandalaksha
Umba
Kuzomen
Ponoi
Beloye More
Severodvinsk
Arkhangelsk
Mezen
Kamenka
Pinega
Severnaya Dvina
Bereznik
Sura
Yarensk
Koslan
Ust Tsilma
Novy Bor
Naryan Mar
Pechora
Usa
Ust Usa
Ust Izhma
Izhma
Ukhta
KOMI
Vorkuta
Khalmer Yu
Ust Vorkuta
Novyy Port
Yar Sale
Salekhard
Labytnangi
Aksarka
Nyda
Nadym
1894
1617
Muzhi
Azovy
Berezovo
Sartynya
Polnovat
Kazym
Oktyabrskoye
Sergino
Ob
Bolshoy Atlym
Kotlas
Pinyug
Murashi
Vychegda
Syktyvkar
Troitsko Pechorsk
Kurya
Kama
Cherdyn
Berezniki
Kudymkar
Glazov
Solikamsk
Izhevsk
Votkinsk
Perm
(Molotov)
Chusovoy
1569
Sarapul
Yekaterinburg
Kungur
Yanaul
Krasnoufimsk
Birsk
Ufa
Zlatoust
Miass
Kamensk-Uralskiy
Pervouralsk
Nizhniy Tagil
Alapayevsk
Krasnouralsk
Novaya Lyalya
Serov
Krasnoturinsk
Polunochnoye
Ivdel
Tavda
Uray
Khanty-Mansiysk
Surgut
Nizhne-Vartovsk
Gorno-Slinkino
Uvat
Irtysh
Tobolsk
Tyumen
Bachelina
Taylakovy
Aleksandrovskoye
Strezhevoy
Laryak
Vach
Urengoy
Pur
Tarko Sale
Krasnoselkupsk
Taz
Tazovskiy (Khalmer-Sede)
Plakhino
Karasino
Yenisey
Sym
SSIA
RUSSIA
20
40
50
60
80
70

71

72

KAZAKSTAN AND CENTRAL ASIA

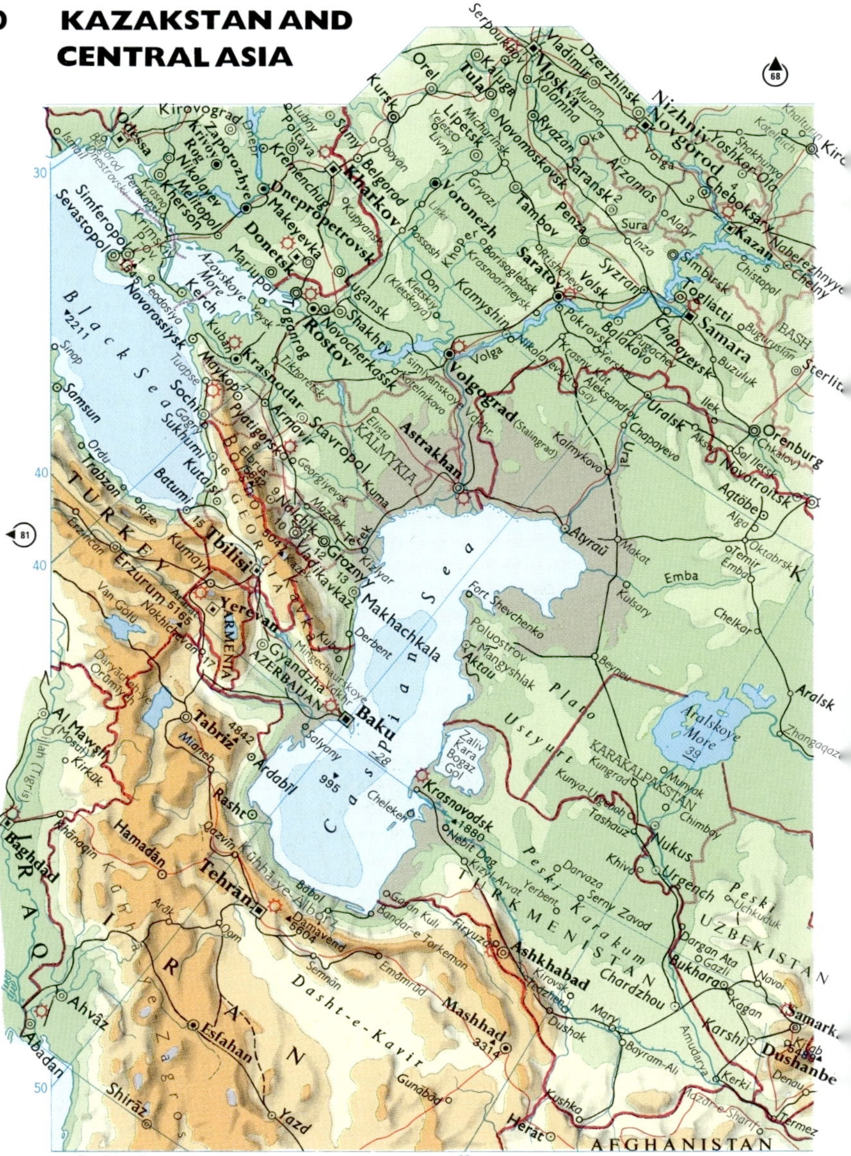
Moskva
Vladimir
Dzerzhinsk
Nizhniy Novgorod
Serpukhov
Kaluga
Tula
Orel
Kolomna
Murom
Ryazan
Kursk
Lipetsk
Novomoskovsk
Michurinsk
Yoshkar-Ola
Cheboksary
Kazan
Naberezhnyye Chelny
Arzamas
Saransk
Penza
Tambov
Voronezh
Belgorod
Kharkov
Sumy
Poltava
Kremenchug
Dnepropetrovsk
Zaporozhye
Krivoy Rog
Nikolayev
Kherson
Melitopol
Odessa
Kirovograd
Simferopol
Sevastopol
Donetsk
Makeyevka
Lugansk
Mariupol
Taganrog
Rostov
Novocherkassk
Shakhty
Kerch
Feodosiya
Azovskoye More
Novorossiysk
Krasnodar
Maykop
Sochi
Sukhumi
Batumi
Kutaisi
Tbilisi
Armavir
Stavropol
Pyatigorsk
Elbrus
Nalchik
Vladikavkaz
Groznyy
Makhachkala
Derbent
Kizlyar
Elista
KALMYKIA
Astrakhan
Volgograd (Stalingrad)
Kamyshin
Saratov
Volsk
Syzran
Simbirsk
Togliatti
Samara
Chapayevsk
Balakovo
Pokrovsk
Uralsk
Orenburg (Chkalov)
Novotroitsk
Aqtöbe
Atyraū
Makat
Kulsary
Emba
Chelkar
Aralsk
Aralskoye More
Fort Shevchenko
Poluostrov Mangyshlak
Aktau
Beyneu
Plato Ustyurt
KARAKALPAKSTAN
Kungrad
Muynak
Nukus
Urgench
Khiva
Tashauz
Kara Bogaz Gol
Krasnovodsk
Nebit Dag
Kizyl-Arvat
Peski Karakum
TURKMENISTAN
Ashkhabad
Mary
Chardzhou
Bukhara
UZBEKISTAN
Samarkand
Karshi
Dushanbe
Termez
Kushka
Herat
AFGHANISTAN
Mashhad
Dasht-e-Kavir
Tehrān
Damāvand
Qazvin
Rasht
Ardabīl
Tabrīz
Hamadān
Esfahan
Shīrāz
Yazd
IRAN
Baku
AZERBAIJAN
Gyandzha
Yerevan
ARMENIA
GEORGIA
Erzurum
Van Gölü
TURKEY
Trabzon
Samsun
Sinop
Black Sea
Caspian Sea
Al Mawsil (Mosul)
Kirkūk
Baghdād
IRAQ
Ahvāz
Ābādān
East from Greenwich
60

1 : 20 000 000

69

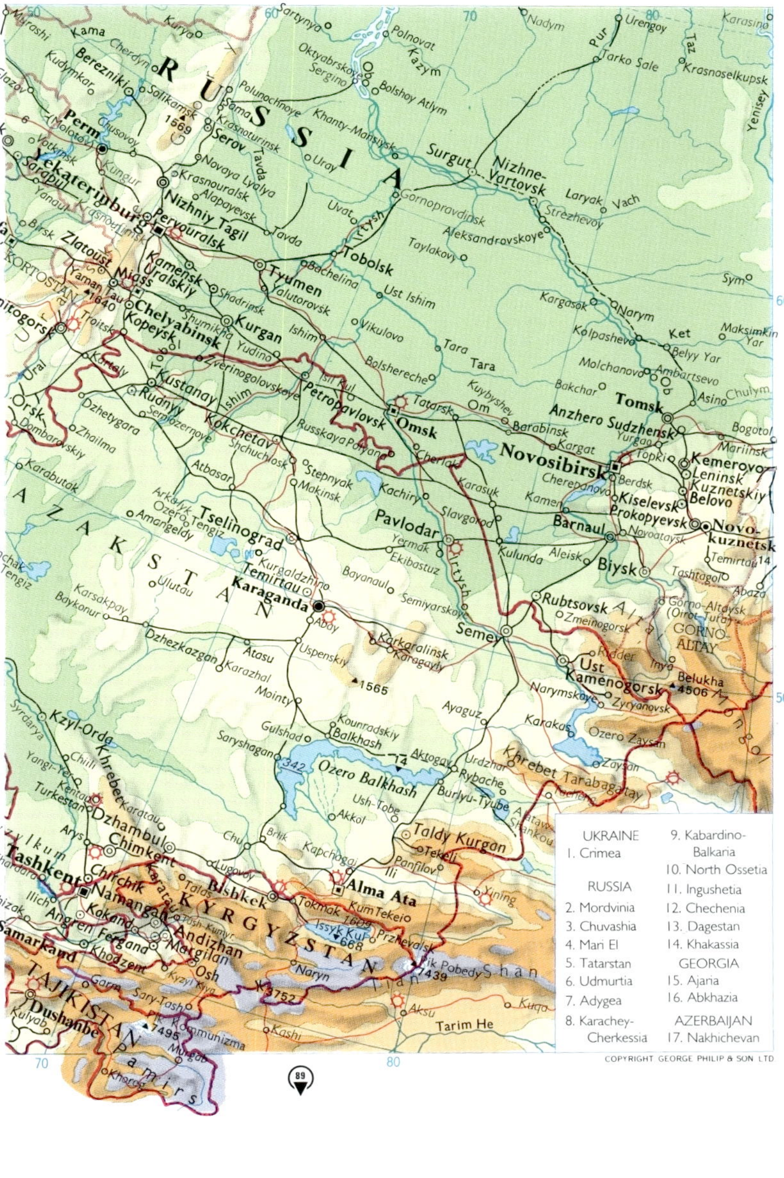

UKRAINE
1. Crimea

RUSSIA
2. Mordvinia
3. Chuvashia
4. Mari El
5. Tatarstan
6. Udmurtia
7. Adygea
8. Karachey-Cherkessia
9. Kabardino-Balkaria
10. North Ossetia
11. Ingushetia
12. Chechenia
13. Dagestan
14. Khakassia

GEORGIA
15. Ajaria
16. Abkhazia

AZERBAIJAN
17. Nakhichevan

74

89

12

69

ARCTIC OCEAN
3800
Ostrov Henrietta
Ostrov Jeanette
Ostrova Delong
Ostrov Zhokhova
Ostrov Bennett
Novosibirskiye Ostrova
Ostrov Faddeyevskiy
Ostrov Novaya Sibir
374
Ostrov Shmidta
Mys Arkticheskiy
Ostrov Komsomolets
Ostrov Pioner
Ostrov Oktyabrskoy Revolyutsii
965
Ostrov Bolshevik
Severnaya Zemlya
Proliv Vilskutskogo
Laptev Sea
Ostrov Belkovskiy
Ostrov Kotelnyy
Ostrov Stolbovoy
Ostrov Malyy Lyakhovskiy
Ostrov Bolshoy Lyakhovskiy
Lyakhovskiye Ostrova
Proliv Dmitriya Lapteva
Kokuora
Poluostrov Taymyr
Gory Byrranga
1146
Oz. Taymyr
Ostrov Bolshoy Begichev
Mys Buorkhaya
Nizhneyansk
Kazachye
Ust Kuyga
Nordvik
Ust Olenek
Olenek
Tit-Ary
Tiksi
Uryung-Khaya
Saskylakh
Novorybnoye
Khatanga
Popigay
Bulun
Kyusyur
Yana
Deputatskiy
Pyasina
Agapa
Volochanka
Kheta
Kotuy
Anabar
Kel (Bysyttakh)
Verkhoyansk
Batagay
Chernoye
Dzhelinde
Dzhardzhan
2389
Verkhoyanskiy Khrebet
Norilsk
Dudinka
Gory Putorana
1701
Potapovo
Yessey
Kystatyam
Zhigansk
Bilir
Moyyero
Igarka
962
Arctic Circle
Kytal ktakh
Lepikha
Lena
Batamay (Ust-Aldan)
Shologontsy
Ugolyak
Sangar
Srednevilyuysk
Bulus
Namtsy
Turukhansk
Vilyuy
Vilyuysk
Verkhnevilyuysk
Nyurba
Pokrovsk
Yelanskoye
Noginsk
Nizhnyaya Tunguska
Tura
Syul'dzhyukyor
Chernyshevskiy
Mirnyy
Pavlovo
Suntar
Sinskoye
Yukti
Tuay-Khaya
Simenga
Lensk (Mukhtuya)
Olekminsk
Verkhnyaya Amga
Tommot
Yerbogachen
Kurya
Baykit
Podkamennaya Tunguska
Kuyumba
Mutaray
Dzhikimde
Aldan
Nokhtuysk
Roman
Vitim
Kropotkin
Yenyuka
Malyy Nimnyr
Chulman
Yartsevo
Severo-Yeniseyskiy
1104
Vanavara
Verkhneye Kalinino
RUSSIA
SAKHA
70
80
90
100
110
120
130
140
150
East from Greenwich

74

1 : 20 000 000

Mys Dezhneva
(East C.)
Uelen
Lavrentiya
Provideniya
Anadyrskiy Zaliv
St. Lawrence I.
(U.S.A.)
Chukotskoye
More
Ostrov Vrangelya
East Siberian Sea
Vankarem
Amen
1843
Rene
Egvekinot
Chukotskiy Khrebet
Pevek
Ust Chaun
Ostrov
Ayon
Ostrova
Medvezhi
Ambarchik
Cherskiy
1853
Bilibino
Anadyr
Beringovskiy
Koryakskiy Khrebet
Khatyrka
2562
Nizhne Kolymsk
Bolshoy Anyuy
1742
Veropol
Markovo
Penzhino
Oloy
Omolon
Kamenskoye
Machevna
Kavacha
Tilichiki
Chokurdakh
Kondakovo
Shamanovo
Indigirka
Srednekolymsk
Uyandi
(Otur-Kyuyel)
Druzhina
Okhotsko Kolymskoye
Paren
Gizhiga
Penzhinskaya Guba
Rekinniki
Kichiga
Ossora
Ostrov
Karaginskiy
Bering Sea
Stolbovaya
Abkit
Evensk
Nayakhan
Kolyma
Zyryanka
Balygychan
Seymchan
Omsukchan
Zashiversk
Khonu
Pobeda
3147
Taskan
Orotukan
Vilìga
Gizhiginskaya
Guba
Palana
Sredinnyy Khrebet
Uka
Komandorskiye
Ostrova
Nikolskoye
Ust-Kamchatsk
Gora Chen
2682
Ust Nera
Khrebet Cherskogo
Yagodnoye
Iret
Zaliv
Shelikhova
Tigil
Poluostrov Kamchatka
4750
Alyaskitovyy
Kyulyunken
Susuman
Loshkalakh
Sanga-Tolon
Atka
Palatka
Magadan
Oymyakon
2959
Ust-Omchugo
Staryy Kheydzhan
Ust-Khayryuzovo
Icha
G. Klyuchevskaya
3621
Pushchino
Zhupanovo
3456
Petropavlovsk-
Kamchatskiy
Sobolev
Khrebet
Aldan
Khandyga
Okhotskiy
Perevoz
Borogontsy
Ytyk-Kel
Allakh-Yun
Arka
Okhotsk
Vorovskoye
Kirovskiy
Bolsheretsk
Opala
Ust Bolsheretsk
Severo-
Kurilsk
Ynykchanskiy
Ulya
Sea of Okhotsk
Yakutsk
Mayya
Amga
Yur
Dzhugdzur
Ust Maya
Ust-Mil
Ostrov
Paramushir
Ostrov
Onekotan
1780
Aim
Maya
Nelkan
Chagda
Chasovnya-
Uchurskaya
Uchur
Ayan
Ostrov Bolshoy
Shantar
Sakhalinskiy
Zaliv
Okha
2246
Kankunskiy
Nemuy
Nikolayevsk-
na-Amure
Susanino
Bogorodskoye
Sakhalin
Aleksandrovsk-
Sakhalinskiy
G. Lopatina
1609
Katangli
Chumikan
Tugur
2482
Kurilskiye Ostrova
Ostrov
Simushir
170
60
180
170
160
50
130
140

75

72

71

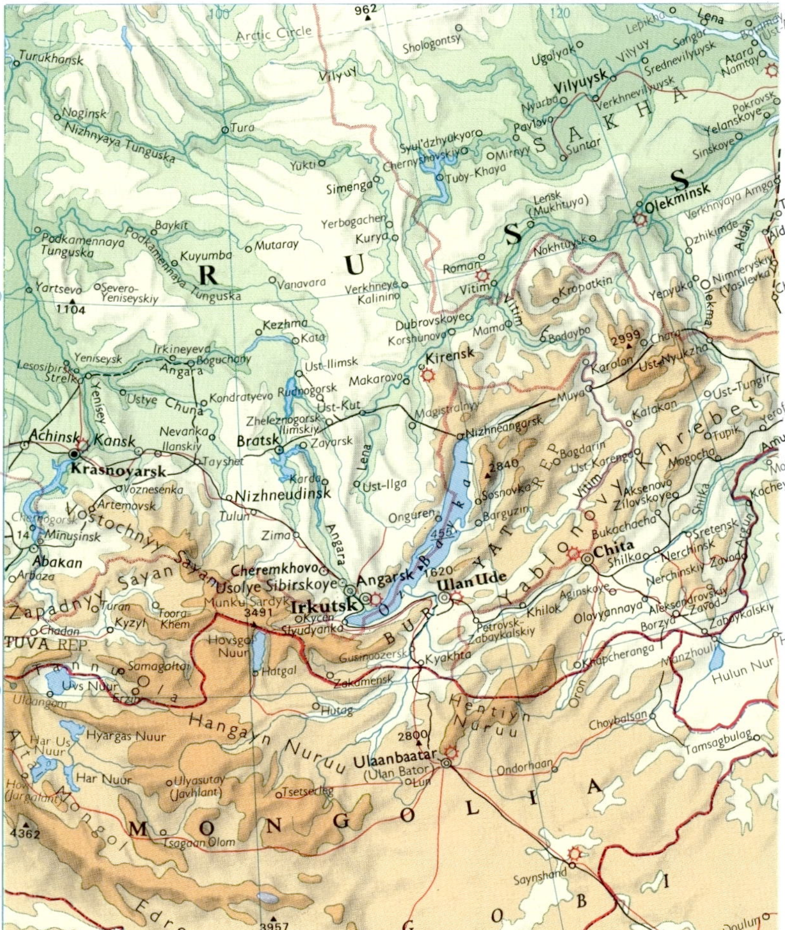

962
Arctic Circle
100
120
Shologontsy
Lena
Turukhansk
Vilyuy
Ugolyak
Vilyuysk
Srednevilyuysk
Sangar
Atara
Namtsy
Verkhnevilyuysk
Nyurba
Pavlovo
S A K H A
Noginsk
Nizhnyaya Tunguska
Tura
Syul'dzhyukyor
Chernyshevskiy
Mirnyy
Suntar
Yukti
Tuoy-Khaya
Simenga
Lensk (Mukhtuya)
Olekminsk
Verkhnyaya Amga
Pokrovsk
Yelanskoye
Sinskoye
Baykit
Yerbogachen
Kurya
Podkamennaya Tunguska
Mutaray
Kuyumba
R U S S
Roman
Nokhtuysk
Dzhikimde
Aldan
Vanavara
Verkhneye Kalinino
Vitim
Kropotkin
Yenyuka
Nimneryskiy (Vasilevka)
Yartsevo
Severo-Yeniseyskiy
1104
60
Dubrovskoye
Mama
Korshunovo
Bodaybo
2999
Chara
Kezhma
Kata
Irkineyeva
Boguchany
Yeniseysk
Lesosibirsk
Strelka
Angara
Ust-Ilimsk
Kirensk
Karalon
Ust-Nyukzha
Makarovo
Rudnogorsk
Kondratyevo
Ustye Chuna
Ust-Kut
Magistralnyy
Muya
Ust-Tungir
Yerofey
Zheleznogorsk-Ilimskiy
Kalakan
Achinsk
Kansk
Nevanka
Ilanskiy
Bratsk
Zayarsk
Nizhneangarsk
Tupik
Amur
Krasnoyarsk
Tayshet
Bagdarin
2840
Ust-Karenga
Mogocha
Karda
Ust-Ilga
Voznesenka
Nizhneudinsk
Sosnovka
Aksenovo
Zilovskoye
Artemovsk
Vostochnyy Sayan
Tulun
Onguren
Barguzin
Baykal
Bukachacha
Sretensk
Chernogorsk
Minusinsk
Zima
1455
Nerchinsk
Abakan
Cheremkhovo
1620
Chita
Shilka
Nerchinskiy Zavod
Arbaza
Angarsk
Ulan Ude
Usolye Sibirskoye
Irkutsk
Aginskoye
Aleksandrovskiy Zavod
Zapadnyy Sayan
Turan
Toora-Khem
Munku Sardyk
3491
Khilok
Olovyannaya
Zabaykalskiy
Kyzyl
Chadan
Slyudyanka
Petrovsk-Zabaykalskiy
Borzya
TUVA REP.
Hovsgol Nuur
Gusinoozersk
Kyakhta
Khapcheranga
Manzhouli
Samagaltay
Hatgal
Zakamensk
Hulun Nur
50
Uvs Nuur
Erzin
Ulaangom
Hutag
Hentiyn Nuruu
Hangayn Nuruu
Choybalsan
Hyargas Nuur
2800
Tamsagbulag
Har Us Nuur
Ulaanbaatar (Ulan Bator)
Har Nuur
Ulyasutay (Javhlant)
Lun
Ondorhaan
Tsetserleg
Hovd (Jargalant)
M O N G O L I A
4362
Altay Mongol
Tsagaan Olom
Saynshand
G O B I
Edrengiyn Nuruu
3957
Doulun
4266
Dalandzadgad
Hami
Gaxun Nur
C H I N A
Baotou
Hohhot
Zhangjiakou
100
110

East from Greenwich

1 : 20 000 000

73

Sea of Okhotsk
Sea of Japan
Poluostrov Kamchatka
Ust Bolsheretsk
Ozernaya
Severo-Kurilsk
Ostrov Paramushir
Ostrov Onekotan
Ostrov Simushir
Ostrov Urup
Kurilskiye Ostrova
Ostrov Iturup
Kurilsk
Ostrov Kunashir
Okhotsk
Ulya
Arka
Yakutsk
Borogontsy
Ytyk-Kel
Okhotskiy Perevoz
Allakh-Yun
Ynykchanskiy
Yur
Amga
Mayya
Ust Maya
Ust-Mil
Aim
Maya
Nelkan
Khrebet Dzhugdzur
Chagda
Uchur
Chasovnya-Uchurskaya
Ayan
Kankunskiy
2246
2482
Stanovoy Khrebet
Nemuy
Chumikan
Tugur
Nagornyy
Tynda
Zeya
Pavlovich
Skovorodino
Dzhalinda
Ushumun
Yermakovo
Uda
Selemdzha
Ekimchan
Norsk
Bureya
Sofiyski
Ostrov Bolshoy Shantar
Sakhalinskiy Zaliv
Nikolayevsk-na-Am.
imeni Poliny Osipenko
Amgun
Okha
Sakhalin
Susanino
Bogorodskoye
Katangli
Aleksandrovsk-Sakhalinskiy
G. Lopatina
1609
Pobedino
Poronaysk
Uglegorsk
Sovetskaya Gavan
Yuzhno-Sakhalinsk
Kholmsk
Korsakov
Sredne Tambovskoye
Amur
2640
Komsomolsk
Amursk
Malamyzh
2078
Khrebet Sikhote Alin
Chegdomyn
Belogorsk
Shimanovsk
Svobodnyy
Zavitinsk
Raychikhinsk
Obluchye
Birobidzhan
Smidovich
Khabarovsk
Nelma
Volochayevka
Leninskoye
Vyazemskiy
Bikin
Blagoveshchensk
Aihui
Poyarkovo
1054
Da Hinggan Ling
Amurzet
Hegang
Songhua Jiang
Jiamusi
Nenjiang
Qiqihar
Suihua
Dalnerechensk
Lesozavodsk
Amgu
Terney
Dalnegorsk
3669
Spassk-Dalnij
Olga
Ozero Khanka
Ussuriysk
Artem
Vladivostok
Nakhodka
Harbin
Ang'angxi
Nen Jiang
Dongbei
Mudanjiang
Kraskino
Tao'an
Jilin
Yanji
Unggi
Chongjin
Changchun
Siping
Songhua Hu
2744
Tonghua
Kilchu
1949
Linxi
Fushun
Shenyang
Anshan
Chifeng
Dandong
NORTH KOREA
Wŏnsan
Kansŏng
Chinnampo
P'yongyang
Yingkou
Chengde
Dalian
Beijing
Sŏul (Seoul)
Inch'on
SOUTH KOREA
Taejŏn
Taegu
Pusan
Wakkanai
Rumoi
Abashiri
2290
Kushiro
Obihiro
Hokkaidō
Sapporo
Otaru
Muroran
Hakodate
Okushiri-shima
Aomori
Hachinohe
Akita
Honshū
Niigata
Toyama
Kanazawa
50
40
120
130
Boundaries of Republics

104

98

ASIA : PHYSICAL

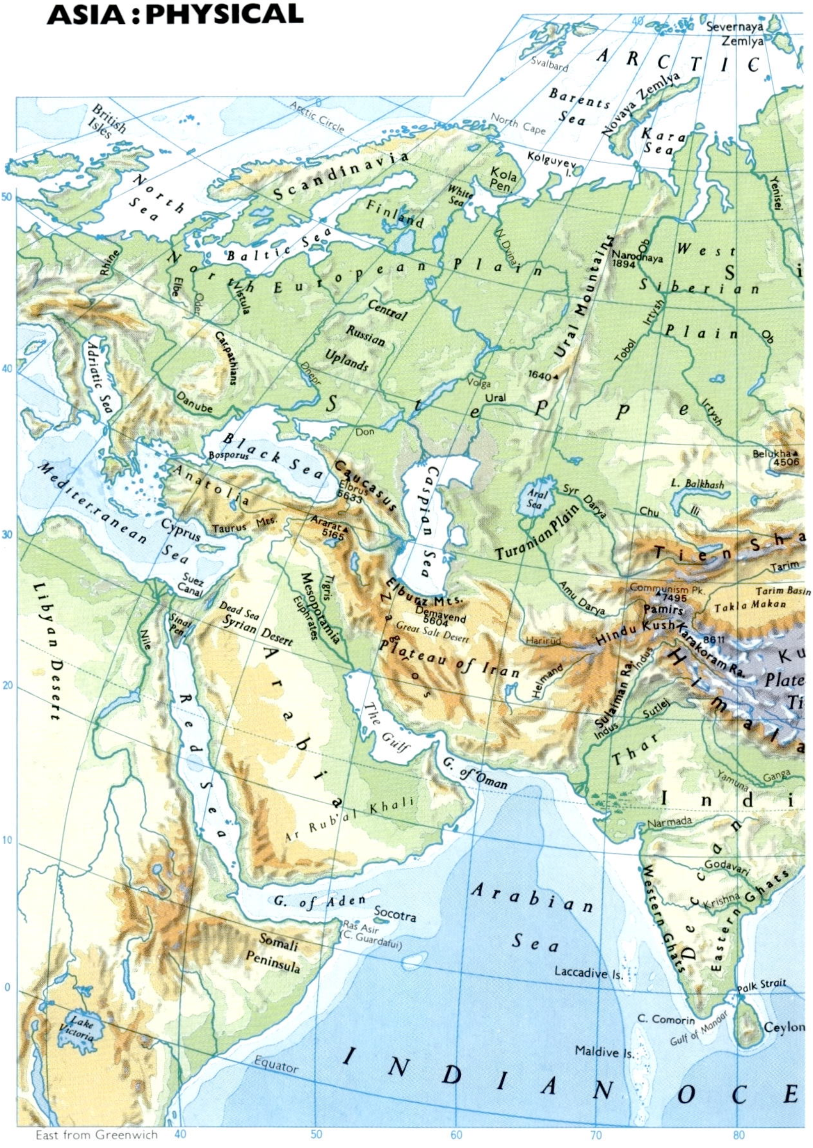
Severnaya Zemlya
Svalbard
ARCTIC
Barents Sea
Novaya Zemlya
Kara Sea
North Cape
Arctic Circle
British Isles
Kolguyev I.
Kola Pen.
White Sea
Scandinavia
North Sea
Finland
Yenisei
Baltic Sea
N. Dvina
Ural Mountains
Narodnaya 1894
Ob
West Siberian Plain
North European Plain
Rhine
Elbe
Oder
Vistula
Central Russian Uplands
Irtysh
Tobol
Carpathians
Adriatic Sea
Dnepr
1640
Volga
Ural
Danube
Steppe
Don
Black Sea
Bosporus
Caucasus
Elbrus 5633
Caspian Sea
Belukha 4506
Mediterranean Sea
Anatolia
Aral Sea
Syr Darya
L. Balkhash
Chu
Ili
Cyprus
Taurus Mts.
Ararat 5165
Turanian Plain
Tien Sha
Tarim
Suez Canal
Libyan Desert
Tigris
Mesopotamia
Euphrates
Elburz Mts.
Demavend 5604
Great Salt Desert
Amu Darya
Communism Pk. 7495
Pamirs
Tarim Basin
Takla Makan
Dead Sea
Syrian Desert
Sinai Pen.
Nile
Arabia
Zagros
Plateau of Iran
Harirud
Hindu Kush
Karakoram Ra.
8611
Helmand
Indus
Himalaya
Ku
Plate
Ti
Red Sea
The Gulf
Sulaiman Ra.
Sutlej
Thar
G. of Oman
Yamuna
Ganga
India
Ar Rub'al Khali
Narmada
Deccan
Godavari
Krishna
Eastern Ghats
Western Ghats
G. of Aden
Socotra
Arabian Sea
Ras Asir (C. Guardafui)
Somali Peninsula
Laccadive Is.
Palk Strait
Lake Victoria
C. Comorin
Gulf of Manaar
Ceylon
Maldive Is.
Equator
INDIAN OCE
East from Greenwich
40
50
60
70
80
30
20
10
0

1 : 60 000 000

C. Chelyuskin
OCEAN
Laptev Sea
New Siberian Is.
Wrangel I.
C. Dezhneva
Bering Strait
Taimyr Peninsula
Kotuy
Olenek
Lena
Verkhoyansk Range
Indigirka
Kolyma
Gydan Ra. (Kolyma)
Kamchatka Peninsula
Bering Sea
Aleutian Is.
7822
Klyuchevsk Vol.
4750
Sredinny Ra.
Central Siberian Plateau
Lower Tunguska
Aldan
Stanovoy Ra.
Sea of Okhotsk
Sakhalin
Kuril Is.
10,542
PACIFIC OCEAN
Yablonovy Ra.
Amur
Angara
L. Baikal
Sayan Mts.
Sikhote Alin Ra.
La Pérouse Str.
Hokkaidō
Great Khingan Mts.
Manchurian Plain
Sungari
Selenga
Altai
Plateau of Mongolia
Gobi
Sea of Japan
Korea
Honshū
Fuji-san
3776
10,554
Japan
Turfan Basin
Po Hai
Yellow Sea
Korea Str.
Shikoku
Kyūshū
Bonin Is.
Lop Nor
Koko Nor
Great Plain of China
Hwang
East China Sea
Ryūkyū Is.
Kunlun Shan
China
Tropic of Cancer
Plateau of Tibet
Yangtze Kiang
Tsangpo
Everest
8848
Himalaya
Brahmaputra
Formosa
Guam
11,022
Si-kiang
Hong (Red)
G. of Tonkin
Hainan
Luzon
Philippine Is.
Caroline Is.
Salween
Irrawaddy
Menam
Mekong
South China Sea
Cape Johnson Deep
10,497
Pelew Is.
Bay of Bengal
Mindanao
Palawan
Sulu Sea
Andaman Is.
G. of Siam
Kinabalu
4101
Halmahera
Celebes Sea
Moluccas
Nicobar Is.
New Guinea
Str. of Malacca
Malay Peninsula
Borneo
Celebes
Ceram
Makasar Strait
Banda Sea
Sunda Is.
Sumatra
East Indies
Arafura Sea
Java Sea
Flores
Timor
Sunda Str.
Java
Bali
Australia

ARCTIC
Severnaya Zemlya
Svalbard
Barents Sea
Novaya Zemlya
Kara Sea
Arctic Circle
UNITED KINGDOM
London
North Sea
Murmansk
Beloje More
Arkhangelsk
Igarka
Yenisey
Baltic Sea
Berlin
Paris
Rhine
St. Peterburg
Ural Mts.
Ob
Irtysh
Tobolsk
EUROPE
Wisła
Warszawa
Moskva
RU
Wien
Yekaterinburg
Novosibirsk
Tomsk
Roma
Beograd
Dnepr
Volga
Orenburg
Chelyabinsk
Omsk
Ken.
Barnaul
Danube
Odessa
Magnitogorsk
Thessaloníki
Rostov
Don
Ural
Semey
Black Sea
Astrakhan
KAZAKSTAN
Istanbul
Bursa
Ankara
Batumi
Tbilisi
Caspian Sea
Aral'skoye More
Syr Darya
Ozero Balkhash
Athínai
Izmir
TURKEY
Erzurum
Yerevan
Baku
UZBEK.
Khiva
Tashkent
Alma Ata
Ining
Mediterranean Sea
El Iskandarîya
Halab
Krasnovodsk
Kokand
KYRGYZSTAN
Tarim
LIBYA
Bayrût
LEB.
SYRIA
Euphrates
Tigris
Tabrīz
TURKMEN.
Bukhara
Ashkhabad
Samarkand
TAJIK.
Kashi
XINJI UYG
ISRAEL
El Qâhira
Dimashq
IRAQ
Mary
Shache
Jerusalem
JORDAN
Baghdād
Tehrān
Mashhad
IRAN
Esfahān
Herāt
Kabul
Peshawar
KASHMIR
Nile
EGYPT
Al Basrah
AFGHANISTAN
Himalaya
XIZ (TI
Aswân
Kuwait
Shīrāz
Qandahār
Lahore
Red Sea
SAUDI ARABIA
Bahrain
Bandar e Bushehr
Zāhedān
Quetta
PAKISTAN
Simla
Al Madīnah
Ar Riyād
The Gulf
Indus
Delhi
NEP
Bûr Sûdân
Suakin
Makkah (Mecca)
U.A.E.
Gwādar
Agra
Lucknow
G. of Oman
Kanpur
Varanasi
El Khartûm
Muscat
Karachi
Allahabad
El Obeid
SUDAN
INDIA
ERITREA
Kamaran
OMAN
Ahmadabad
Narmada
Gondera
YEMEN
Bombay
Godavari
Djibouti
Addis Abeba
Zeila
G. of Aden
Socotra (Yemen)
Arabian Sea
Hyderabad
ETHIOPIA
Harer
Goa
SOMALI REP
Madras
Laccadive Is. (India)
Calicut
Pondicherry
UGANDA
Kampala
KENYA
Obbia
Giuba
RWANDA
BURUNDI
SRI LANK (CEYLON
Colombo
MALDIVES
Muqdisho
Nairobi
Kigoma
INDIAN OC
ZAÏRE
Equator
AFRICA
TANZANIA
Mombasa
East from Greenwich
40
50
60
70
80
10
20
30

1 : 60 000 000

Chelyuskin
OCEAN
Laptev Sea
Novosibirskiye Ostrova
Ostrova Vrangelya
Bering Sea
Aleutian Is.
Lena
Aldan
Yakutsk
Okhotsk
Sea of Okhotsk
Petropavlovsk-Kamchatskiy
Nizhnyaya Tunguska
ASIA
Sakhalin
Kuril Is.
Nikolayevsk
Angara
Amur
Ozero Baykal
Krasnoyarsk
Khabarovsk
Chita
Irkutsk
Kyakhta
Manchuria
Hokkaidō
Sapporo
Hakodate
Harbin
Vladivostok
Ulaanbaatar (Ulan Bator)
Changchun
Sea of Japan
Hovd
MONGOLIA
INNER MONGOLIA
Shenyang (Mukden)
N. KOREA
Tōkyō
Yokohama
Kyōto
Ōsaka
Honshu
Ürümqi (Urumchi)
Beijing
Dalian
Soul
S. KOREA
Pusan
Kitakyūshū
JAPAN
Tianjin
Qingdao
Yellow Sea
Nagasaki
Bonin Is.
Huang
Shanghai
Xi'an
Nanjing
East China Sea
Ryūkyū-rettō
CHINA
Wuhan
Suzhou
Chang
Tropic of Cancer
PACIFIC OCEAN
Chengdu
Chongqing
Xiangtan
Fuzhou
Lhasa
Taiwan (Formosa)
Guangzhou
HONG KONG (Br.)
Macau (Port.)
Guam (U.S.)
BHU.
Brahmaputra
Myitkyina
Kunming
Ganga
BANGLADESH
Dhaka
Calcutta
BURMA
Mandalay
Hanoi
Zhanjiang
G. of Tongking
Hainan
Luzon
PHILIPPINES
Caroline Is.
LAOS
VIETNAM
Hué
Manila
Erawadi
Myit
Thanlwin Myit
Bay of Bengal
THAILAND
Belau
Rangon (Rangoon)
Bangkok
CAMBODIA
South China Sea
Palawan
Mindanao
Davao
Andaman Is. (India)
Gulf of Thailand
Thanh Pho Ho Chi Minh
Sulu Sea
Zamboanga
Sulu Arch
Sabah
BRUNEI
Celebes Sea
Halmahera
New Guinea
Nicobar Is. (India)
George Town
MALAYSIA
Sarawak
Maluku (Moluccas)
Str. of Malacca
Kuala Lumpur
Melaka
Kuching
Borneo
Sulawesi
Ceram
Sumatra
Singapore
INDONESIA
Banda Sea
Thursday I.
Ujung Pandang
Java Sea
Jakarta
Flores
Timor
Selat Sunda
Java
Darwin
AUSTRALIA

53

55

128

Division between Greeks and Turks in Cyprus ; Turks to the North.

1 : 10 000 000

70

Tuapse
Sochi
Sukhumi
Poti
Batumi
Kutaisi
Tskhinvali
Tbilisi
Rustavi
Cherkessk
Georgievsk
Pyatigorsk
Kizlovodsk
Prokhladnyy
Mozdok
Elbrus 5642
Nalchik
Malgobek
Vladikavkaz
Groznyy
Kizlyar
Lopatin
Makhachkala
Buynaksk
Derbent
Fort Shevchenko
CASPIAN
SEA
S E A
R U S S I A
G E O R G I A
Bolshoi Kavkas (Caucasus Mts.)
5047
Kazbek
Terek
Gori
Telavi
Akhaltsikhe
Makharadze
Ardahan
Kura
Artvin
Kackar 3937
Rize
Pazar
Trabzon
Akçaabat
Tirebolu
Giresun
Ordu
(Pontic Mts.)
Kelkit Çayi
Şebinkarahisar
Zara
Gümüşane
Çoruh
Bayburt
Oltu
Kars
Kumayri
Sarikamiş
Kağizman
Keşiş Dağ 3537
Erzincan
Hasankale
Erzurum
Kemah
Mamahatun
Kemaliye
Arapkir
Ağri
Karaköse
Iğdir
Ağri Daği (Ararat) 5165
Doğubayazit
Hekimhan
Elâziğ
Kalan
Bingöl
Murat
Malazgirt
Süphan Daği 4434
Van Gölü
Van
Palu
Ergani
Muş
Tatvan
Bitlis
Siirt
Diyarbakır
Siverek
Firat (Euphrates)
Batman
Misriç
Midyat
Mardin
Sanliurfa
Viranşehir
Cizre
Al Qamishli
Zakhu
Qarachuk
Al 'Amadiyah
Al Hasakah
Zhalah
Ar Raqqah
1547
Sinjar
Tall 'Afar
Ninawa (Nineveh)
Al Mawşil (Mosul)
Zab al Kabir
Arbil
Rawanduz
Qal'at Dizah
Kuysanjaq
Zab aş Şağir
Al Hadr
As Sumaymaniyah
Kirkuk
Halabjah
Dayr az Zawr
Khabur
Abu Kamal
'Anah
Ba'ij
Tuz Khurmatu
Kifri
Tikrit
Samarra'
Diyala
Al Hadithah
Al Miqdadiyah
Al Khalis
Ba'qubah
Khanaqin
Naftshahr
Mandali
W. Hawran
Ar Ramadi
Al Fallujah
Baghdad
Ar Rutbah
Nahr al Furat (Euphrates)
Al Musayyib
Bahr al Milh
Karbala
Babylon
Al Hindiyah
Al Hillah
Al Kufah
An Najaf
Ash Shamiyah
(MESOPOTAMIA)
W. al Ubayyid
Nukhayb
Al Jalamid
W. 'Ar'ar
W. al Khur
Badanah
S H A M
Ad Diwaniyah
Ash Shatrah
As Samawah
Al Kut
Al Hayy
Ar Rifa'
Al Amarah
Badrah
As Suwayrah
Ilam
I L A M
Kabir Kuh
Susangerd
Qal'at Salih
Ahvaz
AL JAZIRAH
I R A Q
S Y R I A
K U R D I S T A N
T U R K E Y
A R M E N I A
Karaklis
Dashkesan
Ozero Sevan
Yerevan
Gyandzha
Mingechaurskoye Vdkhr.
Mirzaani
Sheki
Kuba
Sumgait
Mashtagi
Baku
Yevlakh
Agdam
Stepanakert
Kura
Kazi-Magomed
Alyat
A Z E R B A I J A N
AZER.
Nakhichevan
Kafan
Maku
Khvoy
Marand
Sufian
Ahar
Khiyav
Rud-e Aras (Araks)
Qareh
Im. 26 Bakinskikh Komissarov
Kurinskaya Kosa
Zaliv Kirova
Lenkoran
Astara
Ardabil
Salmas
Tabriz
Kuhha-ye Sabalan 4824
Sarab
SHARQI
Daryacheh-ye Orumiyeh (L. Urmia)
Orumiyeh
4168
Kuh-e Sahand 3722
Azaran
Maragheh
Kargan Rud
GILAN
Khalkhal
Bandar-e Anzali
Rasht
Fowman
Safid
Manjil
Mianeh
Zanjan
ZANJAN
Sa'in Dezh
Miandow Ab
Mahabad
Saqqez
AZARBAYJAN-E GHARBI
AZARBAYJAN-E SHARQI
Sa'idiyeh
Qazvin
Takestan
Bijar
KORDESTAN
Marivan
Avej
I R A N
Sanandaj
Qareh
Saveh
Hamadan
HAMADAN
Kangavar
BAKHTARAN
Bakhtaran
Tafresh
Malayer
Nahavand
Eslamabad-e Gharb
Borujerd
Arak
Khomeyn
Khorramabad
LORESTAN
Aligudarz
Kuhha-ye Zagros
Kuhha-ye Talesh
Kuhha-ye Talesh
Karkheh
Dez
Dezful
Karun
Lali
Shushtar
Masjed Soleyman
Zard Kuh 4548
Meydan-e Naftun
Naft-e-Safid
Veys
Haft Gel
40
44
48
36
32

86

82

80
81

Tel Aviv-Jafo
ISRAEL
Bûr Saîd
Gaza
El 'Arîsh
Jerusalem
Bahr el Miyet (Dead Sea)
Ammān
JORDAN
Ma'ān
Turayf
1128
TRANS-ARABIAN OIL PIPELINE ('TAPLINE')
Bādiyat ash Sham
Badanah
Al 'Amārah
Al Qurna
An Nāṣirīyah
Hawr' al Hammār
El Qantara
Ismâ'ilîya
Gebel el Tîh
El Suweis (Suez)
Al Aqabah
Es Sînâ'
2637
2578
Khalîg el Suweis
Khalîj al Aqabah
Al Jawf
Rafḥā
An Nafūd
Ḥafar al Bāṭin
Tabūk
Qal'at al Akhḍar
Al Muwayliḥ
Taymā'
Ḥā'il
Ṭābah
Mada'in Salih
Es Sahrâ Esh Sharqîya
Bûr Safâga
Quseir
Qena
Qûs
El Uqsur (Luxor)
Isna
Idfu
Nahr en Nîl
Kôm Ombo
Al Wajh
W. Hamd
Hadiyah
Buraydah
'Unayzah
Az Zilfi
Al Majma'
S A U D I
A R A B I A
N A J D
Shaqrā'
25
E G Y P T
Aswân
Sadd el Aali
1st Cataract
El Shallal
Buheiret en Naser (Lake Nasser)
Jazâ'ir Qul'ân
Umm Lajj
1814
Al Madīnah
Yanbu'al Bahr
Duwādimī
Ras Bânâs
Bîr Shalatein
R E D S E A
Tropic of Cancer
Mastūrah
Rābigh
Dafīnah
Bir Ungât
Halaib
2216
Ras Hadarba
'Usfān
2nd Cataract
Wadi Halfa
Es Sahrâ en Nûbîya (Nubian Desert)
Jiddah
Makkah (Mecca)
At Tā'if
2565
Turabah
Gebel Mine
Ras Abu Shagara
Muhammad Qol
BAHR EL AHMAR
Abri
Delgo
AN
3rd Cataract
Argo
El Kab
Abu Hamed
Abû Dis
2635
Al Līth
Bûr Sûdân (Port Sudan)
Suakin
Sinkat
NÎL
'ASĪR
Al Qunfudhah
Kareima
4th Cataract
5th Cataract
Merowe
Trinkitat
Berber
Korti
Musmar
Tokar
Adîg
Ras Kasar
Abhā
Atbara
Derudub
2780
Karora
Ed Damer
Adarama
Abū 'Arīsh
Abā as Sa'ūd
Jazā'ir Farasān
Jīzān
3200
Wad Hamid
6th Cataract
Shendî
Nahr 'Atbara
Nakfa
Khamir
Al Luḥayyah
KASSALA
Keren
Mitsiwa
Dahlak Kebir
Kamarān
Omdurmân
El Khartûm Bahrî
El Khartûm (Khartoum)
Kassala
Akordat
Asmera (Asmara)
Zula
3666
Sana
S U D A N
E R I T R E A
15
El Kamlin
Khashm el Girba
Barentu
Mersa Fatma
Al Ḥudaydah
El Geteina
Wâd Medanî
EL GEZIRA
Adwa
Ḥanish
Edd
Zabīd
AN NÎL EL ABYAD
Ed Dueim
Gedaref
Aksum
Umm Dam
El Mafâza
Mekele
Sennâr
Ras Dashen
4620
Al Mukhā
Kôstî
Singa
Gallabat
Metema
E T H I O P I A
Aseb
El Jebelein
Dabat
Gonder
Sekota
Umm Ruwaba
35
40
45

East from Greenwich

128
129

1 : 15 000 000

86
88
IRAN (PERSIA)
Dasht-e Lūt
Yazd
Masjed Soleyman
Qomsheh
Ahvāz
Khorramshahr
Bandār-e Khomeynī
Başrah
Ābādān
Al Fāw
Umm Qasr
Būbiyān
Faylakah
KUWAIT
Al Kuwayt (Kuwait)
Bandār-e Deyam
Kāzerūn
Khārk
Būshehr
Shīrāz
Neyrīz
Kermān
Kūh-e Hazārān
4419
Bam
Bāft
Zābol
Zāhedān
Jahrom
Mand
Deyyer
Tāherī
Bandār 'Abbās
Mīnāb
Bampūr
Khamīr
Bandar Nakhīlū
Wari'ah
As Saffānīyah
Manīfah
Abū Ḩadrīyah
Al Kharsānīyah
THE GULF
Al Qaţīf
Ad Dammam
Az Ẓahrān
BAHRAIN
102
Al Mubarraz
Al Hufūf
Al 'Uqayr
QATAR
Ad Dawḩah
Musay'īd
Riyāḑ (Riyadh)
Harad
As Sulaymānīyah
Al Ḩarīq
Al Ḩillah
1143
Ghayl
Laylā
Jabal Ţuwayq
Tamrah
2057
Oman
Gābrīk
Jāsk
Ash Shāriqah
Dubayy (Dubai)
UNITED ARAB EMIRATES (TRUCIAL STATES)
Abū Ẓaby (Abu Dhabi)
Abū Ẓaby
Gulf of Oman
Şuḩār
Al Buraymī
Al Khābūra
Maskin
Wudham
Alwa
Maţraḩ
3019
Masqaţ (Muscat)
2151
Şūr
Al 'Ubaylah
Maşīrah
Khalūf
OMAN
Rub 'al Khali
Ẓufār
1678
Jazā'ir Khurīyā Murīyā
Mirbāţ
Salālah
Ghubbat al Qamar
Shibām
Al Ḩawţah
W. Masila
Ḩaḑramawt
Ma'rib
YEMEN
2469
Sayhūt
Dhamār
Nişāb
3350
Al Mukallā
Ra's al Kalb
Ta'izz
Al Ḩawrah
Shaqra
Aḩwar
'inat al Shaab
Al 'Adan (Aden)
INDIAN OCEAN
5143
'Abd al Kūrī
Ḩadībū
1503
Socotra (Yemen)
30
25
20
15
45
50
55
60
COPYRIGHT GEORGE PHILIP & SON LTD

81

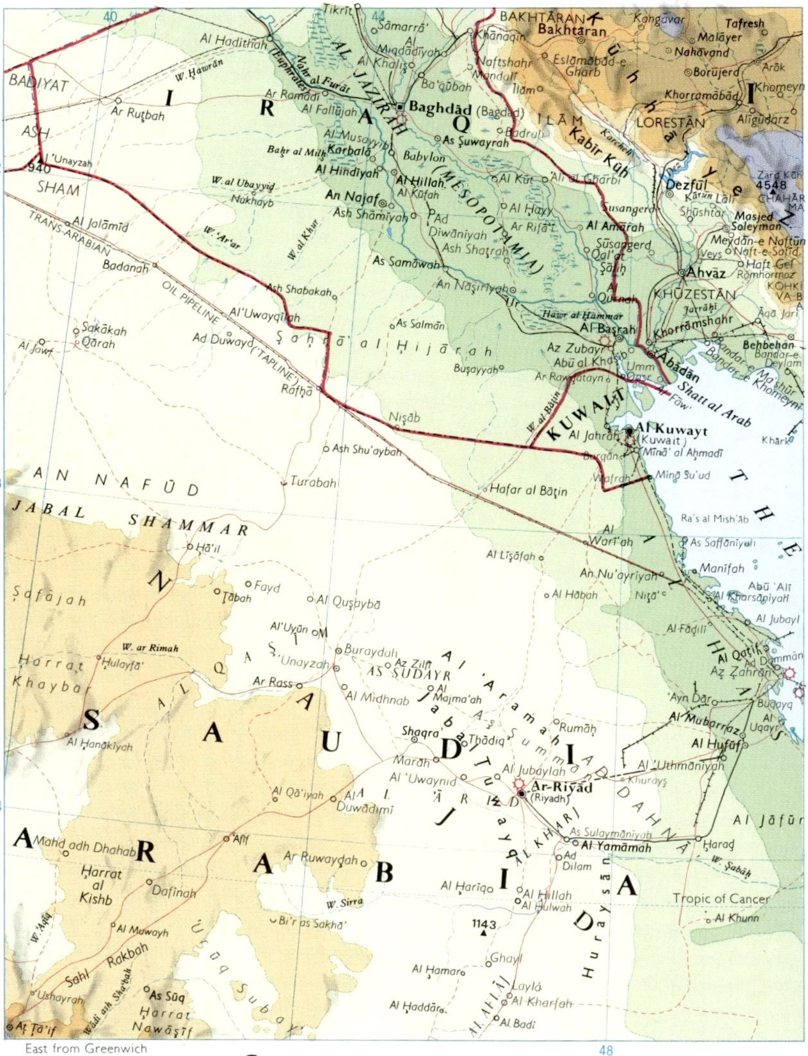

IRAQ
SAUDI ARABIA
KUWAIT
IRAN
Baghdād (Bagdad)
Al Kuwayt (Kuwait)
Ar-Riyād (Riyadh)
Al Basrah
Abādān
Khorramshahr
Ahvāz
Dezful
Bakhtaran
BAKHTARAN
Kangavar
Tafresh
Malāyer
Nahāvand
Borūjerd
Arāk
Khomeyn
Khorramābād
Alīgūdarz
LORESTĀN
Kabīr Kūh
Kūh-ha-ye Zāgros
Zard Kūh
4548
CHAHAR
Masjed Soleymān
Shūshtar
Meydān-e Naftūn
Naft-e Safīd
Haft Gel
Rāmhormoz
KOHKI
KHŪZESTĀN
Behbehān
Bandar-e Deylam
Bandar-e Māshur
Bandar-e Khomeynī
Khārk
Shatt al Arab
Al Fāw
Tikrīt
Sāmarrā'
Al Miqdādīyah
Al Khālis
Khānaqīn
Ba'qūbah
Naftshahr
Mandalī
Eslāmābād-e Gharb
Īlām
ĪLĀM
Badrah
Al Hadīthah
Nahr al Furāt
(Euphrates)
AL JAZĪRAH
(MESOPOTAMIA)
Ar Ramādī
Al Fallūjah
Al Musayyib
As Suwayrah
Bahr al Milh
Karbalā
Babylon
Al Hindīyah
Al Hillah
Al Kūfah
An Najaf
Ash Shāmīyah
Ad Dīwānīyah
Ash Shatrah
Al Kūt
'Alī al Gharbī
Al Hayy
Ar Rifā'
Al 'Amārah
Sūsangerd
Qal'at Sālih
Al Qurnah
As Samāwah
An Nāsirīyah
Ur
Hawr al Hammar
Az Zubayr
Abū al Khasīb
Umm Qasr
Ar Rawdatayn
W. Hawrān
BĀDIYAT ASH SHĀM
Ar Rutbah
Al 'Unayzah
940
W. al Ubayyid
Nukhayb
W. 'Ar'ar
W. al Khur
Al Jalāmīd
TRANS-ARABIAN
OIL PIPELINE
('TAPLINE')
Badanah
Ash Shabakah
Al 'Uwayqīlah
Sakākah
Qārah
Al Jawf
Ad Duwayd
Rafhā
As Salmān
Sahrā' al Hijārah
Busayyah
Nisāb
W. al Bātin
Al Jahrah
Mīnā' al Ahmadī
Burgan
Wafrah
Mīnā Su'ud
Ash Shu'aybah
Hafar al Bātin
Turabah
AN NAFŪD
JABAL SHAMMAR
Hā'il
Fayd
Tābah
Al Qusaybā
Safājah
Al Wari'ah
Al Līsāfah
An Nu'ayrīyah
Al Hābah
Nitā'
Ras al Mish'āb
As Saffānīyah
Manīfah
Abū 'Alī
Al Kharsānīyah
Al Jubayl
Al Fādilī
Al Qatīf
Ad Dammām
Az Zahrān
'Ayn Dār
Buqayq
Al Mubarraz
Al Uqayr
Al Hufūf
Al 'Uthmānīyah
Khurays
Al Jāfūrah
Harad
W. Sabāh
Tropic of Cancer
Al Khunn
THE GULF
Al 'Uyūn
AL QASĪM
Buraydah
'Unayzah
Az Zilfī
AS SUDAYR
Ar Rass
Al Midhnab
Majma'ah
W. ar Rimah
Hulayfā'
Harrat Khaybar
Al Hanākīyah
AL 'ARAMAH
AS SUMMĀN
JABAL TUWAYQ
AD DAHNĀ
Shaqra'
Rumāh
Thādiq
Marāh
Al Jubaylah
Al 'Uwaynid
AL 'ĀRID
Al Qā'īyah
Al Duwādimī
AL KHARJ
As Sulaymānīyah
Al Yamāmah
Ad Dilam
Afīf
Mahd adh Dhahab
Ar Ruwaydah
Harrat al Kishb
Dafīnah
Al Harīq
Al Hillah
Al Hulwah
W. Sirra
Bi'r as Sakhā'
Al Muwayh
W. 'Aqīq
'Urūq Subay'
1143
Hurays ān
Sahl Rakbah
Ghayl
Al Hamar
Laylā
Al Kharfah
Al Haddār
Al Badi
AL AFLĀJ
Ushayrah
As Sūq
Wādī ash Sha'bah
Harrat Nawāsīf
At Tā'if
40
44
48
32
28
24
East from Greenwich

82

82

1 : 10 000 000

86

Qom
Daryācheh-ye Namak
Kāshān
Maḩallāt
Jandaq
Khvor
Nagīneh
Gonābād
KHORĀSĀN
Boshrūyeh
Ferdows
Qāyen
Daryācheh-i-Namakzar
Yazdān
Shīndand
AFGHANISTAN
Harūt Rūd
IRAN
Naţanz
Zavāreh
Anārak
Ardestān
Ţabas
Deyhūk
2886
Khūr
Bīrjand
Ţabas
Mazhān
Sarbīsheh
EŞFAHĀN
Nā'īn
Tīrān
Eşfahan
Najafābād
Kūhpāyeh
Zāyandeh Rūd
Dasht-e Lut (Great Sand Desert)
Nāy Band
Shahr Kord
Varzaneh
Ardakān
Kharānaq
Shūsf
BAKHTĪĀRĪ
Qomsheh
Bātlāq-e Gāvkhūnī
Nadūshan
YAZD
Yazd
Bāfq
Nehbandān
Daryācheh-ye Seistan
Lāsh-e Joveyn
Shīr Kūh
4075
Kūh-e Alījūq
3723
Izad Khvāst
Zagros
Shūr
Rāvar
Shūr Rūd
Zābol
Seistan
LŪYEH
ĀBādeh
Abarqū
Anār
Zarand
Kūh-e Bol
3660
Kūh-e Dīnār
4431
Deh Bīd
Rafsanjān
Kermān
Shahdād
Namakzār-e Shahdād
Kūh-e Seh Konj
Gachsārān
Ardakān
Sīvand
Sa'ādatābād
Lāvar Meydān
Shahr-e Bābak
3992
KERMĀN
Nosratābād
Persepolis
Kāzerūn
Shīrāz
Daryācheh-ye Tashk
Kūh-e Hazārān
4419
Zāhedān (Duzdab)
Mīrjāveh
Ganāveh
Bandar-e Rīg
Borāzjān
FARS
Sarvestān
Neyrīz
Sa'īdābād
Tahrūd
Bam
Fahraj
Lādīz
4042
Kūh-e Taftān
Bāft
Kūh-e Jebal Bārez
3962
Meydān-e Gel
Farrāshband
Fasā
Dārāb
Sabzvārān
Bīābān-e Kermān
Khāsh
BŪSHEHR
Fīrūzābād
Khvormūj
Jahrom
Dowlatābād
Sīāreh
Mand
Shūr
Ţārom
Kahnūj
SĪSTĀN
Deyyer
Kūh-e Furgun
3280
Halīl Rūd
Hāmūn-e Jāz Mūrīān
Īrānshahr
Tāherī
'Alāmarvdasht
Lār
Hormoz
2804
Kūh-e Hormoz
Shamīl
Bampūr
BALŪCHESTĀN
Nāy Band
Bastak
Bandar 'Abbās
HORMOZGĀN
Mīnāb
Remeshk
Kūhhā-ye Bashākerd
Pīp
Qeshm
Jaz. ye Hormoz
Bandar-e Nakhīlū
Bandar-e Chārak
Qeshm
Kūh-e Kūhrān
2163
Qaşr-e Qand
Jazīreh-ye-Lāvān
GULF
Str. of Hormuz
Bent
Nīkshahr
Hendorābī
Qeys
102
Forūr
Bāsa'īdū
Ra's Musandam
Al Muharraq
Al Manāmah
Bandar-e Lengeh
Oman
Al Khaşab
Ra's Rakan
J. al Harīm
2057
BAHRAIN
Sirrī
Abū Mūsā
Ra's al Khaymah
Jāsk
Jaghīn
Rāpch
'Awālī
Ḩālūl
Ash Shāriqah (Sharjah)
Umm al Qaywayn
QATAR
'Ajmān
Ra's-e Meydanī
Ra's-e Tang
Dukhān
Dubayy (Dubay)
Chāh Bahār
Ad Dawhah
Al Fujayrah
Gulf of Oman
Al Wakrah
Dās
Musay'īd
As Zarqā
Shināş
AL SĀHIL
Abū Zaby (Abu Dhabi)
Khawr Duwayhin
Dalmā
Şuḩār
Al Khābūra
Abū al Abyaḑ
Al Buraymī
Şīr Banī Yās
Ţarīf
Al Wāḩāt al Buraymī
Wudham 'Alwā'
Barkā'
Maţraḩ
Masqaţ (Muscat)
J. Ḩafīt
1372
AL BĀŢINAH
Habshān
Murban
AZ ZĀHIRAH
Maskin
Al Qurayyāt
Abū Zaby
UNITED ARAB EMIRATES
(TRUCIAL STATES)
AḌ DAFRAH
Muḑaddah
J. ash Shām
3019
AL ḨAJAR
Bū Hasa
Ţīwī
W. 'Ayn
Izkī
Ibrā'
Şūr
Bunayyān
W. Aswad
Wadim
2151
Ra's al Hadd
'Aziz
'Arādah
W. Batha
JIWA
As Suwayḩ
Adam
Al Kāmil
W. 'Umrayri
W. Ḩalfayn
W. Andām
Al Ashkharah
Al Qurayni
OMAN
32
28
24
52
56
60

88

83

52
56
38
Zaliv
Kara Bogaz Gol
Sartas
Kara Bogaz Gol
CASPIAN SEA
TURKESTAN
Urgench
Turtkul
Khiva
Amu Darya (Oxus)
Darganata
Serny Zavod
Krasnovodski Poluostrov
Krasnovodsk
Krasnovodski Zaliv
Khrebet Bolshoy Balkhan
1880
Nebit Dag
Uzboi
TURKMENISTAN
KARA KUM
Kazandzhik
Kizyl Arvat
Poluostrov Cheleken
im 26 Bakinskikh Komissarov
Ostrov Ogurchinski
995
40
Kopet Dagh
Ashkhabad
Mary (Mery)
Bairam Ali
Iolotan
Murgab
Mohammadābād
Tedzhen
Dushak
Serakhs
Atrak
Ashkhāneh
Shirvān
Bojnūrd
Qūchān
3117
Kizyl Atrek
Gonbab-e Kāvūs
Bandar-e-Torkeman
Behshahr
Tonekābon
Now Shahr
Bābol Sar
Bābol
Gorgān
Qā'emshahr
Sārī
MĀZANDARĀN
Reshteh-ye Kūhhā-ye Alborz
Emāmrūd
Mazīnān
Kūh-e Bīnālūd
3314
Mashhad (Meshed)
Kashaf
Farīmān
Soltānābād
Sabzevār
Neyshābūr
Kūh-e Sorkh
3020
5604
Qolleh-ye Damāvand
Fīrūzkūh
Karaj
Dāmghān
Tūrān
36
TEHRAN
Damāvand
Semnān
SEMNĀN
Torūd
Torbat-e Heydarīyeh
Torbat-e Jām
Kāshmar
Harirud
Garmsār
Khvāf
Ghūriān
HERAT
Qom
Daryācheh-ye Namak
DASHT-E-KAVĪR (Great Salt Desert)
Kavīr-e Namak
Bejestān
Gonābād
Nāgīneh
KHORĀSĀN
Daryacheh-i-Namakzar
Jandaq
Ferdows
Qāyen
Yazdān
Kāshān
Boshrūyeh
Mahallāt
IRAN
Khvor
Tabas
Deyhūk
2886
Zavāreh
Anārak
Natanz
Ardestān
ESFAHĀN
Khūr
Bīrjand
Tabas
Harūt Rūd
Mazhān
Sarbīsheh
(Great Sand Desert)
DASHT-E-LUT
Tirān
Esfahan
Nā'īn
Kūhpāyeh
Nay Band
Najafābād
Zāyandeh Rūd
Ardakān
Kharānaq
Shūsf
Lāsh
Shahr Kord
Varzaneh
BAKHTIARI
Qomsheh
Bātlāq-e Gāvkhūnī
YAZD
Nadūshan
Yazd
Nehbandān
Daryācheh-ye Seistān
32
Shīr Kūh
4075
Bāfq
Zābol
Kūh-e Alījūq
3723
Izad Khvāst
Shūr
Rāvar
Shūr Rūd
Seistan
Kheirsan
Ābādeh
Abarqū
Anār
Zarand
Namakzār-e Shahdād
Kūh-e Bol
3660
Kūh-e Dīnār
4431
Deh Bīd
Rafsanjān
Shahdād
Kermān
Kūh-e Seh Konj
Nosratābād
Gachsarān
Ardakān
Sīvand
Sa'ādatābād
Lāvar Meydān
Shahr-e Bābak
3992
KERMĀN
Zāhedān (Duzdab)
Persepolis
Kāzerūn
Shīrāz
Daryācheh-ye Tashk
Sa'īdābād
Kūh-e Hazārān
4419
Tahrūd
Bandar-e Rīg
FARS
Bāft
Bam
Fahraj
Borazjān
Sarvestān
Neyrīz
Kūh-e Jebāl Bārez
3962
4042
Kūh-e Taftān
Farrāshband
Fasā
Meydān-e Gel
Sabzvārān
Bīābān-e Kermān
BŪSHEHR
Fīrūzābād
Dārāb
East from Greenwich
56
60

81

85

1 : 10 000 000

70

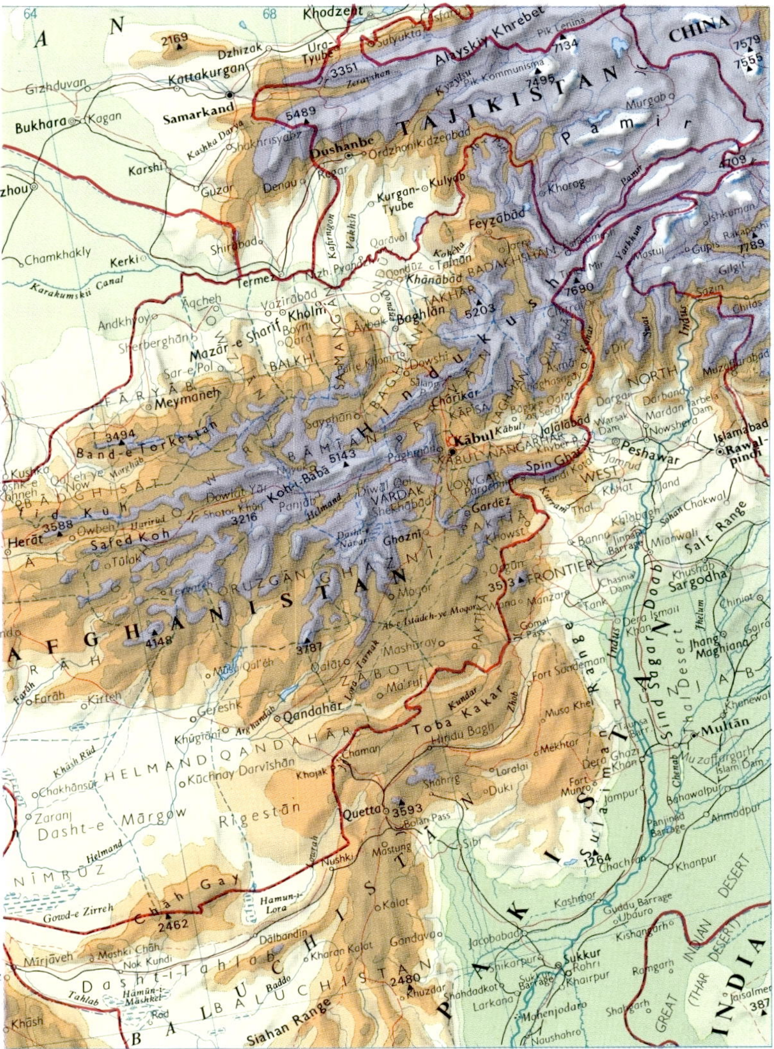
TAJIKISTAN
AFGHANISTAN
PAKISTAN
CHINA
INDIA
BALUCHISTAN
Pamir
Hindu Kush
Alayskiy Khrebet
Pik Lenina
Pik Kommunisma
Khodzent
Dzhizak
Ura-Tyube
Kattakurgan
Samarkand
Bukhara
Kagan
Gizhduvan
Karshi
Guzar
Chardzhou
Shakhrisyabz
Dushanbe
Ordzhonikidzeabad
Regar
Denau
Kurgan-Tyube
Kulyab
Khorog
Murgab
Shirabad
Kerki
Chamkhakly
Karakumskii Canal
Termez
Feyzabad
Khanabad
Kholm
Baghlan
Aqcheh
Andkhvoy
Mazar-e Sharif
Sherberghan
Sar-e Pol
BALKHI
Meymaneh
Band-e Torkestan
Salang
Charikar
Kabul
Jalalabad
Peshawar
Islamabad
Rawalpindi
Nowshera
Mardan
Gilgit
Chilas
Muzaffarabad
Kushka
Herat
Safed Koh
Koh-i-Baba
Band-e Bayan
Bamian
Panjao
Gardez
Ghazni
Khowst
Kohat
Bannu
Spin Ghar
Salt Range
Sargodha
Jhang Maghiana
Multan
Dera Ismail Khan
Dera Ghazi Khan
Fort Sandeman
Musa Khel
Toba Kakar
Hindu Bagh
Qandahar
Gereshk
Farah
Chaman
Quetta
Bolan Pass
Sibi
Mastung
Kalat
Nushki
Dalbandin
Chagai
Khuzdar
Siahan Range
Sukkur
Shikarpur
Jacobabad
Larkana
Mohenjodaro
Khairpur
Rohri
Bahawalpur
Khanpur
Sulaiman Range
HELMAND
NIMRUZ
Dasht-e Margow
Rigestan
Zaranj
Gowd-e Zirreh
Hamun-i-Lora
Hamun-i-Mashkel
Dasht-i-Tahlab
Mirjaveh
Khash
GREAT INDIAN (THAR DESERT)
Jaisalmer
Ramgarh
Thal Desert
Sind Sagar Doab
Indus
Chenab
Jhelum
Helmand
Farah Rud
FRONTIER
NORTH WEST
7134
7495
7579
7555
7690
7789
5489
4709
5203
5143
3351
3494
3588
3216
3513
3787
4148
3593
2462
2480
1264
2169
64
68
36
32
28

89

88

70

87

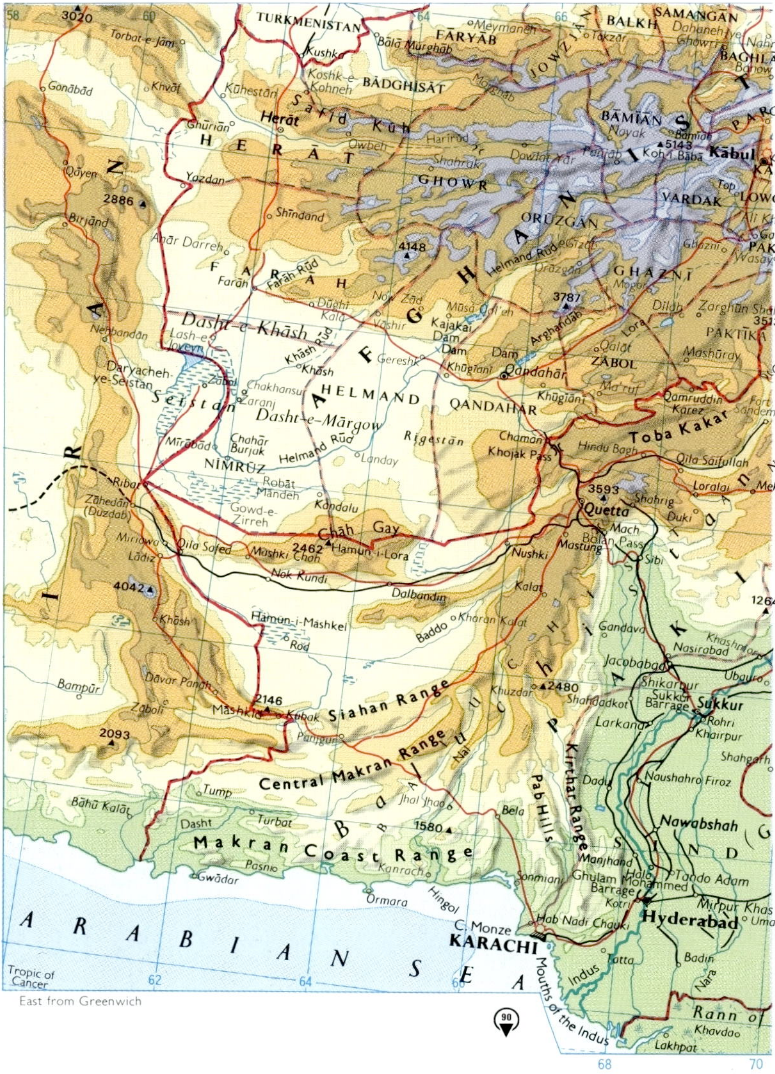

TURKMENISTAN
Torbat-e-Jām
Kushk
Bālā Murghāb
FĀRYĀB
Meymaneh
JOWZJĀN
Tokzār
BALKH
SAMANGĀN
Dahaneh-ye Ghowri
Nahrin
BAGHLĀN
Banow
Charikar
Gonābād
Khvāf
Kūhestān
Koshk-e-Kohneh
BĀDGHĪSĀT
Morghāb
Ghūriān
Herāt
Safid Kūh
HERĀT
Owbeh
Harirud
Shahrak
Dowlat Yar
BĀMIĀN
Nayak
Panjāb
Koh-i Bābā
Bamiān
Kābul
KĀBUL
Qāyen
Yazdan
GHOWR
VARDAK
LOWGAR
Top
Shīndand
Bīrjand
ORŪZGĀN
Ali Khēl
Gardēz
PAKTIĀ
Wasay
Anār Darreh
Helmand Rūd
Gizāb
Orūzgān
Ghaznī
GHAZNĪ
Mogor
FARĀH
Farāh
Farāh Rūd
Now Zād
Dūghī Kala
Mūsā Qal'eh
Dilāh
Zarghūn Shahr
PAKTĪKA
Wana
Nehbandān
Dasht-e-Khāsh
Lash-e-Joveyn
Vashir
Kajakai Dam
Arghandāb
Lora
Qalāt
ZĀBOL
Mashūray
Gomal
Daryacheh-ye-Seistan
Khāsh
Khāsh Rūd
Gereshk
Khūgiānī
Qandahār
Ma'rūf
Zābol
Seistan
Chakhansur
Zaranj
HELMAND
QANDAHĀR
Qamruddin Karez
Fort Sandeman
Dasht-e-Mārgow
Chaman
Khojak Pass
Toba Kakar
Hindu Bagh
Qila Saifullah
Mīrābād
Chahār Burjak
NĪMRŪZ
Helmand Rūd
Rigestān
Landay
Ribat
Robāt Māndeh
Gowd-e-Zirreh
Loralai
Mekhtar
Zāhedān (Duzdab)
Kondalu
Quetta
Shahrig
Duki
Chāh Gay
Mach
Bolan Pass
Sibi
Mīrjāwa
Qila Safed
Mashki Chah
Hamun-i-Lora
Nushki
Mastung
Lādiz
Nok Kundi
Dalbandin
Kalat
Khāsh
Hāmūn-i-Māshkel
Baddo
Kharan Kalat
Gandava
Rod
Khashmor
Nasirabad
Jacobabad
Ubauro
Bampūr
Dāvar Panāh
Khuzdar
Shikarpur
Shahdadkot
Sukkur Barrage
Sukkur
Rohri
Khairpur
Zābolī
Māshkīd
Kubak
Siahan Range
Larkana
Panjgur
Central Makran Range
Kirthar Range
Shahgarh
Dadu
Naushahro Firoz
Tump
Nal
Bāhū Kalāt
Jhal Jhao
Bela
Pab Hills
Nawabshah
Dasht
Turbat
Makran Coast Range
Manjhand
Pasni
Kanrach
Sonmiani
Ghulam Mohammed Barrage
Hala
Tando Adam
Gwādar
Ormara
Hingol
Kotri
Mirpur Khas
Hyderabad
C. Monze
Hab Nadi Chauki
Umarkot
KARACHI
Badin
Tatta
Indus
Nara
Mouths of the Indus
Rann of
Khavdao
Lakhpat
IRAN
AFGHANISTAN
PAKISTAN
BALUCHISTAN
SIND
ARABIAN SEA
Tropic of Cancer
3020
2886
4148
5143
3787
3513
3593
2462
4042
1264
2480
2146
2093
1580
58
60
62
64
66
68
70
34
32
30
28
26
24
East from Greenwich

90

1 : 10 000 000

CHINA
Hindu Kush
BADAKHSHAN
TAKHAR
KAPISA
LAGHMAN
KONARHA
NANGARHAR
NORTH WEST FRONTIER
Mintaka P. 4709
Ishkuman
Tirich Mir 7690
Yarkhun
Mastuj
Gupis
Chitral
Gilgit
Disteghil Sar 7885
Rakaposhi 7788
Aghil Pass 4779
K 2 8611
Aghil Mountains
Karakoram
Karakoram Pass 5575
Haji Langar
Aksai Chin
Indus
Skardu
Shyok
Deosai Mountains
Sazin
Bunji
Chilas
Nanga Parbat 8126
JAMMU AND KASHMIR
Saser 7672
Kargil
Ladakh
Dir
Saidu
Malakand
Kohat-e Khas
Jalalabad
Dargai
Warsak Dam
Landi Kotal
Khyber Pass
Peshawar
Mardan
Tarbela Dam
Naushahra
Attock
Darband
Muzaffarabad
Baramula
Abbotabad
CEASE FIRE LINE 1949
Srinagar
Nunkun 7135
Lanak P. 5486
Leh
Shyok
Pangong Tso
Pal
Zaskar Mountains
Range
Chushul
Rudok
Murree
Punch
Anantnag
Thal
Kohat
Rawalpindi
Islamabad
Khost
Jand
Miram Shah
Bannu
Kalabagh
Jinnah Barrage
Mangla Dam
Jhelum
Riasi
Kishtwar
Himalaya
Hanle
Demchok
Chakwal
Rasul Dam
Chenab
Udhampur
Jammu
Chamba
Brahmaur
Mianwali
Manzai
Sind Sagar Doab
Gujrat
Wazirabad
Sialkot
Pathankot
Gurdaspur
Palampur
7026
Dankhar Gompa
Gar Dzong
Khushab
Sargodha
Hafizabad
Gujranwala
Dera Ismail Khan
Chiniot
Shekhupura
Amritsar
Hoshiarpur
Mandi
HIMACHAL PRADESH
Shipki La
Gartok
Lanchen Khambab
Jhang Maghiana
Trimmu Dam
Gojra
Lahore
Faisalabad
Bhakra Dam
Kasur
Jullundur
Simla
Nangal Dam
Musa Khel
Thal Desert
Phagwara
Ludhiana
Kandaghat
Kamet 7756
Ravi
Firozpur
Sahiwal
(Montgomery)
Bari Doab
PUNJAB
Chakrata
Badrinath
Dera Ghazi Khan
Multan
Khanewal
Fazilka
Muktsar
Jagraon
Chandigarh
Ambala
Mussoorie
Dehra Dun
Nanda Devi 7817
Munro
Jampur
Muzaffargarh
Sutlej
Abohar
Bhatinda
Patiala
Jagadhri
Pauri
Haridwar Dam
Lodhran
Alipur
Ganganagar
Saharanpur
Haridwar
Roorkee
Karnal
Muzaffarnagar
Najibabad
Almora
Panjnad Barrage
Bahawalpur
Suratgarh
Sirsa
Chachran
Ahmadpur
Anupgarh
Hansi
Hisar
HARYANA
Bijnor
Meerut
Haldwani
Moradabad
Amroha
Rampur
Sonipat
New Delhi
Rohtak
Bhiwani
DELHI
Hapur
Guddu Barrage
Thar Desert
Great Indian Desert
Rajasthan Canal
Sardarshahr
Churu
Gurgaon
Ghaziabad
Sambhal
Pilibhit
Bulandshahr
Rewari
Bareilly
Jhunjhunu
Ratangarh
Kishangarh
Bikaner
Kolayat
INDIA
Fatehpur
Nawalgarh
Aligarh
Budaun
Ramgarh
Sikar
1052
Alwar
Hathras
UTTAR PRADESH
Nagaur
Phalodi
Mathura
Bharatpur
Fatehgarh
Mainpuri
Hardoi
Pokaran
Sambhar
Jaipur
Agra
Firozabad
Kannauj
RAJASTHAN
387
Ajmer
Daulpur
Etawah
Ganga
Jodhpur
Luni
Bilara
Malpura
Chambal
Bhind
Kanpur
Munabao
Pachpadra
Nasirabad
Tonk
Sawai Madhopur
Gwalior
Beawar
Kekri
Orai
Barmer
Pali
Marwar
Kunch
Hamirpur
Sheopur Kalan
Datia
Jalor
Bhilwara
Bundi
Shivpuri
Mau Ranipur
Banda
Nathdwara
Kota
Baran
Jhansi
Sirohi
Raniwara
1722
521
Nagar Parkar
Tharad
Chittaurgarh
Gandhi Sagar
Chhatarpur
Kachchh
72
74
76
78
80
36
34
32
30
28
26

101
92
91

88

PAKISTAN
Makran Coast Range
Bāhū Kalāt
Tump
Dasht
Turbat
Pasni
Gwādar
Ormara
Kanrach
Hingol
Jhal Jhao
1580
Bela
Pab Hills
Kirthar Ra.
Dadu
Naushahro Firoz
Nawabshah
SIND
Manjhand
Hala
Tando Adam
Sonmiani
Ghulam Mohammed Barrage
Kotri
Hyderabad
Mirpur Khas
Umarkot
Munabao
Hab Nadi Chauki
C. Monze
KARACHI
Mouths of the Indus
Indus
Tatta
Badin
Nara
Rann of
Khavdao
Lakhpat
Kori Creek
Gulf of Kachchh
GUJ
Bhuj
Bhachau
Mandvi
Kandla
Okha
Dhrol
Dwarka
Jamnagar
Gop
Kathia
Porbandar
Saradiya
1117
Junagadh
Veraval
Diu
Gulf of
ARABIAN SEA
Tropic of Cancer
Goa
GOA
Gadag
Dharwad
Dandeli
Karwar
Hospet
Tungabhadra
Kurnool
Adoni
Bellary
1100
Erramala Hills
Nallamalai Hills
Velikonda Ra.
Cumbum
Chirala
Ongole
Nandyal
Guntakal
Kavali
Kotturu
Rayadrug
Proddatur
Penner
Ranibennur
Davangere
Cuddapah
Nellore
Talguppa
Shimoga
Bhadravati
Gudur
Hindupur
1151
Tirupati
Pulicat Lake
Coondapoor
KARNATAKA
Udupi
1923
Birur
Chikmagalur
Tumkur
1255
Chik Bollapur
Chittoor
Mangalore
Hassan
Bangalore
Kolar
Kolar Gold Fields
Arcot
Vellore
Madras
Saidapet
Kanchipuram (Conjeeveram)
Kasaragod
Madikeri
Mandya
Channapatna
Melagiri Hills
Tiruvannamalai
Madurantakam
1745
Mysore
Dharmapuri
Cannanore
Tellicherry
Pondicherry
Mettur Dam
1628
Cuddalore
Badagara
Ootacamund
2637
Salem
Attur
Calicut (Kozhikode)
TAMIL
Chidambaram
Coimbatore
Erode
Cauvery
Ponnani
Palghat
Karur
Thanjavur
Karikal
Pollachi
Tiruchchirappalli
Nagappattinam
Trichur
Pudukkottai
Palani Hills
2698
Dindigul
Ernakulam
NADU
Karaikkudi
Mattancheri
Madurai
Devakottai
Palk Strait
Point Pedro
Kottayam
Virudhunagar
Jaffna
Alleppey
Cardamon Hills
Ramnad
Palk Bay
Changanacheri
Rajapalaiyam
Mullaittivu
Mannar
Mankulam
Adam's Bridge
Mannar I.
Tenkasi
Quilon
Gulf of Mannar (Manaar)
Tirunelveli
Palayankottai
Trincomalee
Trivandrum
1654
Foul Pt.
Kulasekarappattinam
Nagercoil
Anuradhapura
766
Galoya
Cape Comorin
Puttalam
Batticaloa
Maho
SRI LANKA (CEYLON)
Chilaw
Matale
Kalmunai
Kurunegala
Kandy
Negombo
Pidurutalagala
Colombo
Ragama
2524
Badulla
Mt. Lavinia
Adam's Peak
Moratuwa
2243
Pottuvil
Kalutara
Opanake
Galle
Matara
Hambantota
Dondra Head
Malabar Coast
Western Ghats
Eastern Ghats
KERALA
Coromandel Coast
Continuation Southwards on same scale
East from Greenwich
26
24
14
12
10
8
22
20
18
16
62
64
66
68
70
76
78
80
82

1 : 10 000 000

89

RAJASTHAN
INDIA
MADHYA PRADESH
MAHARASHTRA
ANDHRA PRADESH
GUJARAT
DADRA & NAGAR HAVELI
GOA
BOMBAY
Pokaran
387
Phalodi
Nagaur
Sambhar
Jaipur
Bharatpur
Agra
Mainpuri
Kannauj
Firozabad
Etawah
Kanpur
Ganga
Ajmer
Malpura
Tonk
Daulpur
Chambal
Bhind
Gwalior
Jodhpur
Luni
Bilara
Nasirabad
Sawai Madhopur
Orai
Pachpadra
Beawar
Kekri
Kunch
Hamirpur
Barmer
Pali
Sheopur Kalan
Datia
Marwar
Bhilwara
Bundi
Shivpuri
Jhansi
Mau Ranipur
Banda
Jalor
Sirohi
Nathdwara
Kota
Baran
521
Raniwara
1722
Chittaurgarh
Gandhi Sagar
Chhatarpur
Nagar Parkar
Tharad
Guna
Lalitpur
Tikamgarh
Panna
Disa
Udaipur
Nimach
Jhalawar
Kachchh
Palanpur
Bari Sadri
Taranga Hill
Khed Brahma
Mandsaur
Rajgarh
Sironj
Bina Etawa
Banda
Patan
Himatnagar
Sagar
Damoh
Mahesana
Banswara
Jaora
Vidisha
Little Rann
Ratlam
Shajapur
Bhanrer Range
Jabalpur
Kuda
Viramgam
Ujjain
Sehore
Bhopal
Halvad
Ahmadabad
Dahod
Dewas
Narsinghpur
Jhabua
Indore
Kannod
Hoshangabad
Chotila
Nadiad
Godhra
Dhar
Mhow
Gadarwara
Petlad
Vadodara
(Baroda)
Khambhat
Narmada
Nainpur
Gadhada
1353
Makrai
Bhavnagar
Rajpipla
Khargon
Amreli
1325
Khandwa
Betul
Chhindwara
Balaghat
Palitana
Bharuch
Satpura Range
Tirodi
Katangi
Nandurbar
Ramtek
Gondia
Surat
Tapi
Bhusawal
Gawilgarh Hills
Achalpur
Nagpur
Victor
Navsari
Amalner
Amravati
Dhule
Jalgaon
Bhandara
Valsad
Bramhapuri
Khambhat
Daman
Malegaon
Akola
Wardha
Wainganga
Ajanta Range
Satmala Hills
Chalisgaon
741
Hinganghat
Manmad
Darwha
Yavatmal
Nasik
Yeola
Aurangabad
Washim
Penganga
Wani
Ghugus
Chanda
1646
Deolali
Jalna
Hingoli
Godavari
Adilabad
Sangamner
Asifabad
Bhiwandi
Thane
Ulhasnagar
Parbhani
665
Ahmadnagar
Nander
Pranhita
Bir
Palam
Nirmal
Balaghat Range
Godavari
Jagtial
Kirkee
Kharda
Bodhan
Nizamabad
Manthani
Pune
(Poona)
796
Latur
Udgir
Karimnagar
Barsi
Western Ghats
Mahabaleshwar
1438
Osmanabad
Madha
Manjra
Siddipet
Warangal
Bidar
Satara
Bhima
Solapur
Secunderabad
Pandharpur
Karad
Gulbarga
Hyderabad
Ratnagiri
Nalgonda
Suriapet
Sangli
Kolhapur
Miraj
Bijapur
Yadgir
Narayanpet
Mahbubnagar
Krishna
Jamkhandi
Krishna
Malvan
Raichur
Gadwal
Vengurla
Tenali
917
Belgaum
Eastern Ghats
Nallamalai Hills
Khanapur
Tungabhadra
Kurnool
Chirala
Panaji (Panjim)
Goa
Adoni
Erramala Hills
Cumbum
Marmagao
Gadag
Ongole
Velikonda Ra.
1053
Dharwad
Hospet
Bellary
Nandyal
Savanur
1100
Swamihalli
Guntakal
Karwar
Anjidiv I.
Ranibennur
Kotturu
Proddatur
DECCAN
72
74
76
78
16
18
20
22
24
26

92

EASTERN INDIA, BANGLADESH AND BURMA

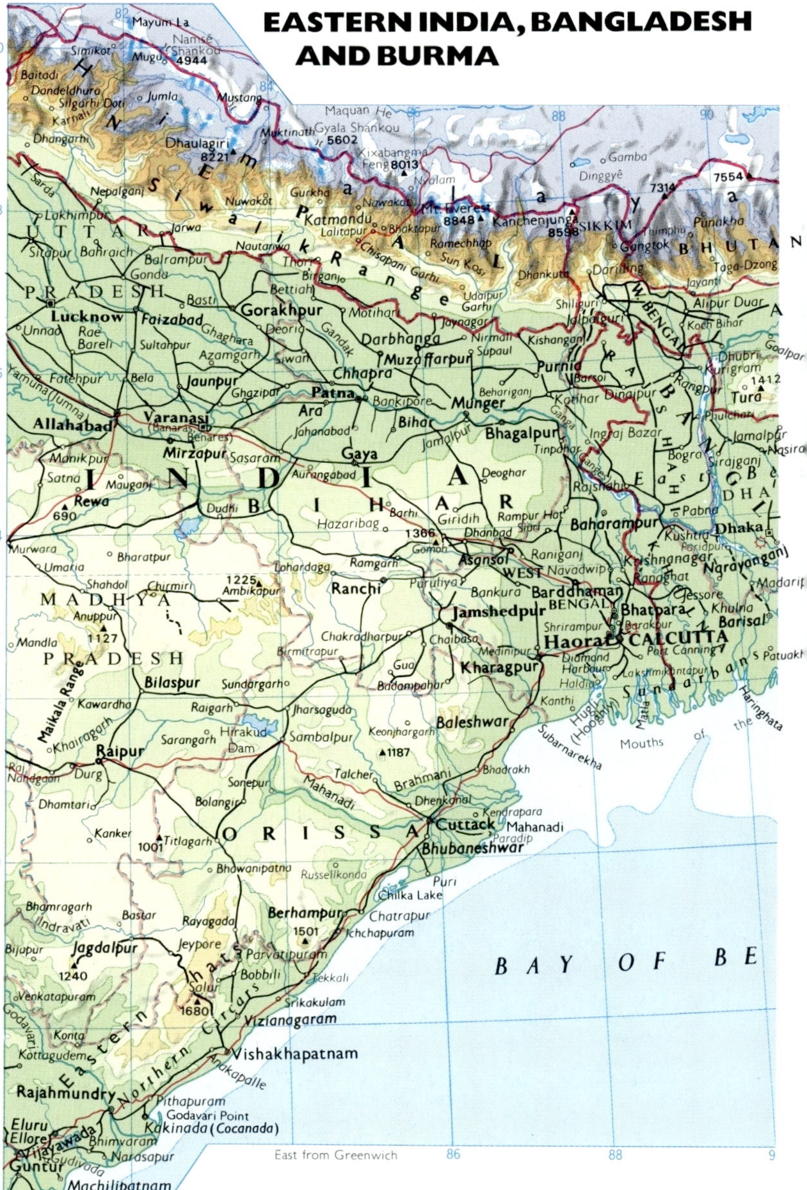
Mayum La
Simikot
Mugu
Namse Shankou
4944
Baitadi
Dandeldhura
Silgarhi Doti
Jumla
Mustang
Karnali
Dhangarhi
Maquan He
Gyala Shankou
5602
Muktinath
Dhaulagiri
8221
Xixabangma Feng
8013
Nyalam
Gamba
Dingyê
7554
7314
Sarda
Nepalganj
Gurkha
Nuwakot
Nawakot
Mt. Everest
8848
Kanchenjunga
8598
SIKKIM
Thimphu
Punakha
Lakhimpur
Jarwa
Katmandu
Lalitapur
Bhaktapur
Ramechhap
Sun Kosi
Gangtok
BHUTAN
UTTAR PRADESH
Sitapur
Bahraich
Nautanwa
Chisapani Garhi
Balrampur
Gonda
Thori
Birganj
Bettiah
Dhankuta
Darjiling
Taga-Dzong
Jayanti
Lucknow
Faizabad
Basti
Gorakhpur
Motihari
Udaipur Garhi
Jaynagar
Shiliguri
Jalpaiguri
Alipur Duar
Koch Bihar
W. BENGAL
Unnao
Rae Bareli
Sultanpur
Ghaghara
Deoria
Gandak
Darbhanga
Nirmali
Kishanganj
Azamgarh
Siwan
Muzaffarpur
Supaul
Dhubri
Goalpara
Kurigram
1412
Yamuna (Jumna)
Fatehpur
Bela
Jaunpur
Chhapra
Purnia
Barsoi
Rangpur
Tura
Ghazipur
Patna
Bankipore
Munger
Behariganj
Katihar
Dinajpur
Allahabad
Varanasi (Banaras, Benares)
Ara
Bihar
Bhagalpur
Ingraj Bazar
Phulchari
Jamalpur
Nasirabad
Mirzapur
Sasaram
Jahanabad
Gaya
Jamalpur
Tinpahar
Bogra
Sirajganj
Manikpur
Satna
Maugani
INDIA
Aurangabad
Deoghar
Ganges
Rajshahi
Rewa
690
Dudhi
BIHAR
Barhi
Giridih
Rampur Hat
Suri
Baharampur
Pabna
Dhaka
Kushtia
Faridpur
Murwara
Hazaribag
1366
Dhanbad
Gomoh
Asansol
Raniganj
Krishnanagar
Narayanganj
Madaripur
Bharatpur
Umaria
Lohardaga
Ramgarh
WEST
Navadwip
Ranaghat
Shahdol
Chirmiri
1225
Ambikapur
Ranchi
Puruliya
Bankura
Barddhaman
Jessore
Khulna
MADHYA PRADESH
BENGAL
Bhatpara
Anuppur
1127
Jamshedpur
Shrirampur
Barakpur
Barisal
Mandla
Chakradharpur
Chaibasa
Haora
CALCUTTA
Birmitrapur
Medinipur
Diamond Harbour
Port Canning
Patuakhali
Maikala Range
Gua
Kharagpur
Lakshmikantapur
Bilaspur
Sundargarh
Badampahar
Haldia
Sundarbans
Kawardha
Raigarh
Jharsaguda
Baleshwar
Kanthi
Hugli (Hooghly)
Matla
Haringhata
Khairagarh
Sarangarh
Hirakud Dam
Sambalpur
Keonjhargarh
Subarnarekha
Mouths of the
Raipur
1187
Raj Nandgaon
Durg
Talcher
Brahmani
Bhadrakh
Sonepur
Mahanadi
Dhamtari
Bolangir
Dhenkanal
Kendrapara
ORISSA
Cuttack
Mahanadi
Kanker
1001
Titlagarh
Paradip
Bhubaneshwar
Bhawanipatna
Russellkonda
Puri
Chilka Lake
Bhamragarh
Indravati
Bastar
Rayagada
Berhampur
Chatrapur
1501
Ichchapuram
Bijapur
Jagdalpur
Jeypore
Parvatipuram
1240
BAY OF BE
Bobbili
Tekkali
Salur
Venkatapuram
1680
Srikakulam
Eastern Ghats
Godavari
Vizianagaram
Konta
Northern Circars
Kottagudem
Vishakhapatnam
Anakapalle
Rajahmundry
Pithapuram
Godavari Point
Kakinada (Cocanada)
Eluru
Ellore
Vijayawada
Bhimvaram
Narasapur
Guntur
Gudivada
Machilipatnam (Bandar)
Bapatla
East from Greenwich
30
28
26
24
22
20
16
82
84
86
88
90
89
91

1 : 10 000 000

CHINA
YUNNAN
BURMA
THAILAND
ARUNACHAL PRADESH
ASSAM
NAGALAND
MEGHALAYA
MANIPUR
MIZORAM
TRIPURA
CHITTAGONG
KACHIN
CHIN
SHAN
KAYAH
KAWTHOOLEI
BENGAL
Tropic of Cancer
Patkai Bum
Kumon Bum
Barail Range
Hukawng Valley
Ponnyadaung
Arakan Yoma
Pegu Yoma
Arakan Coast
Gulf of Martaban
Rambre Kyun
Manaung Kyun
Brahmaputra
Chindwin
Irrawaddy
Salween
Mekong
Sittang Myit
Rangon Myit
Ganga
Karnaphuli Res.
Rima
Jida
Tunga La
Chigu
Lhunze
Comai
Cona
Subansiri
Dihang
Nizamghat
Minutang
Ch'ayu
5881
Thala La
Zhongdian
Zizhixian
Weixi
5500
Lijiang
Jianchuan
Yunlong
Baoshan
Tengchong
Changning
Lancang
Thunkar
7089 Kangto
Tongsa Dzong
Towang
Rupa
Balipara
Saikhoa Ghat
Dum Duma
Tipongpani
Dibrugarh
North Lakhimpur
Sibsagar
Jorhat
Dergaon
Tezpur
Silghat
Rangia
Mairabari
Barpeta
Nowgong
Gauhati
Mokokchung
Kohima
3824
Hpungan La
3072
Putao (Ft. Hertz)
Konglu
Chaukan La
2432
Kawngtim
3411 Bumhpa Bum
Maingkwan
Singkaling Hkamti
2424
Mogaung
Myitkyina
Sadon
Longling
Bhamo
1961 Shillong
Cherrapunji
Haflong
Ukhrul
Tamenglong
Imphal
Barakhola
Sylhet
Silchar
Mohanganj
Lala Ghat
Churachandpur
Kolosib
Tamu
Homalin
Thaungdut
Katha
Indaw
Shwegu
Tigyaing
Wuntho
Man Na
Kunlong
Hsenwi
Pang-Long
Kawnro
Meng-so
Shweli
Namtu
Bawdwin
Lashio
Mawlaik
Kyunhla
Kalewa
Balla
Agartala
Amarpur
Sairang
Aijal
Tiddim
Kennedy Taungdeik 2704
Chandpur
Comilla
Dighinala
Belonia
Lungleh
Falam
Mogok
2299
Mingin
Shwebo
Budalin
Madaya
Gokteik
Mong Yai
Pangyang
2693
Mong Pawk
Bhola
Maijdi (Noakhali)
Hatia
Sandwip Chan.
Chittagong
Dohazari
Gangaw
Alon
Monywa
Mandalay
Mong Hsu
Yinmabin
Sagaing
Mong Kung
Kyaukse
Mong Wa
Keng Tung
Cox's Bazar
Kaladan
Paletwa
Victoria Taungdeik (Mt. Victoria)
3053
Kanpetlet
Pauk
Pakokku
Myingyan
Meiktila
Thazi
2519
Taunggyi
Keng Tawng
Mong Nai
Kyaukpadaung
Yenangyaung
Yamethin
Inle Aing
Mong Pan
Mong Ton
2296
Mon
Minbu
Magwe
Taungdwingyi
Mawkmai
Chiang Rai
Akyab
Loi-kaw
2163
Mae Hong Son
Pyinmana
Kyaukpyu
Letpan
Thayetmyo
Bawlake
Chiengmai
Lamphun
Taungoo
2576
Prome
2620
Taungup
Taunggya
1168
Sandoway
Pyu
Papun
Lampang
Myanaung
Madauk
Letpadan
Henzada
Tharrawaddy
Gwa
Kyonpyaw
Pegu
Tak (Rahaeng)
Rangoon
Yandoon
Thaton
Pa-an
Insein
Martaban
Bassein
Maulamyaing (Moulmein)
2080
Myaungmya
Pyapon
Amherst
Bassein Myit
Maudin Sun
Erawadi
Myitwanya
92
94
96
98
26
24
22
20
18
16
101
99
94
COPYRIGHT GEORGE PHILIP & SON. LTD.

93

BANGLADESH
Cox's Bazar
Paletwa
B U R M A
S H A N
Victoria Taungdeik (Mt. Victoria) 3053
Kanpetlet
Kyauktaw
Minbya
Akyab
Boronga Kyumya
Kyaukpyu
Rambre Kyun
Manaung Kyun
Taungup
Arakan Coast
Sandoway
Gongaw
Ponnyadaung
Monywa
Alon
Mandalay
Madaya
Gokteik
Yinmabin
Sagaing
Maymyo
Pauk
Kyaukse
Myogi
Pakokku
Myingyan
Chauk
Kyaukpadaung
Meiktila
Thazi
Taunggyi
Mon
Yenangyuang
Yamethin
Inle Aing
2519
Mong Nai
Minbu
Magwe
Taungdwingyi
Pyinmana
Mawk Mai
Arakan Yoma
Letpan
Thayetmyo
1168
Allanmyo
Prome
Pegu Yoma
Paungde
Kyangin
Myanaung
Irawaddy
Nyaunglebin
Henzada
Letpadan
Gwa
Bassein
Kyonpyaw
Insein
Taikkyi
Pegu
Rangoon
Syriam
Thongwa
Myaungmya
Wakema
Ma-ubin
Bogale
Pyapon
Maudin Sun
Gulf of Martaban
Loikaw
KAYAH
Bawlake
Toungoo
2620
Sittang
Salween
Papun
KAWTHOOLEI
Madauk
Kyaikto
Thaton
Pa-an
Martaban
Maulamyaing (Moulmein)
Mudon
2080
Dan
Tanen Tong Dan
Moei
Mong Hsu
Mong Lang
Kengtung
Mong Wa
2563
Pangyang
2693
Mong Pawk
Mengwang
Reng Tawng
Mong Hsat
Mong Pan
Mong Ton
2296
Ban Houei Sa
2163
Muang Chiang Rai
Mae Hong San
Phrao
Chiengmai
Ban Khun Yuam
Doi Inthanon 2576
Muang Lamphun
Lampang
Ban Mae Sariang
Phrae
Nan
Uttaradit
Ping
Yanhee
Sawankhalok
Phichai
Sam Ngao
Khuan Phumiphon
Sukhothai
Tak
Phitsanulok
THA
Ban Mae Sot
Muang Phichit
Umpang
Nakhon Sawan
Ban Non Pling
Uthai Thani
Chainat
Kalegauk Kyun
Anin
Ye
Phra Chedi Sam Ong
Kroeng Krai
Khlong
Taling Sung
Noi
Chao Phraya
Ang Thong
Suphan Buri
Phra Nakhon Si Ayutthaya
Natkyizin
Nam Tok
Heinze Is.
Moscos Islands
Maungmagan Is.
Launglon Bok Is.
Yebyu
Tavoy
Kanchanaburi
Thonburi
Bangkok (Krung Thep)
Rat Buri
Samut Sakhon
Samut Songkhram
Bilauk Taungdan
2075
Mali Kyun (Tavoy I.)
Palauk
Phetchaburi
Palaw
1531
Kadan Kyun (King I.)
Ban Hua Hin
Mergui
Tenasserim
1247
Prachuap Khiri Khan
Myeik Kyunzu (Mergui Archipelago)
Letsôk-aw Kyun (Domel I.)
Bokpyin
Bang Saphan
Kho Khot Kra
Lambi Kyun (Sullivan I.)
Chumphon
Kawthaung (Victoria Point)
Kra Buri
Zadetkyi Kyun
Ranong
Preparis North Channel
Pariparit Kyun
Preparis South Channel
Koko Kyunzu
Coco Channel
North Andaman
732
Interview I.
Andaman (India) Islands
Middle Andaman
Karen
Andaman Strait
ANDAMAN SEA
Barren I.
Ritchies Archipelago
Havelock I.
South Andaman
Port Blair
N. Sentinel
Rutland I.
S. Sentinel
Duncan Passage
Little Andaman
22
20
18
16
14
12
92
94
96
98
100
East from Greenwich

96

1 : 10 000 000

99

CHINA
Gejiu
Mengzi
Jinping
Hekou
Ha Giang
Cao Bang
Bac Quang
Lao Cai
Cha Pa
Lai Chau
3076
3143
2431
Bac Kan
Bac-Phan
(Tongking)
Langson
Pingxiang
Ningming
Longzhou
Qinzhou
Hepu
Beihai
Mong Cai
Loc Binh
Thai Nguyen
Phu Doan
Nghia Lo
Luan Chau
Phong Saly
Mengla
Yibang
Jinghong
Dien Bien
Son La
Muong Sing
Nam Tha
Vien Pou Kha
Muong Ngoi
Sam Neua
Phu Loi
2257
Hanoi
Ha Dong
Bac Ninh
Quang Yen
Haiphong
Hoa Binh
Phu Ly
Nam Dinh
Ninh Binh
Hoi Xuan
Haikang
Leizhou Bandao
Gulf of
Tongking
Luang Prabang
Cao Nguyen
Tran Ninh
Xieng Khouang
2820
Ban Ban
Muong Pak Beng
Nam Dong
Muong Soui
2061
Nan
Vang Vieng
Ngum
Mekong
Doi Luang
Thanh Hoa
Chu
Thai Hoa
Ban Khe Bo
2711
Vinh
Linh Cam
Ha Tinh
Pak Sane
Kam Keut
Theun
Lingao
Xinzhou
Dan Xian
Changjiang
Hainan Dao
Dongfang
Wuzhi Shan
1867
Gancheng
Ledong
Huangliu
Yacheng
Yulin
Tianya
Chinmu Chiao
Pak Lay
Vientiane
Pa Mong
Nong Khai
Loei
Wang Saphung
Udon Thani
2300
2320
Tuyen Hoa
Ba Don
Dong Hoi
Nakhon Phanom
Thakhek
Se
Chaîne Annamitique
L A O S
VIETNAM
Quang Tri
Hué
1701
Dong Hene
Savannakhet
Sepone
Bang Hieng
Da Nang (Tourane)
Hoi An
Thang Binh
Sakon Nakhon
Ubolratna
Phong
Nam Phong
Lam Pao
Khon Kaen
Kalasin
Phetchabun
THAILAND
Cao Nguyen
Roi Et
Ban Phai
Khemmarat
Yasothon
Chi
Chaiyaphum
Ban Bua Yai
Mun
Khorat
Ubon Ratchathani
Se Done
Pakse
Saravane
Ban Thateng
1572
Cao Nguyen
Boloven
Hat Nhao
Attopeu
3280
Binh Son
Quang Ngai
Hoai Nhon
(Bong Son)
Pa Sak
Ban Bua Chum
Nakhon Ratchasima
(Khorat)
Buriram
Surin
Sisaket
Thiu Khao Phetchabun
1328
Nong Khae
Prachin Buri
Phanom Dang Rek
761
Cheom Ksan
Phnom Tbeng Meanchey
Khong
Kontum
An Nhon
(Binh Dinh)
Qui Nhon
Pleiku
(Gia Lai)
San
Srepok
Cheo Reo
Song Cau
Tuy Hoa
Ba
Chachoengsao
Samut Prakan (Paknam)
Chon Buri
Si Racha
Ban Lamung
Rayong
Ban Aranyaprathet
Sisophon
Koulen
Sen
Angkor
Siem Reap
Mekong
Stung-Treng
Battambang
Tonle Sap
CAMBODIA
Pailin
Sang Ke
Pursat
Sandan (Sanbor)
Kratie
Senmonorom
Buon Me Thuot
2405
Chanthaburi
Trat
Ko Chang
1744
Phnom Kravanh
Kompong Chhnang
1813
Kompong Cham
Chhlong
Nha Trang
Cam Ranh
Cao Nguyen
Gia Nghia
Da Lat
Di Linh
Djiring
Budop
Loc Ninh
Ko Kut
G. of Thailand
Koh Kong
Kas Kong
Phnom Penh
Prek Thnot
Prey-Veng
Banam
Svay Rieng
Kompong Speu
Takeo
Tay Ninh
Phan Rang
Hoa Da
(Phan Ri)
Phan Thiet
Bien Hoa
Sre Umbell
Kompong Som
Koh Rong
1075
Kampot
Thanh Pho Ho Chi Minh (Saigon)
My Tho
Ba Ria
Vung Tau
Go Cong
Ream
Phu Quoc
Hon Chong
Long Xuyen
Sa Dec
Rach Gia
Can Tho
Khanh Hung
(Soc Trang)
Nam Phan
Cochin China
Bac Lieu
Ca Mau
Mui Ca Mau
Con Dao
102
104
106
108
110
22
20
18
16
14
12
COPYRIGHT
GEORGE PHILIP & SON LTD

94

Koko Kyunzu (Burma)
Coco Channel
North Andaman
Interview I.
732
Andaman (India) Islands
Middle Andaman
Karen
Andaman Strait
Barren I.
South Andaman
Ritchies Archipelago
Havelock I.
Port Blair
N. Sentinel
Rutland I.
S. Sentinel
Duncan Passage
Little Andaman
ANDAMAN SEA
Heinze Is.
Moscos Islands
Maungmagan Is.
Launglon Bok Is.
Mali Kyun (Tavoy I.)
Kadan Kyun (King I.)
Myeik Kyunzu (Mergui Archipelago)
Letsôk-aw Kyun (Domel I.)
Lambi Kyun (Sullivan I.)
Kawthaung (Victoria Point)
Zadetkyi Kyun (St. Mathews I.)
Tavoy
Kanchanaburi
Thonburi
Bangkok (Krung Thep)
Samut Sakhon
Samut Songkhram (Mekong)
Bilauk Taungdan
2075
1531
Mergui
Tenasserim
1247
Bokpyin
Prachuap Khiri Khan
Bang Saphan
Ban Hua Hin
THA
Kho Khot Kra
Chumphon
Kra Buri
Ranong
(Isthmus of Kra)
Kau Tao
Ko Phangan
Ko Samui
1420
Ko Phra Thong
Ban Takua Pa
Surat Thani
1786
Nakhon Si Thammarat
Phangnga
Thung Song
Ban Pak Phanang
Phuket
Trang
Phatthalung
Ban Kantang
Songkhla
Tarutao
Satun
Pulau Langkawi
Alor Setar
George Town
Pulau Pinang
Butterworth
Port Weld
SUM
IN
THAILAND
Satun
Kangar
Sadao
PERLIS
Batong Group
Arau
Jitra
Alor Setar
Yala
Pattani
Narathiwat
Tumpat
Kota Baharu
Pasir Mas
1452
KEDAH
Betong
Sungai Patani
Gurun
Baling
Pasir Puteh
Kelantan
Guchil
Kuala Kerai
George Town
Butterworth
Bukit Mertajam
Gerik
PINANG
Parit Buntar
2170
KELANTAN
Kuala Trengganu
PERAK
Lenggong
Selama
Port Weld
Simpang
Taiping
TRENGGANU
G. Tahan
Kuala Kangsar
2182
2190
Kuala Dungun
Ipoh
PENINSULAR MALAYSIA
Cameron Highlands
Ringlet Falls Dam
Batu Gajah
Kampar
Tapah
Bidor
Telom
S. Tembeling
Kuala Lipis
Bruas
Teluk Anson
Cukai
Sungai Lembing
Jerantut
2108
PAHANG
Raub
Bukit Fraser
Bernam
Sabak
Beserah
Kuantan
Tanjong Malim
Kuala Kubu Baharu
SELANGOR
Bentung
Temerloh
Pahang
Pekan
Strait of Malacca
Kuala Selangor
Rawang
Teriang
Kelang
Kuala Lumpur
Shah Alam
Kepulauan Aroa
Port Kelang
Kajang
NEGERI SEMBILAN
Kuala Pilah
Bahau
Pulau Tioman
Seremban
Gemas
Segamat
Endau
Mersing
Port Dickson
Tampin
1276
Labis
Bekok
SUMATERA
Jasin
Tangkak
MELAKA
Muar
JOHOR
INDONESIA
(Malacca) Melaka
Paya Bakri
Keluang
Pulau Rupat
Bandar Maharani (Muar)
Bandar Penggaram
Yong Peng
Johore
Kg. Sedili Besar
Kota Tinggi
Kulai
Senai
Johor Baharu
Pontian Kecil
Straits of Singapore
SINGAPORE
PENINSULAR MALAYSIA AND SINGAPORE
1:6 000 000
50 0 50 100 km
East from Greenwich
92
96
98
14
12
6
5
4
3
2
100
101
102
103
104

1 : 10 000 000

95

Phanom Dang Raek
1328
Nong Khae
Prachin Buri
Chachoengsao
Samut Prakan (Paknam)
Chon Buri
Si Racha
Ban Lamung
Rayong
Sattahip
Chanthaburi
ILAND
Ko Chang
Ko Kut
G. of Thailand
Koh Kong
Sre Umbell
Koh Rong
Kompong Som
(Sihanoukville)
Ream
Phu Quoc
Ban Aranyaprathet
Sisophon
Battambang
Pailin
Sang Ke
Pursat
Phnom Kravanh
1744
Kas Kong
Angkor
Siem Reap
Tonlé Sap
CAMBODIA
Kompong Chhnang
1813
Kompong Cham
Phnom Penh
Prek Thnot
Kompong Speu
Takeo
1075
Kampot
Cheom Ksan
761
Phnom Tbeng Meanchey
Khong
Koulen
Sen
Mekong
Stung-Treng
Srépok
San
Khong
Sandan (Sanbor)
Kratie
Senmonorom
Chhlong
Prey-Veng
Banam
Svay Rieng
Tay Ninh
Loc Ninh
Budop
Long Xuyen
Hon Chong
Rach Gia
Sa Dec
Can Tho
Khanh Hung (Soc Trang)
Bac Lieu
Ca Mau
Mui Ca Mau
Côn Dao
Nam Phan
Cochin China
My Tho
Go Công
Vung Tau
Ba Ria
Bien Hoa
Thanh Pho
Ho Chi Minh (Saigon)
Cu Lao Hon
Phan Thiet
Hoa Da (Phan Ri)
Phan Rang
Cam Lam (Ba Ngoi)
Cam Rhan
Nha Trang
Djiringne
Di Linh
Gia Nghia
Da Lat
Cao Nguyen
2405
Buon Me Thuot
Cheo Reo
Pleiku (Gia Lai)
Kontum
An Nhon (Binh Dinh)
Qui Nhon
Song Cau
Tuy Hoa
Ba
VIETNAM
SOUTH CHINA SEA
Pattani
Yala
Narathiwat
Tumpat
Kota Baharu
Betong
Kelantan
Kepulauan Perhentian
Kuala Trengganu
Gerik
2170
Taiping
2182
Ipoh
Perak
Gunong Tahan
2190
Cameron Highlands
Kuala Dungun
PENINSULAR
MALAYSIA
Teluk Anson
Kuala Lipis
Raub
Pahang
Kuantan
Kuala Selangor
Port Kelang
Kuala Lumpur
Kelang
Seremban
Gemas
Port Dickson
Melaka
Bandar Maharani
Bandar Penggaram
Keluang
Mersing
Tioman
Johor Baharu
SINGAPORE
Str. of Malacca
ATERA
DONESIA
INDONESIA
Jemaja
Kuala
Siantan
Matak
Kepulauan Anambas
Laut
Telukbutun
959
Kepulauan Natuna Besar
Binjai
Midai
Subi
Kepulauan Natuna Selatan
Kepulauan Tambelan
102
104
106
108
14
12
10
8
6
4
2

111

74

R U S S I A
M O N G O L I A
NORTH KOREA
SOUTH KOREA
Y E L L O W
Ozero Baikal
Irkutsk
Angarsk
Cheremkhovo
Ulan Ude
Chita
Khrebet
Yablonovyy
Hentiyn Nuruu
Ulaanbaatar
Hangayn Nuruu
Tannu Ola
Bayanhongor
Choybalsan
Hailar
Blagoveshchensk
Khabarovsk
Vladivostok
Ussuriysk
Xiao Hinggan Ling
Yilehuli Shan
Qiqihar
HARBIN
Mudanjiang
Jiamusi
Changchun
Jilin
Yanji
SHENYANG
Fushun
Benxi
Anshan
Liaoyang
Dandong
Siping
Liaoyuan
Fuxin
Jinzhou
Yingkou
Qinhuangdao
Chengde
Tangshan
TIANJIN
(Tientsin)
BEIJING
(Peking)
Zhangjiakou
Xuanhua
Datong
Jining
Hohhot
BAOTOU
Baotou
Mu Us Shamo
Yinchuan
Baiyin
Xining
TAIYUAN
Shijiazhuang
Baoding
Yangquan
Jinan
Zibo
Weifang
QINGDAO
Yantai
DALIAN
(Lüda)
Bo Hai
Korea Bay
P'yongyang
Sŏul
Inch'on
Taejon
Taegu
Pusan
Masan
Chŏnju
Kwangju
Mokpo
Alxa Zuoqi
Dzamin Üüd
Saynshand
Erenhot

100

1 : 20 000 000

Lanzhou
Linxia
Lintan
Maqên Gangri
6 282
Min Xian
Maqên
Songpan
Min
Garzê
Yalong
Pingliang
Tongchuan
Tianshui
Baoji
Dali
XI'AN
Qin Ling
4107
Yongji
Jiaozuo
Xinxiang
Luoyang
Kaifeng
Zhengzhou
Shangqiu
Jining
Yanzhou
Teng Xian
Xuzhou
Lianyungang
Hai'an
JIANGSU
Xuchang
HENAN
Nanyang
Shangshui
Huainan
Bengbu
Hongze Hu
NANJING
Zhenjiang
Changzhou
Chang
Suzhou
SHANGHAI
Wuxi
Hefei
Ma'anshan
Wuhu
ANHUI
Anqing
Jiaxing
Shaoxing
Hangzhou
Ningbo
Zhumadian
Xinyang
WUHAN
Hanzhong
Yun Xian
Ankang
Daba Shan
Xiangfan
Xiangyang
HUBEI
Zigui
Yichang
Fengjie
Langzhong
Daxian
Nanchong
Wanxian
Santai
CHENGDU
Guan Xian
Hechuan
Beibei
CHONGQING
Neijiang
Ya'an
Minya Konka
7 556
Wutongqiao
Zigong
Luzhou
Yibin
Daliang Shan
Xichang
Zhaotong
Huize
Zunyi
GUIZHOU
Guiyang
Anshun
Duyun
Zhenyuan
Tongren
2 494
Yuanling
Jianli
Shashi
Jinshi
Dongting Hu
Changde
Yiyang
Xiangtan
HUNAN
Shaoyang
Hengyang
Zhuzhou
Changsha
Ji'an
Nanchang
Jiujiang
Poyang Hu
Huangshi
Jingdezhen
Tunxi
ZHEJIANG
Qu Xian
Jinhua
Linhai
Wenzhou
Shangrao
Lishui
Yingtan
2120
Fuzhou
Shaowu
Jian'ou
Ningde
Fuzhou
Nanping
JIANGXI
Wuyi Shan
Ganzhou
FUJIAN
Min
Quanzhou
Changting
Zhangzhou
Xiamen
Mei Xian
GUANGDONG
Chao'an
Shantou
GUANGZHOU
(Canton)
Shilong
Foshan
Jiangmen
Macao
(PORT.)
Kowloon
Hong Kong (Br.)
Sanshui
Wuzhou
Shaoguan
Guilin
Liuzhou
GUANGXI
ZHUANGZU
Guiping
Hechi
Yishan
Hongshui
Lingyun
Nanning
Pingxiang
Lang Son
Qinzhou
Beihai
Zhanjiang
Leizhou Bandao
Haikou
Hainan Dao
Changjiang
Wuzhi Shan
1867
Huangliu
G. of Tonkin
Haiphong
Hanoi
Nam Dinh
Ninh Binh
Than Hoa
Vinh
VIETNAM
LAOS
Luang Prabang
Xieng Khouang
Nan
Lao Cai
Phong Saly
Lai Chau
Lancang
Simao
Gejiu
Mengzi
Kunming
Xiaguan
Chuxiong
YUNNAN
Anning
Chengjiang
Xingren
Zhanyi
Taibei
(Taipei)
Jilong
Yilan
Xinzhu
Miaoli
Taizhong
Zhanghua
Jiayi
TAIWAN
(FORMOSA)
Yu Shan
3 950
Tainan
Taidong
Gaoxiong
Pingdong
Bashi Channel
Batan Is.
PHILIPPINES
Luzon
Laoag
SOUTH CHINA SEA
EAST CHINA SEA
SEA
Ryūkyū-Rettō
Okinawa
7507
Sakishima-Guntō
Tropic of Cancer
JAPAN
Cheju
Cheju Do
1950
Korea Str.
Tsushima
Fukuoka
Sasebo
Nagasaki
30
20
110
120
East from Greenwich

101
104
97
112

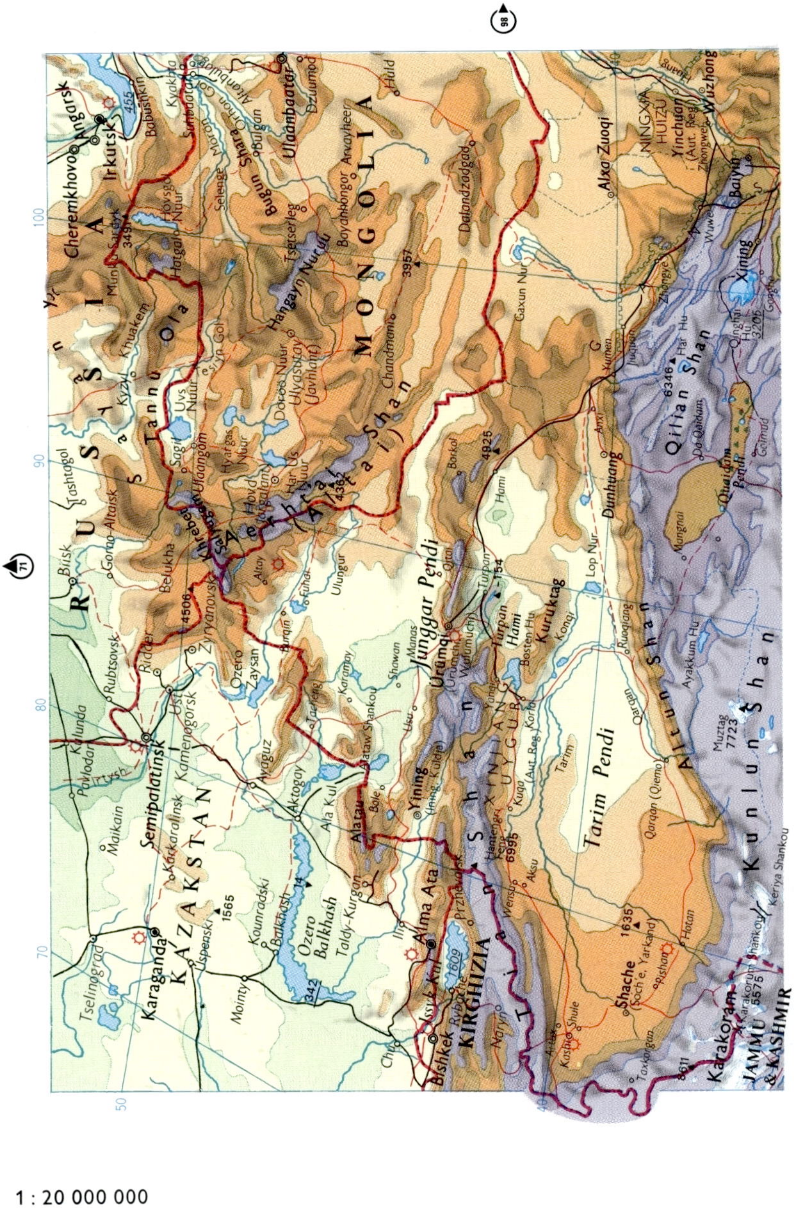
R U S S I A
M O N G O L I A
K A Z A K S T A N
KIRGHIZIA
JAMMU & KASHMIR
NINGXIA HUIZU
X I N J I A N G U Y G U R
Irkutsk
Angarsk
Cheremkhovo
Ulaanbaatar
Kyzyl
Tannu Ola
Hangayn Nuruu
Altai
Altay Shan
Gorno-Altaisk
Biisk
Rubtsovsk
Semipalatinsk
Pavlodar
Karaganda
Ozero Balkhash
Ozero Zaysan
Alma Ata
Bishkek
Issyk Kul
Yining
Ürümqi
Junggar Pendi
Turpan
Hami
Kuruktag
Lop Nur
Dunhuang
Tarim Pendi
Altun Shan
Kunlun Shan
Qilian Shan
Qaidam Pendi
Xining
Yinchuan
Wuzhong
Baiyin
Alxa Zuoqi
Dalandzadgad
Karakoram
Shache
Hotan
Aksu
Kashi
T i a n S h a n
Tselinograd
Ust-Kamenogorsk
Uliastay
Hovd
Ulaangom
Bulgan
Gaxun Nur
Yumen
Anxi
Barkol
Korla
Kuqa
Karamay
Taldy-Kurgan
Przhevalsk
Qiemo
7723
6995
6346
4925
4506
4362
3957
70
80
90
100
50
40
71
98

1 : 20 000 000

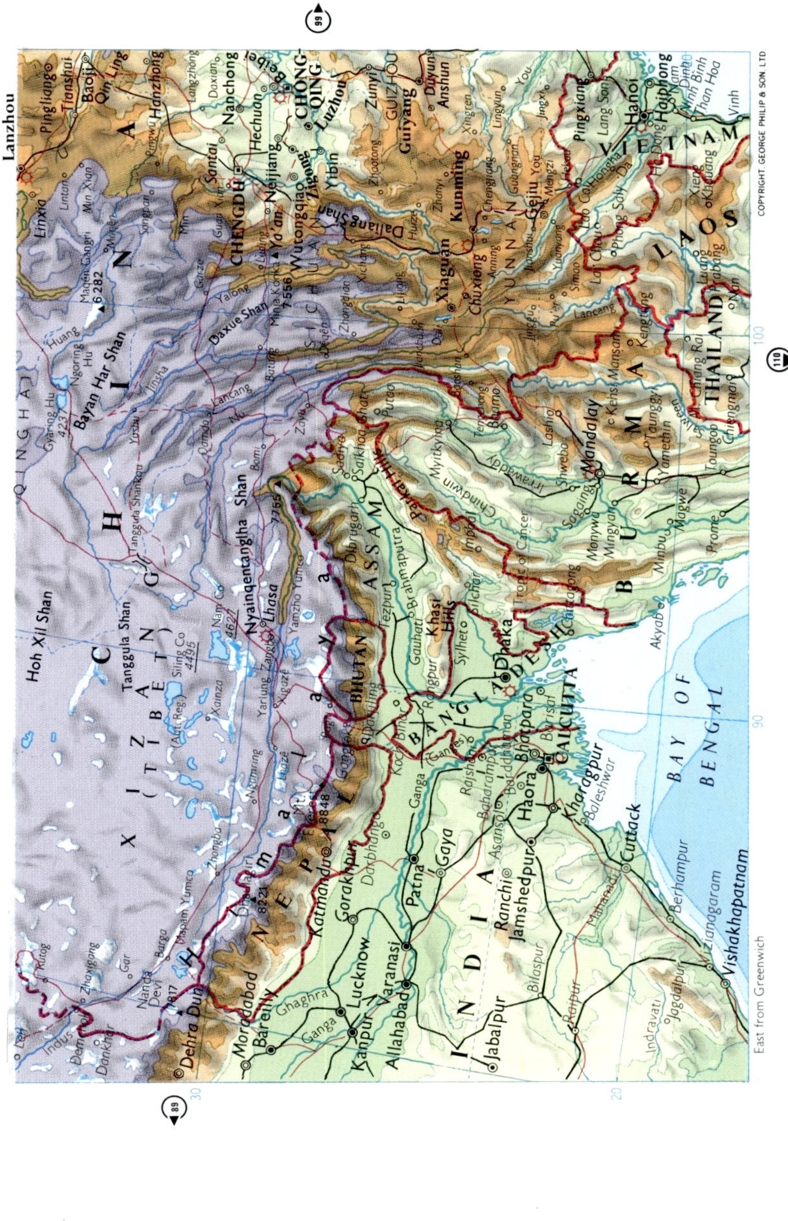

Lanzhou
CHINA
XIZANG (TIBET)
QINGHAI
SICHUAN
YUNNAN
GUIZHOU
Hoh Xil Shan
Tanggula Shan
Bayan Har Shan
Nyainqentanglha Shan
Daxue Shan
Daliang Shan
Qin Ling
Lhasa
CHENGDU
CHONGQING
Kunming
Guiyang
Xiaguan
Chuxiong
Gejiu
Luzhou
Yibin
Zigong
Neijiang
Nanchong
Hanzhong
Tianshui
Baoji
Pingliang
Linxia
Ya'an
Wutongqiao
Leshan
Xigazê
Yarlung Zangbo
Siling Co
Nam Co
Nanda Devi
Dhaulagiri
Mt. Everest 8848
NEPAL
Katmandu
BHUTAN
ASSAM
BANGLADESH
Dhaka
Chittagong
CALCUTTA
Haora
INDIA
Dehra Dun
Moradabad
Bareilly
Lucknow
Kanpur
Allahabad
Varanasi
Patna
Gaya
Gorakhpur
Ranchi
Jamshedpur
Jabalpur
Cuttack
Kharagpur
Berhampur
Vishakhapatnam
Brahmaputra
Ganga
Ghaghra
Indus
BAY OF BENGAL
BURMA
Mandalay
Irrawaddy
Chindwin
Sagaing
Monywa
Magwe
Prome
Toungoo
Akyab
Myitkyina
Lashio
Tropic of Cancer
THAILAND
LAOS
VIETNAM
Hanoi
Haiphong
East from Greenwich
COPYRIGHT GEORGE PHILIP & SON LTD

75

98

East from Greenwich

The numbers refer to prefectures which are listed on page 105.

1 : 7 500 000

Sea of Okhotsk
Rebun-Tō
Rishiri-Tō
Wakkanai
Teshio
Otoineppu
Enbetsu
HOKKAIDŌ
Monbetsu
Yūbetsu
Abashiri-Wan
Nemuro-Kaikyō
Shibetsu
Kitami
Abashiri
Rumoi
Ishikari-Wan (Otaru-Wan)
Daisetsu-Zan 2290
Asahikawa
Atsuta
HOKKAIDŌ
Nemuro
Kamui-Misaki
Bibai
Honbetsu
Otaru
Iwamisawa
Obihiro
Iwanai
Yūbari
Tokachi
Kushiro
Sapporo
Tomakomai
2052
Poroshiri Dake
Shiraoi
Setana
Mombetsu
Uchiura-Wan
Muroran
Urakawa
Samani
Okushiri-Tō
Erimo-Misaki
Esashi
Hakodate
Esan-Misaki
Tsugaru-Kaikyō
Shiriya-Zaki
Matsumae
Mutsu
Mutsu-Wan
Aomori
Hirosaki
Towada-Ko
Hachinohe
F
Odate
Kuji
Noshiro
Yoneshiro
40
Oga-Hantō
Iwate San 2041
Akita
Morioka
Miyako
Omono
Hanamaki
Kamaishi
Honjō
Yokote
Kitakami
Ichinoseki
Sakata
TŌHOKU
Tsuruoka
Mogami
Shinjō
Kogota
N
Ishinomaki
Shiogama
Sendai
Yamagata
Iwanuma
Sado
Niigata
Shibata
Yonezawa
Agano
Fukushima
Bandai San 1819
Suzu-Misaki
Nagaoka
Wajima
Kashiwazaki
Aizuwakamatsu
Koriyama
Naoetsu
Tajima
Nanao
Toyama-Wan
Takada
Iwaki
Himi
Nikkō
Takaoka
Nagano
Hitachi
Toyama
Shinano
Maebashi
Kiryū
Utsunomiya
Ueda
Tochigi
Nakaminato
Matsumoto
Takasaki
Gyoda
Mito
Chichibu
Omiya
Tsuchiura
Takayama
Kawagoe
KANTŌ
Suwa
Urawa
Shin-Tone
Sawara
Kawaguchi
Ichikawa
Chōshi
TŌKYŌ
HONSHU
140
145
45
10

130
135
35
30
SOUTH KOREA
Samchok
Pusan
KOREA STRAIT
Ullung Do
SEA OF JAPAN
Oki-Shotō
Tsushima
Tsushima-Kaikyō
Iki
CHŪGOKU
Hi-no-Misaki
Izumo
Matsue
Yonago 31
Tottori
Toyooka
24
25
Kyō-ga-Saki
Wakasa-Wan
Kanazawa
9
CHUBU
Fukui
11
Takefu
Tsuruga
Maizuru
Ayabe
28
26
Hikone
Biwa Ko
Kuwana
Yokkaichi
Tsu
Matsu
HONSHU
32 Tsuyama
Kyoto
Otsu
Himeji
Amagasaki
Kobe
Osaka
Hamada
33
Masuda
Kurashiki
Okayama
Akashi
Nara
Fukuyama
34
Onomichi
Mihara
Hiroshima
Hagi
Yamaguchi
35
Tokuyama
Kure
Shimonoseki
Ube
Suō-Nada
Seto-naikai
Takamatsu
Marugame
36
Tokushima
Sakai
27
Kishiwada
29
Wakayama
Owase
KINKI
30
Shingū
Shio-no-Misaki
Kii-Suidō
Niihama
37
Matsuyama
SHIKOKU
38
39
Kōchi
Yawatahama
Uwajima
Tosa-Wan
Nakamura
Ashizuri-zaki
Muroto-Misaki
SHIKOKU
Fukuoka
40
Kitakyūshū
Karatsu
41
Nakatsu
Sasebo
Saga
Kurume
Beppu
Ōita
Nakadori-Jima
Omuta
42
Kashima
Aso-zan 1592
44
Usuki
Saiki
Bungo-Suidō
Isahaya
Nagasaki
Kumamoto
Fukue-Jima
Shimabara
Shimō-Jima
Yatsushiro
Nobeoka
43
Minamata
45
KYUSHU
Sendai
46
Miyazaki
Kobayashi
Kagoshima
Miyakonojō
KYŪSHŪ
Kanoya
Makurazaki
Shibushi-Wan
Kagoshima-Wan
Ōsumi-Kaikyō
Nishinoomote
Ōsumi-Shotō
Tane-ga-Shima
Kuchinoerabu-Jima
Yaku-Jima
Tokara-Kaikyō
Naka-no-Shima
Suwanose-Jima
PACIFIC OCEAN
98
East from Greenwich

1 : 7 500 000

103

Sado
Niigata
Shibata
Agano
Yamagata
Sendai
Shiogama
Iwanuma
Yonezawa
Fukushima
Bandai-San
1819
Suzu-Misaki
Wajima
Nagaoka
Kashiwazaki
Aizuwakamatsu
Koriyama
Naoetsu
Tajima
Nanao
Himi
Takaoka
Toyama-Wan
Takada
Iwaki
Nikkō
Toyama
Nagano
Shinano
Hitachi
Maebashi
Kiryū
Utsunomiya
Matsumoto
Ueda
Tochigi
Nakaminato
Takasaki
Gyoda
Mito
Takayama
Chichibu
Ōmiya
Tsuchiura
KANTŌ
Suwa
Kawagoe
Urawa
Shin-Tone
Sawara
Ontake-San
3063
Ina
Kawaguchi
Ichikawa
Chōshi
Kofu
TŌKYŌ
Kiso
Iida
Kawasaki
Chiba
Gifu
Fuji-San
3776
Yokohama
Yokosuka
Fuji-no-miya
Fujisawa
Ichinomiya
Nagoya
Numazu
Katsuura
Shimizu
Atami
Okazaki
Shizuoka
Ito
Tateyama
Suruga-Wan
Ō-Shima
Shimada
Hamamatsu
Toyohashi
Tenryū
Ise-Wan
Toba
Daiō-Misaki
Nii-Jima
Miyake-Jima
Mikura-Jima
Hachijo-Jima
Aoga-Shima
140
145
35
30
HOKKAIDŌ
1 Hokkaidō
TOHŌKU
2 Aomori
3 Akita
4 Iwate
5 Yamagata
6 Miyagi
7 Fukushima
CHŪBU
8 Niigata
9 Ishikawa
10 Toyama
11 Fukui
12 Gifu
13 Nagano
14 Yamanashi
15 Aichi
16 Shizuoka
KANTŌ
17 Gumma
18 Tochigi
19 Saitama
20 Ibaraki
21 Tōkyō
22 Chiba
23 Kanagawa
KINKI
24 Hyōgo
25 Kyōto
26 Shiga
27 Ōsaka
28 Nara
29 Mie
30 Wakayama
CHŪGOKU
31 Tottori
32 Okayama
33 Shimane
34 Hiroshima
35 Yamaguchi
SHIKOKU
36 Kagawa
37 Tokushima
38 Ehime
39 Kōchi
KYŪ SHŪ
40 Fukuoka
41 Saga
42 Nagasaki
43 Kumamoto
44 Ōita
45 Miyazaki
46 Kagoshima

CHŪBU-DISTRICT
KINKI-DISTRICT
Kanazawa
Takaoka
Toyama
Fukui
Kyōto
Ōsaka
Kōbe
Nagoya
Wakayama
Biwa-Ko
Wakasa-Wan
Ise-Wan
Kumano-Nada
Kii-Hantō
East from Greenwich
136
137
35
34
36

1 : 2 500 000

105

Nagano
Nakano
Suzaka
Kōshoku
Ōmachi
Ueda
Komoro
Asama Yama
Chikuma-Gawa
Matsumoto
Saku
Shiojiri
Okaya
Suwa
Suwa-Ko
Chino
Tateshina-Yama
2530
Ina
Komagene
Kiso-Sammyaku
Iida
Tenryū-Gawa
Akaishi-Sammyaku
Akaishi-Dake
3120
Shirane-San
3192
Minobu-Sanchi
Sakuma
Tenryū
Shimada
Hamakita
Kakegawa
Fukuroi
Iwata
Sagara
Omae-Zaki
Nada
Shizuoka
Fujieda
Yaizu
Shimizu
Fuji
Fuji-no-miya
Numazu
Mishima
Atami
Gotemba
Fuji-San
3776
Fuji-yoshida
Tsuru
Minobu
Kōfu
Nirasaki
Enzan
Kobuchizawa
Yamanashi
YAMANASHI
Ōtsuki
Kumotori-Yama
2018
Kantō-Sanchi
Chichibu
Higashi-matsuyama
Kumagaya
Fukaya
Fujioka
Shimonita
Tomioka
Takasaki
Annaka
Maebashi
Shibukawa
Nakanojō
Numata
Minakami
Shirane-San
2578
Chuzenji-Ko
Imaichi
Nikkō
Kanuma
Kiryū
Ashikaga
Ōta
Isesaki
Honjō
Tone-Gawa
Sano
Oyama
Tochigi
Utsunomiya
Hanyu
Kazo
Koga
Gyoda
Kōnosu
Kantō-Heiya
Ageo
Kawagoe
Omiya
Urawa
Kawaguchi
Warabi
Tokorozawa
Ōme
Kodaira
Musashino
Tachikawa
Hachiōji
Mitaka
Fuchū
Sagamihara
Machida
Yamato
Atsugi
Tanzawa-Sanchi
Hatano
Hiratsuka
Fujisawa
Chigasaki
Odawara
Kamakura
Yokosuka
Miura
KAWASAKI
YOKOHAMA
TŌKYŌ
Tōkyō-Wan
Uraga-Suidō
Sagami-Wan
Matsudo
Ichikawa
Funabashi
Chiba
Ichihara
Kisarazu
Kashiwa
Noda
Kasukabe
Koshigaya
Mitsukaidō
Ryūgasaki
Tsuchiura
Kasumi-ga-Ura
Kita-Ura
Itako
Kashima
Sawara
Narita
Sakura
Asahi
Chōshi
Yokaichiba
Narutō
Tōgane
Ōamishirasato
Mobara
Ōtaki
Ōhara
Katsuura
Kamogawa
Bōsō-Hantō
Tateyama
Su-no-Saki
Nojima-Zaki
Shimodate
Shimotsuma
Yūki
Kinu-Gawa
Mo'oka
Motegi
Kasama
Iwase
Mito
Tomobe
Ishioka
Hokota
Katsuta
Nakaminato
Ōarai
Kashima-Nada
Hitachi
Hitachi-ota
Daigo
Karasuyama
Naka-Gawa
Kuriha-shi
Tatebayashi
IBARAKI
CHIBA
SAITAMA
TOKYO
KANAGAWA
SHIZUOKA
GUMMA
TOCHIGI
NAGANO
KANTŌ DISTRICT
Izu-Hantō
Shuzenji
Ito
Toi
1407
Matsuzaki
Shimoda
Irō-Zaki
Suraga-Wan
Sagami-Nada
Mihara-Yama
755
Ō-Shima
To-Shima
Nii-Jima
Shikine-Jima
Kōzu-Shima
Miyake-Jima
Mikura-Jima
138
139
140
34
35
36

105

Masuda
Hagi
Aono-Yama 908
Kanmuri-Yama 1339
Tsuno-Shima
Nagato
YAMAGUCHI
Yamaguchi
Mine
Tokuji
Ōtake
Iwakuni
Hibiki-Nada
Toyoura
Hōfu
Nan'yō
Tokuyama
Genkai-Nada
Shimonoseki
Onoda
Ube
Kudamatsu
Yanai
Hikari
Higasi-Suidō
Ō-Shima
KITAKYŪSHŪ
Katsumoto
Iki
Gō-no-ura
Fukuma
Nakama
Nōgata
Suō-Nada
Naga-Shima
Iwai-Jima
Iki-Kaikyō
Miyuta
Iizuka
Yukuhashi
FUKUOKA
Hime-Jima
Ō-Shima
Yobuko
Maebaru
Umi
Takawa
Nakatsu
Futago-Yama 721
Kunisaki
Iyo-Nada
FUKUOKA
Yamada
Buzen
Karatsu
Tsukushi
Sefuri-San 1055
Sanchi
1200
Usa
Bungotakada
Hōgo-Kaikyō
Hirado
Hirado-Shima
Matsuura
Imari
SAGA
Amagi
Tosu
Hita
Hiji
Kitsuki
Sada-Misaki-Hantō
Kurume
Yame
Yufu-Dake 1584
Beppu-Wan
Sasebo
Takeo
Taku
Saga
Kurogi
Kusu
Beppu
Ōita
Tsurusaki
Saganoseki
Arita
Kashima
Ōkawa
Yanagawa
Chikugo
Setaka
ŌITA
Usuki
Omura-Wan
Ureshino 983
Tara
Ōmuta
Yamaga
Oguni
Kujū-San 1787
Bungo-Suidō
NAGASAKI
Tara-Dake
Arao
Aso
Tsukumi
Ōmura
Kikuchi
Ōzu
Taketa
Saiki
Isahaya
Tamana
Kumamoto
Ichinomiya
Aso-zan 1592
Sobo-Yama 1758
Tsurumi-Saki
Nishi-Sonogi-Hantō
Nagasaki
Unzen-Dake 1360
Shimabara
Mashiki
KUMAMOTO
Kamae
Tachibana-Wan
Obama
Uto
Takachiho
Nomo-Zaki
Kuchinotsu
Oyano
Misumi
Hinokage
Amakusa-Nada
Hondo
Kami-Jima
Kunimi-Dake 1739
Nobeoka
Yatsushiro
Amakusa-Shotō
Shimo-Jima
Yatsushiro-Kai
Itsuki
Shiiba
Kyūshū-Sanchi
Hyūga
Hososhima
Ushibuka
Yunomae
MIYAZAKI
Hitoyoshi
Naga-Shima
Minamata
KYŪSHŪ
Izumi
Saito
Takanabe
Akune
Ōkuchi
Ebino
KYŪSHŪ-DISTRICT
Kami-koshiki-Jima
Yoshimatsu
Kobayashi
Miyanojō
Kurino
1700
Kirishima-Yama
Miyazaki
Sendai
Koshiki-Rettō
Kajiki
Kushikino
Kokubu
Miyakonojō
Ijūin
Hayato
Shimo-koshiki-Jima
Kagoshima
On-Take 1118
Nichinan
KAGOSHIMA
Aburatsu
Taniyama
Fukiage
Shibushi
Tarumizu
Noma-Saki
Kaseda
Kagoshima-Wan
Kushima
Satsuma-Hantō
Kanoya
Chiran
Shibushi-Wan
Makurazaki
Kōyama
Ibusuki
Bō-no-Misaki
Ōsumi-Hantō
Kaimon-Dake 924
Yamagawa
Sata-Misaki
East from Greenwich
130
131
132
34
33
32
31
99
104
109
COPYRIGHT GEORGE PHILIP & SON LTD.

1 : 2 500 000

HONSHŪ
SHIKOKU
SHIKOKU-DISTRICT
CHŪGOKU-DISTRICT
SETO-NAIKAI
Oki-Shotō
Dōgo
Daimanji-San 608
Saigō
Shimane-Hantō
Jizō-Zaki
Sakaiminato
Matsue
Shinji-Ko
Hirata
Hi-no-Misaki
Taisha
Izumo
Shinji
Yasugi
Yonago
Daito
Kisuki
Dai-Sen 1712
TOTTORI
Kurayoshi
Iwami
Kasumi
Tottori
Toyooka
Hidaka
1510
Suga-no-Sen
Wakasa
Wadayama
Ikuno
HYŌGO
Chūgoku-Sanchi
Ōda
1126
Sanbe-San
Yunotsu
Gōtsu
Gō-Gawa
SHIMANE
Hamada
Dōgo-San 1269
Katsuyama
Tsuyama
Ochiai
Niimi
OKAYAMA
Yamazaki
Nishiwaki
Kasai
Tōjō
Shōbara
Miyoshi
Takahashi
Asahi-Gawa
Yanahara
Sayō
Tatsuno
Aioi
Himeji
Ono
Wake
Takasago
Miki
Kakogawa
Akashi
Akō
Bizen
Saidaiji
HIROSHIMA
Kake
Kanmuri-Yama 1339
Ōta-Gawa
Kabe
Fuchū
Ibara
Yakage
Sōja
Okayama
Kurashiki
Kojō
Tamashima
Tamano
Kojima
Kannabe
Fukuyama
Saijō
HIROSHIMA
Itsukaichi
Kaita
Takehara
Mihara
Onomichi
Kasaoka
Tomo
In'no-shima
Marugame
Sakaide
Takamatsu
Shōdo-Shima
Tonoshō
Ieshima-Shotō
Harima-Nada
Awaji-Shima
Sumoto
Tsuna
Nandan
Naruto-Kaikyō
Ōtake
Kure
Ondo
Nigata
Ōmi-Shima
Tadotsu
Zentsūji
Kotohira
Shido
Miki
KAGAWA
Hiketa
Naruto
Itano
Iwakuni
Hiroshima-Wan
Kurahashi-Jima
Aki-Nada
Takuma
Takase
Hiuchi-Nada
Kan onji
Sanyuki-Sammyaku
Kamita
Tokushima
Yanai
Imabari
Kawanoe
Ikeda
Kamojima
Anabuki
Komatsujima
Ōshima
Yashiro-Jima
Hōjō
Niihama
Iyo-mishima
TOKUSHIMA
Anan
Kii-Suidō
Nyūgawa
Saijō
Matsuyama
Matsusaki
Heigun-To
Ishizuchi-Yama 1981
Shikoku-Sanchi
Tsurugi-San 1955
Gamoda-Saki
Iyo
Ōtoyo
KŌCHI
Kuma
Nagahama
Iyo-Nada
EHIME
Tosa-yamada
Mugi
Ozu
Uchiko
Oda
Ino
Kōchi
Nankoku
Aki
Sada-Misaki-Hantō
Yawatahama
Uwa
Sagawa
Tosa
Heiya
Kochi-
Tōyō
Susaki
Tosa-Wan
Hiromi
Uwajima
Kubokawa
Muroto
Muroto-Misaki
Ekawasaki
Bungo-Suidō
Sagc
Jōhen
Tsurumi-Saki
Nakamura
Sukumo
Tosa-shimizu
Oki-no-Shima
Ashizuri-Zaki
East from Greenwich
132
133
134
33
34
35
36
106

1 : 2 500 000

112

99

93

BURMA
THAILAND
LAOS
VIET-NAM
CAMBODIA
CHINA
HONG KONG
(Br.)
Kowloon
Macau
(Port.)
Zhanjiang
Haikou
Hainan
C. Bastion
Beihai
Pingxiang
Haiphong
Hanoi
G. of Tonkin
Nam Dinh
Thanh Hoa
Vinh
Ha Tinh
Quang Tri
Hué
Da-Nang
(Tourane)
An Nhon
Qui Nhon
Nha Trang
Phan Rang
Phan Thiet
THANH PHO HO CHI MINH
(Saigon)
Con Son
Phnom Penh
Kratié
Tonle Sap
Battambang
Kompong Som
Long Xuyen
Can Tho
Pakse
Khong
Srepot
Mekong
Vientiane
Luang Prabang
Phu Loi
2257
Udon Thani
M. Ubon
Nakhon Ratchasima
(Khorat)
Phanom Dang Raek
BANGKOK
Ayutthaya
Chanthaburi
M. Phitsanulok
Uttaradit
Tak
(Raheng)
Chiangmai
Moulmein
Amherst
Ye
Tavoy
Mergui
Myeik
Kyunzu
Taunggyi
Salween
Toungoo
Yamethin
Prome
RANGOON
Bassein
G. of Martaban
Mouths of Irrawaddy
Ramree I.
Cheduba I.
Middle Andaman
Andaman Islands
(India)
Pt. Blair
Little Andaman
ANDAMAN SEA
Ten Degree Channel
Car Nicobar
Nicobar Islands
(India)
Great Nicobar
Gulf of Thailand
Kho Khot Kra
Chumphon
Nakhon Si Thammarat
Mui Bai Bung
Phuket
Trang
Songkhla
(Singora)
Kota Baharu
Kuala Trengganu
G. Tahan
2190
Butterworth
Taiping
Ipoh
George Town
Pinang
Strait of Mala
Banda Aceh
(Kutaraja)
SOUTH CHINA SEA
Hsisha Chuntao
Spratly
Amboyna
Natuna Besar
Palawan
Balabac Str.
Banggi
Kudat
Kinabalu
4101
SABAH
Kota Kinabalu
(Jesselton)
Labuan
Victoria
Bandar Seri Begawan
Sandakan
Labuk
100
110
10
20

1 : 20 000 000

MALAYSIA
INDONESIA
SUMATERA
BORNEO
KALIMANTAN
JAVA
SARAWAK
BRUNEI
SINGAPORE
JAKARTA
BANDUNG
SURABAJA
Medan
Kelang
Kuala Lumpur
Seremban
Telok Anson
Port Kelang
Tanjungbalai
Tebingtinggi
Pematangsiantar
L. Toba
Simeulue
Banjak Is.
Sibolga
Nias
Rupat
Melaka
Bandar Maharani
Johor Baharu
Kepulauan Riau
Pekanbaru
Equator
Batu Is.
Bukittinggi
Sawahlunto
Siberut
Padang
Kerinci
3800
Sipora
P. Pagai Selatan
P. Pagai Utara
Kep. Mentawai
Hari
Jambi
Selat Berhala
Kepulauan Lingga
Selat Bangka
Pangkalpinang
Bangka
Musi
Palembang
Manggar
Pulau Belitung
Karimata Is.
Bengkulu
Enggano
Telukbetung
Selat Sunda
Anambas
Kepulauan Natuna Besar
Natuna Selatan
Kucing
Sibu
Miri
Pontianak
Kapuas
Kapuas
Peg. Muller
Peg. Iran
Peg. Tama Abu
Kajan
Peg. Brassy
Tawau
Teluk Gioeng
Teluk Sebuku
Tarakan
Mahakam
Balikpapan
Peg. Schwaner
Barito
Kualakapuas
Banjarmasin
Pulau Laut
Selat Makasar
Greater Sunda Islands
JAVA SEA
Kepulauan Laut Ketil
Ujung Pandang
Karimunjawa Is.
Bawean
Madura
Kangean Is.
Nusa Tenggara
(Lesser Sunda Islands)
Bali
Lombok
Sumbawa
3726
Raba
Denpasar
Bogor
BARAT
Cirebon
Tegal
Pekalongan
Slamet
3428
TENGAH
Semarang
Madiun
TIMUR
Magelang
Yogyakarta
Surakarta
Kediri
Blitar
Malang
INDIAN OCEAN
Christmas I. (Austral.)
Cocos or Keeling Is. (Austral.)
East from Greenwich
0
10
100
110
COPYRIGHT GEORGE PHILIP & SON LTD

113

99

PACIFIC OCEAN
SOUTH CHINA SEA
SULU SEA
PHILIPPINES
Caroline Is.
Belau
Caroline Islands
(U.S. Trust Territory)
Macau
(Port.)
Kowloon
HONG KONG
(Br.)
TAIWAN
(FORMOSA)
Bashi Channel
Batan Is.
Babuyan Is.
Babuyan Chan.
Aparri
Laoag
2928
Baguio
Dagupan
LUZON
Quezon City
MANILA
Manila B.
Batangas
Polillo Islands
Lamon B.
Calapan
Mindoro
Mindoro Str.
Calamian Group
Tablas
Sibuyan
Catanduanes
Lagonoy G.
Sorsogon
S. Bernardino Str.
Samar
Masbate
Tacloban
Surigao Strait
Leyte
Ormoc
Panay
Iloilo
Bacolod
Cebu
Negros
Bohol
Bohol Sea
Butuan
Cagayan
Mindanao
Davao
Davao Gulf
C. S. Agustin
2965
Ozamiz
Moro Gulf
Zamboanga
Basilan
Jolo
Sulu Arch.
Sarangani B.
Tinaca Point
Palawan
Balabac Str.
Banggi
Labuk
Labuk B.
Sandakan
SABAH
Kinabalu
4101
Kudat
Kota Kinabalu
(Jesselton)
Labuan
Victoria
Bandar Seri Begawan
Amboyna
20
10
120
130

110

1 : 20 000 000

CELEBES SEA
MOLUCCA SEA
INDONESIA
SARAWAK
BRUNEI
BORNEO
KALIMANTAN
SULAWESI (CELEBES)
Greater Sunda Islands
Nusa Tenggara (Lesser Sunda Islands)
FLORES SEA
BANDA SEA
SERAM SEA
TIMOR SEA
ARAFURA SEA
IRIAN JAYA
AUSTRALIA
JAVA
Miri
Sibu
Tawau
Teluk Sebuku
Tarakan
Kajan
Mahakam
Balikpapan
Barito
Kualakapuas
Banjarmasin
Pulau Laut
Kepulauan Laut Ketil
Bawean
Madura
Kangean
SURABAJA
Malang
Kediri
Blitar
Denpasar
Bali
Lombok
Sumbawa
3726
Raba
Flores
Ruteng
Maumere
Sumba
Waingapu
Sawu
Sawu Sea
Timor
Kupang
Dili
Selat Ombai
Wetar
Alor
Pantar
Lomblen
Selat Makasar
Teluk Tomini
Manado
Gorontalo
Palau Sangihe
Kep. Talaud
Rantemario
3455
Pare Pare
Ujung Pandang
Salayar
Muna
Butung
Kendari
Kep. Banggai
Peleng
Taliabu
Mangole
Maluku
Namlea
Buru
Ambon
Ceram
Kep. Obi
Kep. Banda
Morotai
Halmahera
Ternate
Gebe
Waigeo
Misoöl
Sorong
Vogelkop
Wassian
Manokwari
Kepulauan Schouten
Yapen
Teluk Cenderawasih
Teluk Berau
Fakfak
Kep. Watubela
Kepulauan Kai
Wokam
Kobroor
Kepulauan Aru
Trangan
Kepulauan Tanimbar
Yamdena
Selaru
Kep. Leti
Melville I.
Bathurst I.
Van Diemen G.
Darwin
Wessel Is.
C. Arnhem
0
10
120
130
East from Greenwich
111
115
114

AUSTRALIA, NEW ZEALAND AND PAPUA NEW GUINEA

1 : 24 000 000

113

Torres Str.
Thursday I.
C. York
Cape
York
Peninsula
Gulf of
Carpentaria
Barkly Tableland
Mitchell
Laura
Cooktown
Cairns
Gilbert
Normanton
Georgetown
Croydon
Forsayth
Leichhardt
Flinders
Dobbyn
Kajabbi
Mt. Isa
Cloncurry
Dajarra
Burdekin
Townsville
Charters
Towers
Great Barrier Reef
QUEENSLAND
Great Dividing
Mackay
Winton
Capricorn
Longreach
Mackenzie
Rockhampton
Mt. Morgan
Gladstone
Barcoo
Diamantina
Yaraka
Bundaberg
Sandy C.
Charleville
Maryborough
Quilpie
Great Divide
Gympie
Cooper
Thargomindah
Warrego
Cunnamulla
Culgoa
Darling
Darling
Downs
Toowoomba
Ipswich
Brisbane
Dirranbandi
Warwick
C. Byron
Lismore
Marree
Barwon
Walgett
Bourke
L. Frome
Flinders Ranges
New England Ra.
Grafton
Tamworth
Round Mt. 1615
Armidale
Broken Hill
NEW SOUTH WALES
Darling
Cobar
Macquarie
Augusta
P. Pirie
Lofty Ranges
Murray
Mildura
Lachlan
Bathurst
Lithgow
Maitland
Newcastle
Parramatta
Sydney
& Port Jackson
Botany Bay
Katoomba
Blue Mts.
Adelaide
Hay
St. Vincent Gulf
Murrumbidgee
Riverina
Wollongong
Goulburn
Jervis Bay
Encounter B.
Albury
Wagga Wagga
Canberra
Austral. Cap. Terr.
Kingston S.E.
VICTORIA
Maryborough
Bendigo
Australian Alps
Mt. Kosciusko 2230
Bombala
Ballarat
Melbourne
Geelong
C. Howe
Orbost
Portland
Warrnambool
Port Phillip B.
Port Albert
Wilson's Promontory
Bass Strait
King I.
Flinders I.
TASMANIA
Mt. Ossa 1617
Launceston
Queenstown
Hobart
Admiralty Is.
Wewak
Sepik
Schouten Is.
Bismarck
Archipelago
New
Ireland
Rabaul
Kokopo
NEW GUINEA
Madang
Muller Ra.
Lae
New Britain
Huon G.
Wau
Fly
Gulf of
Papua
Mt. Victoria 4035
Owen Stanley Ra.
D'Entrecasteaux
Is.
Daru
P. Moresby
PAPUA NEW GUINEA
On same scale as general map
Samarai
China Strait
Coral Sea
PACIFIC
OCEAN
C. Maria van Diemen
North C.
Russell
Whangarei
Hauraki Gulf
Kaipara Harb.
Gt. Barrier I.
Auckland
Thames
Hamilton
Bay of Plenty
NORTH
ISLAND
Waikato
East C.
New Plymouth
L. Taupo
Gisborne
Mt. Egmont 2518
Ruapehu 2796
Mahia Pen.
Hawke B.
Wanganui
Napier
Hastings
Palmerston N.
C. Farewell
Cook Strait
Nelson
Picton
Wellington
C. Palliser
Greymouth
Hokitika
Southern Alps
Plains
PACIFIC
SOUTH
ISLAND
Christchurch
& Lyttelton
Bank's Pen.
Mt. Cook 3753
Canterbury
Timaru
OCEAN
Waitaki
Doubtful Sd.
Oamaru
Te Anau
Dunedin
& P. Chalmers
West C.
Foveaux Strait
Invercargill
Stewart I.
Bluff Hr.
Southwest C.
NEW ZEALAND
On same scale as main map

QUEENSLAND
NEW SOUTH WALES
Great Dividing Range
Darling Downs
Grey Range
Mc Gregor Ra.
New England Ra.
Liverpool Ra.
Liverpool Plains
Nandewar Range
Richmond Ra.
McPherson Ra.
Lynd Range
Mt. Hutton 984
Mt. Domville 645
Bundaberg
Fraser Island
Maryborough
Gympie
Nambour
Maroochydore
Caloundra
Caboolture
Redcliffe
Sandgate
Wynnum
BRISBANE
Beenleigh
Southport
Gold Coast
Coolangatta
Tweed Heads
Murwillumbah
Mullumbimby
Byron Bay
Lismore
Ballina
Casino
Kyogle
Evans Head
Yamba
Maclean
Grafton
Woolgoolga
Coffs Harbour
Nambucca Heads
Macksville
Kempsey
Port Macquarie
Wauchope
Taree
Ipswich
Toowoomba
Dalby
Kingaroy
Warwick
Stanthorpe
Tenterfield
Glenn Innes
Inverell
Armidale
Tamworth
Gunnedah
Narrabri
Moree
Goondiwindi
Boggabilla
Muswellbrook
Mudgee
Dubbo
Wellington
Narromine
Gilgandra
Coonamble
Coonabarabran
Walgett
Warren
Nyngan
Cobar
Bourke
Brewarrina
Wilcannia
Menindee
Cunnamulla
Charleville
Quilpie
Mitchell
Roma
Miles
St. George
Chinchilla
Bollon
Dirranbandi
Mungindi
Darling
Warrego
Paroo
Barwon
Macquarie
Castlereagh
Bogan
Culgoa
Balonne
Maranoa
Bulloo
Cooper Cr.
L. Numalla
L. Wyara
Bulloo L.
The Salt L.

121

118

1 : 8 000 000

122

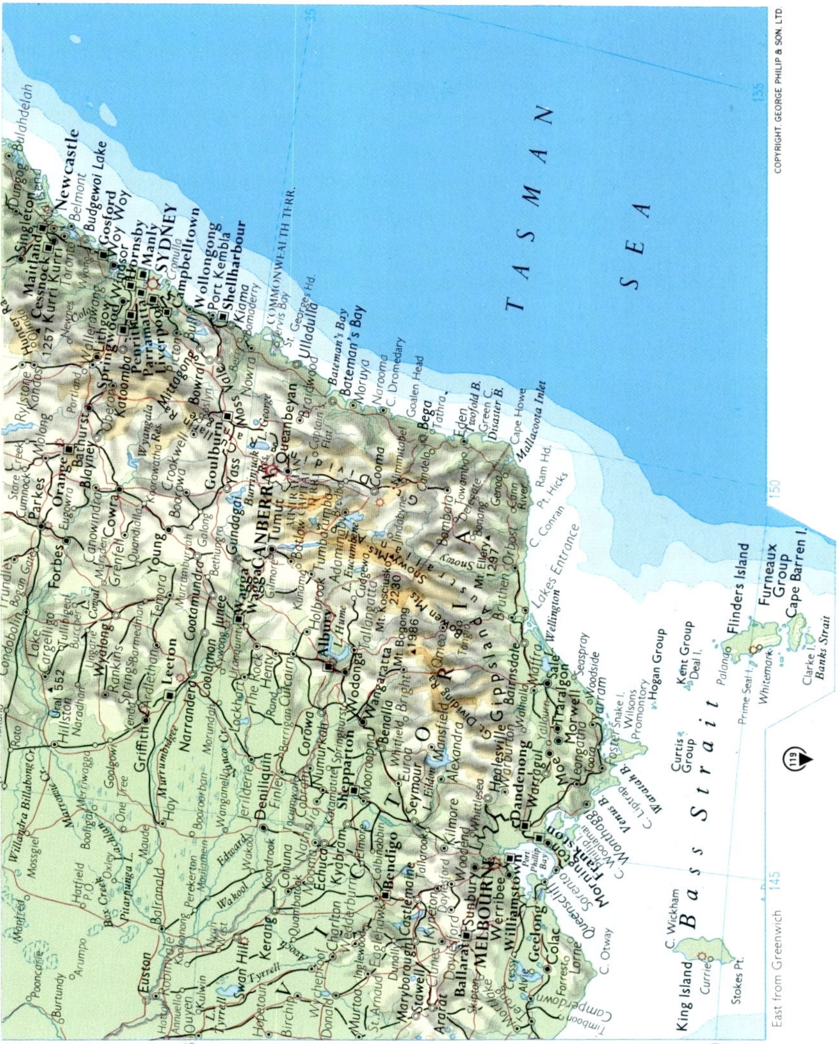
TASMAN
SEA
Bass Strait
SYDNEY
MELBOURNE
CANBERRA
Newcastle
Wollongong
Geelong
Ballarat
Bendigo
Albury
Wagga Wagga
Goulburn
Orange
Bathurst
Dubbo
Griffith
Shepparton
Wangaratta
Cooma
Bega
Eden
Queanbeyan
Gosford
Woy Woy
Maitland
Cessnock
Kurri Kurri
Singleton
Campbelltown
Liverpool
Parramatta
Penrith
Hornsby
Manly
Shellharbour
Port Kembla
Kiama
Nowra
Ulladulla
Bateman's Bay
Moruya
Narooma
Goulburn
Yass
Young
Cowra
Parkes
Forbes
Leeton
Narrandera
Deniliquin
Echuca
Swan Hill
Kerang
Euston
Balranald
Hay
Mildura
Castlemaine
Maryborough
Stawell
Ararat
Colac
Williamstown
Werribee
Sunbury
Dandenong
Frankston
Mornington
Warragul
Moe
Morwell
Traralgon
Sale
Bairnsdale
Lakes Entrance
Wodonga
Benalla
Seymour
Tumut
Mt. Kosciusko 2230
Snowy Mts.
King Island
Flinders Island
Furneaux Group
Cape Barren I.
Wilsons Promontory
COMMONWEALTH TERR.
East from Greenwich
COPYRIGHT. GEORGE PHILIP & SON. LTD.

119
119

AUSTRALIA : ADELAIDE, MELBOURNE, TASMANIA

116

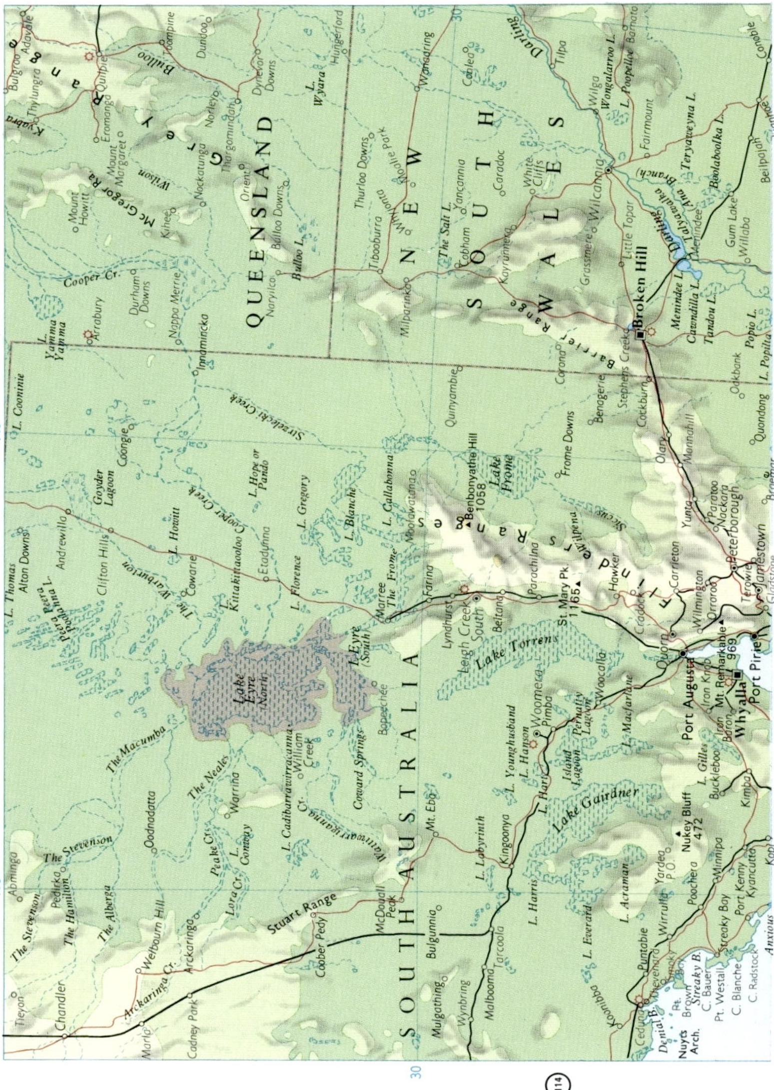

115

114

1 : 8 000 000

117

ADELAIDE
Port Adelaide
Glenelg
Brighton
Elizabeth
Gawler
Murray Bridge
Mannum
Berri
Renmark
Loxton
Barmera
Waikerie
Mildura
Wentworth
Euston
Robinvale
Ouyen
Hopetoun
Swan Hill
Kerang
Balranald
Hay
Deniliquin
Echuca
Kyabram
Shepparton
Bendigo
Castlemaine
Maryborough
Stawell
Ararat
Ballarat
Sunbury
MELBOURNE
Werribee
Williamstown
Geelong
Colac
Lorne
Dandenong
Frankston
Mornington
Seymour
Healesville
Warragul
Warracknabeal
Horsham
Nhill
Dimboola
Hamilton
Portland
Warrnambool
Port Fairy
Mount Gambier
Millicent
Naracoorte
Bordertown
Keith
Kingston South East
Penola
Casterton
Coleraine
Heywood
Port Lincoln
Eyre Peninsula
Cowell
Tumby Bay
Whyalla
Port Broughton
Crystal Brook
Clare
Kapunda
Burra
Kadina
Wallaroo
Moonta
Maitland
Yorke Pen.
Spencer Gulf
Gulf St. Vincent
Kangaroo I.
Kingscote
Victor Harbor
Encounter Bay
L. Alexandrina
The Coorong
Lacepede Bay
Discovery Bay
Portland B.
Bass Strait
King Island
Currie
C. Wickham
Stokes Pt.
C. Otway
TASMANIA
Flinders Island
Furneaux Group
Cape Barren I.
Launceston
Devonport
Burnie
Wynyard
Smithton
Queenstown
Zeehan
Strahan
New Norfolk
Hobart
Glenorchy
Huonville
Storm Bay
Bruny I.
S.E. Cape
S.W. Cape
Port Davey
Macquarie Harb.
Mt. Ossa 1617
Ben Lomond 1527
St. Helens
Maria I.
Tasman Pen.
Port Arthur
East from Greenwich
COPYRIGHT GEORGE PHILIP & SON LTD.

117

114

Carnarvon
Yalbalgo
Dairy Creek
Shark Bay
C. Peron
Peron Pen.
Faure I.
Denham
Denham Sound
Nanga
Hamelin Pool
Wooramel
Gladstone
Tamala
Meadow
Glenburgh
Byro
Mount Narryer
Meeberrie
Errabiddy
Mt. Fraser 799
Peak Hill
Robinson Ra.
New Springs
L. Nabberu
Wongawol
Murchison
Moorarie
Mooloogool
Mt. Eureka 499
Wiluna
L. Way
Mileura
Meekatharra
Murchison Downs
Barr Smith Ra.
Montague Ra.
Bates Ra.
Mt. Keith
Yandal
L. Annean
Taincrow
Nicholson Ra.
Coodardy
Cue
L. Austin
Sanford
Murgoo
Meka
Billabalong
Wandarrie
Mount Magnet
Sandstone
Depot Springs
Leinster
Melrose
Pinnacles
Mt. Redcliffe 576
Murchison House
Gantheaume B.
Bluff Pt.
Kalbarri
Ajana
Dividing Ra.
Tallering Peak 439
Edah
Yoweragabbie
Wyemandoo 543
Ida Valley
Maynard Hills
Leonora
Mt. Alexander
Youanmi Downs
Cashmere Downs
Gwalia
Malcolm
Yuna
Greenough
Northampton
Nabawa
Pindar
Mullewa
Yalgoo
Thundelarra
Geelvink Ch.
Houtman Abrolhos
Geraldton
Greenough
Dongara
Mingenew
Yandanooka
Irwin
Gutha
Morawa
Perenjori
Arrino
WESTERN AUSTRALIA
L. Monger
Paynes Find
Mt. Singleton 677
Earoo
Mt. Elvire
L. Barlee
Mt. Marmion
L. Ballard
Menzies
Riverina
Yarra Yarra Lakes
Latham
Eneabba
Coorow
Wubin
L. Moore
Beacon
Bonnie Rock
Ora Banda
Credo
Kalgoorlie-Boulder
Mt. Burges 554
Coolgardie
L. Deborah East
L. Deborah West
Koolyanobbing
L. Seabrook
North Hd.
Watheroo
Pithara
Dalwallinu
Kalannie
Kulja
Mollerin
Bencubbin
Mukinbudin
Hill
Miling
Ballidu
Bindi Bindi
Cadoux
Koorda
Cowcowing Lakes
L. Wallambin
L. Brown
Southern Cross
Moora
Dandaragan
Yerecoin
Wongan Hills
Amery
Trayning
Moore
Mogumber
Lancelin
Wyalkatchem
Goomalling
Dowerin
Doodlakine
Merredin
Marvel Loch
Mooliabeenee
Gingin
Northam
Kellerberrin
Muntadgin
Yunchep Beach
Clackline
Avon
Cunderdin
Bruce Rock
Wadderin Hill
L. Johnston
Wooroloo
Quairading
Narembeen
PERTH
Swan
Rottnest I.
Fremantle
Kwinana New Town
Rockingham
York
Babakin
Beverley
Corrigin
Bendering
Brookton
Hyden
L. Hope
Darling Ra.
Jarrahdale
Pingelly
Kondinin
Bullaring
Pingaring
L. Tay
Peak Eleanora 503
Serpentine
N. Dandalup
Kulin
Popanyinning
Yealering
Jitarning
Mandurah
Pinjarra
Wickepin
Burngup
L. King
Lake King
Dwellingup
Tinkurrin
Lake Grace
L. Grace
Newdegate
Waroona
Boddington
Cuballing
Narrogin
L. Lockhart
Harvey
Williams
Kukerin
L. Magenta
Ravensthorpe
Worsley
Darkan
Dumbleyung
Brunswick Junction
Collie
Wagin
Bunbury
Bowelling
Duranillin
Nyabing
Pingrup
Geographe B.
Woodanilling
Katanning
Donnybrook
Noggerup
Broomehill
Gnowangerup
Needilup
Jerramungup
Hopetoun
Busselton
Kirup
Boyup Brook
Qualeup
Kojonup
Ongerup
Borden
Bridgetown
Mayanup
Tambellup
Pallinup
Hood Pt.
Nannup
Cranbrook
Bluff Knoll
Margaret River
Yornup
Stirling Ra. 1073
Manjimup
Donnelly
Kendenup
Cheyne B.
C. Knob
C. Riche
Augusta
C. Leeuwin
L. Muir
Frankland
Rocky Gully
Mt. Barker
Flinders B.
Pemberton
Northcliffe
Redmond
Bald I.
C. Vancouver
Albany
Bald Hd.
Walpole
Pt. D'Entrecasteaux
Cliffy Hd.
Pt. Nuyts
Denmark
Wilson Inlet
West C. Howe
25
30
35
115
120
East from Greenwich

1 : 8 000 000

115

CORAL SEA
Great Barrier Reef
QUEENSLAND
Great Dividing Range
Bougainville Reef
Moore Reefs
Holmes Reefs
Willis Group
Magdelaine Cays
Herald Cays
Coringa Is.
Flinders Reefs
Diamond Is.
Lihou Reefs & Cays
Abington Reef
Tregrosse Is.
Palmer
Lakeland
1148
Rossville
Bloomfield
C. Tribulation
Daintree
Miallo
Mossman
Rumula
Port Douglas
Mount Molloy
Clifton Beach
Walsh P.O.
Walsh
Mt. Mulligan
Biboohra
Kuranda
Mungana
Mareeba
Cairns
Chillagoe
Dimbulah
Edmonton
Gordonvale
Almaden
Atherton
Tolga
Deeral
Lynd
Petford
1612
Babinda
Herberton
Bullock Creek
Mount Garnet
Innisfail
Fossilbrook
South Johnstone
Mourilyan
Ravenshoe
Tully
El Arish
Herbert
Dunk I.
Mount Surprise
Bilyana
Rockingham Bay
Cardwell
C. Sandwich
Einasleigh
Hinchinbrook I.
Conjuboy
Halifax
Kidston
Carpentaria Downs
Palm Is.
The Lynd
Ingham
Gt. Palm I.
Greenvale Mine
Bambaroo
Greenvale
Seaview Ra.
Halifax Bay
Rollingstone
C. Cleveland
Burdekin
Clarke River P.O.
Townsville
Giru
C. Bowling Green
Brandon
Toonpan
Woodstock
Ayr
Reid River
Home Hill
Mingela
C. Upstart
Gumlu
Guthalungra
Charters Towers
Ravenswood
Bowen
Gloucester I.
Balfes Creek
Homestead
Binbee
Hook I.
Whitsunday I.
Leichhardt Ra.
Collinsville
Airlie Beach
Hughenden
Pentland
Dalbeg
Shaw I.
Proserpine
Prairie
Torrens Creek
Clarke Ra.
Cumberland Islands
Longton
Cape
Burdekin River Project
Yalboroo
1259
Kungurri
Kuttabul
Yarrowmere
Mackay
Towerhill Cr.
Torrens Cr.
Mount Coolon
Netherdale
Mirani
L. Buchanan
Uanda
Sarina
Prudhoe I.
Suttor
Mount Douglas
Connors Ra.
Northumberland Islands
Landsborough Cr.
Goonyella
Koumala
Percy Is.
Denham Ra.
Nebo
Ilbilbie
L. Galilee
Moranbah
Carmila
Isaac
Broad Sd.
Long I.
Peak Downs
Arthur Pt.
Muttaburra
Mine
Belyando
St. Lawrence
Miclere
Townshend I.
Blair Athol
Dysart
Aramac
Marlborough
May Downs
Darr
Clermont
Peak Ra.
Ogmore
C. Clinton
Longreach
Ilfracombe
Peak Downs
C. Manifold
Barcaldine
Cramsie
Capella
Lochnagar
Fitzroy
Kunwarara
Water Park Pt.
Brixton
Dartmouth
Mt. Tabletop 823
Rubyvale
Yaamba
Yeppoon
Jericho
Drummond Range
Anakie
Mackenzie
Emu Park
Alpha
Emerald
Ridgelands
Alice
Pinehill
Willows
Comet
Blackwater
Bluff
Dingo
Rockhampton
Bogantungan
Yalleroi
Gindie
Gogango
Mount Morgan
Tropic of Capricorn
Nogoa
Duaringa
Isisford
Fernlees
Dululu
Bajool
Pt. Alma
Curtis I.
Blackall
Dawson
Benlidi
Laleham
Raglan
Northampton Downs
Mt. Larcom
Gladstone
Barcoo
Springsure
Emmet
Calliope
P. Curtis
Gowan Range
Terrick Terrick
Expedition Range
Baralaba
Callide
Boyne
Castlevale
Tambo
Rolleston
Biloela
Miriam Vale
Yaraka
Range
Thangool
Warrego
Carnarvon
Banana
Nagoorin
1312
Bauhinia Downs
Moura
Dawes Ra.
Blackwater Cr.
Langlo
Barngo
Mt. King 868
Carnarvon Ra.
Cannondale Mt. 734
Theodore
Rosedale
Bulloo
Monto
Bargara
145
150
20
25
East from Greenwich

15

116

1 : 8 000 000

NEW ZEALAND, CENTRAL AND SOUTH WEST PACIFIC

NORTH ISLAND
PACIFIC
Three Kings Is.
C. Reinga
C. Maria van Diemen
North C.
Houhora
Kaitaia
Whangarei
Dargaville
Auckland
Manukau
Devonport
Takapuna
Hauraki Gulf
Gt. Barrier I.
Coromandel
Thames
Hamilton
Tauranga
Bay of Plenty
Whakatane
Rotorua
Taupo
L. Taupo
Gisborne
Napier
Hastings
Hawke Bay
Wairoa
Mahia Peninsula
New Plymouth
North Taranaki Bight
South Taranaki Bight
Mt. Egmont
Hawera
Wanganui
Palmerston N.
Levin
Dannevirke
Ruahine Ra.
Kaimanawa Mts.
Raukumara Ra.
East C.
C. Turnagain
Golden Bay
C. Farewell
Collingwood
D'Urville I.

SOUTH WEST PACIFIC
1:54 000 000
East 160 from Greenwich
International Date Line
Micronesia
Melanesia
FEDERATED STATES OF MICRONESIA
NAURU
KIRIBATI
Gilbert Is.
Baker I. (U.S.)
SOLOMON ISLANDS
Honiara
Guadalcanal
Bismarck Arch.
TUVALU (Ellice Is.)
Funafuti
Tokelau Is. (N.Z.)
WESTERN SAMOA
Apia
Wallis Arch.
Futuna (Fr.)
VANUATU
FIJI
Suva
Viti Levu
Vanua Levu
Rotuma
TONGA
Tonga Trench
Niue
Kermadec Is. (N.Z.)
Kermadec Trench
10,822
10,047
Coral Sea
New Caledonia (Fr.)
Nouméa
Loyalty Is. (Fr.)
Chesterfield Is. (Fr.)
Norfolk I. (Aust.)
Lord Howe I. (Aust.)
Lord Howe Ridge
Tasman Sea
Brisbane
Ipswich
Newcastle
Sydney
Wollongong
Auckland
NEW ZEALAND

CENTRAL PACIFIC
1:54 000 000
TASMAN SEA
SOUTH ISLAND
WELLINGTON OCEAN
Cook Strait
Foveaux Str.
Westland Bight
Canterbury Bight
Canterbury Plains
SOUTHERN ALPS
NELSON
MARLBOROUGH
Tasman Bay
Pegasus Bay
Karamea Bight
Kaikoura Ra.
Spenser Mts.
Lyell Ra.
Tasman Mts.
Kakanui Mts.
Garvie Mts.
Umbrella Mts.
Dunstan Mts.
Mt. Cook 3753
Mt. Aspiring 3036
Mt. Earnslaw 2819
Mt. Travers 2337
Tapuaenuku 2885
WELLINGTON
Lr. Hutt
Up. Hutt
Petone
Masterton
Carterton
Greytown
Martinborough
Featherston
Eastbourne
Te Horo
Castle Pt.
Nelson
Motueka
Takaka
Richmond
Wakefield
Blenheim
Picton
Havelock
Seddon
Ward
Kaikoura
Westport
Greymouth
Hokitika
Reefton
Christchurch
New Brighton
Lyttelton
Riccarton
Kaiapoi
Rangiora
Akaroa
Banks Penin.
L. Ellesmere
Ashburton
Timaru
Temuka
Oamaru
Dunedin
Mosgiel
Port Chalmers
St. Kilda
Balclutha
Milton
Invercargill
Bluff
Gore
Queenstown
Cromwell
Alexandra
Clyde
Wanaka
Te Anau
Manapouri
Riverton
Stewart I.
Oban
Port Pegasus
S.W. Cape
Ruapuke I.
Resolution I.
Secretary I.
Milford Sd.
Doubtful Sd.
Dusky Sd.
Bligh Sd.
George Sd.
Jackson B.
Chalky Inlet
Preservation Inlet
Te Waewae B.
Otago Harbour
C. Saunders
Nugget Pt.
Waikawa Harb.
Tautuku
L. Tekapo
L. Pukaki
L. Ohau
L. Hawea
L. Wanaka
L. Wakatipu
L. Manapouri
L. Te Anau
L. Poteriteri
L. Hauroko
KIRIBATI
Teraina
Tabuaeran
Kiritimati
Jarvis I. (U.S.)
Malden I.
Starbuck I.
Phoenix Is.
Enderbury I.
Tokelau Is. (N.Z.)
WESTERN SAMOA
Apia
Tutuila (U.S.)
AMER. SAMOA
Wallis Arch.
Futuna (Fr.)
Rotuma
Vanua Levu
Viti Levu
Suva
FIJI
TONGA
Friendly Is.
Tonga Trench
10,822
Kermadec Is. (N.Z.)
Niue (Savage I.) (N.Z.)
Pukapuka
Suwarrow Is. (Suvorov)
Manihiki
Tongareva
Penrhyn Is.
Cook Islands (N.Z.)
Manuae
Rarotonga
Caroline I.
Vostok I.
Flint I.
Marquesas Is. (Fr.)
Tuamotu Archipelago (Fr.)
Society Is. (Fr.)
Leeward Is.
Windward Is.
Tahiti (Fr.)
FRENCH POLYNESIA
Tubuai Is. (Austral Is.) (Fr.)
Rapa Iti (Fr.)
Austral Seamount Chain
Polynesia
International Date Line
East from Greenwich
West from Greenwich
COPYRIGHT. GEORGE PHILIP & SON. LTD.

1 : 7 000 000

115

AFRICA : PHYSICAL

West from Greenwich East from Greenwich

1 : 70 000 000

NORTH ATLANTIC OCEAN
Bay of Biscay
London
UNITED KINGDOM
NETHERLANDS
BELGIUM
GERMANY
POLAND
Warsaw
Prague
CZECH REP.
SLOVAK REP.
Paris
FRANCE
Vienna
AUSTRIA
SWITZ.
HUNGARY
CROAT.
B.-H.
YUG.
ROMANIA
BULGARIA
Kiev
Odessa
Crimea
Black Sea
Volgograd
Caspian Sea
Aral Sea
Tbilisi
Istanbul
Ankara
TURKEY
Madrid
SPAIN
PORTUGAL
Lisbon
Rome
ITALY
Adriatic Sea
MAC.
ALBANIA
GREECE
Athens
Mediterranean Sea
Tangier
Gibraltar
Rabat
Casablanca
Fès
MOROCCO
Marrakech
Oran
Algiers
Tunis
MALTA
TUNISIA
Sfax
Tripoli
Benghazi
Beida
Alexandria
CYPRUS
Aleppo
SYRIA
Damascus
Tel Aviv-Yafo
ISRAEL
Jerusalem
JORDAN
Port Said
Suez
Cairo
IRAQ
Baghdad
Tehran
IRAN
Esfahan
Basra
The Gulf
Madeira (Port.)
Canary Is. (Sp.)
Tenerife
Ifni
El Aaiún
W. SAHARA
MAURITANIA
ALGERIA
LIBYA
Libyan Desert
EGYPT
Nile
L. Nasser
Aswan
Red Sea
SAUDI ARABIA
Medina
Mecca
Bahrain
QATAR
U.A.E.
Ar Riyad
Tropic of Cancer
Sahara
Nouakchott
MALI
Timbuktu
Agades
NIGER
CHAD
SUDAN
Pt. Sudan
Atbara
Omdurman
Khartoum
Kassala
Asmera
Mesewa
YEMEN
ERITREA
Aden
Perim I.
DJIBOUTI
Djibouti
Berbera
St. Louis
Senegal
SENEGAL
Dakar
GAMBIA
Banjul
GUINEA-BISSAU
Bissau
Kayes
Bamako
Niamey
BURKINA FASO
Ouagadougou
Kano
Abeshr
Ndjamena
El Fasher
El Obeid
Kodok
Addis Ababa
Harer
ETHIOPIA
SOMALI REPUBLIC
GUINEA
Freetown
SIERRA LEONE
Monrovia
LIBERIA
IVORY COAST
Abidjan
GHANA
TOGO
BENIN
NIGERIA
Ibadan
Lagos
Accra
Takoradi
CENTRAL AFRICAN REP.
Bangui
Mongalla
CAMEROON
Yaoundé
Buea
Bioko
Gulf of Guinea
EQUATORIAL GUINEA
Mbini
Libreville
GABON
Equator
SAO TOMÉ & PRINCIPE
Annobon
CONGO
Brazzaville
Pte. Noire
Kinshasa
ZAÏRE (CONGO)
Kisangani
Ilebo (P. Francqui)
Kigoma
UGANDA
Kampala
RWANDA
BURUNDI
Victoria
KENYA
Kisumu
Nairobi
Mombasa
Mogadisho
SOUTH ATLANTIC OCEAN
Ascension (Br.)
Boma
Luanda
Kananga
TANZANIA
Pemba
Zanzibar
Dar-es-Salaam
INDIAN OCEAN
Aldabra Is.
Bukama
Lobito
Benguela
ANGOLA
Huambo
Namibe
Lubumbashi
ZAMBIA
Lilongwe
MALAWI
Lusaka
Zambezi
Blantyre
MOZAMBIQUE
COMORO IS.
Mozambique Channel
Mozambique
St. Helena (Br.)
Harare
ZIMBABWE
Bulawayo
Quelimane
Beira
MADAGASCAR
Antananarivo
NAMIBIA (SOUTH WEST AFRICA)
Walvis Bay
Windhoek
BOTSWANA
Gaborone
Tropic of Capricorn
Pretoria
Johannesburg
SWAZ.
Maputo
SOUTH AFRICA
LES.
Bloemfontein
Durban
East London
Cape Town
Port Elizabeth
West from Greenwich
East from Greenwich
COPYRIGHT. GEORGE PHILIP & SON. LTD

1 : 70 000 000

50

A T L A N T I C
O C E A N
Azores
(Port.)
Madeira
(Port.)
Funchal
Is. Canarias
(Sp.)
Sta. Cruz
Tenerife
3718
Las Palmas
C. Juby
Lisboa
PORTUGAL
SPAI
Salamanca
Douro
Tajo
Sevilla
Guadalquivir
Málaga
Str. of Gibraltar
Gibraltar
Tanger
Ceuta (Br.)
(Sp.)
Tetouan
Er Rif
Melill
(Sp.)
Kenitra
Rabat
Fès
Casablanca
Meknès
El Jadida
MOROCCO
Safi
Essaouira
Marrakech
Dj. Toubkal
4165
Haut Atlas
Béchar
Abadla
Agadir
Anti Atlas
Tiznit
Dra
Tindouf
Tarfaya
(Villa Bens)
El Aaiún
Semara
WESTERN SAHARA
Ain Ben Tili
Chegga
Bir Mogrein
Erg Chech
Dakhla
Fdérik
S
a
Nouadhibou
(Port Etienne)
Ras Nouadhibou
El Djouf
MAURITANIA
Tidjikja
Bou Djébéha
MALI
Nouakchott
Senegal
St. Louis
Kaedi
Néma
Goundam
Tombouctou
(Timbuktu)
Bourem
Gao
West from Greenwich

130

1 : 20 000 000

48

ITALY
Nápoli
Bari
Taranto
Brindisi
Tyrrhenian Sea
Sardegna
Cagliari
Madrid
Valencia
Palma
Is. Baleares
Murcia
MEDITERRANEAN SEA
Palermo
Réggio
Etna
3340
Catánia
Sicilia
Ionian Sea
MALTA
Alger (Algiers)
Blida
Skikda
Annaba
Bizerte
C. Bon
Tunis
Bejaia
Setif
Constantine
Oran
Mostaganem
Tiaret
Batna
Khenchela
Mahdia
Sidi Bel Abbès
Biskra
Sfax
Tlemcen
Atlas Saharien
Tolga
Tozeur
Chott Djerid
G. de Gabès
Gabès
Djelfa
Laghouat
Touggourt
TUNISIA
Tarābulus (Tripoli)
Ghardaia
Zuwarah
Misrātah
Gharyān
Ouargla
Hassi Messaoud
Khalij Surt
ALGERIA
Surt
Ghudāmes
Plateau du Tademait
Adrar
Brach
LIBYA
In Salah
Sabhah
Arak
Marzūq
Ghat
Ahaggar
Tropic of Cancer
Tahat 2918
Tamanrasset
Toummo
Bardaï
Tibesti
Emi Koussi
3415
Mts. Tamgak
1800
Aïr
Bilma
Borkou
Agadez
NIGER
CHAD
Ménaka
5
10
15
20
25
30
35
40
East from Greenwich

128

131

86

80

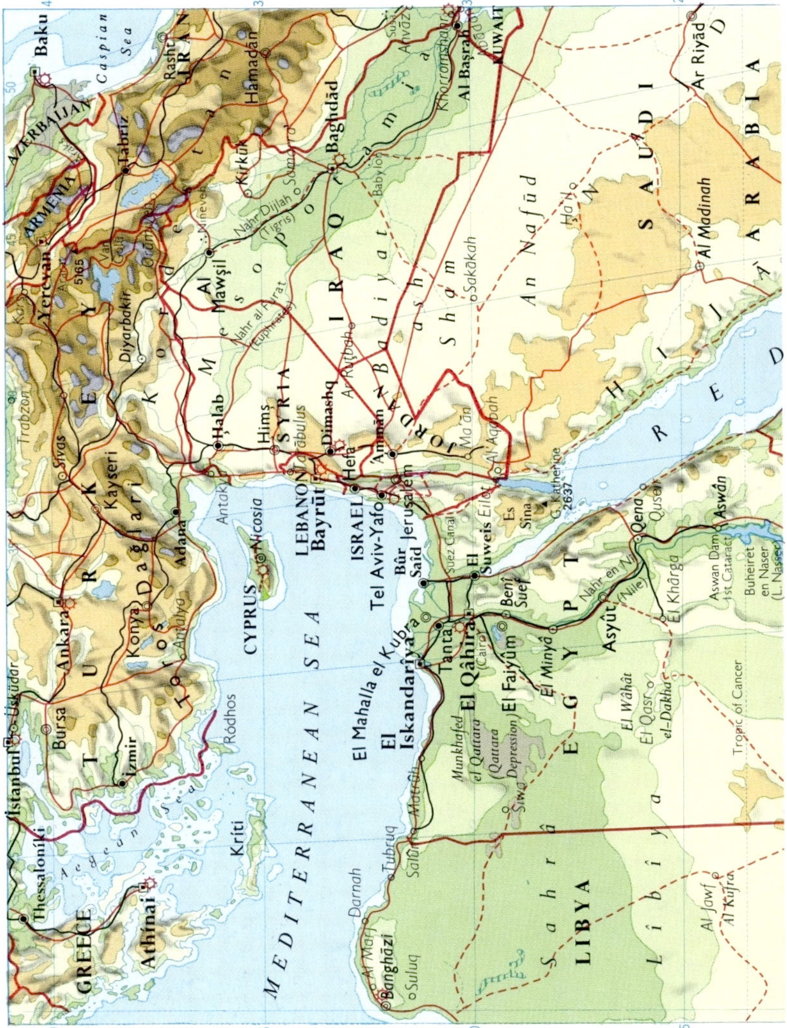

GREECE
Thessaloniki
Athínai
Aegean Sea
Kríti
Ródhos
İstanbul
Üsküdar
Bursa
İzmir
Ankara
Konya
Antalya
Adana
Kayseri
Sivas
Trabzon
Diyarbakır
T U R K E Y
Toros Dağları
Yerevan
ARMENIA
AZERBAIJAN
Baku
Caspian Sea
Tabrīz
Rasht
Hamadān
IRAN
Kurdistan
CYPRUS
Nicosia
Antakya
Halab
Hims
SYRIA
Tarābulus
LEBANON
Bayrūt
Dimashq
Hefa
ISRAEL
Tel Aviv-Yafo
Jerusalem
'Ammān
JORDAN
Ma'ān
Al 'Aqabah
Al Mawşil
Kirkūk
Baghdād
IRAQ
Nahr Dijlah (Tigris)
Nahr al Furat (Euphrates)
Mesopotamia
Badiyat ash Sham
Al Başrah
KUWAIT
Sakākah
An Nafūd
Ḩā'il
SAUDI ARABIA
Al Madīnah
Ar Riyād
Hijaz
RED SEA
MEDITERRANEAN SEA
Bûr Saïd
Suez Canal
El Suweis
El Iskandarîya
El Mahalla el Kubra
Tanta
El Qâhira (Cairo)
El Faiyûm
Benî Suef
El Minyâ
Asyût
Nahr en Nil (Nile)
Qena
Qoseir
Aswân
Aswan Dam
1st Cataract
Buheiret en Naser (L. Nasser)
El Khârga
El Qasr el-Dakhla
El Wâhât
Tropic of Cancer
Es Sînâ
G. Katherîne 2637
Munkhafed el Qattâra (Qattara Depression)
Siwa
Matrûh
E G Y P T
Salûm
Tubruq
Darnah
Al Marj
Banghāzī
Suluq
LIBYA
Sahrâ Lîbîya
Al Jawf
Al Kufra
40
35
30
25
50
45

127

1 : 20 000 000

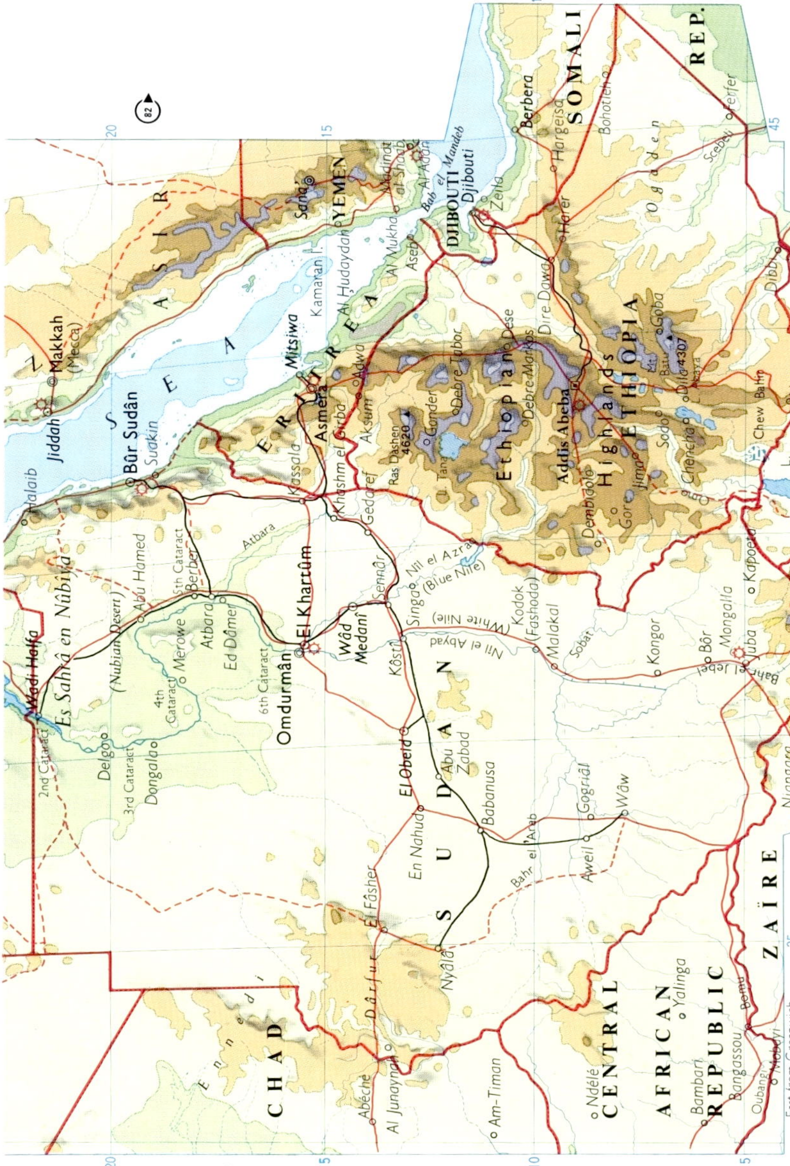
SUDAN
ETHIOPIA
ERITREA
CHAD
CENTRAL AFRICAN REPUBLIC
ZAÏRE
UGANDA
KENYA
SOMALI REP.
DJIBOUTI
YEMEN
ASIA
RED SEA
Es Sahrâ en Nûbîya
(Nubian Desert)
Ethiopian Highlands
Dârfur
Ennedi
Ogaden
Bab el Mandeb
El Khartûm
Omdurmân
Bûr Sudân
Suakin
Halaib
Wadi Halfa
Delgo
Dongala
Merowe
Abu Hamed
Berber
Atbara
Ed Dâmer
Kassala
Khashm el Girba
Gedaref
Sennâr
Wad Medani
Singa
Kôsti
El Obeid
En Nahud
Abu Zabad
Babanusa
El Fâsher
Nyala
Al Junaynah
Kodok (Fashoda)
Malakal
Kongor
Bôr
Mongalla
Juba
Kapoeta
Nimule
Aweil
Gogrial
Wâw
Niangara
Nil el Azraq (Blue Nile)
Nil el Abyad (White Nile)
Bahr el Jebel
Bahr el 'Arab
Sobat
Atbara
2nd Cataract
3rd Cataract
4th Cataract
5th Cataract
6th Cataract
Asmera
Mitsiwa
Aksum
Adwa
Gonder
Ras Dashen 4620
L. Tana
Debre Tabor
Dese
Debre Markos
Addis Abeba
Dembidolo
Gore
Jima
Sodo
Chencha
Dila
Goba
Bura 4307
Dire Dawa
Harer
Hargeisa
Berbera
Bohotleh
Ferfer
Scebeli
Zeila
Djibouti
Aseb
Kamaran I.
Al Hudaydah
Al Mukha
Madinat ash Shab
Al Adan
Sana'
Jiddah
Makkah (Meca)
L. Turkana
Chew Bahir
Mega
Moyale
Dibbi
Abéché
Am-Timan
Ndélé
Bambari
Bangassou
Mobaye
Bomu
Yalinga
Oubangi
East from Greenwich
5
10
15
20
25
30
35
40
45
131
134
135
82

126

Fdérik
Nouadhibou
(Port
Etienne)
Ras Nouadhibou
S
a
El Djouf
MAURITANIA
Tidjikja
Nouakchott
Bou Djébéha
MALI
Senegal
Kaedi
Néma
Goundam
Tombouctou
(Timbuktu)
Bourem
Gao
St.
Louis
Linguére
Selibabi
Nioro
du Sahel
Nara
Hombori
Thiès
Dakar
C.
Vert
SENEGAL
Kaolack
GAMBIA
Banjul
Kayes
Bafoulabé
Mopti
Niger
Dori
Ségou
Gambia
Kita
Koulikoro
BURKINA FASO
Ouagadougou
Koudougou
(UPPER VOLTA)
GUINEA-
BISSAU
Bissau
Arq. dos
Bijagós
Fouta
Djalon
Bamako
GUINEA
Siguiri
Bobo-Dioulasso
Boké
Bawku
Bolgatanga
Kindia
Mamou
Kankan
Wa
Korhogo
Conakry
Kabala
G
Kong
u
Tamale
SIERRA LEONE
Freetown
Pendembu
Séguela
IVORY
L.
Volta
TOGO
Bonthe
Sherbro I.
Bo
Man
Bouaké
COAST
GHANA
Daloa
Kumasi
LIBERIA
Monrovia
Buchanan
Gagnoa
Asamankese
Abidjan
Bingerville
Tema
Accra
Lomé
Nyaake
Grand Cess
Sassandra
Grand
Bassam
Sekondi-
Takoradi
Cape Coast
C. Palmas
Gulf of Gui
15
10
5
0
20
West from Greenwich

1 : 20 000 000

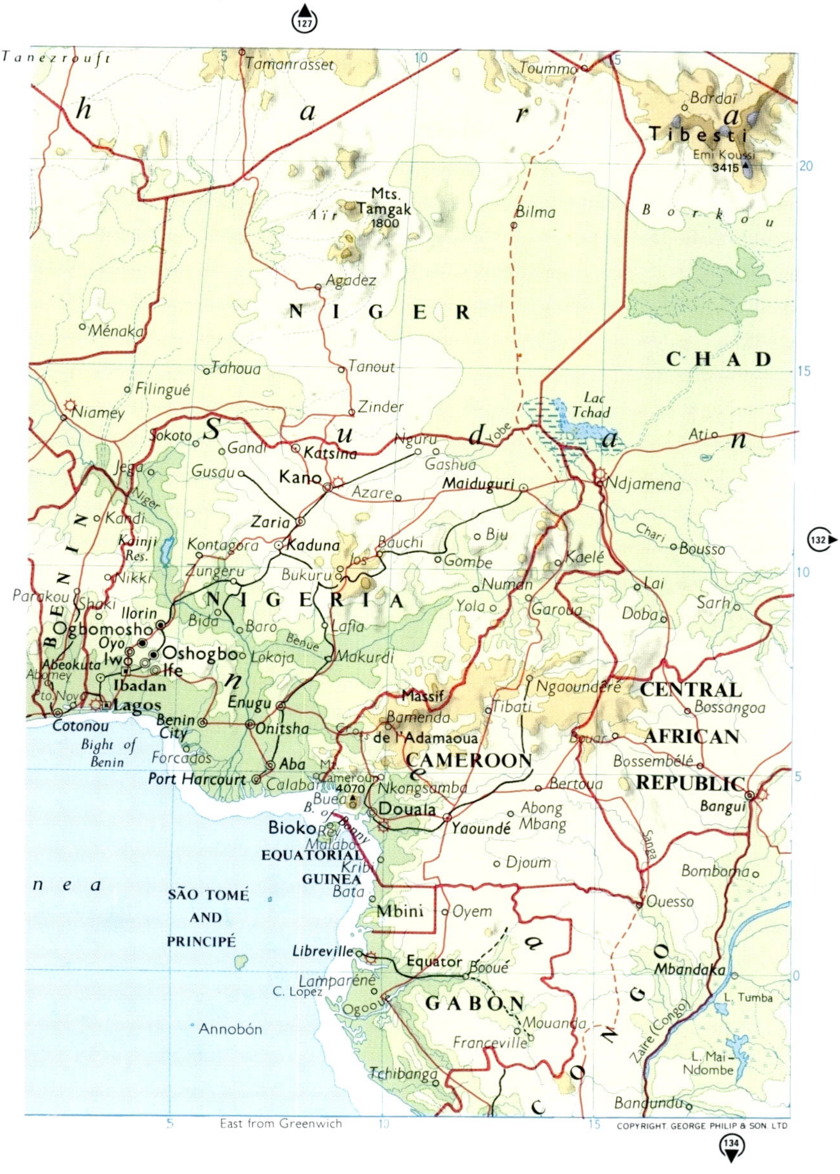
127
Tanezrouft
Tamanrasset
Toummo
Bardaï
Tibesti
Emi Koussi
3415
Mts. Tamgak
1800
Aïr
Bilma
Borkou
Agadez
NIGER
Ménaka
CHAD
Tahoua
Tanout
Filingué
Zinder
Niamey
Lac Tchad
Sokoto
Gandi
Katsina
Nguru
Yobe
Ati
Gashua
Jega
Gusau
Kano
Maiduguri
Ndjamena
Azare
Niger
Kandi
Zaria
Biu
Chari
Bousso
Kainji Res.
Kontagora
Kaduna
Bauchi
Gombe
Kaelé
132
Nikki
Zungeru
Bukuru
Jos
Numan
Lai
Parakou
Shaki
NIGERIA
Yola
Garoua
Doba
Sarh
Ilorin
Bida
Baro
Lafia
BENIN
Ogbomosho
Benue
Oyo
Makurdi
Iwo
Oshogbo
Lokoja
Abeokuta
Ife
Ngaoundéré
CENTRAL
Abomey
Ibadan
Massif
Tibati
Bossangoa
Pto. Novo
Lagos
Enugu
Cotonou
Benin City
Onitsha
Bamenda
de l'Adamaoua
Bouar
AFRICAN
Bight of Benin
Forcados
Aba
Cross
CAMEROON
Bossembélé
Mt. Cameroun
Port Harcourt
Calabar
4070
Nkongsamba
Bertoua
REPUBLIC
Buea
Bangui
B. of Bonny
Douala
Abong Mbang
Bioko
Rey Malabo
Yaoundé
Sanga
EQUATORIAL GUINEA
Kribi
Djoum
Guinea
Bata
Bomboma
SÃO TOMÉ AND PRINCIPÉ
Mbini
Oyem
Ouesso
Libreville
Equator
Booué
Mbandaka
Lambaréné
C. Lopez
Ogooué
GABON
L. Tumba
CONGO
Annobón
Mouanda
Franceville
Zaïre (Congo)
L. Mai-Ndombe
Tchibanga
Bandundu
Sahara
Sudan
5
10
15
20
0
East from Greenwich
COPYRIGHT GEORGE PHILIP & SON, LTD.
134

128

131

Es Sahrâ en Nûbîya
(Nubian Desert)
Delgo
3rd Cataract
Dongala
4th Cataract
Merowe
Abû Hamed
5th Cataract
Berber
Atbara
Ed Dâmer
6th Cataract
Bûr Sudân
Suakin
Omdurmân
El Khartûm
Kassala
Khashm el Girba
Wâd Medanî
Gedaref
Sennâr
Kôstî
El Obeid
En Nahud
El Fâsher
Dârfur
Abéché
Al Junaynah
Nyâlâ
S U D A N
Abu Zabad
Babanusa
Singa
Nîl el Azraq (Blue Nile)
Nîl el Abyad (White Nile)
Kodok (Fashoda)
Malakal
Sobat
Bahr el 'Arab
Aweil
Gogriâl
Wâw
Kongor
Bôr
Mongalla
Juba
Kapoeta
Bahr el Jebel
C H A D
Ennedi
Am-Timan
Ndélé
CENTRAL AFRICAN REPUBLIC
Yalinga
Bambari
Bangassou
Bomu
Oubangi
Mobayi
Bondo
Uere
Titule
Niangara
Isiro
Aketi
Buta
Lisala
Zaïre
Bumba
Basoka
Aruwimi
Kisangani
Chutes Boyoma
Befale
Isangi
Bokote
Z A Ï R E
Ubundu
Lomami
Lomela
Ikela
Monkoto
Lualaba
Kindu
Dekese
Ras Dashen 4620
Gonder
L. Tana
Debre Tabor
Ethio
Debre Marko
Dembidolo
Gore
Jima
Highl
Sodo
Chencha
Omo
L. Turkana 375
Nimule
Arua
Kabarega Falls
L. Mobutu Sese Seko 619
Irumu
Butiaba
Semliki
UGANDA
Kyoga
Mt. Elgon 4321
Kitale
5120
Kampala
Entebbe
Jinja
Eldoret
Mt. Kenya 5200
Ruwenzori
L. Edward
L. George
Lake Victoria 1134
Kisumu
Nakuru
Naivasha
Nairobi
RWANDA
Kigali
Bukoba
Bukavu
Kagera
Mwanza
BURUNDI
Bujumbura
TANZANIA
L. Eyasi
Arusha
Kilimanjaro 5895
Moshi
20
25
30
35
15
10
5
0
East from Greenwich

135

1 : 20 000 000

82

SAUDI ARABIA
ASIR
RED SEA
Rub 'al Khali
OMAN
YEMEN
Hadramawt
Mitsiwa
Asmera
ERITREA
Kamaran I.
Sana'
Al Hudaydah
Adwa
Aksum
Al Mukallā
Al Mukha
Madinat ash Sha'b
Al 'Adan (Aden)
Aseb
Bab el Mandeb
Gulf of Aden
Socotra
(Yemen)
Ras Asir
(C. Guardafui)
Candala
DJIBOUTI
Djibouti
Zeila
Dese
Berbera
Dire Dawa
Addis Abeba
Harer
Hargeisa
Bender Beila
SOMALI REPUBLIC
Bohotleh
ETHIOPIA
Eil
Mt. Batu
4307
Goba
Ogaden
Dila
L. Abaya
Scebeli
Ferfer
Obbia
Dibbi
Mega
Moyale
El Dere
INDIAN OCEAN
Marsabit
Bardera
Wajir
Giuba
Merca
Muqdisho
(Mogadishu)
Brava
Equator
Chisimaio
KENYA
Tana
Lamu
Malindi
Voi
40
45
50
55
20
15
10
5
0

131

NIGERIA
CAMEROON
CENTRAL AFRICAN REPUBLIC
Cross
Cameroon Pk. 4070
Douala
Yaounde
B. of Bonny
Buea
Bioko
Bangui
Ubangi
Bangassu
M. Bomu
Uele
Sanga
Lisala
Aketi
Buta
Zaire (Congo)
Basoko
Bata
RIO MUNI
EQUATORIAL GUINEA
Libreville
Equator
Mbandaka
C. Lopez
Ogowe
GABON
CONGO
Lomami
Franceville
Congo
L. Mai Ndombe
ZAÏRE
Kwa
Brazzaville
Pool Malebo
Kinshasa
(Léopoldville)
Pointe Noire
Sankuru
Ilebo
Lusambo
Cabinda
Boma
Muanda
Matadi
Kananga
Kabinda
Lulua
Kasai
Cuango
Ambriz
Kamina
Luanda
Cuanza
Malanje
Sandoa
Luau
ATLANTIC OCEAN
ANGOLA
Lobito
Benguela
Bié
Huambo
Plateau
Zambesi
Lubango
Namibe
Lealui
Mongu
Cuando
Barotse
Gt. Fish Bay
Cubango
Cunene
Owambo
Seshéke
C. Frio
East from Greenwich

136

1 : 20 000 000

132

133

SUDAN
ETHIOPIA
SOMALI REP.
UGANDA
KENYA
RWANDA
BURUNDI
TANZANIA
MALAWI
ZAMBIA
MOZAMBIQUE
ZIMBABWE
Shaba
land
Mongalla
Juba
Bahr el Jebel
Nile
Nimule
Niangara
Isiro
Wadelai
Kabarega Falls
Aruwimi
L. Mobutu Sese Seko
Irumu
Semliki
Kisangani (Stanleyville)
Stanley Falls
Ubundi
5109
Ruwenzori
L. Edward
L. George
Kampala
Entebbe
Jinja
Owen Falls
Butiaba
L. Kioga
Mt. Elgon
4321
Kitale
Eldoret
Kisumu
Nakuru
Naivasha
Mt. Kenya
5199
Nairobi
Lake Victoria
Bukoba
Kigali
Bukavu (Costermansville)
Kindu
Bujumbura
Kagera
Mwanza
Kilimanjaro
5895
Moshi
Arusha
Voi
L. Eyasi
L. Manyara
Omo
Chew Bahir (L. Stefanie)
L. Turkana
Marsabit
Giuba
Chisimaio
Tana
Lamu
Malindi
Mombasa and Kilindini
Tanga
Pangani
Pemba
Zanzibar
Bagamoyo
Dar-es-Salaam
Mafia
Kilwa
Rufiji
Lindi
Mikindani
C. Delgado
Kasongo
Kongolo
Kigoma
Tabora
Lukuga
L. Tanganyika
Kabalo
Kalemie (Albertville)
Mpanda
Dodoma
Kongwa
Mpwapwa
Morogoro
Iringa
Luvua
Lualaba
L. Rukwa
Kasanga
Mbala
Mbeya
Tukuyu
L. Mweru
Bukama
Karonga
Livingstonia
Nyasa (L. Malawi)
Manda
L. Bangweulu
Chambeshi
Luangwa
Ruvuma
Likasi
Lubumbashi (Elisabethville)
Kitwe
Ndola
Chipata
Lilongwe
Salima
Kafue
Kabwe
Lusaka
Zumbo
Zambesi
Cabora Bassa Dam
Tete
Blantyre
Zomba
L. Shirwa
Limbe
Shire
Nampula
Mozambique
L. Kariba
Livingstone
Victoria Falls
Harare (Salisbury)
Sena
Quelimane
30
35
40
5
10
15

137

134

ANGOLA
ATLANTIC OCEAN
Lobito
Benguela
Bié
Plateau
Huambo
Luau
Zambesi
Lubango
Namibe
Gt. Fish Bay
Cunene
Cubango
Cuando
Lealui
Mongu
Barotse
Sesheke
Owambo
C. Frio
Etosha Pan
Otavi
Grootfontein
Botletle
Makgadikgadi Salt pan
Damaraland
Windhoek
Swakopmund
Walvis Bay
BOTSWA
Tropic of Capricorn
Kalahari
NAMIBIA
Nossob
Hardap Dam
Mafikeng
Molopo
Namaland
Lüderitz
Possession I.
Keetmanshoop
Karas Mts.
Vryburg
Upington
Kimberley
Orange
Port Nolloth
Bushmanland
Namaqualand
De Aar
Calvinia
Stor
Kompasberg 2504
SOUTH AFRICA
St. Helena Bay
Nuweveldberge
Graaff-Reinet
Karoo
Swartberg
Cape Town
Paarl
Oudtshoorn
Table Mountain
C. of Good Hope
Mosselbaai
Port Elizabeth
Algoa
C. Agulhas
10
15
20
25
30
35
East from Greenwich

1 : 20 000 000

135
ZAMBIA
MALAWI
MOZAMBIQUE
ZIMBABWE
SWAZILAND
LESOTHO
Matabeleland
Lubumbashi (Elisabethville)
Likasi
Kitwe
Ndola
Kabwe
Lusaka
Kafue
Chipata
Lilongwe
Salima
Karonga
Livingstonia
Manda
Blantyre
Zomba
Limbe
L. Shirwa
Nampula
Mozambique
C. Delgado
Ruvuma
Bangweulu
Chameshi
Luangwa
Nyasa (L. Malawi)
Zumbo
Zambesi
Cabora Bassa Dam
Tete
Shire
L. Kariba
Livingstone
Victoria Falls
Hwange
Harare (Salisbury)
Sena
Quelimane
Chinde
Zambesi
Mutare
Gweru
Beira
Sofala
Sabi
Bulawayo
Matopo Hills
Masvingo
Zimbabwe
Gwanda
West Nicholson
Serowe
Palapye
Shoshong
Messina
Limpopo
Pietersburg
Olifants
Gaborone
Inhambane
Mozambique Channel
Lydenburg
Barberton
Pretoria
Brakpan
Springs
Krugersdorp
Johannesburg
Germiston
Vereeniging
Vaal
Potchefstroom
Kroonstad
Maputo
Delagoa Bay
Mt. aux Sources
Ladysmith
St. Lucia Bay
3298
Thabana Ntlenyana 3482
Bloemfontein
Maseru
Drakensberg
Stormberge
Pietermaritzburg
Durban
Umtata
INDIAN OCEAN
East London
K. William's Town
Grahamstown
C. Bobraomby
Antsiranana
Nossi-Bé
Andoany
Vohimarina
2876
Tsaratanana
Andapa
Maroantsetra
Mahajanga
Marovoay
Besalampy
Maevatanana
Betsiboka
Fenoarivo
L. Alaotra
Ambatondrazaka
Toamasina
Maintirano
2643
Antananarivo
Belo-Tsiribihina
Mahanoro
Antsirabe
Morondava
Mananjary
Morombé
Fianarantsoa
Mangoky
Ihosy
Manakara
Ankazoabo
Toliara
Betroka
Farafangana
Tropic of Capricorn
Bekily
1956
Ambovombé
Faradofay
C. Vohimena
Madagascar
MADAGASCAR
On same scale.
15
20
25
30
35
40
45
50

ASIA
ARCTIC OCEAN
Beaufort Sea
C. Dezhnev
Wrangel I.
Pt. Barrow
Bering Str.
Pr. of Wales C.
St. Lawrence I.
Yukon
Alaska
Mt. McKinley 6194
Arctic Circle
Mackenzie B.
Banks I.
Parry Is.
M'Clure Str.
Sverdrup Is.
Axel Heiberg Land
Ellesmere I.
Queen Elizabeth Is.
N. Mag. Pole
Viscount Melville Sd.
Devon I.
Lancaster Sound
Victoria I.
G. of Boothia
Baffin Bay
Baffin Island
Greenland
Petermann's Pk. 2940
Denmark Str.
Davis Strait
Cumberland Sd.
C. Farewell
Tundra
Gt. Bear L.
Mackenzie
Foxe Basin
Southampton I.
Chesterfield Inlet
Hudson Strait
C. Chidley
Ungava Peninsula
Hudson Bay
James Bay
Labrador
Hamilton Inlet
Belle Isle Str.
Laurentian Plateau
Kodiak I.
St. Elias Mts.
St. Elias 5489
Mt. Logan 5959
Coast Range
Rocky Mountains
Queen Charlotte Is.
Mt. Waddington 4041
Vancouver I.
Fraser
Peace
Gt. Slave L.
Athabasca L.
Athabasca
Great Plains
Robson Pk. 3954
Yellowhead P.
Kicking Horse P.
Saskatchewan
Nelson
L. Winnipeg
Columbia
Cascade Ra.
Mt. Rainier 4392
Crowsnest P.
Missouri
L. Superior
G. of St. Lawrence
Cabot Str.
St. Lawrence
Ottawa
Nova Scotia
C. Sable
Coast Ra.
Mt. Shasta 4317
C. Mendocino
Snake
Gt. Salt L.
Black Hills 2207
Gannett Pk. 4202
Mississippi
L. Michigan
L. Huron
L. Ontario
Niagara Falls
C. Cod
L. Erie
Sierra Nevada
Great Basin
Platte
Long's Pk. 4345
Mt. Whitney 4418
Death Valley
Mt. Elbert 4399
Ohio
Allegheny Mts.
Appalachian Mts.
Cumberland Plat.
Blue Ridge
Chesapeake B.
C. Hatteras
Colorado
Colorado Plat.
Blanca Pk. 4378
Ozark Plateau
Arkansas
Tennessee
Red
Llano Estacado
Rio Grande
PACIFIC OCEAN
ATLANTIC OCEAN
Lower California
G. of California
Sierra Madre
Mexican Plateau
Florida
Mississippi Delta
Gulf of Mexico
Florida Str.
Bahama Is.
Tropic of Cancer
C. San Lucas
Santiago
Cuba
Greater Antilles
Hispaniola
P. Rico
Yucatan Strait
Gulf of Campêche
Yucatan
Revilla Gigedo
Citlaltepetl 5700
Popocatepetl 5452
Jamaica
G. of Honduras
Caribbean Sea
Central America
Isthmus of Tehuantepec
Vol. Fuego 3734
L. Nicaragua
SOUTH AMERICA
West from Greenwich
70
80
60
50
40
30
20
10
120
100
90

1 : 60 000 000

ASIA
ARCTIC OCEAN
Beaufort Sea
Bering Sea
Bering Str.
Ostrov Vrangelya
Pt. Barrow
Parry Is.
Banks I.
M'Clure Str.
Viscount Melville Sd.
Victoria I.
Ellesmere I.
GREENLAND (Denmark)
Denmark Str.
ICELAND
Lancaster Sd.
Baffin Bay
Upernavik
Baffin Island
Disko I.
Davis Strait
Godthaab
Limit of pack ice (Spring)
C. Farewell
Yukon
ALASKA
Fairbanks
Arctic Circle
Dawson
Klondike
Anchorage
Mackenzie
Gt. Bear L.
Whitehorse
Skagway
Juneau
Yellowknife
Gt. Slave L.
Chesterfield Inlet
Southampton I.
Hudson Strait
Hudson Bay
CANADA
Pr. Rupert
Queen Charlotte Is.
Athabasca L.
Churchill
Dawson Creek
Nelson
Flin Flon
Labrador
Newfoundland
St. John's
Edmonton
Prince Albert
James Bay
Vancouver I.
Fraser
Calgary
Saskatoon
Sept Iles
Corner Brook
C. Breton I.
Victoria
Lethbridge
Moose Jaw
Regina
L. Winnipeg
Vancouver
Medicine Hat
Winnipeg
Thunder Bay
Timmins
Québec
Montreal
Halifax
Nova Scotia
Seattle
Spokane
Portland
Tacoma
Duluth
Sault Ste. Marie
Ottawa
Missouri
Billings
St Paul
Eugene
Snake
Minneapolis
Toronto
Boston
Gt. Salt L.
Milwaukee
Detroit
Buffalo
New York
Sacramento
Reno
Chicago
Cleveland
Philadelphia
San Francisco
Oakland
Salt Lake City
Omaha
Pittsburgh
Baltimore
Platte
Fresno
Denver
Cincinnati
Colorado
Pueblo
Kansas City
St. Louis
Washington
UNITED STATES
C. Hatteras
Los Angeles
San Diego
Amarillo
Memphis
Charlotte
Bermuda (Br.)
Phoenix
Alburquerque
Red
Mississippi
Atlanta
Birmingham
Savannah
ATLANTIC OCEAN
Tucson
El Paso
Dallas
Ciudad Juarez
Baton Rouge
Mobile
Jacksonville
PACIFIC OCEAN
Hermosillo
Baja California
Houston
New Orleans
Florida
Chihuahua
San Antonio
Galveston
Tampa
Gulf of Mexico
BAHAMAS
Miami
Torréon
Monterrey
Tropic of Cancer
MEXICO
La Habana
CUBA
Mazatlán
Tampico
Yucatan Strait
DOM. REP.
S. Luis Potosí
HAITI
Port-au-Prince
Revilla Gigedo (Mex.)
Guadalajara
León
Mérida
Santiago de Cuba
P. Rico (U.S.)
México
Veracruz
JAMAICA
Kingston
Puebla
Coatzacoalcos
BELIZE
Caribbean Sea
Acapulco
GUATEMALA
HONDURAS
Guatemala
Salina Cruz
EL SALVADOR
NICARAGUA
CENTRAL AMERICA
Managua
Cartagena
COSTA RICA
San José
Panama
PANAMA
Canal
SOUTH AMERICA
West from Greenwich
1 : 60 000 000

146

90
80
70
55
50
Ottawa Is.
257
Hudson Bay
Portland Promontory
Inoucdjouac (Port Harrison)
Feuilles
Koksoak
Ft. Chimo
George
Whale
Kaniapiskau
L. Minto
Mélèzes
Sleeper Is.
King George Is.
King George Is.
Baker's Dozen Is.
C. Tatnam
Belcher Is.
L. à L'Eau Claire
Lac Bienville
Schefferville
Grand Baleine
Poste-de-la-Baleine (Great Whale River)
Ft. Severn
Severn
C. Henrietta Maria
Pte. Louis-XIV
Kanaaupscow
La Grande
Kaniapiskau
Winisk
C A N A D A
Ft. George
James Bay
1128
Big Trout L.
Attawapiskat
Akimiski I.
Nouveau Comptoir (Paint Hills)
Eastmain
Q U É
Ft. Albany
Charlton I.
Fort Rupert (Rupert House)
Rupert
L. Mistassini
L. Albanel
ONTARIO
Albany
Albany
Moosonee
Nottaway
Harricana
Péribonca
L. St. Joseph
Missinaibi
Chibougamau
Armstrong
Nakina
Kenogami
Matagami
Dolbeau
L. St-Jean
Saguenay
L. Nipigon
Longlac
Hearst
Cochrane
Rés. de Gouin
Roberval
Jonquière
Chicoutimi
Nipigon
L. Abitibi
Toschereau
Senneterre
Mattagami
1190
Oba
Timmins
Noranda
Rouyn
Heron Bay
Val d'Or
La Tuque
Thunder Bay
Franz
Kirkland Lake
Québec
Lévis
Shawinigan
Michipicoten
Haileybury
L. Témiscamingue
Trois-Rivières
Lake Superior
Cobalt
Rés. de Cabonga
Joliette
Sorel
St. Hyacinthe
Calumet
Keweenaw Bay
Laurium
Sault Ste. Marie
Sudbury
MONTRÉAL
Bessemer
Marquette
North Bay
Ottawa
Lachine
Sherbrook
Copper Cliff
Hull
Granby
Ironwood
Sault Ste. Marie
North Chan.
Parry Sound
Pembroke
L. Champlain
Escanaba
Georgian Bay
Arnprior
Ottawa
Cornwall
Rhinelander
Manistique
Cheboygan
Belleville
Burlington
Iron Mt.
Gladstone
Lake Huron
Orillia
Peterboro'
Kingston
VERMONT
Merrill
Antigo
Menominee
Petoskey
Watertown
Rutland
Wisconsin
Wausau
Green Bay
Traverse City
Owen Sound
Shawa
Cobourg
Glens Falls
Appleton
Cadillac
Saginaw B.
TORONTO
L. Ontario
Syracuse
Utica
Manitowoc
Ludington
Guelph
Niagara Falls
Rochester
Sheboygan
L. Michigan
Saginaw
Kitchener
Stratford
Albany
Milwaukee
Muskegon
London
Brantford
Hamilton
St. Catharines
Buffalo
NEW YORK
Springfield
Madison
Racine
Grand Rapids
Sarnia
Elmira
Binghamton
CONN.
Kenosha
Kalamazoo
DETROIT
Chatham
Lake Erie
Jamestown
Waterbury
Scranton
Rockford
Evanston
Windsor
Erie
Williamsport
Bridgeport
NEW
CHICAGO
Toledo
Cleveland
PENNSYLVANIA
Newark
Jersey City
NEW JERSEY
ILLINOIS
Gary
South Bend
INDIANA
OHIO
Akron
Youngstown
Allentown
Reading
Trenton
80
West from Greenwich

143

157

1 : 15 000 000

147

COAST OF LABRADOR
NEWFOUNDLAND
QUEBEC
NEW BRUNSWICK
NOVA SCOTIA
PR. EDWARD I.
MAINE
NEW HAMPSHIRE
MASS.
RHODE I.
YORK
ATLANTIC OCEAN
Gulf of St. Lawrence
R. St. Lawrence
Nain
Hopedale
C. Harrison
Indian Harbour
Rigolet
Cartwright
L. Melville
Petitsikapau L.
Michikamau Lake
North West R.
Goose Bay
Battle Harb.
Belle Isle
Str. of Belle Isle
Lobstick L.
Churchill Falls
Churchill
Ashuanipi L.
Natashquan
Romaine
St-Augustin-Saguenay
Moisie
Mingan
Sept Îles
Port-Cartier
Manicouagan
Î. d'Anticosti
Notre Dame B.
Twillingate
Lewisporte
Gander
Grand Falls
Bonavista
Trinity B.
Carbonear
St. John's
Harbour Grace
Placentia
Placentia B.
Trepassey
C. Race
Corner Brook
Buchans
814
P. aux Basques
C. Ray
Cabot Str.
C. North
ST.-PIERRE et MIQUELON (Fr.)
Gaspé
C. de Gaspé
Pén. de Gaspé
Matane
Rimouski
Campbellton
Dalhousie
Bathurst
Îs. de la Madeleine
Chatham
Tignish
Summerside
Charlottetown
Cape Breton I.
Glace Bay
Sydney
Port Hawkesbury
Mulgrave
Northumberland Str.
Pictou
New Glasgow
Truro
Rivière-du-Loup
Newcastle
Edmundston
St. Leonard
Moncton
Amherst
Springhill
Windsor
Kentville
Dartmouth
Halifax
Bridgewater
Liverpool
Shelburne
C. Sable
Yarmouth
Digby
B. of Fundy
Saint John
Fredericton
Woodstock
Sable I. (Nova Scotia)
6309
Bangor
Augusta
Lewiston
Portland
1917
Manchester
Lowell
Boston
C. Cod
Worcester
Providence
Haven
Baie-Comeau
Esiamites
60
50
40
70

144

PACIFIC OCEAN
BRITISH COLUMBIA
ALBERTA
WASHINGTON
Kitimat
Babine L.
Stuart L.
Francois L.
McLeod Lake
Hines Ck.
Dawson Creek
Peace R.
Grande Prairie
McLennan
Grouard
Smoky
Rocky Mountains
Prince George
Cariboo Mtns.
Quesnel
Alexandria
Bella Coola
Mt. Waddington 3994
Q. Charlotte Sd.
Quatsino
Vancouver I.
Williams L.
Fraser
Mt. Robson 3954
Edson
Yellowhead P. 1131
Lacombe
Nordegg
Red Deer
Innisfail
Kicking Horse P. 1622
Calgary
Drumheller
Lillooet
Clinton
Ashcroft
Thompson
Revelstoke
Selkirk Mts.
Kamloops
Vernon
Kelowna
Penticton
Nelson
Kaslo
Kootenay
Trail
Rossland
Grand Forks
Comox
Squamish
Cumberland
Port Alberni
Nanaimo
Ladysmith
Juan de Fuca Str.
C. Flattery
Vancouver
New Westminster
Victoria
Bellingham
Everett
Chelan
Hoquiam
Gray's Harb.
Aberdeen
Chehalis
Olympia
Centralia
Seattle
Tacoma
Yakima
Ellensburg
Wenatchee
Spokane
Coeur d'Alene
Sandpoint
Kalispell
Cranbrook
Coleman
Blairmore
Crowsnest P. 1357
Fort Macleod
High River
Bow
Lethbri
Raymond
Cardston
Astoria
St. Helens
Vancouver
Adams
3751

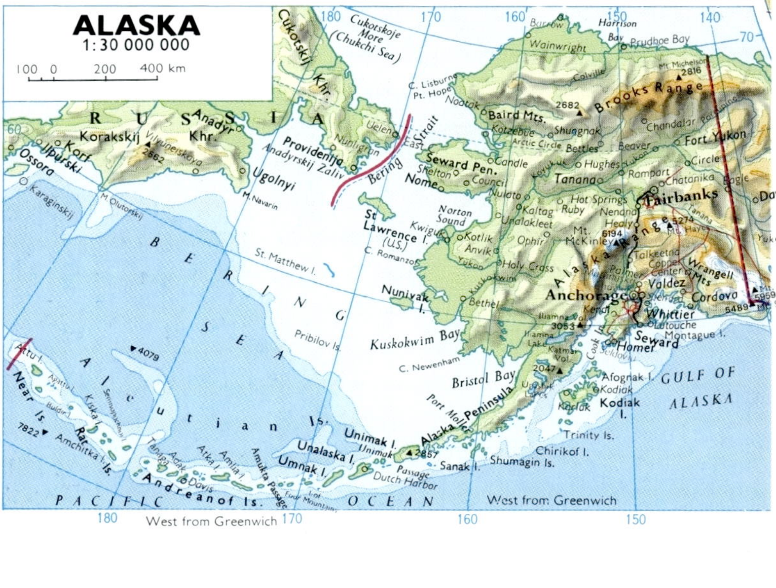
ALASKA
1: 30 000 000
100 0 200 400 km
Cukotskoje More (Chukchi Sea)
Cukotskij Khr.
RUSSIA
Anadyr
Korakskij Khr.
Korf
Ilpurskij
Ossora
Karaginskij
M. Olutorskij
2562
Providenija
Anadyrskij Zaliv
Ugolnyi
M. Navarin
Uelen
Bering Strait
St. Lawrence I. (U.S.)
C. Romanzof
St. Matthew I.
Nunivak I.
BERING SEA
Pribilov Is.
Aleutian Is.
Attu I.
Near Is.
Kiska I.
Rat Is.
Amchitka I.
7822
4079
Andreanof Is.
Adak
Atka I.
Amlia I.
Amukta Passage
Unimak I.
Unalaska I.
Umnak I.
Dutch Harbor
PACIFIC OCEAN
West from Greenwich
Barrow
Wainwright
Harrison Bay
Prudhoe Bay
C. Lisburne
Pt. Hope
Noatak
Colville
Mt. Michelson 2816
Brooks Range
2682
Baird Mts.
Kotzebue
Arctic Circle
Shungnak
Bettles
Beaver
Chandalar
Fort Yukon
Circle
Seward Pen.
Candle
Shelton
Nome
Council
Hughes
Rampart
Tanana
Chatanika
Eagle
Fairbanks
Dawson
Nulato
Kaltag
Ruby
Hot Springs
Nenana
Healy
5274
Unalakleet
Norton Sound
Kwiguk
Kotlik
Anvik
Ophir
Mt. McKinley 6194
Alaska Range
Yukon
Holy Cross
Talkeetna
Copper Center
Palmer
Wrangell Mts.
Valdez
Cordova
5959
5489
Anchorage
Kuskokwim
Bethel
Kenai
Whittier
La Touche
Montague I.
Seward
Iliamna
3053
Iliamna Lake
Kuskokwim Bay
C. Newenham
Bristol Bay
Katmai Vol.
Cook Inlet
Homer
Seldovia
2047
Afognak I.
Kodiak
Kodiak I.
GULF OF ALASKA
Trinity Is.
Alaska Peninsula
Port Moller
Chirikof I.
Shumagin Is.
Sanak I.
2857
Unimak Passage
180
170
160
150
140
70
60
50

1 : 15 000 000

145

Hudson Bay
C. Churchill
Churchill
Seal
Port Nelson
York Factory
Nelson
Amery
Hayes
Gods
Gods L.
Island L.
Sandy L.
Thompson
Southern Indian L.
Reindeer Lake
Brochet
Lynn Lake
Wollaston L.
Cree
Cree L.
Chipewyan
Athabasca
Fort McMurray
Fort Mackay
Lesser Slave L.
Frobisher L.
Churchill L.
Beauval
Lac la Biche
Stanley
L. la Ronge
Sherridon
Flin Flon
Edmonton
Leduc
N. Saskatchewan
Vegreville
Vermilion
Wetaskiwin
Camrose
Stettler
Wainwright
Lloydminster
N. Battleford
Battleford
Beaver
Prince Albert
Rosthern
Hanna
Wilkie
Kerrobert
Biggar
Saskatoon
Humboldt
Melfort
Tisdale
Nipawin
Saskatchewan
The Pas
Cedar Lake
Grand Rapids
Norway Ho.
Bassano
Alsask
Rosetown
L. Diefenbaker
Watrous
Nokomis
Winnipegosis
L. Winnipegosis
Gypsumville
Lake Winnipeg
Medicine Hat
Swift Current
S. Saskatchewan
Canora
Kamsack
831
Yorkton
Melville
Dauphin
Hodgson
Moose Jaw
Regina
Indian Hd.
L. Manitoba
Riverton
ONTARIO
Red. L.
Assiniboia
Shaunavon
Assiniboine
Neepawa
Victoria Beach
Havre
Weyburn
Moosomin
Minnedosa
Stonewall
Selkirk
English
Lac Seul
Marias
Virden
Brandon
Portage la Prairie
St. Boniface
Sioux Lookout
Milk
Estevan
Souris
Winnipeg
Kenora
Fort Peck
Missouri
Glasgow
Carman
Morden
Emerson
L. of the Woods
MONTANA
Lewistown
Minot
Devils Lake
Grafton
Fort Frances
Rainy L.
Thief River Falls
Red
Yellowstone
Glendive
NORTH DAKOTA
Grand Forks
Crookston
Red Lake
Ely
Miles City
Mandan
Dickinson
Jamestown
Valley City
Bemidji
Hibbing
Virginia
Eveleth
2362
Tongue
Bismarck
Moorhead
Fargo
Leech L.
MINNESOTA
Duluth
Lake Superior
Powder
Little Missouri
Wahpeton
Brainerd
Superior
Ashland
UNITED STATES
Kluane
WYOMING
Moreau
Mobridge
Aberdeen
Bigstone L.
Little Falls
St. Cloud
Whitehorse
White Pass
Black Hills
SOUTH DAKOTA
Redfield
Willmar
Anoka
Skagway
Juneau
Admiralty I.
Cheyenne
Pierre
Minneapolis
St. Paul
Fairweather
4663
2207
Rapid City
White
Huron
Brookings
New Ulm
Faribault
Chichagof I.
Sitka
Petersburg
Wrangell
Madison
Mankato
Rochester
Winona
Alexander Archipelago
Baranof I.
Mitchell
Sioux Falls
Fairmont
Ketchikan
Chadron
Niobrara
Missouri
Des Moines
La Crosse
Prince of Wales I.
Prince Rupert
Yankton
Austin
Dall I.
Dixon Entrance
Hecate Strait
Alliance
Cherokee
Mason City
Graham I.
North Platte
Sioux City
Fort Dodge
Webster City
Dubuque
Queen Charlotte Is.
NEBRASKA
Norfolk
IOWA
Cedar Falls
Waterloo
Moresby I.
Sidney
North Platte
Grand Island
Platte
Ames
Cedar Rapids
Sterling
Omaha
Des Moines
Council Bluffs
Davenport
CANADA
ALBERTA
SASKATCHEWAN
MANITOBA
55
50
110
100
60

140 West from Greenwich 100

140

163

142

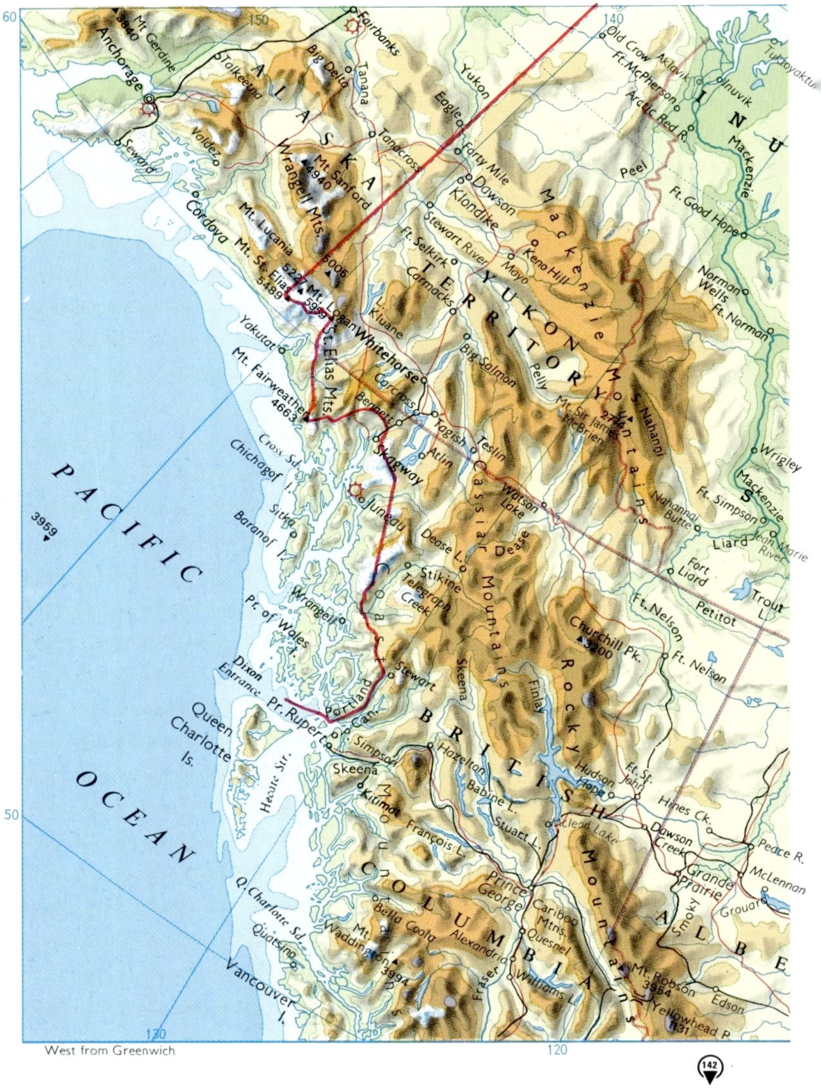
60
150
140
50
130
120
West from Greenwich
PACIFIC
OCEAN
ALASKA
YUKON
TERRITORY
BRITISH
COLUMBIA
ALBE
INU
Fairbanks
Anchorage
Mt. Gerdine
3640
Talkeetna
Big Delta
Tanana
Seward
Valdez
Cordova
Mt. Sanford
4940
Wrangell Mts.
Mt. Lucania
5227
Mt. St. Elias
5489
Mt. Logan
5959
6006
St. Elias Mts.
Yakutat
Mt. Fairweather
4663
Tanacross
Eagle
Yukon
Forty Mile
Dawson
Klondike
Stewart River
Ft. Selkirk
Carmacks
Kluane
Whitehorse
Carcross
Bennett
Tagish
Atlin
Teslin
Skagway
Juneau
Cross Sd.
Chichagof I.
Sitka
Baranof I.
3959
Wrangell
Pr. of Wales I.
Dixon Entrance
Queen Charlotte Is.
Hecate Str.
Pr. Rupert
Portland Can.
Stewart
Simpson
Skeena
Kitimat
Coast Mts.
Stikine
Telegraph Creek
Dease L.
Dease
Cassiar Mountains
Watson Lake
Big Salmon
Pelly
Mayo
Keno Hill
Mackenzie Mountains
Mt. Sir James McBrien
2760
S. Nahanni
Old Crow
Aklavik
Ft. McPherson
Arctic Red R.
Inuvik
Tuktoyaktuk
Mackenzie
Peel
Ft. Good Hope
Norman Wells
Ft. Norman
Wrigley
Mackenzie
Ft. Simpson
Nahanni Butte
Liard
Jean Marie River
Fort Liard
Petitot
Trout L.
Ft. Nelson
Churchill Pk.
3200
Rocky
Finlay
Hazelton
Babine L.
Stuart L.
François L.
Mcleod Lake
Hudson Hope
Ft. St. John
Hines Ck.
Dawson Creek
Peace R.
McLennan
Grande Prairie
Grouard
Smoky
Prince George
Cariboo Mtns.
Quesnel
Alexandria
Bella Coola
Mt. Waddington
3994
Fraser
Williams L.
Q. Charlotte Sd.
Quatsino
Vancouver I.
Mt. Robson
3954
Mountains
Edson
Yellowhead P.
1131

142

1 : 15 000 000

12

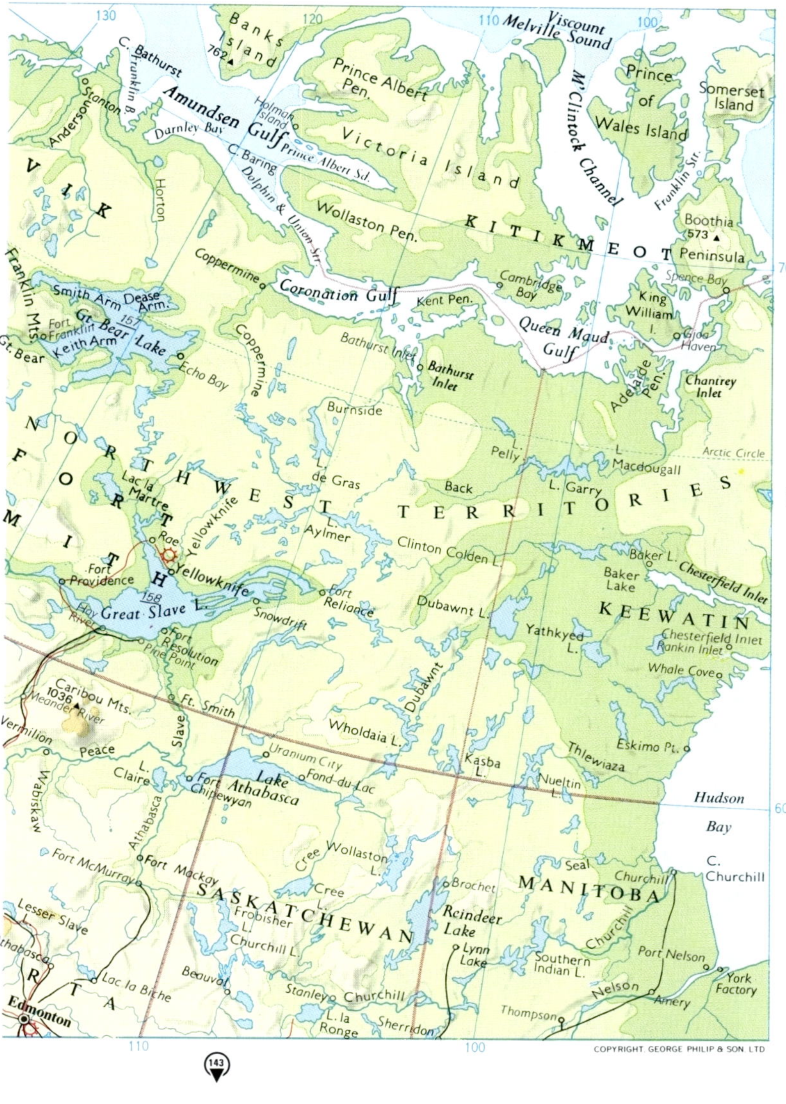
Banks Island
762
C. Bathurst
Franklin B.
Stanton
Anderson
Amundsen Gulf
Darnley Bay
C. Baring
Holman Island
Prince Albert Sd.
Prince Albert Pen.
Victoria Island
Dolphin & Union Str.
Wollaston Pen.
Viscount Melville Sound
M'Clintock Channel
Prince of Wales Island
Somerset Island
Franklin Str.
Boothia Peninsula
573
K I T I K M E O T
Horton
Coppermine
Coronation Gulf
Kent Pen.
Cambridge Bay
Spence Bay
King William I.
Gjoa Haven
Queen Maud Gulf
Chantrey Inlet
Adelaide Pen.
Bathurst Inlet
Franklin Mts.
Smith Arm
Dease Arm
Gt. Bear Lake
157
Fort Franklin
Keith Arm
Gt. Bear
Echo Bay
Burnside
L. Pelly
Arctic Circle
L. Macdougall
L. de Gras
Back
L. Garry
N O R T H W E S T   T E R R I T O R I E S
Lac la Martre
Yellowknife
Rae
Fort Providence
158
Great Slave L.
Hay River
L. Aylmer
Clinton Colden L.
Baker L.
Chesterfield Inlet
Baker Lake
Fort Reliance
Dubawnt L.
Snowdrift
K E E W A T I N
Yathkyed L.
Rankin Inlet
Whale Cove
Fort Resolution
Pine Point
Dubawnt
Caribou Mts.
1036
Meander River
Ft. Smith
Ft. Vermilion
Slave
Wholdaia L.
Eskimo Pt.
Peace
L. Claire
Uranium City
Kasba L.
Thlewiaza
Wabiskaw
Fort Chipewyan
Lake Athabasca
Fond-du-Lac
Nueltin L.
Hudson Bay
Athabasca
Fort McMurray
Fort Mackay
Cree
Wollaston L.
Cree L.
Seal
Churchill
C. Churchill
Brochet
M A N I T O B A
S A S K A T C H E W A N
Reindeer Lake
Frobisher L.
Churchill L.
Lesser Slave
Lynn Lake
Southern Indian L.
Port Nelson
York Factory
Lac la Biche
Beauval
Stanley
Churchill
Nelson
Amery
Thompson
Edmonton
L. la Ronge
Sherridon
130
120
110
100
70
60

146

143

12

Devon Island
Lancaster Sound
1890
Bylot I.
Arctic Bay
Pond Inlet
Pond Inlet
Brodeur
Peninsula
Milne Inlet
Gulf of Boothia
Baffin Bay
2136
Svartenhuk Halvø
Disko
Scott I.
Clyde
C. Hewett
Davis St
Home B.
Broughton Island
Padloping Island
C. Dyer
Cape Dyer
Cumberland Peninsula
2591
Pangnirtung
Hoare B.
Cumberland Sd.
C. Mercy
Fury & Hecla Str.
Igloolik Island
Hall Lake
Pelly Bay
Committee B.
Melville Peninsula
Prince Charles I.
Foxe Basin
NORTHWEST TERRITORIES
Nettilling L.
BAFFIN
Baffin I.
Rae Isthmus
Repulse Bay
Arctic Circle
Foxe
Wager Bay
Wager B.
Roes Welcome Sd.
C. Dorchester
Channel
Foxe Penin.
Amadjuak L.
Amadjuak
Frobisher Bay
Frobisher Bay
Cape Dorset
Southampton I.
Coral Harbour
Bell Pen.
Lake Harbour
Hudson Strait
Resolution
Digges Is.
Coats I.
Mansel I.
Ivujivik
Saglouc (Sugluk)
Maricourt (Wakeham)
Koartac (Notre Dame de Koartac)
Akpatok I.
C. Chidl
Arnaud
Bellin (Payne Bay)
Ungava Bay
Ungava Peninsula
Payne L.
Port Nouveau Québec (George R.)
Ft. Chimo
Koksoak
Feuilles
Whale
Kaniapiskau
Hudson Bay
257
Ottawa Is.
Portland Promontory
Inoucdjouac (Port Harrison)
Mélèzes
L. Minto
Sleeper Is.
King George Is.
King George Is.
Baker's Dozen Is.
Belcher Is.
C. Tatnam
L. à L'Eau Claire
Lac Bienville
Grand Baleine
Poste-de-la-Baleine (Great Whale River)
L. Kaniapiskau
Ft. Severn
ONTARIO
C. Henrietta Maria
West from Greenwich
90
80
70
60
50

145

140

1 : 15 000 000

GREENLAND
ATLANTIC OCEAN
Angmagssalik
Christianshåb
Disko B.
Søndre Strømfjord
Holsteinsborg
Sukkertoppen
2850
Kong Frederik VI's Kyst
Godthåb
Fiskenæsset
Frederikshåb
Ivigtut
Julianehåb
Sydprøven
Nanortalik
Kap Farvel
3809
1676
Hebron
Nutak
George
Nain
NEWFOUNDLAND
C. Harrison
Indian Harbour
Hopedale
Rigolet
Cartwright
L. Melville
COAST OF LABRADOR
Belle Isle
Battle Harb.
North West R.
Goose Bay
Michikamau Lake
Churchill Falls
Churchill
Lobstick L.
Ashuanipi L.
St-Augustin
Str. of Belle Isle
Notre Dame B.
Twillingate
40
30
60
50
141

140

151

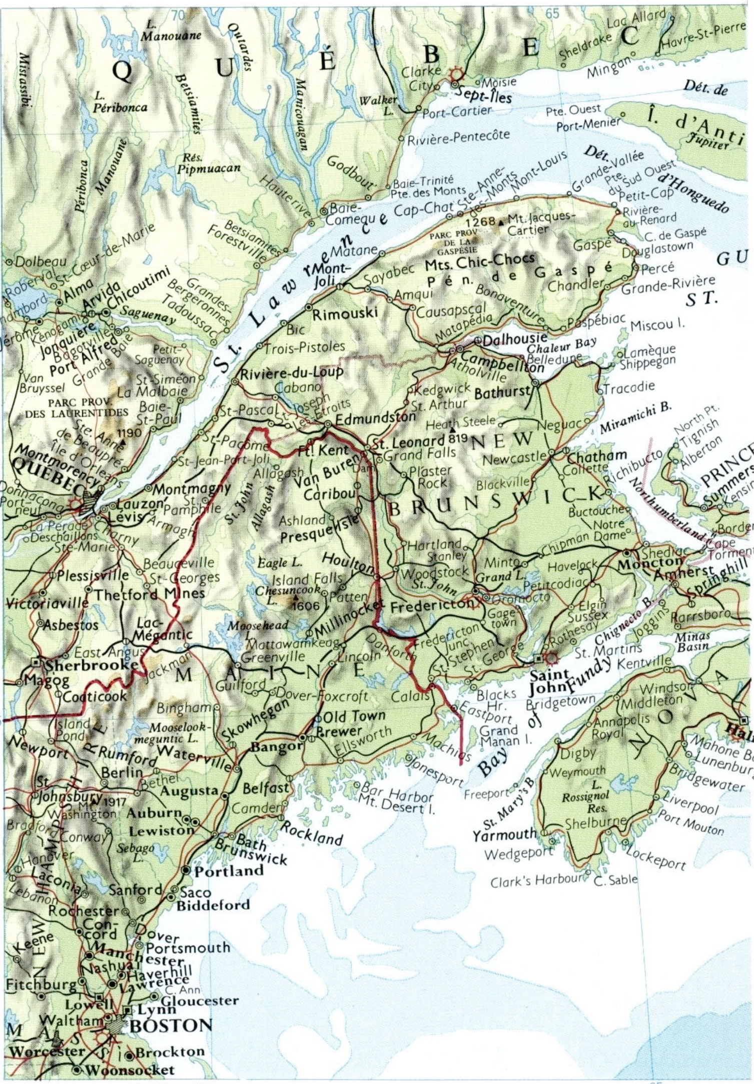
Q U É B E C
L. Manouane
Outardes
Mistassibi
Betsiamites
Manicouagan
L. Péribonca
Walker L.
Clarke City
Moisie
Sept-Îles
Port-Cartier
Sheldrake
Lac Allard
Havre-St-Pierre
Mingan
Dét. de
Pte. Ouest
Port-Menier
Î. d'Anti
Jupiter
Rivière-Pentecôte
Rés. Pipmuacan
Godbout
Baie-Trinité
Pte. des Monts
Dét. d'Honguedo
Grande-Vallée
Pte. du Sud Ouest
Petit-Cap
Rivière-au-Renard
Mont-Louis
Ste-Anne-des-Monts
Cap-Chat
Hauterive
Baie-Comeau
Péribonca
Manouane
Betsiamites
Forestville
1268 Mt. Jacques-Cartier
PARC PROV. DE LA GASPÉSIE
C. de Gaspé
Gaspé
Douglastown
Matane
Dolbeau
St-Cœur-de-Marie
Roberval
Alma
Chambord
Arvida
Chicoutimi
Saguenay
Grandes-Bergeronnes
Tadoussac
Mont-Joli
Sayabec
Amqui
Mts. Chic-Chocs
Pén. de Gaspé
Percé
Chandler
Grande-Rivière
Bonaventure
Causapscal
Matapédia
Rimouski
Bic
Jérôme
Kénogami
Jonquière
Bagotville
Port Alfred
Grande Baie
Petit-Saguenay
Trois-Pistoles
Dalhousie
Chaleur Bay
Paspébiac
Miscou I.
Lamèque
Shippegan
Belledune
Campbellton
Atholville
St. Lawrence
Van Bruyssel
St-Siméon
La Malbaie
Rivière-du-Loup
Cabano
Kedgwick
Bathurst
Tracadie
PARC PROV. DES LAURENTIDES
Baie-St-Paul
St-Pascal
St-Joseph
Les Étroits
St. Arthur
Edmundston
Heath Steele
819
Neguac
Miramichi B.
North Pt.
Tignish
Alberton
1190
Ste-Anne-de-Beaupré
Île d'Orléans
Montmorency
QUEBEC
St-Pacôme
St-Jean-Port-Joli
Ft. Kent
St. Leonard
Grand Falls
NEW BRUNSWICK
Newcastle
Chatham
Collette
Richibucto
PRINCE
Summerside
Kensington
Allagash
Van Buren
Plaster Rock
Blackville
Northumberland
Donnacona
Portneuf
Montmagny
St. Pamphile
Lauzon
Lévis
Caribou
St. John
Allagash
Buctouche
Notre Dame
La Pérade
Deschaillons
Charny
Armagh
Ashland
Presque Isle
Borden
Cape Tormentine
Ste-Marie
Beauceville
St-Georges
Hartland
Stanley
Chipman
Minto
Shediac
Moncton
Eagle L.
Houlton
Woodstock
Havelock
Amherst
Springhill
Plessisville
Thetford Mines
Island Falls
Grand L.
St. John
Petitcodiac
Victoriaville
Chesuncook L.
1606
Patten
Fredericton
Oromocto
Elgin
Sussex
Gagetown
Parrsboro
Asbestos
Lac-Mégantic
Moosehead L.
Millinocket
Mattawamkeag
Fredericton Junc.
St. Stephen
St. George
Rothesay
Chignecto B.
Joggins
Minas Basin
Sherbrooke
East Angus
Jackman
Greenville
Lincoln
Danforth
MAINE
Saint John
St. Martins
Fundy
Kentville
Magog
Coaticook
Guilford
Dover-Foxcroft
Calais
Blacks Hr.
Bridgetown
Windsor
Middleton
Bingham
Old Town
Eastport
Grand Manan I.
Annapolis Royal
NOVA
Halifa
Island Pond
Mooselookmeguntic L.
Skowhegan
Brewer
Ellsworth
Machias
Bay of
Digby
Mahone Bay
Lunenburg
Newport
Rumford
Waterville
Bangor
Jonesport
Weymouth
Bridgewater
Berlin
Bethel
Augusta
Belfast
Bar Harbor
Mt. Desert I.
Freeport
St. Mary's B.
L. Rossignol Res.
Liverpool
St. Johnsbury
1917 Mt. Washington
Auburn
Camden
Port Mouton
Bradford
Conway
Lewiston
Rockland
Shelburne
Yarmouth
Hanover
Sebago L.
Bath
Brunswick
Wedgeport
Lockeport
NEW HAMPSHIRE
Laconia
Portland
Clark's Harbour
C. Sable
Lebanon
Sanford
Saco
Biddeford
Rochester
Concord
Dover
Portsmouth
Keene
Manchester
Nashua
Haverhill
Lawrence
Fitchburg
C. Ann
Gloucester
Lowell
Lynn
Waltham
BOSTON
MASS.
Worcester
Brockton
Woonsocket
70
65
50
45

West from Greenwich

164

1 : 7 000 000

141

Kegaska
Etamamu
Aguanish
Natashquan
Gethsémani
Jacques-Cartier
costi
Heath Pt.
Pte. Sud
572
LF OF
LAWRENCE
Î. Brion
Grande-Entrée
Îs. de la
Madeleine
(Quebec)
Fatima
Cap-aux-Meules
Havre-Aubert
St. Paul
I.
C. North
EDWARD
ISLAND
Charlottetown
East Pt.
Souris
St. Peters
Georgetown
Montague
Murray Hr.
Str.
Pleasant Bay
CAPE BRETON
NAT. PARK
532
Ingonish
Chéticamp
St. Anns B.
Sydney Mines
New Waterford
Glace Bay
Inverness
N. Sydney
Sydney
Cape Breton
Island
Louisbourg
Port
Hood
Bras d'Or
L.
Pt.
Hawkesbury
Fourchu
Antigonish
Pictou
New
Glasgow
Stellarton
St. Peters
I. Madame
Chedabucto B.
Canso
Mulgrave
Sherbrooke
S C O T I A
Upper
Musquodoboit
Dartmouth
Sheet Hr.
Musquodoboit Hr.
A T L A N T I C
O C E A N
Sable I.
(Nova Scotia)
Cabot Strait
Trout River
Bay of Islands
Corner Brook
814
Long Pt.
Port au Port B.
Stephenville
C. St. George
St. George's B.
St. George's
Mts.
Long Range
St. David's
South Branch
St. Andrew's
C. Ray
Channel-Port
aux Basques
Isle aux Morts
Rose Blanche
Burgeo
Ramea
Deer
Lake
Cox's
Cove
Grand
L.
Howley
Buchans
Red Indian
L.
Sop's
Arm
Springdale
South Brook
Botwood
Windsor
Badger
Grand Falls
Bishop's Falls
Gander
L.
Lewisporte
Glenwood
Carmanville
C. Freels
Wesleyville
Bonavista
B.
C. Bonavista
Bonavista
Catalina
Trinity B.
Trinity
Dark Cove
Glovertown
NEWFOUNDLAND
Victoria
Res.
Grey Res.
Salmon
Res.
Port Blandford
381
Clarenville
White
Bear
Res.
Grey
St. Alban's
Terrenceville
Belleoram
Fortune B.
François
Harbour Breton
Grand Bank
Marystown
Burin
St. Lawrence
Miquelon
Langlade
St. Pierre
SAINT-PIERRE
ET MIQUELON
(Fr.)
Placentia
B.
Argentia
Placentia
C. St. Mary's
St. Mary's B.
St.
Bride's
C. Pine
Trepassey
C.
Race
Ferryland
Avalon
Peninsula
Bay Bulls
Holyrood
Mt.
Pearl
Torbay
Wabana
Conception B.
Bay de Verde
Heart's Content
Carbonear
Harbour Grace
Spaniard's Bay
St.
John's
55
45
60

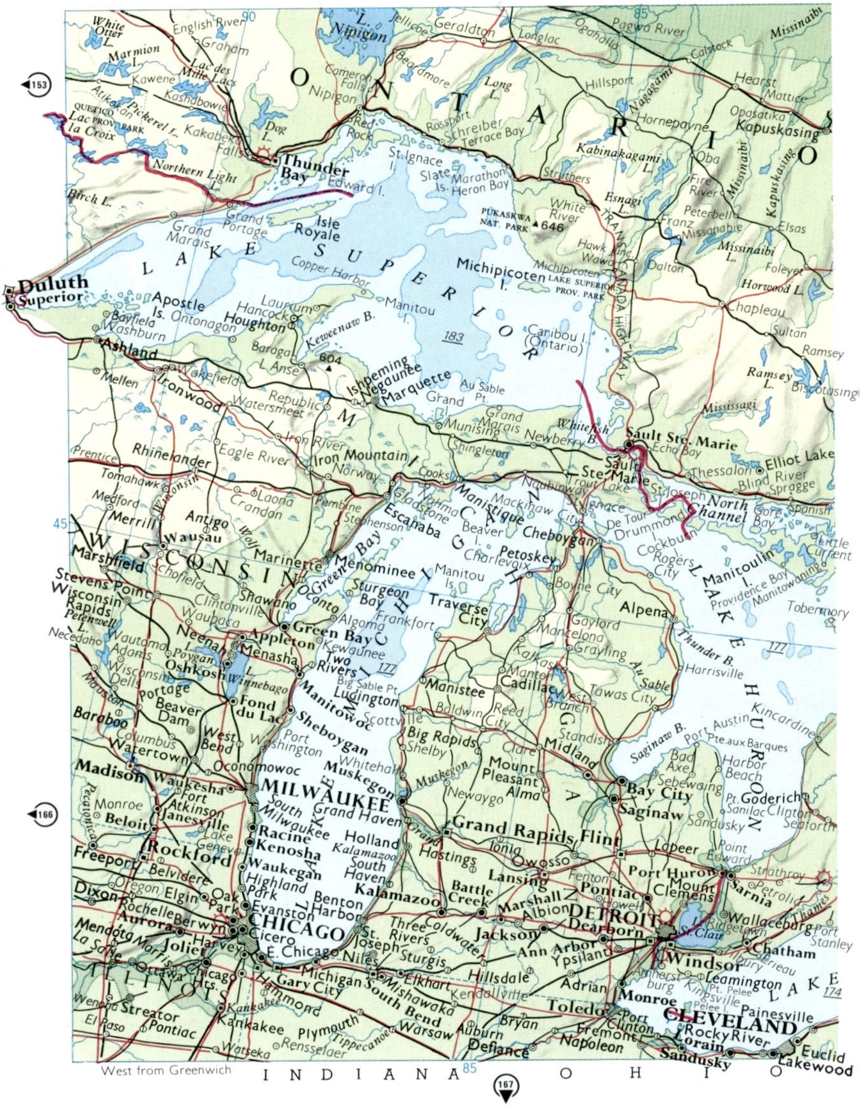
153
166
167
ONTARIO
LAKE SUPERIOR
LAKE MICHIGAN
LAKE HURON
LAKE ERIE
MICHIGAN
WISCONSIN
ILLINOIS
INDIANA
OHIO
West from Greenwich
90
85
45
183
177
174
L. Nipigon
Nipigon
Geraldton
Jellicoe
Longlac
Pagwa River
Missinaibi
Calstock
Hearst
Mattice
Opasatika
Kapuskasing
Hornepayne
Hillsport
Nagagami
Kabinakagami L.
Oba
Fire River
Peterbell
Franz
Missanabie
Missinaibi L.
Elsas
Foleyet
Horwood L.
Chapleau
Sultan
Ramsey
Ramsey L.
Biscotasing
Mississagi
Dalton
Esnagi L.
Struthers
White River
Hawk Junc.
Wawa
Michipicoten
LAKE SUPERIOR PROV. PARK
PUKASKWA NAT. PARK
646
TRANS CANADA HIGHWAY
Marathon
Heron Bay
Slate Is.
Schreiber
Terrace Bay
Rossport
Long L.
Beardmore
Cameron Falls
Red Rock
Dog L.
Thunder Bay
St. Ignace I.
Edward I.
Isle Royale
Grand Portage
Grand Marais
White Otter L.
English River
Graham
Marmion L.
Lac des Mille Lacs
Kawene
Kashabowie
Atikokan
Pickerel L.
QUETICO PROV. PARK
Lac la Croix
Kakabeka Falls
Northern Light L.
Birch L.
Duluth
Superior
Apostle Is.
Bayfield
Washburn
Ashland
Ontonagon
Copper Harbor
Laurium
Hancock
Houghton
Keweenaw B.
Manitou I.
Baraga
L'Anse
604
Caribou I. (Ontario)
Michipicoten I.
Mellen
Wakefield
Ironwood
Watersmeet
Republic
Ishpeming
Negaunee
Marquette
Au Sable Pt.
Grand I.
Grand Marais
Munising
Newberry
Whitefish B.
Sault Ste. Marie
Echo Bay
Thessalon
Elliot Lake
Blind River
Spragge
North Channel
Spanish
Gore Bay
Little Current
Manitoulin I.
Providence Bay
Manitowaning
Tobermory
St. Joseph I.
Drummond I.
Cockburn I.
De Tour
Rogers City
Alpena
Thunder B.
Harrisville
Au Sable
Tawas City
Kincardine
Shingleton
Trout Lake
Naubinway
Ste. Marie
Iron River
Iron Mountain
Norway
Cooks
Prentice
Rhinelander
Eagle River
Tomahawk
Wisconsin
Medford
Merrill
Laona
Crandon
Antigo
Wausau
Wolf
Pembine
Stephenson
Nahma
Gladstone
Escanaba
Manistique
Mackinaw City
St. Ignace
Beaver I.
Charlevoix
Petoskey
Cheboygan
Boyne City
Gaylord
Mancelona
Grayling
Kalkaska
Manton
Cadillac
West Branch
Marshfield
Schofield
Stevens Point
Wisconsin Rapids
Petenwell L.
Necedah
Marinette
Menominee
Green Bay
Oconto
Shawano
Clintonville
Waupaca
Sturgeon Bay
Manitou Is.
Traverse City
Frankfort
Algoma
Kewaunee
Two Rivers
Appleton
Menasha
Neenah
Oshkosh
Poygan L.
L. Winnebago
Wautoma
Adams
Wisconsin Dells
Mauston
Portage
Baraboo
Beaver Dam
Fond du Lac
Manitowoc
Big Sable Pt.
Ludington
Scottville
Manistee
Baldwin
Reed City
Standish
Clare
Midland
Big Rapids
Shelby
Sheboygan
Port Washington
West Bend
Columbus
Watertown
Madison
Oconomowoc
Waukesha
Milwaukee
South Milwaukee
Whitehall
Muskegon
Newaygo
Mount Pleasant
Alma
Saginaw B.
Port Austin
Pte. aux Barques
Bad Axe
Harbor Beach
Sebewaing
Bay City
Saginaw
Goderich
Clinton
Seaforth
Sanilac
Sandusky
Pecatonica
Monroe
Fort Atkinson
Janesville
Beloit
Lake Geneva
Racine
Kenosha
Grand Haven
Holland
Kalamazoo
Grand
Grand Rapids
Flint
Hastings
Ionia
Owosso
Lapeer
Point Edward
Sarnia
Strathroy
Petrolia
Freeport
Rockford
Belvidere
Waukegan
Highland Park
South Haven
Lansing
Fenton
Port Huron
Mount Clemens
Pontiac
Howell
Dixon
Oregon
Elgin
Oak Park
Evanston
Benton Harbor
Battle Creek
Marshall
Albion
Detroit
Dearborn
St. Clair
Wallaceburg
Thames
Ridgetown
Port Stanley
Chatham
Rochelle
Aurora
Berwyn
Chicago
Cicero
Three Rivers
St. Joseph
Coldwater
Jackson
Ann Arbor
Ypsilanti
Windsor
Tilbury
Erieau
Mendota
La Salle
Morris
Joliet
Harvey
E. Chicago
Niles
Sturgis
Hillsdale
Adrian
Amherstburg
Kingsville
Leamington
Pt. Pelee
Pelee I.
Wenona
Ottawa
Chicago Hts.
Gary
Michigan City
Elkhart
Mishawaka
South Bend
Kendallville
Hammond
Streator
El Paso
Pontiac
Kankakee
Plymouth
Tippecanoe
Warsaw
Auburn
Bryan
Toledo
Monroe
Port Clinton
Fremont
Defiance
Napoleon
Watseka
Rensselaer
Sandusky
Lorain
Rocky River
Cleveland
Painesville
Euclid
Lakewood

1 : 7 000 000

140

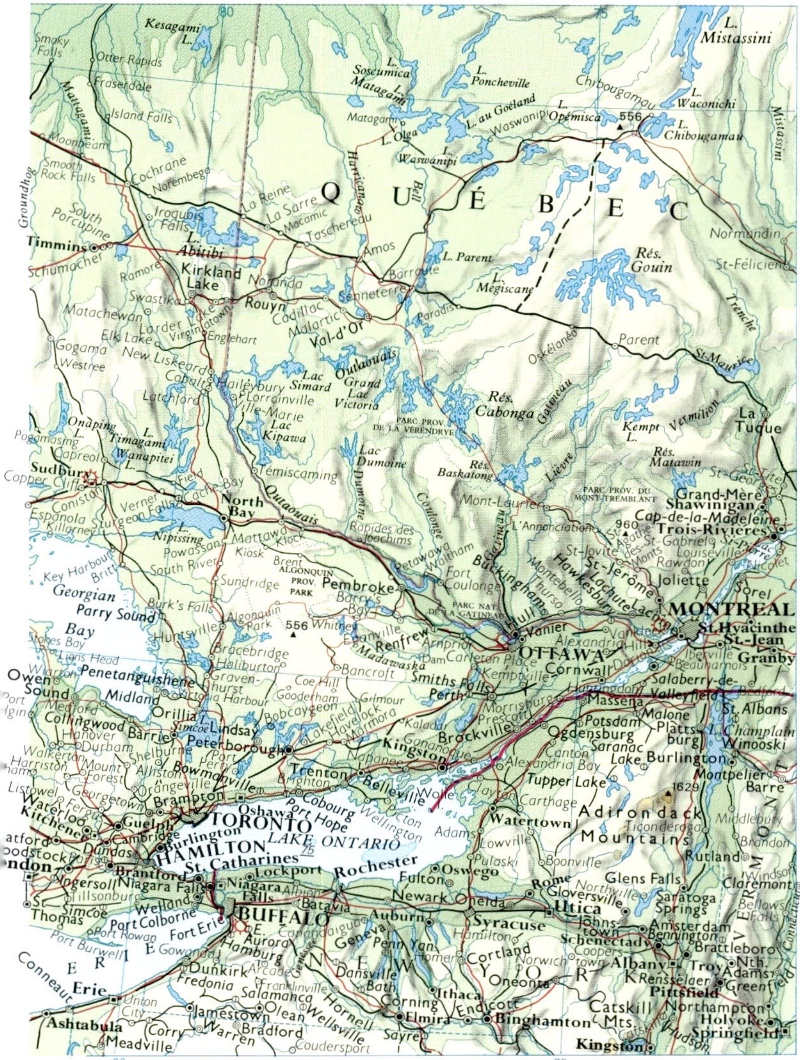

Q U É B E C
Kesagami L.
Smoky Falls
Otter Rapids
Fraserdale
Island Falls
Mattagami
Moonbeam
Smooth Rock Falls
Cochrane
Norembega
Groundhog
South Porcupine
Timmins
Schumacher
Iroquois Falls
L. Abitibi
La Reine
La Sarre
Macamic
Taschereau
Amos
Ramore
Kirkland Lake
Swastika
Matachewan
Larder Lake
Virginiatown
Noranda
Rouyn
Cadillac
Malartic
Val-d'Or
Senneterre
Barraute
Englehart
Elk Lake
Gogama
Westree
New Liskeard
Cobalt
Haileybury
Latchford
Lorrainville
Ville-Marie
Lac Simard
Outaouais
Grand Lac Victoria
Lac Kipawa
Onaping L.
Pogamasing
L. Timagami
L. Wanapitei
Capreol
Sudbury
Copper Cliff
Coniston
Témiscaming
Verner
Sturgeon Falls
Cache Bay
North Bay
Espanola
Killarney
L. Nipissing
Mattawa
Powassan
Kiosk
South River
Key Harbour
Britt
Georgian Bay
Parry Sound
Sundridge
Burk's Falls
Algonquin Park
ALGONQUIN PROV. PARK
Brent
556
Huntsville
Stokes Bay
Lions Head
Wiarton
Owen Sound
Port Elgin
Penetanguishene
Midland
Bracebridge
Haliburton
Gravenhurst
Victoria Harbour
Meaford
Collingwood
Orillia
L. Simcoe
Barrie
Lindsay
Peterborough
Hanover
Durham
Walkerton
Shelburne
Mount Forest
Alliston
Port Perry
Bowmanville
Harriston
Listowel
Orangeville
Georgetown
Brampton
Waterloo
Fergus
Kitchener
Guelph
Cambridge
Oshawa
TORONTO
Burlington
HAMILTON
Dundas
Woodstock
Paris
Brantford
London
Ingersoll
Tillsonburg
St. Thomas
Simcoe
Port Rowan
Port Burwell
Welland
Port Colborne
Fort Erie
St. Catharines
Niagara Falls
E R I E
Conneaut
Erie
Ashtabula
Union City
Corry
Meadville
Matagami
L. Soscumica
L. Matagami
L. Olga
Harricana
L. Waswanipi
Bell
L. Poncheville
L. au Goéland
Waswanipi
L. Opémisca
Chibougamau
556
L. Chibougamau
L. Waconichi
L. Mistassini
Mistassini
Normandin
St-Félicien
L. Parent
L. Megiscane
Paradis
Rés. Gouin
Trenche
Parent
Oskélanéo
St-Maurice
Rés. Cabonga
Gatineau
PARC PROV. DE LA VÉRENDRYE
Kempt L.
Vermilion
La Tuque
Rés. Matawin
Lac Dumoine
Dumoine
Rés. Baskatong
Lièvre
Coulonge
Mont-Laurier
PARC PROV. DU MONT-TREMBLANT
St-Georges
Grand-Mère
Shawinigan
Cap-de-la-Madeleine
Trois-Rivières
960
L'Annonciation
Ste-Agathe-des-Monts
St-Gabriel
St-Jovite
Louiseville
Rapides des Joachims
Petawawa
Waltham
Fort Coulonge
Buckingham
Montebello
Thurso
Hawkesbury
Lachute
St-Jérôme
Rawdon
Joliette
Nicolet
Sorel
Pembroke
Barry's Bay
PARC NAT. DE LA GATINEAU
Hull
Vanier
OTTAWA
MONTREAL
St. Hyacinthe
St-Jean
Granby
Whitney
Eganville
Renfrew
Arnprior
Madawaska
Carleton Place
Kemptville
Alexandria
Vaudreuil
Dorion
Cornwall
Iberville
Beauharnois
Salaberry-de-Valleyfield
Bancroft
Coe Hill
Gooderham
Gilmour
Smiths Falls
Perth
Huntingdon
Massena
Bedford
Morrisburg
Prescott
Potsdam
Malone
St. Albans
Bobcaygeon
Lakefield
Havelock
Marmora
Kaladar
Brockville
Ogdensburg
Plattsburg
L. Champlain
Winooski
Gananoque
Kingston
Canton
Saranac Lake
Burlington
Napanee
Alexandria Bay
Montpelier
Barre
Trenton
Brighton
Belleville
Clayton
Tupper Lake
1629
Cobourg
Port Hope
Picton
Wellington
Wolfe I.
Carthage
Watertown
Adirondack Mountains
Middlebury
Ticonderoga
Brandon
LAKE ONTARIO
Adams
Lowville
Rutland
Pulaski
Boonville
Windsor
Lockport
Rochester
Oswego
Fulton
Rome
Northville
Glens Falls
Claremont
Niagara Falls
Albion
Batavia
Newark
Oneida
Gloversville
Saratoga Springs
Bellows Falls
BUFFALO
Auburn
Syracuse
Utica
Johnstown
Amsterdam
Bennington
E. Aurora
Canandaigua
Geneva
Hamilton
Schenectady
Brattleboro
Hamburg
Penn Yan
Cortland
Coopers-town
Genesee
Dunkirk
Arcade
Homer
Norwich
Albany
Troy
Nth. Adams
Greenfield
Fredonia
Franklinville
Dansville
Oneonta
Rensselaer
Salamanca
Bath
Hornell
Corning
Ithaca
Pittsfield
Jamestown
Olean
Wellsville
Elmira
Endicott
Binghamton
Catskill Mts.
Northampton
Holyoke
Springfield
Warren
Bradford
Sayre
Coudersport
Kingston
Hudson
Connecticut
Hartford
N E W Y O R K
V E R M O N T
P E N N S Y L V A N I A
80
75
50
45

148

164

CANADA : SOUTHERN SASKATCHEWAN AND MANITOBA

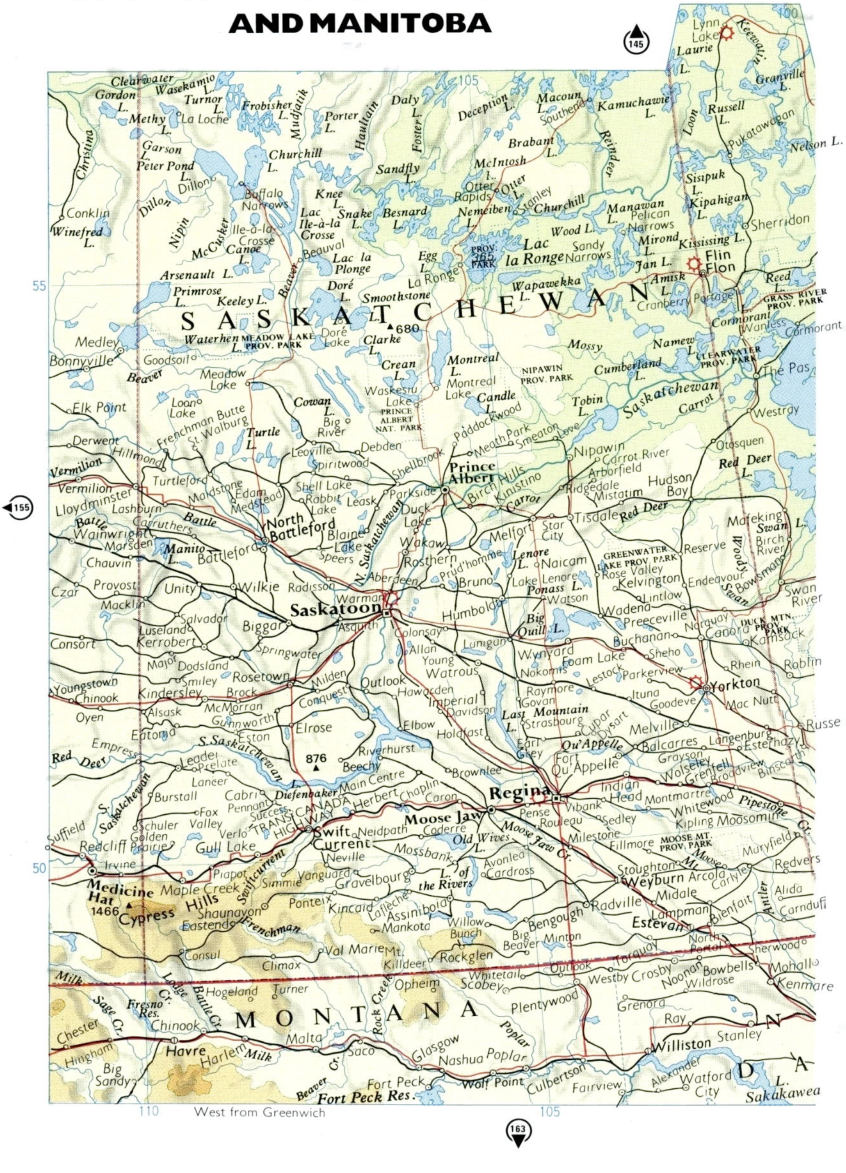

1 : 7 000 000

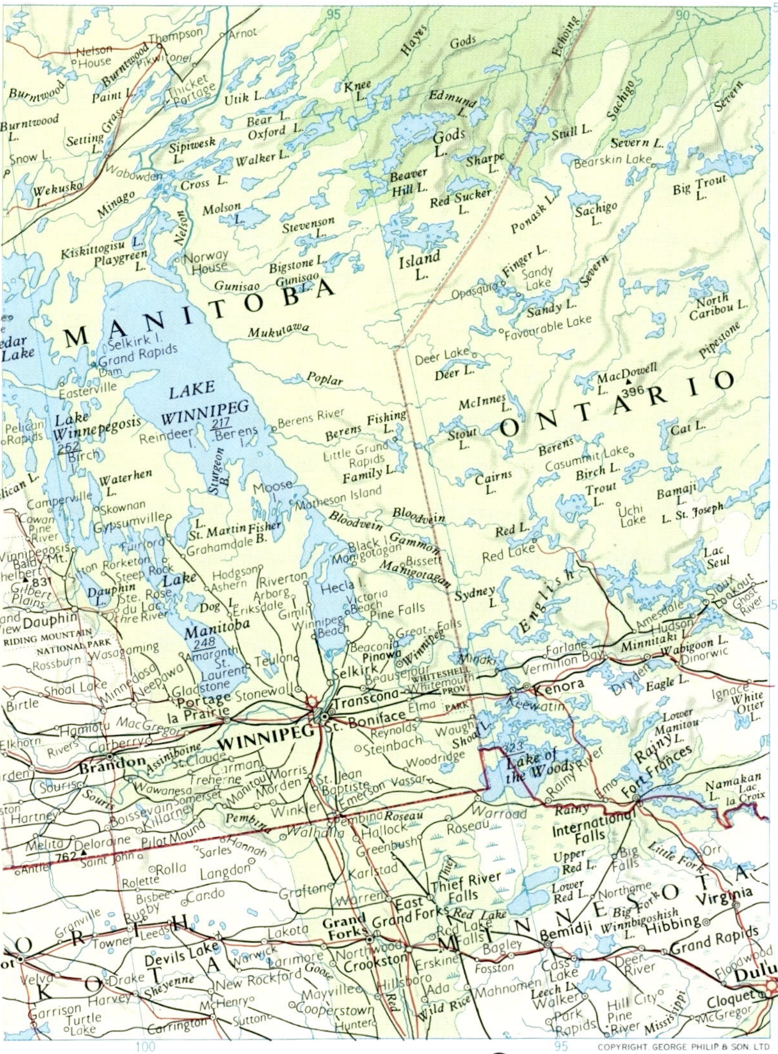
MANITOBA
ONTARIO
LAKE WINNIPEG
217
Lake Winnepegosis
252
Manitoba
248
Cedar Lake
Moose Lake
Thompson
Arnot
Nelson House
Burntwood
Pikwitonei
Thicket Portage
Paint L.
Grass
Burntwood L.
Setting L.
Snow L.
Wekusko L.
Wabowden
Minago
Utik L.
Knee L.
Hayes
Gods
Echoing
Edmund L.
Bear L.
Oxford L.
Sipiwesk L.
Walker L.
Cross L.
Gods L.
Sharpe L.
Stull L.
Sachigo
Severn
Severn L.
Bearskin Lake
Beaver Hill L.
Red Sucker L.
Big Trout L.
Molson L.
Nelson
Stevenson L.
Ponask L.
Sachigo L.
Kiskittogisu L.
Playgreen L.
Norway House
Bigstone L.
Gunisao L.
Gunisao
Island L.
Finger L.
Opasquia
Sandy Lake
Sandy L.
North Caribou L.
Mukutawa
Favourable Lake
Selkirk I.
Grand Rapids
Dam
Easterville
Deer Lake
Deer L.
Pipestone
Poplar
MacDowell L.
396
McInnes L.
Pelican Rapids
Reindeer I.
Berens I.
Berens River
Berens
Fishing L.
Stout L.
Cat L.
Birch
Little Grand Rapids
Family L.
Casummit Lake
Birch L.
Waterhen L.
Sturgeon B.
Moose I.
Matheson Island
Cairns L.
Trout L.
Bamaji L.
Pelican L.
Camperville
Skownan
Bloodvein
Uchi Lake
L. St. Joseph
Cowan
Pine River
Gypsumville
St. Martin L.
Fisher B.
Red L.
Winnipegosis
Fairford
Grahamdale
Black I.
Manigotagan
Gammon
Bissett
Red Lake
Lac Seul
Baldy Mt.
Ethelbert
Siglunes
Rorketon
Steep Rock
Hodgson
Riverton
Sioux Lookout
Ghost River
831
Gilbert Plains
Dauphin L.
Ste. Rose du Lac
Ochre River
Ashern
Dog L.
Arborg
Eriksdale
Hecla I.
Victoria Beach
Sydney L.
English
Amesdale
Grand View
Dauphin
Gimli
Pine Falls
Hudson
RIDING MOUNTAIN NATIONAL PARK
Winnipeg Beach
Great Falls
Minnitaki L.
Wabigoon L.
Dinorwic
Rossburn
Wasagaming
Amaranth
Beaconia
Pinawa
Winnipeg
Minaki
Farlane
Vermilion Bay
Dryden
Eagle L.
Ignace
White Otter L.
St. Laurent
Teulon
Selkirk
Beausejour
WHITESHELL PROV. PARK
Whitemouth
Shoal Lake
Minnedosa
Neepawa
Gladstone
Stonewall
Transcona
Kenora
Keewatin
Birtle
Portage la Prairie
St. Boniface
Elma
Lower Manitou L.
Hamiota
MacGregor
WINNIPEG
Reynolds
Waugh
Shoal L.
Elkhorn
Rivers
Carberry
Steinbach
323
Lake of the Woods
Rainy L.
Rainy River
Fort Frances
Virden
Brandon
Assiniboine
St. Claude
Carman
Treherne
Woodridge
Souris
Wawanesa
Manitou
Morris
St. Jean Baptiste
Morden
Emerson
Vassar
Emo
Namakan L.
Lac la Croix
Reston
Hartney
Boissevain
Somerset
Killarney
Winkler
Warroad
Rainy
International Falls
Melita
Deloraine
Pilot Mound
Pembina
Walhalla
Hallock
Roseau
762
Saint John
Sarles
Hannah
Greenbush
Little Fork
Orr
Antler
Rolla
Langdon
Karlstad
Upper Red L.
Big Falls
Rolette
Thief
Thief River Falls
Bisbee
Cando
Grafton
Lower Red L.
Northome
Virginia
Rugby
Warren
East Grand Forks
Big Fork
Granville
Grand Forks
Red Lake Falls
Winnibigoshish L.
Hibbing
Towner
Leeds
Lakota
Bemidji
Grand Rapids
Minot
Bagley
Devils Lake
Warwick
Larimore
Northwood
Crookston
Erskine
Fosston
Cass Lake
Deer River
Floodwood
Duluth
Velva
Drake
Sheyenne
New Rockford
Goose
Hillsboro
Mahnomen
Leech L.
Walker
Cloquet
Mayville
Ada
Garrison
Harvey
McHenry
Cooperstown
Red
Wild Rice
Hill City
Mississippi
Park Rapids
Pine River
McGregor
Turtle Lake
Carrington
Sutton
Hunter
NORTH DAKOTA
MINNESOTA
55
50
90
95
100

140
150
156

144

130
125
50
West from Greenwich
BRITISH COLUMBIA
COAST MOUNTAINS
QUEEN CHARLOTTE ISLANDS
PACIFIC OCEAN
VANCOUVER ISLAND
Dixon Entrance
Hecate Strait
Queen Charlotte Str.
Johnstone Str.
Str. of Georgia
Juan de Fuca Str.
Puget Sound
C. Muzon
C. Knox
Langara I.
Virago Sd.
Graham I.
Masset
Port Clements
Tlell
Queen Charlotte
Sandspit
Rennell Sd.
Louise I.
Tasu Sd.
Moresby I.
Lyell I.
Burnaby I.
Jedway
Kunghit I.
Rose Harbour
Duke I.
C. Chacon
Dundas I.
Rose Pt.
Stephens I.
Porcher I.
McCauley I.
Metlakatla
Pearse I.
Alice Arm
Inlet
Nass
Aiyansh
Arrandale
Port Simpson
Prince Rupert
Port Edward
Oona River
Cedarvale
Hazelton
New Hazelton
Seven Sisters 2755
Pacific
Terrace
Skeena
Zymoetz
Kitimat
Grenville Channel
Pitt I.
Principe Chan.
Banks I.
Hartley Bay
Hawkesbury I.
2755
Gil I.
Gribbell I.
Gardner Canal
Kemano
Estevan Group
Caamaño Sd.
Princess Royal I.
Aristazabal I.
Swindle I.
Laredo Sd.
Price I.
Pooley I.
Roderick I.
Kimsquit
Milbanke Sd.
Bella Bella
Hunter I.
King I.
Bella Coola
Firvale
Namu
Rivers Inlet
Calvert I.
Wadhams
Margaret Bay
Scott Is.
Sullivan Bay
Port Hardy
Quatsino
Quatsino Sd.
Brooks B.
Alert Bay
Port Alice
Gilford I.
Kelsey Bay
Checleset B.
Kyuquot
Zeballos
Campbell River
Nootka I.
Nootka
STRATHCONA PROV. PARK
Golden Hinde 2200
Courtenay
Comox
Cumberland
Fanny Bay
Flores I.
Great Central L.
Tofino
Port Alberni
Ucluelet
Barkley Sd.
Bamfield
Parksville
Nanaimo
Ladysmith
Youbou
Chemainus
Duncan
Saltspring I.
Port Renfrew
C. Flattery
C. Alava
Sekiu
Victoria
Sidney
Anacortes
Whidbey I.
Forks
Port Angeles
Port Townsend
OLYMPIC NATIONAL PARK
2428
Mt. Olympus
Bremerton
Nielton
SEATTLE
Babine
Takla Landing
Takla L.
Babine L.
Bulkley
Smithers
Telkwa
Quick
Perow
Topley
Houston
Burns Lake
Priestly
Morice L.
François L.
Ootsa
Fraser Lake
Cheslatta L.
Nechako
Eutsuk L.
TWEEDSMUIR PROV. PARK
Dean
Tetachuck L.
West Road
Mt. Downton 2365
Anahim Lake
Chilcotin
Charlotte L.
Kleena Kleene
Tatla Lake
Monarch Mt. 3533
Klinaklini
Mt. Waddington 3994
3289
Chilko L.
Chilko
Taseko
Knight Inlet
Bute Inlet
Bralorne
Powell River
Pemberton
Alta Lake
Lang Bay
Texada
Squamish
Sechelt
Gibsons
Port Mellon
GARIBALDI PROV. PARK
2957
Gott Pk.
Lillooet
Harrison L.
VANCOUVER
North Vancouver
New Westminster
Port Coquitlam
Haney
Mission City
Abbotsford
Blaine
Chilliwack
Hope
Bellingham
Mt. Baker 3284
Burlington
Newhalem
Concrete
Mount Vernon
Darrington
Arlington
Glacier Pk. 3211
Everett
Snohomish
Skykomish
Williston Lake
Germansen Landing
Manson Creek
Tchentlo L.
Nation
Chuchi L.
Inzana L.
Mackenzie
McLeod Lake
Tezzeron L.
Pinchi L.
Stuart L.
Fort St. James
Salmon
Stuart
Vanderhoof
Crooked
Summit Lake
Prince George
Chilako
Woodpecker
Strathnaver
Nazko
Quesnel
Alexandria
Marguerite
Williams Lake
Alexis Creek
Springhouse
Big Cr.
Dog Creek
Fraser
Lillooet
Lytton
Boston Bar
North Bend
Spuzzum

171

1 : 7 000 000

145

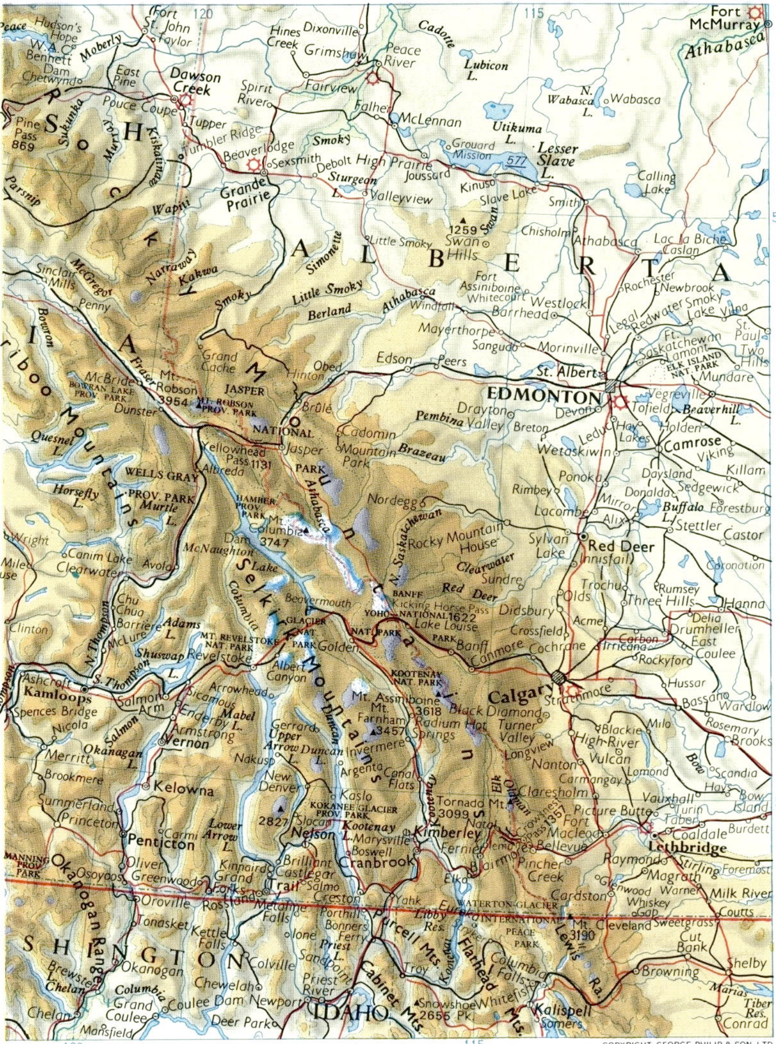

Peace
Hudson's Hope
W.A.C. Bennett Dam
Chetwynd
Moberly
Fort St. John
Taylor
120
Dawson Creek
East Pine
Pouce Coupe
Tupper
Pine Pass 869
Sukunka
Murray
Kiskatinaw
Tumbler Ridge
Parsnip
Hines Creek
Dixonville
Grimshaw
Peace River
Cadotte
Lubicon L.
Fairview
Spirit River
Falher
McLennan
Beaverlodge
Sexsmith
Debolt
High Prairie
Joussard
Smoky
Sturgeon L.
Grande Prairie
Valleyview
Grouard Mission
Utikuma L.
Lesser Slave L.
N. Wabasca L.
Wabasca
115
Fort McMurray
Athabasca
Calling Lake
Smith
Kinuso
Slave Lake
Swan
1259
Swan Hills
Chisholm
Athabasca
Lac la Biche
Caslan
Little Smoky
Wapiti
Simonette
Narraway
Kakwa
Smoky
Little Smoky
Berland
Athabasca
Windfall
Fort Assiniboine
Whitecourt
Westlock
Barrhead
Rochester
Newbrook
Redwater
Smoky Lake
Vilna
St. Paul
Two Hills
Legal
Ft. Saskatchewan
Lamont
ELK ISLAND NAT. PARK
Mundare
Mayerthorpe
Sanguda
Morinville
St. Albert
EDMONTON
Vegreville
Tofield
Beaverhill L.
Holden
Devon
Edson
Peers
Obed
Hinton
Grand Cache
ALBERTA
Sinclair Mills
McGregor
Penny
Bowron
Fraser
McBride
BOWRAN LAKE PROV. PARK
Dunster
Mt. Robson 3954
MT. ROBSON PROV. PARK
JASPER NATIONAL PARK
Brûlé
Drayton Valley
Breton
Pembina
Cadomin
Mountain Park
Brazeau
Jasper
Yellowhead Pass 1131
Albreda
Leduc
Hay Lakes
Camrose
Viking
Killam
Wetaskiwin
Daysland
Sedgewick
Ponoka
Rimbey
Donalda
Forestburg
Buffalo L.
Mirror
Alix
Stettler
Castor
Lacombe
Nordegg
Rocky Mountain House
Sylvan Lake
Red Deer
Innisfail
Coronation
Quesnel L.
Cariboo Mountains
WELLS GRAY PROV. PARK
Horsefly L.
Murtle L.
HAMBER PROV. PARK
Mt. Columbia 3747
Athabasca
N. Saskatchewan
Clearwater
Red Deer
Sundre
Wright
100 Mile House
Canim Lake
Clearwater
Avola
McNaughton Lake
Mica Dam
Selkirk Mountains
Columbia
Beavermouth
BANFF NATIONAL PARK
Kicking Horse Pass 1622
Lake Louise
Didsbury
Olds
Trochu
Rumsey
Three Hills
Hanna
Chu Chua
Barriere
N. Thompson
Adams L.
Clinton
McLure
GLACIER NAT. PARK
YOHO NATIONAL PARK
Golden
MT. REVELSTOKE NAT. PARK
Revelstoke
Shuswap L.
Crossfield
Acme
Delia
Drumheller
East Coulee
Carbon
Irricana
Rockyford
Cochrane
Banff
Canmore
Thompson
Ashcroft
Kamloops
S. Thompson
Spences Bridge
Salmon Arm
Sicamous
Albert Canyon
Arrowhead
KOOTENAY NAT. PARK
Calgary
Strathmore
Hussar
Bassano
Wardlow
Nicola
Salmon
Enderby
Mabel L.
Armstrong
Vernon
Mt. Assiniboine 3618
Black Diamond
Turner Valley
Mt. Farnham 3457
Radium Hot Springs
Gerrard
Upper Arrow L.
Duncan L.
Duncan
Invermere
Blackie
Milo
High River
Rosemary
Brooks
Longview
Merritt
Okanagan L.
Nakusp
Argenta
Vulcan
Nanton
Bow
Scandia
Brookmere
Kelowna
New Denver
Canal Flats
Kootenay
Lomond
Carmangay
Claresholm
Hays
Vauxhall
Bow Island
Summerland
Kaslo
KOKANEE GLACIER PROV. PARK
2827
Tornado Mt. 3099
Elk
Oldman
Turin
Taber
Picture Butte
Princeton
Slocan
Kootenay L.
Nelson
Marysville
Kimberley
Crowsnest Pass 1357
Fort Macleod
Coaldale
Burdett
Lethbridge
Penticton
Carmi
Lower Arrow L.
Fernie
Blairmore
Bellevue
Pincher Creek
Raymond
Stirling
Foremost
MANNING PROV. PARK
Okanogan Range
Oliver
Osoyoos
Greenwood
Kinnaird
Grand Forks
Brilliant
Castlegar
Trail
Salmo
Boswell
Cranbrook
Creston
Elko
Magrath
Warner
Milk River
Glenwood
Cardston
WATERTON-GLACIER INTERNATIONAL PEACE PARK
Whiskey Gap
Coutts
Oroville
Rossland
Metaline Falls
Porthill
Bonners Ferry
Yahk
Libby Res.
Eureka
Mt. Cleveland 3190
Sweetgrass
Tonasket
Kettle Falls
Ione
Purcell Mts.
Kootenai
Flathead
Lewis Ra.
Cut Bank
WASHINGTON
Colville
Priest L.
Sandpoint
Troy
Columbia Falls
Shelby
Browning
Brewster
Okanogan
Chewelah
Cabinet Mts.
Marias
Chelan
Columbia
Grand Coulee
Coulee Dam
Newport
Priest River
Snowshoe Pk. 2655
Whitefish
Kalispell
Tiber Res.
Chelan
Mansfield
Deer Park
IDAHO
Flathead Mts.
Somers
Conrad
120
115
50
55

152

162

140

163

Berens
Lake Winnipeg
MANITOBA
Gimli
Winnipeg
Winnipeg
Emerson
Lake of the Woods
Kenora
Trout Lake
L. St. Joseph
Albany
English
L. Seul
Sioux Lookout
Lake Nipigon
Nakina
Kenogami
Longlac
Hearst
Missinaibi
Abitibi
Mattagami
Moosonee
Moose
O N T A R I O
C A N A D A
Oba
Nipigon
White River
Franz
Timmins
Ignace
Seine
Rainy L.
Fort Frances
Thunder Bay
I. St. Ignace
Wawa
Michipicoten
Michipicoten I.
I. Royale
Lake Superior
183 above S. L.
Calumet
Laurium
Keweenaw Bay
Whitefish Bay
Sault Ste. Marie
Sault Ste. Marie
North Chan.
Grafton
Red
Thief River Falls
Grand Forks
Red Lake
Bemidji
Hibbing
Virginia
Two Harbors
Leech L.
Apostle Is.
Moorhead
Fargo
MINNESOTA
Duluth
Superior
Bessemer
Ironwood
Ishpeming
Marquette
Ashland
Escanaba
Manistique
Cheboygan
Fergus Falls
Mississippi
Brainerd
Rhinelander
Iron Mt.
Big Stone Lake
St. Cloud
Anoka
Merrill
Antigo
Menominee
Lake Huron
Saginaw Bay
177
Coteau des Prairies
Willmar
Stillwater
Chippewa Falls
Wausau
Traverse City
Watertown
Minneapolis
St. Paul
Red Wing
Eau Claire
Stevens Point
Green Bay
Manistee
Cadillac
Minnesota
New Ulm
Brookings
Faribault
Winona
Wisconsin Rapids
Appleton
Ludington
Mankato
WISCONSIN
Manitowoc
Muskegon
Midland
Bay City
Madison
Owatonna
Rochester
La Crosse
Fond du Lac
Saginaw
Flint
Port Huron
Fairmont
Austin
Sheboygan
177
Lake Michigan
Muskegon
Baraboo
Beaver Dam
Owosso
Pontiac
Sioux Falls
Worthington
Albert Lea
Watertown
Milwaukee
Grand Rapids
Lansing
Yankton
Spencer
Des Moines
Mason City
Charles City
Wisconsin
Madison
Racine
Battle Creek
Ann Arbor
Windsor
Big Sioux
Cherokee
Webster City
Waterloo
Janesville
Beloit
Kenosha
Kalamazoo
Jackson
Monroe
Sioux City
Fort Dodge
Cedar Falls
Cedar Rapids
Dubuque
Rockford
Waukegan
Evanston
St. Joseph
I O W A
Elgin
CHICAGO
Toledo
Norfolk
Ames
Marshalltown
Iowa City
Clinton
Dixon
Aurora
Joliet
South Bend
Elkhart
Columbus
Fremont
Des Moines
Newton
Davenport
Moline
Ottawa
Hammond
Gary
Ft. Wayne
Findlay
Omaha
Council Bluffs
Oskaloosa
Rock Island
Kewanee
Streator
Kankakee
Wabash
Huntington
Lima
Marion
Ottumwa
Galesburg
Kokomo
Marion
Lincoln
Red Oak
Creston
Burlington
Peoria
Bloomington
Lafayette
Muncie
Piqua
Nebraska City
Shenandoah
Keokuk
Pekin
Danville
Anderson
Dayton
Illinois
Champaign
Urbana
Frankfort
Richmond
Springfield
Beatrice
Kirksville
Jacksonville
Springfield
Decatur
Indianapolis
Kettering
St. Joseph
Chillicothe
Quincy
Hannibal
Mississippi
ILLINOIS
INDIANA
Terre Haute
Hamilton
Cincinnati
Atchison
Moberly
Mattoon
Covington
Newport
Manhattan
Leavenworth
Kansas City
Marshall
Columbia
Mexico
Alton
Granite City
Bloomington
Bedford
Maysville
Junction City
Topeka
Kansas
Lawrence
Kansas City
Missouri
St. Charles
St. Louis
E. St. Louis
Wabash
Vincennes
Jeffersonville
Frankfort
Winchester
Sedalia
Jefferson City
Centralia
New Albany
Lexington
Ottawa
Belleville
Mt. Vernon
Evansville
Louisville
Emporia
MISSOURI
W. Frankfort
Danville
Richmond
KANSAS
Osage
L. of the Ozarks
Rolla
Henderson
Owensboro
KENTUCKY
Newton
El Dorado
Fort Scott
Nevada
Plateau
Marion
Somerset
Wichita
Lebanon
Cape Girardeau
Ohio
Green
Bowling Green
Winfield
Parsons
Pittsburg
Springfield
Ozark
Cairo
Hopkinsville
Middlesboro
Paducah
50
45
40
95
90
85
West from Greenwich

158

1 : 12 000 000

141

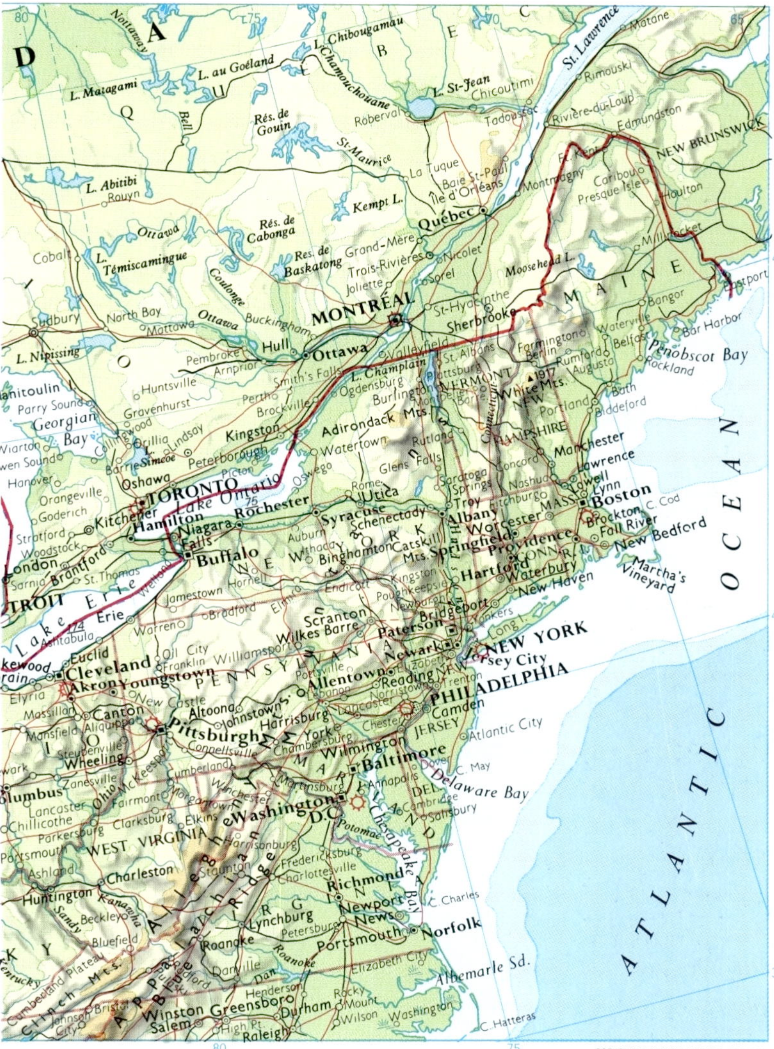

ATLANTIC OCEAN
NEW YORK
PHILADELPHIA
MONTREAL
TORONTO
Boston
Québec
Ottawa
Baltimore
Washington D.C.
Pittsburgh
Cleveland
Buffalo
Rochester
Syracuse
Albany
Hartford
Providence
Richmond
Norfolk
Newport News
Portsmouth
Hamilton
Kingston
Sherbrooke
Trois-Rivières
Chicoutimi
Rimouski
Rivière-du-Loup
Edmundston
NEW BRUNSWICK
MAINE
VERMONT
NEW HAMPSHIRE
MASS.
CONN.
R.I.
NEW JERSEY
PENNSYLVANIA
MARYLAND
DEL.
VIRGINIA
WEST VIRGINIA
St. Lawrence
Lake Ontario
Lake Erie
L. Champlain
L. St-Jean
L. Abitibi
L. Nipissing
Georgian Bay
Manitoulin I.
Adirondack Mts.
White Mts.
Catskill Mts.
Appalachian Mts.
Blue Ridge
Allegheny Mts.
Cumberland Plateau
Chesapeake Bay
Delaware Bay
Penobscot Bay
Albemarle Sd.
Long I.
Martha's Vineyard
C. Cod
C. May
C. Charles
C. Hatteras
Bar Harbor
Bangor
Moosehead L.
Portland
Manchester
Lawrence
Lowell
Lynn
Worcester
Springfield
New Haven
Bridgeport
Paterson
Newark
Jersey City
Trenton
Camden
Atlantic City
Wilmington
Annapolis
Allentown
Reading
Harrisburg
Lancaster
York
Scranton
Wilkes Barre
Binghamton
Utica
Schenectady
Troy
Erie
Youngstown
Akron
Canton
Wheeling
Columbus
Charleston
Huntington
Roanoke
Lynchburg
Winston Salem
Greensboro
Durham
Raleigh
Kitchener
London
Niagara Falls
Sudbury
North Bay
Hull
Oshawa
Peterborough
COPYRIGHT. GEORGE PHILIP & SON. LTD.

159

156

161

95
90
40
35
30
Nebraska City
Shenandoah
Beatrice
Kirksville
St. Joseph
Chillicothe
Atchison
Manhattan
Junction City
Leavenworth
Topeka
Kansas
Kansas City
Lawrence
Ottawa
Emporia
KANSAS
Newton
El Dorado
Fort Scott
Wichita
Winfield
Parsons
Arkansas City
Bartlesville
Ponca City
Tulsa
Stillwater
Cushing
OKLAHOMA
Shawnee
Seminole
Canadian
Ardmore
Durant
Sherman
Denton
Fort Worth
Dallas
Ennis
Waxahachie
Corsicana
Hillsboro
Waco
Temple
TEXAS
Brazos
Bryan
Houston
Pasadena
Galveston
Cuero
Victoria
Freeport
Port Lavaca
Matagorda I.
Aransas Pass
Padre I.
Laguna Madre
San Benito
Brownsville
Rio Grande
West from Greenwich
Keokuk
Quincy
Hannibal
Moberly
Marshall
Mexico
Columbia
Missouri
Sedalia
Jefferson City
St. Charles
St. Louis
E. St. Louis
MISSOURI
Osage
L. of the Ozarks
Rolla
Nevada
Lebanon
Springfield
Pittsburg
Joplin
Carthage
Ozark Plateau
Neosho
Muskogee
Fayetteville
Boston Mts.
Van Buren
Russellville
Fort Smith
McAlester
ARKANSAS
Little Rock
Ouachita Mts.
Hot Springs
Arkansas
Stuttgart
Pine Bluff
White
Newport
Conway
Hope
Red River
Paris
Texarkana
Camden
El Dorado
Ouachita
Greenville
Terrell
Marshall
Tyler
Longview
Jacksonville
Palestine
Nacogdoches
Lufkin
Trinity
Neches
Huntsville
Sabine
Minden
Shreveport
Monroe
Natchitoches
Alexandria
De Ridder
LOUISIANA
Jennings
Lafayette
Baton Rouge
Lake Charles
Beaumont
Orange
Port Arthur
New Iberia
Marsh I.
Atchafalaya B.
Morgan City
Houma
New Orleans
Lake Pontchartrain
Chandeleur Is.
Breton Sd.
Delta of the Mississippi
Choctawhatchee B.
Mississippi
Illinois
Pekin
Bloomington
Champaign
Danville
Urbana
Springfield
Decatur
ILLINOIS
Mattoon
Alton
Granite City
Belleville
Centralia
Mt. Vernon
W. Frankfort
Marion
Cape Girardeau
Cairo
Poplar Bluff
Paragould
Jonesboro
Blytheville
Union City
Memphis
Wabash
Vincennes
Evansville
Henderson
Owensboro
Ohio
Paducah
Mayfield
Hopkinsville
Clarksville
Frankfort
Anderson
Dayton
Richmond
Springfield
Kettering
Indianapolis
INDIANA
Terre Haute
Hamilton
Cincinnati
Newport
Covington
Bloomington
Bedford
Maysville
Jeffersonville
New Albany
Frankfort
Louisville
Winchester
Lexington
Richmond
Danville
KENTUCKY
Somerset
Green
Bowling Green
Cumberland
Middlesboro
Oak Ridge
Knoxville
Nashville
Lebanon
Dyersburg
TENNESSEE
Jackson
Columbia
Athens
Cleveland
Chattanooga
Florence
Huntsville
Dalton
Corinth
Decatur
Tennessee
Cumberland Plateau
Rome
Gadsden
Marietta
Atlanta
East
Tupelo
Clarksdale
Cleveland
Greenwood
Columbus
Anniston
Birmingham
Bessemer
Newnan
Tuscaloosa
La Grange
Greenville
MISSISSIPPI
ALABAMA
Yazoo
Yazoo City
Canton
Meridian
Demopolis
Selma
Phenix City
Columbus
Montgomery
Vicksburg
Jackson
Tombigbee
Alabama
Troy
Brookhaven
Laurel
Greenville
Natchez
McComb
Hattiesburg
Chattahoochee
Andalusia
Dothan
Bogalusa
Picayune
Gulfport
Biloxi
Mobile
Pascagoula
Pensacola
Panama City
C. S. Blas
Apalachicola
St. Georges I.
GULF OF MEXICO

1 : 12 000 000

157

Columbus
Lancaster
Ohio
Chillicothe
Parkersburg
Portsmouth
Ashland
Huntington
Fairmont
Clarksburg
Elkins
WEST VIRGINIA
Charleston
Kanawha
Sandy
Beckley
Bluefield
Allegheny Mts.
Washington
D.C.
MARYLAND
DEL.
Cambridge
Salisbury
Potomac
Chesapeake Bay
Harrisonburg
Staunton
Charlottesville
Fredericksburg
Richmond
Newport News
C. Charles
Norfolk
Portsmouth
Petersburg
Lynchburg
Roanoke
Danville
Dan
Elizabeth City
Albemarle Sd.
Henderson
Rocky Mount
Durham
Winston Salem
Greensboro
High Pt.
Raleigh
Wilson
Washington
Pamlico Sd.
C. Hatteras
Kinston
Goldsboro
Neuse
New Bern
Raleigh Bay
Salisbury
NORTH CAROLINA
Concord
Fayetteville
Charlotte
Asheville
2037
Johnson City
Bristol
Morristown
Clinch Mts.
Kentucky
Spartanburg
Greenville
Union
Rock Hill
Cape Fear
Onslow Bay
Wilmington
C. Fear
Pedee
Florence
Anderson
Gainesville
Greenwood
Columbia
Sumter
SOUTH CAROLINA
Long Bay
Georgetown
Santee
C. Royal
Athens
Decatur
Augusta
Orangeburg
Charleston
Charleston Harb.
Griffin
Milledgeville
Savannah
Macon
Dublin
Oconee
Altamaha
Savannah
Cordele
Albany
Fitzgerald
Waycross
Brunswick
Flint
Moultrie
Bainbridge
Valdosta
Thomasville
St. Johns R.
Jacksonville
Tallahassee
Lake City
St. Augustine
Palatka
Daytona Beach
Apalachee B.
Gainesville
L. George
Ocala
C. Canaveral
Sanford
Orlando
Indian River
Lakeland
Tampa
Plant City
Clearwater
St. Petersburg
Tampa B.
Bradenton
Sarasota
Arcadia
L. Okeechobee
Ft. Pierce
West Palm Beach
Charlotte Harb.
Ft. Myers
Everglades
Fort Lauderdale
Miami
Coral Gables
C. Sable
Florida Bay
Florida Keys
Key West
Florida Str.
Grand Bahama I.
Freeport
Little Abaco
Gt. Abaco
N.W. Providence Chan.
N.E. Providence Channel
BAHAMAS
Nassau
New Providence
Eleuthera I.
Cat I.
Exuma Sound
Andros I.
Long I.
ATLANTIC OCEAN
75
70
35
30
25
85
80

178

162

PACIFIC OCEAN
San Francisco
Golden Gate
Vallejo
Richmond
Berkeley
Oakland
San Mateo
Santa Clara
San Jose
Santa Cruz
Monterey
Salinas
Sacramento
Stockton
Modesto
Merced
Yosemite National Park
Sierra Nevada
Fresno
Hanford
Visalia
Sequoia Nat. Park
Tulare
Mt. Whitney
4418
Coast Ranges
Santa Lucia Ra.
Paso Robles
San Luis Obispo
Sta. Maria
CALIFORNIA
Bakersfield
Tehachapi Pass
1216
Santa Barbara
Pt. Conception
S. Cruz I.
Sta. Rosa I.
Hollywood
Santa Monica
LOS ANGELES
Glendale
Pasadena
Alhambra
Mojave Desert
Barstow
3506
San Bernardino
Redlands
Riverside
Santa Barbara Is.
Long Beach
Anaheim
Santa Ana
S. Nicolas I.
Sta. Catalina
S. Clemente I.
San Diego
Tijuana
Salton Sea
-72
Brawley
El Centro
Mexicali
Yuma
B. de Todos Santos
Ensenada
Walker Lake
Hawthorne
White Mts.
Owens Lake
Death Valley
-86
NEVADA
Tonopah
Ely
3982
Wheeler Pk.
Las Vegas
Lake Mead
Virgin
Colorado
Colorado Desert
Havasu Lake
UTAH
Sevier
Sevier L.
Richfield
Nephi
3710
Cedar City
St. George
Zion Nat. Park
Page
Grand Canyon Nat. Park
Grand Canyon
Painted Desert
Humphreys Pk.
3851
Flagstaff
Kingman
Prescott
Verde
Mogollon
ARIZONA
Phoenix
Salt
Mesa
Gila
Globe
Tucson
Nogales
Magdalena
SONORA
Ures
Hermosillo
Guaymas
Ciudad Obregón
Golfo de California
I. Ángel de la Guarda
I. Tiburón
BAJA CALIFORNIA
BAJA CALIFORNIA NORTE
BAJA CALIFORNIA SUR
3078
S. Quintín
C. S. Quintín
Guadalupe (Mex.)
Bahía Sebastián Vizcaíno
I. de Cedros
Punta Eugenia
Sta. Rosalía
Mulejé
Punta Concepción
La Purísima
125
120
115
110
35
30
HAWAII
1:10 000 000
0
100
200 km
Kauai
Mana
Lihue
Niihau
Kaula
Kauai Channel
Oahu
Kahana
Wahiawa
Honolulu
Pearl City
Pearl Harbor
Kaiwi Channel
Molokai
Kalaupapa
Lanai
Lahaina
Maui
Paia
Hana
Haleakala 3056
Makena
Kahoolawe
Hawaiian Islands
Alenuihaha Channel
Mahukona
Kawaihae
4205
Mauna Kea
Mauna Loa
4170
Hawaii
Hilo
Keaau
Kailua
Glenwood
Kilauea Crater
1247
Pahala
158
156
160
22
20
West from Greenwich

1 : 12 000 000

163

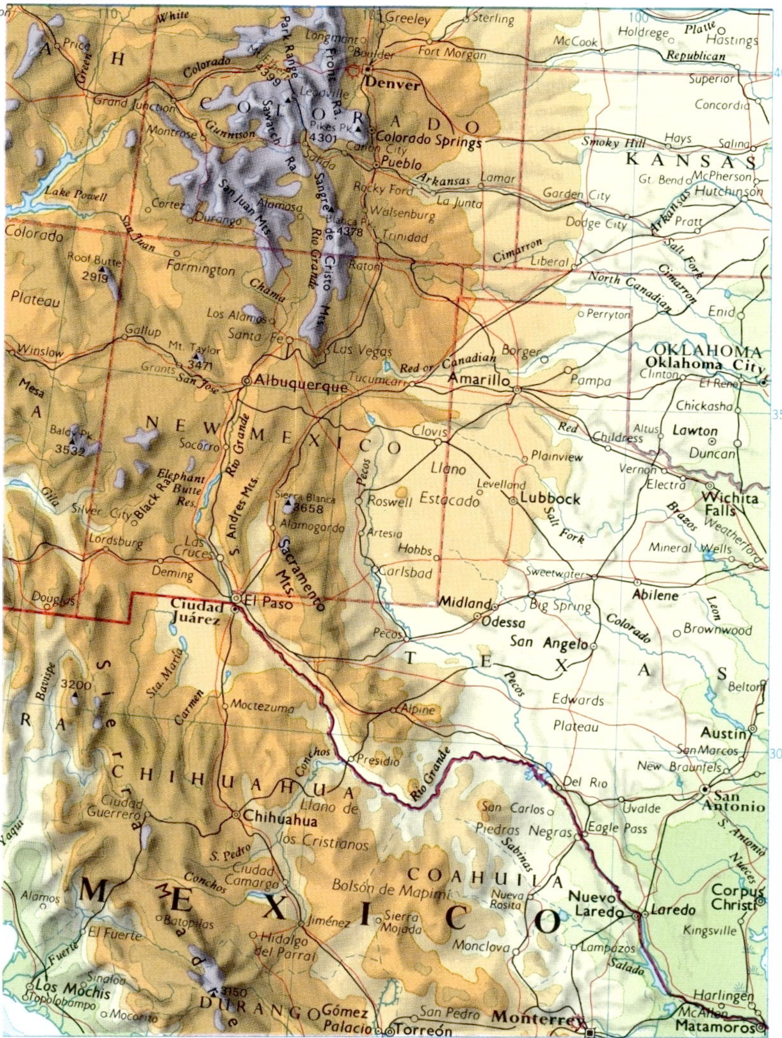
Greeley
Sterling
Holdrege
Platte
Hastings
Longmont
Boulder
Fort Morgan
McCook
Republican
Denver
Superior
Concordia
Price
Green
White
Colorado
Mt. Elbert 4399
Park Range
Front Ra.
Leadville
Grand Junction
C O L O R A D O
Sawatch Ra.
Pikes Pk. 4301
Colorado Springs
Smoky Hill
Hays
Salina
Montrose
Gunnison
Cañon City
Pueblo
K A N S A S
Salida
Sangre
Arkansas
Lamar
Gt. Bend
McPherson
Lake Powell
San Juan Mts.
Alamosa
Rocky Ford
La Junta
Garden City
Hutchinson
Cortez
Durango
Blanca Pk. 4378
Walsenburg
Dodge City
Arkansas
Pratt
Colorado
San Juan
de
Cristo
Mts.
Trinidad
Salt Fork
Rio Grande
Cimarron
Liberal
Roof Butte 2919
Farmington
Raton
North Canadian
Cimarron
Chama
Plateau
Los Alamos
Perryton
Enid
Gallup
Santa Fe
Las Vegas
Borger
OKLAHOMA
Winslow
Mt. Taylor 3471
Red or Canadian
Oklahoma City
Grants
San Jose
Albuquerque
Tucumcari
Amarillo
Pampa
Clinton
El Reno
Mesa
Chickasha
A
Baldy Pk. 3532
N E W
M E X I C O
Clovis
Red
Childress
Altus
Lawton
Socorro
Plainview
Duncan
Rio Grande
Llano
Vernon
Electra
Elephant Butte Res.
S. Andres Mts.
Levelland
Wichita Falls
Gila
Black Ra.
Pecos
Sierra Blanca 3658
Roswell
Estacado
Lubbock
Silver City
Alamogordo
Salt Fork
Brazos
Weatherford
Lordsburg
Las Cruces
Sacramento Mts.
Artesia
Hobbs
Mineral Wells
Deming
Carlsbad
Sweetwater
Douglas
Ciudad Juárez
El Paso
Midland
Big Spring
Abilene
Leon
Odessa
Colorado
Brownwood
Pecos
San Angelo
T E X A S
Sta. María
Pecos
Bavispe
3200
S i e r r a
Belton
Edwards
Carmen
Moctezuma
Alpine
Plateau
R A
Austin
Conchos
Presidio
San Marcos
C H I H U A H U A
Rio Grande
New Braunfels
Del Rio
San Antonio
Ciudad Guerrero
Llano de
Chihuahua
San Carlos
Uvalde
Yaqui
los Cristianos
Piedras Negras
Eagle Pass
S. Antonio
S. Pedro
Sabinas
Nueces
Conchos
Ciudad Camargo
C O A H U I L A
Bolsón de Mapimí
Nuevo Rosita
Nuevo Laredo
Laredo
Corpus Christi
Alamos
M E X I C O
Batopilas
Jiménez
Sierra Mojada
Kingsville
El Fuerte
Madre
Hidalgo del Parral
Monclova
Lampazos
Fuerte
Salada
Sinaloa
Los Mochis
Topolobampo
3150
Harlingen
DURANGO
Gómez Palacio
San Pedro
McAllen
Mocorito
Torreón
Monterrey
Matamoros
110
100
40
35
30
105
West from Greenwich

158

174

142

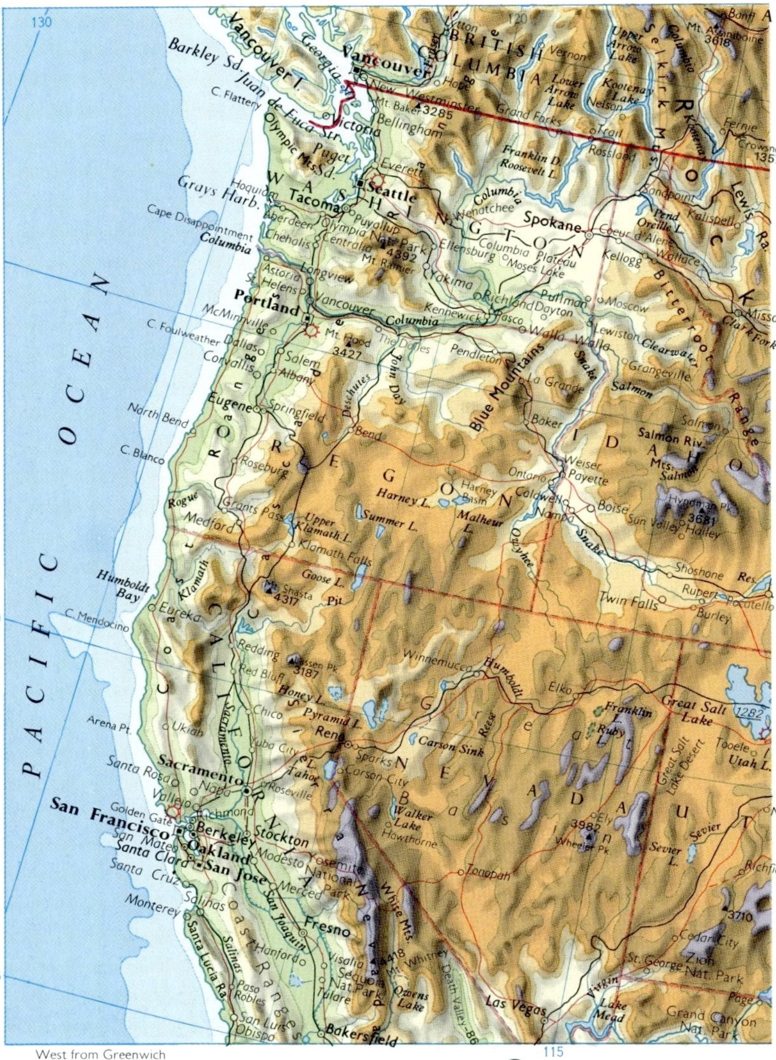
130
120
115
45
40
35
PACIFIC OCEAN
BRITISH COLUMBIA
WASHINGTON
OREGON
IDAHO
CALIFORNIA
NEVADA
UTAH
Vancouver I.
Vancouver
Victoria
Barkley Sd.
Juan de Fuca Str.
Georgia Str.
C. Flattery
New Westminster
Mt. Baker 3285
Bellingham
Olympic Mts.
Puget Sd.
Everett
Seattle
Tacoma
Grays Harb.
Hoquiam
Aberdeen
Olympia
Puyallup
Cape Disappointment
Columbia
Chehalis
Centralia
Mt. Rainier Nat. Park
4392
Mt. Rainier
Ellensburg
Wenatchee
Columbia Plateau
Moses Lake
Yakima
Spokane
Coeur d'Alene
Kellogg
Wallace
Astoria
St. Helens
Longview
Vancouver
Portland
McMinnville
Kennewick
Richland
Pasco
Dayton
Pullman
Moscow
Lewiston
Clearwater
Walla Walla
C. Foulweather
Dallas
Corvallis
Salem
Albany
Mt. Hood
3427
The Dalles
Pendleton
John Day
Deschutes
Blue Mountains
La Grande
Snake
Salmon
Grangeville
Eugene
Springfield
North Bend
C. Blanco
Roseburg
Bend
Baker
Salmon Riv. Mts.
Salmon
Weiser
Payette
Ontario
Harney L.
Harney Basin
Malheur L.
Caldwell
Nampa
Boise
Hyndman Pk.
3681
Sun Valley
Hailey
Rogue
Grants Pass
Medford
Upper Klamath L.
Klamath Falls
Summer L.
Owyhee
Goose L.
Humboldt Bay
Klamath
Mt. Shasta
4317
Pit
Eureka
C. Mendocino
Redding
Lassen Pk.
3187
Red Bluff
Honey L.
Chico
Pyramid L.
Winnemucca
Humboldt
Elko
Great Salt Lake
1282
Franklin L.
Ruby L.
Arena Pt.
Ukiah
Yuba City
Sacramento
Reno
Sparks
Carson City
Carson Sink
Reese
Tooele
Utah L.
Great Salt Lake Desert
Santa Rosa
Napa
Vallejo
Roseville
L. Tahoe
Golden Gate
Richmond
San Francisco
Berkeley
Oakland
San Mateo
Stockton
Walker Lake
Hawthorne
Ely
3982
Wheeler Pk.
Sevier L.
Sevier
Santa Clara
San Jose
Modesto
Yosemite National Park
Merced
Tonopah
Richfield
Santa Cruz
Monterey
Salinas
San Joaquin
Fresno
White Mts.
3710
Cedar City
Zion Nat. Park
St. George
Hanford
Visalia
Sequoia Nat. Park
Tulare
4418
Mt. Whitney
Owens Lake
Death Valley
Santa Lucia Ra.
Paso Robles
San Luis Obispo
Coast Ranges
Bakersfield
Las Vegas
Virgin
Lake Mead
Grand Canyon Nat. Park
Page
Sierra Nevada
Great Basin
Cascade Range
Coast Ra.
Lytton
Vernon
Hope
Grand Forks
Upper Arrow Lake
Lower Arrow Lake
Kootenay Lake
Nelson
Trail
Rossland
Franklin D. Roosevelt L.
Columbia
Selkirk Mts.
Mt. Assiniboine
3618
Banff
Fernie
Crowsnest
1357
Sandpoint
Pend Oreille L.
Kalispell
Lewis Ra.
Bitterroot Range
Clark Fork
Missoula
ROCKY
Shoshone
Rupert
Twin Falls
Burley
Pocatello

West from Greenwich

160

1 : 12 000 000

143

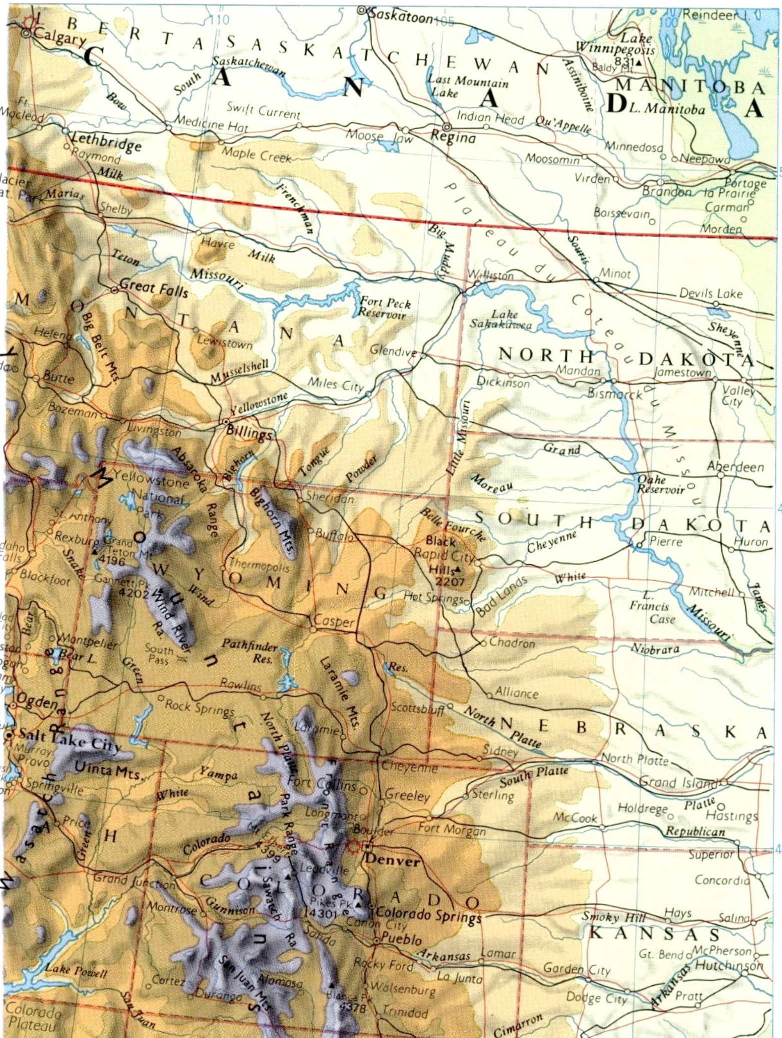

Calgary
Saskatoon
Reindeer L.
Lake Winnipegosis
Baldy Mt.
831
MANITOBA
SASKATCHEWAN
CANADA
South Saskatchewan
Bow
Last Mountain Lake
Assiniboine
L. Manitoba
Swift Current
Medicine Hat
Indian Head
Qu'Appelle
Ft. Macleod
Lethbridge
Raymond
Moose Jaw
Regina
Maple Creek
Moosomin
Minnedosa
Neepawa
Virden
Brandon
Portage la Prairie
Carman
Boissevain
Morden
Milk
Glacier Nat. Park
Marias
Shelby
Frenchman
plateau du Coteau du Missouri
Big Muddy
Souris
Havre
Milk
Teton
Missouri
Williston
Minot
Devils Lake
Great Falls
Fort Peck Reservoir
Lake Sakakawea
Sheyenne
MONTANA
Big Belt Mts.
Helena
Lewistown
Glendive
NORTH DAKOTA
Butte
Musselshell
Miles City
Mandan
Dickinson
Bismarck
Jamestown
Valley City
Bozeman
Yellowstone
Livingston
Billings
Little Missouri
Grand
Absaroka Range
Bighorn
Tongue
Powder
Aberdeen
Yellowstone National Park
Oahe Reservoir
Moreau
Sheridan
Bighorn Mts.
Belle Fourche
SOUTH DAKOTA
St. Anthony
Rexburg
Buffalo
Black Hills
Rapid City
2207
Cheyenne
Pierre
Huron
Idaho Falls
Grand Teton Mt.
4196
Snake
Thermopolis
Blackfoot
Gannett Pk.
4202
WYOMING
Wind
Hot Springs
Bad Lands
White
Mitchell
James
Wind River Ra.
L. Francis Case
Missouri
Malad City
Bear
Casper
Chadron
Montpelier
Preston
Logan
Bear L.
South Pass
Pathfinder Res.
Laramie Mts.
Res.
Niobrara
Green
Rawlins
Alliance
Ogden
Rock Springs
Scottsbluff
North Platte
NEBRASKA
Salt Lake City
Murray
Provo
Laramie
Sidney
North Platte
Uinta Mts.
Cheyenne
Springville
Yampa
South Platte
Grand Island
White
Fort Collins
Greeley
Sterling
Holdrege
Platte
Hastings
Longmont
McCook
Wasatch Range
Price
Boulder
Fort Morgan
Republican
UTAH
Green
Colorado
Park Range
Front Range
Denver
Superior
Mt. Elbert
4399
Leadville
Grand Junction
Sawatch Ra.
ROCKY MOUNTAINS
COLORADO
Concordia
Montrose
Gunnison
Pikes Pk.
14301
Colorado Springs
Smoky Hill
Hays
Salina
Cañon City
KANSAS
Salida
Pueblo
Arkansas
Lamar
Gt. Bend
McPherson
Rocky Ford
Lake Powell
La Junta
Garden City
Hutchinson
Alamosa
Cortez
Durango
San Juan Mts.
Walsenburg
Arkansas
Blanca Pk.
4378
Dodge City
Pratt
Colorado Plateau
San Juan
Trinidad
Cimarron
110
105
100
50
45
40

156

161

BOSTON, NEW YORK, WASHINGTON

148
151
167

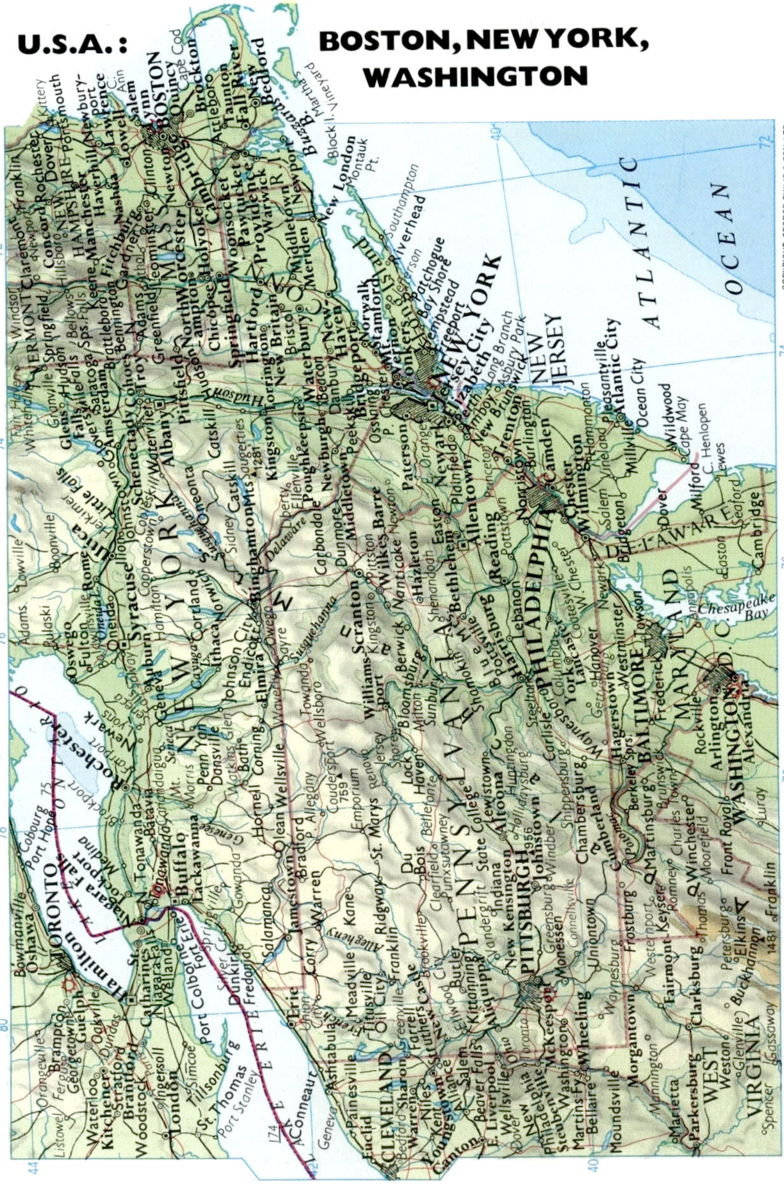
ATLANTIC
OCEAN
NEW YORK
PENNSYLVANIA
NEW JERSEY
MARYLAND
DELAWARE
WEST VIRGINIA
MASS.
VERMONT
NEW HAMPSHIRE
D.C.
BOSTON
NEW YORK
PHILADELPHIA
BALTIMORE
WASHINGTON
PITTSBURGH
CLEVELAND
BUFFALO
TORONTO
Hamilton
Rochester
Syracuse
Albany
Hartford
Providence
Worcester
Springfield
Scranton
Harrisburg
Trenton
Newark
Camden
Wilmington
Erie
Youngstown
Akron
Canton
Binghamton
Utica
LAKE ERIE
LAKE ONTARIO
Long Island
Cape Cod
Chesapeake Bay
West from Greenwich

1 : 6 000 000

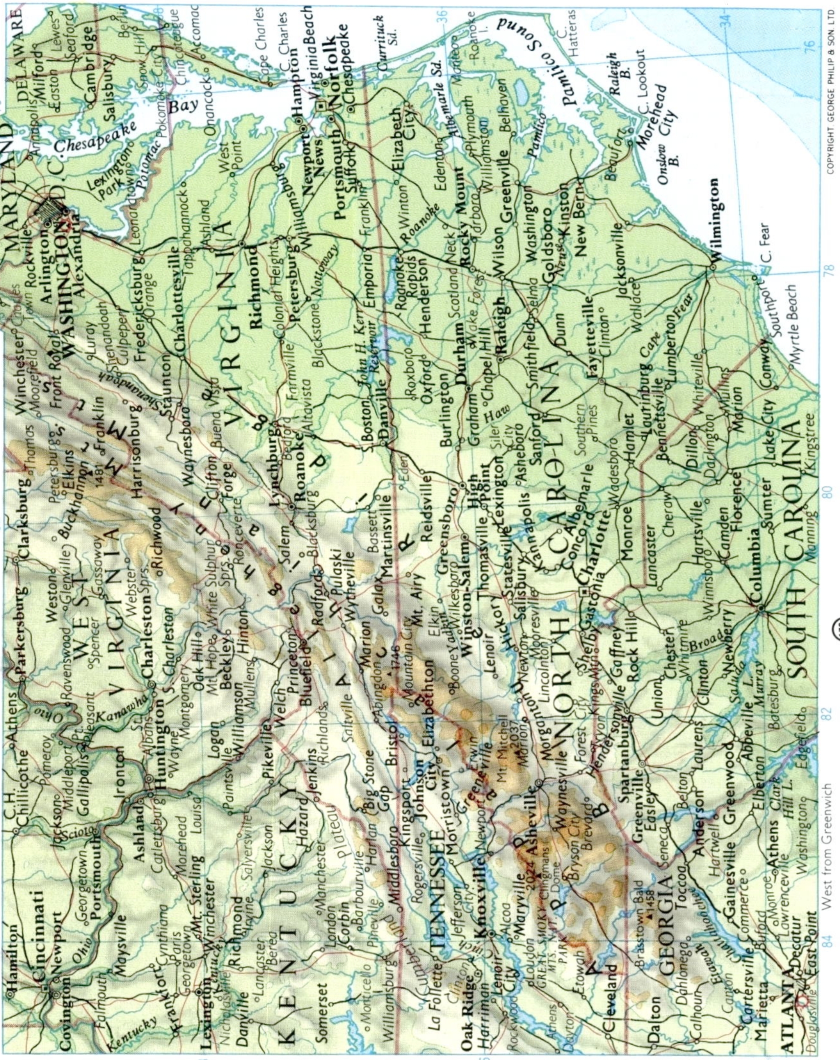
DELAWARE
MARYLAND
WASHINGTON D.C.
Chesapeake Bay
Baltimore
Arlington
Alexandria
Annapolis
Cambridge
Salisbury
Norfolk
Virginia Beach
Chesapeake
Portsmouth
Newport News
Hampton
Richmond
Petersburg
Charlottesville
Fredericksburg
Lynchburg
Roanoke
Danville
Staunton
VIRGINIA
WEST VIRGINIA
Charleston
Huntington
Parkersburg
Clarksburg
KENTUCKY
Lexington
Cincinnati
Covington
Newport
Frankfort
TENNESSEE
Knoxville
Oak Ridge
Kingsport
Johnson City
Bristol
NORTH CAROLINA
Raleigh
Durham
Greensboro
Winston-Salem
Charlotte
Asheville
Wilmington
Fayetteville
Rocky Mount
Greenville
SOUTH CAROLINA
Columbia
Spartanburg
Greenville
Rock Hill
GEORGIA
ATLANTA
Athens
Decatur
Marietta
Pamlico Sound
Albemarle Sd.
Currituck Sd.
C. Hatteras
C. Lookout
C. Fear
C. Charles
Mt. Mitchell 2037
West from Greenwich
COPYRIGHT GEORGE PHILIP & SON LTD.

1 : 6 000 000

156

163

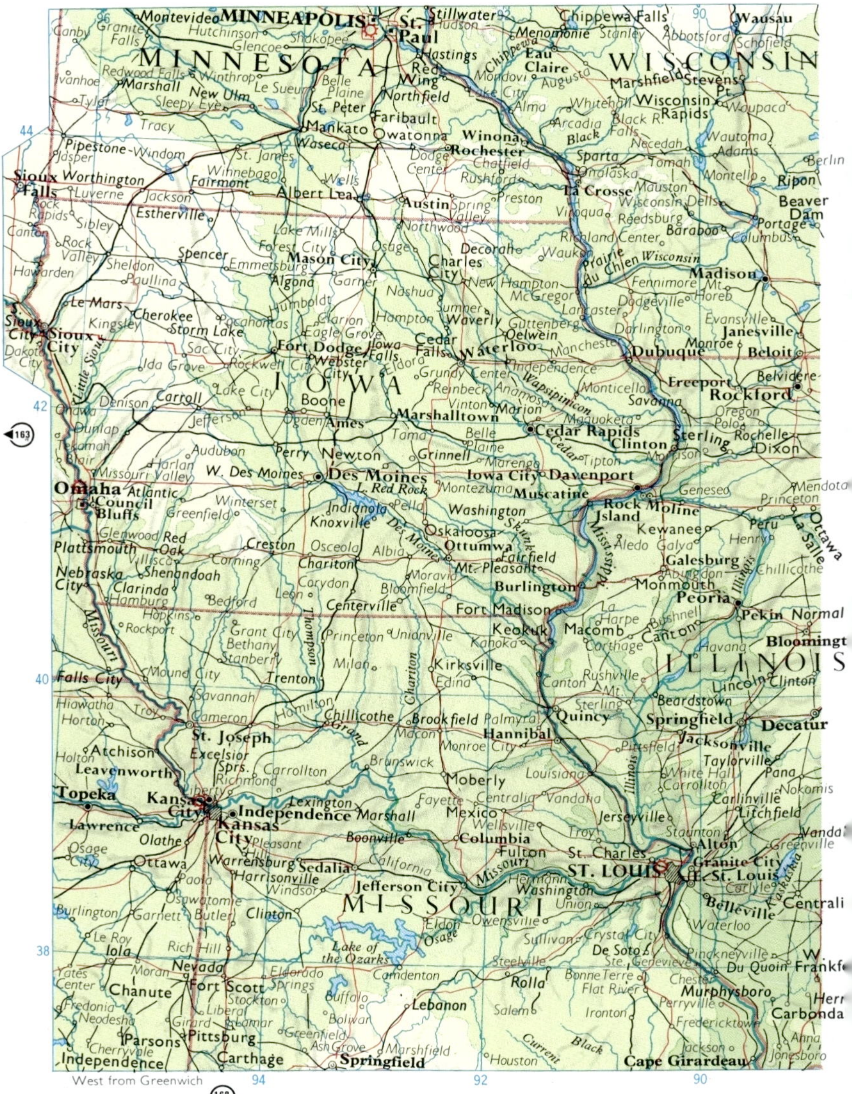
MINNESOTA
WISCONSIN
IOWA
ILLINOIS
MISSOURI
MINNEAPOLIS
St. Paul
Montevideo
Granite Falls
Canby
Hutchinson
Glencoe
Shakopee
Stillwater
Hudson
Hastings
Red Wing
Northfield
Faribault
Owatonna
Mankato
Waseca
St. Peter
Le Sueur
Belle Plaine
New Ulm
Sleepy Eye
Redwood Falls
Winthrop
Marshall
Ivanhoe
Tyler
Tracy
Pipestone
Windom
Jasper
St. James
Winnebago
Fairmont
Wells
Albert Lea
Austin
Dodge Center
Rochester
Winona
Chatfield
Rushford
Preston
Spring Valley
Worthington
Luverne
Jackson
Sioux Falls
Rock Rapids
Sibley
Estherville
Canton
Rock Valley
Hawarden
Sheldon
Paullina
Spencer
Emmetsburg
Lake Mills
Forest City
Mason City
Northwood
Osage
Charles City
Decorah
Algona
Garner
Nashua
New Hampton
Le Mars
Cherokee
Kingsley
Pocahontas
Storm Lake
Humboldt
Clarion
Eagle Grove
Hampton
Sumner
Waverly
Iowa Falls
Cedar Falls
Waterloo
Oelwein
Sioux City
Dakota City
Sac City
Ida Grove
Fort Dodge
Webster City
Rockwell City
Eldora
Grundy Center
Reinbeck
Independence
Manchester
Anamosa
Wapsipinicon
Vinton
Marion
Monticello
Maquoketa
Little Sioux
Denison
Carroll
Lake City
Boone
Jefferson
Ogden
Ames
Marshalltown
Tama
Belle Plaine
Cedar Rapids
Cedar
Onawa
Dunlap
Tekamah
Blair
Harlan
Audubon
Perry
Newton
Grinnell
Marengo
Iowa City
Tipton
Davenport
Clinton
Missouri Valley
Omaha
Council Bluffs
Atlantic
W. Des Moines
Des Moines
L. Red Rock
Montezuma
Muscatine
Winterset
Greenfield
Indianola
Pella
Knoxville
Oskaloosa
Washington
Skunk
Ottumwa
Fairfield
Mt. Pleasant
Glenwood
Red Oak
Plattsmouth
Villisca
Corning
Creston
Osceola
Chariton
Albia
Moravia
Nebraska City
Shenandoah
Clarinda
Hamburg
Bedford
Corydon
Leon
Centerville
Bloomfield
Burlington
Fort Madison
Keokuk
Kahoka
Hopkins
Rockport
Grant City
Bethany
Stanberry
Princeton
Unionville
Thompson
Milan
Kirksville
Edina
Chariton
Falls City
Mound City
Trenton
Savannah
Hiawatha
Horton
Troy
Cameron
Hamilton
Chillicothe
Brookfield
Palmyra
Grand
Macon
Hannibal
Quincy
St. Joseph
Atchison
Holton
Excelsior Sprs.
Richmond
Carrollton
Brunswick
Monroe City
Leavenworth
Liberty
Moberly
Louisiana
Topeka
Kansas City
Independence
Lexington
Marshall
Fayette
Centralia
Mexico
Vandalia
Lawrence
Olathe
Boonville
Wellsville
Columbia
Fulton
Osage City
Ottawa
Pleasant Hill
Warrensburg
Sedalia
California
Missouri
Hermann
Washington
St. Charles
ST. LOUIS
Paola
Harrisonville
Jefferson City
Osawatomie
Windsor
Burlington
Garnett
Butler
Clinton
Eldon
Owensville
Union
Osage
Le Roy
Iola
Rich Hill
Lake of the Ozarks
Sullivan
Crystal City
De Soto
Ste. Genevieve
Yates Center
Moran
Nevada
Eldorado Springs
Camdenton
Rolla
Bonne Terre
Flat River
Chanute
Fort Scott
Stockton
Buffalo
Lebanon
Salem
Ironton
Fredonia
Neodesha
Liberal
Girard
Lamar
Bolivar
Parsons
Cherryvale
Pittsburg
Greenfield
Ash Grove
Marshfield
Houston
Current
Black
Independence
Carthage
Springfield
Cape Girardeau
Chippewa Falls
Menomonie
Chippewa
Stanley
Abbotsford
Wausau
Schofield
Eau Claire
Augusta
Mondovi
Lake City
Alma
Marshfield
Stevens Pt.
Wisconsin Rapids
Waupaca
Whitehall
Arcadia
Black
Black R. Falls
Necedah
Wautoma
Adams
Berlin
Sparta
Tomah
Onalaska
La Crosse
Mauston
Montello
Ripon
Wisconsin Dells
Beaver Dam
Viroqua
Reedsburg
Portage
Columbus
Baraboo
Richland Center
Waukon
Prairie du Chien
Wisconsin
Madison
Fennimore
Mt. Horeb
McGregor
Lancaster
Dodgeville
Guttenberg
Evansville
Darlington
Janesville
Monroe
Beloit
Dubuque
Freeport
Belvidere
Rockford
Savanna
Oregon
Polo
Sterling
Rochelle
Dixon
Morrison
Geneseo
Mendota
Princeton
Rock Island
Moline
Kewanee
Peru
La Salle
Ottawa
Aledo
Galva
Henry
Mississippi
Galesburg
Abingdon
Illinois
Chillicothe
Monmouth
Peoria
La Harpe
Bushnell
Pekin
Normal
Macomb
Canton
Bloomington
Carthage
Havana
Rushville
Lincoln
Clinton
Canton
Mt. Sterling
Beardstown
Springfield
Decatur
Pittsfield
Jacksonville
Taylorville
Illinois
White Hall
Pana
Carrollton
Nokomis
Carlinville
Litchfield
Jerseyville
Staunton
Vandalia
Alton
Greenville
Granite City
E. St. Louis
Carlyle
Kaskaskia
Belleville
Centralia
Waterloo
Pinckneyville
Du Quoin
W. Frankfort
Chester
Murphysboro
Perryville
Herrin
Carbondale
Fredericktown
Jackson
Anna
Jonesboro
44
42
40
38
96
92
90
West from Greenwich
94
92
90

168

1 : 6 000 000

150

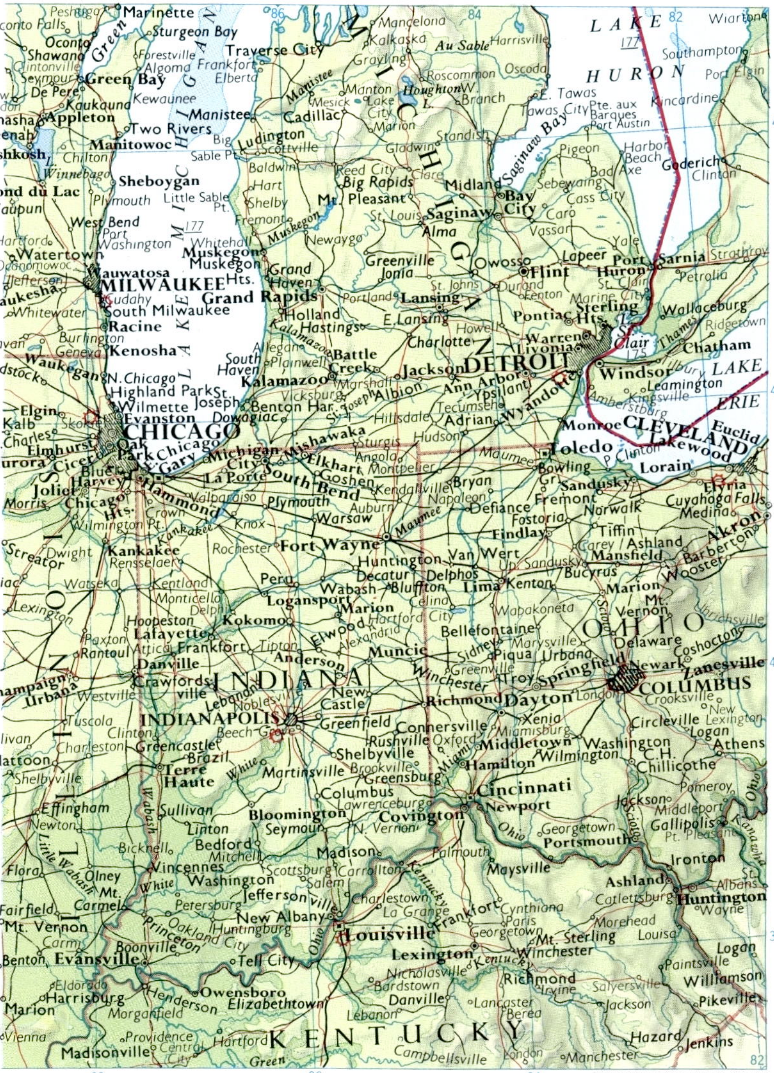
LAKE HURON
LAKE MICHIGAN
LAKE ERIE
MICHIGAN
INDIANA
OHIO
KENTUCKY
ILLINOIS
Green Bay
Saginaw Bay
St. Clair
177
175
86
84
82
88
44
42
40
38
Peshtigo
Marinette
Oconto Falls
Oconto
Shawano
Sturgeon Bay
Forestville
Algoma
Clintonville
Seymour
De Pere
Green Bay
Kewaunee
New London
Kaukauna
Menasha
Appleton
Neenah
Two Rivers
Manitowoc
Oshkosh
Chilton
Winnebago
Sheboygan
Fond du Lac
Plymouth
Waupun
West Bend
Port Washington
Hartford
Watertown
Oconomowoc
Jefferson
Wauwatosa
MILWAUKEE
Waukesha
Cudahy
South Milwaukee
Whitewater
Racine
Burlington
Delavan
Geneva
Kenosha
Woodstock
Waukegan
N. Chicago
Highland Park
Wilmette
Elgin
Evanston
De Kalb
Skokie
CHICAGO
St. Charles
Elmhurst
Oak Park
Aurora
Cicero
Blue Is.
Harvey
Joliet
Chicago Hts.
Morris
Wilmington
Crown Pt.
Streator
Dwight
Kankakee
Rensselaer
Pontiac
Watseka
Kentland
Lexington
Monticello
Delphi
Hoopeston
Paxton
Lafayette
Rantoul
Attica
Frankfort
Danville
Champaign
Urbana
Crawfordsville
Westville
Tuscola
Sullivan
Clinton
Charleston
Mattoon
Greencastle
Brazil
Terre Haute
Shelbyville
Effingham
Newton
Sullivan
Linton
Bicknell
Flora
Olney
Vincennes
Mt. Carmel
Fairfield
Mt. Vernon
Carmi
Benton
Evansville
Eldorado
Harrisburg
Marion
Vienna
Henderson
Morganfield
Providence
Madisonville
Central City
Hartford
Green
Boonville
Princeton
Oakland City
Petersburg
Huntingburg
Tell City
Owensboro
Elizabethtown
Washington
Jefferson ville
New Albany
Louisville
Scottsburg
Salem
Charlestown
Carrollton
La Grange
Madison
Bedford
Mitchell
Seymour
N. Vernon
Bloomington
Martinsville
Columbus
Lawrenceburg
Covington
Greensburg
Brookville
Shelbyville
Rushville
Connersville
Greenfield
INDIANAPOLIS
Beech Grove
Lebanon
Noblesville
New Castle
Richmond
Muncie
Anderson
Elwood
Alexandria
Tipton
Kokomo
Logansport
Peru
Wabash
Marion
Hartford City
Bluffton
Huntington
Decatur
Celina
Fort Wayne
Rochester
Warsaw
Knox
Plymouth
Valparaiso
Hammond
Gary
La Porte
Michigan City
South Bend
Mishawaka
Elkhart
Goshen
Kendallville
Auburn
Angola
Sturgis
Montpelier
Bryan
Napoleon
Defiance
Maumee
Van Wert
Delphos
Lima
Wapakoneta
Kenton
Findlay
Fostoria
Tiffin
Fremont
Sandusky
Norwalk
Bowling Gr.
Toledo
Monroe
Port Clinton
Lorain
CLEVELAND
Lakewood
Euclid
Elyria
Cuyahoga Falls
Medina
Akron
Barberton
Ashland
Mansfield
Wooster
Carey
Up. Sandusky
Bucyrus
Marion
Mt. Vernon
Uhrichsville
Delaware
Coshocton
Newark
Zanesville
COLUMBUS
Crooksville
New Lexington
Logan
Athens
Circleville
Washington C.H.
Chillicothe
Pomeroy
Middleport
Gallipolis
Pt. Pleasant
Jackson
Portsmouth
Ironton
Ashland
Catlettsburg
Huntington
St. Albans
Wayne
Louisa
Morehead
Mt. Sterling
Winchester
Paintsville
Logan
Williamson
Pikeville
Salyersville
Jackson
Hazard
Jenkins
Manchester
London
Berea
Lancaster
Richmond
Irvine
Lexington
Nicholasville
Georgetown
Paris
Cynthiana
Frankfort
Bardstown
Danville
Lebanon
Campbellsville
Maysville
Falmouth
Georgetown
Cincinnati
Newport
Hamilton
Middletown
Oxford
Miamisburg
Wilmington
Xenia
Dayton
Springfield
London
Troy
Piqua
Urbana
Sidney
Greenville
Winchester
Bellefontaine
Marysville
Hillsdale
Hudson
Adrian
Tecumseh
Ypsilanti
Ann Arbor
Wyandotte
DETROIT
Warren
Livonia
Sterling Hts.
Pontiac
Howell
Fenton
Durand
Flint
Lapeer
Port Huron
Marine City
St. Clair
Owosso
St. Johns
Lansing
E. Lansing
Portland
Ionia
Greenville
Charlotte
Jackson
Albion
Marshall
Battle Creek
Hastings
Kalamazoo
Vicksburg
Plainwell
Allegan
South Haven
Holland
Grand Rapids
Grand Haven
Muskegon
Muskegon Hts.
Whitehall
Little Sable Pt.
Benton Har.
St. Joseph
Dowagiac
Newaygo
Fremont
Shelby
Hart
Baldwin
Ludington
Big Sable Pt.
Scottville
Manistee
Frankfort
Elberta
Traverse City
Cadillac
Manton
Mesick
Lake City
Marion
Reed City
Big Rapids
Mt. Pleasant
St. Louis
Alma
Saginaw
Midland
Bay City
Clare
Gladwin
Standish
Grayling
Kalkaska
Mancelona
Roscommon
Houghton L.
W. Branch
Au Sable
Harrisville
Oscoda
E. Tawas
Tawas City
Pte. aux Barques
Port Austin
Pigeon
Harbor Beach
Bad Axe
Sebewaing
Caro
Cass City
Vassar
Yale
Sarnia
Strathroy
Petrolia
Wallaceburg
Ridgetown
Chatham
Thames
Windsor
Tilbury
Leamington
Kingsville
Amherstburg
Goderich
Clinton
Kincardine
Port Elgin
Southampton
Wiarton
Manistee
Muskegon
Kalamazoo
St. Joseph
Maumee
Kankakee
Wabash
White
Little Wabash
Ohio
Kentucky
Miami
Scioto
Kanawha
Green

164

165

169

U.S.A.: LOWER MISSISSIPPI AND GULF COAST

166

161

176

1 : 6 000 000

167

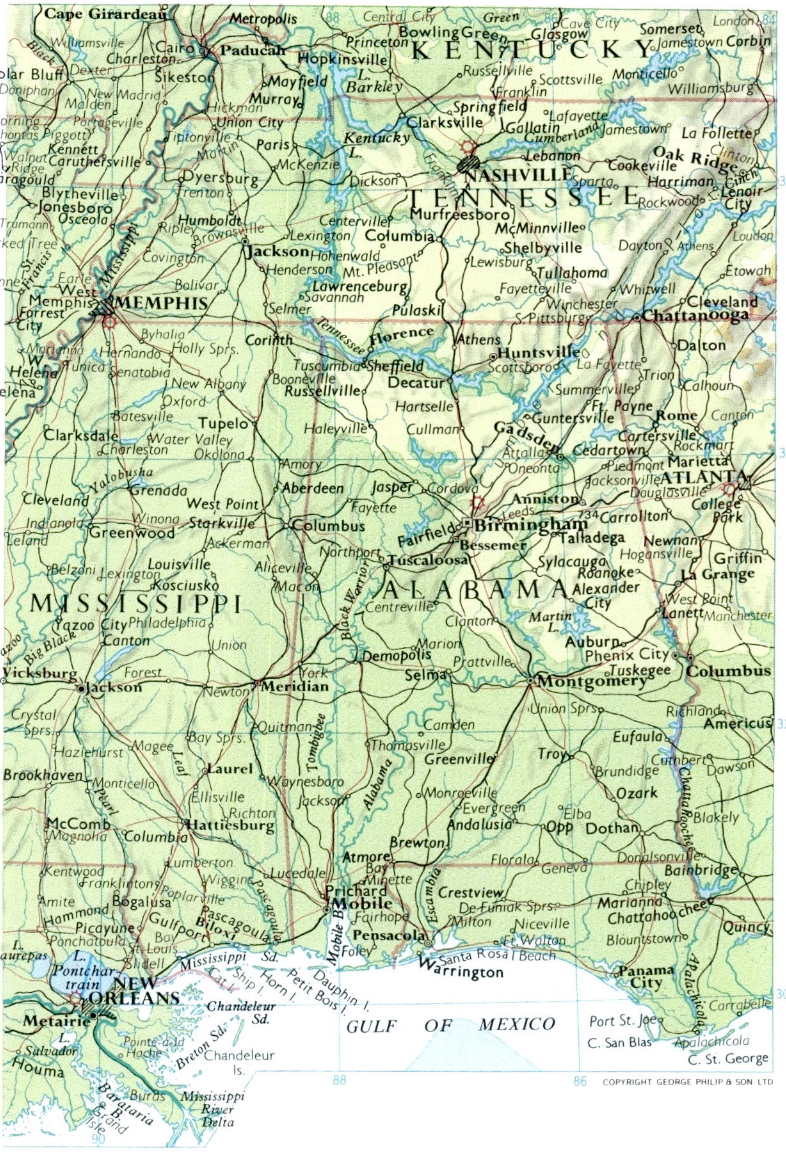
KENTUCKY
TENNESSEE
MISSISSIPPI
ALABAMA
GULF OF MEXICO
Cape Girardeau
Metropolis
Central City
Green
Cave City
Somerset
London
Corbin
Williamsville
Cairo
Paducah
Princeton
Bowling Green
Glasgow
Jamestown
Poplar Bluff
Dexter
Charleston
Sikeston
Hopkinsville
Russellville
Scottsville
Monticello
Williamsburg
Doniphan
New Madrid
Mayfield
L. Barkley
Franklin
Malden
Murray
Springfield
Lafayette
Corning
Portageville
Hickman
Union City
Clarksville
Gallatin
Cumberland
Jamestown
La Follette
Pocahontas
Piggott
Tiptonville
Kentucky L.
Kennett
Caruthersville
Paris
Lebanon
Cookeville
Oak Ridge
Walnut Ridge
McKenzie
NASHVILLE
Paragould
Dyersburg
Dickson
Sparta
Harriman
Lenoir City
Blytheville
Trenton
Murfreesboro
Rockwood
Jonesboro
Osceola
Humboldt
Centerville
McMinnville
Trumann
Ripley
Brownsville
Lexington
Columbia
Marked Tree
Jackson
Hohenwald
Shelbyville
Loudon
St. Francis
Covington
Henderson
Mt. Pleasant
Lewisburg
Dayton
Athens
Wynne
Earle
Mississippi
Tullahoma
Etowah
West Memphis
Bolivar
Lawrenceburg
Savannah
Fayetteville
Whitwell
MEMPHIS
Selmer
Pulaski
Winchester
Cleveland
Forrest City
S. Pittsburg
Chattanooga
Byhalia
Corinth
Florence
Athens
Marianna
Hernando
Holly Sprs.
Tennessee
Dalton
W. Helena
Tunica
Senatobia
Tuscumbia
Sheffield
Huntsville
Scottsboro
La Fayette
Trion
Booneville
Decatur
Summerville
Calhoun
Helena
New Albany
Russellville
Oxford
Hartselle
Ft. Payne
Batesville
Tupelo
Haleyville
Guntersville
Rome
Canton
Clarksdale
Water Valley
Cullman
Gadsden
Cartersville
Charleston
Okolona
Attalla
Cedartown
Rockmart
Amory
Oneonta
Piedmont
Marietta
Yalobusha
Aberdeen
Jasper
Cordova
Jacksonville
ATLANTA
Grenada
Douglasville
Cleveland
West Point
Fayette
Anniston
College Park
Indianola
Winona
Starkville
Columbus
Leeds
Carrollton
Leland
Greenwood
Birmingham
Ackerman
Fairfield
Talladega
Newnan
Bessemer
Northport
Tuscaloosa
Sylacauga
Hogansville
Griffin
Belzoni
Lexington
Louisville
Aliceville
Roanoke
La Grange
Kosciusko
Macon
Black Warrior
Alexander City
Centreville
West Point
Yazoo City
Philadelphia
Clanton
Martin L.
Lanett
Manchester
Big Black
Canton
Yazoo
Union
Marion
Auburn
Phenix City
Vicksburg
Demopolis
Prattville
Forest
York
Selma
Tuskegee
Columbus
Jackson
Newton
Meridian
Montgomery
Crystal Sprs.
Quitman
Camden
Union Sprs.
Richland
Americus
Bay Sprs.
Tombigbee
Thomasville
Eufaula
Hazlehurst
Magee
Leaf
Greenville
Troy
Cuthbert
Dawson
Brookhaven
Laurel
Alabama
Brundidge
Monticello
Waynesboro
Chattahoochee
Pearl
Ellisville
Monroeville
Ozark
Richton
Jackson
Evergreen
Elba
Blakely
McComb
Hattiesburg
Andalusia
Opp
Dothan
Magnolia
Columbia
Brewton
Atmore
Florala
Donalsonville
Kentwood
Lumberton
Lucedale
Geneva
Bainbridge
Franklinton
Wiggins
Bay Minette
Chipley
Poplarville
Prichard
Crestview
Amite
Bogalusa
Pascagoula
Mobile
De Funiak Sprs.
Marianna
Hammond
Picayune
Gulfport
Biloxi
Fairhope
Escambia
Milton
Niceville
Chattahoochee
Quincy
Ponchatoula
Bay St. Louis
Mobile B.
Pensacola
Ft. Walton
Blountstown
L. Maurepas
Slidell
Foley
Santa Rosa I. Beach
Mississippi Sd.
Warrington
L. Pontchartrain
Cat I.
Ship I.
Horn I.
Petit Bois I.
Dauphin I.
Panama City
Apalachicola
NEW ORLEANS
Chandeleur Sd.
Carrabelle
Metairie
Port St. Joe
L. Salvador
Pointe-a-la Hache
Breton Sd.
Chandeleur Is.
C. San Blas
Apalachicola
C. St. George
Houma
Barataria B.
Buras
Mississippi River Delta
Grand Isle
734
88
86
84
90
36
34
32
30
165
170

165
169
178
ATLANTA
Decatur
Douglasville
East Point
College Park
Carrollton
Covington
Greensboro
Augusta
Aiken
Orangeburg
L. Marion
Andrews
Georgetown
Eatonton
Sparta
Bamberg
L. Moultrie
Newnan
Griffin
Wrens
St. George
GEORGIA
Savannah
Summerville
Cooper
La Grange
Barnesville
Forsyth
Milledgeville
Tennille
Waynesboro
Walterboro
West Point
Thomaston
Millen
Hampton
Charleston
Mt. Pleasant
Lanett
Manchester
Macon
Sylvania
Combahee
Phenix City
Warner Robins
Swainsboro
Ogeechee
Ridgeland
Fort Valley
Dublin
Beaufort
Columbus
Perry
Cochran
Oconee
Statesboro
Parris I.
Hawkinsville
Vidalia
Ocmulgee
Eastman
Lyons
Pembroke
Richland
Savannah
Americus
32
Eufaula
Cordele
Altamaha
Cuthbert
Hazlehurst
Baxley
Ossabaw I.
Dawson
Ashburn
Fitzgerald
Jesup
St. Catherines I.
Albany
Ocilla
Alma
Sylvester
Sapelo I.
Chattahoochee
Flint
Tifton
Douglas
Blakely
St. Simons I.
Nashville
Satilla
Brunswick
Moultrie
Waycross
Jekyll I.
Adel
Donalsonville
Pelham
Okefenokee Swamp
Bainbridge
Cairo
Folkston
Cumberland I.
Thomasville
Valdosta
Quitman
Fernandina Beach
Chattahoochee
ATLANTIC
Quincy
Monticello
Jasper
Madison
JACKSONVILLE
St. Johns
Tallahassee
Live Oak
Baldwin
Jacksonville Beach
Apalachicola
Suwannee
Lake City
Perry
Starke
30
Apalachee B.
Green Cove Sprs.
St. Augustine
Carrabelle
High Sprs.
Palatka
Apalachicola
Gainesville
FLORIDA
C. St. George
Cross City
Bunnell
Williston
L. George
Ormond Beach
Holly Hill
OCEAN
Ocala
Daytona Beach
Cedar Key
New Smyrna Beach
De Land
Dunnellon
Eustis
Sanford
Crystal River
Mt. Dora
Inverness
Leesburg
Titusville
Winter Garden
Winter Park
GULF
Brooksville
Orlando
C. Canaveral
Cocoa
Dade City
Kissimmee
St. Cloud
Auburndale
Haines City
Tarpon Sprs.
Melbourne
Dunedin
Lakeland
Plant City
Winter Haven
28
Clearwater
Tampa
Lake Wales
Indian River
Bartow
St. Petersburg
Ft Meade
Vero Beach
OF
Tampa Bay
Palmetto
Wauchula
Kissimmee
Ft. Pierce
Bradenton
Sebring
Sarasota
L. Istokpoga
Okeechobee
Stuart
Arcadia
L. Okeechobee
Punta Gorda
Pahokee
Palm Beach
La Belle
Belle Glade
West Palm Beach
MEXICO
Charlotte Harb.
Ft. Myers
Clewiston
Lake Worth
Boynton Beach
Delray Beach
Immokalee
Boca Raton
Everglades
Pompano Beach
Naples
Big Cypress Swamp
Ft. Lauderdale
Carol City
Hollywood
26
84
West from Greenwich
82
Everglades City
Hialeah
Miami Beach
Miami
EVERGLADES NAT. PARK
Biscayne B.
Coral Gables
Homestead
80

1 : 6 000 000

154
162
172
CANADA
VANCOUVER
New Westminster
Chilliwack
Blaine
Ferndale
Lynden
Everson
Mt. Baker 3285
Bellingham
Ross L.
Grand Forks
Oroville
Okanogan
Tonasket
Republic
Northport
Metaline Falls
Ione
Pend Oreille
Kettle Falls
Colville
Priest L.
Sandpoint
Port Renfrew
Duncan
Juan de Fuca Strait
Victoria
C. Flattery
Anacortes
Burlington
Sedro Woolley
Concrete
La Conner
Oak Hr.
Clear Lake
Mt. Vernon
Winthrop
Twisp
Okanogan
Omak
Franklin D. Roosevelt L.
Chewelah
Newport
Priest River
Pend Oreille L.
Sekiu
Port Angeles
Port Townsend
Sequim
Darrington
Arlington
Glacier Pk 3213
L. Chelan
Pateros
Brewster
Mason City
Keller
Grand Coulee Dam
Springdale
Deer Park
Rathdrum
Coeur d'Alene
Forks
Olympic Mts.
Mt. Olympus 2428
OLYMPIC NAT. PARK
Chimacum
Poulsbo
Admiralty Inlet
Puget Sd.
Everett
Snohomish
Edmonds
Skykomish
Leavenworth
Chelan
Mansfield
Grand Coulee
Waterville
Coulee City
Creston
Davenport
Spokane
Medical Lake
Cheney
Cœur d'Alene L.
St. Maries
Bremerton
Port Orchard
Nelton
Hoodsport
SEATTLE
WASHINGTON
Renton
Tacoma
Cashmere
Wenatchee
Soap Lake
Columbia Basin
Ephrata
Odessa
Sprague
Rosalia
Plummer
Tekoa
Moclips
Shelton
Puyallup
Easton
Cle Elum
Quincy
Moses Lake
Ritzville
Oakesdale
Hoquiam
Aberdeen
Elma
Montesano
Olympia
Tumwater
Enumclaw
Buckley
Mt. Rainier 4392
Ellensburg
Yakima
Beverly
Lind
Endicott
Garfield
Palouse
Westport
Willapa B.
Raymond
South Bend
Centralia
Chehalis
Ashford
MT. RAINIER NAT. PARK
Morton
Naches
Othello
Lacrosse
Colfax
Pullman
Moscow
Troy
Ocean Park
Long Beach
Pe Ell
Winlock
Toledo
Selah
Connell
Colton
Astoria
Cathlamet
Union Gap
Wapato
Granger
Snake
Pomeroy
Genesee
Warrenton
Castle Rock
Toppenish
Sunnyside
Richland
Dayton
Clarkston
Asotin
Lewiston
Clatskanie
Kelso
Longview
Mt. St. Helens 2550
Mt. Adams 3751
Mabton
Grandview
Prosser
Pasco
Waitsburg
Anatone
Seaside
Rainier
St. Helens
Kalama
Kennewick
Umatilla
Wallula
Walla Walla
Salmon
PACIFIC OCEAN
Wheeler
Bay City
Vancouver
Klickitat
Goldendale
Columbia
Hermiston
Milton-Freewater
PORTLAND
Camas
Hood River
Weston
Tillamook
Forest Gro.
Hillsboro
Cascade Locks
The Dalles
Wasco
Arlington
Pendleton
Elgin
Wallowa
Gresham
Milwaukie
Deschutes
Lexington
Heppner
Pilot Rock
Imbler
Enterprise
Joseph
McMinnville
Newberg
Oregon City
Mt Hood 3427
Grass Valley
La Grande
Willamina
Canby
Condon
Hardman
Blue Mountains
Wallowa Mts. 3058
Mt. Angel
Maupin
Kent
Dallas
Salem
Falls City
Independence
Shaniko
Fossil
North Powder
Homestead
Corvallis
Newport
Mill City
John Day
Spray
Haines
Halfway
Toledo
Mt. Jefferson 3200
Long Creek
Baker
Richland
Council
Albany
Philomath
Lebanon
Madras
Mitchell
Waldport
Brownsville
Dayville
Cambridge
Harrisburg
Crooked
Prineville
Sweet Home
Sisters
Prairie City
Junction City
Three Sisters 3156
Redmond
John Day 2926
Huntington
Mapleton
Springfield
McKenzie
OREGON
Seneca
Brogan
Weiser
Florence
Eugene
Bend
Ontario
Payette
Cottage Grove
Oakridge
Brothers
Silvies
Malheur
Vale
Nyssa
New Plymouth
Parma
Reedsport
Drain
La Pine
Silver Cr.
Riley
Burns
Juntura
Caldwell
Homedale
Coos Bay
Oakland
Sutherlin
Harney Basin
Crane
Nampa
Coquille
Crescent
Chemult
Owyhee Res.
Roseburg
Umpqua
Cascade Ra.
Camas Valley
Myrtle Creek
Silver Lake
Harney L.
Malheur L.
Murphy
Powers
Crater L.
Owyhee
Jordan Valley
Port Orford
Canyonville
Summer L.
Frenchglen
Rogue
Glendale
Ft. Klamath
Paisley
Gold Hill
L. Abert
2962
Grants Pass
Mt. McLoughlin 2894
Valley Falls
Gold Beach
Jacksonville
Sprague River
Algoma
Medford
Upper Klamath L.
Bly
Klamath Falls
Brookings
Ashland
Lakeview
Warner Ra.
Merrill
Goose L.
Hornbrook
Dorris
Clear Lake Res.
McDermitt
Happy Camp
Crescent City
Klamath
Yreka
Montague
Upper L.
NEVADA
Santa Rosa Mts.
CALIFORNIA
Mt. Shasta 4317
Alturas
Cedarville
124
122
120
118
48
46
44
42
West from Greenwich
COPYRIGHT GEORGE PHILIP & SON LTD

1 : 6 000 000

163

171

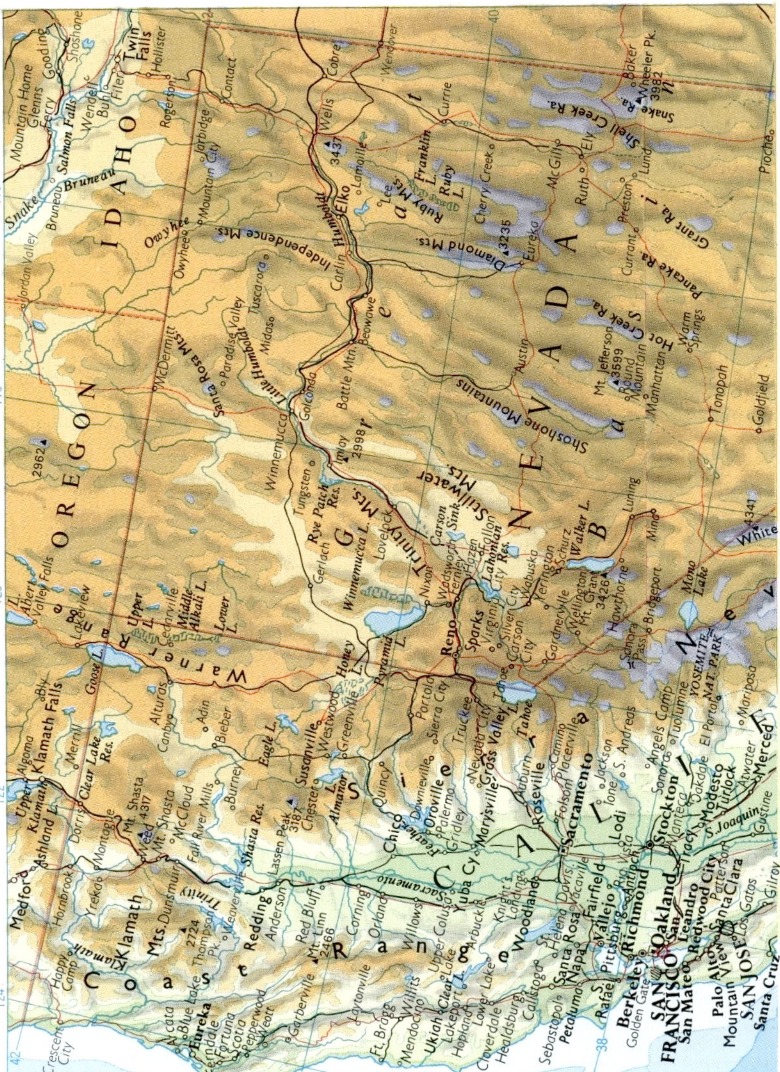
OREGON
IDAHO
NEVADA
CALIFORNIA
Coast Ranges
Klamath Mts.
Warner Ra.
Great Basin
Sierra Nevada
Medford
Klamath Falls
Redding
Eureka
Chico
Sacramento
Reno
Carson City
Stockton
Modesto
Merced
Oakland
Berkeley
SAN FRANCISCO
SAN JOSE
Santa Cruz
Elko
Winnemucca
Tonopah
Ely
Twin Falls
Pyramid L.
Walker L.
Mono Lake
L. Tahoe
Shasta Res.
Mt. Shasta 4317
Lassen Peak 3187
YOSEMITE NAT. PARK

1 : 6 000 000

160

C a l i f o r n i a
O r a n g e
C o a s t R a n g e
ARIZONA
NEVADA
MEXICO
PACIFIC
OCEAN
LOS ANGELES
SAN DIEGO
SAN BERNARDINO
Los Angeles
Santa Monica
Beverly Hills
Inglewood
Alhambra
Pasadena
Glendale
Burbank
Long Beach
Redondo Beach
Huntington Beach
Huntington Park
Santa Ana
Fullerton
Riverside
Pomona
Ontario
Corona
Redlands
Newport Beach
Laguna Beach
Oceanside
Carlsbad
Escondido
Coronado
Chula Vista
National City
El Cajon
La Mesa
Tijuana
Tecate
Mexicali
Calexico
El Centro
Brawley
Imperial
Holtville
Calipatria
Niland
Westmorland
Salton Sea
-72
Palm Springs
Banning
Hemet
Indio
Coachella
Mecca
Blythe
Desert Center
Twentynine Palms
Bristol L.
Danby L.
Havasu L.
Amboy
Needles
Topock
Lake Havasu City
Parker Dam
Parker
Colorado
Colorado Aqueduct
Imperial Dam
Laguna Dam
All American Canal
Yuma
Somerton
Wellton
Mohawk
Gila
Gila Bend Mts.
Gila Bend
Sentinel
Buckeye
Quartzsite
Salome
Wickenburg
Morristown
Congress
Octave
Kingman
Oatman
Hualpai Pk.
2519
Yucca
Davis Dam
Peach Sprs
Seligman
Nelson
Hoover Dam
Lake Mead
MEAD NAT. REC. AREA
Mt. Trumbull
2447
Bunkerville
St. George
Sta. Clara
Hurricane
Virgin
Overton
Moapa
Boulder City
Henderson
Las Vegas
N. Las Vegas
Spring Mts.
3633
Pahrump
Goodsprings
Jean
Nelson
Searchlight
Providence Mts.
Soda L.
Baker
Ludlow
Barstow
Yermo
Mojave Desert
Victorville
Hesperia
Lancaster
Palmdale
Mojave
Kramer
Randsburg
Inyokern
Searles L.
Little Lake
Telescope Pk.
3366
Panamint Mts.
Death Valley
-86
DEATH VALLEY NAT. MON.
Death Valley Junc.
Beatty
Lida
Bishop
Big Pine
North Palisade
Mts.
Inyo Ra.
Independence
Lone Pine
Olancha
Owens L.
Mt. Whitney
4418
KINGS CANYON NAT. PARK
4341
SEQUOIA NAT. PARK
Kings
Kern
Aqueduct
Bakersfield
Buena Vista
Taft
Maricopa
McKittrick
Tehachapi
Tehachapi Mts.
Lebec
2692
Los Angeles Aqueduct
Fillmore
Ojai
Sta. Paula
San Fernando
Hollywood
Oxnard
Ventura
Santa Barbara
Carpinteria
Los Olivos
Lompoc
Santa Maria
Nipomo
Arroyo Grande
Guadalupe
Pt. Arguello
Pt. Concepcion
S. Luis Obispo
Morro Bay
Atascadero
Paso Robles
San Miguel
Cambria
Piedras Blancas Pt.
1787
Santa Lucia Range
Pt. Sur
Carmel
Monterey
Pacific Grove
Pt. Pinos
Salinas
Watsonville
Hollister
S. Juan Bautista
Gonzales
Soledad
King City
Salinas
Coalinga
Mendota
Los Banos
Madera
Chowchilla
S. Joaquin
Fresno
Clovis
Fowler
Selma
Kingsburg
Sanger
Reedley
Dinuba
Visalia
Hanford
Lemoore
Stratford
Corcoran
Tulare
Tulare Lake
Exeter
Lindsay
Porterville
Tipton
Earlimart
Delano
Wasco
Shafter
Santa Rosa I.
Santa Cruz I.
Channel Is.
San Nicolas I.
Santa Catalina I.
Santa Catalina
San Clemente I.
Gulf of Santa Catalina
Elsinore
S. Juan Capistrano
San Clemente
Temecula
Fall Brook
Julian
Ramona
Caliente
Panaca
Modena
Newcastle
Enterprise
Meadow Valley Wash
Elgin
Hiko
Alamo
36
34
32
38
118
116
114
120
West from Greenwich

174

176

161

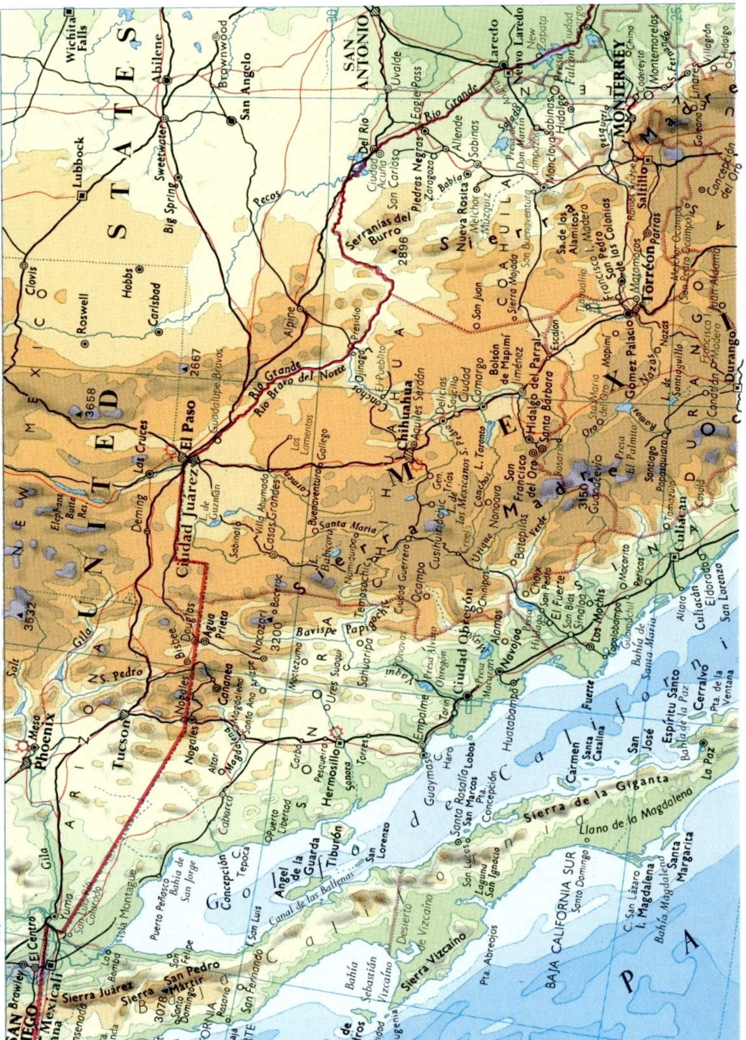
UNITED STATES
MEXICO
NEW MEXICO
ARIZONA
SONORA
CHIHUAHUA
COAHUILA
DURANGO
SINALOA
BAJA CALIFORNIA NORTE
BAJA CALIFORNIA SUR
SAN DIEGO
Tijuana
Mexicali
Ensenada
El Centro
Brawley
Yuma
Phoenix
Tucson
Nogales
Cananea
Agua Prieta
Douglas
Bisbee
Deming
Las Cruces
El Paso
Ciudad Juárez
Chihuahua
Hermosillo
Guaymas
Empalme
Ciudad Obregón
Navojoa
Los Mochis
Culiacán
Durango
Gómez Palacio
Torreón
Saltillo
MONTERREY
Laredo
Nuevo Laredo
SAN ANTONIO
San Angelo
Abilene
Lubbock
Wichita Falls
Roswell
Clovis
Hobbs
Carlsbad
Big Spring
Sweetwater
Brownwood
Pecos
Alpine
Del Rio
Ciudad Acuña
Piedras Negras
Eagle Pass
Uvalde
Hidalgo del Parral
La Paz
Santa Rosalía
Río Grande
Río Bravo del Norte
Gila
Sierra Juárez
Sierra de la Giganta
Sierra Vizcaíno
Desierto de Vizcaíno
Llano de la Magdalena
I. de Cedros
Tiburón
Ángel de la Guarda
I. Magdalena
Serranías del Burro
Bolsón de Mapimí
3658
3532
2667
3200
3150
2896
3078
100
105
110
115
30
25

1 : 12 000 000

REFERENCE TO NUMBERS
1 Distrito Federal
2 Aguascalientes
3 Guanajuato
4 Hidalgo
5 México
6 Morelos
7 Querétaro
8 Tlaxcala
PACIFIC OCEAN
Tropic of Cancer
Mazatlán
Tepic
Guadalajara
Aguascalientes
Zacatecas
San Luis Potosí
León
Guanajuato
Querétaro
Celaya
Morelia
Toluca
México
Cuernavaca
Pachuca
Colima
Manzanillo
Acapulco
Ciudad Victoria
Matehuala
Fresnillo
Les Tres Marías
San José del Cabo
C. de San Lucas
Todos Santos
San Lázaro
PANAMA CANAL
1:1 000 000
0 5 10 15 km
ATLANTIC OCEAN
PACIFIC OC.
REPUBLIC OF PANAMÁ
Colón
Cristóbal
Silver City
Gatun
Gatun Locks
Gatun Dam
Gatun Lake
Gamboa
Madden L.
Madden Dam
Culebra
Pedro Miguel Locks
Miraflores Locks
Balboa
La Boca
Panamá
La Chorrera
Arraiján
West from Greenwich
COPYRIGHT, GEORGE PHILIP & SON LTD.

158

GULF OF MEXICO
UNITED STATES
MISSISSIPPI
ALABAMA
ARKANSAS
LOUISIANA
COAHUILA
NEW ORLEANS
HOUSTON
DALLAS
FORT WORTH
SAN ANTONIO
BIRMINGHAM
MONTERREY
Corpus Christi
Galveston
Beaumont
Port Arthur
Austin
Waco
Tyler
Shreveport
Jackson
Baton Rouge
Mobile
Pensacola
Panama City
Montgomery
Little Rock
Lubbock
Abilene
San Angelo
Laredo
Nuevo Laredo
Brownsville
Matamoros
Saltillo
Torreón
Mississippi Delta
Terrebonne B.
Mobile B.
Rio Grande
5203
2896
884
85
90
95
100
30
25

174

1 : 12 000 000

178

Tropic of Cancer
Isla Desterrada
Isla Pérez
Progreso
Mérida
Y U C A T Á N
C. Catoche
Isla de Cozumel
QUINTANA ROO
Chetumal
Ambergris Cay
Turneffe Is.
BELIZE
Belize City
Belmopan
Golfo de Honduras
Campeche
C A M P E C H E
Ciudad del Carmen
Laguna de Términos
Champotón
Bahía de Campeche
T A B A S C O
Villahermosa
Coatzacoalcos
Minatitlán
Istmo de Tehuantepec
C H I A P A S
Tuxtla Gutiérrez
Tapachula
GUATEMALA
Guatemala
Puerto Barrios
HONDURAS
San Pedro Sula
EL SALVADOR
San Salvador
Veracruz
Jalapa
Córdoba
Orizaba
Puebla
México
Toluca
Cuernavaca
Pachuca
Tampico
Ciudad Madero
Laguna de Tamiahua
Tuxpan
Sierra de Tamaulipas
Ciudad Victoria
San Luis Potosí
Zacatecas
Aguascalientes
León
Guanajuato
Querétaro
Celaya
Guadalajara
Morelia
Uruapan
G U E R R E R O
Sierra Madre del Sur
Acapulco
Chilpancingo
Oaxaca
O A X A C A
Tehuantepec
Salina Cruz
Golfo de Tehuantepec
P A C I F I C   O C E A N
6662
5448
95
20
15

175

West from Greenwich

180

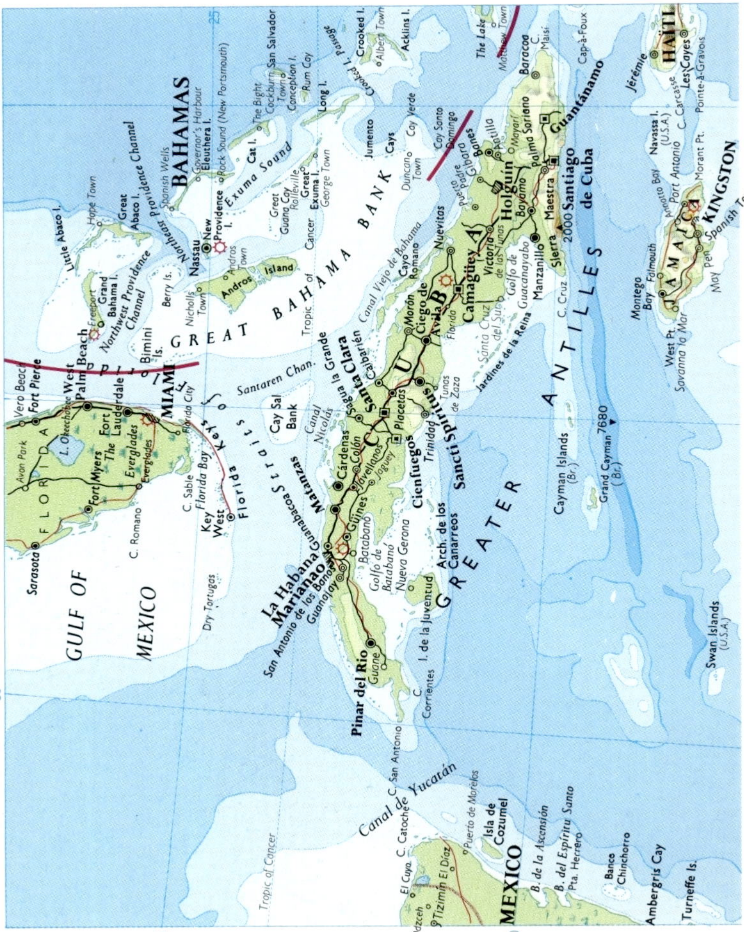

GULF OF MEXICO
FLORIDA
Sarasota
Fort Myers
Avon Park
L. Okeechobee
Vero Beach
Fort Pierce
West Palm Beach
Fort Lauderdale
MIAMI
The Everglades
Florida City
Florida Bay
C. Sable
C. Romano
Key West
Florida Keys
Dry Tortugas
Straits of Florida
BAHAMAS
Little Abaco I.
Great Abaco I.
Hope Town
Grand Bahama I.
Freeport
Northwest Providence Channel
Northeast Providence Channel
Bimini Is.
Berry Is.
Nassau
New Providence I.
Andros Island
Andros Town
Nicholls Town
Eleuthera I.
Governor's Harbour
Spanish Wells
Rock Sound (New Portsmouth)
Exuma Sound
Cat I.
The Bight
Great Exuma I.
George Town
Great Guana Cay
Rolleville
Long I.
Conception I.
Rum Cay
Cockburn Town
San Salvador
Crooked I.
Crooked I. Passage
Albert Town
Acklins I.
GREAT BAHAMA BANK
Tropic of Cancer
Santaren Chan.
Cay Sal Bank
Jumento Cays
Duncano Town
Cay Verde
Cay Santo Domingo
The Lake
Matthew Town
CUBA
La Habana
Marianao
Guanajay
San Antonio de los Baños
Güines
Matanzas
Cárdenas
Jovellanos
Colón
Jagüey
Batabanó
Golfo de Batabanó
Nueva Gerona
I. de la Juventud
Arch. de los Canarreos
Pinar del Rio
Guane
C. Corrientes
C. San Antonio
Santa Clara
Sagua la Grande
Caibarién
Placetas
Cienfuegos
Trinidad
Sancti Spíritus
Tunas de Zaza
Canal Nicolás
Canal Viejo de Bahama
Morón
Ciego de Avila
Cayo Romano
Camagüey
Nuevitas
Florida
Santa Cruz del Sur
Jardines de la Reina
Golfo de Guacanayabo
Victoria de las Tunas
Puerto Padre
Gibara
Holguín
Banes
Antilla
Mayarí
Bayamo
Manzanillo
Palma Soriano
Sierra Maestra
2000
Santiago de Cuba
Guantánamo
Baracoa
C. Maisí
C. Cruz
GREATER ANTILLES
Cayman Islands (Br.)
Grand Cayman (Br.)
7680
HAITI
Jérémie
Les Cayes
Cap-à-Foux
Navassa I. (U.S.A.)
C. Carcasse
Pointe-à-Gravois
JAMAICA
KINGSTON
Spanish Town
Montego Bay
Falmouth
Port Antonio
Annotto Bay
Morant Pt.
May Pen
Savanna la Mar
West Pt.
Swan Islands (U.S.A.)
MEXICO
Canal de Yucatán
C. Catoche
El Cuyo
Tizimín
El Díaz
Puerto de Morelos
Isla de Cozumel
B. de la Ascensión
B. del Espíritu Santo
Pta. Herrero
Banco Chinchorro
Ambergris Cay
Turneffe Is.
Odzceh
75
80
85
25
20

159

177

1 : 12 000 000

C A R I B B E A N
S E A
P A C I F I C   O C E A N
HONDURAS
NICARAGUA
COSTA RICA
PANAMA
COLOMBIA
Golfo de Honduras
Islas de la Bahía
I. de Roatán
Tela
La Ceiba
Trujillo
Puerto Castilla
C. Camarón
Pta. Patuca
Laguna Caratasca
C. Falso
C. Gracias a Dios
Olanchito
Juticalpa
Tegucigalpa
Yuscarán
Danlí
Choluteca
Sulaco
Patuca
Coco
Ocotal
Somoto
Estelí
Jinotega
Matagalpa
Cord. Isabella
Tuma
Bonanza
Tungla
Siquia
Puerto Cabezas
Pta. Gorda
Cayos Miskitos (Nicaragua)
Chinandega
El Sauce
León
Corinto
Managua
Lago de Managua
Boaco
Masaya
Granada
Diriamba
Jinotepe
Rivas
Pto. Sandino (Pto. Somoza)
San Juan del Sur
Bahía de Salinas
C. Sta. Elena
Lago de Nicaragua
Isla de Ometepe
San Carlos
San Juan
Santo Domingo
Juigalpa
Cord. de Yolaina
Bluefields
El Bluff
Pta. de Perlas
Corn Is. (Leased by Nicaragua to U.S.A.)
Pta. del Mono
Bahía de San Juan del Norte
I. de San Andrés (Colombia)
Cayos de Albuquerque (Colombia)
I. de Providencia (Colombia)
Roncador Cay (U.S.A. & Colombia)
Bajo Nuevo (Colombia)
Pedro Cays (Jamaica)
Morant Cays (Jamaica)
Golfo del Papagayo
Guanacaste (Liberia)
Santa Cruz
Cord. del Guanacaste
Pen. de Nicoya
C. Blanco
Golfo de Nicoya
Puntarenas
Alajuela
Cord. Central
Guápiles
San José
Cartago
Limón
Pta. Mona
Puerto Quepos
Chirripó Grande 3837
Bahía de Coronado
Pen. de Osa
Golfito
Golfo Dulce
Pta. Burica
Cord. de Talamanca
Puerto Cortés
Vol. Barú 3374
Almirante
Bocas del Toro
Boca de Chiriquí
Laguna de Chiriquí
Golfo de los Mosquitos
Bajo Boquete
David
Pedregal
Puerto Armuelles
Golfo de Chiriquí
Isla Coiba
Sa. de Tabasará
Santiago
Chitré
Pen. de Azuero
Pta. Mariato
Las Tablas
Pta. Mala
Penonomé
PANAMA CANAL
Gatun L.
Colón
Balboa
Panamá
Golfo de Panamá
Arch. de las Perlas
Garachiné
Chepo
Cordillera de San Blas
Archipiélago de San Blas
Pta. Manzanillo
La Palma
Golfo de Urabá
G. del Darién
Turbo
I. de San Bernardo
Golfo de Morrosquillo
Lorica
Montería
Sinú
Cáceres
Nudo del Paramillo 3960
Dabeiba
Yarumal
Barranca bermeja
Puerto Wilches
Simití
Nechí
Cauca
Sahagún
Sincé
Sincelejo
El Carmen
Magangué
Mompós
Banco
Magdalena
Plato
Ariguaní
Cesar
Fundación
Calamar
Arjona
Cartagena
BARRANQUILLA
Sabanalarga
Santa Marta
Ciénaga
5800
C. de la Aguja
West from Greenwich
15
10
85
80
75

184

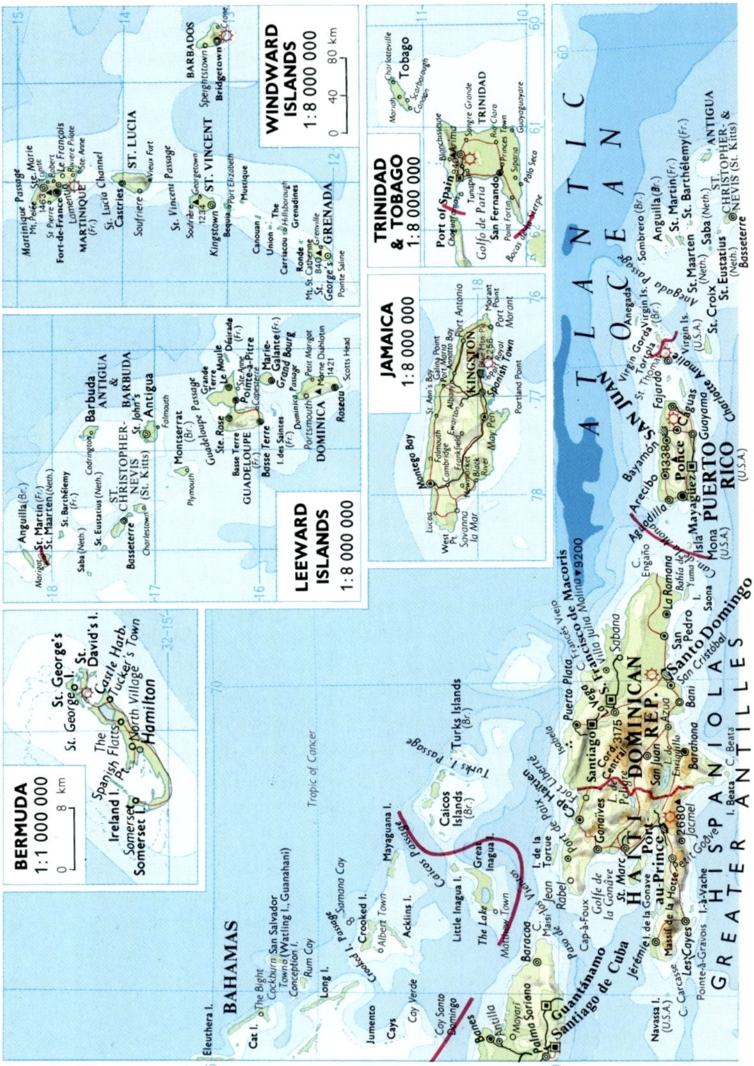

BERMUDA
1:1 000 000
St. George's
St. David's I.
Castle Harb.
Tucker's Town
Hamilton
The Flatts
North Village
Spanish Pt.
Ireland I.
Somerset
Somerset I.
LEEWARD ISLANDS
1:8 000 000
Anguilla (Br.)
St. Martin (Fr.)
St. Maarten (Neth.)
Saba (Neth.)
St. Barthélemy (Fr.)
St. Eustatius (Neth.)
ST. CHRISTOPHER-NEVIS (St. Kitts)
Basseterre
Charlestown
Barbuda
Codrington
ANTIGUA & BARBUDA
St. John's
Antigua
Montserrat (Br.)
Plymouth
Guadeloupe Passage
GUADELOUPE (Fr.)
Basse Terre
Ste. Rose
Grande Terre
Le Moule
Pointe-à-Pitre
Désirade (Fr.)
Marie-Galante (Fr.)
Grand Bourg
I. des Saintes (Fr.)
Dominica Passage
Portsmouth
DOMINICA
Morne Diablotin 1421
Roseau
Scotts Head
WINDWARD ISLANDS
1:8 000 000
0 40 80 km
Martinique Passage
Mt. Pelée 1463
Ste. Marie
Fort-de-France
Le François
Lamentin
MARTINIQUE (Fr.)
St. Lucia Channel
Castries
ST. LUCIA
Soufrière
Vieux Fort
St. Vincent Passage
Soufrière 1234
Georgetown
ST. VINCENT
Kingstown
Bequia
Mustique
The Grenadines
Canouan
Union
Carriacou
Hillsborough
Ronde
Mt. St. Catherine 840
Grenville
St. George's
GRENADA
Pointe Saline
BARBADOS
Speightstown
Bridgetown
TRINIDAD & TOBAGO
1:8 000 000
Tobago
Charlotteville
Scarborough
Port of Spain
Arima
Sangre Grande
TRINIDAD
Golfo de Paria
San Fernando
Rio Claro
Princes Town
Point Fortin
Bocas del Dragon
Boca de la Sierpe
JAMAICA
1:8 000 000
Montego Bay
St. Ann's Bay
Port Antonio
Falmouth
Lucea
Savanna la Mar
Black River
May Pen
Spanish Town
KINGSTON
Port Royal
Port Morant
Morant Point
Portland Point
BAHAMAS
Eleuthera I.
Cat I.
The Bight
Cockburn Town
San Salvador (Watling I., Guanahani)
Conception I.
Rum Cay
Long I.
Crooked I. Passage
Samana Cay
Crooked I.
Albert Town
Acklins I.
Mayaguana I.
Jumento Cays
Cay Verde
Cay Santo Domingo
Little Inagua I.
Great Inagua I.
The Lake
Matthew Town
Caicos Passage
Caicos Islands (Br.)
Turks Islands (Br.)
Turks I. Passage
Tropic of Cancer
Windward Passage
Baracoa
C. Maisí
Guantánamo
Santiago de Cuba
Palma Soriano
Banes
Antilla
Mayarí
HAITI
I. de la Tortue
Port de Paix
Cap Haïtien
Fort Liberté
Gonaïves
St. Marc
Golfe de la Gonâve
I. de la Gonave
Port-au-Prince
Jacmel
Jérémie
Les Cayes
Massif de la Hotte
I. à-Vache
Navassa I. (U.S.A.)
DOMINICAN REP.
Santiago
Puerto Plata
San Francisco de Macorís
Cord. Central
3175
San Juan
Barahona
C. Beata
I. Beata
Santo Domingo
San Cristóbal
San Pedro de Macorís
La Romana
Saona I.
C. Engaño
Samaná
Mona Passage
Isla Mona (U.S.A.)
PUERTO RICO (U.S.A.)
Aguadilla
Arecibo
Bayamón
SAN JUAN
Mayagüez
Ponce
Guayama
Caguas
Fajardo
Virgin Is. (U.S.A.)
St. Thomas
Tortola
Virgin Gorda
Anegada
Anegada Passage
St. Croix
Sombrero (Br.)
HISPANIOLA
GREATER ANTILLES
ATLANTIC OCEAN
Milwaukee Deep
9200

178

1 : 12 000 000

CARIBBEAN SEA
LESSER ANTILLES
LEEWARD ISLANDS
WINDWARD ISLANDS
Morant Cays (Jamaica)
St. Johns
BARBUDA
Montserrat (Br.)
Guadeloupe Passage
Ste. Rose
Le Moule
(Fr.) GUADELOUPE
Pointe-à-Pitre
Basse Terre
Marie-Galante (Fr.)
Grand Bourg
Aves (Ven.)
DOMINICA
Roseau
Martinique Passage
Mt. Pelée 1463
Sainte Marie
Le François
Fort-de-France
MARTINIQUE (Fr.)
St. Lucia Channel
Castries
ST. LUCIA
St. Vincent Passage
ST. VINCENT
Speightstown
Bridgetown
BARBADOS
Kingstown
The Grenadines
St. George's
GRENADA
NETH. ANTILLES
Aruba
Curaçao
Bonaire
Willemstad
La Blanquilla (Ven.)
Los Hermanos (Venezuela)
Isla Orchila (Ven.)
Islas de Aves (Ven.)
Islas Los Roques (Ven.)
Isla La Tortuga (Ven.)
Isla de Margarita
La Asunción
Porlamar
Los Testigos (Ven.)
Tobago
Port of Spain
Arima
Galera Pt.
TRINIDAD & TOBAGO
San Fernando
Río Claro
Siparia
Bocas de la Sierpe
Pta. Peñas
Bocas del Dragón
Pen. de Paria
Güiria
Golfo de Paria
Delta del Orinoco
Pta. Gallinas
Pen. de la Guajira
Uribia
Riohacha
C. de la Aguja
Santa Marta
BARRANQUILLA
Ciénaga
Sa. Nevada de Santa Marta
5800
Cartagena
Sabanalarga
Fundación
Calamar
Arjona
El Carmen
Plato
Sincelejo
Magangué
Mompós
Sincé
Sahagún
Ariguaní
Cesar
El Banco
Magdalena
Cauca
Nechí
Simití
Cáceres
Puerto Wilches
Yarumal
Barrancabermeja
COLOMBIA
Sierra de Perijá
Codazzi
3630
Machiques
MARACAIBO
La Concepción
Lago de Maracaibo
Catatumbo
Zulia
Ocaña
Cúcuta
San Cristóbal
Colón
Rubio
Pamplona
4100
Bucaramanga
Arauca
C. San Román
Península de Paraguaná
Punto Fijo
Bahía de Amuay
Cardón
Golfo de Venezuela
Puerto Cumarebo
Coro
Capatárida
Altagracia
Mene de Mauroa
Santa Rita
Cabimas
Churuguara
Tocuyo
Carora
Barquisimeto
San Felipe
Aroa
Palma Sola
Tucacas
Triste G.
Puerto Cabello
Maiquetía
La Guaira
CARACAS
Guatire
Maracay
L. de Valencia
Valencia
Yaritagua
El Tocuyo
Betijoque
Trujillo
Valera
Timotes
San Carlos
5007
Ejido
Cord. de Mérida
Mérida
Acarigua
San Carlos
Guanare
Portuguesa
Barinas
Libertad
Los Teques
Villa de Cura
S. Juan de los Morros
Ocumare del Tuy
C. Codera
Carenero
El Guapo
Pen. de Araya
Puerto La Cruz
Cumaná
Cumanacoa
Barcelona
Caicara
2596
Clarines
Carúpano
Río Caribe
Caripito
Maturín
Aragua de Barcelona
Cantaura
El Tigre
Unare
Tigre
Tucupita
Valle de Pascua
Calabozo
Guarico
Manapire
Pariaguán
Barrancas
Soledad
Ciudad Guayana (Santo Tomé)
Ciudad Bolívar
Upata
Sierra Imataca
Guasipati
El Callao
Ciudad Piar
Caroní
La Paragua
Apure
Orinoco
San Fernando
Caicara
La Urbana
Capanaparo
Arauca
VENEZUELA
GUYANA
15
10
75
70
65
60
West from Greenwich

179
184
185

SOUTH AMERICA : PHYSICAL

Curaçao (Neth.)
Trinidad
G. of Darien
5800
Cord. de Mérida
Llanos
Orinoco
Magdalena
Demerara
Courantyne
Surinam
Kaieteur Falls
Roraima
2810
Guiana
Sa. Pacaraima
Orinoco
Casiquiare
Essequibo
Sa. de Tumucumaque
Amazon
Marajó I.
Pará
Equator
Cotopaxi 5897
Chimborazo 6267
Putumayo
Japurá
Negro
Amazon
Marañón
Pta. Pariñas
Selvas
Tapajós
Tocantins
Purus
Madeira
S. Antônio Falls
Aripuanã
Xingu
Araguaia
Parnaíba
C. de São Roque
C. Branco
Ucayali
6768
São Francisco
Guaporé
Plateau of Mato Grosso
Brazilian Highlands
L. Titicaca
Illampu Ancohuma
6550
Bolivian Plateau
Pilcomayo
Gran Chaco
Paraguay
Paraná
Sa. da Mantiqueira
2890
C. Frio
8050
Tropic of Capricorn
Atacama Desert
Iguaçu Falls
Sa. do Mar
PACIFIC OCEAN
Ojos del Salado 6863
Uruguay
Entre Rios
Paraná
Lagoa dos Patos
Aconcagua 6960
Juan Fernández
Andes
Pampas
Rio de la Plata
Colorado
Pta. Mogotes
ATLANTIC OCEAN
Negro
G. of San Matías
Valdés Pen.
Chiloé
Chubut
Chonos Arch.
G. of San Jorge
4058
Patagonia
6212
Falkland Is.
Magellan's Str.
West from Greenwich
COPYRIGHT. GEORGE PHILIP & SON. LTD.
Tierra del Fuego
Staten I.
C. Froward
C. Horn

1 : 50 000 000

Curaçao (Neth.)
Trinidad & Tobago
Maracaibo
Barranquilla
G. of Darien
Cartagena
La Guaira
Caracas
Barquisimeto
Orinoco
Bucaramanga
G. of Panama
VENEZUELA
Magdalena
Medellín
Manizales
Bogotá
Cali
COLOMBIA
Georgetown
GUYANA
Paramaribo
SURINAM
FR. GUIANA
Cayenne
Orinoco
Casiquiare
Amazon
Pará
Equator
Quito
ECUADOR
Guayaquil
Cuenca
Putumayo
Japurá
Negro
Manaus
Amazon
Belém
São Luís (Maranhão)
Tocantins
Marañon
Iquitos
Teresina
Fortaleza (Ceará)
Natal
João Pessoa
Recife (Pernambuco)
Maceió
Parnaíba
Paulistana
São Francisco
Chiclayo
Trujillo
Ucayali
Purus
Madeira
Aripuana
Tapajós
Xingu
Araguaia
PERU
Callão
Lima
Cuzco
Andes
B R A Z I L
Guaporé
Salvador (Bahia)
L. Titicaca
BOLIVIA
La Paz
Cochabamba
Oruro
Santa Cruz
Sucre
Cuiabá
Goiânia
Brasília
Arequipa
Mollendo
Tacna
Arica
Iquique
Corumbá
Paraguay
Pirapora
Belo Horizonte
PARAGUAY
Paraná
Ribeirão Preto
Campinas
São Paulo
Santos
Niteroi
Rio de Janeiro
Tropic of Capricorn
Antofagasta
Pilcomayo
Asunción
Curitiba
Iguaçu Falls
Tucumán
Paraná
Uruguay
PACIFIC OCEAN
ARGENTINA
Córdoba
Mendoza
Santa Fé
Paraná
Rosario
URUGUAY
Pôrto Alegre
Lagoa dos Patos
Rio Grande do Sul
Viña del Mar
Valparaíso
Santiago
Juan Fernández (Chile)
Buenos Aires
La Plata
Montevideo
Rio de la Plata
Talca
Concepción
CHILE
Colorado
Pta. Mogotes
Temuco
Bahía Blanca
Negro
Valdivia
G. of San Matías
ATLANTIC OCEAN
Puerto Montt
Chiloé
Chubut
Patagonia
Chonos Arch.
G. of San Jorge
Falkland Is. (Br.)
Stanley
Punta Arenas
Magellan's Str.
Tierra del Fuego
Staten I.
C. Horn
West from Greenwich
COPYRIGHT GEORGE PHILIP & SON LTD

1 : 50 000 000

181

179

Barranquilla
Santa Marta
Ciénaga
Riohacha
Soledad
Cartagena
Sabanalarga
Turbaco
Calamar
Fundación
Aracataca
Maracaibo
Cabimas
Machiques
Lago de Maracaibo
Barquisimeto
Valencia
Maracay
Maiquetía
La Guaira
CARACAS
Puerto Cabello
Tucacas
Coro
Punto Fijo
La Vela
Puerto Cumarebo
Altagracia
Mene de Mauroa
Tocuyo
San Felipe
Aruba (Neth.)
Curaçao
Willemstad
Bonaire (Neth.)
I. Los Roques (Ven.)
I. Orchila (Ven.)
Is. de Aves (Ven.)
Pta. Gallinas
Pen. de Paraguana
Pen. de la Guajira
Uribia
G. de Venezuela
Sa. Nevada de Sta. Marta
Ocumare del Tuy
Tuy
San Juan de los Morros
Valle de Pascua
Calabozo
San Carlos
El Tocuyo
Trujillo
Valera
Guanare
Portuguesa
Barinas
Mérida
5007
El Vigía
Tachira
Encontrados
Catatumbo
Sta. Carlos del Zulia
La Ceiba
Mene Grande
San Fernando de Apure
Apure
Orinoco
Caicara
La Urbana
Colón
Portobelo
Pta. Manzanillo
PANAMA
Panamá
La Chorrera
Arch. de las Perlas
La Palma
El Real
Golfo de Panamá
Pta. Mala
Jaque
Jurado
Is. de S. Bernardo
G. de Morrosquillo
Golfo del Darién
Arjona
El Carmen
Plato
Sincelejo
Magangué
Mompós
Montería
El Banco
Magdalena
Turbo
Riosucio
Atrato
Antioquia
Yarumal
Cauca
Pto. Willches
Ocaña
Cúcuta
San Cristóbal
Rubio
Pamplona
4100
Guasdualito
Arauca
Capanaparo
VENEZ
Medellín
Barrancabermeja
Bucaramanga
San Gil
Socorro
Pto. Berrío
Vélez
Sogamoso
Tunja
Chiquinquira
Trinidad
Meta
Pto. Páez
Pto. Carreño
2285
Pto. Ayacucho
Ventuari
Tomo
Vichada
G. de Cupica
PACIFIC
OCEAN
C. Corrientes
Quibdó
Riosucio
Aguadas
Honda
La Dorada
Manizales
Pereira
Cartago
Armenia
Tulua
Facatativa
Tolima
5215
Zipaquira
BOGOTA
Villavicencio
Fusagasuga
Girardot
Espinal
Ibagué
Orocué
S. José de Ocune
San Fernando de Atabapo
Pta. Charambira
Buenaventura
Buga
Palmira
Cali
COLOMBIA
Natagaima
Huila
5750
Neiva
Guaviare
Inírida
Guainía
I. Gorgona
Mosquera
Popayán
Puracé
4646
Garzón
Campoalegre
San José del Guaviare
Tumaco
Patia
Barbacoas
Bolívar
Florencia
S. Lorenzo
El Diviso
Pasto
Mocoa
Túquerres
Ipiales
Caquetá
Caguan
Vaupés
Yarí
Isana
San Carlos
Cucuí
Sa. Imeri
Esmeraldas
Tulcán
Pto. Asís
Putumayo
Mitú
Otavalo
Ibarra
La Tagua
Iauretê
Uaupés
Içana
Cojimies
Equator
Cayambe
Cuhimbe
Pto. Leguizamo
Bahía de Caráquez
Chone
Quito
Cotopaxi 5896
Latacunga
Aguarico
Napo
Cabo Pantoja
Apaporis
Marié
Manta
Portoviejo
Ambato
ECUADOR
Nuevo Rocafuerte
Montecristi
Jipijapa
Sta. Ana
Chimborazo
6267
Riobamba
La Pedrera
Japurá
Guayaquil
Babahoyo
Curaray
Arica
Putumayo
Salinas
Santa Elena
Milagro
Sangay
Alausí
5230
Solimões
G. de Guayaquil
Azogues
Cuenca
Sigsig
Santa Clotilde
Tonantins
Fonte Boa
Pto. Bolívar
Machala
Saraguro
Pastaza
Corrientes
Pebas
Amazonas (Amazon)
Iça
Tarapaca
Santo Antônio do Içá
Tumbes
Zorritos
Loja
Zamora
Santiago
Morona
Tigre
Mazán
Iquitos
Leticia
São Paulo de Olivença
Borja
Nauta
Benjamin Constant
Yavari
Talara
Ayabaca
3934
Chira
Barranca
Marañón
Parinari
Jandiatuba
Jutaí
A M
Concórdia
Sullana
Paita
Piura
Catacaos
Chulucanas
Huancabamba
Jaén
PERU
Lagunas
Requena
Cahuapanas
Yurimaguas
Ucayali
B
Juruá
Tapauá
Bayovar
P. Negra
Reventazón
Desierto de Sechura
Ferreñafe
Chiclayo
Moyobamba
Lamas
Tarapoto
Chachapoyas
Saposoa
Eirunepé
Pimentel
Chepén
Cajamarca
Chilete
Pacasmayo
San Pedro de Lloc
Foz do Gregório
Ipixuna
Contamana
Cruzeiro do Sul
Tarauacá
Pauini
75
70
10
5
0
West from Greenwich

186

1 : 16 000 000

The Grenadines
St.George's
GRENADA
I. Blanquilla (Ven.)
Los Hermanos (Ven.)
I. La Tortuga (Ven.)
I. Margarita
La Asunción
Los Testigos
Porlamar
Carúpano
Tobago
Scarborough
Port of Spain
TRINIDAD & TOBAGO
Pen. de Araya
Cumaná
Guiria
S. Fernando
Rio Claro
ATLANTIC
OCEAN
Pto. Piritu
Barcelona
Puerto La Cruz
2596
Caripito
Maturín
Guanipa
El Tigre
Tigre
Tucupita
Barrancas
Pariaguan
Ciudad Guayana
Cariapo
Morawhanna
Soledad
(Santo Tomé)
Upata
Ciudad Bolivar
Guasipati
Barima
Waini
Matthew's Ridge
Ciudad Piar
El Callao
Tumeremo
U E L A
Cuyuni
La Paragua
El Dorado
Georgetown
Caura
Mazaruni
Parika
Rosignol
New Amsterdam
Paramaribo
Nieuw Amsterdam
Bartica
Nieuw Nickerie
Pakaraima
Essequibo
Skeldon
Totness
Paragua
2560
Linden
Moengo
Mana
Iracoubo
Caroni
Nickerie
Kwakoegron
Albina
Sinnamary
Kourou
2810
Mt. Roraima
Kaieteur Falls
Berbice
Brokopondo
St. Laurent
Tumatumari
Coppename
Suriname
Cayenne
G U Y A N A
Mts.
Courantyne
Kaw
Approuague
Sierra Pacaraima
Apoteri
SURINAM
FR. GUIANA
C. Orange
Oiapoque
St. Georges
Julianatop
1280
Marowijne
Tacutu
Lethem
Rupununi
Tapanahoni
Camopi
Serra Parima
Uraricoera
Rewa
Mucajai
Boa Vista
Dadanawa
Litani
Orinoco
New
Essequibo
Amapá
Ilha de Maracá
Serra
Tumucumaque
C. do Norte
RORAIMA
Serra Acaraí
AMAPÁ
Sa. Tapirapecó
Catrimani
Branco
Demini
Meriruma
Araguari
Serra do Navio
Pto. Grande
Jari
Padauiri
Catrimani
Macapá
Ilha Caviana
Jauaperi
Mapuera
Trombetas
Cuminá
Curuápanema
Paru
Mazagão
Afuá
Chaves
Boiacu
Negro
Maicuru
I. Grande de Gurupá
Ilha de Marajó
Barcelos
Carvoeira
Moura
Nhamundá
Monte Alegre
Prainha
Almeirim
Gurupá
Breves
Muaná
Marañ
Unini
Uatumã
Uracara
Óbidos
Curralinho
Faro
Juruti
Pôrto de Moz
Cametá
L. Amaná
Amazonas (Amazon)
Xingu
(Amazonas)
Itaquatiara
Santarém
Sousel
Anapu
Jacundá
Manaus
Parintins
Belterra
Pacajá
Baião
L. Badajós
Tupinambaranas
Altamira
L. Piorini
Tefé
Manacapuru
Maués
Aveiro
P A R Á
Brasília Legal
Coari
Codajás
Ilha Tupinambaranas
Tefé
A Z O N A S
Borba
Tapajós
Itaituba
Iriri
R A Z I L
Abacaxis
Purus
Madeira
Bacabal
Itatuba
Manicoré
Sucunduri
Jamanxim
Curuá
Xingu
Sa. dos Carajás
Canutama
Ipixuna
Prainha
das Canudos
Fresco
Iriri
Lábrea
Humaitá
65
60
55
10
5
5

188

187

184

PACIFIC OCEAN
ECUADOR
PERU
Salinas
Santa Elena
Guayaquil
Milagro
Alausí
5230
Azogues
Cuenca
Sigsig
Pto. Bolívar
Machala
G. de Guayaquil
Tumbes
Zorritos
Zaruma
Saraguro
Loja
Zamora
Santiago
Morona
Pastaza
Corrientes
Tigre
Napo
Santa Clotilde
Mazán
Pebas
Iquitos
Nauta
Yavari
Talara
Ayabaca
3934
Borja
Barranca
Marañón
Parinari
Requena
Sullana
Chira
Chulucanas
Paita
Piura
Catacaos
Huancabamba
Jaén
Cahuapanas
Lagunas
Yurimaguas
Ucayali
Bayovar
Desierto de Sechura
Pta Negra
Reventazón
Ferreñafe
Moyobamba
Lamas
Tarapoto
Chiclayo
Chachapoyas
Saposoa
Pimentel
Chepén
Cajamarca
Contamana
Cruzeiro do Sul
Pacasmayo
Chilete
San Pedro de Lloc
Ascope
Pto. Chicama
Trujillo
Huallaga
Juruá
Porto Valter
Milne Edwards Trench
Salaverry
Tayabamba
Pucallpa
Masisea
Chimbote
Caras
Huascarán
6768
Tingo María
Pachitea
Taumaturgo
Casma
Huaraz
Santa
Aija
Huánuco
Panao
Huarmey
Chiquián
Ambo
Cerro de Pasco
Pto. Bermúdez
Goyllarisquisga
Huachón
Atalaya
Perené
Urubamba
Barranca
Sayán
Huacho
Huayllay
6369
Peru
La Oroya
Tarma
Morococha
Mantaro
Jauja
Ancón
Callao
Huancayo
Apurímac
I. San Lorenzo
Matucana
Pampas
LIMA
Yauyos
Huancavelica
Ayacucho
Quillabamba
Machupicchu
Cañete
Urubamba
Chincha Alta
Tambo de Mora
Huancapi
Cuzco
Pisco
Abancay
Icá
Chalhuanca
Santo Tomás
Puquio
Antabamba
Peru–Chile Trench
Coracora
Nudo Coropuna
6425
Chuquibamba
San Juan
Chala
Caravelí
Atico
Aplao
Camaná
Matarani
6866
Krümmel Trench
85
80
75
5
10
15
20

West from Greenwich

1 : 16 000 000

185

AMAZONAS
BRAZIL
ACRE
RONDÔNIA
BOLIVIA
CHILE
ARGENTINA
PARAGUAY
Solimões (Amazonas)
Amazonas (Amazon)
Manaus
Tonantins
Iça
Tarapacá
Santo Antônio do Içá
Fonte Boa
L. Amanã
L. Badajós
Itaquatiara
Uracara
Maués
Ilha Tupinambaranas
Manacapuru
Codajás
Coari
Tefé
L. Piorini
São Paulo de Olivença
Leticia
Benjamin Constant
Concórdia
Jandiatuba
Jutaí
Juruá
Purus
Tapauá
Itatuba
Madeira
Manicoré
Borba
Abacaxis
Canutama
Eirunepé
Ipixuna
Tarauacá
Feijó
Pauini
Lábrea
Ipixuna
Humaitá
Calama
Prainha
Aripuanã
Canudos
Sucunduri
Teles Pires
Serra dos Apiacas
Bôca do Acre
Ituxi
Sena Madureira
Porto Velho
Caritianas
Aripuanã
Roosevelt
Juruena
Rio Branco
Abunã
Ariquemes
Iaco
Acre
Xapuri
Brasiléia
Sta. Rosa
Villa Bella
Guajará-Mirim
Orton
Iñapari
Cobija
Tahuamanu
Riberalta
Yata
Beni
Madre de Dios
Presidente Hermes
Pimenta Bueno
Barão de Melgaço
Serra dos Parecis
Serra do Norte
Arinos
Serra do Tombador
Sangue
Piedras
Manuripi
Manu
Puerto Heath
Principe da Beira
Guaporé
Vilhena
Juruena
Utiariti
Saturnina
Pto. Maldonado
Madidi
L. Rogoaguado
Exaltación
Mamoré
Itonamas
San Martin
Calca
Urcos
6384
Macusani
Ixiamas
Sta. Ana
L. Rogagua
Magdalena
Paraguá
Paruro
Sicuani
Sandia
Apolo
Rurrenabaque
Coiro
Trinidad
Blanco
Mato Grosso
1995
Guaporé
Paraguai
Azangaro
Ayaviri
Lampa
Huancane
Juliaca
3812
Lago Titicaca
San Borja
San Miguel
Puno
Sorata
Ancohuma
6550
Coroico
Concepción
San Javier
San Ignacio
San Matías
Cáceres
Arequipa
Juli
La Paz
Inquisivi
Ichilo
Omate
Guaqui
Illimani
6462
El Cerro
Mollendo
Viacha
Corocoro
Moquegua
Torata
Umala
Desaguadero
Sicasica
Cochabamba
Portachuelo
L. Concepción
San José
Ilo
Charaña
Punata
Santa Cruz
Tacna
Sajama
6520
Corque
Oruro
Grande
Roboré
Arica
Lauca
L. Poopó
Uncia
Challapata
Sucre
Corumbá
Puerto Suárez
Porto Esperança
Pisagua
Sillajhuay
Sal. de Coipasa
Rio Mulatos
Potosí
Pilcomayo
Charagua
Parapetí
Coimbra
5995
Iquique
Pozo Almonte
Pintados
Salar de Uyuni
Cuzco 5950
Huanchaca
San Lucas
Camiri
Cuevo
Bahia Negra
Pica
Uyuni
Pulacayo
Cotagaita
Lagunas
Collaguasi
Chiguana
Atocha
Pilaya
Villa Montes
Fuerto Olimpo
Ollagüe
Tarija
Porto Murtinho
Loa
Quillagua
Tupiza
Mariscal Estigarribia
Punta Rieles
Tocopilla
Taco
Villazón
Yacuiba
Pto. Sastre
Chuquicamata
La Quiaca
Chaco Boreal
Pto. Casado
Apa
Calama
5970
Rinconada
Tartagal
Filadelfia
Pto. Pinasco
Sierra Gorda
Pta. Angamos
Cerro Sairecabur
Trench
70
65
60
5
10
15
20

188

190

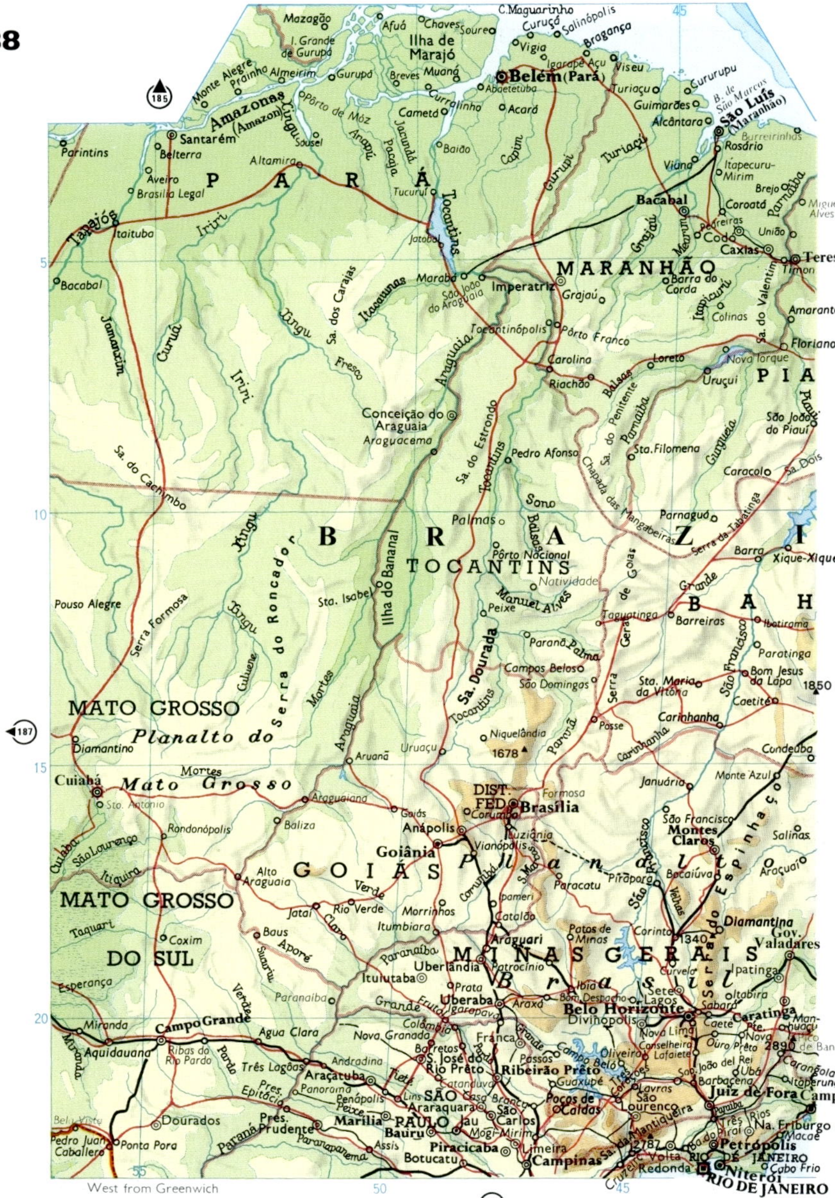
185
187
191
West from Greenwich
5
10
15
20
45
50
55
PARÁ
MARANHÃO
PIA
B R A Z I
TOCANTINS
BAH
MATO GROSSO
Planalto do Mato Grosso
GOIÁS
MINAS GERAIS
MATO GROSSO DO SUL
Planalto Brasil
Espinhaço
C. Maguarinho
Mazagão
Afuá
Chaves
Soure
Curuçá
Salinópolis
Vigia
Bragança
I. Grande de Gurupá
Ilha de Marajó
Monte Alegre
Prainha
Almeirim
Gurupá
Breves
Muaná
Belém (Pará)
Abaetetuba
Viseu
Turiaçu
Gururupu
B. de São Marcos
São Luís (Maranhão)
Guimarães
Alcântara
Amazonas (Amazon)
Xingu
Pôrto de Móz
Cametá
Curralinho
Acará
Santarém
Belterra
Parintins
Sousel
Baião
Capim
Turiaçu
Rosário
Itapecuru-Mirim
Brejo
Parnaíba
Miguel Alves
Altamira
Aveiro
Brasília Legal
Tucuruí
Tocantins
Gurupi
Bacabal
Coroatá
Pedreiras
Codó
União
Caxias
Teresina
Timon
Tapajós
Itaituba
Iriri
Jatobal
Marabá
São João do Araguaia
Imperatriz
Grajaú
Barra do Corda
Bacabal
Jamanxim
Curuá
Xingu
Sa. dos Carajás
Itacaiunas
Fresco
Tocantinópolis
Pôrto Franco
Colinas
Amarante
Floriano
Nova Iorque
Carolina
Riachão
Balsas
Loreto
Uruçuí
Araguaia
Conceição do Araguaia
Araguacema
Sa. do Estrondo
Pedro Afonso
Sa. do Penitente
Parnaíba
Sta. Filomena
Gurguéia
São João do Piauí
Caracol
Sa. do Cachimbo
Sono
Palmas
Chapada das Mangabeiras
Parnaguá
Serra da Tabatinga
Barra
Xique-Xique
Serra do Roncador
Ilha do Bananal
Pôrto Nacional
Natividade
Manuel Alves
Grande
Sta. Isabel
Pouso Alegre
Serra Formosa
Culuene
Mortes
Peixe
Taguatinga
Barreiras
Ibotirama
Paratinga
Paranã
Palma
Campos Belos
São Domingos
Sa. Dourada
Bom Jesus da Lapa
Sta. Maria da Vitória
São Francisco
1850
Caetité
Diamantino
Niquelândia
1678
Uruaçu
Aruanã
Posse
Carinhanha
Condeúba
Cuiabá
Sto. Antonio
Araguaiana
Goiás
DIST. FED.
Brasília
Formosa
Corumbá
Januária
Monte Azul
Baliza
Rondonópolis
São Lourenço
Itiquira
Anápolis
Goiânia
Luziânia
Vianópolis
São Francisco
Montes Claros
Salinas
Alto Araguaia
Verde
Paracatu
Pirapora
Bocaiúva
Araçuaí
Jataí
Rio Verde
Morrinhos
Ipameri
Catalão
Itumbiara
Taquari
Coxim
Baus
Aporé
Araguari
Patos de Minas
Corinto
1340
Diamantina
Gov. Valadares
Paranaíba
Uberlândia
Patrocínio
Curvelo
Ipatinga
Ituiutaba
Prata
Ibiá
Sete Lagoas
Esperança
Paranaíba
Uberaba
Araxá
Bom Despacho
Sabará
Itabira
Belo Horizonte
Divinópolis
Caeté
Caratinga
Manhuaçu
Miranda
Campo Grande
Água Clara
Colômbia
Igarapava
Nova Granada
Franca
Nova Lima
Conselheiro Lafaiete
Ouro Prêto
Aquidauana
Ribas do Rio Pardo
Pardo
Barretos
S. José do Rio Prêto
Ribeirão Prêto
Passos
Oliveira
2890
Três Lagoas
Andradina
Araçatuba
Tietê
Catanduva
Guaxupé
São João del Rei
Ubá
Itaperuna
Panorama
Pres. Epitácio
Peixe
Penápolis
Lins
SÃO PAULO
Araraquara
Casa Branca
Poços de Caldas
Lavras
São Lourenço
Barbacena
Juiz de Fora
Campos
Bela Vista
Dourados
Pres. Prudente
Marília
Bauru
Jaú
São Carlos
Mogi-Mirim
Sa. da Mantiqueira
2787
Três Rios
Nova Friburgo
Macaé
Pedro Juan Caballero
Ponta Porã
Paraná
Paranapanema
Assis
Botucatu
Piracicaba
Limeira
Campinas
Volta Redonda
Petrópolis
RIO DE JANEIRO
Niterói
Cabo Frio

1 : 16 000 000

Fortaleza (Ceará)
Fernando de Noronha (Braz.)
Rocas
CEARÁ
RIO GRANDE DO NORTE
Natal
PARAÍBA
João Pessoa (Paraiba)
Olinda
RECIFE (Pernambuco)
PERNAMBUCO
Maceió
ALAGOAS
SERGIPE
Aracaju
Salvador (Bahia)
Vitória
ATLANTIC OCEAN
Trindade (Braz.)
6059

187

BOLIVIA
PARA
Chaco Boreal
Chaco Central
Gran Chaco
Chaco Austral
ARGENTINA
CHILE
Desierto de Atacama
Puna de Atacama
Peru – Chile Trench
Richards Trench
Tropic of Capricorn
Lagunas
Collaguasi
Ollagüe
Chiguana
Tupiza
Tarija
Villa Montes
Loa
Quillagua
Toco
Tocopilla
Chuquicamata
Villazón
Yacuiba
La Quiaca
Punta Rieles
Filadelfia
Pilcomayo
5970
Rinconada
Tartagal
Sierra Gorda
Calama
Cerro Sairecábur
Iturbe
Embarcación
Pta. Angamos
8050
Mejillones
Salar de Atacama
Humahuaca
Orán
Bermejo
Los Blancos
Pta. Tetas
Antofagasta
Susques
Tabacal
Confuso
Portezuelo de Socompo
Rivadavia
Aguas Blancas
S. Salvador de Jujuy
Perico
Llullaillaco
6723
Salta
Güemes
Las Lomitas
Cachinal
Teuco
25
Taltal
Catalina
Joaquín V. Gonzalez
Pirané
Metán
Guachipas
Rosario de la Frontera
San José del Boquerón
Trancas
Potrerillos
Formosa
Chañaral
Pueblo Hundido
Burruyacú
Campo Gallo
San Miguel de Tucumán
Avió Terai
Pres. R. S. Peña
Pilar
P. de San Francisco
4722
5500
Sa. de Aconquija
Caldera
Ojos del Salado
6863
G. Pinedo
Resistencia
Copiapo
Copiapó
Tres Puentes
Andalgalá
La Cocha
La Banda
Va. Angela
Charadai
Barranqueras
Corrientes
Punta de Díaz
Santiago del Estero
Quimilí
Empedrado
Carrizal Bajo
Tinogasta
Añatuya
Bella Vista
Huasco
Catamarca
Va. Ocampo
Vallenar
Frias
Col. Dora
Intiyaco
San Roque
Mercedes
Va. Mazán
Chilecito
Chumbicha
Bandera
Co. del Toro
6380
6250
La Rioja
Ceballar
Tostado
Reconquista
Goya
Guandacol
Recreo
Selva
Salado
Vera
La Serena
Coquimbo
Rivadavia
Patquia
Villa de María
Ceres
Esquina
30
Vicuña
San José de Jáchal
Bermejo
S. Cristóbal
Tongoy
Ovalle
Chamical
Dean Funes
L. Mar Chiquita
Monteros
S. Javier
La Paz
Serrezuela
Cruz del Eje
S. Justa
Calingasta
Córdoba
Rafaela
Albardón
Villa Colón
S. Francisco
Esperanza
Illapel
San Juan
Chepes
Alta Gracia
Las Varillas
Santa Fe
Paraná
Salamanca
Va. Dolores
Gálvez
Villaguay
Los Vilos
San Felipe
Quines
Villa María
Bell Ville
Diamante
Concepción del Uruguay
Papudo
Quintero
Los Andes
Aconcagua
6960
Sta. Rosa
Las Rosas
Viña del Mar
Valparaíso
Quillota
Mendoza
S. Francisco del Monte de Oro
Cañada de Gómez
Rosario
SANTIAGO
Paso Uspallata
Tupungato
6800
La Paz
Río Cuarto
Casilda
Gualeguay
Gualeguaychú
San Antonio
S. Bernardo
Tunuyán
San Luis
S. Nicolás
Pergamino
Ibicuy
Rancagua
Puente Alto
S. Carlos
Mercedes
Justo Daract
La Carlota
Venado Tuerto
Pichilemú
San Fernando
San Rafael
Mte. Comán
Laboulaye
Rufino
BUENOS AIRES
Curicó
Junín
Mercedes
Luján
Licantén
Huinca Renancó
Gral. Villegas
Lincoln
Chivilcoy
Avellaneda
35
Gral. Alvear
Realicó
Constitución
Talca
Atuel
Gral. Pico
Nueve de Julio
Linares
Sal. Llancanelo
Malargüe
Arizona
Trenque Lauquen
Pehuajó
Saladillo
Cauquenes
Victorica
Bolívar
S. Carlos
Parral
Sta. Isabel
Catriló
Gral. Alvear
Las Flores
Talcahuano
Concepción
Chillán
Santa Rosa
Azul
Coronel
Chos Malal
Toay
Olavarría
Arauco
Lota
Polcura
Limay Mahuida
Doblas
Carhué
Gral. La Madrid
Tandil
Rosenda
Los Angeles
Gral. Acha
Puán
Cor. Suárez
Lebu
Angol
Colorado
Colonia 25 de Mayo
Sa. de la Ventana
Sa. de Tandil
Cañete
Mulchén
Puelches
Pigüé
Cor. Pringles
Balcarce
Victoria
Tornquist
Traiguén
Las Lajas
Añelo
Lobería
Temuco
Cherquenco
Gral. Roca
Chelforó
Bahía Blanca
Quequén
Puerto Saavedra
Paso Pino Hachado
Neuquén
Tres Arroyos
Necochea
Nueva Imperial
Freire
Zapala
R. Colorado
Choele Choel
Colorado
Punta Alta
Cor. Dorrego
Loncoche
Villarrica
Bahía Blanca
Valdivia
Junín de los Andes
Picún Leufú
I. Trinidad
El Cuy
40
Los Lagos
Negro
La Unión
L. Ranco
Osorno
Sa. Colorada
Valcheta
San Antonio Oeste
Carmen de Patagones
L. Llanquihue
L. Nahuel Huapi
Comallo
Pta. Rasa
Pto. Varas
Viedma
Puerto Montt
Maquinchao
Tronador
3554
S. Carlos de Bariloche
Golfo San Matías
75
70
65
60
West from Greenwich

192

1 : 16 000 000

188
MATO GROSSO DO SUL
Pôrto Murtinho
Bela Vista
Pedro Juan Caballero
Ponta Pora
Dourados
Concepción
Horqueta
Belén
San Pedro
Rosario
Villa Hayes
Asunción
Paraguarí
Villarrica
Abai
Caazapá
Yegros
San Pedro del Paraná
S. Ignacio
Encarnación
Posadas
Gral. Paz
Apóstoles
Sto. Tomé
São Borja
Alvear
Itaqui
Alegrete
Uruguaiana
Quaraí
Rosario do Sul
Artigas
Santana do Livramento
Rivera
Concordia
Salto
Tacuarembó
Paysandú
URUGUAY
Durazno
Mercedes
Trinidad
Colonia del Sacramento
Florida
Minas
S. José de Mayo
MONTEVIDEO
Maldonado
Rocha
Treinta y Tres
José Batlle y Ordóñez
Melo
Jaguarão
Pelotas
Rio Grande
Bagé
Cangussu
Mostardas
Lagoa dos Patos
L. Mirim
L. Mangueira
Sta. Vitória do Palmar
Río de la Plata
La Plata
Magdalena
Pipinas
Chascomús
C.S. Antonio
Dolores
Gral. Guido
Gral. Juan Madariago
Mar del Plata
RIO GRANDE DO SUL
Santa Maria
Sta. Cruz do Sul
Cachoeira do Sul
S. Gabriel
Santiago
Cruz Alta
Sto. Ângelo
Santa Rosa
Passo Fundo
Erechim
Joaçaba
Pôrto Alegre
S. Leopoldo
Osorio
Caxias do Sul
Araranguá
Criciúma
Tubarão
Laguna
Lajes
SANTA CATARINA
Rio do Sul
Blumenau
Itajaí
Joinvile
Florianópolis
São Francisco do Sul
Mafra
Rio Negro
União da Vitória
Pto. União
Bernardo de Irigoyen
Iguaçu Falls
Foz de Iguaçu
Hernandarias
Itaipú Dam
Pto. Mendes
Guaira
PARANÁ
Guarapuava
Ponta Grossa
Curitiba
Paranaguá
Castro
Jaguariaíva
Maringá
Londrina
Rolândia
Arapongas
Apucarana
Jacarèzinho
Pres. Prudente
Pres. Epitacio
Marília
Assis
Araçatuba
Penapolis
Lins
Catanduva
Araraquara
Jau
São Carlos
Ribeirão Prêto
Guaxupé
Poços de Caldas
Piracicaba
Limeira
Botucatu
Campinas
Itu
Jundiaí
Sorocaba
Tatuí
SÃO PAULO
Mogi das Cruzes
Santos
Iguape
Juquiá
Taubaté
Jacareí
RIO DE JANEIRO
Barbacena
São João del Rei
Lavras
São Lourenço
2787
Angra dos Reis
Baía da Ilha Grande
I. de São Sebastião
BRAZIL
Serra do Mar
ATLANTIC OCEAN
1888
5830
25
30
35
40
55
50
45

190

Talcahuano
Concepción
Coronel
Arauco
Lota
Lebu
Cañete
S. Carlos
Parral
Chillán
Los Angeles
Angol
Mulchén
Victoria
Traiguén
Temuco
Puerto Saavedra
Nueva Imperial
Freire
Loncoche
Villarrica
Valdivia
Los Lagos
La Unión
Osorno
L. Llanquihue
Pto. Varas
Puerto Montt
Ancud
G. de Ancud
Castro
I. de Chiloé
Pto. Quellón
C. Quilán
Boca del Guafo
Islas Guaitecas
Archipiélago de los Chonos
I. Magdalena
Pto. Aisén
Coihaique
Balmaceda
Pen. de Taitao
C. Tres Montes
G. de Penas
San Valentín
4058
Lago Buenos Aires
L. Pueyrredon
L. Cochrane
San Lorenzo
3700
I. Campana
L. O'Higgins
L. S. Martín
L. Viedma
I. Wellington
I. Mornington
Murallón
3600
Argentino
I. Madre de Dios
Calafate
Canal Concepción
I. Hanover
Estrecho Nelson
El Turbio
Pto. Natales
Arch. Reina Adelaida
Estrecho de Magallanes
(Magellan's Str.)
I. Desolación
B. Otway
I. Santa Inés
Seno Skyring
Seno de Otway
Punta Arenas
Porvenir
S. Sebastián
Tierra del Fuego
Rio Grande
I. Dawson
2469
Canal Beagle
Ushuaia
L. Fagnano
I. Clarence
Canal Cockburn
Pen. Brecknock
I. Stewart
I. Londonderry
Bahía Cook
I. Hoste
B. Nassau
I. Navarino
Pen. Hardy
I. Hermite
Islas Wollaston
Cabo de Hornos (C. Horn)
Islas Diego Ramirez
C. San Diego
I. de los Estados (Staten I.)
Estrecho de Le Maire
Sta. Isabel
Victorica
Santa Rosa
Catriló
Toay
Limay Mahuida
Doblas
Gral. Acha
Colonia 25 de Mayo
Chos-Malal
Neuquén
Colorado
Las Lajas
Añelo
Puelches
Chadileuvú
Paso Pino Hachado
Zapala
Gral. Roca
Chelforó
R. Colorado
Choele Choel
Junín de los Andes
Limay
Picún Leufú
El Cuy
L. Ranco
L. Nahuel Huapi
Tronador
3554
S. Carlos de Bariloche
Sa. Colorada
Comallo
Maquinchao
Ñorquinco
Gastre
Leleque
Esquel
Chubut
Telsen
Paso de Indios
Las Plumas
José de San Martín
L. Musters
L. Colhué Huapi
Sarmiento
Chico
Valcheta
San Antonio Oeste
Carmen de Patagones
Pta. Rasa
Viedma
Negro
Golfo San Matías
Verde
Puerto Lobos
G. San José
Pirámides
Península Valdés
Punta Delgada
Pto. Madryn
Golfo Nuevo
Trelew
Rawson
Camarones
C. Dos Bahías
Golfo San Jorge
Comodoro Rivadavia
Las Heras
Pico Truncado
Mazarredo
C. Tres Puntas
Deseado
Fitz Roy
Jaramillo
C. Blanco
Pto. Deseado
Bahía Laura
Pta. Medanosa
San Julián
Santa Cruz
Sta. Cruz
Bahía Grande
Pto. Coyle
Coig
Gallegos
Rio Gallegos
C. Vírgenes
Olavarría
Azul
Dolores
C. S. Anto
Gral. Guido
Gral. Juan Madariago
Tandil
Carhué
Gral. La Madrid
Cor. Suárez
Puán
Pigüé
Sa. de la Ventana
Tornquist
Cor. Pringles
Sa. de Tandil
Juárez
Balcarce
Ayacucho
Maipú
Mar del Pl
Lobería
Quequén
Necochea
Tres Arroyos
Cor. Dorrego
Bahía Blanca
Punta Alta
I. Trinidad
ATLANTIC OCEAN
FALKLAND ISLANDS
(ISLAS MALVINAS)
Jason Is
C. Dolphin (Br.)
K. George B.
West Falkland
700
705
Stanley
East Falkland
Weddell I.
Port Darwin
C. Meredith
Falkland Sound
A N D E S
C O R D I L L E R A
P A T A G O N I A
A R G E N T I N A
C H I L E

West from Greenwich

1 : 16 000 000

INDEX

Abbreviations used

Ala. – *Alabama*
Arch. – *Archipelago*
Ark. – *Arkansas*
Austral. – *Australia*
B. – *Baie, Bahia, Bay, Boca, Bucht, Bugt*
B.C. – *British Columbia*
Bangla. – *Bangladesh*
Br. – *British*
C. – *Cabo, Cap, Cape, Coast, Costa*
C. Rica – *Costa Rica*
Calif. – *California*
Cap. Terr. – *Capital Territory*
Cat. – *Cataract*
Cent. – *Central*
Chan. – *Channel*
Colo. – *Colorado*
Conn. – *Connecticut*
Cord. – *Cordillera*
D.C. – *District of Columbia*
Del. – *Delaware*
Dét. – *Détroit*
Dom. Rep. – *Dominican Republic*
Domin. – *Dominica*
E. – *East, Eastern*
Est. – *Estrecho*
Falk. Is. – *Falkland Islands*
Fla. – *Florida*
Fr. Gui. – *French Guiana*
G. – *Golfe, Golfo, Gulf, Guba, Gebel*
Ga. – *Georgia*
Gt. – *Great*
Guat. – *Guatemala*
Hants. – *Hampshire*
Hd. – *Head*
Hond. – *Honduras*
Hts. – *Heights*
I. (s) – *Ile, Ilha, Insel, Isla, Island(s)*
I. of W. – *Isle of Wight*
Ill. – *Illinois*
Ind. – *Indiana*
Ind. Oc. – *Indian Ocean*
J. – *Jabal, Jazira*
K. – *Kap, Kapp*
Kans. – *Kansas*
Ky. – *Kentucky*
L. – *Lac, Lacul, Lago, Lagoa, Lake, Limni, Loch, Lough*
La. – *Louisiana*
Lag. – *Laguna*
Lancs. – *Lancashire*
Man. – *Manitoba*
Mass. – *Massachusetts*
Md. – *Maryland*
Mich. – *Michigan*
Minn. – *Minnesota*
Miss. – *Mississippi*
Mo. – *Missouri*
Mont. – *Montana*
Mt.(s) – *Mont, Monta, Monti, Muntii, Montaña, Mount, Mountain(s)*
N. – *North, Northern*
N.B. – *New Brunswick*
M.C. – *North Carolina*
N. Dak. – *North Dakota*
N.H. – *New Hampshire*
N.J. – *New Jersey*
N. Mex. – *New Mexico*
N.S.W. – *New South Wales*
N.W.T. – *North West Territories*
N.Y. – *New York*
N.Z. – *New Zealand*
Nebr. – *Nebraska*
Neth. – *Netherlands*
Nev. – *Nevada*
Nfld. – *Newfoundland*
Nic. – *Nicaragua*
Okla. – *Oklahoma*
Ont. – *Ontario*
Oreg. – *Oregon*
Os. – *Ostrov*
Oz. – *Ozero*
P. – *Pass, Passo, Pasul, Pulau*
P.E.I. – *Prince Edward Island*
Pa. – *Pennsylvania*
Pac. Oc. – *Pacific Ocean*
Papua N.G. – *Papua New Guinea*
Pen. – *Peninsula*
Pk. – *Peak*
Plat. – *Plateau*
P-ov. – *Poluostrov*
Pt. – *Point*
Pta. – *Ponta, Punta*
Queens. – *Queensland*
R. – *Rio, River, Rivière*
R.I. – *Rhode Island*
Ra.(s) – *Range(s)*
Raj. – *Rajasthan*
Rep. – *Republic*
Res. – *Reserve, Reservoir*
S. – *South, Southern, Sea, Sur*
S.C. – *South Carolina*
S. Africa – *South Africa*
S. Dak. – *South Dakota*
Sa. – *Serra, Sierra*
Salop. – *Shropshire*
Sard. – *Sardinia*
Sask. – *Saskatchewan*
Sd. – *Sound*
Sev. – *Severnaya*
Si. Arabia – *Saudi Arabia*
St. – *Saint*
Sta. – *Santa*
Ste. – *Sainte*
Str. – *Strait, Stretto*
Switz. – *Switzerland*
Tas. – *Tasmania*
Tenn. – *Tennessee*
Terr. – *Territory*
Tex. – *Texas*
Tipp. – *Tipperary*
Trin. & Tob. – *Trinidad and Tobago*
U.K. – *United Kingdom*
U.S.A. – *United States of America*
Ut. P. – *Uttar Pradesh*
Va. – *Virginia*
Vic. – *Victoria*
Vol. – *Volcano*
Vt. – *Vermont*
Wash. – *Washington*
W. – *West, Western, Wadi*
W. Va. – *West Virginia*
Wis. – *Wisconsin*
Worcs. – *Worcestershire*
Yorks. – *Yorkshire*

Introduction to Index

The number printed in bold type against each entry indicates the map page where the feature can be found. This is followed by its geographical coordinates. The first coordinate indicates latitude, i.e. distance north or south of the Equator. The second coordinate indicates longitude, i.e. distance east or west of the meridian of Greenwich in England (shown as 0° longitude). Both latitude and longitude are measured in degrees and minutes (with 60 minutes in a degree), and appear on the map as horizontal and vertical gridlines respectively. Thus the entry for Paris in France reads:

Paris, France . . . . **39** 48 50N 2 20 E

This entry indicates that Paris is on page **39**, at latitude 48 degrees 50 minutes north (approximately five-sixths of the distance between horizontal gridlines 48 and 49, marked on either side of the page) and at longitude 2 degrees 20 minutes east (approximately one-third of the distance between vertical gridlines 2 and 3, marked at top and bottom of the page). Paris can be found where lines extended from these two points cross on the page. The geographical coordinates are sometimes only approximate but are close enough for the place to be located. Rivers have been indexed to their mouth or confluence.

An open square □ signifies that the name refers to an administrative subdivision of a country while a solid square ■ follows the name of a country. An arrow → follows the name of a river.

The alphabetical order of names composed of two or more words is governed primarily by the first word and then by the second. This rule applies even if the second word is a description or its abbreviation, R., L., I., for example:

North Walsham
Northallerton
Northampton
Northern Circars
Northumberland Is.
Northumberland Str.

Names composed of a proper name (Gibraltar) and a description (Strait of) are positioned alphabetically by the proper name. This is the case where the definite article follows a proper name (Mans, Le). If the same word occurs in the name of a town and a geographical feature, the town name is listed first followed by the name or names of the geographical features.

Names beginning with M', Mc are all indexed as if they were spelt Mac. All names beginning St. are alphabetised under Saint, but Sankt, Sint, Santa and San are all spelt in full and are alphabetised accordingly.

If the same place name occurs twice or more times in the index and all are in the same country, each is followed by the name of the administrative subdivision in which it is located. The names are placed in the alphabetical order of the subdivisions. If the same place name occurs twice or more in the index and the places are in different countries they will be followed by their country names, the latter governing the alphabetical order. In a mixture of these situations the primary order is fixed by the alphabetical sequence of the countries and the secondary order by that of the country subdivisions.

The index shows Welsh and Scottish administrative names prior to April 1996. The maps on pages 24 to 33 show the new administrative areas and names.

A

Aachen	**42**	50	47N	6	4 E
Aalborg = Ålborg	**61**	57	2N	9	54 E
Aalsmeer	**40**	52	17N	4	43 E
Aalst	**42**	50	56N	4	2 E
Aalten	**41**	51	56N	6	35 E
Aarhus = Århus	**61**	56	8N	10	11 E
Aba	**131**	5	10N	7	19 E
Ābādān	**84**	30	22N	48	20 E
Ābādeh	**85**	31	8N	52	40 E
Abadla	**126**	31	2N	2	45W
Abai	**191**	25	58S	55	54W
Abakan	**74**	53	40N	91	10 E
Abancay	**186**	13	35S	72	55W
Abariringa I.	**122**	2	50S	171	40W
Abashiri	**103**	44	0N	144	15 E
Abashiri-Wan	**103**	44	0N	144	30 E
Abaya, L.	**133**	6	30N	37	50 E
Abbay = Nîl el Azraq →	**129**	15	38N	32	31 E
Abbeville, France	**38**	50	6N	1	49 E
Abbeville, U.S.A.	**165**	34	12N	82	21W
Abéché	**129**	13	50N	20	35 E
Abeokuta	**131**	7	3N	3	19 E
Aberaeron	**26**	52	15N	4	16W
Aberayron = Aberaeron	**26**	52	15N	4	16W
Aberdare	**27**	51	43N	3	27W
Aberdeen, U.K.	**33**	57	9N	2	6W
Aberdeen, S. Dak., U.S.A.	**163**	45	30N	98	30W
Aberdeen, Wash., U.S.A.	**171**	47	0N	123	50W
Aberdovey	**26**	52	33N	4	3W
Aberfeldy	**33**	56	37N	3	50W
Abergavenny	**26**	51	49N	3	1W
Aberystwyth	**26**	52	25N	4	6W
Abha	**82**	18	0N	42	34 E
Abidjan	**130**	5	26N	3	58W
Abilene	**161**	32	22N	99	40W
Abington	**25**	55	30N	3	42W
Abkhazia □	**70**	43	12N	41	5 E
Abohar	**89**	30	10N	74	10 E
Abomey	**131**	7	10N	2	5 E
Abong-Mbang	**131**	4	0N	13	8 E
Abrud	**56**	46	19N	23	5 E
Abruzzi □	**47**	42	15N	14	0 E
Absaroka Ra.	**163**	44	40N	110	0W
Abū al Khaşīb	**84**	30	25N	48	0 E
Abū 'Alī	**84**	27	20N	49	27 E
Abū 'Arīsh	**82**	16	58N	45	20 E
Abu Dhabi = Abū Z̧āby	**85**	24	28N	54	22 E
Abu Hamed	**129**	19	32N	33	13 E
Abū Z̧āby	**85**	24	28N	54	22 E
Abunã	**187**	9	40S	65	20W
Abunã →	**187**	9	41S	65	20W
Abut Hd.	**123**	43	7S	170	15 E
Acámbaro	**177**	20	2N	100	44W
Acaponeta	**175**	22	30N	105	22W
Acapulco	**177**	16	51N	99	56W
Acatlán	**177**	18	10N	98	3W
Acayucan	**177**	17	57N	94	55W
Accra	**130**	5	35N	0	6W
Accrington	**28**	53	46N	2	22W
Achill I.	**34**	53	58N	10	5W
Achinsk	**74**	56	20N	90	20 E
Aconcagua, Cerro	**190**	32	39S	70	0W
Aconquija, Mt.	**190**	27	0S	66	0W
Açores, Is. dos = Azores	**126**	38	44N	29	0W
Acre = 'Akko	**80**	32	55N	35	4 E
Acre □	**187**	9	1S	71	0W
Ad Dawhah	**85**	25	15N	51	35 E
Ada	**168**	34	50N	96	45W
Adamaoua, Massif de l'	**131**	7	20N	12	20 E
Adamawa Highlands = Adamaoua, Massif de l'	**131**	7	20N	12	20 E
Adaminaby	**117**	36	0S	148	45 E
Adams, Mt.	**171**	46	10N	121	28W
Adam's Bridge	**90**	9	15N	79	40 E
Adana	**80**	37	0N	35	16 E
Adapazarı	**80**	40	48N	30	25 E
Adare, C.	**15**	71	0S	171	0 E
Addis Ababa = Addis Abeba	**133**	9	2N	38	42 E
Addis Abeba	**133**	9	2N	38	42 E
Adelaide	**119**	34	52S	138	30 E
Adelaide Pen.	**145**	68	15N	97	30W
Adélie, Terre	**15**	68	0S	140	0 E
Aden = Al 'Adan	**83**	12	45N	45	0 E
Aden, G. of	**133**	13	0N	50	0 E
Adige →	**47**	45	9N	12	20 E
Adirondack Mts.	**151**	44	0N	74	15W
Admiralty Is.	**115**	2	0S	147	0 E
Adoni	**90**	15	33N	77	18W
Adrian	**167**	41	55N	84	0W
Adriatic Sea	**52**	43	0N	16	0 E
Adwa	**132**	14	15N	38	52 E
Ægean Sea	**55**	37	0N	25	0 E
Æolian Is. = Eólie, I.	**49**	38	30N	14	50 E
Aerht'ai Shan	**100**	46	40N	92	45 E
Afars & Issas, Terr. of = Djibouti ■	**133**	12	0N	43	0 E
Afghanistan ■	**87**	33	0N	65	0 E
Afuá	**188**	0	15S	50	20W
Afyonkarahisar	**80**	38	45N	30	33 E
Agadir	**126**	30	28N	9	35W
Agano →	**103**	37	57N	139	8 E
Agartala	**93**	23	50N	91	23 E
Agen	**36**	44	12N	0	38 E
Ageo	**107**	35	58N	139	36 E
Aghil Pass	**89**	36	15N	76	35 E
Agra	**89**	27	17N	77	58 E
Ağri Daği	**81**	39	50N	44	15 E
Água Clara	**188**	20	25S	52	45W
Agua Prieta	**174**	31	18N	109	34W
Aguadas	**184**	5	40N	75	38W
Aguadilla	**180**	18	27N	67	10W
Aguas Blancas	**190**	24	15S	69	55W
Aguascalientes	**175**	21	53N	102	18W
Aguascalientes □	**175**	22	0N	102	30W
Agulhas, Kaap	**136**	34	52S	20	0 E
Ahaggar	**127**	23	0N	6	30 E
Ahaura →	**123**	42	21S	171	34 E
Ahmadabad	**91**	23	0N	72	40 E
Ahmadnagar	**91**	19	7N	74	46 E
Ahmedabad = Ahmadabad	**91**	23	0N	72	40 E
Ahmednagar = Ahmadnagar	**91**	19	7N	74	46 E
Ahvāz	**84**	31	20N	48	40 E
Ahvenanmaa = Åland	**66**	60	15N	20	0 E
Ahwar	**83**	13	30N	46	40 E
Aigle, L'	**39**	48	46N	0	38 E
Aigues-Mortes	**37**	43	35N	4	12 E
Aiken	**170**	33	34N	81	50W
Ailsa Craig	**30**	55	15N	5	7W
Aimorés	**189**	19	30S	41	4W
Aïn Ben Tili	**126**	25	59N	9	27W
Aioi	**109**	34	48N	134	28 E
Aïr	**127**	18	30N	8	0 E
Airdrie	**31**	55	53N	3	57W
Aire →	**29**	53	42N	0	55W
Airlie Beach	**121**	20	16S	148	43 E
Aisne →	**37**	49	26N	2	50 E
Aix-en-Provence	**37**	43	32N	5	27 E
Aix-la-Chapelle = Aachen	**42**	50	47N	6	4 E
Aix-les-Bains	**37**	45	41N	5	53 E
Aizuwakamatsu	**105**	37	30N	139	56 E
Ajaccio	**36**	41	55N	8	40 E
Ajanta Ra.	**91**	20	28N	75	50 E
Ajaria □	**70**	41	30N	42	0 E
Ajmer	**91**	26	28N	74	37 E
Akaishi-Dake	**107**	35	27N	138	9 E
Akaishi-Sammyaku	**107**	35	25N	138	10 E
Akashi	**109**	34	45N	135	0 E
Akershus fylke □	**60**	60	0N	11	10 E
Akhelóös →	**54**	38	36N	21	14 E
Akhisar	**80**	38	56N	27	48 E
Aki	**109**	33	30N	133	54 E
Aki-Nada	**109**	34	5N	132	40 E
Akita	**103**	39	45N	140	7 E
'Akko	**80**	32	55N	35	4 E
Aklavik	**144**	68	12N	135	0W
Akō	**109**	34	45N	134	24 E
Akola	**91**	20	42N	77	2 E
Akranes	**64**	64	19N	21	58W
Akron	**167**	41	7N	81	31W

Aksaray **80** 38 25N 34 2 E
Aksarka **69** 66 31N 67 50 E
Akşehir **80** 38 18N 31 30 E
Aksum **132** 14 5N 38 40 E
Aktyubinsk = Aqtöbe **70** 50 17N 57 10 E
Akune **108** 32 1N 130 12 E
Akureyri **64** 65 40N 18 6W
Al 'Adan **83** 12 45N 45 0 E
Al Amādīyah **81** 37 5N 43 30 E
Al Amārah **84** 31 55N 47 15 E
Al 'Aqabah **80** 29 31N 35 0 E
Al Başrah **84** 30 30N 47 50 E
Al Ḥadīthah **81** 31 28N 37 8 E
Al Hāmad **80** 31 30N 39 30 E
Al Ḥasakah **81** 36 35N 40 45 E
Al Ḥawrah **83** 13 50N 47 35 E
Al Ḥayy **84** 32 5N 46 5 E
Al Ḥillah, Iraq **84** 32 30N 44 25 E
Al Ḥillah, Si. Arabia **83** 23 35N 46 50 E
Al Hindīyah **84** 32 30N 44 10 E
Al Ḥudaydah **82** 14 50N 43 0 E
Al Hūfuf **84** 25 25N 49 45 E
Al Jāfūrah **84** 25 0N 50 15 E
Al Jawf, Libya **128** 24 10N 23 24 E
Al Jawf, Si. Arabia **82** 29 55N 39 40 E
Al Jazirah **81** 33 30N 44 0 E
Al Khalīl **80** 31 32N 35 6 E
Al Kūt **84** 32 30N 46 0 E
Al Kuwayt **84** 29 30N 47 30 E
Al Lādhiqīyah **80** 35 30N 35 45 E
Al Lidām **82** 20 33N 44 45 E
Al Luḥayyah **82** 15 45N 42 40 E
Al Madīnah **82** 24 35N 39 52 E
Al Manāmāh **85** 26 10N 50 30 E
Al Marj **128** 32 25N 20 30 E
Al Mawşil **81** 36 15N 43 5 E
Al Mubarraz **84** 25 30N 49 40 E
Al Muḥarraq **85** 26 15N 50 40 E
Al Mukallā **83** 14 33N 49 2 E
Al Qaţīf **84** 26 35N 50 0 E
Al Quds = Jerusalem **80** 31 47N 35 10 E
Al Qunfudhah **82** 19 3N 41 4 E
Al Qurnah **84** 31 1N 47 25 E
Al 'Ubaylah **83** 21 59N 50 57 E
Al 'Uthmānīyah **84** 25 5N 49 22 E
Al Wajh **82** 26 10N 36 30 E
Alabama □ **169** 33 0N 87 0W
Alabama → **169** 31 8N 87 57W
Alagoas □ **189** 9 0S 36 0W
Alagoinhas **189** 12 7S 38 20W
Alajuela **179** 10 2N 84 8W
Alamogordo **161** 32 59N 106 0W
Álamos **174** 27 1N 108 56W
Alamosa **163** 37 30N 106 0W
Åland **66** 60 15N 20 0 E
Alaska □ **142** 65 0N 150 0W
Alaska, G. of **142** 58 0N 145 0W
Alaska Pen. **142** 56 0N 160 0W
Alaska Range **142** 62 50N 151 0W
Alba Iulia **56** 46 8N 23 39 E
Albacete **51** 39 0N 1 50W
Albania ■ **52** 41 0N 20 0 E
Albany, Australia **120** 35 1S 117 58 E
Albany, Ga., U.S.A. **170** 31 40N 84 10W
Albany, N.Y., U.S.A. **164** 42 35N 73 47W
Albany, Oreg., U.S.A. **171** 44 41N 123 0W
Albany → **140** 52 17N 81 31W
Albemarle **165** 35 27N 80 15W
Albemarle Sd. **165** 36 0N 76 30W
Albert **38** 50 0N 2 38 E
Albert, L. = Mobutu Sese Seko, L. **132** 1 30N 31 0 E
Albert Lea **166** 43 32N 93 20W
Alberta □ **155** 54 40N 115 0W
Albertville = Kalemie **135** 5 55S 29 9 E
Albi **37** 43 56N 2 9 E
Albion **167** 42 15N 84 45W
Ålborg **61** 57 2N 9 54 E
Alborz, Reshteh-ye Kūhhā-ye **86** 36 0N 52 0 E
Albuquerque **161** 35 5N 106 47W
Alburquerque **50** 39 15N 6 59W
Albury **117** 36 3S 146 56 E
Alcântara **188** 2 20S 44 30W
Alcázar de San Juan **50** 39 24N 3 12W
Alcira **51** 39 9N 0 30W
Aldan → **75** 63 28N 129 35 E
Aldeburgh **25** 52 9N 1 35 E
Alderney **36** 49 42N 2 12W
Aldershot **25** 51 15N 0 43W
Alençon **39** 48 27N 0 4 E
Aleppo = Ḥalab **80** 36 10N 37 15 E
Alès **37** 44 9N 4 5 E
Alessándria **46** 44 54N 8 37 E
Ålesund **65** 62 28N 6 12 E
Aleutian Is. **142** 52 0N 175 0W
Alexander Arch. **143** 57 0N 135 0W
Alexander City **169** 32 58N 85 57W
Alexandra, Australia **117** 37 8S 145 40 E
Alexandra, N.Z. **123** 45 14S 169 25 E
Alexandretta = İskenderun **80** 36 32N 36 10 E
Alexandria = El Iskandarîya **128** 31 0N 30 0 E
Alexandria, La., U.S.A. **168** 31 20N 92 30W
Alexandria, Va., U.S.A. **164** 38 47N 77 1W
Alexandrina, L. **119** 35 25S 139 10 E
Alexandroúpolis **55** 40 50N 25 54 E
Alexis Creek **154** 52 10N 123 20W
Alfreton **29** 53 6N 1 22W
Algarve **50** 36 58N 8 20W
Alger **127** 36 42N 3 8 E
Algeria ■ **127** 35 10N 3 11 E
Algiers = Alger **127** 36 42N 3 8 E
Algoa B. **136** 33 50S 25 45 E
Alhambra **173** 34 2N 118 10W
Alicante **51** 38 23N 0 30W
Alice Springs **114** 23 40S 133 50 E
Aligarh **89** 27 55N 78 10 E
Alipur Duar **92** 26 30N 89 35 E
Aliquippa **164** 40 38N 80 18W
Alkmaar **40** 52 37N 4 45 E
Allahabad **92** 25 25N 81 58 E
Allegheny Mts. **165** 38 0N 80 0W
Allen, Bog of **35** 53 15N 7 0W
Allende **174** 28 20N 100 51W
Allentown **164** 40 36N 75 30W
Alleppey **90** 9 30N 76 28 E
Aller → **42** 52 57N 9 10 E
Allier → **37** 46 57N 3 4 E
Alloa **31** 56 7N 3 49W
Alma, Canada **148** 48 35N 71 40W
Alma, U.S.A. **167** 43 25N 84 40W
Alma Ata **71** 43 15N 76 57 E
Almada **50** 38 40N 9 9W
Almelo **41** 52 22N 6 42 E
Almería **51** 36 52N 2 27W
Almirante **179** 9 10N 82 30W
Alor **113** 8 15S 124 30 E
Alor Setar **96** 6 7N 100 22 E
Alpena **150** 45 6N 83 24W
Alphen **40** 51 29N 4 58 E
Alpine **161** 30 25N 103 35W
Alps **16** 47 0N 8 0 E
Alsace **37** 48 15N 7 25 E
Alsask **152** 51 21N 109 59W
Alston **28** 54 48N 2 26W
Alta Gracia **190** 31 40S 64 30W
Altagracia **184** 10 45N 71 30W
Altai = Aerht'ai Shan **100** 46 40N 92 45 E
Altamaha → **170** 31 19N 81 17W
Altamira **188** 3 12S 52 10W
Alto Adige = Trentino-Alto Adige □ **47** 46 30N 11 0 E
Alton **166** 38 55N 90 5W
Altona **43** 53 32N 9 56 E
Altoona **164** 40 32N 78 24W
Altun Shan **100** 38 30N 88 0 E
Alvarado **177** 18 46N 95 46W
Älvsborgs län □ **60** 58 30N 12 30 E
Alwar **89** 27 38N 76 34 E
Alxa Zuoqi **98** 38 50N 105 40 E
Am-Timan **129** 11 0N 20 10 E
Amadjuak **146** 64 0N 72 39W
Amadjuak L. **146** 65 0N 71 8W

Amagasaki	**106**	34 42N	135 20 E
Amagi	**108**	33 25N	130 39 E
Amakusa-Nada	**108**	32 35N	130 5 E
Amalner	**91**	21 5N	75 5 E
Amapá	**185**	2 5N	50 50W
Amapá □	**185**	1 40N	52 0W
Amarillo	**161**	35 14N	101 46W
Amasya	**80**	40 40N	35 50 E
Amatitlán	**177**	14 29N	90 38W
Amazon = Amazonas →	**185**	0 5S	50 0W
Amazonas □	**185**	4 0S	62 0W
Amazonas →	**185**	0 5S	50 0W
Ambala	**89**	30 23N	76 56 E
Ambato	**184**	1 5S	78 42W
Ambikapur	**92**	23 15N	83 15 E
Ambleside	**28**	54 26N	2 58W
Ambo	**186**	10 5S	76 10W
Ambon	**113**	3 35S	128 20 E
Amboyna I.	**112**	7 50N	112 50 E
Amderma	**69**	69 45N	61 30 E
Ameca	**175**	20 33N	104 2W
Ameca, R. →	**175**	20 41N	105 18W
Ameland	**41**	53 27N	5 45 E
American Highland	**14**	73 0S	75 0 E
American Samoa ■	**123**	14 20S	170 40W
Americus	**170**	32 0N	84 10W
Amersfoort	**40**	52 9N	5 23 E
Amery	**143**	56 34N	94 3W
Ames	**166**	42 0N	93 40W
Amga →	**75**	62 38N	134 32 E
Amgu	**75**	45 45N	137 15 E
Amgun →	**75**	52 56N	139 38 E
Amherst	**148**	45 48N	64 8W
Amherstburg	**150**	42 6N	83 6W
Amiens	**38**	49 54N	2 16 E
Amlwch	**26**	53 24N	4 21W
'Ammān	**80**	31 57N	35 52 E
Amorgós	**55**	36 50N	25 57 E
Amos	**151**	48 35N	78 5W
Amoy = Xiamen	**99**	24 25N	118 4 E
Amravati	**91**	20 55N	77 45 E
Amreli	**91**	21 35N	71 17 E
Amritsar	**89**	31 35N	74 57 E
Amsterdam, Neths.	**40**	52 23N	4 54 E
Amsterdam, U.S.A.	**164**	42 58N	74 10W
Amudarya →	**70**	43 40N	59 0 E
Amundsen Gulf	**145**	71 0N	124 0W
Amundsen Sea	**15**	72 0S	115 0W
Amur →	**75**	52 56N	141 10 E
An Nafūd	**82**	28 15N	41 0 E
An Najaf	**84**	32 3N	44 15 E
An Nāşirīyah	**84**	31 0N	46 15 E
An Nhon	**95**	13 55N	109 7 E
An Nu'ayrīyah	**84**	27 30N	48 30 E
An Uaimh	**34**	53 39N	6 40W
Anabar →	**72**	73 8N	113 36 E
Anaconda	**163**	46 7N	113 0W
Anacortes	**171**	48 30N	122 40W
Anadolu	**80**	38 0N	30 0 E
Anadyr →	**73**	64 55N	176 5 E
Anadyrskiy Zaliv	**73**	64 0N	180 0 E
Anaheim	**173**	33 50N	118 0W
Anambas Is.	**111**	3 20N	106 30 E
Anamur	**80**	36 8N	32 58 E
Anan	**109**	33 54N	134 40 E
Anápolis	**188**	16 15S	48 50W
Anārak	**85**	33 25N	53 40 E
Anatolia = Anadolu	**80**	38 0N	30 0 E
Añatuya	**190**	28 20S	62 50W
Anchorage	**142**	61 10N	149 50W
Ancohuma, Nevada	**187**	16 0S	68 50W
Ancona	**47**	43 37N	13 30 E
Ancud	**192**	42 0S	73 50W
Ancud, G. de	**192**	42 0S	73 0W
Åndalsnes	**65**	62 35N	7 43 E
Andalucía □	**50**	37 35N	5 0W
Andalusia	**169**	31 19N	86 30W
Andalusia □ = Andalucía □	**50**	37 35N	5 0W
Andaman Is.	**94**	12 30N	92 30 E
Andaman Sea	**94**	13 0N	96 0 E
Andaman Str.	**94**	12 15N	92 20 E
Andelys, Les	**39**	49 15N	1 25 E
Anderson, Ind., U.S.A.	**167**	40 5N	85 40W
Anderson, S.C., U.S.A.	**165**	34 32N	82 40W
Andes, Cord. de los	**182**	20 0S	68 0W
Andhra Pradesh □	**91**	16 0N	79 0 E
Andikíthira	**55**	35 52N	23 15 E
Andizhan	**71**	41 10N	72 0 E
Andorra ■	**36**	42 30N	1 30 E
Andover	**24**	51 13N	1 29W
Andreanof Is.	**142**	52 0N	178 0W
Andrewilla	**118**	26 31S	139 17 E
Ándria	**49**	41 13N	16 17 E
Andropov = Rybinsk	**68**	58 5N	38 50 E
Ándros	**55**	37 50N	24 57 E
Andros I.	**178**	24 30N	78 0W
Angara →	**74**	58 30N	97 0 E
Angarsk	**74**	52 30N	104 0 E
Angaston	**119**	34 30S	139 8 E
Ånge	**66**	62 31N	15 35 E
Ängelholm	**61**	56 15N	12 58 E
Angels Camp	**172**	38 8N	120 30W
Ångerman →	**66**	64 0N	17 20 E
Angers	**36**	47 30N	0 35W
Angkor	**95**	13 22N	103 50 E
Anglesey	**26**	53 17N	4 20W
Angmagssalik	**147**	65 40N	37 20W
Angol	**190**	37 56S	72 45W
Angola ■	**134**	12 0S	18 0 E
Angoulême	**36**	45 39N	0 10 E
Angoumois	**36**	45 50N	0 25 E
Anguilla	**180**	18 14N	63 5W
Angus, Braes of	**33**	56 51N	3 10W
Anhui □	**99**	32 0N	117 0 E
Anhwei □ = Anhui □	**99**	32 0N	117 0 E
Anin	**94**	15 36N	97 50 E
Anjō	**106**	34 57N	137 5 E
Anjou	**36**	47 20N	0 15W
Anju	**98**	39 36N	125 40 E
Ankang	**99**	32 40N	109 1 E
Ankara	**80**	40 0N	32 54 E
Ann Arbor	**167**	42 17N	83 45W
Annaba	**127**	36 50N	7 46 E
Annam = Trung-Phan	**95**	16 0N	108 0 E
Annamitique, Chaîne	**95**	17 0N	106 0 E
Annan	**31**	55 0N	3 17W
Annapolis	**164**	39 0N	76 30W
Annecy	**37**	45 55N	6 8 E
Anniston	**169**	33 45N	85 50W
Annobón	**131**	1 25S	5 36 E
Annonay	**37**	45 15N	4 40 E
Annotto Bay	**180**	18 17N	77 3W
Anqing	**99**	30 30N	117 3 E
Anse, L'	**150**	46 47N	88 28W
Anshan	**98**	41 3N	122 58 E
Anshun	**99**	26 18N	105 57 E
Anstruther	**31**	56 14N	2 40W
Antabamba	**186**	14 40S	73 0W
Antakya	**80**	36 14N	36 10 E
Antalya	**80**	36 52N	30 45 E
Antalya Körfezi	**80**	36 15N	31 30 E
Antananarivo	**137**	18 55S	47 31 E
Antarctic Pen.	**14**	67 0S	60 0W
Antarctica	**14**	90 0S	0 0 E
Anti Atlas	**126**	30 0N	8 30W
Antibes	**37**	43 34N	7 6 E
Anticosti, Î. d'	**148**	49 30N	63 0W
Antigo	**150**	45 8N	89 5W
Antigua, Guatemala	**177**	14 34N	90 41W
Antigua, W. Indies	**180**	17 0N	61 50W
Antigua and Barbuda ■	**180**	17 20N	61 48W
Antilla	**178**	20 40N	75 50W
Antioch	**172**	38 7N	121 45W
Antioquia	**184**	6 40N	75 55W
Antipodes Is.	**11**	49 45S	178 40 E
Antofagasta	**190**	23 50S	70 30W
Antrim	**34**	54 43N	6 13W
Antrim, Mts. of	**34**	54 57N	6 8W
Antsiranana	**137**	12 25S	49 20 E
Antwerp = Antwerpen	**42**	51 13N	4 25 E
Antwerpen	**42**	51 13N	4 25 E
Anvers = Antwerpen	**42**	51 13N	4 25 E

Anvik	**142**	62 37N	160 20W
Anxious B.	**119**	33 24S	134 45 E
Anyang	**98**	36 5N	114 21 E
Anzhero-Sudzhensk	**71**	56 10N	86 0 E
Ánzio	**46**	41 28N	12 37 E
Aoga-Shima	**105**	32 28N	139 46 E
Aomori	**103**	40 45N	140 45 E
Apalachee B.	**170**	30 0N	84 0W
Apalachicola	**170**	29 40N	85 0W
Apalachicola →	**170**	29 40N	85 0W
Aparri	**112**	18 22N	121 38 E
Apeldoorn	**41**	52 13N	5 57 E
Apennines	**16**	44 20N	10 20 E
Apizaco	**177**	19 25N	98 9W
Aplao	**186**	16 0S	72 40W
Apolo	**187**	14 30S	68 30W
Apostle Is.	**150**	47 0N	90 30W
Apostolos Andreas, C.	**80**	35 42N	34 35 E
Appalachian Mts.	**138**	38 0N	80 0W
Appingedam	**41**	53 19N	6 51 E
Appleby	**28**	54 35N	2 29W
Appleton	**167**	44 17N	88 25W
Apulia = Púglia □	**49**	41 0N	16 30 E
Apure →	**184**	7 37N	66 25W
Aqabah = Al 'Aqabah	**80**	29 31N	35 0 E
Aqtöbe	**70**	50 17N	57 10 E
Aquidauana	**188**	20 30S	55 50W
Áquila, L'	**47**	42 21N	13 24 E
Aquiles Serdán	**174**	28 36N	105 53W
Ar Riyāḍ	**83**	24 41N	46 42 E
Ar Ruṭbah	**81**	33 0N	40 15 E
Ara	**92**	25 35N	84 32 E
Arab, Bahr el →	**129**	9 50N	29 0 E
Arab, Shatt al	**84**	30 0N	48 31 E
Arabia	**76**	25 0N	45 0 E
Arabian Gulf = Gulf, The	**85**	27 0N	50 0 E
Arabian Sea	**76**	16 0N	65 0 E
Aracaju	**189**	10 55S	37 4W
Aracati	**189**	4 30S	37 44W
Araçatuba	**188**	21 10S	50 30W
Arad	**56**	46 10N	21 20 E
Arafura Sea	**113**	9 0S	135 0 E
Aragón □	**51**	41 25N	1 0W
Araguacema	**188**	8 50S	49 20W
Araguaia →	**188**	5 21S	48 41W
Araguari	**188**	18 38S	48 11W
Arāk	**84**	34 0N	49 40 E
Arakan Coast	**93**	19 0N	94 0 E
Arakan Yoma	**93**	20 0N	94 40 E
Araks = Aras, Rūd-e →	**81**	39 10N	47 10 E
Aral Sea = Aralskoye More	**70**	44 30N	60 0 E
Aralsk	**70**	46 50N	61 20 E
Aralskoye More	**70**	44 30N	60 0 E
Aran I.	**34**	55 0N	8 30W
Aran Is.	**35**	53 5N	9 42W
Aranjuez	**50**	40 1N	3 40W
Aransas Pass	**158**	27 55N	97 9W
Arao	**108**	32 59N	130 25 E
Araraquara	**188**	21 50S	48 0W
Ararat	**119**	37 16S	143 0 E
Ararat, Mt. = Ağri Daği	**81**	39 50N	44 15 E
Aras, Rūd-e →	**81**	39 10N	47 10 E
Araya, Pen. de	**185**	10 40N	64 0W
Arbīl	**81**	36 15N	44 5 E
Arbroath	**31**	56 34N	2 35W
Arcachon	**36**	44 40N	1 10W
Arcadia	**170**	27 20N	81 50W
Archangel = Arkhangelsk	**69**	64 40N	41 0 E
Arcot	**90**	12 53N	79 20 E
Arctic Bay	**146**	73 1N	85 7W
Arctic Ocean	**12**	78 0N	160 0W
Arctic Red River	**144**	67 15N	134 0W
Ardabīl	**81**	38 15N	48 18 E
Ardennes	**42**	50 0N	5 10 E
Ardgour	**32**	56 45N	5 25W
Ardlethan	**117**	34 22S	146 53 E
Ardmore	**168**	34 10N	97 5W
Ardnacrusha	**35**	52 43N	8 38W
Ardnamurchan, Pt. of	**32**	56 44N	6 14W
Ards Pen.	**34**	54 30N	5 25W
Arecibo	**180**	18 29N	66 42W
Arequipa	**187**	16 20S	71 30W
Arezzo	**46**	43 28N	11 50 E
Argentan	**39**	48 45N	0 1W
Argentário, Mte.	**46**	42 23N	11 11 E
Argentina ■	**190**	35 0S	66 0W
Argentino, L.	**192**	50 10S	73 0W
Árgos	**54**	37 40N	22 43 E
Argostólion	**54**	38 12N	20 33 E
Argun →	**74**	53 20N	121 28 E
Århus	**61**	56 8N	10 11 E
Arica, Chile	**187**	18 32S	70 20W
Arica, Colombia	**184**	2 0S	71 50W
Arida	**106**	34 5N	135 8 E
Arima	**180**	10 38N	61 17W
Ario de Rosales	**175**	19 12N	101 43W
Aripuanã	**187**	9 25S	60 30W
Aripuanã →	**187**	5 7S	60 25W
Ariquemes	**187**	9 55S	63 6W
Arisaig	**32**	56 55N	5 50W
Aristazabal I.	**154**	52 40N	129 10W
Arizona □	**160**	34 20N	111 30W
Arjona	**184**	10 14N	75 22W
Arkadelphia	**168**	34 5N	93 0W
Arkansas □	**168**	35 0N	92 30W
Arkansas →	**168**	33 48N	91 4W
Arkansas City	**158**	37 4N	97 3W
Arkhangelsk	**69**	64 40N	41 0 E
Arklow	**35**	52 48N	6 10W
Arkticheskiy, Mys	**72**	81 10N	95 0 E
Arles	**37**	43 41N	4 40 E
Arlington	**164**	38 52N	77 5W
Armagh	**34**	54 22N	6 40W
Armavir	**70**	45 2N	41 7 E
Armenia	**184**	4 35N	75 45W
Armenia ■	**70**	40 0N	41 0 E
Armentières	**38**	50 40N	2 50 E
Armidale	**116**	30 30S	151 40 E
Armstrong	**155**	50 25N	119 10W
Arnaouti, C.	**80**	35 6N	32 17 E
Arnaud →	**146**	59 59N	69 46W
Arnhem	**41**	51 58N	5 55 E
Arnhem, C.	**115**	12 20S	137 30 E
Arnhem Land	**114**	13 10S	134 30 E
Arnprior	**151**	45 26N	76 21W
Arran	**30**	55 34N	5 12W
Arras	**38**	50 17N	2 46 E
Arriaga	**177**	16 14N	93 54W
Árta	**54**	39 8N	21 2 E
Artigas	**191**	30 20S	56 30W
Artois	**38**	50 20N	2 30 E
Aru, Kepulauan	**113**	6 0S	134 30 E
Arua	**132**	3 1N	30 58 E
Aruanã	**188**	14 54S	51 10W
Aruba	**181**	12 30N	70 0W
Arusha	**135**	3 20S	36 40 E
Arvida	**148**	48 25N	71 14W
Arys	**71**	42 26N	68 48 E
'As Saffānīyah	**84**	28 5N	48 50 E
As Samāwah	**84**	31 15N	45 15 E
As Sulaymānīyah	**83**	24 9N	47 18 E
As Sumaymānīyah	**81**	35 35N	45 29 E
As Suwaydā'	**80**	32 40N	36 30 E
As Şuwayrah	**84**	32 55N	45 0 E
Asahi	**107**	35 43N	140 39 E
Asahi-Gawa →	**109**	34 36N	133 58 E
Asahigawa	**103**	43 46N	142 22 E
Asama-Yama	**107**	36 24N	138 31 E
Asamankese	**130**	5 50N	0 40W
Asansol	**92**	23 40N	87 1 E
Asbestos	**148**	45 47N	71 58W
Ascension I.	**125**	8 0S	14 15W
Áscoli Piceno	**47**	42 51N	13 34 E
Aseb	**133**	13 0N	42 40 E
Ash Shām, Bādiyat	**80**	32 0N	40 0 E
Ash Shāmīyah	**84**	31 55N	44 35 E
Ash Shāriqah	**85**	25 23N	55 26 E
Ash Shaṭrah	**84**	31 30N	46 10 E
Ashburton	**123**	43 53S	171 48 E
Ashby-de-la-Zouch	**28**	52 45N	1 29W
Ashcroft	**155**	50 40N	121 20W
Asheboro	**165**	35 43N	79 46W

Asheville 165 35 39N 82 30W
Ashford, Australia . . . . . 116 29 15S 151 3 E
Ashford, U.K. . . . . . 25 51 8N 0 53 E
Ashikaga . . . . . 107 36 28N 139 29 E
Ashizuri-Zaki . . . . . 109 32 44N 133 0 E
Ashkhabad . . . . . 70 38 0N 57 50 E
Ashland, Kans., U.S.A. 156 37 13N 99 43W
Ashland, Ky., U.S.A. 165 38 25N 82 40W
Ashland, Oreg., U.S.A. 171 42 10N 122 38W
Ashland, Wis., U.S.A. 150 46 40N 90 52W
Ashq'elon . . . . . 80 31 42N 34 35 E
Ashtabula 164 41 52N 80 50W
Ashton-under-Lyne 28 53 30N 2 8W
Ashuanipi, L. 147 52 45N 66 15W
Asinara I. . . . . . 48 41 5N 8 15 E
'Asīr □ . . . . . 82 18 40N 42 30 E
Asir, Ras . . . . . 133 11 55N 51 10 E
Asmara = Asmera . . . . . 132 15 19N 38 55 E
Asmera . . . . . 132 15 19N 38 55 E
Aso . . . . . 108 33 0N 131 5 E
Aso-Zan . . . . . 108 32 53N 131 6 E
Aspiring, Mt. . . . . . 123 44 23S 168 46 E
Assam □ . . . . . 93 26 0N 93 0 E
Assen . . . . . 41 53 0N 6 35 E
Assiniboia 152 49 40N 105 59W
Assiniboine → 153 49 53N 97 8W
Assisi . . . . . 46 43 4N 12 36 E
Asti . . . . . 46 44 54N 8 11 E
Astipálaia . . . . . 55 36 32N 26 22 E
Astoria 171 46 16N 123 50W
Astrakhan . . . . . 70 46 25N 48 5 E
Asturias □ 50 43 15N 6 0W
Asunción 191 25 10S 57 30W
Aswân . . . . . 128 24 4N 32 57 E
Asyût . . . . . 128 27 11N 31 4 E
At Ţafīlah . . . . . 80 30 45N 35 30 E
At Ta'if . . . . . 82 21 5N 40 27 E
Atacama, Desierto de 190 24 0S 69 20W
Atalaya 186 10 45S 73 50W
Atami . . . . . 107 35 5N 139 4 E
Atbara . . . . . 129 17 42N 33 59 E
'Atbara → . . . . . 129 17 40N 33 56 E
Atchafalaya B. 168 29 30N 91 20W
Atchison 166 39 40N 95 10W
Athabasca 155 54 45N 113 20W
Athabasca → 145 58 40N 110 50W
Athabasca, L. 145 59 15N 109 15W
Athenry 35 53 18N 8 45W
Athens = Athínai . . . . . 55 37 58N 23 46 E
Athens, Ala., U.S.A. 169 34 49N 86 58W
Athens, Ga., U.S.A. 165 33 56N 83 24W
Athens, Ohio, U.S.A. 167 39 25N 82 6W
Athens, Tenn., U.S.A. 169 35 45N 84 38W
Athens, Tex., U.S.A. 168 32 11N 95 48W
Atherton . . . . . 121 17 17S 145 30 E
Athínai . . . . . 55 37 58N 23 46 E
Athlone 34 53 26N 7 57W
Atholl, Forest of 33 56 51N 3 50W
Áthos . . . . . 55 40 9N 24 22 E
Athy 35 53 0N 7 0W
Atico 186 16 14S 73 40W
Atlanta 170 33 50N 84 24W
Atlantic 166 41 25N 95 0W
Atlantic City 164 39 25N 74 25W
Atlantic Ocean 9 0 0 20 0W
Atlas Mts. = Haut Atlas 126 32 30N 5 0W
Atmore 169 31 2N 87 30W
Atsugi . . . . . 107 35 25N 139 21 E
Atsumi . . . . . 106 34 35N 137 4 E
Atsumi-Wan . . . . . 106 34 44N 137 13 E
Attawapiskat → 140 52 57N 82 18W
Attleboro 164 41 56N 71 18W
Atyraū . . . . . 70 47 5N 52 0 E
Aubagne . . . . . 37 43 17N 5 37 E
Aube → . . . . . 37 48 34N 3 43 E
Aubenas . . . . . 37 44 37N 4 24 E
Auburn, Ala., U.S.A. 169 32 37N 85 30W
Auburn, N.Y., U.S.A. 164 42 57N 76 39W
Auckland . . . . . 122 36 52S 174 46 E
Auckland Is. . . . . . 15 50 40S 166 5 E
Aude → . . . . . 37 43 13N 3 14 E
Augsburg . . . . . 43 48 22N 10 54 E
Augusta, Ga., U.S.A. 170 33 29N 81 59W
Augusta, Maine, U.S.A. 148 44 20N 69 46W
Aunis 36 46 5N 0 50W
Aurangabad . . . . . 91 19 50N 75 23 E
Aurillac . . . . . 37 44 55N 2 26 E
Aurora 167 41 42N 88 12W
Aust-Agder fylke □ . . . . . 60 58 55N 7 40 E
Austin, Minn., U.S.A. 166 43 37N 92 59W
Austin, Tex., U.S.A. 161 30 20N 97 45W
Austral Is. = Tubuai Is. 123 25 0S 150 0W
Australia ■ . . . . . 114 23 0S 135 0 E
Australian Alps . . . . . 117 36 30S 148 30 E
Australian Cap. Terr. □ . . . . . 117 35 30S 149 0 E
Austria ■ . . . . . 45 47 0N 14 0 E
Autlán 175 19 40N 104 30W
Auvergne . . . . . 37 45 20N 3 15 E
Auxerre . . . . . 39 47 48N 3 32 E
Avalon Pen. 149 47 30N 53 20W
Aveiro 185 3 10S 55 5W
Avellaneda 190 34 50S 58 10W
Aves, I. de 181 15 45N 63 55W
Avesnes-sur-Helpe . . . . . 38 50 8N 3 55 E
Aveyron → . . . . . 36 44 7N 1 5 E
Aviemore 33 57 11N 3 50W
Avignon . . . . . 37 43 57N 4 50 E
Ávila 50 40 39N 4 43W
Avon □ 27 51 30N 2 40W
Avon →, Avon, U.K. 24 51 30N 2 43W
Avon →, Hants., U.K. 24 50 44N 1 45W
Avonmouth 27 51 30N 2 42W
Avranches 36 48 40N 1 20W
Awaji-Shima . . . . . 109 34 30N 134 50 E
Aweil . . . . . 129 8 42N 27 20 E
Axel Heiberg I. 12 80 0N 90 0W
Axminster 27 50 47N 3 1W
Ayabe . . . . . 106 35 20N 135 20 E
Ayacucho 186 13 0S 74 0W
Ayíos Evstrátios . . . . . 55 39 34N 24 58 E
Ayon, Ostrov . . . . . 73 69 50N 169 0 E
Ayr, Australia . . . . . 121 19 35S 147 25 E
Ayr, U.K. 31 55 28N 4 37W
Ayre, Pt. of 28 54 27N 4 21W
Aytos . . . . . 53 42 42N 27 16 E
Ayutla 177 16 58N 99 17W
Az Zahrān . . . . . 84 26 10N 50 7 E
Az Zubayr . . . . . 84 30 20N 47 50 E
Azamgarh . . . . . 92 26 5N 83 13 E
Azbine = Aïr . . . . . 127 18 30N 8 0 E
Azerbaijan ■ . . . . . 70 40 20N 48 0 E
Azores 126 38 44N 29 0W
Azov Sea = Azovskoye More . . . . . 68 46 0N 36 30 E
Azovskoye More . . . . . 68 46 0N 36 30 E
Azúa de Compostela 180 18 25N 70 44W
Azuero, Pen. de 179 7 30N 80 30W
Azul 190 36 42S 59 43W

B

Ba Ngoi = Cam Lam . . . . . 95 11 54N 109 10 E
Baarn . . . . . 40 52 12N 5 17 E
Bāb el Māndeb . . . . . 133 12 35N 43 25 E
Babahoyo 184 1 40S 79 30W
Babinda . . . . . 121 17 20S 145 56 E
Babine L. 154 54 48N 126 0W
Bābol . . . . . 86 36 40N 52 50 E
Babuyan Is. . . . . . 112 19 10N 121 40 E
Babylon . . . . . 84 32 40N 44 30 E
Bac Ninh . . . . . 95 21 13N 106 4 E
Bac Phan . . . . . 95 22 0N 105 0 E
Bac Quang . . . . . 95 22 30N 104 48 E
Bacabal 188 4 15S 44 45W
Bacău . . . . . 57 46 35N 26 55 E
Back → 145 65 10N 104 0W
Bacolod . . . . . 112 10 40N 122 57 E
Bad Lands 163 43 40N 102 10W
Badajoz 50 38 50N 6 59W
Badakhshān □ . . . . . 87 36 30N 71 0 E

Badalona	**51**	41 26N	2 15 E
Badanah	**82**	30 58N	41 30 E
Baden-Baden	**42**	48 45N	8 15 E
Baden-Württemberg □	**42**	48 40N	9 0 E
Bādghīsāt □	**87**	35 0N	63 0 E
Badin	**88**	24 38N	68 54 E
Baffin □	**146**	70 0N	80 0W
Baffin B.	**13**	72 0N	64 0W
Baffin I.	**146**	68 0N	75 0W
Bafra	**80**	41 34N	35 54 E
Bāft	**85**	29 15N	56 38 E
Bagé	**191**	31 20S	54 15W
Baghdād	**84**	33 20N	44 30 E
Baghlān	**87**	36 12N	69 0 E
Baghlān □	**87**	36 0N	68 30 E
Bahamas ■	**178**	24 0N	75 0W
Baharampur	**92**	24 2N	88 27 E
Bahawalpur	**89**	29 24N	71 40 E
Bahía = Salvador	**189**	13 0S	38 30W
Bahía □	**189**	12 0S	42 0W
Bahía Blanca	**190**	38 35S	62 13W
Bahr el Jebel →	**129**	7 30N	30 30 E
Bahraich	**92**	27 38N	81 37 E
Bahrain ■	**85**	26 0N	50 35 E
Baia Mare	**56**	47 40N	23 35 E
Baie Comeau	**148**	49 12N	68 10W
Baie-St-Paul	**148**	47 28N	70 32W
Ba'ījī	**81**	35 0N	43 30 E
Baikal, L. = Baykal, Oz.	**74**	53 0N	108 0 E
Baile Atha Cliath = Dublin	**35**	53 20N	6 18W
Bailleul	**38**	50 44N	2 41 E
Bainbridge	**170**	30 53N	84 34W
Baird Mts.	**142**	67 10N	160 15W
Bairnsdale	**117**	37 48S	147 36 E
Baiyin	**98**	36 45N	104 14 E
Baja	**59**	46 12N	18 59 E
Baja California	**174**	31 10N	115 12W
Baja California Norte □	**174**	30 0N	115 0W
Baja California Sur □	**174**	25 50N	111 50W
Bajimba, Mt.	**116**	29 17S	152 6 E
Baker	**171**	44 50N	117 55W
Baker I.	**122**	0 10N	176 35W
Baker Lake	**145**	64 20N	96 3W
Bakersfield	**173**	35 25N	119 0W
Bākhtarān	**84**	34 23N	47 0 E
Bakony Forest = Bakony Hegység	**59**	47 10N	17 30 E
Bakony Hegység	**59**	47 10N	17 30 E
Baku	**70**	40 25N	49 45 E
Bala	**26**	52 54N	3 36W
Balabac, Str.	**112**	7 53N	117 5 E
Balabakk	**80**	34 0N	36 10 E
Balaghat	**91**	21 49N	80 12 E
Balaghat Ra.	**91**	18 50N	76 30 E
Balaklava	**119**	34 7S	138 22 E
Balakovo	**68**	52 4N	47 55 E
Balaton	**59**	46 50N	17 40 E
Balboa	**179**	9 0N	79 30W
Balbriggan	**34**	53 35N	6 10W
Balcarce	**190**	38 0S	58 10W
Balclutha	**123**	46 15S	169 45 E
Baldy Peak	**161**	33 50N	109 30W
Baleares, Islas	**51**	39 30N	3 0 E
Balearic Is. = Baleares, Islas	**51**	39 30N	3 0 E
Bali	**111**	8 20S	115 0 E
Balikesir	**80**	39 35N	27 58 E
Balikpapan	**111**	1 10S	116 55 E
Balkan Mts. = Stara Planina	**53**	43 15N	23 0 E
Balkan Pen.	**17**	42 0N	22 0 E
Balkh □	**87**	36 30N	67 0 E
Balkhash	**71**	46 50N	74 50 E
Balkhash, Ozero	**71**	46 0N	74 50 E
Ballachulish	**32**	56 40N	5 10W
Ballarat	**117**	37 33S	143 50 E
Ballard, L.	**120**	29 20S	120 10 E
Ballater	**33**	57 2N	3 2W
Ballina, Australia	**116**	28 50S	153 31 E
Ballina, Mayo, Ireland	**34**	54 7N	9 10W
Ballina, Tipp., Ireland	**35**	52 49N	8 27W
Ballinasloe	**35**	53 20N	8 12W
Ballinrobe	**34**	53 36N	9 13W
Ballycastle	**34**	55 12N	6 15W
Ballymena	**34**	54 53N	6 18W
Ballymoney	**34**	55 5N	6 30W
Ballyshannon	**34**	54 30N	8 10W
Balmaceda	**192**	46 0S	71 50W
Balmoral	**33**	57 3N	3 13W
Balrampur	**92**	27 30N	82 20 E
Balranald	**117**	34 38S	143 33 E
Balsas, R. →	**177**	17 55N	102 10W
Baltic Sea	**16**	56 0N	20 0 E
Baltimore	**164**	39 18N	76 37W
Baluchistan □	**88**	27 30N	65 0 E
Bamako	**130**	12 34N	7 55W
Bambari	**129**	5 40N	20 35 E
Bamberg	**43**	49 54N	10 53 E
Bāmīān □	**87**	35 0N	67 0 E
Ban Aranyaprathet	**95**	13 41N	102 30 E
Ban Don = Surat Thani	**96**	9 6N	99 20 E
Ban Houei Sai	**95**	20 22N	100 32 E
Ban Khe Bo	**95**	19 10N	104 39 E
Ban Khun Yuam	**94**	18 49N	97 57 E
Ban Nong Pling	**94**	15 40N	100 10 E
Ban Phai	**95**	16 4N	102 44 E
Banaras = Varanasi	**92**	25 22N	83 0 E
Banbridge	**34**	54 21N	6 17W
Banbury	**25**	52 4N	1 21W
Bancroft	**151**	45 3N	77 51W
Banda	**91**	25 30N	80 26 E
Banda, Kepulauan	**113**	4 37S	129 50 E
Banda Aceh	**111**	5 35N	95 20 E
Banda Banda, Mt.	**116**	31 10S	152 28 E
Banda Sea	**113**	6 0S	130 0 E
Bandar = Machilipatnam	**92**	16 12N	81 8 E
Bandār 'Abbās	**85**	27 15N	56 15 E
Bandar-e Anzalī	**81**	37 30N	49 30 E
Bandar-e Khomeyni	**84**	30 30N	49 5 E
Bandar-e Lengeh	**85**	26 35N	54 58 E
Bandar-e Nakhīlū	**85**	26 58N	53 30 E
Bandar-e Torkeman	**86**	37 0N	54 10 E
Bandar Seri Begawan	**112**	4 52N	115 0 E
Bandeira, Pico da	**188**	20 26S	41 47W
Bandırma	**80**	40 20N	28 0 E
Bandon	**35**	51 44N	8 45W
Bandung	**111**	6 54S	107 36 E
Banes	**178**	21 0N	75 42W
Banff, Canada	**155**	51 10N	115 34W
Banff, U.K.	**33**	57 40N	2 32W
Bangalore	**90**	12 59N	77 40 E
Bangassou	**129**	4 55N	23 7 E
Banggai	**113**	1 40S	123 30 E
Banghāzī	**128**	32 11N	20 3 E
Bangka, Selat	**111**	2 30S	105 30 E
Bangkok	**94**	13 45N	100 35 E
Bangladesh ■	**92**	24 0N	90 0 E
Bangor, N. Ireland, U.K.	**34**	54 40N	5 40W
Bangor, Wales, U.K.	**26**	53 13N	4 9W
Bangor, U.S.A.	**148**	44 48N	68 42W
Bangui	**131**	4 23N	18 35 E
Bangweulu, L.	**135**	11 0S	30 0 E
Bani	**180**	18 16N	70 22W
Banja Luka	**52**	44 49N	17 11 E
Banjarmasin	**111**	3 20S	114 35 E
Banjul	**130**	13 28N	16 40W
Bankipore	**92**	25 35N	85 10 E
Banks I., B.C., Canada	**154**	53 20N	130 0W
Banks I., N.W.T., Canada	**145**	73 15N	121 30W
Banks Pen.	**123**	43 45S	173 15 E
Banks Str.	**119**	40 40S	148 10 E
Bann →	**34**	54 30N	6 31W
Banning	**173**	33 58N	116 52W
Bannockburn	**31**	56 5N	3 55W
Bannu	**89**	33 0N	70 18 E
Bantry	**35**	51 40N	9 28W
Baoding	**98**	38 50N	115 28 E
Baoji	**99**	34 20N	107 5 E
Baotou	**98**	40 32N	110 2 E
Ba'qūbah	**81**	33 45N	44 50 E
Bar	**52**	42 8N	19 8 E
Bar Harbor	**148**	44 15N	68 20W
Baraboo	**166**	43 28N	89 46W
Baracoa	**178**	20 20N	74 30W

Barahona	**180**	18 13N	71 7W
Barail Range	**93**	25 15N	93 20 E
Baramula	**89**	34 15N	74 20 E
Baran	**91**	25 9N	76 40 E
Baranof I.	**143**	57 0N	135 10W
Baranovichi	**68**	53 10N	26 0 E
Barbacoas	**184**	1 45N	78 0W
Barbados ■	**180**	13 0N	59 30W
Barbuda I.	**180**	17 30N	61 40W
Barca, La	**175**	20 17N	102 34W
Barcaldine	**121**	23 43S	145 6 E
Barcelona, Spain	**51**	41 21N	2 10 E
Barcelona, Venezuela	**185**	10 10N	64 40W
Barcelos	**185**	1 0S	63 0W
Barddhaman	**92**	23 14N	87 39 E
Bardera	**133**	2 20N	42 27 E
Bardsey I.	**26**	52 46N	4 47W
Bareilly	**89**	28 22N	79 27 E
Barentin	**38**	49 33N	0 58 E
Barents Sea	**13**	73 0N	39 0 E
Bargara	**121**	24 50S	152 25 E
Bari	**49**	41 6N	16 52 E
Bari Doab	**89**	30 20N	73 0 E
Barīm	**82**	12 39N	43 25 E
Barinas	**184**	8 36N	70 15W
Barisal	**92**	22 45N	90 20 E
Barito →	**111**	4 0S	114 50 E
Barlee, L.	**120**	29 15S	119 30 E
Barletta	**49**	41 20N	16 17 E
Barmer	**91**	25 45N	71 20 E
Barmera	**119**	34 15S	140 28 E
Barmouth	**26**	52 44N	4 3W
Barnard Castle	**28**	54 33N	1 55W
Barnaul	**71**	53 20N	83 40 E
Barneveld	**41**	52 7N	5 36 E
Barnsley	**28**	53 33N	1 29W
Barnstaple	**27**	51 5N	4 3W
Baro	**131**	8 35N	6 18 E
Baroda = Vadodara	**91**	22 20N	73 10 E
Barpeta	**93**	26 20N	91 10 E
Barquísimeto	**184**	10 4N	69 19W
Barra	**32**	57 0N	7 30W
Barra Hd.	**32**	56 47N	7 40W
Barraba	**116**	30 21S	150 35 E
Barranca	**186**	10 45S	77 50W
Barrancabermeja	**184**	7 0N	73 50W
Barrancas	**185**	8 55N	62 5W
Barranqueras	**190**	27 30S	59 0W
Barranquilla	**184**	11 0N	74 50W
Barre	**151**	44 15N	72 30W
Barreiros	**188**	8 49S	35 12W
Barrhead	**155**	54 10N	114 24W
Barrie	**151**	44 24N	79 40W
Barrier Ra.	**118**	31 0S	141 30 E
Barrington Tops	**116**	32 6S	151 28 E
Barrow →	**35**	52 10N	6 57W
Barrow, Pt.	**138**	71 22N	156 30W
Barrow-in-Furness	**28**	54 8N	3 15W
Barry	**27**	51 23N	3 19W
Barry's Bay	**151**	45 29N	77 41W
Barsi	**91**	18 10N	75 50 E
Barstow	**173**	34 58N	117 2W
Bartica	**185**	6 25N	58 40W
Bartow	**170**	27 53N	81 49W
Basel	**44**	47 35N	7 35 E
Bashi Channel	**99**	21 15N	122 0 E
Bashkortostan □	**69**	54 0N	57 0 E
Basilan	**112**	6 35N	122 0 E
Basildon	**25**	51 34N	0 29 E
Basilicata □	**49**	40 30N	16 0 E
Basim = Washim	**91**	20 3N	77 0 E
Basle = Basel	**44**	47 35N	7 35 E
Basoka	**134**	1 16N	23 40 E
Basque Provinces = Vascongadas	**50**	42 50N	2 45W
Basra = Al Başrah	**84**	30 30N	47 50 E
Bass Rock	**31**	56 5N	2 40W
Bass Str.	**117**	39 15S	146 30 E
Bassano	**155**	50 48N	112 20W
Basse-Terre	**180**	16 0N	61 40W
Bassein	**93**	16 45N	94 30 E
Basseterre	**180**	17 17N	62 43W
Basti	**92**	26 52N	82 55 E
Bastia	**36**	42 40N	9 30 E
Batabanó	**178**	22 40N	82 20W
Batamay	**74**	63 30N	129 15 E
Batan Is.	**112**	20 25N	121 59 E
Batang	**101**	30 1N	99 0 E
Batavia	**164**	43 0N	78 10W
Batemans Bay	**117**	35 44S	150 11 E
Batesville	**168**	35 48N	91 40W
Bath, U.K.	**27**	51 22N	2 22W
Bath, Maine, U.S.A.	**148**	43 50N	69 49W
Bath, N.Y., U.S.A.	**164**	42 20N	77 17W
Bathurst = Banjul	**130**	13 28N	16 40W
Bathurst, Australia	**117**	33 25S	149 31 E
Bathurst, Canada	**148**	47 37N	65 43W
Bathurst, C.	**145**	70 34N	128 0W
Bathurst Inlet	**145**	66 50N	108 1W
Batlow	**117**	35 31S	148 9 E
Batman	**81**	37 55N	41 5 E
Batna	**127**	35 34N	6 15 E
Baton Rouge	**168**	30 30N	91 5W
Batopilas	**174**	27 1N	107 44W
Battambang	**95**	13 7N	103 12 E
Batticaloa	**90**	7 43N	81 45 E
Battle	**25**	50 55N	0 30 E
Battle Creek	**167**	42 20N	85 6W
Battle Harbour	**147**	52 16N	55 35W
Battleford	**152**	52 45N	108 15W
Batu Gajah	**96**	4 28N	101 3 E
Batu Is.	**111**	0 30S	98 25 E
Batumi	**70**	41 30N	41 30 E
Bauchi	**131**	10 22N	9 48 E
Bauru	**188**	22 10S	49 0W
Bavaria = Bayern □	**43**	49 7N	11 30 E
Bawdwin	**93**	23 5N	97 20 E
Bawean	**111**	5 46S	112 35 E
Bawku	**130**	11 3N	0 19W
Bay City	**167**	43 35N	83 51W
Bay Shore	**164**	40 44N	73 15W
Bayamo	**178**	20 20N	76 40W
Bayamón	**180**	18 24N	66 10W
Bayan Har Shan	**101**	34 0N	98 0 E
Bayan Hot = Alxa Zuoqi	**98**	38 50N	105 40 E
Bayern □	**43**	49 7N	11 30 E
Bayeux	**36**	49 17N	0 42W
Bayfield	**150**	43 34N	81 42W
Baykal, Oz.	**74**	53 0N	108 0 E
Baykonur	**71**	47 48N	65 50 E
Bayonne	**36**	43 30N	1 28W
Bayreuth	**43**	49 56N	11 35 E
Bayrūt	**80**	33 53N	35 31 E
Baytown	**168**	29 42N	94 57W
Beachy Head	**25**	50 44N	0 16 E
Beagle, Canal	**192**	55 0S	68 30W
Béarn	**36**	43 8N	0 36W
Beauce, Plaine de la	**37**	48 10N	1 45 E
Beaudesert	**116**	27 59S	153 0 E
Beaufort	**170**	32 25N	80 40W
Beaufort Sea	**12**	72 0N	140 0W
Beaugency	**39**	47 47N	1 38 E
Beauharnois	**151**	45 20N	73 52W
Beauly	**33**	57 29N	4 27W
Beaumaris	**26**	53 16N	4 7W
Beaumont	**168**	30 5N	94 8W
Beaumont-sur-Oise	**39**	49 9N	2 17 E
Beauséjour	**153**	50 5N	96 35W
Beauvais	**38**	49 25N	2 8 E
Beauval	**152**	55 9N	107 37W
Beaver	**142**	66 20N	147 30W
Beaver →	**152**	55 26N	107 45W
Beaver Falls	**164**	40 44N	80 20W
Beaverlodge	**155**	55 11N	119 29W
Beawar	**91**	26 3N	74 18 E
Bečej	**52**	45 36N	20 3 E
Béchar	**127**	31 38N	2 18W
Beckley	**165**	37 50N	81 8W
Bedford, U.K.	**25**	52 8N	0 29W
Bedford, U.S.A.	**167**	38 50N	86 30W
Bedford □	**25**	52 4N	0 28W
Beenleigh	**116**	27 43S	153 10 E

Be'er Sheva' 80 31 15N 34 48 E
Beersheba = Be'er Sheva' 80 31 15N 34 48 E
Beeston 29 52 55N 1 11W
Bega 117 36 41S 149 51 E
Behbehān 84 30 30N 50 15 E
Beibei 99 29 47N 106 22 E
Beihai 99 21 28N 109 6 E
Beijing 98 39 55N 116 20 E
Beira 137 19 50S 34 52 E
Beira-Alta 50 40 35N 7 35W
Beira-Baixa 50 40 2N 7 30W
Beira-Litoral 50 40 5N 8 30W
Beirut = Bayrūt 80 33 53N 35 31 E
Bejaia 127 36 42N 5 2 E
Békéscsaba 59 46 40N 21 5 E
Bela 92 25 50N 82 0 E
Bela Crkva 52 44 55N 21 27 E
Belarus ■ 68 53 30N 27 0 E
Belaya Tserkov 68 49 45N 30 10 E
Belcher Is. 140 56 15N 78 45W
Belém 188 1 20S 48 30W
Belfast, U.K. 34 54 35N 5 56W
Belfast, U.S.A. 148 44 30N 69 0W
Belfort 37 47 38N 6 50 E
Belgaum 91 15 55N 74 35 E
Belgium ■ 42 50 30N 5 0 E
Belgorod 68 50 35N 36 35 E
Belgrade = Beograd 52 44 50N 20 37 E
Belitung 111 3 10S 107 50 E
Belize ■ 177 17 0N 88 30W
Belize City 177 17 25N 88 0W
Bell Peninsula 146 63 50N 82 0W
Bell Ville 190 32 40S 62 40W
Bella Coola 154 52 25N 126 40W
Bellaire 164 40 1N 80 46W
Bellary 90 15 10N 76 56 E
Belle Fourche → 163 44 25N 102 19W
Belle Glade 170 26 43N 80 38W
Belle Isle 147 51 57N 55 25W
Belle Isle, Str. of 141 51 30N 56 30W
Bellefontaine 167 40 20N 83 45W
Belleville, Canada 151 44 10N 77 23W
Belleville, U.S.A. 166 38 30N 90 0W
Bellevue 155 49 35N 114 22W
Bellin 146 60 0N 70 0W
Bellingham 171 48 45N 122 27W
Bellingshausen Sea 14 66 0S 80 0W
Belmont 117 33 4S 151 42 E
Belmopan 177 17 18N 88 30W
Belo Horizonte 188 19 55S 43 56W
Belogorsk 75 51 0N 128 20 E
Beloit 166 42 35N 89 0W
Belomorsk 68 64 35N 34 30 E
Belovo 71 54 30N 86 0 E
Beloye More 69 66 30N 38 0 E
Beloye Ozero 68 45 15N 46 50 E
Belper 28 53 2N 1 29W
Belukha 71 49 50N 86 50 E
Belyy, Ostrov 69 73 30N 71 0 E
Bemidji 156 47 30N 94 50W
Ben Lomond, N.S.W., Australia 116 30 1S 151 40 E
Ben Lomond, Tas., Australia 119 41 38S 147 42 E
Ben Macdhui 33 57 4N 3 40W
Ben More, Central, U.K. 32 56 23N 4 31W
Ben More, Strath., U.K. 30 56 26N 6 2W
Ben More Assynt 32 58 7N 4 51W
Ben Nevis 32 56 48N 5 0W
Benalla 117 36 30S 146 0 E
Benares = Varanasi 92 25 22N 83 0 E
Benbecula 32 57 26N 7 21W
Benbonyathe, Mt. 118 30 25S 139 11 E
Bencubbin 120 30 48S 117 52 E
Bend 171 44 2N 121 15W
Bendemeer 116 30 53S 151 8 E
Bender Beila 133 9 30N 50 48 E
Bendigo 117 36 40S 144 15 E
Benevento 49 41 7N 14 45 E
Bengal, Bay of 92 15 0N 90 0 E
Bengbu 99 32 58N 117 20 E
Benghazi = Banghāzī 128 32 11N 20 3 E
Benguela 134 12 37S 13 25 E
Beni → 187 10 23S 65 24W
Beni Suef 128 29 5N 31 6 E
Benidorm 51 38 33N 0 9W
Benin ■ 131 10 0N 2 0 E
Benin, Bight of 131 5 0N 3 0 E
Benin City 131 6 20N 5 31 E
Benjamin Constant 187 4 40S 70 15W
Bennett 144 59 56N 134 53W
Bennettsville 165 34 38N 79 39W
Benton 168 34 30N 92 35W
Benue → 131 7 48N 6 46 E
Benxi 98 41 20N 123 48 E
Beograd 52 44 50N 20 37 E
Beppu 108 33 15N 131 30 E
Berau, Teluk 113 2 30S 132 30 E
Berber 129 18 0N 34 0 E
Berbera 133 10 30N 45 2 E
Berck-sur-Mer 38 50 25N 1 36 E
Berezniki 69 59 24N 56 46 E
Bérgamo 46 45 42N 9 40 E
Bergen, Neths. 40 52 40N 4 43 E
Bergen, Norway 60 60 23N 5 20 E
Bergen-op-Zoom 40 51 30N 4 18 E
Bergerac 36 44 51N 0 30 E
Berhala, Selat 111 1 0S 104 15 E
Berhampore = Baharampur 92 24 2N 88 27 E
Berhampur 92 19 15N 84 54 E
Bering Sea 142 58 0N 167 0 E
Bering Str. 142 66 0N 170 0W
Berkeley 172 37 52N 122 20W
Berkshire □ 25 51 30N 1 20W
Berkshire Downs 24 51 30N 1 30W
Berlin, Germany 43 52 32N 13 24 E
Berlin, U.S.A. 148 44 29N 71 10W
Bermuda ■ 180 32 45N 65 0W
Bern 44 46 57N 7 28 E
Bernay 39 49 5N 0 35 E
Berne = Bern 44 46 57N 7 28 E
Berri 119 34 14S 140 35 E
Berry 37 47 0N 2 0 E
Bertoua 131 4 30N 13 45 E
Berwick-upon-Tweed 31 55 47N 2 0W
Berwyn Mts. 26 52 54N 3 26W
Besançon 37 47 15N 6 0 E
Bessemer, Ala., U.S.A. 169 33 25N 86 57W
Bessemer, Mich., U.S.A. 156 46 27N 90 0W
Bethel 142 60 50N 161 50W
Bethlehem 164 40 39N 75 24W
Béthune 38 50 30N 2 38 E
Betsiboka → 137 16 3S 46 36 E
Beverley 29 53 52N 0 26W
Beverly Hills 173 34 4N 118 29W
Beverwijk 40 52 28N 4 38 E
Bexhill 24 50 51N 0 29 E
Beyneu 70 45 10N 55 3 E
Beyşehir Gölü 80 37 40N 31 45 E
Béziers 37 43 20N 3 12 E
Bezwada = Vijayawada 92 16 31N 80 39 E
Bhadravati 90 13 49N 75 40 E
Bhagalpur 92 25 10N 87 0 E
Bhakra Dam 89 31 30N 76 45 E
Bhandara 91 21 5N 79 42 E
Bhanrer Ra. 91 23 40N 79 45 E
Bharat = India ■ 78 20 0N 78 0 E
Bharatpur 89 27 15N 77 30 E
Bharuch 91 21 47N 73 0 E
Bhatpara 92 22 50N 88 25 E
Bhaunagar = Bhavnagar 91 21 45N 72 10 E
Bhavnagar 91 21 45N 72 10 E
Bhilwara 91 25 25N 74 38 E
Bhima → 91 16 25N 77 17 E
Bhiwandi 91 19 20N 73 0 E
Bhiwani 89 28 50N 76 9 E
Bhopal 91 23 20N 77 30 E
Bhubaneshwar 92 20 15N 85 50 E
Bhusaval 91 21 3N 75 46 E
Bhutan ■ 92 27 25N 90 30 E
Biafra, B. of = Bonny, Bight of 131 3 30N 9 20 E
Biała Podlaska 58 52 4N 23 6 E

Białystok	**58**	53 10N	23 10 E
Biarritz	**36**	43 29N	1 33W
Bibai	**103**	43 19N	141 52 E
Bicester	**25**	51 53N	1 9W
Biche, L. la	**155**	54 50N	112 3W
Bidar	**91**	17 55N	77 35 E
Biddeford	**148**	43 30N	70 28W
Bideford	**27**	51 1N	4 13W
Bié, Planalto de	**136**	12 0S	16 0 E
Bieber	**172**	41 4N	121 6W
Biel	**44**	47 8N	7 14 E
Bielé Karpaty	**59**	49 5N	18 0 E
Bielefeld	**42**	52 2N	8 31 E
Bielsko-Biała	**59**	49 50N	19 2 E
Bien Hoa	**95**	10 57N	106 49 E
Bienne = Biel	**44**	47 8N	7 14 E
Bienville, L.	**146**	55 5N	72 40W
Big Belt Mts.	**163**	46 50N	111 30W
Big Cypress Swamp	**170**	26 12N	81 10W
Big Horn Mts. = Bighorn Mts.	**163**	44 30N	107 30W
Big Rapids	**167**	43 42N	85 27W
Big Sioux →	**156**	42 30N	96 25W
Big Spring	**161**	32 10N	101 25W
Big Stone Gap	**165**	36 52N	82 45W
Big Trout L.	**153**	53 40N	90 0W
Biggar, Canada	**152**	52 4N	108 0W
Biggar, U.K.	**31**	55 38N	3 31W
Bighorn →	**163**	46 9N	107 28W
Bighorn Mts.	**163**	44 30N	107 30W
Bihar	**92**	25 5N	85 40 E
Bihar □	**92**	25 0N	86 0 E
Bijagós, Arquipélago dos	**130**	11 15N	16 10W
Bijapur	**91**	16 50N	75 55 E
Bijeljina	**52**	44 46N	19 17 E
Bikaner	**89**	28 2N	73 18 E
Bikin	**75**	46 50N	134 20 E
Bilaspur	**92**	22 2N	82 15 E
Bilauk Taungdan	**94**	13 0N	99 0 E
Bilbao	**50**	43 16N	2 56W
Billingham	**29**	54 36N	1 18W
Billings	**163**	45 43N	108 29W
Billiton Is. = Belitung	**111**	3 10S	107 50 E
Bilma	**127**	18 50N	13 30 E
Biloela	**121**	24 24S	150 31 E
Biloxi	**169**	30 24N	88 53W
Bina-Etawah	**91**	24 13N	78 14 E
Bīnālūd, Kūh-e	**86**	36 30N	58 30 E
Bindi Bindi	**120**	30 37S	116 22 E
Bingara	**116**	29 52S	150 36 E
Bingerville	**130**	5 18N	3 49W
Bingham	**148**	45 5N	69 50W
Binghamton	**164**	42 9N	75 54W
Binh Dinh = An Nhon	**95**	13 55N	109 7 E
Binnaway	**116**	31 28S	149 24 E
Binzert = Bizerte	**127**	37 15N	9 50 E
Bioko	**131**	3 30N	8 40 E
Bir Mogrein	**126**	25 10N	11 25W
Birchip	**119**	35 56S	142 55 E
Bird I. = Aves, I. de	**181**	15 45N	63 55W
Birdum	**114**	15 39S	133 13 E
Birkenhead	**28**	53 24N	3 1W
Birmingham, U.K.	**24**	52 30N	1 55W
Birmingham, U.S.A.	**169**	33 31N	86 50W
Birobidzhan	**75**	48 50N	132 50 E
Birr	**35**	53 7N	7 55W
Bisai	**106**	35 16N	136 44 E
Biscay, B. of	**36**	45 0N	2 0W
Biscostasing	**150**	47 18N	82 9W
Bishkek	**71**	42 54N	74 46 E
Bishop Auckland	**28**	54 40N	1 40W
Bishop's Stortford	**25**	51 52N	0 11 E
Bismarck	**163**	46 49N	100 49W
Bismarck Arch.	**115**	2 30S	150 0 E
Bissagos = Bijagós, Arquipélago dos	**130**	11 15N	16 10W
Bissau	**130**	11 45N	15 45W
Bitola	**52**	41 5N	21 10 E
Bitolj = Bitola	**52**	41 5N	21 10 E
Bitterroot Range	**162**	46 0N	114 20W
Biu	**131**	10 40N	12 3 E
Biwa-Ko	**106**	35 15N	136 10 E

Biysk	**71**	52 40N	85 0 E
Bizen	**109**	34 43N	134 8 E
Bizerte	**127**	37 15N	9 50 E
Bjørnøya	**13**	74 30N	19 0 E
Black → = Da →	**95**	21 15N	105 20 E
Black Diamond	**155**	50 45N	114 14W
Black Forest = Schwarzwald	**42**	48 0N	8 0 E
Black Hills	**163**	44 0N	103 50W
Black Mts.	**26**	51 52N	3 5W
Black Sea	**17**	43 30N	35 0 E
Blackall	**121**	24 25S	145 45 E
Blackburn	**28**	53 44N	2 30W
Blackpool	**28**	53 48N	3 3W
Blackwater	**121**	23 35S	148 53 E
Blackwater →, Meath, Ireland	**34**	53 46N	7 0W
Blackwater →, Munster, Ireland	**35**	51 55N	7 50W
Blackwater →, U.K.	**34**	54 31N	6 35W
Blackwell	**168**	36 55N	97 20W
Blaenau Ffestiniog	**26**	53 0N	3 57W
Blagoveshchensk	**75**	50 20N	127 30 E
Blair Atholl	**33**	56 46N	3 50W
Blairmore	**155**	49 40N	114 25W
Blanc, Mont	**37**	45 48N	6 50 E
Blanca Peak	**163**	37 35N	105 29W
Blanche L.	**118**	29 15S	139 40 E
Blanco, C.	**171**	42 50N	124 40W
Blandford Forum	**24**	50 52N	2 10W
Blantyre	**137**	15 45S	35 0 E
Blarney	**35**	51 57N	8 35W
Blaydon	**28**	54 56N	1 47W
Blayney	**117**	33 32S	149 14 E
Blekinge län □	**61**	56 20N	15 20 E
Blenheim	**123**	41 38S	173 57 E
Bletchley	**25**	51 59N	0 44W
Blida	**127**	36 30N	2 49 E
Blind River	**150**	46 10N	82 58W
Blitar	**111**	8 5S	112 11 E
Bloemfontein	**137**	29 6S	26 14 E
Blois	**36**	47 35N	1 20 E
Bloody Foreland	**34**	55 10N	8 18W
Bloomington, Ill., U.S.A.	**166**	40 27N	89 0W
Bloomington, Ind., U.S.A.	**167**	39 10N	86 30W
Bloomsburg	**164**	41 0N	76 30W
Blue Mts., Oreg., U.S.A.	**171**	45 15N	119 0W
Blue Mts., Pa., U.S.A.	**164**	40 30N	76 30W
Blue Nile = Nîl el Azraq →	**129**	15 38N	32 31 E
Blue Ridge Mts.	**165**	36 30N	80 15W
Bluefield	**165**	37 18N	81 14W
Bluefields	**179**	12 20N	83 50W
Bluestack, mt.	**34**	54 46N	8 5W
Bluff	**123**	46 37S	168 20 E
Blumenau	**191**	27 0S	49 0W
Blyth	**28**	55 8N	1 32W
Bo	**130**	7 55N	11 50W
Bo Hai	**98**	39 0N	120 0 E
Boa Vista	**185**	2 48N	60 30W
Boaco	**179**	12 29N	85 35W
Bobadah	**116**	32 19S	146 41 E
Bobcaygeon	**151**	44 33N	78 33W
Bobo-Dioulasso	**130**	11 8N	4 13W
Bobraomby, Tanjon' i	**137**	12 40S	49 10 E
Bobruysk	**68**	53 10N	29 15 E
Bôca do Acre	**187**	8 50S	67 27W
Boca Raton	**170**	26 21N	80 5W
Bocas del Toro	**179**	9 15N	82 20W
Bocholt	**42**	51 50N	6 35 E
Bochum	**42**	51 28N	7 12 E
Boden	**67**	65 50N	21 42 E
Bodensee	**44**	47 35N	9 25 E
Bodhan	**91**	18 40N	77 44 E
Bodmin	**27**	50 28N	4 44W
Bodmin Moor	**27**	50 33N	4 36W
Bodø	**64**	67 17N	14 24 E
Bogalusa	**169**	30 50N	89 55W
Boggabilla	**116**	28 36S	150 24 E
Boggabri	**116**	30 45S	150 0 E
Boggeragh Mts.	**35**	52 2N	8 55W
Bognor Regis	**25**	50 47N	0 40W
Bogong, Mt.	**117**	36 47S	147 17 E

Bogor	**111**	6 36S	106 48 E
Bogota	**184**	4 34N	74 0W
Boguchany	**74**	58 40N	97 30 E
Bohain	**38**	49 59N	3 28 E
Bohemian Forest = Böhmerwald	**43**	49 30N	12 40 E
Böhmerwald	**43**	49 30N	12 40 E
Bohol	**112**	9 50N	124 10 E
Bohol Sea	**112**	9 0N	124 0 E
Bohotleh	**133**	8 20N	46 25 E
Boise	**162**	43 43N	116 9W
Boissevain	**153**	49 15N	100 5W
Boké	**130**	10 56N	14 17W
Bolan Pass	**88**	29 50N	67 20 E
Bolaños, R. →	**175**	21 12N	104 5W
Bolbec	**38**	49 30N	0 30 E
Bolgatanga	**130**	10 44N	0 53W
Bolívar	**190**	36 15S	60 53W
Bolivia ■	**187**	17 6S	64 0W
Bollnäs	**60**	61 21N	16 24 E
Bollon	**116**	28 2S	147 29 E
Bologna	**47**	44 30N	11 20 E
Boloven, Cao Nguyen	**95**	15 10N	106 30 E
Bolsena, L. di	**46**	42 35N	11 55 E
Bolshevik, Ostrov	**72**	78 30N	102 0 E
Bolshoi Kavkas	**70**	42 50N	44 0 E
Bolshoy Begichev, Ostrov	**72**	74 20N	112 30 E
Bolsward	**41**	53 3N	5 32 E
Bolton	**28**	53 35N	2 26W
Bolzano	**47**	46 30N	11 20 E
Boma	**134**	5 50S	13 4 E
Bombala	**117**	36 56S	149 15 E
Bombay	**91**	18 55N	72 50 E
Bomu →	**129**	4 40N	23 30 E
Bon, C.	**127**	37 1N	11 2 E
Bonaire	**181**	12 10N	68 15W
Bonavista	**149**	48 40N	53 5W
Bonifacio, Bouches de	**48**	41 12N	9 15 E
Bonn	**42**	50 43N	7 6 E
Bonneval	**39**	48 11N	1 24 E
Bonnie Rock	**120**	30 29S	118 22 E
Bonny, Bight of	**131**	3 30N	9 20 E
Bonnyville	**152**	54 20N	110 45W
Bonthe	**130**	7 30N	12 33W
Boonah	**116**	27 58S	152 41 E
Boone	**166**	42 5N	93 53W
Boonville	**167**	38 3N	87 13W
Boorowa	**117**	34 28S	148 44 E
Boothia, Gulf of	**146**	71 0N	90 0W
Boothia Pen.	**145**	71 0N	94 0W
Bootle	**28**	53 28N	3 1W
Bôr	**129**	6 10N	31 40 E
Borås	**60**	57 43N	12 56 E
Borāzjān	**85**	29 22N	51 10 E
Bordeaux	**36**	44 50N	0 36W
Borders □	**31**	55 35N	2 50W
Bordertown	**119**	36 19S	140 45 E
Bordj Omar Driss	**127**	28 10N	6 40 E
Borger	**161**	35 40N	101 20W
Borja	**186**	4 20S	77 40W
Borlänge	**60**	60 29N	15 26 E
Borneo	**111**	1 0N	115 0 E
Bornholm	**61**	55 10N	15 0 E
Borujerd	**84**	33 55N	48 50 E
Borzya	**74**	50 24N	116 31 E
Boscastle	**27**	50 42N	4 42W
Boshan	**98**	36 28N	117 49 E
Bosna →	**52**	45 4N	18 29 E
Bosnia-Herzegovina ■	**52**	44 0N	18 0 E
Bōsō-Hantō	**107**	35 20N	140 20 E
Bosporus = Karadeniz Boğazı	**80**	41 10N	29 10 E
Bossangoa	**131**	6 35N	17 30 E
Bossembélé	**131**	5 25N	17 40 E
Bossier City	**168**	32 28N	93 48W
Bosten Hu	**100**	41 55N	87 40 E
Boston, U.K.	**29**	52 59N	0 2W
Boston, U.S.A.	**164**	42 20N	71 0W
Bothnia, G. of	**67**	63 0N	20 0 E
Botletle →	**136**	20 10S	23 15 E
Botoşani	**57**	47 42N	26 41 E
Botswana ■	**136**	22 0S	24 0 E
Botucatu	**188**	22 55S	48 30W
Bou Djébéha	**126**	18 25N	2 45W
Bouaké	**130**	7 40N	5 2W
Bougie = Bejaia	**127**	36 42N	5 2 E
Boulogne-sur-Mer	**38**	50 42N	1 36 E
Bourbonnais	**37**	46 28N	3 0 E
Bourem	**130**	17 0N	0 24W
Bourg-en-Bresse	**37**	46 13N	5 12 E
Bourges	**37**	47 9N	2 25 E
Bourgogne	**37**	47 0N	4 30 E
Bourke	**116**	30 8S	145 55 E
Bournemouth	**24**	50 43N	1 53W
Bousso	**131**	10 34N	16 52 E
Bouvet I. = Bouvetøya	**14**	54 26S	3 24 E
Bouvetøya	**14**	54 26S	3 24 E
Bowen	**121**	20 0S	148 16 E
Bowland, Forest of	**28**	54 0N	2 30W
Bowling Green, Ky., U.S.A.	**169**	37 0N	86 25W
Bowling Green, Ohio, U.S.A.	**167**	41 22N	83 40W
Bowling Green, C.	**121**	19 19S	147 25 E
Bowmanville	**151**	43 55N	78 41W
Bowral	**117**	34 26S	150 27 E
Boyle	**34**	53 58N	8 19W
Boyne →	**34**	53 43N	6 15W
Boyne City	**150**	45 13N	85 1W
Boyup Brook	**120**	33 50S	116 23 E
Bozeman	**163**	45 40N	111 0W
Bozen = Bolzano	**47**	46 30N	11 20 E
Brač	**52**	43 20N	16 40 E
Bracciano, L. di	**46**	42 8N	12 11 E
Bracebridge	**151**	45 2N	79 19W
Bräcke	**66**	62 45N	15 26 E
Brad	**56**	46 10N	22 50 E
Bradenton	**170**	27 25N	82 35W
Bradford, U.K.	**28**	53 47N	1 45W
Bradford, U.S.A.	**164**	41 58N	78 41W
Braemar	**33**	57 2N	3 20W
Braga	**50**	41 35N	8 25W
Bragança, Brazil	**188**	1 0S	47 2W
Bragança, Portugal	**50**	41 48N	6 50W
Brahmanbaria	**93**	23 58N	91 15 E
Brahmani →	**92**	20 39N	86 46 E
Brahmaputra →	**93**	24 2N	90 59 E
Braidwood	**117**	35 27S	149 49 E
Brăila	**57**	45 19N	27 59 E
Brainerd	**156**	46 20N	94 10W
Braintree	**25**	51 53N	0 34 E
Brampton	**151**	43 45N	79 45W
Branco →	**185**	1 20S	61 50W
Branco, Cabo	**182**	7 9S	34 47W
Brandenburg	**43**	52 24N	12 33 E
Brandon	**153**	49 50N	99 57W
Brantford	**151**	43 10N	80 15W
Brasil, Planalto	**188**	18 0S	46 30W
Brasília	**188**	15 47S	47 55 E
Braşov	**57**	45 38N	25 35 E
Brassey, Banjaran	**111**	5 0N	117 15 E
Brasstown Bald, Mt.	**165**	34 54N	83 45W
Bratislava	**59**	48 10N	17 7 E
Bratsk	**74**	56 10N	101 30 E
Brattleboro	**164**	42 53N	72 37W
Braunschweig	**43**	52 17N	10 28 E
Brava	**133**	1 20N	44 8 E
Bravo del Norte →	**174**	25 57N	97 9W
Brawley	**173**	32 58N	115 30W
Bray	**35**	53 12N	6 6W
Brazil	**167**	39 32N	87 8W
Brazil ■	**188**	10 0S	50 0W
Brazilian Highlands = Brasil, Planalto	**188**	18 0S	46 30W
Brazos →	**168**	28 53N	95 23W
Brazzaville	**134**	4 9S	15 12 E
Brčko	**52**	44 54N	18 46 E
Breadalbane	**31**	56 30N	4 15W
Bream Bay	**122**	35 56S	174 28 E
Brecon	**26**	51 57N	3 23W
Brecon Beacons	**26**	51 53N	3 27W
Breda	**40**	51 35N	4 45 E
Breiðafjörður	**64**	65 15N	23 15W
Bremen	**42**	53 4N	8 47 E

Bremerhaven	**42**	53 34N	8 35 E
Bremerton	**171**	47 30N	122 38W
Brenham	**168**	30 5N	96 27W
Brentwood	**25**	51 37N	0 19 E
Bréscia	**46**	45 33N	10 13 E
Breslau = Wrocław	**58**	51 5N	17 5 E
Brest, France	**36**	48 24N	4 31W
Brest, U.S.S.R.	**68**	52 10N	23 40 E
Bretagne	**36**	48 0N	3 0W
Bretçu	**57**	46 7N	26 18 E
Breton Sd.	**169**	29 40N	89 12W
Brett, C.	**122**	35 10S	174 20 E
Brewer	**148**	44 43N	68 50W
Brewster	**171**	48 10N	119 51W
Brewton	**169**	31 9N	87 2W
Brezhnev = Naberezhnyye Chelny	**68**	55 42N	52 19 E
Briançon	**37**	44 54N	6 39 E
Bridgend	**27**	51 30N	3 35W
Bridgeport	**164**	41 12N	73 12W
Bridgeton	**164**	39 29N	75 10W
Bridgetown, Australia	**120**	33 58S	116 7 E
Bridgetown, Barbados	**180**	13 0N	59 30W
Bridgnorth	**24**	52 33N	2 25W
Bridgwater	**27**	51 7N	3 0W
Bridlington	**29**	54 6N	0 11W
Bridport	**27**	50 43N	2 45W
Brigham City	**163**	41 30N	112 1W
Bright	**117**	36 42S	146 56 E
Brighton, Australia	**119**	42 42S	147 16 E
Brighton, U.K.	**25**	50 50N	0 9W
Bríndisi	**49**	40 39N	17 55 E
Brisbane	**116**	27 25S	153 2 E
Bristol, U.K.	**27**	51 26N	2 35W
Bristol, Conn., U.S.A.	**164**	41 44N	72 57W
Bristol, Tenn., U.S.A.	**165**	36 36N	82 11W
Bristol B.	**142**	58 0N	160 0W
Bristol Channel	**27**	51 18N	4 30W
Bristow	**168**	35 55N	96 28W
British Columbia □	**154**	55 0N	125 15W
British Guiana = Guyana ■	**185**	5 0N	59 0W
British Honduras = Belize ■	**177**	17 0N	88 30W
British Isles	**18**	55 0N	4 0W
Brittany = Bretagne	**36**	48 0N	3 0W
Brive-la-Gaillarde	**36**	45 10N	1 32 E
Brlik	**71**	44 0N	74 5 E
Brno	**59**	49 10N	16 35 E
Broach = Bharuch	**91**	21 47N	73 0 E
Broad Law	**31**	55 30N	3 22W
Broad Sd.	**121**	22 0S	149 45 E
Broads, The	**29**	52 45N	1 30 E
Brochet	**145**	57 53N	101 40W
Brockton	**164**	42 8N	71 2W
Brockville	**151**	44 35N	75 41W
Brod	**52**	41 35N	21 17 E
Brodeur Pen.	**146**	72 30N	88 10W
Broken Hill = Kabwe	**135**	14 30S	28 29 E
Broken Hill	**118**	31 58S	141 29 E
Bromley	**25**	51 20N	0 5 E
Brookhaven	**169**	31 40N	90 25W
Brooks	**155**	50 35N	111 55W
Brooks Ra.	**142**	68 40N	147 0W
Brosna →	**35**	53 8N	8 0W
Brough	**28**	54 32N	2 19W
Broughty Ferry	**31**	56 29N	2 50W
Brouwershaven	**40**	51 45N	3 55 E
Brownsville	**158**	25 56N	97 25W
Brownwood	**161**	31 45N	99 0W
Bruay-en-Artois	**38**	50 29N	2 33 E
Bruce, Mt.	**114**	22 37S	118 8 E
Bruce Rock	**120**	31 52S	118 8 E
Bruck an der Leitha	**45**	48 1N	16 47 E
Bruges = Brugge	**42**	51 13N	3 13 E
Brugge	**42**	51 13N	3 13 E
Brunei = Bandar Seri Begawan	**112**	4 52N	115 0 E
Brunei ■	**111**	4 50N	115 0 E
Bruno	**152**	52 20N	105 30W
Brunswick = Braunschweig	**43**	52 17N	10 28 E
Brunswick, Ga., U.S.A.	**170**	31 10N	81 30W
Brunswick, Maine, U.S.A.	**148**	43 53N	69 50W
Bruny I.	**119**	43 20S	147 15 E
Brussel	**42**	50 51N	4 21 E
Bruthen	**117**	37 42S	147 50 E
Bruton	**27**	51 6N	2 28W
Bryan, Ohio, U.S.A.	**167**	41 30N	84 30W
Bryan, Tex., U.S.A.	**168**	30 40N	96 27W
Bryan, Mt.	**119**	33 30S	139 0 E
Bryansk	**68**	53 13N	34 25 E
Brzeg	**58**	50 52N	17 30 E
Bucaramanga	**184**	7 0N	73 0W
Buchan	**33**	57 32N	2 8W
Buchan Ness	**33**	57 29N	1 48W
Buchanan	**130**	5 57N	10 2W
Buchans	**149**	48 50N	56 52W
Bucharest = Bucureşti	**57**	44 27N	26 10 E
Buckhannon	**165**	39 2N	80 10W
Buckhaven	**31**	56 10N	3 2W
Buckingham, Canada	**151**	45 37N	75 24W
Buckingham, U.K.	**25**	52 0N	0 59W
Buckingham □	**25**	51 50N	0 55W
Buckleboo	**118**	32 54S	136 12 E
Bucureşti	**57**	44 27N	26 10 E
Bucyrus	**167**	40 48N	83 0W
Budalin	**93**	22 20N	95 10 E
Budapest	**59**	47 29N	19 5 E
Budaun	**89**	28 5N	79 10 E
Bude	**27**	50 49N	4 33W
Budgewoi Lake	**117**	33 13S	151 34 E
Buenaventura, Colombia	**184**	3 53N	77 4W
Buenaventura, Mexico	**174**	29 51N	107 29W
Buenos Aires	**190**	34 30S	58 20W
Buffalo	**164**	42 55N	78 50W
Bug →	**58**	52 31N	21 5 E
Buga	**184**	4 0N	76 15W
Bugun Shara	**100**	49 0N	104 0 E
Builth Wells	**26**	52 10N	3 26W
Buir Nur	**98**	47 50N	117 42 E
Bujumbura	**135**	3 16S	29 18 E
Bukachacha	**74**	52 55N	116 50 E
Bukavu	**23**	2 20S	28 52 E
Bukhara	**70**	39 48N	64 25 E
Bukit Mertajam	**96**	5 22N	100 28 E
Bukittinggi	**111**	0 20S	100 20 E
Bukoba	**135**	1 20S	31 49 E
Bukuru	**131**	9 42N	8 48 E
Bulahdelah	**117**	32 23S	152 13 E
Bulandshahr	**89**	28 28N	77 51 E
Bulawayo	**137**	20 7S	28 32 E
Bulgaria ■	**53**	42 35N	25 30 E
Bull Shoals L.	**168**	36 40N	93 5W
Bully-les-Mines	**38**	50 27N	2 44 E
Bulsar = Valsad	**91**	20 40N	72 58 E
Bulun	**72**	70 37N	127 30 E
Bunbury	**120**	33 20S	115 35 E
Buncrana	**34**	55 8N	7 28W
Bundaberg	**116**	24 54S	152 22 E
Bundi	**91**	25 30N	75 35 E
Bundoran	**34**	54 24N	8 17W
Bungo-Suidō	**109**	33 0N	132 15 E
Buorkhaya, Mys	**72**	71 50N	132 40 E
Bûr Sa'îd	**128**	31 16N	32 18 E
Bûr Sûdân	**129**	19 32N	37 9 E
Buraymī, Al Wāhāt al	**83**	24 10N	55 43 E
Burbank	**173**	34 9N	118 23W
Burdur	**80**	37 45N	30 22 E
Burdwan = Barddhaman	**92**	23 14N	87 39 E
Burgas	**53**	42 33N	27 29 E
Burgenland □	**45**	47 20N	16 20 E
Burgos	**50**	42 21N	3 41W
Burgundy = Bourgogne	**37**	47 0N	4 30 E
Burin	**149**	47 1N	55 14W
Burkina Faso ■	**130**	12 0N	1 0W
Burlington, Canada	**151**	43 18N	79 45W
Burlington, Iowa, U.S.A.	**166**	40 50N	91 5W
Burlington, N.C., U.S.A.	**165**	36 7N	79 27W
Burlington, N.J., U.S.A.	**164**	40 5N	74 50W
Burlington, Vt., U.S.A.	**151**	44 27N	73 14W
Burma ■	**93**	21 0N	96 30 E
Burnie	**119**	41 4S	145 56 E
Burnley	**28**	53 47N	2 15W
Burns	**171**	43 40N	119 4W

Burns Lake	**154**	54 20N	125 45W
Burra	**119**	33 40S	138 55 E
Bursa	**80**	40 15N	29 5 E
Burton-upon-Trent	**28**	52 48N	1 39W
Buru	**113**	3 30S	126 30 E
Burundi ■	**135**	3 15S	30 0 E
Bury	**28**	53 36N	2 19W
Bury St. Edmunds	**25**	52 15N	0 42 E
Buryat Rep. □	**74**	53 0N	110 0 E
Buskerud fylke □	**60**	60 13N	9 0 E
Busselton	**120**	33 42S	115 15 E
Bussum	**40**	52 16N	5 10 E
Bute	**30**	55 48N	5 2W
Butiaba	**132**	1 50N	31 20 E
Butler	**164**	40 52N	79 52W
Butte	**163**	46 0N	112 31W
Butterworth	**96**	5 24N	100 23 E
Butuan	**112**	8 57N	125 33 E
Butung	**113**	5 0S	122 45 E
Buxton	**28**	53 16N	1 54W
Buyaga	**74**	59 50N	127 0 E
Buzău	**57**	45 10N	26 50 E
Buzen	**108**	33 35N	131 5 E
Buzzards Bay	**164**	41 45N	70 38W
Bydgoszcz	**58**	53 10N	18 0 E
Byelorussia = Belorussia ■	**68**	53 30N	27 0 E
Bylot I.	**146**	73 13N	78 34W
Byrd Land	**15**	79 30S	125 0W
Byron Bay	**116**	28 43S	153 37 E
Byrranga, Gory	**72**	75 0N	100 0 E
Bytom	**58**	50 25N	18 54 E

C

Cabimas	**184**	10 23N	71 25W
Cabinda	**134**	5 33S	12 11 E
Cabinda □	**134**	5 0S	12 30 E
Cabo Pantoja	**184**	1 0S	75 10W
Cabonga, Réservoir	**151**	47 20N	76 40W
Caboolture	**116**	27 5S	152 58 E
Cabora Bassa Dam	**137**	15 20S	32 50 E
Caborca	**174**	30 40N	112 10W
Cabot Strait	**149**	47 15N	59 40W
Cabrera, I.	**51**	39 8N	2 57 E
Cabri	**152**	50 35N	108 25W
Čačak	**52**	43 54N	20 20 E
Cáceres	**50**	39 26N	6 23W
Cache Bay	**151**	46 22N	80 0W
Cachoeira	**189**	12 30S	39 0W
Cachoeira de Itapemirim	**189**	20 51S	41 7W
Cachoeira do Sul	**191**	30 3S	52 53W
Cader Idris	**26**	52 43N	3 56W
Cadibarrawirracanna, L.	**118**	28 52S	135 27 E
Cadillac, Canada	**151**	48 14N	78 23W
Cadillac, U.S.A.	**167**	44 16N	85 25W
Cádiz	**50**	36 30N	6 20W
Cádiz, G. de	**50**	36 40N	7 0W
Caen	**36**	49 10N	0 22W
Caernarfon	**26**	53 8N	4 17W
Caernarfon B.	**26**	53 4N	4 40W
Caernarvon = Caernarfon	**26**	53 8N	4 17W
Caerphilly	**27**	51 34N	3 13W
Cagayan de Oro	**112**	8 30N	124 40 E
Cágliari	**48**	39 15N	9 6 E
Caguas	**180**	18 14N	66 4W
Caha Mts.	**35**	51 45N	9 40W
Caher	**35**	52 23N	7 56W
Cahors	**36**	44 27N	1 27 E
Cahuapanas	**186**	5 15S	77 0W
Caibarién	**178**	22 30N	79 30W
Caicos Is.	**180**	21 40N	71 40W
Cairngorm Mts.	**33**	57 6N	3 42W
Cairns	**121**	16 57S	145 45 E
Cairo = El Qâhira	**128**	30 1N	31 14 E
Cairo	**169**	37 0N	89 10W
Cajamarca	**186**	7 5S	78 28W
Calabar	**131**	4 57N	8 20 E
Calabozo	**184**	9 0N	67 28W
Calábria □	**49**	39 24N	16 30 E
Calais, France	**38**	50 57N	1 56 E
Calais, U.S.A.	**148**	45 11N	67 20W
Calama, Brazil	**187**	8 0S	62 50W
Calama, Chile	**190**	22 30S	68 55W
Calamar	**184**	10 15N	74 55W
Calamian Group	**112**	11 50N	119 55 E
Calca	**187**	13 22S	72 0W
Calcutta	**92**	22 36N	88 24 E
Caldwell	**171**	43 45N	116 42W
Calgary	**155**	51 0N	114 10W
Cali	**184**	3 25N	76 35W
Calicut	**90**	11 15N	75 43 E
California □	**172**	37 25N	120 0W
California, Golfo de	**174**	28 0N	112 0W
Callander	**31**	56 15N	4 14W
Callao	**186**	12 0S	77 0W
Caloundra	**116**	26 45S	153 10 E
Caltanissetta	**49**	37 30N	14 3 E
Cam Lam	**95**	11 54N	109 10 E
Cam Ranh	**95**	11 54N	109 12 E
Camagüey	**178**	21 20N	78 0W
Camaná	**186**	16 30S	72 50W
Camargue	**37**	43 34N	4 34 E
Camarones	**192**	44 50S	65 40W
Cambay = Khambhat	**91**	22 23N	72 33 E
Cambodia ■	**95**	12 15N	105 0 E
Camborne	**27**	50 13N	5 18W
Cambrai	**38**	50 11N	3 14 E
Cambrian Mts.	**26**	52 25N	3 52W
Cambridge, Canada	**151**	43 23N	80 15W
Cambridge, N.Z.	**122**	37 54S	175 29 E
Cambridge, U.K.	**25**	52 13N	0 8 E
Cambridge, Mass., U.S.A.	**164**	42 20N	71 8W
Cambridge, Md., U.S.A.	**164**	38 33N	76 2W
Cambridge, Ohio, U.S.A.	**167**	40 1N	81 35W
Cambridge Bay	**145**	69 10N	105 0W
Cambridge Gulf	**114**	14 55S	128 15 E
Cambridgeshire □	**25**	52 12N	0 7 E
Camden, Ark., U.S.A.	**168**	33 40N	92 50W
Camden, N.J., U.S.A.	**164**	39 57N	75 7W
Camden, S.C., U.S.A.	**165**	34 17N	80 34W
Cameroon ■	**131**	6 0N	12 30 E
Cameroun, Mt.	**131**	4 13N	9 10 E
Cametá	**188**	2 12S	49 30W
Camiri	**187**	20 3S	63 31W
Camocim	**189**	2 55S	40 50W
Campagna	**46**	40 40N	15 5 E
Campania □	**49**	40 50N	14 45 E
Campbell I.	**15**	52 30S	169 0 E
Campbell River	**154**	50 5N	125 20W
Campbellton	**148**	47 57N	66 43W
Campbelltown, Australia	**117**	34 4S	150 49 E
Campbelltown, U.K.	**30**	57 34N	4 2W
Campeche	**177**	19 51N	90 32W
Campeche □	**177**	19 0N	90 30W
Campeche, B. de	**177**	20 0N	94 0W
Camperdown	**119**	38 14S	143 9 E
Camperville	**153**	51 59N	100 9W
Campina Grande	**189**	7 20S	35 47W
Campinas	**188**	22 50S	47 0W
Campo Grande	**188**	20 25S	54 40W
Campos	**188**	21 50S	41 20W
Camrose	**155**	53 0N	112 50W
Can Tho	**95**	10 2N	105 46 E
Canada ■	**139**	60 0N	100 0W
Cañada de Gómez	**190**	32 40S	61 30W
Canadian →	**158**	35 27N	95 3W
Çanakkale Boğazi	**80**	40 0N	26 0 E
Cananea	**174**	30 57N	110 18W
Canarias, Islas	**126**	28 30N	16 0W
Canary Is. = Canarias, Islas	**126**	28 30N	16 0W
Canaveral, C.	**170**	28 28N	80 31W
Canberra	**117**	35 15S	149 8 E
Candala	**133**	11 30N	49 58 E
Candia = Iráklion	**55**	35 20N	25 12 E
Canea = Khaniá	**55**	35 30N	24 4 E
Çankırı	**80**	40 40N	33 37 E
Canmore	**155**	51 7N	115 18W
Canna	**32**	57 3N	6 33W
Cannanore	**90**	11 53N	75 27 E

Cannes	**37**	43 32N	7 0 E
Cannock	**28**	52 42N	2 2W
Canora	**152**	51 40N	102 30W
Canowindra	**117**	33 35S	148 38 E
Canso	**149**	45 20N	61 0W
Cantabrian Mts. = Cantábrica, Cordillera	**50**	43 0N	5 10W
Cantábrica, Cordillera	**50**	43 0N	5 10W
Canterbury	**25**	51 17N	1 5 E
Canterbury □	**123**	43 45S	171 19 E
Canterbury Bight	**123**	44 16S	171 55 E
Canterbury Plains	**123**	43 55S	171 22 E
Canton = Guangzhou	**99**	23 5N	113 10 E
Canton, Ill., U.S.A.	**166**	40 32N	90 0W
Canton, Miss., U.S.A.	**169**	32 40N	90 1W
Canton, Ohio, U.S.A.	**167**	40 47N	81 22W
Canutama	**185**	6 30S	64 20W
Cap-Chat	**148**	49 6N	66 40W
Cap-de-la-Madeleine	**151**	46 22N	72 31W
Cap-Haïtien	**180**	19 40N	72 20W
Cape Barren I.	**119**	40 25S	148 15 E
Cape Breton I.	**149**	46 0N	60 30W
Cape Coast	**130**	5 5N	1 15W
Cape Dorset	**146**	64 14N	76 32W
Cape Fear ⟶	**165**	34 30N	78 25W
Cape Girardeau	**169**	37 20N	89 30W
Cape May	**164**	39 1N	74 53W
Cape Montague	**149**	46 5N	62 25W
Cape Town	**136**	33 55S	18 22 E
Cape Verde Is. ■	**9**	17 10N	25 20W
Cape York Peninsula	**115**	12 0S	142 30 E
Caquetá ⟶	**184**	1 15S	69 15W
Caracal	**57**	44 8N	24 22 E
Caracas	**184**	10 30N	66 55W
Caratinga	**188**	19 50S	42 10W
Carberry	**153**	49 50N	99 25W
Carbonara, C.	**48**	39 8N	9 30 E
Carbondale	**166**	37 45N	89 10W
Carbonear	**149**	47 42N	53 13W
Carcassonne	**37**	43 13N	2 20 E
Carcross	**144**	60 13N	134 45W
Cárdenas, Cuba	**178**	23 0N	81 30W
Cárdenas, Mexico	**177**	21 0N	99 40W
Cardiff	**27**	51 28N	3 11W
Cardigan	**26**	52 6N	4 41W
Cardigan B.	**26**	52 30N	4 30W
Cardston	**155**	49 15N	113 20W
Cardwell	**121**	18 14S	146 2 E
Caribbean Sea	**181**	15 0N	75 0W
Cariboo Mts.	**155**	53 0N	121 0W
Caribou	**148**	46 55N	68 0W
Caribou Mts.	**145**	59 12N	115 40W
Carinhanha	**188**	14 15S	44 46W
Carinthia = Kärnten □	**45**	46 52N	13 30 E
Carlisle, U.K.	**28**	54 54N	2 55W
Carlisle, U.S.A.	**164**	40 12N	77 10W
Carlow	**35**	52 50N	6 58W
Carlow □	**35**	52 43N	6 50W
Carlsbad, Calif., U.S.A.	**173**	33 11N	117 25W
Carlsbad, N. Mex., U.S.A.	**161**	32 20N	104 14W
Carlyle	**152**	49 40N	102 20W
Carmacks	**144**	62 5N	136 16W
Carman	**153**	49 30N	98 0W
Carmarthen	**26**	51 52N	4 20W
Carmarthen B.	**27**	51 40N	4 30W
Carnarvon	**120**	24 51S	113 42 E
Carnegie, L.	**114**	26 5S	122 30 E
Carniche, Alpi	**47**	46 36N	13 0 E
Carnsore Pt.	**35**	52 10N	6 20W
Caroline Is.	**122**	8 0N	150 0 E
Caroona	**116**	31 24S	150 26 E
Carpathians, Mts.	**17**	49 50N	21 0 E
Carpaţii Meridionali	**57**	45 30N	25 0 E
Carpentaria, G. of	**115**	14 0S	139 0 E
Carrara	**46**	44 5N	10 7 E
Carrick-on-Shannon	**34**	53 57N	8 7W
Carrick-on-Suir	**35**	52 22N	7 30W
Carrickfergus	**34**	54 43N	5 50W
Carrickmacross	**34**	54 0N	6 43W
Carroll	**166**	42 2N	94 55W
Carrollton	**170**	33 36N	85 5W
Carse of Gowrie	**31**	56 30N	3 10W
Carson City	**172**	39 12N	119 46W
Carstairs	**31**	55 42N	3 41W
Cartagena, Colombia	**184**	10 25N	75 33W
Cartagena, Spain	**51**	37 38N	0 59W
Cartago, Colombia	**184**	4 45N	75 55W
Cartago, Costa Rica	**179**	9 50N	85 52W
Cartersville	**169**	34 11N	84 48W
Carthage	**168**	37 10N	94 20W
Cartwright	**147**	53 41N	56 58W
Caruaru	**189**	8 15S	35 55W
Carúpano	**185**	10 39N	63 15W
Caruthersville	**169**	36 10N	89 40W
Carvin	**38**	50 30N	2 57 E
Casablanca	**126**	33 36N	7 36W
Casas Grandes	**174**	30 22N	107 57W
Cascade Ra.	**171**	47 0N	121 30W
Casilda	**190**	33 10S	61 10W
Casino	**116**	28 52S	153 3 E
Casiquiare ⟶	**184**	2 1N	67 7W
Casma	**186**	9 30S	78 20W
Casper	**163**	42 52N	106 20W
Caspian Sea	**70**	43 0N	50 0 E
Cassiar Mts.	**144**	59 30N	130 30W
Castellón de la Plana	**51**	39 58N	0 3W
Castelsarrasin	**36**	44 2N	1 7 E
Casterton	**119**	37 30S	141 30 E
Castilla La Nueva	**50**	39 45N	3 20W
Castilla La Vieja	**50**	41 55N	4 0W
Castle Douglas	**31**	54 57N	3 57W
Castlebar	**34**	53 52N	9 17W
Castleblaney	**34**	54 7N	6 44W
Castlegar	**155**	49 20N	117 40W
Castlemaine	**117**	37 2S	144 12 E
Castlereagh	**34**	53 47N	8 30W
Castletown	**28**	58 35N	3 22W
Castletown Bearhaven	**35**	51 40N	9 54W
Castor	**155**	52 15N	111 50W
Castres	**37**	43 37N	2 13 E
Castricum	**40**	52 33N	4 40 E
Castries	**180**	14 0N	60 50W
Castro	**192**	42 30S	73 50W
Cat I.	**178**	24 30N	75 30W
Catacáos	**186**	5 20S	80 45W
Catalonia = Cataluña □	**51**	41 40N	1 15 E
Cataluña □	**51**	41 40N	1 15 E
Catamarca	**190**	28 30S	65 50W
Catanduanes	**112**	13 50N	124 20 E
Catánia	**49**	37 31N	15 4 E
Catanzaro	**49**	38 54N	16 38 E
Catoche, C.	**177**	21 35N	87 5W
Catskill Mts.	**164**	42 15N	74 15W
Cauca ⟶	**184**	8 54N	74 28W
Caucasus Mts. = Bolshoi Kavkas	**70**	42 50N	44 0 E
Caudry	**38**	50 7N	3 22 E
Cauquenes	**190**	36 0S	72 22W
Cavaillon	**37**	43 50N	5 2 E
Cavan	**34**	54 0N	7 22W
Cawnpore = Kanpur	**91**	26 28N	80 20 E
Caxias	**188**	4 55S	43 20W
Caxias do Sul	**191**	29 10S	51 10W
Cayenne	**185**	5 0N	52 18W
Cayes, Les	**180**	18 15N	73 46W
Cayman Is.	**178**	19 40N	80 30W
Ceanannus Mor	**34**	53 42N	6 53W
Ceará = Fortaleza	**189**	3 45S	38 35W
Ceará □	**189**	5 0S	40 0W
Cebu	**112**	10 18N	123 54 E
Cedar ⟶	**166**	41 17N	91 21W
Cedar City	**162**	37 41N	113 3W
Cedar Falls	**166**	42 39N	92 29W
Cedar L.	**152**	53 10N	100 0W
Cedar Rapids	**166**	42 0N	91 38W
Cedartown	**169**	34 1N	85 15W
Ceduna	**118**	32 7S	133 46 E
Cegléd	**59**	47 11N	19 47 E
Ceiba, La	**179**	15 40N	86 50W
Celaya	**177**	20 31N	100 37W
Celebes = Sulawesi □	**113**	2 0S	120 0 E

Celebes Sea	**113**	3 0N	123 0 E
Center	**168**	31 50N	94 10W
Centerville	**166**	40 45N	92 57W
Central □	**31**	56 10N	4 30W
Central, Cordillera	**184**	5 0N	75 0W
Central African Republic ■	**129**	7 0N	20 0 E
Central Makran Range	**88**	26 30N	64 15 E
Central Russian Uplands	**17**	54 0N	36 0 E
Central Siberian Plateau	**77**	65 0N	105 0 E
Centralia	**166**	38 32N	89 5W
Cephalonia = Kefallinía	**54**	38 20N	20 30 E
Ceram = Seram	**113**	3 10S	129 0 E
Ceram Sea = Seram Sea	**113**	2 30S	128 30 E
Cerignola	**49**	41 17N	15 53 E
Cerigo = Kíthira	**55**	36 9N	23 0 E
Cerritos	**177**	22 26N	100 17W
Cesena	**47**	44 9N	12 14 E
Českomoravská Vrchovina	**59**	49 30N	15 40 E
Český Těšin	**59**	49 45N	18 39 E
Cessnock	**117**	32 50S	151 21 E
Cetinje	**52**	42 23N	18 59 E
Ceuta	**126**	35 52N	5 18W
Cévennes	**37**	44 10N	3 50 E
Ceylon = Sri Lanka ■	**90**	7 30N	80 50 E
Chachapoyas	**186**	6 15S	77 50W
Chachoengsao	**95**	13 42N	101 5 E
Chad ■	**131**	15 0N	17 15 E
Chad, L. = Tchad, L.	**131**	13 30N	14 30 E
Chadron	**163**	42 50N	103 0W
Chagos Arch.	**76**	6 0S	72 0 E
Chāh Bahār	**85**	25 20N	60 40 E
Chakradharpur	**92**	22 45N	85 40 E
Chala	**186**	15 48S	74 20W
Chalcis = Khalkís	**55**	38 27N	23 42 E
Chalhuanca	**186**	14 15S	73 15W
Chalisgaon	**91**	20 30N	75 10 E
Challapata	**187**	18 53S	66 50W
Chalon-sur-Saône	**37**	46 48N	4 50 E
Châlons-sur-Marne	**37**	48 58N	4 20 E
Chambal →	**91**	26 29N	79 15 E
Chambersburg	**164**	39 53N	77 41W
Chambéry	**37**	45 34N	5 55 E
Chamonix	**37**	45 55N	6 51 E
Champagne	**37**	49 0N	4 40 E
Champaign	**167**	40 8N	88 14W
Champlain, L.	**151**	44 30N	73 20W
Chañaral	**190**	26 23S	70 40W
Chandigarh	**89**	30 43N	76 47 E
Chandler	**118**	27 0S	133 19 E
Chang Jiang →	**99**	31 48N	121 10 E
Changchiak'ou = Zhangjiakou	**98**	40 48N	114 55 E
Ch'angchou = Changzhou	**99**	31 47N	119 58 E
Changchun	**98**	43 57N	125 17 E
Changde	**99**	29 4N	111 35 E
Changhai = Shanghai	**99**	31 15N	121 26 E
Changsha	**99**	28 12N	113 0 E
Changzhi	**98**	36 10N	113 6 E
Changzhou	**99**	31 47N	119 58 E
Channel Is.	**36**	49 30N	2 40W
Channel-Port aux Basques	**149**	47 30N	59 9W
Chanthaburi	**95**	12 38N	102 12 E
Chantilly	**39**	49 12N	2 29 E
Chanute	**166**	37 45N	95 25W
Chao Phraya →	**94**	13 32N	100 36 E
Ch'aoan	**99**	23 41N	116 33 E
Chapala, L. de	**175**	20 15N	103 0W
Chapayevsk	**68**	53 0N	49 40 E
Chapel Hill	**165**	35 53N	79 3W
Chapleau	**150**	47 50N	83 24W
Charagua	**187**	19 45S	63 10W
Charaña	**187**	17 30S	69 25W
Chard	**27**	50 52N	2 59W
Chardzhou	**70**	39 6N	63 34 E
Chari →	**131**	12 58N	14 31 E
Chārīkār	**87**	35 0N	69 10 E
Charleroi	**42**	50 24N	4 27 E
Charles, C.	**165**	37 10N	75 59W
Charles City	**166**	43 2N	92 41W
Charleston, S.C., U.S.A.	**170**	32 47N	79 56W
Charleston, W. Va., U.S.A.	**165**	38 24N	81 36W
Charleville = Rath Luirc	**35**	52 21N	8 40W
Charleville	**116**	26 24S	146 15 E
Charleville-Mézières	**37**	49 44N	4 40 E
Charlotte, Mich., U.S.A.	**167**	42 36N	84 48W
Charlotte, N.C., U.S.A.	**165**	35 16N	80 46W
Charlotte Amalie	**180**	18 22N	64 56W
Charlotte Harbor	**170**	26 58N	82 4W
Charlottenburg	**43**	52 31N	13 15 E
Charlottesville	**165**	38 1N	78 30W
Charlottetown	**149**	46 14N	63 8W
Charlton, Australia	**117**	36 16S	143 24 E
Charlton, U.S.A.	**166**	40 59N	93 20W
Charters Towers	**121**	20 5S	146 13 E
Chartres	**39**	48 29N	1 30 E
Chascomús	**191**	35 30S	58 0W
Château-du-Loir	**39**	47 40N	0 25 E
Château-Thierry	**39**	49 3N	3 20 E
Châteaubriant	**36**	47 43N	1 23W
Châteaudun	**39**	48 3N	1 20 E
Châteauroux	**37**	46 50N	1 40 E
Châtellerault	**36**	46 50N	0 30 E
Chatham, N.B., Canada	**148**	47 2N	65 28W
Chatham, Ont., Canada	**141**	42 24N	82 11W
Chatham, U.K.	**25**	51 22N	0 32 E
Chatta-Hantō	**106**	34 45N	136 55 E
Chattahoochee →	**170**	30 43N	84 51W
Chattanooga	**169**	35 2N	85 17W
Chaumont	**37**	48 7N	5 8 E
Chauny	**38**	49 37N	3 12 E
Cheboksary	**68**	56 8N	47 12 E
Cheboygan	**150**	45 38N	84 29W
Chechenia □	**70**	43 30N	45 29 E
Chegdomyn	**75**	51 7N	133 1 E
Chegga	**126**	25 27N	5 40W
Chehalis	**171**	46 44N	122 59W
Cheju Do	**99**	33 29N	126 34 E
Chekiang = Zhejiang □	**99**	29 0N	120 0 E
Chelforó	**190**	39 0S	66 33W
Chelkar Tengiz, Solonchak	**70**	48 0N	62 30 E
Chełm	**58**	51 8N	23 30 E
Chełmża	**58**	53 10N	18 39 E
Cheltenham	**24**	51 55N	2 5W
Chelyabinsk	**71**	55 10N	61 24 E
Chemainus	**154**	48 55N	123 42W
Chemnitz	**43**	50 50N	12 55 E
Chemult	**171**	43 14N	121 47W
Chen, Gora	**73**	65 16N	141 50 E
Chencha	**132**	6 15N	37 32 E
Chenchiang = Zhenjiang	**99**	32 11N	119 26 E
Chengchou = Zhengzhou	**99**	34 45N	113 34 E
Chengde	**98**	40 59N	117 58 E
Chengdu	**99**	30 38N	104 2 E
Ch'engtu = Chengdu	**99**	30 38N	104 2 E
Cheo Reo	**95**	13 25N	108 28 E
Chepstow	**27**	51 38N	2 40W
Cher →	**36**	47 21N	0 29 E
Cherbourg	**36**	49 39N	1 40W
Cheremkhovo	**74**	53 8N	103 1 E
Cherepovets	**68**	59 5N	37 55 E
Cherkassy	**68**	49 27N	32 4 E
Chernigov	**68**	51 28N	31 20 E
Chernovtsy	**68**	48 15N	25 52 E
Chernoye	**72**	70 30N	89 10 E
Cherokee	**166**	42 40N	95 30W
Cherrapunji	**93**	25 17N	91 47 E
Cherskiy	**73**	68 45N	161 18 E
Cherskogo Khrebet	**73**	65 0N	143 0 E
Cherwell →	**25**	51 46N	1 18W
Chesapeake	**165**	36 43N	76 15W
Chesapeake Bay	**165**	38 0N	76 12W
Cheshire □	**28**	53 14N	2 30W
Cheshskaya Guba	**69**	67 20N	47 0 E
Chester, U.K.	**28**	53 12N	2 53W
Chester, Pa., U.S.A.	**164**	39 54N	75 20W
Chester, S.C., U.S.A.	**165**	34 44N	81 13W
Chesterfield	**28**	53 14N	1 26W
Chesterfield Inlet	**145**	63 30N	90 45W
Chetumal	**177**	18 30N	88 18W
Cheviot, The	**31**	55 29N	2 8W
Cheviot Hills	**31**	55 20N	2 30W
Chew Bahir	**132**	4 40N	36 50 E

Cheyenne	**163**	41 9N	104 49W
Cheyenne →	**163**	44 40N	101 15W
Chhapra	**92**	25 48N	84 44 E
Chiamussu = Jiamusi	**98**	46 40N	130 26 E
Chiang Mai	**94**	18 47N	98 59 E
Chiapa →	**177**	16 42N	93 0W
Chiapas □	**177**	16 30N	92 30W
Chiba	**107**	35 30N	140 7 E
Chibougamau	**151**	49 56N	74 24W
Chicago	**167**	41 53N	87 40W
Chicago Heights	**167**	41 29N	87 37W
Chichagof I.	**143**	58 0N	136 0W
Chichester	**25**	50 50N	0 47W
Chichibu	**107**	36 5N	139 10 E
Ch'ich'ihaerh = Qiqihar	**98**	47 26N	124 0 E
Chiclayo	**186**	6 42S	79 50W
Chico	**172**	39 45N	121 54W
Chicopee	**164**	42 6N	72 37W
Chicoutimi	**148**	48 28N	71 5W
Chidambaram	**90**	11 20N	79 45 E
Chidley C.	**146**	60 23N	64 26W
Chigasaki	**107**	35 19N	139 24 E
Chihli, G. of = Bo Hai	**98**	39 0N	120 0 E
Chihuahua	**174**	28 38N	106 5W
Chihuahua □	**174**	28 30N	106 0W
Chikugo	**108**	33 14N	130 28 E
Chilapa	**177**	17 40N	99 11W
Childress	**161**	34 30N	100 15W
Chile ■	**190**	35 0S	72 0W
Chilin = Jilin	**98**	43 44N	126 30 E
Chilka L.	**92**	19 40N	85 25 E
Chillán	**190**	36 40S	72 10W
Chillicothe, Mo., U.S.A.	**166**	39 45N	93 30W
Chillicothe, Ohio, U.S.A.	**167**	39 20N	82 58W
Chilliwack	**154**	49 10N	121 54W
Chiloé, I. de	**192**	42 30S	73 50W
Chilpancingo	**177**	17 30N	99 30W
Chiltern Hills	**25**	51 44N	0 42W
Chimborazo	**184**	1 29S	78 55W
Chimbote	**186**	9 0S	78 35W
Chimkent	**71**	42 18N	69 36 E
Chin □	**93**	22 0N	93 0 E
China ■	**79**	30 0N	110 0 E
Chinan = Jinan	**98**	36 38N	117 1 E
Chinandega	**179**	12 35N	87 12W
Chincha Alta	**186**	13 25S	76 7W
Chinchilla	**116**	26 45S	150 38 E
Chinchou = Jinzhou	**98**	41 5N	121 3 E
Chindwin →	**93**	21 26N	95 15 E
Ch'ingtao = Qingdao	**98**	36 5N	120 20 E
Chinju	**98**	35 12N	128 2 E
Chinnampo	**98**	38 52N	125 10 E
Chino	**107**	35 59N	138 9 E
Chinon	**36**	47 10N	0 15 E
Chippenham	**24**	51 27N	2 7W
Chippewa Falls	**166**	44 55N	91 22W
Chiquián	**186**	10 10S	77 0W
Chiquimula	**177**	14 51N	89 37W
Chiquinquira	**184**	5 37N	73 50W
Chirala	**90**	15 50N	80 26 E
Chirchik	**71**	41 29N	69 35 E
Chita	**74**	52 0N	113 35 E
Chitral	**89**	35 50N	71 56 E
Chitré	**179**	7 59N	80 27W
Chittagong	**93**	22 19N	91 48 E
Chittagong □	**93**	24 5N	91 0 E
Chivilcoy	**190**	34 55S	60 0W
Chkalov = Orenburg	**70**	51 45N	55 6 E
Chōfu	**107**	35 39N	139 33 E
Choix	**174**	26 43N	108 17W
Chojnice	**58**	53 42N	17 32 E
Cholet	**36**	47 4N	0 52W
Choluteca	**179**	13 20N	87 14W
Chon Buri	**95**	13 21N	101 1 E
Chongjin	**98**	41 47N	129 50 E
Chŏngju	**98**	36 39N	127 27 E
Chongqing	**99**	29 35N	106 25 E
Chŏnju	**98**	35 50N	127 4 E
Chonos, Arch. de los	**192**	45 0S	75 0W
Chorley	**28**	53 39N	2 39W
Chorzów	**58**	50 18N	18 57 E
Chōshi	**107**	35 45N	140 51 E
Christchurch, N.Z.	**123**	43 33S	172 47 E
Christchurch, U.K.	**24**	50 44N	1 33W
Christianshåb	**147**	68 50N	51 18W
Christmas I. = Kiritimati	**123**	1 58N	157 27W
Christmas I.	**111**	10 30S	105 40 E
Ch'uanchou = Quanzhou	**99**	24 55N	118 34 E
Chūbu □	**106**	36 45N	137 30 E
Chubut →	**192**	43 20S	65 5W
Chūgoku □	**109**	35 0N	133 0 E
Chūgoku-Sanchi	**109**	35 0N	133 0 E
Chukotskiy Khrebet	**73**	68 0N	175 0 E
Chukotskoye More	**73**	68 0N	175 0W
Chula Vista	**173**	32 39N	117 8W
Chulman	**74**	56 52N	124 52 E
Chulucanas	**186**	5 8S	80 10W
Chumikan	**75**	54 40N	135 10 E
Chumphon	**94**	10 35N	99 14 E
Chunchŏn	**98**	37 58N	127 44 E
Chungking = Chongqing	**99**	29 35N	106 25 E
Chuquibamba	**186**	15 47S	72 44W
Chur	**44**	46 52N	9 32 E
Churchill →, Man., Canada	**143**	58 47N	94 12W
Churchill →, Nfld., Canada	**147**	53 19N	60 10W
Churchill, C.	**143**	58 46N	93 12W
Churchill Falls	**147**	53 36N	64 19W
Churchill Pk.	**144**	58 10N	125 10W
Churu	**89**	28 20N	74 50 E
Chuvashia □	**68**	55 30N	47 0 E
Chuxiong	**101**	25 2N	101 28 E
Cicero	**167**	41 48N	87 48W
Ciego de Avila	**178**	21 50N	78 50W
Ciénaga	**184**	11 1N	74 15W
Cienfuegos	**178**	22 10N	80 30W
Cimarron →	**161**	36 10N	96 17W
Cincinnati	**167**	39 10N	84 26W
Cinto, Mt.	**36**	42 24N	8 54 E
Ciotat, La	**37**	43 12N	5 36 E
Circle	**142**	65 50N	144 10W
Circleville	**167**	39 35N	82 57W
Cirebon	**111**	6 45S	108 32 E
Cirencester	**24**	51 43N	1 59W
Citlaltépetl, Volcán	**177**	19 1N	97 16W
Ciudad Acuña	**174**	29 20N	100 58W
Ciudad Bolívar	**185**	8 5N	63 36W
Ciudad Camargo, Chihuahua, Mexico	**174**	27 40N	105 10W
Ciudad Camargo, Tamaulipas, Mexico	**176**	26 19N	98 50W
Ciudad de Valles	**177**	21 59N	99 1W
Ciudad del Carmen	**177**	18 38N	91 50W
Ciudad Guayana	**185**	8 0N	62 30W
Ciudad Guzmán	**175**	19 41N	103 29W
Ciudad Juárez	**174**	31 44N	106 29W
Ciudad Madero	**177**	22 16N	97 50W
Ciudad Mante	**177**	22 44N	98 57W
Ciudad Obregón	**174**	27 29N	109 56W
Ciudad Real	**50**	38 59N	3 55W
Ciudad Rodrigo	**50**	40 35N	6 32W
Ciudad Trujillo = Santo Domingo	**180**	18 30N	64 54W
Ciudad Victoria	**177**	23 44N	99 8W
Çivril	**80**	38 20N	29 43 E
Cizre	**81**	37 19N	42 10 E
Clare	**119**	33 50S	138 37 E
Clare □	**35**	52 20N	9 0W
Clare →	**35**	53 22N	9 5W
Clare I.	**34**	53 48N	10 0W
Claremont	**164**	43 23N	72 20W
Claremore	**168**	36 40N	95 37W
Claremorris	**34**	53 45N	9 0W
Claresholm	**155**	50 0N	113 33W
Clark Fork →	**162**	48 9N	116 15W
Clarksburg	**164**	39 18N	80 21W
Clarksdale	**169**	34 12N	90 33W
Clarkston	**171**	46 28N	117 2W
Clarksville	**169**	36 32N	87 20W
Clear, C.	**20**	51 26N	9 30W
Clearwater, Canada	**155**	51 38N	120 2W
Clearwater, U.S.A.	**170**	27 58N	82 45W
Cleburne	**168**	32 18N	97 25W

Clee Hills	**24**	52 26N	2 35W
Cleethorpes	**29**	53 33N	0 2W
Cleeve Hill	**24**	51 54N	2 0W
Clermont, Australia	**121**	22 49S	147 39 E
Clermont, France	**39**	49 23N	2 24 E
Clermont-Ferrand	**37**	45 46N	3 4 E
Clevedon	**27**	51 26N	2 52W
Cleveland, Miss., U.S.A.	**169**	33 43N	90 43W
Cleveland, Ohio, U.S.A.	**167**	41 28N	81 43W
Cleveland, Tenn., U.S.A.	**169**	35 9N	84 52W
Cleveland, Tex., U.S.A.	**169**	30 18N	95 0W
Cleveland □	**29**	54 35N	1 8 E
Cleveleys	**28**	53 52N	3 3W
Clew B.	**34**	53 54N	9 50W
Clifton Beach	**121**	16 46S	145 39 E
Clifton Forge	**165**	37 49N	79 51W
Clinton, Canada	**150**	43 37N	81 32W
Clinton, Iowa, U.S.A.	**166**	41 50N	90 12W
Clinton, Mass., U.S.A.	**164**	42 26N	71 40W
Clinton, Mo., U.S.A.	**166**	38 20N	93 46W
Clinton, Okla., U.S.A.	**161**	35 30N	99 0W
Clinton, S.C., U.S.A.	**165**	34 30N	81 54W
Clinton Colden L.	**145**	63 58N	107 27W
Clonakilty	**35**	51 37N	8 53W
Cloncurry	**115**	20 40S	140 28 E
Clones	**34**	54 10N	7 13W
Clonmel	**35**	52 22N	7 42W
Clovis	**161**	34 20N	103 10W
Cluj-Napoca	**56**	46 47N	23 38 E
Clunes	**117**	37 20S	143 45 E
Clwyd □	**26**	53 5N	3 20W
Clyde →	**31**	55 56N	4 29W
Clyde, Firth of	**30**	55 20N	5 0W
Clydebank	**31**	55 54N	4 25W
Coahuila □	**174**	27 20N	102 0W
Coaldale	**155**	49 45N	112 35W
Coalinga	**173**	36 10N	120 21W
Coalville	**29**	52 43N	1 21W
Coast Mts.	**144**	55 0N	129 0W
Coast Ranges	**173**	41 0N	123 0W
Coatbridge	**31**	55 52N	4 2W
Coatepeque	**177**	14 46N	91 55W
Coats I.	**146**	62 30N	83 0W
Coats Land	**14**	77 0S	25 0W
Coatzacoalcos	**177**	18 9N	94 25W
Cobalt	**151**	47 25N	79 42W
Cobán	**177**	15 30N	90 21W
Cobar	**116**	31 27S	145 48 E
Cóbh	**35**	51 50N	8 18W
Cobham	**118**	30 18S	142 7 E
Cobourg	**151**	43 58N	78 10W
Cobram	**117**	35 54S	145 40 E
Cocanada = Kakinada	**92**	16 57N	82 11 E
Cochabamba	**187**	17 26S	66 10W
Cochin China = Nam-Phan	**95**	10 30N	106 0 E
Cochran	**170**	32 25N	83 23W
Cochrane	**151**	49 0N	81 0W
Cockburn, Canal	**192**	54 30S	72 0W
Coco →	**179**	15 0N	83 8W
Coco Chan.	**94**	13 50N	93 25 E
Cocos Is.	**111**	12 10S	96 55 E
Cod, C.	**164**	42 8N	70 10W
Codajás	**185**	3 55S	62 0W
Codó	**185**	4 30S	43 55W
Cœur d'Alene	**171**	47 45N	116 51W
Coffs Harbour	**116**	30 16S	153 5 E
Cohoes	**164**	42 47N	73 42W
Cohuna	**117**	35 45S	144 15 E
Coiba, I.	**179**	7 30N	81 40W
Coihaique	**192**	45 30S	71 45W
Coimbatore	**90**	11 2N	76 59 E
Coimbra	**50**	40 15N	8 27W
Cojimies	**184**	0 20N	80 0W
Cojutepequé	**177**	13 41N	88 54W
Colac	**117**	38 21S	143 35 E
Colchester	**25**	51 54N	0 55 E
Coldstream	**31**	55 39N	2 14W
Coleman	**155**	49 40N	114 30W
Coleraine, Australia	**119**	37 36S	141 40 E
Coleraine, U.K.	**34**	55 8N	6 40W
Colima	**175**	19 14N	103 43W

Colima □	**175**	19 10N	104 0W
Coll	**30**	56 40N	6 35W
College Park	**170**	33 42N	84 27W
Collie	**120**	33 22S	116 8 E
Collingwood	**151**	44 29N	80 13W
Collinsville	**121**	20 30S	147 56 E
Collooney	**34**	54 11N	8 28W
Colmar	**37**	48 5N	7 20 E
Colne	**28**	53 51N	2 11W
Cologne = Köln	**42**	50 56N	6 58 E
Colomb-Béchar = Béchar	**127**	31 38N	2 18W
Colômbia	**188**	20 10S	48 40W
Colombia ■	**184**	3 45N	73 0W
Colombo	**90**	6 56N	79 58 E
Colón, Cuba	**178**	22 42N	80 54W
Colón, Panama	**179**	9 20N	79 54W
Colonia	**191**	34 25S	57 50W
Colonsay	**30**	56 4N	6 12W
Colorado □	**163**	37 40N	106 0W
Colorado →, Argentina	**190**	39 50S	62 8W
Colorado →, Calif., U.S.A.	**173**	34 45N	114 40W
Colorado →, Tex., U.S.A.	**161**	28 36N	95 58W
Colorado Desert	**160**	34 20N	116 0W
Colorado Plateau	**161**	36 40N	110 30W
Colorado Springs	**163**	38 55N	104 50W
Columbia, Miss., U.S.A.	**169**	31 16N	89 50W
Columbia, Mo., U.S.A.	**166**	38 58N	92 20W
Columbia, S.C., U.S.A.	**165**	34 0N	81 0W
Columbia, Tenn., U.S.A.	**169**	35 40N	87 0W
Columbia →	**171**	46 15N	124 5W
Columbia, District of □	**164**	38 55N	77 0W
Columbia Basin	**171**	47 30N	118 30W
Columbretes, Is.	**51**	39 50N	0 50 E
Columbus, Ga., U.S.A.	**170**	32 30N	84 58W
Columbus, Ind., U.S.A.	**167**	39 14N	85 55W
Columbus, Miss., U.S.A.	**169**	33 30N	88 26W
Columbus, Ohio, U.S.A.	**167**	39 57N	83 1W
Colwyn Bay	**26**	53 17N	3 44W
Comeragh Mts.	**35**	52 17N	7 35W
Comilla	**93**	23 28N	91 10 E
Comitán	**177**	16 18N	92 9W
Committee B.	**146**	68 30N	86 30W
Communism Pk. = Kommunizma, Pik	**71**	39 0N	72 2 E
Como	**46**	45 48N	9 5 E
Como, L. di	**46**	46 5N	9 17 E
Comodoro Rivadavia	**192**	45 50S	67 40W
Comorin, C.	**90**	8 3N	77 40 E
Comoro Is. ■	**125**	12 10S	44 15 E
Comox	**154**	49 42N	124 55W
Compiègne	**38**	49 24N	2 50 E
Côn Dao	**95**	8 45N	106 45 E
Conakry	**130**	9 29N	13 49W
Conceição da Barra	**189**	18 35S	39 45W
Concepción, Argentina	**191**	27 20S	65 35W
Concepción, Chile	**190**	36 50S	73 0W
Concepción, Est. de	**192**	50 30S	74 55W
Concepción del Oro	**174**	24 38N	101 25W
Concepción del Uruguay	**190**	32 35S	58 20W
Conchos, R. →	**174**	29 35N	104 25W
Concord, Calif., U.S.A.	**172**	37 59N	122 2W
Concord, N.C., U.S.A.	**165**	35 28N	80 35W
Concord, N.H., U.S.A.	**164**	43 12N	71 30W
Concordia, Argentina	**190**	31 20S	58 2W
Concordia, U.S.A.	**161**	39 35N	97 40W
Condamine	**155**	26 56S	150 9 E
Condé	**38**	50 26N	3 34 E
Condobolin	**117**	33 4S	147 6 E
Congleton	**28**	53 10N	2 12W
Congo = Zaïre →	**134**	6 4S	12 24 E
Congo (Kinshasa) = Zaïre ■	**134**	3 0S	23 0 E
Congo ■	**134**	1 0S	16 0 E
Congo Basin	**124**	0 10S	24 30 E
Conjeeveram = Kanchipuram	**90**	12 52N	79 45 E
Connacht	**34**	53 23N	8 40W
Conneaut	**164**	41 55N	80 32W
Connecticut □	**164**	41 40N	72 40W
Connecticut →	**157**	41 17N	72 21W
Connemara	**34**	53 29N	9 45W
Connors Ra.	**121**	21 40S	149 10 E
Consett	**28**	54 52N	1 50W

Constance = Konstanz	**44**	47 39N	9 10 E
Constance, L. = Bodensee	**44**	47 35N	9 25 E
Constanţa	**57**	44 14N	28 38 E
Constantine	**127**	36 25N	6 42 E
Contamana	**186**	7 19S	74 55W
Conway = Conwy	**26**	53 17N	3 50W
Conway = Conwy →	**26**	53 18N	3 50W
Conway, N.H., U.S.A.	**148**	43 58N	71 8W
Conway, S.C., U.S.A.	**165**	33 49N	79 2W
Conwy	**26**	53 17N	3 50W
Conwy →	**26**	53 18N	3 50W
Cook, Mt.	**123**	43 36S	170 9 E
Cook Inlet	**142**	59 0N	151 0W
Cook Is.	**123**	17 0S	160 0W
Cook Strait	**123**	41 15S	174 29 E
Cookeville	**169**	36 12N	85 30W
Cookstown	**34**	54 40N	6 43W
Coolah	**116**	31 48S	149 41 E
Coolamon	**117**	34 46S	147 8 E
Coolangatta	**116**	28 11S	153 29 E
Coolgardie	**120**	30 55S	121 8 E
Cooma	**117**	36 12S	149 8 E
Coonabarabran	**116**	31 14S	149 18 E
Coonamble	**116**	30 56S	148 27 E
Cooper Cr. →	**118**	12 7S	132 41 E
Coorong, The	**119**	35 50S	139 20 E
Coorow	**120**	29 53S	116 2 E
Coos Bay	**171**	43 26N	124 7W
Cootamundra	**117**	34 36S	148 1 E
Copenhagen = København	**61**	55 41N	12 34 E
Copiapó	**190**	27 30S	70 20W
Copper Center	**142**	62 10N	145 25W
Coppermine	**145**	67 50N	115 5W
Coppermine →	**145**	67 49N	116 4W
Coquilhatville = Mbandaka	**134**	0 1N	18 18 E
Coquimbo	**190**	30 0S	71 20W
Coracora	**186**	15 5S	73 45W
Coral Gables	**170**	25 45N	80 16W
Coral Harbour	**146**	64 8N	83 10W
Coral Sea	**121**	15 0S	150 0 E
Corbeil-Essonnes	**39**	48 36N	2 26 E
Corbin	**165**	37 0N	84 3W
Corby	**25**	52 29N	0 41W
Cordele	**170**	31 55N	83 49W
Córdoba, Argentina	**190**	31 20S	64 10W
Córdoba, Mexico	**177**	18 53N	96 56W
Córdoba, Spain	**50**	37 50N	4 50W
Córdoba, Sierra de	**190**	31 10S	64 25W
Cordova	**142**	60 36N	145 45W
Corfu = Kérkira	**54**	39 38N	19 50 E
Corinth = Kórinthos	**54**	37 56N	22 55 E
Corinth	**169**	34 54N	88 30W
Corinth, G. of = Korinthiakós Kólpos	**54**	38 16N	22 30 E
Corinto, Brazil	**188**	18 20S	44 30W
Corinto, Nic.	**179**	12 30N	87 10W
Cork	**35**	51 54N	8 30W
Cork □	**35**	51 50N	8 50W
Çorlu	**80**	41 11N	27 49 E
Corn Is. = Maiz, Islas del	**179**	12 15N	83 4W
Corner Brook	**140**	48 57N	57 58W
Cornwall	**151**	45 2N	74 44W
Cornwall □	**27**	50 26N	4 40W
Coro	**184**	11 25N	69 41W
Coroatá	**188**	4 8S	44 0W
Corocoro	**187**	17 15S	68 28W
Coroico	**187**	16 0S	67 50W
Coromandel Coast	**90**	12 30N	81 0 E
Corona	**173**	33 49N	117 36W
Coronado	**173**	32 45N	117 9W
Coronation Gulf	**145**	68 25N	110 0W
Coronel	**190**	37 0S	73 10W
Coronel Pringles	**190**	38 0S	61 30W
Corowa	**117**	35 58S	146 21 E
Corozal	**177**	9 19N	75 18W
Corpus Christi	**161**	27 50N	97 28W
Corrib, L.	**34**	53 5N	9 10W
Corrientes	**190**	27 30S	58 45W
Corrientes, C., Colombia	**184**	5 30N	77 34W
Corrientes, C., Cuba	**178**	21 43N	84 30W
Corrientes, C., Mexico	**175**	20 25N	105 42W
Corrigin	**120**	32 20S	117 53 E
Corse	**36**	42 0N	9 0 E
Corsica = Corse	**36**	42 0N	9 0 E
Corsicana	**168**	32 5N	96 30W
Cortez	**163**	37 24N	108 35W
Cortland	**164**	42 35N	76 11W
Çorum	**80**	40 30N	34 57 E
Corumbá	**187**	19 0S	57 30W
Coruña, La	**50**	43 20N	8 25W
Corunna = Coruña, La	**50**	43 20N	8 25W
Corvallis	**171**	44 36N	123 15W
Cosamaloapan	**177**	18 23N	95 50W
Cosenza	**49**	39 17N	16 14 E
Coshocton	**167**	40 17N	81 51W
Costa Blanca	**51**	38 25N	0 10W
Costa Brava	**51**	41 30N	3 0 E
Costa del Sol	**50**	36 30N	4 30W
Costa Dorada	**51**	40 45N	1 15 E
Costa Rica ■	**179**	10 0N	84 0W
Cotagaita	**187**	20 45S	65 40W
Côte d'Or	**37**	47 10N	4 50 E
Coteau des Prairies	**156**	44 30N	97 0W
Cotonou	**131**	6 20N	2 25 E
Cotopaxi, Vol.	**184**	0 40S	78 30W
Cotswold Hills	**24**	51 42N	2 10W
Cottbus	**43**	51 44N	14 20 E
Coulommiers	**39**	48 50N	3 3 E
Council	**142**	64 55N	163 45W
Council Bluffs	**166**	41 20N	95 50W
Courantyne →	**185**	5 55N	57 5W
Courtrai = Kortrijk	**42**	50 50N	3 17 E
Coventry	**24**	52 25N	1 31W
Covington, Ga., U.S.A.	**170**	33 36N	83 50W
Covington, Ky., U.S.A.	**167**	39 5N	84 30W
Cowdenbeath	**31**	56 7N	3 20W
Cowes	**25**	50 45N	1 18W
Cowra	**117**	33 49S	148 42 E
Coxim	**188**	18 30S	54 55W
Cracow = Kraków	**58**	50 4N	19 57 E
Craigavon = Lurgan	**34**	54 28N	6 20W
Craiova	**57**	44 21N	23 48 E
Cranbrook, Australia	**120**	34 18S	117 33 E
Cranbrook, Canada	**155**	49 30N	115 46W
Crateús	**189**	5 10S	40 39W
Crato	**189**	7 10S	39 25W
Crawfordsville	**167**	40 2N	86 51W
Crawley	**24**	51 7N	0 10W
Creil	**39**	49 15N	2 34 E
Cremona	**46**	45 8N	10 2 E
Crépy-en-Valois	**39**	49 14N	2 54 E
Cres	**52**	44 58N	14 25 E
Crescent City	**172**	41 45N	124 12W
Creston, Canada	**155**	49 10N	116 31W
Creston, U.S.A.	**166**	41 0N	94 20W
Crestview	**169**	30 45N	86 35W
Crete = Kríti	**55**	35 15N	25 0 E
Creuse →	**36**	47 0N	0 34 E
Creusot, Le	**37**	46 50N	4 24 E
Crewe	**28**	53 6N	2 28W
Criciúma	**191**	28 40S	49 23W
Crieff	**31**	56 22N	3 50W
Crimea □	**70**	45 30N	33 10 E
Crişul Alb →	**56**	46 42N	21 17 E
Crişul Negru →	**56**	46 38N	22 26 E
Crna Gora = Montenegro □	**52**	42 40N	19 20 E
Crna Gora	**52**	42 10N	21 30 E
Croatia ■	**52**	45 20N	18 0 E
Crockett	**168**	31 20N	95 30W
Cromarty	**33**	57 40N	4 2W
Cromer	**29**	52 56N	1 18 E
Crooked I.	**180**	22 50N	74 10W
Crookwell	**117**	34 28S	149 24 E
Cross Fell	**28**	54 44N	2 29W
Cross L.	**153**	54 45N	97 30W
Crosse, La	**166**	43 48N	91 13W
Crowley	**168**	30 15N	92 20W
Crowsnest Pass	**155**	49 40N	114 40W
Cruz, C.	**178**	19 50N	77 50W
Cruz Alta	**191**	28 45S	53 40W
Cruz del Eje	**190**	30 45S	64 50W
Cruzeiro do Sul	**186**	7 35S	72 35W

Place	Page	Lat	Long
Crystal Brook	**119**	33 21S	138 12 E
Cu Lao Hon	**95**	10 54N	108 18 E
Cuando →	**134**	14 0S	19 30 E
Cuanza →	**134**	9 2S	13 30 E
Cuba ■	**178**	22 0N	79 0W
Cubango →	**134**	18 50S	22 25 E
Cucuí	**184**	1 12N	66 50W
Cúcuta	**184**	7 54N	72 31W
Cuddalore	**90**	11 46N	79 45 E
Cuddapah	**90**	14 30N	78 47 E
Cue	**120**	27 25S	117 54 E
Cuenca, Ecuador	**184**	2 50S	79 9W
Cuenca, Spain	**51**	40 5N	2 10W
Cuenca, Serranía de	**51**	39 55N	1 50W
Cuernavaca	**177**	18 55N	99 15W
Cuevo	**187**	20 15S	63 30W
Cuiabá	**188**	15 30S	56 0W
Cuillin Hills	**32**	57 14N	6 15W
Cuitzeo, L. de	**175**	19 55N	101 5W
Culcairn	**117**	35 41S	147 3 E
Culiacán	**174**	24 48N	107 24W
Cullarin Range	**117**	34 30S	149 30 E
Culloden Moor	**33**	57 29N	4 7W
Culverden	**123**	42 47S	172 49 E
Cumaná	**185**	10 30N	64 5W
Cumberland	**164**	39 40N	78 43W
Cumberland →	**169**	36 15N	87 0W
Cumberland Is.	**121**	20 35S	149 10 E
Cumberland Pen.	**146**	67 0N	64 0W
Cumberland Plat.	**169**	36 0N	84 30W
Cumberland Sd.	**146**	65 30N	66 0W
Cumbria □	**28**	54 35N	2 55W
Cumbrian Mts.	**28**	54 30N	3 0W
Cumbum	**90**	15 40N	79 10 E
Cummins	**119**	34 16S	135 43 E
Cumnock	**31**	55 27N	4 18W
Cunene →	**134**	17 20S	11 50 E
Cunnamulla	**116**	28 2S	145 38 E
Curaçao	**181**	12 10N	69 0W
Curaray →	**184**	2 20S	74 5W
Curiapo	**185**	8 33N	61 5W
Curicó	**190**	34 55S	71 20W
Curitiba	**191**	25 20S	49 10W
Curtis Group	**117**	39 30S	146 37 E
Curuá →	**188**	5 23S	54 22W
Curuçá	**188**	0 43S	47 50W
Curuzú Cuatiá	**191**	29 50S	58 5W
Cushing	**168**	35 59N	96 46W
Cusihuiriáchic	**174**	28 14N	106 50W
Cuthbert	**170**	31 47N	84 47W
Cuttack	**92**	20 25N	85 57 E
Cuxhaven	**42**	53 51N	8 41 E
Cuyahoga Falls	**167**	41 8N	81 30W
Cuzco, Bolivia	**187**	20 0S	66 50W
Cuzco, Peru	**186**	13 32S	72 0W
Cwmbran	**27**	51 39N	3 0W
Cypress Hills	**152**	49 40N	109 30W
Cyprus ■	**80**	35 0N	33 0 E
Cyrenaica	**124**	27 0N	23 0 E
Czech Republic ■	**59**	49 0N	15 0 E
Czeremcha	**58**	52 31N	23 21 E
Częstochowa	**58**	50 49N	19 7 E

D

Place	Page	Lat	Long
Da →	**95**	21 15N	105 20 E
Da Hinggan Ling	**98**	48 0N	121 0 E
Da Nang	**95**	16 4N	108 13 E
Da Yunhe →	**99**	34 25N	120 5 E
Daba Shan	**99**	32 0N	109 0 E
Dacca = Dhaka	**92**	23 43N	90 26 E
Dacca □ = Dhaka □	**93**	24 25N	90 25 E
Dadanawa	**185**	2 50N	59 30W
Dadra and Nagar Haveli □	**91**	20 5N	73 0 E
Daghestan □	**70**	42 30N	47 0 E
Dahomey = Benin ■	**131**	10 0N	2 0 E
Dai-Sen	**109**	35 22N	133 32 E
Daiō-Misaki	**106**	34 15N	136 45 E
Daisetsu-Zan	**103**	43 30N	142 57 E
Daito	**109**	35 19N	132 58 E
Dajarra	**115**	21 42S	139 30 E
Dakar	**130**	14 34N	17 29W
Dakhla	**126**	23 50N	15 53W
Dakhla, El Wâhât el-	**128**	25 30N	28 50 E
Đakovica	**52**	42 22N	20 26 E
Dalandzadgad	**98**	43 27N	104 30 E
Dalbeattie	**31**	54 55N	3 50W
Dalby	**116**	27 10S	151 17 E
Dalhousie	**148**	48 5N	66 26W
Dali	**99**	25 40N	100 10 E
Dalian	**98**	38 50N	121 40 E
Daliang Shan	**99**	28 0N	102 45 E
Dallas, Oreg., U.S.A.	**171**	45 0N	123 15W
Dallas, Tex., U.S.A.	**168**	32 50N	96 50W
Dalmacija	**52**	43 20N	17 0 E
Dalmatia = Dalmacija	**52**	43 20N	17 0 E
Daloa	**130**	7 0N	6 30W
Dalton	**169**	34 47N	84 58W
Daly Waters	**114**	16 15S	133 24 E
Daman	**91**	20 25N	72 57 E
Damaraland	**136**	21 0S	17 0 E
Damascus = Dimashq	**80**	33 30N	36 18 E
Damāvand	**86**	35 47N	52 0 E
Damāvand, Qolleh-ye	**86**	35 56N	52 10 E
Dampier	**114**	20 41S	116 42 E
Dampier Arch.	**114**	20 38S	116 32 E
Danbury	**164**	41 23N	73 29W
Dandenong	**117**	38 0S	145 15 E
Dandong	**98**	40 10N	124 20 E
Dangriga	**177**	17 0N	88 13W
Dannevirke	**122**	40 12S	176 8 E
Dansville	**164**	42 32N	77 41W
Danville, Ill., U.S.A.	**167**	40 10N	87 40W
Danville, Ky., U.S.A.	**167**	37 40N	84 45W
Danville, Va., U.S.A.	**165**	36 40N	79 20W
Danzig = Gdańsk	**58**	54 22N	18 40 E
Dar es Salaam	**135**	6 50S	39 12 E
Darbhanga	**92**	26 15N	85 55 E
Dardanelles = Çanakkale Boğazi	**80**	40 0N	26 0 E
Dârfûr	**129**	13 40N	24 0 E
Dargan Ata	**70**	40 29N	62 10 E
Dargaville	**122**	35 57S	173 52 E
Darién, G. del	**184**	9 0N	77 0W
Darjeeling = Darjiling	**92**	27 3N	88 18 E
Darjiling	**92**	27 3N	88 18 E
Darling →	**119**	34 4S	141 54 E
Darling Downs	**116**	27 30S	150 30 E
Darling Ra.	**120**	32 30S	116 0 E
Darlington	**28**	54 33N	1 33W
Darmstadt	**42**	49 51N	8 40 E
Darnley, C.	**14**	68 0S	69 0 E
Dart →	**27**	50 24N	3 36W
Dartmoor	**27**	50 36N	4 0W
Dartmouth, Canada	**149**	44 40N	63 30W
Dartmouth, U.K.	**27**	50 21N	3 35W
Darwin	**114**	12 25S	130 51 E
Dasht-e Kavīr	**86**	34 30N	55 0 E
Dasht-e Lūt	**85**	31 30N	58 0 E
Dasht-e Mārgow	**87**	30 40N	62 30 E
Datia	**91**	25 39N	78 27 E
Datong	**98**	40 6N	113 18 E
Daugavpils	**68**	55 53N	26 32 E
Dauphin	**153**	51 9N	100 5W
Dauphiné	**37**	45 15N	5 25 E
Davangere	**90**	14 25N	75 55 E
Davao	**112**	7 0N	125 40 E
Davenport	**166**	41 30N	90 40W
Daventry	**24**	52 16N	1 10W
David	**179**	8 30N	82 30W
Davis Sea	**15**	66 0S	92 0 E
Davis Str.	**146**	65 0N	58 0W
Davos	**44**	46 48N	9 49 E
Dawson	**144**	64 10N	139 30W
Dawson Creek	**155**	55 45N	120 15W
Dawson Range	**121**	24 30S	149 48 E
Daylesford	**117**	37 21S	144 9 E
Dayr az Zawr	**81**	35 20N	40 5 E
Dayton, Ohio, U.S.A.	**167**	39 45N	84 10W

Dayton, Wash., U.S.A.	**171**	46 20N	118 10W
Daytona Beach	**170**	29 14N	81 0W
De Aar	**136**	30 39S	24 0 E
De Land	**170**	29 1N	81 19W
De Ridder	**168**	30 48N	93 15W
De Soto	**166**	38 7N	90 33W
Deakin	**114**	30 46S	128 0 E
Deal	**25**	51 13N	1 25 E
Dean, Forest of	**24**	51 50N	2 35W
Deán Funes	**190**	30 20S	64 20W
Dease →	**144**	59 56N	128 32W
Dease Lake	**144**	58 25N	130 6W
Death Valley	**173**	36 19N	116 52W
Deauville	**38**	49 23N	0 2 E
Debar	**52**	41 31N	20 30 E
Debre Markos	**132**	10 20N	37 40 E
Debre Tabor	**132**	11 50N	38 26 E
Debrecen	**59**	47 33N	21 42 E
Decatur, Ala., U.S.A.	**169**	34 35N	87 0W
Decatur, Ga., U.S.A.	**170**	33 47N	84 17W
Decatur, Ill., U.S.A.	**166**	39 50N	89 0W
Deccan	**76**	18 0N	79 0 E
Dedéagach = Alexandroúpolis	**55**	40 50N	25 54 E
Dee →, Scotland, U.K.	**33**	57 4N	2 7W
Dee →, Wales, U.K.	**26**	53 15N	3 7W
Deepwater	**116**	29 25S	151 51 E
Deer Lake	**149**	49 11N	57 27W
Defiance	**167**	41 20N	84 20W
Deh Bīd	**85**	30 39N	53 11 E
Dehra Dun	**89**	30 20N	78 4 E
Dej	**56**	47 10N	23 52 E
Del Rio	**161**	29 23N	100 50W
Delano	**173**	35 48N	119 13W
Delaware □	**164**	39 0N	75 40W
Delaware →	**164**	39 20N	75 25W
Delaware B.	**157**	38 50N	75 0W
Delft	**40**	52 1N	4 22 E
Delfzijl	**41**	53 20N	6 55 E
Delgado, C.	**137**	10 45S	40 40 E
Delgo	**129**	20 6N	30 40 E
Delhi	**89**	28 38N	77 17 E
Delice →	**80**	39 45N	34 15 E
Delicias	**174**	28 13N	105 28W
Delong, Ostrova	**72**	76 40N	149 20 E
Deloraine	**119**	41 30S	146 40 E
Delray Beach	**170**	26 27N	80 4W
Demanda, Sierra de la	**50**	42 15N	3 0W
Dembidolo	**132**	8 34N	34 50 E
Deming	**161**	32 10N	107 50W
Demopolis	**169**	32 30N	87 48W
Den Burg	**40**	53 3N	4 47 E
Den Haag = 's-Gravenhage	**40**	52 7N	4 17 E
Den Helder	**40**	52 57N	4 45 E
Den Oever	**40**	52 56N	5 2 E
Denain	**38**	50 20N	3 22 E
Denbigh	**26**	53 12N	3 26W
Denham	**120**	25 56S	113 31 E
Deniliquin	**117**	35 30S	144 58 E
Denison	**168**	33 50N	96 40W
Denizli	**80**	37 42N	29 2 E
Denmark	**120**	34 59S	117 25 E
Denmark ■	**61**	55 30N	9 0 E
Denmark Str.	**13**	66 0N	30 0W
Denton	**168**	33 12N	97 10W
D'Entrecasteaux Is.	**115**	9 0S	151 0 E
Denver	**163**	39 45N	105 0W
Deolali	**91**	19 58N	73 50 E
Deoria	**92**	26 31N	83 48 E
Deosai Mts.	**89**	35 40N	75 0 E
Dera Ghazi Khan	**89**	30 5N	70 43 E
Dera Ismail Khan	**89**	31 50N	70 50 E
Derby	**28**	52 55N	1 28W
Derby □	**28**	52 55N	1 28W
Derg, L.	**35**	53 0N	8 20W
Derry = Londonderry	**34**	55 0N	7 20W
Derryveagh Mts.	**34**	55 0N	8 40W
Derwent →, Cumb., U.K.	**28**	54 42N	3 22W
Derwent →, Derby, U.K.	**29**	52 53N	1 17W
Derwent →, N. Yorks., U.K.	**29**	53 45N	0 57W
Derwent Water, L.	**28**	54 35N	3 9W

Des Moines	**166**	41 35N	93 37W
Des Moines →	**166**	40 23N	91 25W
Deschutes →	**171**	45 30N	121 0W
Dese	**133**	11 5N	39 40 E
Despeñaperros, Paso	**50**	38 24N	3 30W
Dessau	**43**	51 49N	12 15 E
Dessye = Dese	**133**	11 5N	39 40 E
Desvrès	**38**	50 40N	1 48 E
Detroit	**167**	42 23N	83 5W
Deurne	**41**	51 27N	5 49 E
Deutsche Bucht	**42**	54 10N	7 51 E
Devakottai	**90**	9 55N	78 45 E
Deventer	**41**	52 15N	6 10 E
Devizes	**24**	51 21N	2 0W
Devon I.	**13**	75 10N	85 0W
Devonport, Australia	**119**	41 10S	146 22 E
Devonport, N.Z.	**122**	36 49S	174 49 E
Devonport, U.K.	**27**	50 23N	4 11W
Devonshire □	**27**	50 50N	3 40W
Dewsbury	**28**	53 42N	1 38W
Dezfūl	**84**	32 20N	48 30 E
Dezhneva, Mys	**73**	66 5N	169 40W
Dhahran = Aẓ Ẓahrān	**84**	26 10N	50 7 E
Dhaka	**92**	23 43N	90 26 E
Dhaka □	**93**	24 25N	90 25 E
Dhamar	**83**	14 30N	44 20 E
Dhar	**91**	22 35N	75 26 E
Dharmapuri	**90**	12 10N	78 10 E
Dharwad	**90**	15 22N	75 15 E
Dhidhimótikhon	**55**	41 22N	26 29 E
Dhikti	**55**	35 8N	25 22 E
Dhodhekánisos	**55**	36 35N	27 0 E
Dhuburi	**92**	26 2N	89 59 E
Dhule	**91**	20 58N	74 50 E
Di Linh, Cao Nguyen	**95**	11 30N	108 0 E
Diamantina	**188**	18 17S	43 40W
Diamantina →	**115**	26 45S	139 10 E
Diamantino	**188**	14 30S	56 30W
Dibrugarh	**93**	27 29N	94 55 E
Dickinson	**163**	46 50N	102 48W
Didsbury	**155**	51 35N	114 10W
Diefenbaker L.	**152**	51 0N	106 55W
Dieppe	**38**	49 54N	1 4 E
Dieren	**41**	52 3N	6 6 E
Digby	**148**	44 38N	65 50W
Digne	**37**	44 5N	6 12 E
Dijlah, Nahr →	**81**	31 0N	47 25 E
Dijon	**37**	47 20N	5 0 E
Dila	**133**	6 21N	38 22 E
Dillon	**165**	34 26N	79 20W
Dimashq	**80**	33 30N	36 18 E
Dimboola	**119**	36 28S	142 7 E
Dîmboviţa →	**57**	44 14N	26 13 E
Dimitrovgrad	**53**	42 5N	25 35 E
Dimitrovo = Pernik	**53**	42 35N	23 2 E
Dinan	**36**	48 28N	2 2W
Dinara Planina	**52**	44 0N	16 30 E
Dinaric Alps = Dinara Planina	**52**	44 0N	16 30 E
Dindigul	**90**	10 25N	78 0 E
Dingle	**35**	52 9N	10 17W
Dingle B.	**35**	52 3N	10 20W
Dingwall	**33**	57 36N	4 26W
Dinuba	**173**	36 31N	119 22W
Dire Dawa	**133**	9 35N	41 45 E
Diriamba	**179**	11 51N	86 19W
Dirranbandi	**116**	28 33S	148 17 E
Disappointment L.	**114**	23 20S	122 40 E
Discovery B.	**119**	38 10S	140 40 E
Disko	**146**	69 45N	53 30W
Diss	**25**	52 23N	1 6 E
Diu	**91**	20 45N	70 58 E
Dives-sur-Mer	**39**	49 18N	0 8W
Dixon	**166**	41 50N	89 30W
Dixon Entrance	**154**	54 30N	132 0W
Diyarbakir	**81**	37 55N	40 18 E
Djakarta = Jakarta	**111**	6 9S	106 49 E
Djelfa	**130**	34 40N	3 15 E
Djerid, Chott	**127**	33 42N	8 30 E
Djibouti	**133**	11 30N	43 5 E
Djibouti ■	**133**	12 0N	43 0 E
Djoum	**131**	2 41N	12 35 E

Dmitriya Lapteva, Proliv **72** 73 0N 140 0 E
Dnepr → **68** 46 30N 32 18 E
Dnepropetrovsk **68** 48 30N 35 0 E
Dnestr → **68** 46 18N 30 17 E
Dnestrovski = Belgorod **68** 50 35N 36 35 E
Dnieper = Dnepr → **68** 46 30N 32 18 E
Dniester = Dnestr → **68** 46 18N 30 17 E
Dobrich **53** 43 37N 27 49 E
Dobruja **57** 44 30N 28 15 E
Dodecanese = Dhodhekánisos **55** 36 35N 27 0 E
Dodge City **161** 37 42N 100 0W
Dodoma **135** 6 8S 35 45 E
Doesburg **41** 52 1N 6 9 E
Doetinchem **41** 51 59N 6 18 E
Dogger Bank **124** 54 50N 2 0 E
Doi Luang **95** 18 30N 101 0 E
Dojran **54** 41 10N 22 45 E
Dokkum **41** 53 20N 5 59 E
Dolbeau **148** 48 53N 72 18W
Dole **37** 47 7N 5 31 E
Dolgellau **26** 52 44N 3 53W
Dolgelley = Dolgellau **26** 52 44N 3 53W
Dolomites = Dolomiti **47** 46 30N 11 40 E
Dolomiti **47** 46 30N 11 40 E
Dolores **191** 36 20S 57 40W
Dolphin and Union Str. **145** 69 5N 114 45W
Domel I. = Letsôk-aw Kyun **94** 11 30N 98 25 E
Dominica ■ **180** 15 20N 61 20W
Dominican Rep. ■ **180** 19 0N 70 30W
Don →, Russia **68** 47 4N 39 18 E
Don →, U.K. **33** 57 14N 2 5W
Donaghadee **34** 54 38N 5 32W
Donau → **42** 48 10N 17 0 E
Doncaster **29** 53 31N 1 9W
Dondra Head **90** 5 55N 80 40 E
Donegal **34** 54 39N 8 8W
Donegal □ **34** 54 53N 8 0W
Donegal B. **34** 54 30N 8 35W
Donetsk **68** 48 0N 37 45 E
Dongara **120** 29 14S 114 57 E
Dongen **40** 51 38N 4 56 E
Dongting Hu **99** 29 18N 112 45 E
Donnelly's Crossing **122** 35 42S 173 38 E
Donnybrook **120** 33 34S 115 48 E
Doon → **31** 55 26N 4 41W
Dorada, La **184** 5 30N 74 40W
Dorchester **27** 50 42N 2 28W
Dorchester, C. **146** 65 27N 77 27W
Dordogne □ **36** 45 5N 0 40 E
Dordrecht **40** 51 48N 4 39 E
Dornoch **33** 57 52N 4 0W
Dorrigo **116** 30 20S 152 44 E
Dorris **172** 41 59N 121 58W
Dorset □ **27** 50 48N 2 25W
Dortmund **42** 51 32N 7 28 E
Dothan **169** 31 10N 85 25W
Douai **38** 50 21N 3 4 E
Douala **131** 4 0N 9 45 E
Douarnenez **36** 48 6N 4 21W
Douglas, U.K. **28** 54 9N 4 29W
Douglas, U.S.A. **170** 31 32N 82 52W
Doullens **38** 50 10N 2 20 E
Dounreay **33** 58 34N 3 44W
Dourados **188** 22 9S 54 50W
Douro → **50** 41 8N 8 40W
Douro Litoral □ **50** 41 10N 8 20W
Dove → **28** 52 51N 1 36W
Dover, U.K. **25** 51 7N 1 19 E
Dover, Del., U.S.A. **164** 39 10N 75 31W
Dover, N.H., U.S.A. **164** 43 12N 70 51W
Dover, Str. of **38** 51 0N 1 30 E
Dovey → **26** 52 32N 4 0W
Downham Market **25** 52 36N 0 22 E
Downpatrick **34** 54 20N 5 43W
Drachten **41** 53 7N 6 5 E
Dragoman, Prokhod **53** 43 0N 22 53 E
Draguignan **37** 43 30N 6 27 E
Drakensberg **137** 31 0S 28 0 E
Dráma **55** 41 9N 24 10 E
Drammen **60** 59 42N 10 12 E
Drau = Drava → **59** 45 33N 18 55 E
Drava → **59** 45 33N 18 55 E
Drayton Valley **155** 53 12N 114 58W
Drenthe □ **41** 52 52N 6 40 E
Dresden **43** 51 2N 13 45 E
Dreux **39** 48 44N 1 23 E
Driffield **29** 54 0N 0 25W
Drin i zi → **52** 41 37N 20 28 E
Drina → **52** 44 53N 19 21 E
Drogheda **34** 53 45N 6 20W
Droitwich **24** 52 16N 2 10W
Dronne → **36** 45 2N 0 9W
Dronning Maud Land **14** 72 30S 12 0 E
Drumheller **155** 51 25N 112 40W
Drummond Ra. **121** 23 45S 147 10 E
Drummondville **151** 45 55N 72 25W
Dryden **153** 49 47N 92 50W
Du Bois **164** 41 8N 78 46W
Du Quoin **166** 38 0N 89 10W
Dubai = Dubayy **85** 25 18N 55 20 E
Dubawnt → **145** 64 33N 100 6W
Dubawnt, L. **143** 63 4N 101 42W
Dubayy **85** 25 18N 55 20 E
Dubbo **116** 32 11S 148 35 E
Dublin, Ireland **35** 53 20N 6 18W
Dublin, U.S.A. **170** 32 30N 82 34W
Dublin □ **34** 53 24N 6 20W
Dubrovnik **52** 42 39N 18 6 E
Dubuque **166** 42 30N 90 41W
Dudley **24** 52 30N 2 5W
Dugi Otok **52** 44 0N 15 0 E
Duisburg **42** 51 27N 6 42 E
Duluth **150** 46 48N 92 10W
Dumbarton **31** 55 58N 4 35W
Dumfries **31** 55 4N 3 37W
Dumfries & Galloway □ **31** 55 0N 4 0W
Dun Laoghaire **35** 53 17N 6 9W
Dunărea → **57** 45 30N 8 15 E
Dunaújváros **59** 47 0N 18 57 E
Dunbar **31** 56 0N 2 32W
Dunblane **31** 56 10N 3 58W
Duncan, Canada **154** 48 45N 123 40W
Duncan, U.S.A. **161** 34 25N 98 0W
Duncan Pass. **94** 11 0N 92 30 E
Dundalk **34** 54 1N 6 25W
Dundas, Canada **151** 43 17N 79 59W
Dundas, Greenland **13** 77 0N 69 0W
Dundee **31** 56 29N 3 0W
Dundrum **34** 54 17N 5 50W
Dunedin **123** 45 50S 170 33 E
Dunedoo **116** 32 0S 149 25 E
Dunfermline **31** 56 5N 3 28W
Dungannon **34** 54 30N 6 47W
Dungarvan **35** 52 6N 7 40W
Dungeness **25** 50 54N 0 59 E
Dungog **117** 32 22S 151 46 E
Dunhuang **100** 40 8N 94 36 E
Dunkeld **33** 56 34N 3 36W
Dunkerque **38** 51 2N 2 20 E
Dunkery Beacon **27** 51 15N 3 37W
Dunkirk = Dunkerque **38** 51 2N 2 20 E
Dunkirk **164** 42 30N 79 18W
Dúnleary = Dun Laoghaire **35** 53 17N 6 9W
Dunmore **164** 41 27N 75 38W
Dunn **165** 35 18N 78 36W
Dunnet Hd. **33** 58 38N 3 22W
Duns **31** 55 47N 2 20W
Dunsmuir **172** 41 10N 122 18W
Dunstan Mts. **123** 44 53S 169 35 E
Durance → **37** 43 55N 4 45 E
Durango, Mexico **174** 24 3N 104 39W
Durango, U.S.A. **163** 37 16N 107 50W
Durango □ **174** 24 50N 104 50W
Durant **168** 34 0N 96 25W
Durazno **191** 33 25S 56 31W
Durban **137** 29 49S 31 1 E
Durg **92** 21 15N 81 22 E
Durham, U.K. **28** 54 47N 1 34W
Durham, U.S.A. **165** 36 0N 78 55W
Durham □ **28** 54 42N 1 45W
Durmitor **52** 43 10N 19 0 E

Durness	**32**	58 34N	4 45W
D'Urville I.	**122**	40 50S	173 55 E
Dushanbe	**71**	38 33N	68 48 E
Düsseldorf	**42**	51 15N	6 46 E
Duwādimi	**82**	24 35N	44 15 E
Duyun	**99**	26 18N	107 29 E
Duzce	**80**	40 50N	31 10 E
Duzdab = Zāhedān	**86**	29 30N	60 50 E
Dvina, Sev. →	**69**	64 32N	40 30 E
Dvinsk = Daugavpils	**68**	55 53N	26 32 E
Dyer, C.	**146**	66 40N	61 0W
Dyersburg	**169**	36 2N	89 20W
Dyfed □	**26**	52 0N	4 30W
Dysart	**121**	22 32S	148 23 E
Dzamin Üüd	**98**	43 50N	111 58 E
Dzerzhinsk	**68**	53 40N	27 1 E
Dzhalal-Abad	**71**	40 56N	73 0 E
Dzhalinda	**75**	53 26N	124 0 E
Dzhambul	**71**	42 54N	71 22 E
Dzhardzhan	**72**	68 10N	124 10 E
Dzhetygara	**71**	52 11N	61 12 E
Dzhezkazgan	**71**	47 44N	67 40 E
Dzhugdzur, Khrebet	**75**	57 30N	138 0 E
Dzuumod	**98**	47 45N	106 58 E

E

Eagle	**142**	64 44N	141 7W
Eagle Pass	**161**	28 45N	100 35W
Eagle River	**150**	45 55N	89 17W
Ealing	**25**	51 30N	0 19W
Earn →	**31**	56 20N	3 19W
Easley	**165**	34 52N	82 35W
East Angus	**148**	45 30N	71 40W
East Bengal	**92**	24 0N	90 0 E
East Beskids = Vychodné Beskydy	**59**	49 30N	22 0 E
East C.	**122**	37 42S	178 35 E
East Chicago	**167**	41 40N	87 30W
East China Sea	**99**	30 5N	126 0 E
East Falkland	**192**	51 30S	58 30W
East Indies	**77**	0 0	120 0 E
East Kilbride	**31**	55 46N	4 10W
East Liverpool	**164**	40 39N	80 35W
East London	**137**	33 0S	27 55 E
East Main = Eastmain	**140**	52 10N	78 30W
East Pakistan = Bangladesh ■	**92**	24 0N	90 0 E
East Point	**170**	33 40N	84 28W
East St. Louis	**166**	38 37N	90 4W
East Schelde → = Oosterschelde	**40**	51 33N	4 0 E
East Siberian Sea	**73**	73 0N	160 0 E
East Sussex □	**25**	51 0N	0 20 E
Eastbourne, N.Z.	**123**	41 19S	174 55 E
Eastbourne, U.K.	**25**	50 46N	0 18 E
Eastern Ghats	**90**	14 0N	78 50 E
Eastleigh	**25**	50 58N	1 21W
Eastmain	**140**	52 10N	78 30W
Eastmain →	**140**	52 27N	78 26W
Easton	**164**	40 41N	75 15W
Eau Claire	**166**	44 46N	91 30W
Eau Claire, L. à l'	**146**	56 10N	74 25W
Ebbw Vale	**26**	51 47N	3 12W
Eboli	**49**	40 39N	15 2 E
Ebro →	**51**	40 43N	0 54 E
Echizen-Misaki	**106**	35 59N	135 57 E
Echo Bay	**145**	46 29N	84 4W
Echuca	**117**	36 10S	144 20 E
Ecuador ■	**184**	2 0S	78 0W
Ed Dâmer	**129**	17 27N	34 0 E
Edam	**40**	52 31N	5 3 E
Eddystone	**27**	50 11N	4 16W
Ede	**41**	52 4N	5 40 E
Eden	**117**	37 3S	149 55 E
Eden →	**28**	54 57N	3 2W
Edenhope	**119**	37 4S	141 19 E
Edge Hill	**24**	52 7N	1 28W
Edhessa	**54**	40 48N	22 5 E
Edinburgh	**31**	55 57N	3 12W
Edirne	**80**	41 40N	26 34 E
Edmonton, Australia	**121**	17 2S	145 46 E
Edmonton, Canada	**155**	53 30N	113 30W
Edmundston	**148**	47 23N	68 20W
Edson	**155**	53 35N	116 28W
Edward, L.	**132**	0 25S	29 40 E
Edward VII Land	**15**	80 0S	150 0W
Edwards Plat.	**161**	30 30N	101 5W
Effingham	**167**	39 8N	88 30W
Égadi, Ísole	**48**	37 55N	12 16 E
Eger	**59**	47 53N	20 27 E
Egmont, Mt.	**122**	39 17S	174 5 E
Eğridir Gölü	**80**	37 53N	30 50 E
Egypt ■	**128**	28 0N	31 0 E
Eifel	**42**	50 10N	6 45 E
Eigg	**32**	56 54N	6 10W
Eil	**133**	8 0N	49 50 E
Eindhoven	**41**	51 26N	5 30 E
Eirunepé	**187**	6 35S	69 53W
El Aaiún	**126**	27 9N	13 12W
El Cajon	**173**	32 49N	117 0W
El Callao	**185**	7 18N	61 50W
El Centro	**173**	32 50N	115 40W
El Cerro	**187**	17 30S	61 40W
El Dere	**133**	3 50N	47 8 E
El Djouf	**126**	20 0N	11 30 E
El Dorado	**168**	33 10N	92 40W
El Escorial	**50**	40 35N	4 7W
El Faiyûm	**128**	29 19N	30 50 E
El Fâsher	**129**	13 33N	25 26 E
El Ferrol	**50**	43 29N	8 15W
El Fuerte	**174**	26 25N	108 39W
El Geteina	**129**	14 50N	32 27 E
El Iskandarîya	**128**	31 0N	30 0 E
El Jadida	**126**	33 11N	8 17W
El Khârga	**128**	25 30N	30 33 E
El Khartûm	**129**	15 31N	32 35 E
El Mahalla el Kubra	**128**	31 0N	31 0 E
El Minyâ	**128**	28 7N	30 33 E
El Obeid	**129**	13 8N	30 10 E
El Oro	**177**	27 15N	103 30W
El Paso	**161**	31 50N	106 30W
El Progreso	**177**	15 26N	87 51W
El Qâhira	**128**	30 1N	31 14 E
El Qasr	**128**	25 44N	28 42 E
El Salvador ■	**177**	13 50N	89 0W
El Suweis	**128**	29 58N	32 31 E
El Tigre	**185**	8 44N	64 15W
El Turbio	**192**	51 45S	72 5W
Elat	**80**	29 30N	34 56 E
Elâzığ	**81**	38 37N	39 14 E
Elba	**46**	42 48N	10 15 E
Elbasani	**52**	41 9N	20 9 E
Elbe →	**42**	53 50N	9 0 E
Elbert, Mt.	**163**	39 5N	106 27W
Elberton	**165**	34 7N	82 51W
Elbeuf	**39**	49 17N	1 2 E
Elbing = Elbląg	**58**	54 10N	19 25 E
Elbląg	**58**	54 10N	19 25 E
Elbrus	**70**	43 21N	42 30 E
Elburg	**41**	52 26N	5 50 E
Elburz Mts. = Alborz, Reshteh-ye Kūhhā-ye	**86**	36 0N	52 0 E
Elche	**51**	38 15N	0 42W
Eldorado	**174**	24 20N	107 22W
Eldorado Springs	**166**	37 54N	93 59W
Eldoret	**132**	0 30N	35 17 E
Eleanora, Peak	**120**	32 57S	121 9 E
Electra	**161**	34 0N	99 0W
Elephant Butte Res.	**161**	33 45N	107 30W
Eleuthera	**178**	25 0N	76 20W
Elgin, U.K.	**33**	57 39N	3 20W
Elgin, Ill., U.S.A.	**167**	42 0N	88 20W
Elgin, Oreg., U.S.A.	**171**	45 37N	118 0W
Elgon, Mt.	**132**	1 10N	34 30 E
Elisabethville = Lubumbashi	**135**	11 40S	27 28 E
Elizabeth, Australia	**119**	34 42S	138 41 E
Elizabeth, U.S.A.	**164**	40 37N	74 12W
Elizabeth City	**165**	36 18N	76 16W

Elizabethton	**165**	36 20N	82 13W
Elizabethtown	**167**	37 40N	85 54W
Elk Point	**152**	53 54N	110 55W
Elkhart	**167**	41 42N	85 55W
Elkins	**165**	38 53N	79 53W
Elko	**172**	40 50N	115 50W
Ellensburg	**171**	47 0N	120 30W
Ellery, Mt.	**117**	37 28S	148 47 E
Ellesmere I.	**13**	79 30N	80 0W
Ellesmere Port	**28**	53 17N	2 55W
Ellice Is. = Tuvalu ■	**122**	8 0S	178 0 E
Elliot Lake	**150**	46 25N	82 35W
Ellore = Eluru	**92**	16 48N	81 8 E
Ellsworth Land	**14**	76 0S	89 0W
Ellsworth Mts.	**14**	78 30S	85 0W
Elmhurst	**167**	41 52N	87 58W
Elmira	**164**	42 8N	76 49W
Elrose	**152**	51 12N	108 0W
Eluru	**92**	16 48N	81 8 E
Elvas	**50**	38 50N	7 10W
Elwood	**167**	40 20N	85 50W
Ely	**172**	39 10N	114 50W
Elyria	**167**	41 22N	82 8W
Emāmrūd	**86**	36 30N	55 0 E
Emba →	**70**	46 38N	53 14 E
Emden	**42**	53 22N	7 12 E
Emerald	**121**	23 32S	148 10 E
Emilia-Romagna □	**46**	44 33N	10 40 E
Emmeloord	**41**	52 44N	5 46 E
Emmen	**41**	52 48N	6 57 E
Empalme	**174**	27 58N	110 51W
Emporia, Kans., U.S.A.	**158**	38 25N	96 10W
Emporia, Va., U.S.A.	**165**	36 41N	77 32W
Ems →	**42**	52 37N	9 26 E
En Nahud	**129**	12 45N	28 25 E
Ena	**106**	35 25N	137 25 E
Ena-San	**106**	35 26N	137 36 E
Encarnación	**191**	27 15S	55 50W
Encarnación de Díaz	**175**	21 31N	102 14W
Encontrados	**184**	9 3N	72 14W
Enderby	**155**	50 35N	119 10W
Enderby Land	**14**	66 0S	53 0 E
Endicott	**164**	42 6N	76 2W
Engaño, C.	**180**	18 30N	68 20W
Engels	**68**	51 28N	46 6 E
Enggano	**111**	5 20S	102 40 E
England □	**21**	53 0N	2 0W
English Bazar = Ingraj Bazar	**92**	24 58N	88 10 E
English Channel	**16**	50 0N	2 0W
Enid	**161**	36 26N	97 52W
Enkhuizen	**40**	52 42N	5 17 E
Ennedi	**129**	17 15N	22 0 E
Ennis	**35**	52 51N	8 59W
Enniscorthy	**35**	52 30N	6 35W
Enniskillen	**34**	54 20N	7 40W
Enriquillo, L.	**180**	18 20N	72 5W
Enschede	**41**	52 13N	6 53 E
Ensenada	**174**	31 52N	116 37W
Enshū-Nada	**106**	34 27N	137 38 E
Entebbe	**132**	0 4N	32 28 E
Enterprise	**171**	45 30N	117 18W
Entre Ríos □	**190**	30 30S	58 30W
Enugu	**131**	6 20N	7 30 E
Enzan	**107**	35 42N	138 44 E
Eólie, I.	**49**	38 30N	14 50 E
Epe	**41**	52 21N	5 59 E
Épernay	**39**	49 3N	3 56 E
Ephesus	**80**	37 50N	27 33 E
Épinal	**37**	48 10N	6 27 E
Epping	**25**	51 42N	0 8 E
Equatorial Guinea ■	**134**	2 0S	8 0 E
Er Rif	**126**	35 1N	4 1W
Erāwadī Myit → = Irrawaddy →	**93**	15 50N	95 6 E
Ercha = Shamanovo	**73**	69 45N	147 20 E
Erciyaş Dağı	**80**	38 30N	35 30 E
Erebus, Mt.	**15**	77 35S	167 0 E
Erechim	**191**	27 35S	52 15W
Ereğli	**80**	41 15N	31 30 E
Erfurt	**43**	50 58N	11 2 E
Erg Chech	**126**	50 59N	11 0 E
Erie	**164**	42 10N	80 7W
Erie, L.	**151**	42 15N	81 0W
Erímanthos	**54**	37 57N	21 50 E
Erimo-misaki	**103**	41 50N	143 15 E
Eritrea ■	**132**	14 0N	41 0 E
Ermoúpolis = Síros	**55**	37 28N	24 57 E
Erne, Lough	**34**	54 26N	7 46W
Erode	**90**	11 24N	77 45 E
Erramala Hills	**90**	15 30N	78 15 E
Erris Hd.	**34**	54 19N	10 0W
Erzgebirge	**43**	50 25N	13 0 E
Erzincan	**81**	39 46N	39 30 E
Erzurum	**81**	39 57N	41 15 E
Es Sînâ'	**128**	29 0N	34 0 E
Esan-Misaki	**103**	41 40N	141 10 E
Esashi	**103**	41 52N	140 7 E
Esbjerg	**61**	55 29N	8 29 E
Escanaba	**150**	45 44N	87 5W
Escondido	**173**	33 9N	117 4W
Escuintla	**177**	14 20N	90 48W
Eşfahān	**85**	33 0N	53 0 E
Esh Sham = Dimashq	**80**	33 30N	36 18 E
Esk →	**29**	54 27N	0 36W
Eskilstuna	**60**	59 22N	16 32 E
Eskimo Pt.	**145**	61 10N	94 15W
Eskişehir	**80**	39 50N	30 35 E
Eslāmābād-e Gharb	**84**	34 10N	46 30 E
Esmeraldas	**184**	1 0N	79 40W
Espanola	**151**	46 15N	81 46W
Esperance	**114**	33 45S	121 55 E
Espinazo, Sierra del = Espinhaço, Serra do	**188**	17 30S	43 30W
Espinhaço, Serra do	**188**	17 30S	43 30W
Espírito Santo □	**189**	20 0S	40 45W
Essaouira	**126**	31 32N	9 42W
Essen	**42**	51 28N	6 59 E
Essequibo →	**185**	6 50N	58 30W
Essex □	**25**	51 48N	0 30 E
Estados, I. de los	**192**	54 40S	64 30W
Estelí	**179**	13 9N	86 22W
Estevan	**152**	49 10N	102 59W
Estherville	**166**	43 25N	94 50W
Estonia ■	**68**	58 30N	25 30 E
Estoril	**50**	38 42N	9 23W
Estrêla, Serra da	**50**	40 10N	7 45W
Estremadura	**50**	39 0N	9 0W
Étampes	**39**	48 26N	2 10 E
Étaples	**38**	50 30N	1 39 E
Etawah	**91**	26 48N	79 6 E
Ethiopia ■	**133**	8 0N	40 0 E
Ethiopian Highlands	**132**	10 0N	37 0 E
Etna	**49**	37 45N	15 0 E
Etosha Pan	**136**	18 40S	16 30 E
Etzatlán	**175**	20 46N	104 5W
Euboea = Évvoia	**55**	38 30N	24 0 E
Euclid	**167**	41 32N	81 31W
Eucumbene, L.	**117**	36 2S	148 40 E
Eufaula	**169**	35 20N	95 33W
Eugene	**171**	44 0N	123 8W
Eupen	**42**	50 37N	6 3 E
Euphrates = Furāt, Nahr al →	**84**	31 0N	47 25 E
Eureka, Calif., U.S.A.	**172**	40 50N	124 0W
Eureka, Nev., U.S.A.	**172**	39 32N	116 2W
Euroa	**117**	36 44S	145 35 E
Europa, Pta. de	**50**	36 3N	5 21W
Europa Pt. = Europa, Pta. de	**50**	36 3N	5 21W
Europoort	**40**	51 57N	4 10 E
Euston	**119**	34 30S	142 46 E
Eutsuk L.	**154**	53 20N	126 45W
Evans Head	**116**	29 7S	153 27 E
Evanston	**167**	42 0N	87 40W
Evansville	**167**	38 0N	87 35W
Everard, L.	**118**	31 30S	135 0 E
Everest, Mt.	**92**	28 5N	86 58 E
Everett	**171**	48 0N	122 10W
Everglades	**170**	26 0N	80 30W
Evesham	**24**	52 6N	1 57W
Évora	**50**	38 33N	7 57W
Évreux	**39**	49 0N	1 8 E
Évvoia	**55**	38 30N	24 0 E

Excelsior Springs	**166**	39 20N	94 10W
Exe →	**27**	50 38N	3 27W
Exeter	**27**	50 43N	3 31W
Exmoor	**27**	51 10N	3 59W
Exmouth	**27**	50 37N	3 26W
Extremadura □	**50**	39 30N	6 5W
Eyasi, L.	**135**	3 30S	35 0 E
Eye Pen.	**32**	58 13N	6 10W
Eyre, L.	**118**	29 30S	137 26 E
Eyre Mts.	**123**	45 25S	168 25 E
Eyre Pen.	**119**	33 30S	137 17 E

F

Facatativá	**184**	4 49N	74 22W
Faddeyevskiy, Ostrov	**72**	76 0N	150 0 E
Fair Hd.	**34**	55 14N	6 10W
Fairbanks	**142**	64 50N	147 50W
Fairfield, N.Z.	**123**	45 54S	170 24 E
Fairfield, Ala., U.S.A.	**169**	33 30N	87 0W
Fairfield, Calif., U.S.A.	**172**	38 14N	122 1W
Fairfield, Tex., U.S.A.	**168**	31 40N	96 0W
Fairmont, Minn., U.S.A.	**166**	43 37N	94 30W
Fairmont, W. Va., U.S.A.	**164**	39 29N	80 10W
Fairview	**155**	56 5N	118 25W
Fairweather, Mt.	**143**	58 55N	137 45W
Faisalabad	**89**	31 30N	73 5 E
Faizabad	**92**	26 45N	82 10 E
Fajardo	**180**	18 20N	65 39W
Fakenham	**29**	52 50N	0 51 E
Falam	**93**	23 0N	93 45 E
Falkirk	**31**	56 0N	3 47W
Falkland Is.	**192**	51 30S	59 0W
Falköping	**60**	58 12N	13 33 E
Fall River	**164**	41 45N	71 5W
Falls City	**166**	40 0N	95 40W
Falmouth, Jamaica	**180**	18 30N	77 40W
Falmouth, U.K.	**27**	50 9N	5 5W
Famagusta	**80**	35 8N	33 55 E
Farāh	**87**	32 20N	62 7 E
Farāh □	**87**	32 25N	62 10 E
Fareham	**25**	50 52N	1 11W
Farewell, C.	**122**	40 29S	172 43 E
Farewell C. = Farvel, Kap	**147**	59 48N	43 55W
Fargo	**156**	46 52N	96 40W
Farmington, N.H., U.S.A.	**157**	43 25N	71 3W
Farmington, N. Mex., U.S.A.	**161**	36 45N	108 28W
Farnborough	**25**	51 17N	0 46W
Faro	**50**	37 2N	7 55W
Faroe Is.	**16**	62 0N	7 0W
Fars □	**85**	29 30N	55 0 E
Fársala	**54**	39 17N	22 23 E
Farvel, Kap	**147**	59 48N	43 55W
Fāryāb □	**87**	36 0N	65 0 E
Fatehgarh	**89**	27 25N	79 35 E
Fatehpur, Raj., India	**92**	28 0N	74 40 E
Fatehpur, Ut. P., India	**89**	25 56N	81 13 E
Faxaflói	**64**	64 29N	23 0W
Fayetteville, Ark., U.S.A.	**168**	36 0N	94 5W
Fayetteville, N.C., U.S.A.	**165**	35 0N	78 58W
Fazilka	**89**	30 27N	74 2 E
Fdérik	**126**	22 40N	12 45W
Fear, C.	**165**	33 51N	78 0W
Fécamp	**38**	49 45N	0 22 E
Feilding	**122**	40 13S	175 35 E
Feira de Santana	**189**	12 15S	38 57W
Felixstowe	**25**	51 58N	1 22 E
Fengjie	**99**	31 5N	109 36 E
Fens, The	**29**	52 45N	0 2 E
Fenyang	**98**	37 19N	111 46 E
Ferfer	**133**	5 4N	45 9 E
Fergana	**71**	40 23N	71 19 E
Fergus Falls	**156**	46 18N	96 7W
Fermoy	**35**	52 4N	8 18W
Fernando de Noronha	**189**	4 0S	33 10W
Fernando Póo = Bioko	**131**	3 30N	8 40 E
Fernie	**155**	49 30N	115 5W
Ferrara	**47**	44 50N	11 36 E
Ferté-Bernard, La	**39**	48 10N	0 40 E
Fès	**126**	34 0N	5 0W
Feuilles →	**146**	58 47N	70 4W
Feyzābād	**87**	37 7N	70 33 E
Fezzan	**124**	27 0N	15 0 E
Fianarantsoa	**137**	21 26S	47 5 E
Fichtelgebirge	**43**	50 10N	12 0 E
Fife □	**31**	56 13N	3 2W
Fife Ness	**31**	56 17N	2 35W
Fiji ■	**122**	17 20S	179 0 E
Filey	**29**	54 13N	0 18W
Findlay	**167**	41 0N	83 41W
Finisterre, C.	**50**	42 50N	9 19W
Finland ■	**67**	63 0N	27 0 E
Finland, G. of	**67**	60 0N	26 0 E
Finlay →	**144**	57 0N	125 10W
Finley	**117**	35 38S	145 35 E
Firenze	**47**	43 47N	11 15 E
Firozabad	**89**	27 10N	78 25 E
Fishguard	**26**	51 59N	4 59W
Fiskenæsset	**147**	63 5N	50 45W
Fitchburg	**164**	42 35N	71 47W
Fitzgerald	**170**	31 45N	83 16W
Fitzroy →	**121**	23 32S	150 52 E
Fiume = Rijeka	**52**	45 20N	14 21 E
Flagstaff	**160**	35 10N	111 40W
Flamborough Hd.	**29**	54 8N	0 4W
Flannan Is.	**32**	58 9N	7 52W
Flattery, C.	**171**	48 21N	124 43W
Flèche, La	**39**	47 42N	0 4W
Fleetwood	**28**	53 55N	3 1W
Flekkefjord	**60**	58 18N	6 39 E
Flensburg	**43**	54 46N	9 28 E
Flers	**36**	48 47N	0 33W
Flin Flon	**152**	54 46N	101 53W
Flinders I.	**117**	40 0S	148 0 E
Flinders Ranges	**118**	31 30S	138 30 E
Flinders Reefs	**121**	17 37S	148 31 E
Flint, U.K.	**26**	53 15N	3 7W
Flint, U.S.A.	**167**	43 5N	83 40W
Flint →	**170**	30 52N	84 38W
Flodden	**31**	55 37N	2 8W
Flora	**167**	38 40N	88 30W
Florence = Firenze	**47**	43 47N	11 15 E
Florence, Ala., U.S.A.	**169**	34 50N	87 40W
Florence, S.C., U.S.A.	**165**	34 12N	79 44W
Flores, Guatemala	**177**	16 59N	89 50W
Flores, Indonesia	**113**	8 35S	121 0 E
Flores Sea	**113**	6 30S	124 0 E
Floriano	**188**	6 50S	43 0W
Florianópolis	**191**	27 30S	48 30W
Florida	**191**	34 7S	56 10W
Florida □	**170**	28 30N	82 0W
Florida, Straits of	**159**	25 0N	80 0W
Florida B.	**159**	25 0N	81 20W
Florida Keys	**159**	25 0N	80 40W
Flórina	**54**	40 48N	21 26 E
Flushing = Vlissingen	**40**	51 26N	3 34 E
Fly →	**115**	8 25S	143 0 E
Foam Lake	**152**	51 40N	103 32W
Fóggia	**49**	41 28N	15 31 E
Foix	**36**	42 58N	1 38 E
Folda	**64**	64 41N	10 50 E
Folkestone	**25**	51 5N	1 11 E
Follette, La	**169**	36 23N	84 9W
Fond-du-Lac, Canada	**145**	59 19N	107 12W
Fond du Lac, U.S.A.	**167**	43 46N	88 26W
Fontainebleau	**39**	48 24N	2 40 E
Fonte Boa	**184**	2 33S	66 0W
Foochow = Fuzhou	**99**	26 5N	119 16 E
Forbes	**117**	33 22S	148 0 E
Forestburg	**155**	52 35N	112 1W
Forestville	**148**	48 48N	69 2W
Forfar	**33**	56 40N	2 53W
Forlì	**47**	44 14N	12 2 E
Formby Pt.	**28**	53 33N	3 7W
Formentera	**51**	38 43N	1 27 E
Formosa = Taiwan ■	**99**	23 30N	121 0 E
Formosa	**191**	26 15S	58 10W
Forrest City	**169**	35 0N	90 50W
Fort Albany	**140**	52 15N	81 35W

Fort Augustus 32 57 9N 4 40W
Fort Chipewyan 145 58 42N 111 8W
Fort Collins 163 40 30N 105 4W
Fort-Coulonge 151 45 50N 76 45W
Fort-de-France 180 14 36N 61 2W
Fort Dodge 166 42 29N 94 10W
Fort Frances 153 48 36N 93 24W
Fort Franklin 145 65 10N 123 30W
Fort George 140 53 50N 79 0W
Fort Good-Hope 144 66 14N 128 40W
Fort Hertz = Putao 93 27 28N 97 30 E
Fort Kent 148 47 12N 68 30W
Fort-Lamy = Ndjamena 131 12 10N 14 59 E
Fort Lauderdale 170 26 10N 80 5W
Fort Liard 144 60 14N 123 30W
Fort Mackay 143 57 12N 111 41W
Fort Macleod 155 49 45N 113 30W
Fort McMurray 155 56 44N 111 7W
Fort McPherson 144 67 30N 134 55W
Fort Madison 166 40 39N 91 20W
Fort Morgan 163 40 10N 103 50W
Fort Myers 170 26 39N 81 51W
Fort Nelson 144 58 50N 122 44W
Fort Nelson → 144 59 32N 124 0W
Fort Payne 169 34 25N 85 44W
Fort Peck L. 163 47 40N 107 0W
Fort Pierce 170 27 29N 80 19W
Fort Providence 145 61 3N 117 40W
Fort Qu'Appelle 152 50 45N 103 50W
Fort Resolution 145 61 10N 113 40W
Fort Rupert 140 51 30N 78 40W
Fort St. James 154 54 30N 124 10W
Fort St. John 155 56 15N 120 50W
Fort Sandeman 88 31 20N 69 31 E
Fort Saskatchewan 155 53 40N 113 15W
Fort Scott 166 37 50N 94 40W
Fort Severn 140 56 0N 87 40W
Fort Shevchenko 70 43 40N 51 20 E
Fort Simpson 144 61 45N 121 15W
Fort Smith, Canada 145 60 0N 111 51W
Fort Smith, U.S.A. 168 35 25N 94 25W
Fort Smith Region □ 145 63 0N 120 0W
Fort Trinquet = Bir Mogrein 126 25 10N 11 25W
Fort Valley 170 32 33N 83 52W
Fort Vermilion 145 58 24N 116 0W
Fort Wayne 167 41 5N 85 10W
Fort William 32 56 48N 5 8W
Fort Worth 168 32 45N 97 25W
Fort Yukon 142 66 35N 145 20W
Fortaleza 189 3 45S 38 35W
Forth → 31 56 9N 4 18W
Forth, Firth of 31 56 5N 2 55W
Fortuna 172 40 38N 124 8W
Foshan 99 23 4N 113 5 E
Foster 117 38 40S 146 15 E
Fougères 36 48 21N 1 14W
Foula, I. 30 60 10N 2 5W
Foulness I. 24 51 36N 0 55 E
Fourmies 38 50 1N 4 2 E
Foúrnoi 55 37 36N 26 32 E
Fouta Djalon 130 11 20N 12 10W
Foveaux Str. 123 46 42S 168 10 E
Fowey 27 50 20N 4 39W
Foxe Basin 146 66 0N 77 0W
Foxe Chan. 146 65 0N 80 0W
Foxe Pen. 146 65 0N 76 0W
Foxton 122 40 29S 175 18 E
Foyle, Lough 34 55 6N 7 8W
Foynes 35 52 37N 9 5W
Franca 188 20 33S 47 30W
France ■ 37 47 0N 3 0 E
Franche-Comté 37 46 30N 5 50 E
François 180 14 38N 60 57W
Franeker 41 53 12N 5 33 E
Frankfort, Ind., U.S.A. 167 40 20N 86 33W
Frankfort, Ky., U.S.A. 165 38 12N 84 52W
Frankfurt am Main 42 50 7N 8 40 E
Frankfurt an der Oder 43 52 50N 14 31 E
Fränkische Alb 43 49 20N 11 30 E
Franklin, La., U.S.A. 168 29 45N 91 30W
Franklin, N.H., U.S.A. 164 43 28N 71 39W
Franklin, W. Va., U.S.A. 165 38 38N 79 21W
Franklin D. Roosevelt L. 162 48 30N 118 16W
Franklin Mts. 145 65 0N 125 0W
Franklin Str. 145 72 0N 96 0W
Frankston 117 38 8S 145 8 E
Franz 150 48 25N 84 30W
Fraser → 154 49 7N 123 11W
Fraser, Mt. 120 25 35S 118 20 E
Fraser I. 116 25 15S 153 10 E
Fraserburgh 33 57 41N 2 0W
Fray Bentos 190 33 10S 58 15W
Frederick 164 39 25N 77 23W
Fredericksburg 165 38 16N 77 29W
Fredericton 148 45 57N 66 40W
Frederikshavn 61 57 28N 10 31 E
Fredrikstad 60 59 13N 10 57 E
Freeport, Bahamas 178 26 30N 78 47W
Freeport, Ill., U.S.A. 166 42 18N 89 40W
Freeport, N.Y., U.S.A. 164 40 39N 73 35W
Freeport, Tex., U.S.A. 158 28 55N 95 22W
Freetown 130 8 30N 13 17W
Freiberg 42 50 55N 13 20 E
Freibourg = Fribourg 44 46 49N 7 9 E
Fréjus 37 43 25N 6 44 E
Fremantle 120 32 7S 115 47 E
Fremont, Calif., U.S.A. 172 37 32N 122 1W
Fremont, Nebr., U.S.A. 166 41 30N 96 30W
French Guiana ■ 185 4 0N 53 0W
French Pass 123 40 55S 173 55 E
French Terr. of Afars & Issas = Djibouti ■ 133 12 0N 43 0 E
Fresnillo 175 23 10N 102 53W
Fresno 173 36 47N 119 50W
Fria, C. 136 18 0S 12 0 E
Frias 190 28 40S 65 5W
Fribourg 44 46 49N 7 9 E
Friendly, Is. = Tonga ■ 123 19 50S 174 30W
Friesland □ 41 53 5N 5 50 E
Frio, C. 182 22 50S 41 50W
Friuli-Venezia Giulia □ 47 46 0N 13 0 E
Frobisher B. 146 62 30N 66 0W
Frobisher Bay 146 63 44N 68 31W
Frobisher L. 152 56 20N 108 15W
Frome 27 51 16N 2 17W
Frome, L. 118 30 45S 139 45 E
Frome Downs 118 31 13S 139 45 E
Front Range 163 40 0N 105 40W
Front Royal 164 38 55N 78 10W
Frontera 177 18 32N 92 38W
Frostburg 164 39 43N 78 57W
Frunze = Bishkek 71 42 54N 74 46 E
Frutal 188 20 0S 49 0W
Fuchou = Fuzhou 99 26 5N 119 16 E
Fuchū, Hiroshima, Japan 109 34 34N 133 14 E
Fūchū, Tōkyō, Japan 107 35 40N 139 29 E
Fuerte, R. → 174 25 54N 109 22W
Fuji 107 35 9N 138 39 E
Fuji-no-miya 107 35 10N 138 40 E
Fuji-San 107 35 22N 138 44 E
Fuji-yoshida 107 35 30N 138 46 E
Fujian □ 99 26 0N 118 0 E
Fujieda 107 34 52N 138 16 E
Fujisawa 107 35 22N 139 29 E
Fukaya 107 36 12N 139 12 E
Fukien = Fujian □ 99 26 0N 118 0 E
Fukuchiyama 106 35 19N 135 9 E
Fukue-Shima 104 32 40N 128 45 E
Fukui 106 36 0N 136 10 E
Fukuoka 108 33 39N 130 21 E
Fukushima 103 37 44N 140 28 E
Fukuyama 109 34 35N 133 20 E
Fulton, Mo., U.S.A. 166 38 50N 91 55W
Fulton, N.Y., U.S.A. 164 43 20N 76 22W
Funabashi 107 35 45N 140 0 E
Funchal 126 32 38N 16 54W
Fundación 184 10 31N 74 11W
Fundy, B. of 148 45 0N 66 0W
Furāt, Nahr al → 84 31 0N 47 25 E
Furneaux Group 119 40 10S 147 50 E
Furness 28 54 14N 3 8W
Fürth 43 49 29N 11 0 E

Fury and Hecla Str.	**146**	69 56N	84 0W
Fushun	**98**	41 50N	123 55 E
Fuxin	**98**	42 5N	121 48 E
Fuzhou	**99**	26 5N	119 16 E
Fylde	**28**	53 50N	2 58W
Fyn	**61**	55 20N	10 30 E
Fyne, L.	**30**	56 0N	5 20W

G

Gabès, Golfe de	**127**	34 0N	10 30 E
Gabon ■	**134**	0 10S	10 0 E
Gaborone	**137**	24 45S	25 57 E
Gachsārān	**85**	30 15N	50 45 E
Gadag	**90**	15 30N	75 45 E
Gadsden	**169**	34 1N	86 0W
Gaeta	**49**	41 12N	13 35 E
Gaffney	**165**	35 3N	81 40W
Gagnon	**141**	51 50N	68 5W
Gainesville, Fla., U.S.A.	**170**	29 38N	82 20W
Gainesville, Ga., U.S.A.	**165**	34 17N	83 47W
Gainesville, Tex., U.S.A.	**168**	33 40N	97 10W
Gainsborough	**29**	53 23N	0 46W
Gairdner L.	**118**	31 30S	136 0 E
Galápagos	**10**	0 0	89 0W
Galas →	**96**	4 55N	101 57 E
Galashiels	**31**	55 37N	2 50W
Galaţi	**57**	45 27N	28 2 E
Galatina	**49**	40 10N	18 10 E
Galdhøpiggen	**60**	61 38N	8 18 E
Galesburg	**166**	40 57N	90 23W
Galicia □	**50**	42 43N	7 45W
Galilee, L.	**121**	22 20S	145 50 E
Gallatin	**169**	36 24N	86 27W
Galle	**90**	6 5N	80 10 E
Gallinas, Pta.	**184**	12 28N	71 40W
Gallipoli = Gelibolu	**80**	40 28N	26 43 E
Gallípoli	**49**	40 8N	18 0 E
Gällivare	**66**	67 9N	20 40 E
Galloway	**31**	55 0N	4 25W
Galloway, Mull of	**30**	54 38N	4 50W
Gallup	**161**	35 30N	108 45W
Galty Mts.	**35**	52 22N	8 10W
Galveston	**168**	29 15N	94 48W
Galveston B.	**168**	29 30N	94 50W
Galway	**35**	53 16N	9 4W
Galway □	**34**	53 16N	9 3W
Gamagori	**106**	34 50N	137 14 E
Gambia ■	**130**	13 25N	16 0W
Gambia →	**130**	13 28N	16 34W
Gand = Gent	**42**	51 2N	3 42 E
Gander	**149**	48 58N	54 35W
Gandhi Sagar	**91**	24 40N	75 40 E
Gandi	**131**	12 55N	5 49 E
Ganga →	**92**	23 20N	90 30 E
Ganges = Ganga →	**92**	23 20N	90 30 E
Gangtok	**92**	27 20N	88 37 E
Gannett Pk.	**163**	43 15N	109 38W
Gansu □	**98**	36 0N	104 0 E
Ganzhou	**99**	25 51N	114 56 E
Gao	**130**	16 15N	0 5W
Gaoxiong	**99**	22 38N	120 18 E
Garachiné	**179**	8 0N	78 12W
Garanhuns	**189**	8 50S	36 30W
Garberville	**172**	40 11N	123 50W
Garda, L. di	**46**	45 40N	10 40 E
Garden City	**161**	38 0N	100 45W
Garden Grove	**173**	33 47N	117 55W
Gardēz	**87**	33 37N	69 9 E
Garmsār	**86**	35 20N	52 25 E
Garonne →	**36**	45 2N	0 36W
Garoua	**131**	9 19N	13 21 E
Garrison Res. = Sakakawea, L.	**163**	47 30N	102 0W
Garry L.	**145**	65 58N	100 18W
Garvie Mts.	**123**	45 30S	168 50 E
Garwa = Garoua	**131**	9 19N	13 21 E
Gary	**167**	41 35N	87 20W
Garzón	**184**	2 10N	75 40W
Gascogne	**36**	43 45N	0 20 E
Gascony = Gascogne	**36**	43 45N	0 20 E
Gaspé	**148**	48 52N	64 30W
Gaspé, C. de	**148**	48 48N	64 7W
Gaspé, Pén. de	**148**	48 45N	65 40W
Gastonia	**165**	35 17N	81 10W
Gastre	**192**	42 20S	69 15W
Gata, C. de	**51**	36 41N	2 13W
Gateshead	**28**	54 57N	1 37W
Gauhati	**93**	26 10N	91 45 E
Gävle	**60**	60 40N	17 9 E
Gävleborgs län □	**60**	61 30N	16 15 E
Gawilgarh Hills	**91**	21 15N	76 45 E
Gawler	**119**	34 30S	138 42 E
Gawler Ranges	**114**	32 30S	135 45 E
Gaxun Nur	**100**	42 22N	100 30 E
Gaya	**92**	24 47N	85 4 E
Gaylord	**150**	45 1N	84 41W
Gayndah	**116**	25 35S	151 32 E
Gaza	**80**	31 30N	34 28 E
Gaziantep	**80**	37 6N	37 23 E
Gdańsk	**58**	54 22N	18 40 E
Gdańska, Zatoka	**58**	54 30N	19 20 E
Gdynia	**58**	54 35N	18 33 E
Gedaref	**129**	14 2N	35 28 E
Geelong	**117**	38 10S	144 22 E
Gejiu	**99**	23 20N	103 10 E
Gelderland □	**41**	52 5N	6 10 E
Geldermalsen	**40**	51 53N	5 17 E
Geldrop	**41**	51 25N	5 32 E
Geleen	**41**	50 57N	5 49 E
Gelibolu	**80**	40 28N	26 43 E
Gelsenkirchen	**42**	51 30N	7 5 E
Gemert	**41**	51 33N	5 41 E
General Alvear	**190**	35 0S	67 40W
General Pico	**190**	35 45S	63 50W
Geneva = Genève	**44**	46 12N	6 9 E
Geneva	**164**	42 53N	77 0W
Geneva, L. = Léman, Lac	**44**	46 26N	6 30 E
Genève	**44**	46 12N	6 9 E
Genk	**41**	50 58N	5 32 E
Genkai-Nada	**108**	34 0N	130 0 E
Gennargentu, Mti. del	**48**	40 0N	9 10 E
Genoa = Génova	**46**	44 24N	8 56 E
Génova	**46**	44 24N	8 56 E
Génova, Golfo di	**46**	44 0N	9 0 E
Gent	**42**	51 2N	3 42 E
George, L.	**132**	0 5N	30 10 E
George River = Port Nouveau-Québec	**146**	58 30N	65 59W
George Town	**96**	5 25N	100 15 E
Georgetown, Australia	**119**	18 17S	143 33 E
Georgetown, Canada	**151**	43 40N	79 56W
Georgetown, Guyana	**185**	6 50N	58 12W
Georgetown, U.S.A.	**170**	33 22N	79 15W
Georgia □	**170**	32 0N	82 0W
Georgia ■	**70**	42 0N	43 0 E
Georgian B.	**151**	45 15N	81 0W
Gera	**43**	50 53N	12 11 E
Geraldton, Australia	**120**	28 48S	114 32 E
Geraldton, Canada	**150**	49 44N	86 59W
Gereshk	**87**	31 47N	64 35 E
Germany ■	**18**	52 0N	12 0 E
Germiston	**137**	26 15S	28 10 E
Gerona	**51**	41 58N	2 46 E
Ghana ■	**130**	6 0N	1 0W
Ghat	**127**	24 59N	10 11 E
Ghawdex = Gozo	**49**	36 0N	14 13 E
Ghaziabad	**89**	28 42N	77 26 E
Ghazipur	**92**	25 38N	83 35 E
Ghaznī	**87**	33 30N	68 28 E
Ghaznī □	**87**	32 10N	68 20 E
Ghent = Gent	**42**	51 2N	3 42 E
Ghowr □	**87**	34 0N	64 20 E
Ghulam Mohammad Barrage	**88**	25 30N	68 20 E
Giant's Causeway	**34**	55 15N	6 30W
Gibara	**178**	21 9N	76 11W
Gibraltar	**50**	36 7N	5 22W
Gibraltar, Str. of	**50**	35 55N	5 40W
Gien	**39**	47 40N	2 36 E

Gifu	**106**	35 30N	136 45 E
Gigha	**30**	55 42N	5 45W
Gijón	**50**	43 32N	5 42W
Gila →	**173**	32 43N	114 33W
Gīlān □	**81**	37 0N	50 0 E
Gilbert Is. = Kiribati ■	**122**	1 0N	176 0 E
Gilford I.	**154**	50 40N	126 30W
Gilgandra	**116**	31 43S	148 39 E
Gilgit	**89**	35 50N	74 15 E
Gillingham	**25**	51 23N	0 34 E
Gingin	**120**	31 22S	115 54 E
Gippsland	**117**	37 45S	147 15 E
Girardot	**184**	4 18N	74 48W
Giresun	**81**	40 55N	38 30 E
Gironde →	**36**	45 32N	1 7W
Girvan	**30**	55 15N	4 50W
Gisborne	**122**	38 39S	178 5 E
Gisors	**39**	49 15N	1 47 E
Gizhiga	**73**	62 3N	160 30 E
Gizhiginskaya, Guba	**73**	61 0N	158 0 E
Giżycko	**58**	54 2N	21 48 E
Gjoa Haven	**145**	68 20N	96 8W
Glace Bay	**149**	46 11N	59 58W
Gladstone, Queens., Australia	**121**	23 52S	151 16 E
Gladstone, S. Austral., Australia	**118**	33 15S	138 22 E
Gláma	**64**	65 48N	23 0W
Glasgow, U.K.	**31**	55 52N	4 14W
Glasgow, U.S.A.	**169**	37 2N	85 55W
Glastonbury	**27**	51 9N	2 42W
Gleiwitz = Gliwice	**58**	50 22N	18 41 E
Glen Coe	**32**	56 40N	5 0W
Glen Innes	**116**	29 44S	151 44 E
Glen Mor	**33**	57 12N	4 37 E
Glenburgh	**120**	25 26S	116 6 E
Glendale	**173**	34 7N	118 18W
Glendive	**163**	47 7N	104 40W
Glenelg	**119**	34 58S	138 31 E
Glenns Ferry	**172**	43 0N	115 15W
Glenorchy	**119**	42 49S	147 18 E
Glenrothes	**31**	56 12N	3 11W
Glens Falls	**164**	43 20N	73 40W
Gliwice	**58**	50 22N	18 41 E
Głogów	**58**	51 37N	16 5 E
Glossop	**28**	53 27N	1 56W
Gloucester	**24**	51 52N	2 15W
Gloucestershire □	**24**	51 44N	2 10W
Gloversville	**164**	43 5N	74 18W
Gniezno	**58**	52 30N	17 35 E
Go Cong	**95**	10 22N	106 40 E
Goa	**91**	15 33N	73 59 E
Goa □	**90**	15 33N	73 59 E
Goat Fell	**30**	55 37N	5 11W
Goba	**133**	7 1N	39 59 E
Gobi	**98**	44 0N	111 0 E
Gobō	**106**	33 53N	135 10 E
Godavari →	**91**	16 25N	82 18 E
Godbout	**148**	49 20N	67 38W
Goderich	**150**	43 45N	81 41W
Godhra	**91**	22 49N	73 40 E
Gods L.	**153**	54 40N	94 15W
Godthåb	**147**	64 10N	51 35W
Goeie Hoop, Kaap die	**136**	34 24S	18 30 E
Goeree	**40**	51 50N	4 0 E
Goes	**40**	51 30N	3 55 E
Gogama	**151**	47 35N	81 43W
Goiânia	**188**	16 43S	49 20W
Goiás □	**188**	12 10S	48 0W
Goirle	**40**	51 31N	5 4 E
Gojō	**106**	34 21N	135 42 E
Gökçeada	**55**	40 10N	25 50 E
Gold Coast, Australia	**116**	28 0S	153 25 E
Gold Coast, W. Afr.	**124**	4 0N	1 40W
Golden Bay	**122**	40 40S	172 50 E
Golden Gate	**172**	37 54N	122 30W
Golden Hinde	**154**	49 40N	125 44W
Golden Vale	**35**	52 33N	8 17W
Goldfield	**172**	37 45N	117 13W
Goldsboro	**165**	35 24N	77 59W
Goldsworthy	**114**	20 21S	119 30 E
Golfo Aranci	**48**	41 0N	9 35 E
Gomel	**68**	52 28N	31 0 E
Gómez Palacio	**174**	25 34N	103 30W
Gonābād	**86**	34 15N	58 45 E
Gonaïves	**180**	19 20N	72 42W
Gonda	**92**	27 9N	81 58 E
Gonder	**132**	12 39N	37 30 E
Good Hope, C. of = Goeie Hoop, Kaap die	**136**	34 24S	18 30 E
Goole	**29**	53 42N	0 52W
Goondiwindi	**116**	28 30S	150 21 E
Goose Bay	**147**	53 15N	60 20W
Gorakhpur	**92**	26 47N	83 23 E
Gordonvale	**121**	17 5S	145 50 E
Gore, Ethiopia	**132**	8 12N	35 32 E
Gore, N.Z.	**123**	46 5S	168 58 E
Gorey	**35**	52 41N	6 18W
Gorinchem	**40**	51 50N	4 59 E
Gorkiy = Nizhniy Novgorod	**68**	56 20N	44 0 E
Görlitz	**43**	51 10N	14 59 E
Gorna Oryakhovitsa	**53**	43 7N	25 40 E
Gorno-Altay □	**71**	51 0N	86 0 E
Gorzów Wielkopolski	**58**	52 43N	15 15 E
Gosford	**117**	33 23S	151 18 E
Gospič	**52**	44 35N	15 23 E
Gosport	**25**	50 48N	1 8W
Göteborg	**60**	57 43N	11 59 E
Göteborgs och Bohus län □	**60**	58 30N	11 30 E
Gotemba	**107**	35 18N	138 56 E
Gotha	**43**	50 56N	10 42 E
Gotland	**60**	57 30N	18 33 E
Gōtsu	**109**	35 0N	132 14 E
Gottwaldov = Zlin	**59**	49 14N	17 40 E
Gouda	**40**	52 1N	4 42 E
Gouin, Rés.	**151**	48 35N	74 40W
Goulburn	**117**	34 44S	149 44 E
Goundam	**130**	16 25N	3 45W
Gournay-en-Bray	**38**	49 29N	1 44 E
Governador Valadares	**188**	18 15S	41 57W
Governor's Harbour	**178**	25 10N	76 14W
Gower, The	**27**	51 35N	4 10W
Goya	**190**	29 10S	59 10W
Gozo	**49**	36 0N	14 13 E
Graaff-Reinet	**136**	32 13S	24 32 E
Gracias a Dios, C.	**179**	15 0N	83 10W
Grafton	**116**	29 38S	152 58 E
Graham	**165**	36 5N	79 22W
Graham I.	**154**	53 40N	132 30W
Graham Land	**14**	65 0S	64 0W
Grahamstown	**137**	33 19S	26 31 E
Grain Coast	**124**	4 20N	10 0W
Grampian □	**33**	57 0N	3 0W
Grampian Mts.	**33**	56 50N	4 0W
Grampians, The	**119**	37 0S	142 20 E
Gran Chaco	**190**	25 0S	61 0W
Gran Sasso d'Italia	**47**	42 25N	13 30 E
Granada, Nic.	**179**	11 58N	86 0W
Granada, Spain	**50**	37 10N	3 35W
Granby	**151**	45 25N	72 45W
Grand Bank	**149**	47 6N	55 48W
Grand Bassam	**130**	5 10N	3 49W
Grand Canyon	**160**	36 3N	112 9W
Grand Cayman	**178**	19 20N	81 20W
Grand Cess	**130**	4 40N	8 12W
Grand Falls	**149**	48 56N	55 40W
Grand Forks, Canada	**155**	49 0N	118 30W
Grand Forks, U.S.A.	**156**	48 0N	97 3W
Grand Island	**163**	40 59N	98 25W
Grand Junction	**163**	39 0N	108 30W
Grand Mère	**151**	46 36N	72 40W
Grand Portage	**150**	47 58N	89 41W
Grand Rapids, Canada	**153**	53 12N	99 19W
Grand Rapids, U.S.A.	**167**	42 57N	86 40W
Grand St.-Bernard, Col. du	**44**	45 53N	7 11 E
Grand Teton	**163**	43 54N	111 50W
Grand View	**153**	51 10N	100 42W
Grande →, Bolivia	**187**	15 51S	64 39W
Grande →, Brazil	**188**	20 6S	51 4W
Grande, B.	**192**	50 30S	68 20W
Grande, La	**171**	45 15N	118 0W
Grande, La →	**140**	53 50N	79 0W
Grande Baleine, R. de la →	**140**	55 16N	77 47W

Grande de Santiago, R. →	**175**	21 36N	105 26W
Grande Prairie	**155**	55 10N	118 50W
Grande-Rivière	**148**	48 26N	64 30W
Grange, La	**170**	33 4N	85 0W
Grangemouth	**31**	56 1N	3 43W
Grangeville	**162**	45 57N	116 4W
Granite City	**166**	38 45N	90 3W
Grant, Mt.	**172**	38 34N	118 48W
Grantham	**29**	52 55N	0 39W
Grantown-on-Spey	**33**	57 19N	3 36W
Grants Pass	**171**	42 30N	123 22W
Grass Valley	**172**	39 18N	121 0W
Grasse	**37**	43 38N	6 56 E
Gravelbourg	**152**	49 50N	106 35W
Gravelines	**38**	51 0N	2 10 E
's-Gravenhage	**40**	52 7N	4 17 E
Gravesend	**25**	51 25N	0 22 E
Grayling	**167**	44 40N	84 42W
Graz	**45**	47 4N	15 27 E
Great Abaco I.	**178**	26 25N	77 10W
Great Australian Bight	**114**	33 30S	130 0 E
Great Bahama Bank	**178**	23 15N	78 0W
Great Barrier I.	**122**	36 11S	175 25 E
Great Barrier Reef	**121**	18 0S	146 50 E
Great Basin	**172**	40 0N	116 30W
Great Bear L.	**145**	65 30N	120 0W
Great Britain	**16**	54 0N	2 15W
Great Divide, The	**117**	35 0S	149 17 E
Great Dividing Ra.	**121**	23 0S	146 0 E
Great Exuma I.	**178**	23 30N	75 50W
Great Falls	**163**	47 27N	111 12W
Great Inagua I.	**180**	21 0N	73 20W
Great Indian Desert = Thar Desert	**89**	28 0N	72 0 E
Great Orme's Head	**26**	53 20N	3 52W
Great Ouse →	**29**	52 47N	0 22 E
Great Plains	**138**	47 0N	105 0W
Great Salt Lake	**162**	41 0N	112 30W
Great Salt Lake Desert	**162**	40 20N	113 50W
Great Slave L.	**145**	61 23N	115 38W
Great Wall	**98**	38 30N	109 30 E
Great Whernside	**28**	54 9N	1 59W
Great Yarmouth	**29**	52 40N	1 45 E
Greater Antilles	**181**	17 40N	74 0W
Greater Manchester □	**28**	53 30N	2 15W
Greater Sunda Is.	**111**	2 30S	110 0 E
Gredos, Sierra de	**50**	40 20N	5 0W
Greece ■	**54**	40 0N	23 0 E
Greeley	**163**	40 30N	104 40W
Green →, Ky., U.S.A.	**167**	37 54N	87 30W
Green →, Utah, U.S.A.	**163**	38 11N	109 53W
Green Bay	**167**	44 30N	88 0W
Greenfield	**164**	42 38N	72 38W
Greenland □	**147**	66 0N	45 0W
Greenland Sea	**13**	73 0N	10 0W
Greenock	**30**	55 57N	4 46W
Greensboro	**165**	36 7N	79 46W
Greenville, Ala., U.S.A.	**169**	31 50N	86 37W
Greenville, Mich., U.S.A.	**167**	43 12N	85 14W
Greenville, Miss., U.S.A.	**168**	33 25N	91 0W
Greenville, N.C., U.S.A.	**165**	35 37N	77 26W
Greenville, S.C., U.S.A.	**165**	34 54N	82 24W
Greenville, Tenn., U.S.A.	**165**	36 13N	82 51W
Greenwood, Miss., U.S.A.	**169**	33 30N	90 4W
Greenwood, S.C., U.S.A.	**165**	34 13N	82 13W
Grenada	**169**	33 45N	89 50W
Grenada ■	**180**	12 10N	61 40W
Grenoble	**37**	45 12N	5 42 E
Grenville	**117**	37 46S	143 52 E
Gretna Green	**31**	55 0N	3 3W
Grey Range	**116**	27 0S	143 30 E
Grey Res.	**149**	48 20N	56 30W
Greymouth	**123**	42 29S	171 13 E
Griffin	**170**	33 17N	84 14W
Griffith	**117**	34 18S	146 2 E
Grimsby	**29**	53 35N	0 5W
Grimshaw	**155**	56 10N	117 40W
Grinnell	**166**	41 45N	92 43W
Grodno	**68**	53 42N	23 52 E
Groningen	**41**	53 15N	6 35 E
Groningen □	**41**	53 16N	6 40 E
Grootfontein	**136**	19 31S	18 6 E
Groznyy	**70**	43 20N	45 45 E
Grudziądz	**58**	53 30N	18 47 E
Grytviken	**14**	53 50S	37 10W
Gt. Stour = Stour →	**25**	51 15N	1 20 E
Guadalajara, Mexico	**175**	20 40N	103 20W
Guadalajara, Spain	**50**	40 37N	3 12W
Guadalquivir →	**50**	36 47N	6 22W
Guadalupe = Guadeloupe ■	**180**	16 20N	61 40W
Guadalupe Bravos	**174**	31 23N	106 7W
Guadarrama, Sierra de	**50**	41 0N	4 0W
Guadeloupe ■	**180**	16 20N	61 40W
Guadiana →	**50**	37 14N	7 22W
Guadix	**50**	37 18N	3 11W
Guaíra	**191**	24 5S	54 10W
Guajará-Mirim	**187**	10 50S	65 20W
Gualeguay	**190**	33 10S	59 14W
Gualeguaychú	**190**	33 3S	59 31W
Guam	**10**	13 27N	144 45 E
Guanabacoa	**178**	23 8N	82 18W
Guanacaste, Cordillera del	**179**	10 40N	85 4W
Guanahani = San Salvador	**178**	24 0N	74 40W
Guanajay	**178**	22 56N	82 42W
Guanajuato	**177**	21 1N	101 15W
Guanajuato □	**177**	21 0N	101 0W
Guanare	**184**	8 42N	69 12W
Guangdong □	**99**	23 0N	113 0 E
Guangxi Zhuangzu Zizhiqu □	**99**	24 0N	109 0 E
Guangzhou	**99**	23 5N	113 10 E
Guantánamo	**178**	20 10N	75 14W
Guaporé →	**187**	11 55S	65 4W
Guaqui	**187**	16 41S	68 54W
Guarapuava	**191**	25 20S	51 30W
Guarda	**50**	40 32N	7 20W
Guardafui, C. = Asir, Ras	**133**	11 55N	51 10 E
Guatemala	**177**	14 40N	90 22W
Guatemala ■	**177**	15 40N	90 30W
Guaviare →	**184**	4 3N	67 44W
Guayama	**180**	17 59N	66 7W
Guayaquil	**184**	2 15S	79 52W
Guayaquil, G. de	**186**	3 10S	81 0W
Guaymas	**174**	27 56N	110 54W
Guddu Barrage	**89**	28 30N	69 50 E
Gudur	**90**	14 12N	79 55 E
Guelph	**151**	43 35N	80 20W
Guernica	**50**	43 19N	2 40W
Guernsey	**36**	49 30N	2 35W
Guerrero □	**177**	17 40N	100 0W
Guilin	**99**	25 18N	110 15 E
Guimarães	**188**	2 9S	44 42W
Guinea ■	**130**	10 20N	10 0W
Guinea, Gulf of	**130**	3 0N	2 30 E
Guinea-Bissau ■	**130**	12 0N	15 0W
Güines	**178**	22 50N	82 0W
Guiyang	**99**	26 32N	106 40 E
Guizhou □	**99**	27 0N	107 0 E
Gujarat □	**91**	23 20N	71 0 E
Gujranwala	**89**	32 10N	74 12 E
Gujrat	**89**	32 40N	74 2 E
Gulbarga	**91**	17 20N	76 50 E
Gulf, The	**85**	27 0N	50 0 E
Gulfport	**169**	30 21N	89 3W
Gulgong	**116**	32 20S	149 49 E
Gull Lake	**152**	50 10N	108 29W
Gümüsane	**81**	40 30N	39 30 E
Guna	**91**	24 40N	77 19 E
Gundagai	**117**	35 3S	148 6 E
Gunnedah	**116**	30 59S	150 15 E
Gunningbar Cr. →	**116**	31 14S	147 6 E
Guntakal	**90**	15 11N	77 27 E
Guntersville	**169**	34 18N	86 16W
Guntur	**92**	16 23N	80 30 E
Gurdaspur	**89**	32 5N	75 31 E
Gurgaon	**89**	28 27N	77 1 E
Gurkha	**92**	28 5N	84 40 E
Gurupi →	**188**	1 13S	46 6W
Guryev = Atyraū	**70**	47 5N	52 0 E
Gusau	**131**	12 12N	6 40 E
Guthrie	**168**	35 55N	97 30W
Guyana ■	**185**	5 0N	59 0W
Guyenne	**36**	44 30N	0 40 E

Guyra	**116**	30 15S	151 40 E
Gwalior	**91**	26 12N	78 10 E
Gwent □	**27**	51 45N	2 55W
Gweru	**137**	19 28S	29 45 E
Gwynedd □	**26**	53 0N	4 0W
Gyandzha	**70**	40 45N	46 20 E
Gyaring Hu	**101**	34 50N	97 40 E
Gydanskiy P-ov.	**69**	70 0N	78 0 E
Gympie	**116**	26 11S	152 38 E
Gyoda	**107**	36 10N	139 30 E
Gyöngyös	**59**	47 48N	20 0 E
Győr	**59**	47 41N	17 40 E
Gypsumville	**153**	51 45N	98 40W

H

Ha 'Arava	**80**	30 50N	35 20 E
Ha Giang	**95**	22 50N	104 59 E
Haarlem	**40**	52 23N	4 39 E
Habana, La	**178**	23 8N	82 22W
Hachijō-Jima	**105**	33 5N	139 45 E
Hachinohe	**103**	40 30N	141 29 E
Hachiōji	**107**	35 40N	139 20 E
Ḫadera	**80**	32 27N	34 55 E
Hadhramaut = Haḑramawt	**83**	15 30N	49 30 E
Hadiya	**82**	25 30N	36 56 E
Haḑramawt	**83**	15 30N	49 30 E
Hadrians Wall	**28**	55 0N	2 30W
Haeju	**98**	38 3N	125 45 E
Haerhpin = Harbin	**98**	45 48N	126 40 E
Hafar al Bāţin	**82**	28 25N	46 0 E
Hafnarfjörður	**64**	64 4N	21 57W
Haft-Gel	**84**	31 30N	49 32 E
Hagen	**42**	51 21N	7 29 E
Hagerstown	**164**	39 39N	77 46W
Hagi	**108**	34 30N	131 22 E
Hags Hd.	**35**	52 57N	9 30W
Hague, The = 's-Gravenhage	**40**	52 7N	4 17 E
Hai'an	**99**	32 37N	120 27 E
Haifa = Ḫefa	**80**	32 46N	35 0 E
Haikou	**99**	20 1N	110 16 E
Ḥā'il	**82**	27 28N	41 45 E
Hailar	**98**	49 10N	119 38 E
Hailey	**162**	43 30N	114 15W
Haileybury	**151**	47 30N	79 38W
Hainan	**99**	19 0N	110 0 E
Hainan Dao	**99**	19 0N	109 30 E
Haiphong	**95**	20 47N	106 41 E
Haiti ■	**180**	19 0N	72 30W
Hakken-Zan	**106**	34 10N	135 54 E
Hakodate	**103**	41 45N	140 44 E
Ḥalab	**80**	36 10N	37 15 E
Halaib	**129**	22 12N	36 30 E
Halberstadt	**43**	51 53N	11 2 E
Halfmoon Bay	**123**	46 50S	168 5 E
Halifax, Canada	**148**	44 38N	63 35W
Halifax, U.K.	**28**	53 43N	1 51W
Halifax B.	**121**	18 50S	147 0 E
Hallands län □	**61**	56 50N	12 50 E
Halle	**43**	51 29N	12 0 E
Halls Creek	**114**	18 16S	127 38 E
Halmahera	**113**	0 40N	128 0 E
Halmstad	**61**	56 41N	12 52 E
Hälsingborg = Helsingborg	**61**	56 3N	12 42 E
Hamada	**109**	34 56N	132 4 E
Hamadān	**81**	34 52N	48 32 E
Hamadān □	**81**	35 0N	49 0 E
Hamāh	**80**	35 5N	36 40 E
Hamakita	**107**	34 45N	137 47 E
Hamamatsu	**106**	34 45N	137 45 E
Hamar	**60**	60 48N	11 7 E
Hamburg	**43**	53 32N	9 59 E
Hämeenlinna	**67**	61 0N	24 28 E
Hamelin Pool	**120**	26 22S	114 20 E
Hameln	**42**	52 7N	9 24 E
Hamhung	**98**	39 54N	127 30 E
Hamilton, Australia	**119**	37 45S	142 2 E
Hamilton, Bermuda	**180**	32 15N	64 45W
Hamilton, Canada	**151**	43 15N	79 50W
Hamilton, N.Z.	**122**	37 47S	175 19 E
Hamilton, U.K.	**31**	55 47N	4 2W
Hamilton, U.S.A.	**167**	39 20N	84 35W
Hamm	**42**	51 40N	7 49 E
Hammerfest	**67**	70 39N	23 41 E
Hammond, Ind., U.S.A.	**167**	41 40N	87 30W
Hammond, La., U.S.A.	**169**	30 32N	90 30W
Hampshire □	**25**	51 3N	1 20W
Hampshire Downs	**25**	51 10N	1 10W
Hampton	**165**	37 4N	76 18W
Hanamaki	**103**	39 23N	141 7 E
Hancock	**150**	47 10N	88 40W
Handa	**106**	34 53N	137 0 E
Handan	**98**	36 35N	114 28 E
Haney	**154**	49 12N	122 40W
Hanford	**173**	36 23N	119 39W
Hangayn Nuruu	**100**	47 30N	100 0 E
Hangchou = Hangzhou	**99**	30 18N	120 11 E
Hangö	**67**	59 50N	22 57 E
Hangu	**98**	39 18N	117 53 E
Hangzhou	**99**	30 18N	120 11 E
Hanna	**155**	51 40N	111 54W
Hannibal	**166**	39 42N	91 22W
Hannover	**42**	52 23N	9 43 E
Hanoi	**95**	21 5N	105 55 E
Hanover = Hannover	**42**	52 23N	9 43 E
Hanover, N.H., U.S.A.	**148**	43 43N	72 17W
Hanover, Pa., U.S.A.	**164**	39 46N	76 59W
Hansi	**89**	29 10N	75 57 E
Hanyū	**107**	36 10N	139 32 E
Hanzhong	**99**	33 10N	107 1 E
Haora	**92**	22 37N	88 20 E
Haparanda	**67**	65 52N	24 8 E
Ḥaraḑ, Si. Arabia	**83**	24 22N	49 0 E
Ḥaraḑ, Yemen	**83**	16 26N	43 5 E
Harare	**137**	17 43S	31 2 E
Harbin	**98**	45 48N	126 40 E
Harbour Breton	**149**	47 29N	55 50W
Harbour Grace	**149**	47 40N	53 22W
Hardap Dam	**136**	24 32S	17 50 E
Hardenberg	**41**	52 34N	6 37 E
Harderwijk	**41**	52 21N	5 38 E
Hardinxveld	**40**	51 49N	4 53 E
Hardwar = Haridwar	**89**	29 58N	78 9 E
Harer	**133**	9 20N	42 8 E
Harfleur	**38**	49 30N	0 10 E
Hargeisa	**133**	9 30N	44 2 E
Hari →	**111**	1 16S	104 5 E
Haridwar	**89**	29 58N	78 9 E
Harima-Nada	**109**	34 30N	134 35 E
Harīrūd →	**86**	34 20N	62 30 E
Harlech	**26**	52 52N	4 7W
Harlingen, Neths.	**41**	53 11N	5 25 E
Harlingen, U.S.A.	**161**	26 20N	97 50W
Harlow	**25**	51 47N	0 9 E
Harney Basin	**171**	43 30N	119 0W
Härnösand	**66**	62 38N	18 0 E
Harriman	**169**	36 0N	84 35W
Harris	**32**	57 50N	6 55W
Harris L.	**118**	31 10S	135 10 E
Harrisburg, Ill., U.S.A.	**167**	37 42N	88 30W
Harrisburg, Pa., U.S.A.	**164**	40 18N	76 52W
Harrison	**168**	36 10N	93 4W
Harrison, C.	**147**	54 55N	57 55W
Harrison B.	**142**	70 25N	151 30W
Harrisonburg	**165**	38 28N	78 52W
Harrogate	**28**	53 59N	1 32W
Harrow	**25**	51 35N	0 15W
Hartford	**164**	41 47N	72 41W
Hartland Pt.	**27**	51 2N	4 32W
Hartlepool	**29**	54 42N	1 11W
Hartsville	**165**	34 23N	80 2W
Harvey, Australia	**120**	33 5S	115 54 E
Harvey, U.S.A.	**167**	41 40N	87 40W
Harwich	**25**	51 56N	1 18 E
Haryana □	**89**	29 0N	76 10 E
Hashima	**106**	35 20N	136 40 E
Hashimoto	**106**	34 19N	135 37 E
Hastings, N.Z.	**122**	39 39S	176 52 E
Hastings, U.K.	**25**	50 51N	0 36 E

Hastings, U.S.A.	**163**	40 34N	98 22W
Hastings Ra.	**116**	31 15S	152 14 E
Hatano	**107**	35 22N	139 14 E
Hathras	**89**	27 36N	78 6 E
Hatteras, C.	**165**	35 10N	75 30W
Hattiesburg	**169**	31 20N	89 20W
Hatvan	**59**	47 40N	19 45 E
Hau Bon = Cheo Reo	**95**	13 25N	108 28 E
Hauraki Gulf	**122**	36 35S	175 5 E
Haut Atlas	**126**	32 30N	5 0W
Havana = Habana, La	**178**	23 8N	82 22W
Havant	**25**	50 51N	0 59W
Havelock	**151**	44 26N	77 53W
Haverfordwest	**26**	51 48N	4 59W
Haverhill	**164**	42 50N	71 2W
Havre	**163**	48 34N	109 40W
Havre, Le	**38**	49 30N	0 5 E
Hawaii □	**160**	20 30N	157 0W
Hawaiian Is.	**160**	20 30N	156 0W
Hawea Lake	**123**	44 28S	169 19 E
Hawera	**122**	39 35S	174 19 E
Hawick	**31**	55 25N	2 48W
Hawke B.	**122**	39 25S	177 20 E
Hawkesbury	**151**	45 37N	74 37W
Hawthorne	**172**	38 31N	118 37W
Hay, Australia	**117**	34 30S	144 51 E
Hay, U.K.	**26**	52 4N	3 9W
Hay River	**145**	60 51N	115 44W
Hayward's Heath	**25**	51 0N	0 5W
Hazard	**165**	37 18N	83 10W
Hazaribag	**92**	23 58N	85 26 E
Hazebrouck	**38**	50 42N	2 31 E
Hazelton	**154**	55 20N	127 42W
Hazleton	**164**	40 58N	76 0W
Healdsburg	**172**	38 33N	122 51W
Healesville	**117**	37 35S	145 30 E
Heanor	**29**	53 1N	1 20W
Hearst	**150**	49 40N	83 41W
Hebei □	**98**	39 0N	116 0 E
Hebel	**116**	28 58S	147 47 E
Hebrides	**16**	57 30N	7 0W
Hebron = Al Khalīl	**80**	31 32N	35 6 E
Hebron	**147**	58 5N	62 30W
Hecate Str.	**154**	53 10N	130 30W
Hechuan	**99**	30 2N	106 12 E
Hedmark fylke □	**60**	61 17N	11 40 E
Heemstede	**40**	52 22N	4 37 E
Heerenveen	**41**	52 57N	5 55 E
Heerlen	**41**	50 55N	6 0 E
Ḥefa	**80**	32 46N	35 0 E
Hefei	**99**	31 52N	117 18 E
Hegang	**98**	47 20N	130 19 E
Heidelberg	**42**	49 23N	8 41 E
Heilbronn	**42**	49 8N	9 13 E
Heilongjiang □	**98**	48 0N	126 0 E
Heilunkiang = Heilongjiang □	**98**	48 0N	126 0 E
Heinze Is.	**94**	14 25N	97 45 E
Hekimhan	**81**	38 50N	38 0 E
Hekinan	**106**	34 52N	137 0 E
Hekla	**16**	63 56N	19 35W
Helena, Ark., U.S.A.	**169**	34 30N	90 35W
Helena, Mont., U.S.A.	**163**	46 40N	112 0W
Helensburgh	**30**	56 0N	4 44W
Helmand →	**87**	31 12N	61 34 E
Helmond	**41**	51 29N	5 41 E
Helmsdale	**33**	58 7N	3 40W
Helsingborg	**61**	56 3N	12 42 E
Helsinki	**67**	60 15N	25 3 E
Helston	**27**	50 7N	5 17W
Helvellyn	**28**	54 31N	3 1W
Hemel Hempstead	**25**	51 45N	0 28W
Hempstead	**164**	30 5N	96 5W
Henan □	**99**	34 0N	114 0 E
Henderson	**165**	36 20N	78 25W
Hendersonville	**165**	35 21N	82 28W
Hengelo	**41**	52 16N	6 48 E
Hengyang	**99**	26 51N	112 30 E
Hénin-Beaumont	**38**	50 25N	2 58 E
Hennebont	**36**	47 49N	3 19W
Henrietta Maria C.	**140**	55 9N	82 20W
Henty	**117**	35 30S	147 0 E
Henzada	**93**	17 38N	95 26 E
Herāt	**87**	34 20N	62 7 E
Herāt □	**87**	35 0N	62 0 E
Herbert →	**121**	18 31S	146 17 E
Herbiers, Les	**36**	46 52N	1 0W
Hercegnovi	**52**	42 30N	18 33 E
Hercegovina = Bosnia & Herzegovina □	**52**	44 0N	18 0 E
Hereford	**24**	52 4N	2 42W
Hereford and Worcester □	**24**	52 10N	2 30W
Herford	**42**	52 7N	8 40 E
Hermosillo	**174**	29 4N	110 58W
Heroica = Caborca	**174**	30 40N	112 10W
Heroica Nogales = Nogales	**174**	31 20N	110 56W
Heron Bay	**150**	48 40N	86 25W
Herrin	**166**	37 50N	89 0W
Hertford □	**25**	51 51N	0 5W
's-Hertogenbosch	**40**	51 42N	5 17 E
Hesse = Hessen □	**42**	50 40N	9 20 E
Hessen □	**42**	50 40N	9 20 E
Hewett, C.	**146**	70 16N	67 45W
Hexham	**28**	54 58N	2 7W
Heysham	**28**	54 5N	2 53W
Heywood	**119**	38 8S	141 37 E
Hi-no-Misaki	**109**	35 26N	132 38 E
Hialeach	**170**	25 49N	80 17W
Hibiki-Nada	**108**	34 0N	130 0 E
Hickory	**165**	35 46N	81 17W
Hida-Gawa →	**106**	35 26N	137 3 E
Hida-Sammyaku	**106**	36 30N	137 40 E
Hida-Sanchi	**106**	36 10N	137 0 E
Hidaka	**109**	35 30N	134 44 E
Hidalgo □	**177**	20 30N	99 0W
Hidalgo del Parral	**174**	26 56N	105 40W
Higashi-matsuyama	**107**	36 2N	139 25 E
Higashiōsaka	**106**	34 40N	135 37 E
Higasi-Suidō	**108**	34 0N	129 30 E
High Atlas = Haut Atlas	**126**	32 30N	5 0W
High Point	**165**	35 57N	79 58W
High Prairie	**155**	55 30N	116 30W
Highland □	**32**	57 30N	5 0W
Highland Park	**167**	42 10N	87 50W
Ḥijārah, Ṣaḥrā' al	**84**	30 25N	44 30 E
Hikari	**108**	33 58N	131 58 E
Hikone	**106**	35 15N	136 10 E
Hildesheim	**43**	52 9N	9 55 E
Hillegom	**40**	52 18N	4 35 E
Hillsboro	**171**	45 31N	123 0W
Hillston	**117**	33 30S	145 31 E
Hilo	**160**	19 44N	155 5W
Hilversum	**40**	52 14N	5 10 E
Himachal Pradesh □	**89**	31 30N	77 0 E
Himalaya, Mts.	**101**	29 0N	84 0 E
Hime-Jima	**108**	33 43N	131 40 E
Himeji	**109**	34 50N	134 40 E
Himi	**106**	36 50N	137 0 E
Ḥimṣ	**80**	34 40N	36 45 E
Hinchinbrook I.	**121**	18 20S	146 15 E
Hinckley	**25**	52 33N	1 21W
Hindmarsh	**119**	34 54S	138 34 E
Hindu Kush	**89**	36 0N	71 0 E
Hindupur	**90**	13 49N	77 32 E
Hines Creek	**155**	56 20N	118 40W
Hingoli	**91**	19 41N	77 15 E
Hinton	**165**	37 40N	80 51W
Hirado	**108**	33 22N	129 33 E
Hirakarta	**106**	34 48N	135 40 E
Hirakud Dam	**92**	21 32N	83 45 E
Hirata	**109**	35 24N	132 49 E
Hiratsuka	**107**	35 19N	139 21 E
Hirosaki	**103**	40 34N	140 28 E
Hiroshima	**109**	34 24N	132 30 E
Hirson	**38**	49 55N	4 4 E
Hispaniola	**180**	19 0N	71 0W
Hita	**108**	33 20N	130 58 E
Hitachi	**107**	36 36N	140 39 E
Hitachiota	**107**	36 30N	140 30 E
Hitchin	**25**	51 57N	0 16W
Hitoyoshi	**108**	32 13N	130 45 E
Hitra	**65**	63 30N	8 45 E
Hiuchi-Nada	**109**	34 5N	133 20 E

Ho Chi Minh City = Thanh Pho Ho Chi Minh	**95**	10 58N	106 40 E
Hoa Binh	**95**	20 50N	105 20 E
Hobart	**119**	42 50S	147 21 E
Hobbs	**161**	32 40N	103 3W
Hodaka-Dake	**106**	36 17N	137 39 E
Hódmezövásárhely	**59**	46 28N	20 22 E
Hoek van Holland	**40**	52 0N	4 7 E
Hofsjökull	**64**	64 49N	18 48W
Hōfu	**108**	34 3N	131 34 E
Hogan Group	**117**	39 13S	147 1 E
Hoh Xil Shan	**101**	35 0N	89 0 E
Hohhot	**98**	40 52N	111 40 E
Hōjō	**109**	33 58N	132 46 E
Hokitika	**123**	42 42S	171 0 E
Hokkaidō □	**103**	43 30N	143 0 E
Holbrook	**117**	35 42S	147 18 E
Holderness	**29**	53 45N	0 5W
Holdrege	**163**	40 26N	99 22W
Holguín	**178**	20 50N	76 20W
Holland	**167**	42 47N	86 7W
Holly Springs	**169**	34 45N	89 25W
Hollywood, Calif., U.S.A.	**173**	34 7N	118 25W
Hollywood, Fla., U.S.A.	**170**	26 0N	80 9W
Holsteinsborg	**147**	66 40N	53 30W
Holsworthy	**27**	50 48N	4 21W
Holt	**64**	63 33N	19 48W
Holy I., Scotland, U.K.	**31**	55 31N	5 4W
Holy I., Wales, U.K.	**26**	53 17N	4 37W
Holyhead	**26**	53 18N	4 38W
Holyoke	**164**	42 14N	72 37W
Hombori	**130**	15 20N	1 38W
Home Hill	**121**	19 43S	147 25 E
Homer	**142**	59 40N	151 35W
Homs = Ḥimş	**80**	34 40N	36 45 E
Honan = Henan □	**99**	34 0N	114 0 E
Hondo	**108**	32 27N	130 12 E
Honduras ■	**179**	14 40N	86 30W
Honduras, Golfo de	**177**	16 50N	87 0W
Hong Kong ■	**99**	22 11N	114 14 E
Hongha →	**95**	22 0N	104 0 E
Hongshui He →	**99**	23 48N	109 30 E
Honiton	**27**	50 48N	3 11W
Honolulu	**160**	21 19N	157 52W
Honshū	**106**	36 0N	138 0 E
Hoogeveen	**41**	52 44N	6 30 E
Hook Hd.	**35**	52 8N	6 57W
Hook of Holland = Hoek van Holland	**40**	52 0N	4 7 E
Hoorn	**40**	52 38N	5 4 E
Hope, Canada	**154**	49 25N	121 25 E
Hope, U.S.A.	**168**	33 40N	93 36W
Hope Town	**178**	26 35N	76 57W
Hopedale	**147**	55 28N	60 13W
Hopei = Hebei □	**98**	39 0N	116 0 E
Hopelchén	**177**	19 46N	89 51W
Hopetoun, Vic., Australia	**119**	35 42S	142 22 E
Hopetoun, W. Austral., Australia	**120**	33 57S	120 7 E
Hopkinsville	**169**	36 52N	87 26W
Hoquiam	**171**	46 50N	123 55W
Hordaland fylke □	**60**	60 25N	6 15 E
Hormoz	**85**	27 35N	55 0 E
Hormuz Str.	**85**	26 30N	56 30 E
Horn, Cape = Hornos, Cabo de	**192**	55 50S	67 30W
Hornavan	**66**	66 15N	17 30 E
Hornell	**164**	42 23N	77 41W
Hornos, Cabo de	**192**	55 50S	67 30W
Hornsby	**117**	33 42S	151 2 E
Hornsea	**29**	53 55N	0 10W
Horqin Youyi Qianqi	**98**	46 5N	122 3 E
Horsens	**61**	55 52N	9 51 E
Horsham	**119**	36 44S	142 13 E
Horton →	**145**	69 56N	126 52W
Hoshiarpur	**89**	31 30N	75 58 E
Hospet	**90**	15 15N	76 20 E
Hospitalet de Llobregat	**51**	41 21N	2 6 E
Hoste, I.	**192**	55 0S	69 0W
Hot Springs	**168**	34 30N	93 0W
Houghton	**150**	47 9N	88 39W
Houghton-le-Spring	**28**	54 51N	1 28W
Houhora	**122**	34 49S	173 9 E
Houlton	**148**	46 5N	67 50W
Houma	**169**	29 35N	90 44W
Houston, Canada	**154**	54 25N	126 39W
Houston, U.S.A.	**168**	29 50N	95 20W
Houtman Abrolhos	**120**	28 43S	113 48 E
Hovd	**100**	48 2N	91 37 E
Hove	**25**	50 50N	0 10W
Howe, C.	**117**	37 30S	150 0 E
Howrah = Haora	**92**	22 37N	88 20 E
Hoy I.	**33**	58 50N	3 15W
Hrádec Králové	**58**	50 15N	15 50 E
Hrvatska = Croatia ■	**52**	45 20N	18 0 E
Hsiamen = Xiamen	**99**	24 25N	118 4 E
Hsian = Xi'an	**99**	34 15N	109 0 E
Hsinhailien = Lianyungang	**99**	34 40N	119 11 E
Hsüchou = Xuzhou	**99**	34 18N	117 10 E
Hua Hin	**94**	12 34N	99 58 E
Huacho	**186**	11 10S	77 35W
Huainan	**99**	32 38N	116 58 E
Huallaga →	**186**	5 0S	75 30W
Huambo	**134**	12 42S	15 54 E
Huancane	**187**	15 10S	69 44W
Huancavelica	**186**	12 50S	75 5W
Huancayo	**186**	12 5S	75 12W
Huanchaca	**187**	20 15S	66 40W
Huang Hai = Yellow Sea	**99**	35 0N	123 0 E
Huang Ho →	**98**	37 30N	118 50 E
Huangshi	**99**	30 10N	115 3 E
Huánuco	**186**	9 55S	76 15W
Huaraz	**186**	9 30S	77 32W
Huascarán	**186**	9 8S	77 36W
Huasco	**190**	28 30S	71 15W
Huatabampo	**174**	26 50N	109 38W
Huautla	**177**	17 51N	100 5W
Hubei □	**99**	31 0N	112 0 E
Hubli-Dharwad = Dharwad	**90**	15 22N	75 15 E
Huddersfield	**28**	53 38N	1 49W
Hudiksvall	**66**	61 43N	17 10 E
Hudson	**164**	42 15N	73 46W
Hudson →	**164**	40 42N	74 2W
Hudson Bay	**146**	52 51N	102 23W
Hudson Str.	**146**	62 0N	70 0W
Hudson's Hope	**155**	56 0N	121 54W
Hue	**95**	16 30N	107 35 E
Huehuetenango	**177**	15 20N	91 28W
Huelva	**50**	37 18N	6 57W
Huesca	**51**	42 8N	0 25W
Hughenden	**121**	20 52S	144 10 E
Huila, Nevado del	**184**	3 0N	76 0W
Huinca Renancó	**190**	34 51S	64 22W
Huixtla	**177**	15 9N	92 28W
Huizen	**40**	52 18N	5 14 E
Hukawng Valley	**93**	26 30N	96 30 E
Hull, Canada	**151**	45 25N	75 44W
Hull, U.K.	**29**	53 45N	0 20W
Hulst	**40**	51 17N	4 2 E
Hulun Nur	**98**	49 0N	117 30 E
Humaitá	**187**	27 2S	58 31W
Humber →	**29**	53 40N	0 10W
Humberside □	**29**	53 50N	0 30W
Humboldt, Canada	**152**	52 15N	105 9W
Humboldt, U.S.A.	**169**	35 50N	88 55W
Humboldt →	**172**	40 2N	118 31W
Hume, L.	**117**	36 0S	147 0 E
Húnaflói	**64**	65 50N	20 50W
Hunan □	**99**	27 30N	111 30 E
Hunedoara	**56**	45 40N	22 50 E
Hungary ■	**59**	47 20N	19 20 E
Hungary, Plain of	**17**	47 0N	20 0 E
Hŭngnam	**98**	39 49N	127 45 E
Hunsrück	**42**	49 30N	7 0 E
Hunstanton	**29**	52 57N	0 30 E
Hunter Ra.	**117**	32 45S	150 15 E
Huntingdon	**25**	52 20N	0 11W
Huntington, Ind., U.S.A.	**167**	40 52N	85 30W
Huntington, W. Va., U.S.A.	**165**	38 20N	82 30W
Huntington Beach	**173**	33 40N	118 0W
Huntly	**122**	37 34S	175 11 E
Huntsville, Canada	**151**	45 20N	79 14W

Huntsville, Ala., U.S.A. **169** 34 45N 86 35W
Huntsville, Tex., U.S.A. **168** 30 45N 95 35W
Huonville **119** 43 0S 147 5 E
Hupeh = Hubei □ **99** 31 0N 112 0 E
Huron, L. **150** 45 0N 83 0W
Hurricane **173** 37 10N 113 12W
Húsavík **64** 66 3N 17 21W
Hutchinson **161** 38 3N 97 59W
Hvar **52** 43 11N 16 28 E
Hwang Ho = Huang Ho → **98** 37 30N 118 50 E
Hwange **137** 18 18S 26 30 E
Hyden **120** 32 24S 118 53 E
Hyderabad, India **91** 17 22N 78 29 E
Hyderabad, Pakistan **88** 25 23N 68 24 E
Hyères **37** 43 8N 6 9 E
Hyndman Pk. **162** 43 50N 114 10W
Hythe **24** 51 4N 1 5 E
Hyūga **108** 32 25N 131 35 E

I

Iaşi **57** 47 10N 27 40 E
Ibadan **131** 7 22N 3 58 E
Ibagué **184** 4 20N 75 20W
Ibara **109** 34 36N 133 28 E
Ibaraki **106** 34 49N 135 34 E
Ibarra **184** 0 21N 78 7W
Iberian Peninsula **16** 40 0N 5 0W
Ibiza **51** 38 54N 1 26 E
Ibuki-Sanchi **106** 35 25N 136 18 E
Ibusuki **108** 31 12N 130 40 E
Icá **186** 14 0S 75 48W
Içá → **184** 2 55S 67 58W
Iceland ■ **64** 65 0N 19 0W
Icha **73** 55 30N 156 0 E
Ich'ang = Yichang **99** 30 40N 111 20 E
Ichchapuram **92** 19 10N 84 40 E
Ichihara **107** 35 28N 140 5 E
Ichikawa **107** 35 44N 139 55 E
Ichinomiya **106** 35 18N 136 48 E
Ichinoseki **103** 38 55N 141 8 E
Idaho □ **162** 44 10N 114 0W
Idaho Falls **163** 43 30N 112 1W
Ídhi Óros **55** 35 15N 24 45 E
Ídhra **55** 37 20N 23 28 E
Ierápetra **55** 35 0N 25 44 E
Ife **131** 7 30N 4 31 E
Igloolik **146** 69 20N 81 49W
Iguaçu → **191** 25 36S 54 36W
Iguaçu, Cat. del **191** 25 41S 54 26W
Iguaçu Falls = Iguaçu, Cat. del **191** 25 41S 54 26W
Iguala de la Independencia **177** 18 21N 99 32W
Iguassu = Iguaçu → **191** 25 36S 54 36W
Iida **107** 35 35N 137 50 E
Iisalmi **67** 63 32N 27 10 E
Iizuka **108** 33 38N 130 42 E
IJmuiden **40** 52 28N 4 35 E
IJsselmeer **40** 52 45N 5 20 E
IJsselstein **40** 52 1N 5 2 E
Ikaría **55** 37 35N 26 10 E
Ikeda **109** 34 1N 133 48 E
Iki **108** 33 45N 129 42 E
Iki-Kaikyō **108** 33 40N 129 45 E
Île-de-France **37** 49 0N 2 20 E
Ilebo **134** 4 17S 20 55 E
Ilfracombe **27** 51 13N 4 8W
Ilhéus **189** 14 49S 39 2W
Ili → **71** 45 53N 77 10 E
Iliamna L. **142** 59 35N 155 30W
Iliodhrómia **55** 39 12N 23 50 E
Ilkeston **29** 52 59N 1 19W
Illampu = Ancohuma, Nevada **187** 16 0S 68 50W
Illinois □ **166** 40 15N 89 30W
Illinois → **166** 38 55N 90 28W
Ilo **187** 17 40S 71 20W
Iloilo **112** 10 45N 122 33 E
Ilorin **131** 8 30N 4 35 E
Imabari **109** 34 4N 133 0 E
Imari **108** 33 15N 129 52 E
Imatra **67** 61 12N 28 48 E
Immingham **29** 53 37N 0 12W
Imperial **152** 51 21N 105 28W
Imphal **92** 24 48N 93 56 E
İmroz = Gökçeada **55** 40 10N 25 50 E
Ina **107** 35 50N 138 0 E
Iñapari **187** 11 0S 69 40W
Inari **67** 68 54N 27 5 E
Inarijärvi **67** 69 0N 28 0 E
Inazawa **106** 35 15N 136 47 E
Inchon **98** 37 27N 126 40 E
Indalsälven → **66** 62 36N 17 30 E
Independence, Kans., U.S.A. **166** 37 10N 95 43W
Independence, Mo., U.S.A. **166** 39 3N 94 25W
India ■ **78** 20 0N 78 0 E
Indian Head **152** 50 30N 103 41W
Indiana **164** 40 38N 79 9W
Indiana □ **167** 40 0N 86 0W
Indianapolis **167** 39 42N 86 10W
Indigirka → **73** 70 48N 148 54 E
Indonesia ■ **111** 5 0S 115 0 E
Indore **91** 22 42N 75 53 E
Indre → **36** 47 16N 0 19 E
Indus → **88** 24 20N 67 47 E
Indus, Mouth of the **88** 24 0N 68 0 E
İnebolu **80** 41 55N 33 40 E
İnegöl **80** 40 5N 29 31 E
Ingersoll **151** 43 4N 80 55W
Ingham **121** 18 43S 146 10 E
Ingleborough **28** 54 11N 2 23W
Inglewood, N.Z. **122** 39 9S 174 14 E
Inglewood, U.S.A. **173** 33 58N 118 21W
Ingolstadt **43** 48 45N 11 26 E
Ingushetia □ **70** 43 20N 44 50 E
Inhambane **137** 23 54S 35 30 E
Ining = Yining **100** 43 58N 81 10 E
Inishmore **35** 53 8N 9 45W
Inishowen **34** 55 14N 7 15W
Inn → **43** 48 35N 13 28 E
Innamincka **118** 27 44S 140 46 E
Inner Hebrides **32** 57 0N 6 30W
Inner Mongolia = Nei Monggol Zizhiqu □ **98** 42 0N 112 0 E
Innisfail, Australia **121** 17 33S 146 5 E
Innisfail, Canada **155** 52 0N 113 57W
In'no-shima **109** 34 19N 133 10 E
Innsbruck **45** 47 16N 11 23 E
Inoucdjouac **146** 58 25N 78 15W
Inowrocław **58** 52 50N 18 12 E
Inquisivi **187** 16 50S 67 10W
Insein **93** 16 50N 96 5 E
Interlaken **44** 46 41N 7 50 E
Inuvik **144** 68 16N 133 40W
Inuvik □ **144** 70 0N 130 0W
Inuyama **106** 35 23N 136 56 E
Inveraray **30** 56 13N 5 5W
Invercargill **123** 46 24S 168 24 E
Inverell **116** 29 45S 151 8 E
Invergordon **33** 57 41N 4 10W
Inverness **33** 57 29N 4 12W
Investigator Group **119** 34 45S 134 20 E
Investigator Str. **119** 35 30S 137 0 E
Ioánnina **54** 39 42N 20 47 E
Iola **166** 38 0N 95 20W
Iona **30** 56 20N 6 25W
Ionian Is. = Iónioi Nísoi **54** 38 40N 20 0 E
Ionian Sea **54** 37 30N 17 30 E
Iónioi Nísoi **54** 38 40N 20 0 E
Íos **55** 36 41N 25 20 E
Iowa □ **166** 42 18N 93 30W
Iowa City **166** 41 40N 91 35W
Iowa Falls **166** 42 30N 93 15W
Ipiales **184** 0 50N 77 37W
Ipin = Yibin **99** 28 45N 104 32 E
Ípiros □ **54** 39 30N 20 30 E
Ipoh **96** 4 35N 101 5 E
Ipswich, Australia **116** 27 35S 152 40 E
Ipswich, U.K. **25** 52 4N 1 9 E
Iquique **187** 20 19S 70 5W

Iquitos	**186**	3 45S	73 10W
Iracoubo	**185**	5 30N	53 10W
Iráklion	**55**	35 20N	25 12 E
Iran ■	**86**	33 0N	53 0 E
Iran Ra.	**111**	2 20N	114 50 E
Irapuato	**177**	20 41N	101 28W
Iraq ■	**81**	33 0N	44 0 E
Irbid	**80**	32 35N	35 48 E
Ireland ■	**34**	53 0N	8 0W
Irian Jaya □	**113**	4 0S	137 0 E
Iriri →	**188**	3 52S	52 37W
Irish Republic ■	**20**	53 0N	8 0W
Irish Sea	**20**	54 0N	5 0W
Irkutsk	**74**	52 18N	104 20 E
Irō-Zaki	**107**	34 36N	138 51 E
Iron Gate = Portile de Fier	**56**	44 42N	22 30 E
Iron Knob	**118**	32 46S	137 8 E
Iron Mountain	**150**	45 49N	88 4W
Ironbridge	**24**	52 38N	2 29W
Ironton	**167**	38 35N	82 40W
Ironwood	**150**	46 30N	90 10W
Iroquois Falls	**151**	48 46N	80 41W
Irrawaddy →	**93**	15 50N	95 6 E
Irtysh →	**69**	61 4N	68 52 E
Irumu	**135**	1 32N	29 53 E
Irún	**51**	43 20N	1 52W
Irvine	**31**	55 37N	4 40W
Irvinestown	**34**	54 28N	7 38W
Ísafjörður	**64**	66 5N	23 9W
Isahaya	**108**	32 52N	130 2 E
Íschia	**49**	40 45N	13 51 E
Ise	**106**	34 25N	136 45 E
Ise-Wan	**106**	34 43N	136 43 E
Isère →	**37**	44 59N	4 51 E
Isesaki	**107**	36 19N	139 12 E
Ishikari-Wan	**103**	43 25N	141 1 E
Ishinomaki	**103**	38 32N	141 20 E
Ishioka	**107**	36 11N	140 16 E
Ishkuman	**89**	36 30N	73 50 E
Ishpeming	**150**	46 30N	87 40W
İskenderun	**80**	36 32N	36 10 E
Islamabad	**89**	33 40N	73 10 E
Island L.	**153**	53 47N	94 25W
Island Pond	**148**	48 25N	56 23W
Islay	**30**	55 46N	6 10W
Isle-Adam, L'	**39**	49 6N	2 14 E
Isle Royale	**150**	48 0N	88 50W
Isparta	**80**	37 47N	30 30 E
Israel ■	**80**	32 0N	34 50 E
Issoire	**37**	45 32N	3 15 E
Issyk-Kul, Ozero	**71**	42 25N	77 15 E
İstanbul	**80**	41 0N	29 0 E
Istra	**52**	45 10N	14 0 E
Istria = Istra	**52**	45 10N	14 0 E
Itabuna	**189**	14 48S	39 16W
Itaituba	**185**	4 10S	55 50W
Itajaí	**191**	27 50S	48 39W
Italy ■	**19**	42 0N	13 0 E
Itaquatiara	**185**	2 58S	58 30W
Itaquí	**191**	29 8S	56 30W
Itchen →	**24**	50 57N	1 20W
Ithaca = Itháki	**54**	38 25N	20 40 E
Ithaca	**164**	42 25N	76 30W
Itháki	**54**	38 25N	20 40 E
Ito	**107**	34 58N	139 5 E
Ituaçu	**189**	13 50S	41 18W
Ituiutaba	**188**	19 0S	49 25W
Iturup, Ostrov	**75**	45 0N	148 0 E
Ivano-Frankovsk	**68**	48 40N	24 40 E
Ivanovo, Belorussia	**68**	52 7N	25 29 E
Ivanovo, Russia	**68**	57 5N	41 0 E
Ivigtut	**147**	61 14N	48 12W
Iviza = Ibiza	**51**	38 54N	1 26 E
Ivory Coast ■	**130**	7 30N	5 0W
Iwai-Jima	**108**	33 47N	131 58 E
Iwaki	**105**	37 3N	140 55 E
Iwakuni	**109**	34 15N	132 8 E
Iwami	**109**	35 32N	134 15 E
Iwamizawa	**103**	43 12N	141 46 E
Iwanuma	**103**	38 7N	140 51 E
Iwata	**107**	34 42N	137 51 E
Iwo	**131**	7 39N	4 9 E
Ixiamas	**187**	13 50S	68 5W
Ixtepec	**177**	16 34N	95 6W
Ixtlán	**175**	20 11N	102 24W
Ixtlán de Juárez	**177**	17 23N	96 28W
Iyo	**109**	33 45N	132 45 E
Iyo-mishima	**109**	33 58N	133 30 E
Iyo-Nada	**109**	33 40N	132 20 E
Izamal	**177**	20 56N	89 1W
Izhevsk	**69**	56 51N	53 14 E
İzmir	**80**	38 25N	27 8 E
İzmit	**80**	40 45N	29 50 E
Izu-Hantō	**107**	34 45N	139 0 E
Izumi	**108**	32 5N	130 22 E
Izumi-sano	**106**	34 23N	135 18 E
Izumiotsu	**106**	34 30N	135 24 E
Izumo	**109**	35 20N	132 46 E

J

Jabalpur	**91**	23 9N	79 58 E
Jacarèzinho	**191**	23 5S	50 0W
Jackson, Mich., U.S.A.	**167**	42 18N	84 25W
Jackson, Miss., U.S.A.	**169**	32 20N	90 10W
Jackson, Tenn., U.S.A.	**169**	35 40N	88 50W
Jacksonville, Fla., U.S.A.	**170**	30 15N	81 38W
Jacksonville, Ill., U.S.A.	**166**	39 42N	90 15W
Jacksonville, N.C., U.S.A.	**165**	34 50N	77 29W
Jacksonville, Tex., U.S.A.	**168**	31 58N	95 19W
Jacmel	**180**	18 14N	72 32W
Jacobabad	**88**	28 20N	68 29 E
Jacques Cartier, Dét. de	**149**	50 0N	63 30W
Jadotville = Likasi	**135**	10 55S	26 48 E
Jaén, Peru	**186**	5 25S	78 40W
Jaén, Spain	**50**	37 44N	3 43W
Jaffa = Tel Aviv-Yafo	**80**	32 4N	34 48 E
Jaffna	**90**	9 45N	80 2 E
Jagdalpur	**92**	19 3N	82 0 E
Jaguariaíva	**191**	24 10S	49 50W
Jagüey Grande	**178**	22 35N	81 7W
Jahrom	**85**	28 30N	53 31 E
Jaipur	**91**	27 0N	75 50 E
Jakarta	**111**	6 9S	106 49 E
Jalalabad	**87**	34 30N	70 29 E
Jalapa, Guatemala	**177**	14 39N	89 59W
Jalapa, Mexico	**177**	17 43N	92 49W
Jalgaon	**91**	21 0N	75 42 E
Jalisco □	**175**	20 20N	103 40W
Jalna	**91**	19 48N	75 38 E
Jalón →	**51**	41 47N	1 4W
Jalpaiguri	**92**	26 32N	88 46 E
Jamaica ■	**180**	18 10N	77 30W
Jamalpur, Bangla.	**92**	24 52N	89 56 E
Jamalpur, India	**92**	25 18N	86 28 E
Jambi	**111**	1 38S	103 30 E
James →	**163**	42 52N	97 18W
James B.	**140**	51 30N	80 0W
Jamestown, Australia	**118**	33 10S	138 32 E
Jamestown, N. Dak., U.S.A.	**163**	46 54N	98 42W
Jamestown, N.Y., U.S.A.	**164**	42 5N	79 18W
Jamkhandi	**91**	16 30N	75 15 E
Jammu	**89**	32 43N	74 54 E
Jammu & Kashmir □	**89**	34 25N	77 0 E
Jamnagar	**90**	22 30N	70 6 E
Jamshedpur	**92**	22 44N	86 12 E
Jan Mayen Is.	**13**	71 0N	9 0W
Janesville	**166**	42 39N	89 1W
Januária	**188**	15 25S	44 25W
Jaora	**91**	23 40N	75 10 E
Japan ■	**79**	36 0N	136 0 E
Japan, Sea of	**102**	40 0N	135 0 E
Japurá →	**185**	3 8S	64 46W
Jargalant = Hovd	**100**	48 2N	91 37 E
Jargeau	**39**	47 50N	2 1 E
Jarosław	**58**	50 2N	22 42 E
Jāsk	**85**	25 38N	57 45 E
Jasło	**59**	49 45N	21 30 E
Jasper, Canada	**155**	52 55N	118 5W

Jasper, U.S.A.	**169**	33 48N	87 16W
Jassy = Iaşi	**57**	47 10N	27 40 E
Jataí	**188**	17 58S	51 48W
Jaú	**188**	22 10S	48 30W
Jaunpur	**92**	25 46N	82 44 E
Java, I.	**111**	7 0S	110 0 E
Java Sea	**111**	4 35S	107 15 E
Javhlant = Ulyasutay	**100**	47 56N	97 28 E
Jean Marie River	**144**	61 32N	120 38W
Jean Rabel	**180**	19 50N	73 5W
Jedburgh	**31**	55 28N	2 33W
Jędrzejów	**58**	50 35N	20 15 E
Jefferson, Mt.	**171**	44 45N	121 50W
Jefferson City	**166**	38 34N	92 10W
Jeffersonville	**167**	38 20N	85 42W
Jelenia Góra	**58**	50 50N	15 45 E
Jena	**43**	50 56N	11 33 E
Jenkins	**165**	37 13N	82 41W
Jennings	**168**	30 10N	92 45W
Jeparit	**119**	36 8S	142 1 E
Jequié	**189**	13 51S	40 5W
Jequitinhonha	**189**	16 30S	41 0W
Jérémie	**180**	18 40N	74 10W
Jerez de García Salinas	**175**	22 39N	103 0W
Jerez de la Frontera	**50**	36 41N	6 7W
Jerez de los Caballeros	**50**	38 20N	6 45W
Jericho	**121**	23 38S	146 6 E
Jerilderie	**117**	35 20S	145 41 E
Jerome	**148**	47 37N	82 14W
Jersey, I.	**36**	49 13N	2 7W
Jersey City	**164**	40 41N	74 8W
Jerseyville	**166**	39 5N	90 20W
Jerusalem	**80**	31 47N	35 10 E
Jesselton = Kota Kinabalu	**112**	6 0N	116 4 E
Jhang Maghiana	**89**	31 15N	72 22 E
Jhansi	**91**	25 30N	78 36 E
Jharsuguda	**92**	21 56N	84 5 E
Jhelum →	**89**	31 20N	72 10 E
Jhunjhunu	**89**	28 10N	75 30 E
Jiamusi	**98**	46 40N	130 26 E
Ji'an	**99**	27 6N	114 59 E
Jiangmen	**99**	22 32N	113 0 E
Jiangsu □	**99**	33 0N	120 0 E
Jiangxi □	**99**	27 30N	116 0 E
Jian'ou	**99**	27 3N	118 17 E
Jiao Xian	**98**	36 18N	120 1 E
Jiaozuo	**99**	35 16N	113 12 E
Jiaxing	**99**	30 49N	120 45 E
Jiayi	**99**	23 30N	120 24 E
Jibuti = Djibouti ■	**133**	12 0N	43 0 E
Jiddah	**82**	21 29N	39 10 E
Jido	**93**	29 2N	94 58 E
Jihlava	**59**	49 28N	15 35 E
Jilin	**98**	43 44N	126 30 E
Jilong	**99**	25 8N	121 42 E
Jima	**132**	7 40N	36 47 E
Jiménez	**174**	27 8N	104 54W
Jinan	**98**	36 38N	117 1 E
Jingdezhen	**99**	29 20N	117 11 E
Jining, Nei Mongol Zizhiqu, China	**98**	41 5N	113 0 E
Jining, Shandong, China	**99**	35 22N	116 34 E
Jinja	**132**	0 25N	33 12 E
Jinnah Barrage	**89**	32 58N	71 33 E
Jinotega	**179**	13 6N	85 59W
Jinotepe	**179**	11 50N	86 10W
Jinshi	**99**	29 40N	111 50 E
Jinzhou	**98**	41 5N	121 3 E
Jipijapa	**184**	1 0S	80 40W
Jiquilpan de Juárez	**175**	19 59N	102 43W
Jisr ash Shughūr	**80**	35 49N	36 18 E
Jiujiang	**99**	29 42N	115 58 E
Jixi	**98**	45 20N	130 50 E
João Pessoa	**189**	7 10S	34 52W
Jodhpur	**91**	26 23N	73 8 E
Joensuu	**67**	62 37N	29 49 E
Jogjakarta = Yogyakarta	**111**	7 49S	110 22 E
Jōhana	**106**	36 30N	136 57 E
Johannesburg	**137**	26 10S	28 2 E
John o' Groats	**33**	58 39N	3 3W
Johnson City, N.Y., U.S.A.	**164**	42 7N	75 57W

Johnson City, Tenn., U.S.A.	**165**	36 18N	82 21W
Johnston	**31**	51 45N	5 5W
Johnstown, N.Y., U.S.A.	**164**	43 1N	74 20W
Johnstown, Pa., U.S.A.	**164**	40 19N	78 53W
Johor □	**96**	2 5N	103 20 E
Johor Baharu	**96**	1 28N	103 46 E
Joigny	**39**	48 0N	3 20 E
Joinvile	**191**	26 15S	48 55 E
Joliet	**167**	41 30N	88 0W
Joliette	**151**	46 3N	73 24W
Jolo	**112**	6 0N	121 0 E
Jonesboro	**169**	35 50N	90 45W
Jönköping	**60**	57 45N	14 10 E
Jönköpings län □	**61**	57 30N	14 30 E
Jonquière	**148**	48 27N	71 14W
Joplin	**168**	37 0N	94 31W
Jordan ■	**80**	31 0N	36 0 E
Jordan →	**80**	31 48N	35 32 E
Jorhat	**93**	26 45N	94 12 E
José de San Martín	**192**	44 4S	70 26W
Jowzjān □	**87**	36 10N	66 0 E
Juan de Fuca Str.	**142**	48 15N	124 0W
Juan Fernández, Arch. de	**183**	33 50S	80 0W
Juàzeiro	**189**	9 30S	40 30W
Juàzeiro do Norte	**189**	7 10S	39 18W
Jubbulpore = Jabalpur	**91**	23 9N	79 58 E
Júcar →	**51**	39 5N	0 10W
Juchitán de Zaragoza	**177**	16 26N	95 1W
Jugoslavia = Yugoslavia ■	**52**	44 0N	21 0 E
Juiz de Fora	**188**	21 43S	43 19W
Juli	**187**	16 10S	69 25W
Juliaca	**187**	15 25S	70 10W
Julianehåb	**147**	60 43N	46 0W
Jullundur	**89**	31 20N	75 40 E
Jumla	**92**	29 15N	82 13 E
Jumna = Yamuna →	**92**	25 30N	81 53 E
Junagadh	**91**	21 30N	70 30 E
Jundiaí	**191**	24 30S	47 0W
Juneau	**143**	58 20N	134 20W
Junee	**117**	34 53S	147 35 E
Junggar Pendi	**100**	44 30N	86 0 E
Junín	**190**	34 33S	60 57W
Jura, Europe	**37**	46 35N	6 5 E
Jura, U.K.	**30**	56 0N	5 50W
Jurado	**184**	7 7N	77 46W
Juruá →	**184**	2 37S	65 44W
Juruena	**187**	13 0S	58 10W
Juruena →	**187**	7 20S	58 3W
Juticalpa	**179**	14 40N	86 12W
Jutland = Jylland	**61**	56 25N	9 30 E
Juventud, I. de la	**178**	21 40N	82 40W
Jylland	**61**	56 25N	9 30 E
Jyväskylä	**67**	62 14N	25 50 E

K

Kaapstad = Cape Town	**136**	33 55S	18 22 E
Kabala	**130**	9 38N	11 37W
Kabardino-Balkaria □	**70**	43 30N	43 30 E
Kabarega Falls	**132**	2 15N	31 30 E
Kabīr Kūh	**84**	33 0N	47 30 E
Kābul	**87**	34 28N	69 11 E
Kābul □	**87**	34 30N	69 0 E
Kabwe	**135**	14 30S	28 29 E
Kachin □	**93**	26 0N	97 30 E
Kadan Kyun	**94**	12 30N	98 20 E
Kadina	**119**	34 0S	137 43 E
Kaduna	**131**	10 30N	7 21 E
Kaédi	**126**	16 9N	13 28W
Kāf	**80**	31 25N	37 29 E
Kafirévs, Ákra	**55**	38 9N	24 38 E
Kafue →	**135**	15 30S	26 0 E
Kaga	**106**	36 16N	136 15 E
Kagoshima	**108**	31 35N	130 33 E
Kagoshima-Wan	**108**	31 25N	130 40 E
Kai, Kepulauan	**113**	5 55S	132 45W
Kaieteur Falls	**185**	5 1N	59 10W
Kaifeng	**99**	34 49N	114 30 E

Kaikoura Ra.	**123**	41 59S	173 41 E
Kailua	**160**	19 39N	156 0W
Kaimanawa Mts.	**122**	39 15S	175 56 E
Kainan	**106**	34 9N	135 12 E
Kainji Res.	**131**	10 1N	4 40 E
Kaipara Harbour	**122**	36 25S	174 14 E
Kaiserslautern	**42**	49 30N	7 43 E
Kaitaia	**122**	35 8S	173 17 E
Kajaani	**67**	64 17N	27 46 E
Kajana = Kajaani	**67**	64 17N	27 46 E
Kakabeka Falls	**150**	48 24N	89 37W
Kakamigahara	**106**	35 28N	136 48 E
Kakanui Mts.	**123**	45 10S	170 30 E
Kakegawa	**107**	34 45N	138 1 E
Kakinada	**92**	16 57N	82 11 E
Kakogawa	**109**	34 46N	134 51 E
Kalabáka	**54**	39 42N	21 39 E
Kalahari	**136**	24 0S	21 30 E
Kalamata	**54**	37 3N	22 10 E
Kalamazoo	**167**	42 20N	85 35W
Kalamazoo →	**167**	42 40N	86 12W
Kalat	**88**	29 8N	66 31 E
Kalaupapa	**160**	21 12N	156 59W
Kalemie	**135**	5 55S	29 9 E
Kalgan = Zhangjiakou	**98**	40 48N	114 55 E
Kalgoorlie-Boulder	**120**	30 40S	121 22 E
Kálimnos	**55**	37 0N	27 0 E
Kalinin = Tver	**68**	56 55N	35 55 E
Kaliningrad	**68**	54 42N	20 32 E
Kalispell	**162**	48 10N	114 22W
Kalisz	**58**	51 45N	18 8 E
Kalmar	**61**	56 40N	16 20 E
Kalmar län □	**61**	57 25N	16 0 E
Kalmykia □	**70**	46 5N	46 1 E
Kalocsa	**59**	46 32N	19 0 E
Kaluga	**68**	54 35N	36 10 E
Kama →	**68**	55 45N	52 0 E
Kamaishi	**103**	39 16N	141 53 E
Kamakura	**107**	35 19N	139 33 E
Kamaran	**82**	15 21N	42 35 E
Kamchatka, P-ov.	**73**	57 0N	160 0 E
Kamenka	**69**	53 10N	44 5 E
Kamensk Uralskiy	**69**	56 25N	62 2 E
Kamenskoye	**73**	62 45N	165 30 E
Kameoka	**106**	35 0N	135 35 E
Kameyama	**106**	34 51N	136 27 E
Kami-koshiki-Jima	**108**	31 50N	129 52 E
Kamioka	**106**	36 25N	137 15 E
Kamloops	**155**	50 40N	120 20W
Kampala	**132**	0 20N	32 30 E
Kampar	**96**	4 18N	101 9 E
Kampen	**41**	52 33N	5 53 E
Kampot	**95**	10 36N	104 10 E
Kampuchea = Cambodia ■	**95**	12 15N	105 0 E
Kamsack	**152**	51 34N	101 54W
Kamui-Misaki	**103**	43 20N	140 21 E
Kamyshin	**68**	50 10N	45 24 E
Kananga	**134**	5 55S	22 18 E
Kanawha →	**165**	38 50N	82 8W
Kanazawa	**106**	36 30N	136 38 E
Kanchenjunga	**92**	27 50N	88 10 E
Kanchipuram	**90**	12 52N	79 45 E
Kandahar = Qandahār	**87**	31 32N	65 30 E
Kandalaksha	**69**	67 9N	32 30 E
Kandi	**131**	11 7N	2 55 E
Kandos	**117**	32 45S	149 58 E
Kandy	**90**	7 18N	80 43 E
Kangar	**97**	6 27N	100 12 E
Kangaroo I.	**119**	35 45S	137 0 E
Kangean Is.	**113**	6 55S	115 23 E
Kangnŭng	**98**	37 45N	128 54 E
Kangto	**93**	27 50N	92 35 E
Kaniapiskau →	**146**	56 40N	69 30W
Kanin, P-ov.	**69**	68 0N	45 0 E
Kaniva	**119**	36 22S	141 18 E
Kankakee	**167**	41 6N	87 50W
Kankakee →	**167**	41 23N	88 16W
Kankan	**130**	10 23N	9 15W
Kanmuri-Yama	**109**	34 30N	132 4 E
Kannapolis	**165**	35 32N	80 37W
Kano	**131**	12 2N	8 30 E
Kan'onji	**109**	34 7N	133 39 E
Kanoya	**108**	31 25N	130 50 E
Kanpur	**91**	26 28N	80 20 E
Kansas □	**161**	38 40N	98 0W
Kansas →	**158**	39 7N	94 36W
Kansas City, Kans., U.S.A.	**166**	39 0N	94 40W
Kansas City, Mo., U.S.A.	**166**	39 3N	94 30W
Kansk	**74**	56 20N	95 37 E
Kansu = Gansu □	**98**	36 0N	104 0 E
Kantō □	**107**	36 15N	139 30 E
Kantō-Sanchi	**107**	35 59N	138 50 E
Kanuma	**107**	36 34N	139 42 E
Kaohsiung = Gaoxiong	**99**	22 38N	120 18 E
Kaolack	**130**	14 5N	16 8W
Kāpīsā □	**87**	35 0N	69 20 E
Kapoeta	**129**	4 50N	33 35 E
Kapuas →	**111**	0 25S	109 20 E
Kapunda	**119**	34 20S	138 56 E
Kapuskasing	**150**	49 25N	82 30W
Kaputar, Mt.	**116**	30 15S	150 10 E
Kara Bogaz Gol, Zaliv	**70**	41 0N	53 30 E
Kara Kum = Karakum, Peski	**70**	39 30N	60 0 E
Kara Sea	**69**	75 0N	70 0 E
Karabük	**80**	41 12N	32 37 E
Karachi	**88**	24 53N	67 0 E
Karad	**91**	17 15N	74 10 E
Karadeniz Boğazı	**80**	41 10N	29 10 E
Karaganda	**71**	49 50N	73 10 E
Karaj	**86**	35 48N	51 0 E
Karakalpakstan □	**70**	43 0N	58 0 E
Karakoram Pass	**89**	35 33N	77 50 E
Karakoram Ra.	**89**	35 30N	77 0 E
Karakum, Peski	**70**	39 30N	60 0 E
Karaman	**80**	37 14N	33 13 E
Karamea Bight	**123**	41 22S	171 40 E
Karasuk	**71**	53 44N	78 2 E
Karatau, Khrebet	**71**	43 30N	69 30 E
Karbalā	**84**	32 36N	44 3 E
Karelian Rep. □	**68**	65 30N	32 30 E
Karen	**94**	12 49N	92 53 E
Kariba Lake	**137**	16 40S	28 25 E
Karimata I.	**111**	1 40S	109 0 E
Karimnagar	**91**	18 26N	79 10 E
Karimunjawa, Kepulauan	**111**	5 50S	110 30 E
Kariya	**106**	34 58N	137 1 E
Karl-Marx-Stadt = Chemnitz	**43**	50 50N	12 55 E
Karlskrona	**61**	56 10N	15 35 E
Karlsruhe	**42**	49 3N	8 23 E
Karlstad	**60**	59 23N	13 30 E
Karnal	**89**	29 42N	77 2 E
Karnaphuli Res.	**93**	22 40N	92 20 E
Karnataka □	**90**	13 15N	77 0 E
Kärnten □	**45**	46 52N	13 30 E
Kárpathos	**55**	35 37N	27 10 E
Kars	**81**	40 40N	43 5 E
Karshi	**70**	38 53N	65 48 E
Kasai →	**134**	3 30S	16 10 E
Kasaoka	**109**	34 30N	133 30 E
Kaseda	**108**	31 25N	130 19 E
Kāshān	**86**	34 5N	51 30 E
Kashi	**100**	39 30N	76 2 E
Kashihara	**106**	34 27N	135 46 E
Kashima	**108**	33 7N	130 6 E
Kashima-Nada	**107**	36 0N	140 45 E
Kashiwa	**107**	35 52N	139 59 E
Kāshmar	**86**	35 16N	58 26 E
Kashmir	**78**	34 0N	76 0 E
Kashun Noerh = Gaxun Nur	**100**	42 22N	100 30 E
Kásos	**55**	35 20N	26 55 E
Kassala	**129**	16 0N	36 0 E
Kassel	**42**	51 19N	9 32 E
Kastoría	**54**	40 30N	21 19 E
Kasugai	**106**	35 12N	136 59 E
Kasukabe	**107**	35 58N	139 49 E
Kasumiga-Ura	**107**	36 0N	140 25 E
Kasur	**89**	31 5N	74 25 E
Katanning	**120**	33 40S	117 33 E
Katha	**93**	24 10N	96 30 E
Katherîna, Gebel	**128**	28 30N	33 57 E
Katherine	**114**	14 27S	132 20 E
Kathiawar	**91**	22 20N	71 0 E

Katihar **92** 25 34N 87 36 E
Katmandu **92** 27 45N 85 20 E
Katoomba **117** 33 41S 150 19 E
Katowice **58** 50 17N 19 5 E
Katsuta **107** 36 25N 140 31 E
Katsuura **107** 35 10N 140 20 E
Katsuyama **106** 36 3N 136 30 E
Kattegatt **61** 57 0N 11 20 E
Katwijk-aan-Zee **40** 52 12N 4 24 E
Kauai **160** 22 0N 159 30W
Kaukauna **167** 44 20N 88 13W
Kaunas **68** 54 54N 23 54 E
Kawachi-Nagano **106** 34 28N 135 31 E
Kawagoe **107** 35 55N 139 29 E
Kawaguchi **107** 35 52N 139 45 E
Kawanoe **109** 34 1N 133 34 E
Kawarau **122** 45 3S 168 45 E
Kawasaki **107** 35 35N 139 42 E
Kayah □ **93** 19 15N 97 15 E
Kayes **130** 14 25N 11 30W
Kayseri **80** 38 45N 35 30 E
Kazachye **72** 70 52N 135 58 E
Kazakstan ■ **71** 50 0N 70 0 E
Kazan **68** 55 48N 49 3 E
Kazanlúk **53** 42 38N 25 20 E
Kāzerūn **85** 29 38N 51 40 E
Kazo **107** 36 7N 139 36 E
Kéa **55** 37 35N 24 22 E
Keaau **160** 19 37N 155 3W
Kebnekaise **66** 67 53N 18 33 E
Kecskemét **59** 46 57N 19 42 E
Kedah □ **96** 5 50N 100 40 E
Kediri **111** 7 51S 112 1 E
Keeling Is. = Cocos Is. **111** 12 10S 96 55 E
Keene **164** 42 57N 72 17W
Keetmanshoop **136** 26 35S 18 8 E
Keewatin **153** 49 46N 94 34W
Keewatin □ **145** 63 20N 95 0W
Kefallinía **54** 38 20N 20 30 E
Keflavík **64** 64 2N 22 35W
Keighley **28** 53 52N 1 54W
Keith, Australia **119** 36 6S 140 20 E
Keith, U.K. **33** 57 33N 2 58W
Kelang **96** 3 2N 101 26 E
Kelantan □ **96** 5 10N 102 0 E
Kelantan → **96** 6 13N 102 14 E
Kellerberrin **120** 31 36S 117 38 E
Kellogg **162** 47 30N 116 5W
Kells = Ceanannus Mor **34** 53 42N 6 53W
Kelowna **155** 49 50N 119 25W
Kelso, U.K. **31** 55 36N 2 27W
Kelso, U.S.A. **171** 46 10N 122 57W
Keluang **96** 2 3N 103 18 E
Kelvington **152** 52 10N 103 30W
Kemerovo **71** 55 20N 86 5 E
Kemi **67** 65 44N 24 34 E
Kemi → **67** 67 30N 28 30 E
Kempsey **116** 31 1S 152 50 E
Kendal **28** 54 19N 2 44W
Keng Tung **93** 21 0N 99 30 E
Kenitra **126** 34 15N 6 40W
Kenmare **35** 51 52N 9 35W
Kennewick **171** 46 11N 119 2W
Keno Hill **144** 63 57N 135 18W
Kenora **153** 49 47N 94 29W
Kenosha **167** 42 33N 87 48W
Kent **164** 41 8N 81 20W
Kent □ **25** 51 12N 0 40 E
Kent Group **117** 39 30S 147 20 E
Kent Pen. **145** 68 30N 107 0W
Kentucky □ **167** 37 20N 85 0W
Kentucky → **167** 38 41N 85 11W
Kenya ■ **133** 1 0N 38 0 E
Kenya, Mt. **132** 0 10S 37 18 E
Keokuk **166** 40 25N 91 24W
Kepsut **80** 39 40N 28 9 E
Kerala □ **90** 11 0N 76 15 E
Kerang **117** 35 40S 143 55 E
Kerch **68** 45 20N 36 20 E
Kerki **70** 37 50N 65 12 E
Kérkira **54** 39 38N 19 50 E
Kerkrade **41** 50 53N 6 4 E
Kermadec Is. **122** 30 0S 178 15W
Kermān **85** 30 15N 57 1 E
Kermān □ **85** 30 0N 57 0 E
Kermānshāh = Bākhtarān **84** 34 23N 47 0 E
Kerrobert **152** 52 0N 109 11W
Kerry □ **35** 52 7N 9 35W
Kerulen → **98** 48 48N 117 0 E
Kestenga **68** 66 0N 31 50 E
Keswick **28** 54 35N 3 9W
Ketchikan **143** 55 25N 131 40W
Kettering **156** 39 41N 84 10W
Kewanee **166** 41 18N 89 55W
Keweenaw B. **150** 46 56N 88 23W
Key West **159** 24 33N 82 0W
Keyser **164** 39 26N 79 0W
Khabarovsk **75** 48 30N 135 5 E
Khalkhāl **81** 37 37N 48 32 E
Khalkís **55** 38 27N 23 42 E
Khalmer Yu **69** 67 58N 65 1 E
Khambhat **91** 22 23N 72 33 E
Khambhat, G. of **91** 20 45N 72 30 E
Khamir **82** 16 0N 44 0 E
Khānābād **87** 36 45N 69 5 E
Khānaqīn **81** 34 23N 45 25 E
Khandwa **91** 21 49N 76 22 E
Khanewal **89** 30 20N 71 55 E
Khaniá **55** 35 30N 24 4 E
Khanka, Ozero **75** 45 0N 132 24 E
Kharagpur **92** 22 20N 87 25 E
Kharkov **68** 49 58N 36 20 E
Khartoum = El Khartûm **129** 15 31N 32 35 E
Khashm el Girba **129** 14 59N 35 58 E
Khaskovo **53** 41 56N 25 30 E
Khatanga **72** 72 0N 102 20 E
Khatanga → **72** 72 55N 106 0 E
Khenchela **127** 35 28N 7 11 E
Kherson **68** 46 35N 32 35 E
Kheta → **72** 71 54N 102 6 E
Khíos, I. **55** 38 20N 26 0 E
Khmer Rep. = Cambodia ■ **95** 12 15N 105 0 E
Khodzhent **71** 40 17N 69 37 E
Khojak P. **88** 30 55N 66 30 E
Kholm **87** 36 45N 67 40 E
Khon Kaen **95** 16 30N 102 47 E
Khoper → **68** 49 30N 42 20 E
Khorāsān □ **86** 34 0N 58 0 E
Khorat = Nakhon Ratchasima **95** 14 59N 102 12 E
Khorat, Cao Nguyen **95** 15 30N 102 50 E
Khorog **71** 37 30N 71 36 E
Khorramābād **84** 33 30N 48 25 E
Khorrāmshahr **84** 30 29N 48 15 E
Khulna **92** 22 45N 89 34 E
Khulna □ **92** 22 25N 89 35 E
Khushab **89** 32 20N 72 20 E
Khūzestān □ **84** 31 0N 49 0 E
Khvor **86** 33 45N 55 0 E
Khvoy **81** 38 35N 45 0 E
Khyber Pass **89** 34 10N 71 8 E
Kiama **117** 34 40S 150 50 E
Kiangsi = Jiangxi □ **99** 27 30N 116 0 E
Kiangsu = Jiangsu □ **99** 33 0N 120 0 E
Kichiga **73** 59 50N 163 5 E
Kicking Horse Pass **155** 51 28N 116 16W
Kidderminster **24** 52 24N 2 13W
Kidnappers, C. **122** 39 38S 177 5 E
Kiel **43** 54 16N 10 8 E
Kielce **58** 50 52N 20 42 E
Kieler Bucht **42** 54 30N 10 30 E
Kiev = Kiyev **68** 50 30N 30 28 E
Kigali **135** 1 59S 30 4 E
Kii-Hantō **106** 34 0N 135 45 E
Kii-Sanchi **106** 34 20N 136 0 E
Kii-Suidō **109** 33 40N 135 0 E
Kikládhes □ **55** 37 0N 25 0 E
Kikuchi **108** 32 59N 130 47 E
Kilcoy **116** 26 59S 152 30 E
Kildare □ **35** 53 10N 6 50W
Kilimanjaro **132** 3 7S 37 20 E
Kilis **80** 36 50N 37 10 E

Kilkenny	**35**	52 40N	7 17W
Kilkenny □	**35**	52 35N	7 15W
Killala B.	**34**	54 20N	9 12W
Killarney, Canada	**153**	49 10N	99 40W
Killarney, Ireland	**35**	52 2N	9 30W
Killary Harbour	**34**	53 38N	9 52W
Killiecrankie, Pass of	**33**	56 44N	3 46W
Kilmarnock	**31**	55 36N	4 30W
Kilmore	**117**	37 25S	144 53 E
Kilrush	**35**	52 39N	9 30W
Kimba	**118**	33 8S	136 23 E
Kimberley, Australia	**114**	16 20S	127 0 E
Kimberley, Canada	**155**	49 40N	115 59W
Kimberley, S. Africa	**136**	28 43S	24 46 E
Kinabalu	**112**	6 3N	116 14 E
Kincardine	**150**	44 10N	81 40W
Kindersley	**152**	51 30N	109 10W
Kindia	**130**	10 0N	12 52W
King Frederick VI Land = Kong Frederik VI.s Kyst	**147**	63 0N	43 0W
King George Is.	**140**	57 20N	80 30W
King I. = Kadan Kyun	**94**	12 30N	98 20 E
King I., Australia	**119**	39 50S	144 0 E
King I., Canada	**154**	52 10N	127 40W
King Sd.	**114**	16 50S	123 20 E
King William I.	**145**	69 10N	97 25W
Kingaroy	**116**	26 32S	151 51 E
Kingman	**173**	35 12N	114 2W
King's Lynn	**29**	52 45N	0 25 E
Kingscote	**119**	35 40S	137 38 E
Kingsport	**165**	36 33N	82 36W
Kingston, Canada	**151**	44 14N	76 30W
Kingston, Jamaica	**180**	18 0N	76 50W
Kingston, N.Z.	**123**	45 20S	168 43 E
Kingston, U.S.A.	**164**	41 55N	74 0W
Kingston South East	**119**	36 51S	139 55 E
Kingstown	**180**	13 10N	61 10W
Kingsville	**150**	42 2N	82 45W
Kingussie	**33**	57 5N	4 2W
Kinistino	**152**	52 57N	105 2W
Kinki □	**106**	33 30N	136 0 E
Kinnairds Hd.	**33**	57 40N	2 0W
Kinsale, Old Hd. of	**35**	51 37N	8 32W
Kinshasa	**134**	4 20S	15 15 E
Kinston	**165**	35 18N	77 35W
Kintyre	**30**	55 30N	5 35W
Kintyre, Mull of	**30**	55 17N	5 55W
Kinu-Gawa →	**107**	35 36N	139 57 E
Kiparissia	**54**	37 15N	21 40 E
Kirensk	**74**	57 50N	107 55 E
Kirghizia = Kyrgyzstan ■	**71**	42 0N	75 0 E
Kiribati ■	**122**	1 0N	176 0 E
Kırıkkale	**80**	39 51N	33 32 E
Kirin = Jilin	**98**	43 44N	126 30 E
Kiritimati	**123**	1 58N	157 27W
Kirkcaldy	**31**	56 7N	3 10W
Kirkcudbright	**31**	54 50N	4 3W
Kirkee	**91**	18 34N	73 56 E
Kirkintilloch	**31**	55 57N	4 10W
Kirkland Lake	**151**	48 9N	80 2W
Kirksville	**166**	40 8N	92 35W
Kirkūk	**81**	35 30N	44 21 E
Kirkwall	**33**	58 59N	2 59W
Kirov	**69**	58 35N	49 40 E
Kirovabad = Gyandzha	**70**	40 45N	46 20 E
Kirovograd	**68**	48 35N	32 20 E
Kirthar Range	**88**	27 0N	67 0 E
Kiruna	**66**	67 52N	20 15 E
Kiryū	**107**	36 24N	139 20 E
Kisangani	**135**	0 35N	25 15 E
Kisarazu	**107**	35 23N	139 55 E
Kiselevsk	**71**	54 5N	86 39 E
Kishangarh	**89**	27 50N	70 30 E
Kishinev	**68**	47 0N	28 50 E
Kishiwada	**106**	34 28N	135 22 E
Kiskunfelégyháza	**59**	46 42N	19 53 E
Kiso-Gawa →	**106**	35 20N	136 45 E
Kisumu	**132**	0 3S	34 45 E
Kita	**130**	13 5N	9 25W
Kita-Ura	**107**	36 0N	140 34 E
Kitakami-Gawa →	**103**	38 25N	141 19 E
Kitakyūshū	**108**	33 50N	130 50 E
Kitale	**132**	1 0N	35 0 E
Kitami	**103**	43 48N	143 54 E
Kitchener	**151**	43 27N	80 29W
Kíthira	**55**	36 9N	23 0 E
Kíthnos	**55**	37 26N	24 27 E
Kitikmeot □	**145**	70 0N	110 0W
Kitimat	**154**	54 3N	128 38W
Kitsuki	**108**	33 25N	131 37 E
Kittakittaooloo, L.	**118**	28 3S	138 14 E
Kitwe	**135**	12 54S	28 13 E
Kiyev	**68**	50 30N	30 28 E
Klagenfurt	**45**	46 38N	14 20 E
Klaipeda	**68**	55 43N	21 10 E
Klamath →	**172**	41 40N	124 4W
Klamath Falls	**171**	42 20N	121 50W
Klamath Mts.	**172**	41 20N	123 0W
Kleena Kleene	**154**	52 0N	124 59W
Klondike	**144**	64 0N	139 26W
Kluane L.	**144**	61 15N	138 40W
Klyuchevsk	**73**	55 50N	160 30 E
Knaresborough	**28**	54 1N	1 29W
Knockmealdown Mts.	**35**	52 16N	8 0W
Knossos	**55**	35 16N	25 10 E
Knoxville, Iowa, U.S.A.	**166**	41 20N	93 5W
Knoxville, Tenn., U.S.A.	**165**	35 58N	83 57W
Ko Chang	**95**	12 0N	102 20 E
Ko Kut	**95**	11 40N	102 32 E
Koartac	**146**	60 55N	69 40W
Kobarid	**52**	46 15N	13 30 E
Kobayashi	**108**	31 56N	130 59 E
Kobdo = Hovd	**100**	48 2N	91 37 E
Kōbe	**106**	34 45N	135 10 E
København	**61**	55 41N	12 34 E
Koblenz	**42**	50 21N	7 36 E
Kobroor, Kepulauan	**113**	6 10S	134 30 E
Kočani	**53**	41 55N	22 25 E
Kōchi	**109**	33 30N	133 35 E
Kochiu = Gejiu	**99**	23 20N	103 10 E
Kodaira	**107**	35 44N	139 29 E
Kodiak I.	**142**	57 30N	152 45W
Kōfu	**107**	35 40N	138 30 E
Koga	**107**	36 11N	139 43 E
Kogota	**103**	38 33N	141 3 E
Koh-i-Bābā	**87**	34 30N	67 0 E
Kohat	**89**	33 40N	71 29 E
Kokand	**71**	40 30N	70 57 E
Kokchetav	**71**	53 20N	69 25 E
Koko Kyunzu	**94**	14 10N	93 25 E
Kokomo	**167**	40 30N	86 6W
Kokopo	**115**	4 22S	152 19 E
Koksoak →	**146**	58 30N	68 10W
Kokubu	**108**	31 44N	130 46 E
Kola Pen. = Kolskiy Poluostrov	**69**	67 30N	38 0 E
Kolar	**90**	13 12N	78 15 E
Kolar Gold Fields	**90**	12 58N	78 16 E
Kolarovgrad	**53**	43 18N	26 55 E
Kolding	**61**	55 30N	9 29 E
Kolguyev, Ostrov	**69**	69 20N	48 30 E
Kolhapur	**91**	16 43N	74 15 E
Köln	**42**	50 56N	6 58 E
Koło	**58**	52 14N	18 40 E
Kolomna	**68**	55 8N	38 45 E
Kolskiy Poluostrov	**69**	67 30N	38 0 E
Kolyma →	**73**	69 30N	161 0 E
Komagene	**107**	35 44N	137 58 E
Komaki	**106**	35 17N	136 55 E
Komandorskiye, Is.	**73**	55 0N	167 0 E
Komárno	**59**	47 49N	18 5 E
Komatsu	**106**	36 25N	136 30 E
Komatsujima	**109**	34 0N	134 35 E
Komi □	**69**	64 0N	55 0 E
Kommunizma, Pik	**71**	39 0N	72 2 E
Komoro	**107**	36 19N	138 26 E
Kompong Cham	**95**	12 0N	105 30 E
Kompong Chhnang	**95**	12 20N	104 35 E
Kompong Som	**95**	10 38N	103 30 E
Komsomolets, Ostrov	**72**	80 30N	95 0 E
Komsomolsk	**75**	50 30N	137 0 E
Konarhá □	**87**	35 30N	71 3 E

Kong 130 8 54N 4 36W
Kong, Koh 95 11 20N 103 0 E
Kong Christian X.s Land 13 74 0N 29 0W
Kong Frederik VI.s Kyst 147 63 0N 43 0W
Kong Frederik VIII.s Land 13 78 30N 26 0W
Kongor 129 7 1N 31 27 E
Königsberg = Kaliningrad 68 54 42N 20 32 E
Konin 58 52 12N 18 15 E
Konjic 52 43 42N 17 58 E
Konosha 68 61 0N 40 5 E
Konstanz 44 47 39N 9 10 E
Kontagora 131 10 23N 5 27 E
Konya 80 37 52N 32 35 E
Konya Ovasi 80 38 30N 33 0 E
Koolyanobbing 120 30 48S 119 36 E
Kopaonik Planina 52 43 10N 21 50 E
Kopeysk 71 55 7N 61 37 E
Kopparberg 60 59 52N 15 0 E
Koppeh Dāgh 86 38 0N 58 0 E
Korab 52 41 44N 20 40 E
Korça 52 40 37N 20 50 E
Korčula 52 42 57N 17 8 E
Kordestān □ 81 36 0N 47 0 E
Korea Bay 98 39 0N 124 0 E
Korea Strait 104 34 0N 129 30 E
Korhogo 130 9 29N 5 28W
Korinthiakós Kólpos 54 38 16N 22 30 E
Kórinthos 54 37 56N 22 55 E
Kōriyama 105 37 24N 140 23 E
Koroit 119 38 18S 142 24 E
Kortrijk 42 50 50N 3 17 E
Koryakskiy Khrebet 73 61 0N 171 0 E
Kos 55 36 50N 27 15 E
Kosciusko 169 33 3N 89 34W
Kosciusko, Mt. 117 36 27S 148 16 E
Koshigaya 107 35 54N 139 48 E
K'oshih = Kashi 100 39 30N 76 2 E
Koshiki-Rettō 108 31 45N 129 49 E
Kōshoku 107 36 38N 138 6 E
Košice 59 48 42N 21 15 E
Kosovska-Mitrovica 52 42 54N 20 52 E
Kôstî 129 13 8N 32 43 E
Kostroma 68 57 50N 40 58 E
Koszalin 58 53 50N 16 8 E
Kota 91 25 14N 75 49 E
Kota Baharu 96 6 7N 102 14 E
Kota Kinabalu 112 6 0N 116 4 E
Kotelnich 68 58 20N 48 10 E
Kotka 67 60 28N 26 58 E
Kotlas 69 61 15N 47 0 E
Kotor 52 42 25N 18 47 E
Kotuy → 77 71 54N 102 6 E
Kotzebue 142 66 50N 162 40W
Kowloon 99 22 20N 114 15 E
Kōyama 108 31 20N 130 56 E
Koyukuk → 142 64 56N 157 30W
Kozáni 55 40 19N 21 47 E
Kozhikode = Calicut 90 11 15N 75 43 E
Kōzu-Shima 107 34 13N 139 10 E
Kra, Isthmus of = Kra, Kho Khot 94 10 15N 99 30 E
Kra, Kho Khot 94 10 15N 99 30 E
Kragujevac 52 44 2N 20 56 E
Kraków 58 50 4N 19 57 E
Kraljevo 52 43 44N 20 41 E
Krasnodar 68 45 5N 39 0 E
Krasnovodsk 70 40 0N 52 52 E
Krasnoyarsk 74 56 8N 93 0 E
Krasnyy Kut 68 50 50N 47 0 E
Kratie 95 12 32N 106 10 E
Kravanh, Chuor Phnum 95 12 0N 103 32 E
Krefeld 42 51 20N 6 32 E
Kremenchug 68 49 5N 33 25 E
Krishna → 91 15 57N 80 59 E
Krishnanagar 92 23 24N 88 33 E
Kristiansand 60 58 9N 8 1 E
Kristianstad 61 56 2N 14 9 E
Kristianstads län □ 61 56 15N 14 0 E
Kristiansund 65 63 7N 7 45 E
Kríti 55 35 15N 25 0 E
Krivoy Rog 68 47 51N 33 20 E
Krk 52 45 8N 14 40 E
Kronobergs län □ 61 56 45N 14 30 E
Kronshtadt 68 60 5N 29 45 E
Krotoszyn 58 51 42N 17 23 E
Krugersdorp 137 26 5S 27 46 E
Krung Thep = Bangkok 94 13 45N 100 35 E
Kruševac 52 43 35N 21 28 E
Krymskiy P-ov. 68 45 0N 34 0 E
Kuala Dungun 96 4 45N 103 25 E
Kuala Kangsar 96 4 46N 100 56 E
Kuala Lipis 96 4 10N 102 3 E
Kuala Lumpur 96 3 9N 101 41 E
Kuala Pilah 96 2 45N 102 15 E
Kuala Trengganu 96 5 20N 103 8 E
Kuangchou = Guangzhou 99 23 5N 113 10 E
Kuantan 96 3 49N 103 20 E
Kubak 88 27 10N 63 10 E
Kuban → 68 45 20N 37 30 E
Kubokawa 109 33 12N 133 8 E
Kuchinoerabu-Jima 104 30 28N 130 11 E
Kucing 111 1 33N 110 25 E
Kudamatsu 108 34 0N 131 52 E
Kueiyang = Guiyang 99 26 32N 106 40 E
Kūh-e-Jebāl Bārez 85 29 0N 58 0 E
Kūh-e Sorkh 86 35 30N 58 45 E
Kūhhā-ye-Bashākerd 85 26 45N 59 0 E
Kūhhā-ye Sabalān 81 38 15N 47 45 E
Kuji 103 40 11N 141 46 E
Kuldja = Yining 100 43 58N 81 10 E
Kulunda 71 52 35N 78 57 E
Kumagaya 107 36 9N 139 22 E
Kumamoto 108 32 45N 130 45 E
Kumano 106 33 54N 136 5 E
Kumano-Nada 106 33 47N 136 20 E
Kumasi 130 6 41N 1 38W
Kumayri 70 40 47N 43 50 E
Kumon Bum 93 26 30N 97 15 E
Kunashir, Ostrov 75 44 0N 146 0 E
Kunimi-Dake 109 32 33N 131 1 E
Kunlun Shan 100 36 0N 86 30 E
Kunming 101 25 1N 102 41 E
Kunsan 98 35 59N 126 45 E
Kuopio 67 62 53N 27 35 E
Kupang 113 10 19S 123 39 E
Kurashiki 109 34 40N 133 50 E
Kurayoshi 109 35 26N 133 50 E
Kure 109 34 14N 132 32 E
Kurgan 71 55 26N 65 18 E
Kuril Is. = Kurilskiye Ostrova 75 45 0N 150 0 E
Kurilskiye Ostrova 75 45 0N 150 0 E
Kurnool 90 15 45N 78 0 E
Kurobe-Gawe → 106 36 55N 137 25 E
Kurri Kurri 117 32 50S 151 28 E
Kursk 68 51 42N 36 11 E
Kuršumlija 52 43 9N 21 19 E
Kurume 108 33 15N 130 30 E
Kurunegala 90 7 30N 80 23 E
Kusatsu 106 34 58N 135 57 E
Kushikino 108 31 44N 130 16 E
Kushima 108 31 29N 131 14 E
Kushimoto 106 33 28N 135 47 E
Kushiro 103 43 0N 144 25 E
Kushka 70 35 20N 62 18 E
Kushtia 92 23 55N 89 5 E
Kuskokwim Bay 142 59 50N 162 56W
Kustanay 71 53 10N 63 35 E
Kusu 108 33 16N 131 9 E
Kütahya 80 39 30N 30 2 E
Kutaisi 70 42 19N 42 40 E
Kutaraja = Banda Aceh 111 5 35N 95 20 E
Kutno 58 52 15N 19 23 E
Kuujjuaq 146 58 6N 68 15W
Kuwait = Al Kuwayt 84 29 30N 47 30 E
Kuwait ■ 84 29 30N 47 30 E
Kuwana 106 35 0N 136 43 E
Kuybyshev = Samara 68 53 8N 50 6 E
Kwakoegron 185 5 12N 55 25W
Kwangju 98 35 9N 126 54 E
Kwangsi-Chuang = Guangxi Zhuangzu Zizhiqu □ 99 24 0N 109 0 E
Kwangtung = Guangdong □ 99 23 0N 113 0 E

Kweichow = Guizhou □ **99** 27 0N 107 0 E
Kwinana New Town **120** 32 15S 115 47 E
Kyabram **117** 36 19S 145 4 E
Kyaukpadaung **93** 20 52N 95 8 E
Kyle of Lochalsh **32** 57 17N 5 43W
Kyneton **117** 37 10S 144 29 E
Kyō-ga-Saki **106** 35 45N 135 15 E
Kyoga, L. **132** 1 35N 33 0 E
Kyogle **116** 28 40S 153 0 E
Kyōto **106** 35 0N 135 45 E
Kyrenia **80** 35 20N 33 20 E
Kyrgyzstan ■ **71** 42 0N 75 0 E
Kyūshū **108** 33 0N 131 0 E
Kyūshū □ **108** 33 0N 131 0 E
Kyūshū-Sanchi **108** 32 35N 131 17 E
Kyustendil **53** 42 16N 22 41 E
Kyzyl **74** 51 50N 94 30 E
Kyzylkum, Peski **70** 42 30N 65 0 E
Kzyl-Orda **71** 44 48N 65 28 E

L

Labe = Elbe → **42** 53 50N 9 0 E
Laboulaye **190** 34 10S 63 30W
Labrador, Coast of □ **147** 53 20N 61 0W
Lábrea **187** 7 15S 64 51W
Lac la Martre **145** 63 8N 117 16W
Laccadive Is. = Lakshadweep Is. **78** 10 0N 72 30 E
Lachine **151** 45 30N 73 40W
Lachute **151** 45 39N 74 21W
Lackawanna **164** 42 49N 78 50W
Lacombe **155** 52 30N 113 44W
Laconia **148** 43 32N 71 30W
Ladakh Ra. **89** 34 0N 78 0 E
Ladoga, L. = Ladozhskoye Ozero **68** 61 15N 30 30 E
Ladozhskoye Ozero **68** 61 15N 30 30 E
Ladysmith **154** 49 0N 123 49W
Lae **115** 6 40S 147 2 E
Lafayette, Ind., U.S.A. **167** 40 25N 86 54W
Lafayette, La., U.S.A. **168** 30 18N 92 0W
Laghmān □ **87** 34 20N 70 0 E
Laghouat **127** 33 50N 2 59 E
Lagny **39** 48 52N 2 40 E
Lagos, Nigeria **131** 6 25N 3 27 E
Lagos, Portugal **50** 37 5N 8 41W
Lagos de Moreno **175** 21 21N 101 55W
Laguna **191** 28 30S 48 50W
Laguna Beach **173** 33 31N 117 52W
Laguna Madre **158** 27 0N 97 20W
Lagunas, Chile **187** 21 0S 69 45W
Lagunas, Peru **186** 5 10S 75 35W
Lahore **89** 31 32N 74 22 E
Lahti **67** 60 58N 25 40 E
Lahtis = Lahti **67** 60 58N 25 40 E
Laï **131** 9 25N 16 18 E
Laidley **116** 27 39S 152 20 E
Lairg **33** 58 1N 4 24W
Laja, R. de la → **177** 20 55N 100 46W
Lajes **191** 27 48S 50 20W
Lake Cargelligo **117** 33 15S 146 22 E
Lake Charles **168** 30 15N 93 10W
Lake City, Fla., U.S.A. **170** 30 10N 82 40W
Lake City, S.C., U.S.A. **165** 33 51N 79 44W
Lake Grace **120** 33 7S 118 28 E
Lake Harbour **146** 62 50N 69 50W
Lake Worth **170** 26 36N 80 3W
Lakeland **170** 28 0N 82 0W
Lakes Entrance **117** 37 50S 148 0 E
Lakewood **167** 41 28N 81 50W
Lakshadweep Is. **78** 10 0N 72 30 E
Lala Ghat **93** 24 30N 92 40 E
Lalitpur **91** 24 42N 78 28 E
Lamar **163** 38 9N 102 35W
Lambi Kyun **96** 10 50N 98 20 E
Lameroo **119** 35 19S 140 33 E
Lamía **54** 38 55N 22 26 E
Lammermuir Hills **31** 55 50N 2 40W
Lamon Bay **112** 14 30N 122 20 E
Lampa **187** 15 22S 70 22W
Lampang **94** 18 16N 99 32 E
Lampeter **26** 52 6N 4 6W
Lamu **133** 2 16S 40 55 E
Lanark **31** 55 40N 3 48W
Lancang Jiang → **101** 21 40N 101 10 E
Lancashire □ **28** 53 40N 2 30W
Lancaster, U.K. **28** 54 3N 2 48W
Lancaster, U.S.A. **164** 40 4N 76 19W
Lancaster Sd. **146** 74 13N 84 0W
Lanchow = Lanzhou **99** 36 1N 103 52 E
Landes, Les **36** 44 20N 1 0W
Land's End **27** 50 4N 5 43W
Landskrona **61** 55 53N 12 50 E
Lanett **169** 33 0N 85 15W
Langjökull **64** 64 39N 20 12W
Langlade **149** 46 50N 56 20W
Langøya **64** 68 45N 14 50 E
Langres, Plateau de **37** 47 45N 5 3 E
Languedoc **37** 43 58N 4 0 E
Lannion **36** 48 46N 3 29W
Lansing **167** 42 47N 84 40W
Lanzhou **99** 36 1N 103 52 E
Laois □ **35** 53 0N 7 20W
Laon **38** 49 33N 3 35 E
Laona **150** 45 32N 88 41W
Laos ■ **95** 17 45N 105 0 E
Lapeer **167** 43 3N 83 20W
Lapland = Lappland **67** 68 7N 24 0 E
Lappland **67** 68 7N 24 0 E
Laptev Sea **72** 76 0N 125 0 E
Laramie **163** 41 20N 105 38W
Laramie Mts. **163** 42 0N 105 30W
Laredo **161** 27 34N 99 29W
Laren **40** 52 16N 5 14 E
Largs **30** 55 48N 4 51W
Lárisa **54** 39 49N 22 28 E
Larkana **88** 27 32N 68 18 E
Larnaca **80** 35 0N 33 35 E
Larne **34** 54 52N 5 50W
Laryak **69** 61 15N 80 0 E
Las Cruces **161** 32 18N 106 50W
Las Lajas **190** 38 30S 70 25W
Las Palmas **126** 28 7N 15 26W
Las Vegas, N. Mex., U.S.A. **161** 35 35N 105 10W
Las Vegas, Nev., U.S.A. **173** 36 10N 115 5W
Lashio **93** 22 56N 97 45 E
Latacunga **184** 0 50S 78 35W
Latakia = Al Lādhiqīyah **80** 35 30N 35 45 E
Latium = Lazio □ **46** 42 10N 12 30 E
Latrobe **119** 41 14S 146 30 E
Latur **91** 18 25N 76 40 E
Latvia ■ **68** 56 50N 24 0 E
Lauchhammer **43** 51 35N 13 48 E
Launceston, Australia **119** 41 24S 147 8 E
Launceston, U.K. **27** 50 38N 4 21W
Launglon Bok **94** 13 50N 97 54 E
Laurel **169** 31 41N 89 9W
Laurens **165** 34 32N 82 2W
Laurentian Plat. **138** 52 0N 70 0W
Laurinburg **165** 34 50N 79 25W
Lausanne **44** 46 32N 6 38 E
Laut, Pulau **111** 3 40S 116 10 E
Laut Ketil, Kepulauan **113** 4 45S 115 40 E
Lauzon **148** 46 48N 71 10W
Laval **36** 48 4N 0 48W
Lávrion **55** 37 40N 24 4 E
Lawrence, Kans., U.S.A. **166** 39 0N 95 10W
Lawrence, Mass., U.S.A. **164** 42 40N 71 9W
Lawrenceburg **169** 35 12N 87 19W
Lawton **161** 34 33N 98 25W
Lazio □ **46** 42 10N 12 30 E
Lea → **25** 51 30N 0 10W
Leader **152** 50 50N 109 30W
Leadhills **31** 55 25N 3 47W
Leadville **163** 39 17N 106 23W
Leamington, Canada **150** 42 3N 82 36W
Leamington, U.K. **24** 52 18N 1 32W
Leavenworth **166** 39 25N 95 0W
Lebanon, Mo., U.S.A. **166** 37 40N 92 40W

Lebanon, Oreg., U.S.A.	**171**	44 31N	122 57W
Lebanon, Pa., U.S.A.	**164**	40 20N	76 28W
Lebanon, Tenn., U.S.A.	**169**	36 15N	86 20W
Lebanon ■	**80**	34 0N	36 0 E
Lecce	**49**	40 20N	18 10 E
Ledbury	**24**	52 3N	2 25W
Leduc	**155**	53 15N	113 30W
Leeds	**28**	53 48N	1 34W
Leek	**28**	53 7N	2 2W
Leerdam	**40**	51 54N	5 6 E
Leesburg	**170**	28 47N	81 52W
Leeton	**117**	34 33S	146 23 E
Leeuwarden	**41**	53 15N	5 48 E
Leeuwin, C.	**120**	34 20S	115 9 E
Leeward Is.	**181**	16 30N	63 30W
Leghorn = Livorno	**46**	43 32N	10 18 E
Legnica	**58**	51 12N	16 10 E
Leicester	**25**	52 39N	1 9W
Leicester □	**25**	52 40N	1 10W
Leichhardt	**121**	33 53S	151 9 E
Leiden	**40**	52 9N	4 30 E
Leigh Creek South	**118**	30 38S	138 26 E
Leinster	**120**	27 51S	120 36 E
Leinster □	**35**	53 0N	7 10W
Leinster, Mt.	**35**	52 38N	6 47W
Leipzig	**43**	51 20N	12 23 E
Leith	**31**	55 59N	3 10W
Leith Hill	**24**	51 10N	0 23W
Leitrim	**34**	54 0N	8 5W
Lek →	**40**	51 54N	4 35 E
Leleque	**192**	42 28S	71 0W
Léman, Lac	**44**	46 26N	6 30 E
Lemmer	**41**	52 51N	5 43 E
Lena →	**72**	72 52N	126 40 E
Leninabad = Khodzhent	**71**	40 17N	69 37 E
Leninakan = Kumayri	**70**	40 47N	43 50 E
Leningrad = Sankt-Peterburg	**68**	59 55N	30 20 E
Leninsk-Kuznetskiy	**71**	54 44N	86 10 E
Leninskoye	**75**	47 56N	132 38 E
Lenoir City	**165**	35 40N	84 20W
Lens, Belgium	**38**	50 33N	3 54 E
Lens, France	**37**	50 26N	2 50 E
Lensk	**74**	60 48N	114 55 E
Leominster, U.K.	**24**	52 15N	2 43W
Leominster, U.S.A.	**164**	42 32N	71 45W
León, Mexico	**177**	21 7N	101 40W
León, Nic.	**179**	12 20N	86 51W
León, Spain	**50**	42 38N	5 34W
León □	**50**	42 40N	5 55W
Leongatha	**117**	38 30S	145 58 E
Léopold II, Lac = Mai-Ndombe, L.	**134**	2 0S	18 20 E
Léopoldville = Kinshasa	**134**	4 20S	15 15 E
Lérida	**51**	41 37N	0 39 E
Lerwick	**30**	60 10N	1 10W
Lesbos, I. = Lésvos	**55**	39 10N	26 20 E
Lesotho ■	**137**	29 40S	28 0 E
Lesozavodsk	**75**	45 30N	133 29 E
Lesser Antilles	**181**	15 0N	61 0W
Lesser Slave L.	**155**	55 30N	115 25W
Lésvos	**55**	39 10N	26 20 E
Letchworth	**25**	51 58N	0 13W
Lethbridge	**155**	49 45N	112 45W
Leti, Kepulauan	**113**	8 10S	128 0 E
Leticia	**184**	4 9S	70 0W
Letsôk-aw Kyun	**94**	11 30N	98 25 E
Letterkenny	**34**	54 57N	7 42W
Leuven	**42**	50 52N	4 42 E
Levanger	**65**	63 45N	11 19 E
Levin	**122**	40 37S	175 18 E
Lévis	**148**	46 48N	71 9W
Levkás	**54**	38 40N	20 43 E
Levkôsia = Nicosia	**80**	35 10N	33 25 E
Lewes	**25**	50 53N	0 2 E
Lewis	**32**	58 10N	6 40W
Lewis, Butt of	**32**	58 30N	6 12W
Lewis Ra.	**162**	48 0N	113 15W
Lewisporte	**149**	49 15N	55 3W
Lewiston	**148**	44 3N	70 10 E
Lexington, Ky., U.S.A.	**165**	38 6N	84 30W
Lexington, Mo., U.S.A.	**166**	39 7N	93 55W
Lexington, N.C., U.S.A.	**165**	35 50N	80 13W
Lexington, Oreg., U.S.A.	**171**	45 29N	119 46W
Lexington Park	**165**	38 16N	76 27W
Leyte	**112**	11 0N	125 0 E
Lhasa	**101**	29 50N	91 3 E
Lhazê	**101**	29 5N	87 38 E
Lianyungang	**99**	34 40N	119 11 E
Liaoning □	**98**	41 40N	122 30 E
Liaoyuan	**98**	42 58N	125 2 E
Liard →	**144**	61 51N	121 18W
Libau = Liepaja	**68**	56 30N	21 0 E
Liberec	**58**	50 47N	15 7 E
Liberia ■	**130**	6 30N	9 30W
Lîbîya, Sahrâ'	**128**	27 35N	25 0 E
Libreville	**134**	0 25N	9 26 E
Libya ■	**127**	27 0N	17 0 E
Lichfield	**28**	52 40N	1 50W
Liechtenstein ■	**44**	47 8N	9 35 E
Liège	**42**	50 38N	5 35 E
Liegnitz = Legnica	**58**	51 12N	16 10 E
Lienyünchiangshih = Lianyungang	**99**	34 40N	119 11 E
Liepaja	**68**	56 30N	21 0 E
Liévin	**38**	50 24N	2 47 E
Liffey →	**35**	53 21N	6 20W
Lifford	**34**	54 50N	7 30W
Liguria □	**46**	44 30N	9 0 E
Ligurian Sea	**46**	43 20N	9 0 E
Lihou Reefs and Cays	**121**	17 25S	151 40 E
Lihue	**160**	21 59N	159 24W
Likasi	**135**	10 55S	26 48 E
Lille, Belgium	**38**	51 15N	4 50 E
Lille, France	**37**	50 38N	3 3 E
Lille Bælt	**61**	55 20N	9 45 E
Lillehammer	**60**	61 8N	10 30 E
Lillers	**38**	50 35N	2 28 E
Lillooet	**154**	50 44N	121 57W
Lilongwe	**137**	14 0S	33 48 E
Lima, Peru	**186**	12 0S	77 0W
Lima, U.S.A.	**167**	40 42N	84 5W
Limassol	**80**	34 42N	33 1 E
Limavady	**34**	55 3N	6 58W
Limbe	**137**	15 55S	35 2 E
Limburg □	**41**	51 20N	5 55 E
Limeira	**188**	22 35S	47 28W
Limerick	**35**	52 40N	8 38W
Limerick □	**35**	52 30N	8 50W
Limfjorden	**61**	56 55N	9 0 E
Límnos	**55**	39 50N	25 5 E
Limoges	**36**	45 50N	1 15 E
Limón	**179**	10 0N	83 2W
Limousin	**36**	46 0N	1 0 E
Limpopo →	**137**	25 15S	33 30 E
Linares, Chile	**190**	35 50S	71 40W
Linares, Mexico	**176**	24 50N	99 40W
Linares, Spain	**50**	38 10N	3 40W
Lincoln, Argentina	**190**	34 55S	61 30W
Lincoln, U.K.	**29**	53 14N	0 32W
Lincoln, Ill., U.S.A.	**166**	40 10N	89 20W
Lincoln, Maine, U.S.A.	**148**	45 27N	68 29W
Lincoln, Nebr., U.S.A.	**156**	40 50N	96 42W
Lincoln □	**29**	53 14N	0 32W
Lincoln Sea	**12**	84 0N	55 0W
Lincoln Wolds	**29**	53 20N	0 5W
Lindsay, Canada	**151**	44 22N	78 43W
Lindsay, U.S.A.	**173**	36 14N	119 6W
Línea de la Concepción, La	**50**	36 15N	5 23W
Lingga, Kepulauan	**111**	0 10S	104 30 E
Linguéré	**130**	15 25N	15 5W
Linköping	**60**	58 28N	15 36 E
Linlithgow	**31**	55 58N	3 38W
Linxia	**99**	35 36N	103 10 E
Linz	**45**	48 18N	14 18 E
Lion, G. du	**37**	43 0N	4 0 E
Lípari, Is.	**49**	38 30N	14 50 E
Lipetsk	**68**	52 37N	39 35 E
Lippe →	**42**	51 39N	6 38 E
Lisboa	**50**	38 42N	9 10W
Lisbon = Lisboa	**50**	38 42N	9 10W
Lisburn	**34**	54 30N	6 9W
Lisburne, C.	**142**	68 50N	166 0W

Lisieux	**39**	49 10N	0 12 E
Lismore	**116**	28 44S	153 21 E
Lister, Mt.	**15**	78 0S	162 0 E
Listowel	**35**	52 27N	9 30W
Litchfield	**166**	39 10N	89 40W
Lithgow	**117**	33 25S	150 8 E
Lithuania ■	**68**	55 30N	24 0 E
Little Andaman I.	**94**	10 40N	92 15 E
Little Barrier I.	**122**	36 12S	175 8 E
Little Current	**150**	45 55N	82 0W
Little Falls	**164**	43 3N	74 50W
Little Minch	**32**	57 35N	6 45W
Little Rann	**91**	23 25N	71 25 E
Little Rock	**168**	34 41N	92 10W
Littlehampton	**25**	50 48N	0 32W
Liuzhou	**99**	24 22N	109 22 E
Liverpool, Australia	**117**	33 54S	150 58 E
Liverpool, Canada	**148**	44 5N	64 41W
Liverpool, U.K.	**28**	53 25N	3 0W
Liverpool Plains	**116**	31 15S	150 15 E
Livingston, Guatemala	**177**	15 50N	88 50W
Livingston, U.K.	**31**	55 52N	3 33W
Livingston, Mont., U.S.A.	**163**	45 40N	110 40W
Livingston, Tex., U.S.A.	**168**	30 44N	94 54W
Livingstone	**135**	17 46S	25 52 E
Livonia	**167**	42 25N	83 23W
Livorno	**46**	43 32N	10 18 E
Lizard Pt.	**27**	49 57N	5 11W
Ljubljana	**52**	46 4N	14 33 E
Ljusnan →	**66**	61 12N	17 8 E
Llandeilo	**26**	51 53N	4 0W
Llandovery	**26**	51 59N	3 49W
Llandrindod Wells	**26**	52 15N	3 23W
Llandudno	**26**	53 19N	3 51W
Llanelli	**27**	51 41N	4 11W
Llanes	**50**	43 25N	4 50W
Llangollen	**26**	52 58N	3 10W
Llanidloes	**26**	52 28N	3 31W
Llano Estacado	**161**	34 0N	103 0W
Llanos	**184**	5 0N	71 35W
Lloydminster	**152**	53 17N	110 0W
Loc Ninh	**95**	11 50N	106 34 E
Lochaber	**32**	56 55N	5 0W
Lochboisdale	**32**	57 10N	7 20W
Lochem	**41**	52 9N	6 26 E
Lochgilphead	**30**	56 2N	5 37W
Lochinver	**32**	58 9N	5 15W
Lochmaddy	**32**	57 36N	7 10W
Lochy, L.	**32**	56 58N	4 55W
Lock Haven	**164**	41 7N	77 31W
Lockhart	**117**	35 14S	146 40 E
Lockport	**164**	43 12N	78 42W
Lodi	**172**	38 12N	121 16W
Łódź	**58**	51 45N	19 27 E
Lofoten	**64**	68 30N	15 0 E
Logan, Utah, U.S.A.	**163**	41 45N	111 50W
Logan, W. Va., U.S.A.	**165**	37 51N	81 59W
Logan, Mt	**144**	60 31N	140 22W
Logansport	**167**	40 45N	86 21W
Logroño	**51**	42 28N	2 27W
Loire →	**36**	47 16N	2 10W
Loja	**184**	3 59S	79 16W
Lokka	**67**	67 55N	27 35 E
Lolland	**61**	54 45N	11 30 E
Lom	**53**	43 48N	23 12 E
Lomami →	**134**	0 46N	24 16 E
Lombardia □	**46**	45 35N	9 45 E
Lombardy = Lombardia □	**46**	45 35N	9 45 E
Lombok	**113**	8 45S	116 30 E
Lomé	**130**	6 9N	1 20 E
Lomond, L.	**31**	56 8N	4 38W
Lompoc	**173**	34 41N	120 32W
Łomza	**58**	53 10N	22 2 E
London, Canada	**150**	42 59N	81 15W
London, U.K.	**25**	51 30N	0 5W
Londonderry	**34**	55 0N	7 20W
Londrina	**191**	23 18S	51 10W
Long Beach	**173**	33 46N	118 12W
Long I., Bahamas	**178**	23 20N	75 10W
Long I., U.S.A.	**164**	40 50N	73 20W
Long Range Mts.	**149**	49 30N	57 30W
Long Xuyen	**95**	10 19N	105 28 E
Longford, Australia	**119**	41 32S	147 3 E
Longford, Ireland	**34**	53 43N	7 50W
Longford □	**34**	53 42N	7 45W
Longlac	**150**	49 45N	86 25W
Longmont	**163**	40 10N	105 4W
Longreach	**121**	23 28S	144 14 E
Longview, Tex., U.S.A.	**168**	32 30N	94 45W
Longview, Wash., U.S.A.	**171**	46 9N	122 58W
Looe	**27**	50 24N	4 25W
Loop Hd.	**35**	52 34N	9 55W
Lop Nor	**100**	40 20N	90 10 E
Lopez, C.	**134**	0 47S	8 40 E
Lorain	**167**	41 28N	82 55W
Lorca	**51**	37 41N	1 42W
Lord Howe I.	**122**	31 33S	159 6 E
Lordsburg	**161**	32 22N	108 45W
Lorient	**36**	47 45N	3 23W
Lorn	**30**	56 26N	5 10W
Lorn, Firth of	**30**	56 20N	5 40W
Lorraine	**37**	49 0N	6 0 E
Los Alamos	**161**	35 57N	106 17W
Los Andes	**190**	32 50S	70 40W
Los Angeles, Chile	**190**	37 28S	72 23W
Los Angeles, U.S.A.	**173**	34 0N	118 10W
Los Angeles Aqueduct	**173**	35 25N	118 0W
Los Hermanos	**181**	11 45N	84 25W
Los Mochis	**174**	25 45N	108 57W
Los Testigos	**181**	11 23N	63 6W
Lošinj	**52**	44 30N	14 30 E
Lossiemouth	**33**	57 43N	3 17W
Lot →	**36**	44 18N	0 20 E
Lota	**190**	37 5S	73 10W
Lothian □	**31**	55 50N	3 0W
Loughborough	**29**	52 46N	1 11W
Loughrea	**35**	53 11N	8 33W
Louisbourg	**149**	45 55N	60 0W
Louise I.	**154**	52 55N	131 50W
Louisiana □	**168**	30 50N	92 0W
Louisville, Ky., U.S.A.	**167**	38 15N	85 45W
Louisville, Miss., U.S.A.	**169**	33 7N	89 3W
Lourdes	**36**	43 6N	0 3W
Lourenço-Marques = Maputo	**137**	25 58S	32 32 E
Louth	**29**	53 23N	0 0 E
Louth □	**34**	53 55N	6 30W
Louvain = Leuven	**42**	50 52N	4 42 E
Louviers	**39**	49 12N	1 10 E
Lowell	**164**	42 38N	71 19W
Lower Austria = Niederösterreich □	**45**	48 25N	15 40 E
Lower California = Baja California	**174**	31 10N	115 12W
Lower Hutt	**123**	41 10S	174 55 E
Lower Saxony = Niedersachsen □	**42**	52 45N	9 0 E
Lowestoft	**25**	52 29N	1 44 E
Łowicz	**58**	52 6N	19 55 E
Loxton	**119**	34 28S	140 31 E
Loyalty Is. = Loyauté, Is.	**122**	21 0S	167 30 E
Loyang = Luoyang	**99**	34 40N	112 26 E
Loyauté, Is.	**122**	21 0S	167 30 E
Lualaba →	**135**	0 26N	25 20 E
Luan Chau	**95**	21 38N	103 24 E
Luanda	**134**	8 50S	13 15 E
Luang Prabang	**95**	19 52N	102 10 E
Luarca	**50**	43 32N	6 32W
Lubbock	**161**	33 40N	101 53W
Lübeck	**43**	53 52N	10 41 E
Lublin	**58**	51 12N	22 38 E
Lubnān, J.	**80**	33 50N	35 45 E
Lubumbashi	**135**	11 40S	27 28 E
Lucca	**46**	43 50N	10 30 E
Luce Bay	**30**	54 45N	4 48W
Lučenec	**59**	48 18N	19 42 E
Lucerne = Luzern	**44**	47 3N	8 18 E
Lucknow	**92**	26 50N	81 0 E
Lüda = Dalian	**98**	38 50N	121 40 E
Lüderitz	**136**	26 41S	15 8 E
Ludhiana	**89**	30 57N	75 56 E
Ludington	**167**	43 58N	86 27W
Ludlow	**24**	52 23N	2 42W

Ludwigshafen **42** 49 27N 8 27 E
Lufkin **168** 31 25N 94 40W
Lugano **44** 46 0N 8 57 E
Lugansk **68** 48 38N 39 15 E
Lugo **50** 43 2N 7 35W
Lugovoye **71** 42 55N 72 43 E
Luján **190** 34 45S 59 5W
Łuków **58** 51 55N 22 23 E
Lule älv → **67** 65 35N 22 10 E
Luleå **67** 65 35N 22 10 E
Lüleburgaz **80** 41 23N 27 22 E
Lulua → **134** 6 30S 22 50 E
Luluabourg = Kananga **134** 5 55S 22 18 E
Lumberton **165** 34 37N 78 59W
Lundy **27** 51 10N 4 41W
Lune → **28** 54 0N 2 51W
Lüneburg **43** 53 15N 10 23 E
Lüneburg Heath =
Lüneburger Heide **43** 53 0N 10 0 E
Lüneburger Heide **43** 53 0N 10 0 E
Lūni → **91** 24 41N 71 14 E
Luoyang **99** 34 40N 112 26 E
Lurgan **34** 54 28N 6 20W
Lusaka **135** 15 28S 28 16 E
Luta = Dalian **98** 38 50N 121 40 E
Luton **25** 51 53N 0 24W
Lutsk **68** 50 50N 25 15 E
Luvua → **135** 6 50S 27 30 E
Luxembourg **42** 49 37N 6 9 E
Luxembourg ■ **42** 50 0N 6 0 E
Luzern **44** 47 3N 8 18 E
Luzhou **99** 28 52N 105 20 E
Luziânia **188** 16 20S 48 0W
Luzon **112** 16 0N 121 0 E
Lvov **68** 49 50N 24 0 E
Lyakhovskiye, Ostrova **72** 73 40N 141 0 E
Lyallpur = Faisalabad **89** 31 30N 73 5 E
Lyell I. **154** 52 40N 131 35W
Lyell Range **123** 41 38S 172 20 E
Lyme Regis **27** 50 44N 2 57W
Lymington **24** 50 46N 1 32W
Lynchburg **165** 37 23N 79 10W
Lynn **164** 42 28N 70 57W
Lynn Lake **152** 56 51N 101 3W
Lynton **27** 51 14N 3 50W
Lyon **37** 45 46N 4 50 E
Lyons = Lyon **37** 45 46N 4 50 E
Lytham St. Anne's **28** 53 45N 2 58W
Lyttelton **122** 43 35S 172 44 E

M

Ma'ān **80** 30 12N 35 44 E
Ma'anshan **99** 31 44N 118 29 E
Ma'arrat an Nu'mān **80** 35 43N 36 43 E
Maas → **40** 51 45N 4 32 E
Maaseik **41** 51 6N 5 45 E
Maastricht **41** 50 50N 5 40 E
Mablethorpe **29** 53 21N 0 14 E
McAlester **168** 34 57N 95 46W
Macao = Macau ■ **99** 22 16N 113 35 E
Macapá **185** 0 5N 51 4W
Macau **189** 5 0S 36 40W
Macau ■ **99** 22 16N 113 35 E
McBride **155** 53 20N 120 19W
Macclesfield **28** 53 16N 2 9W
McClure Str. **12** 75 0N 119 0W
McComb **169** 31 13N 90 30W
McCook **163** 40 15N 100 35W
McDermitt **172** 42 0N 117 45W
Macdonald L. **114** 23 30S 129 0 E
Macdonnell Ranges **114** 23 40S 133 0 E
McDouall Peak **118** 29 51S 134 55 E
Macduff **33** 57 40N 2 30W
Macedonia ■ **55** 41 39N 22 0 E
Maceió **189** 9 40S 35 41W
Macfarlane, L. **118** 32 0S 136 40 E
Macgillycuddy's Reeks **35** 52 2N 9 45W
Machala **184** 3 20S 79 57W
Machida **107** 35 28N 139 23 E
Machilipatnam **92** 16 12N 81 8 E
Machiques **184** 10 4N 72 34W
Machynlleth **26** 52 36N 3 51W
Mackay **121** 21 8S 149 11 E
Mackay, L. **114** 22 30S 129 0 E
McKeesport **164** 40 21N 79 50W
Mackenzie → **144** 69 10N 134 20W
Mackenzie Bay **12** 69 0N 137 30W
Mackenzie Mts. **144** 64 0N 130 0W
McKinley, Mt. **142** 63 2N 151 0W
McKinley Sea **13** 84 0N 10 0W
McKinney **168** 33 10N 96 40W
Macksville **116** 30 40S 152 56 E
Maclean **116** 29 26S 153 16 E
McLennan **155** 55 42N 116 50W
MacLeod Lake **154** 54 58N 123 0W
M'Clintock Chan. **145** 72 0N 102 0W
McMinnville, Oreg., U.S.A. **171** 45 16N 123 11W
McMinnville, Tenn., U.S.A. **169** 35 43N 85 45W
McMurdo Sd. **15** 77 0S 170 0 E
McMurray = Fort McMurray **155** 56 44N 111 7W
McNaughton L. **155** 52 0N 118 10W
Macomb **166** 40 25N 90 40W
Mâcon, France **37** 46 19N 4 50 E
Macon, U.S.A. **170** 32 50N 83 37W
McPherson **161** 38 25N 97 40W
Macpherson Ra. **116** 28 15S 153 15 E
Macquarie → **116** 30 5S 147 30 E
Macquarie Is. **15** 54 36S 158 55 E
MacRobertson Land **14** 71 0S 64 0 E
Macroom **35** 51 54N 8 57W
Madagascar ■ **137** 20 0S 47 0 E
Madang **115** 5 12S 145 49 E
Madaripur **93** 23 19N 90 15 E
Made **40** 51 41N 4 49 E
Madeira **126** 32 50N 17 0W
Madeira → **185** 3 22S 58 45W
Madeleine, Îs. de la **149** 47 30N 61 40W
Madera **173** 37 0N 120 1W
Madhya Pradesh □ **91** 21 50N 81 0 E
Madison, Fla., U.S.A. **170** 30 29N 83 39W
Madison, Ind., U.S.A. **167** 38 42N 85 20W
Madison, Wis., U.S.A. **166** 43 5N 89 25W
Madisonville **167** 37 20N 87 30W
Madiun **111** 7 38S 111 32 E
Madras = Tamil Nadu □ **90** 11 0N 77 0 E
Madras, India **90** 13 8N 80 19 E
Madras, U.S.A. **171** 44 40N 121 10W
Madre, Laguna **176** 25 0N 97 30W
Madre de Dios → **187** 10 59S 66 8W
Madre del Sur, Sa. **177** 17 0N 100 0W
Madre Occidental, Sa. **174** 25 0N 105 0W
Madre Oriental, Sa. **177** 22 0N 99 30W
Madrid **50** 40 25N 3 45W
Madura, Selat **111** 7 30S 113 20 E
Madurai **90** 9 55N 78 10 E
Madurantakam **90** 12 30N 79 50 E
Mae Rim **94** 18 54N 98 57 E
Maebashi **107** 36 24N 139 4 E
Maesteg **27** 51 36N 3 40W
Maestra, Sierra **178** 20 15N 77 0W
Mafeking **152** 52 40N 101 10W
Maffra **117** 37 53S 146 58 E
Mafia **135** 7 45S 39 50 E
Mafikeng **136** 25 50S 25 38 E
Mafra **191** 26 10S 50 0W
Magadan **73** 59 38N 150 50 E
Magallanes, Estrecho de **192** 52 30S 75 0W
Magangué **184** 9 14N 74 45W
Magdalena, Bolivia **187** 13 13S 63 57W
Magdalena, Mexico **174** 30 38N 110 57W
Magdalena → **184** 11 6N 74 51W
Magdeburg **43** 52 8N 11 36 E
Magelang **111** 7 29S 110 13 E
Magellan's Str. = Magallanes,
Estrecho de **192** 52 30S 75 0W
Magherafelt **34** 54 44N 6 37W
Magnitogorsk **71** 53 27N 59 4 E
Magog **148** 45 18N 72 9W

Magosa = Famagusta ..... 80 35 8N 33 55 E
Magrath 155 49 25N 112 50W
Mahābād ..... 81 36 50N 45 45 E
Mahajanga □ ..... 137 17 0S 47 0 E
Mahakam → ..... 111 0 35S 117 17 E
Maḩallāt ..... 86 33 55N 50 30 E
Mahanadi → ..... 92 20 20N 86 25 E
Maharashtra □ ..... 91 20 30N 75 30 E
Mahbubnagar ..... 91 16 45N 77 59 E
Mahia Pen. ..... 122 39 9S 177 55 E
Mahón ..... 51 39 53N 4 16 E
Mahone Bay 148 44 30N 64 20W
Mahukona 160 20 11N 155 52W
Mai-Ndombe, L. ..... 134 2 0S 18 20 E
Maidenhead 25 51 31N 0 42W
Maiduguri ..... 131 12 0N 13 20 E
Maikala Ra. ..... 92 22 0N 81 0 E
Main → ..... 42 50 0N 8 18 E
Maine ..... 36 48 0N 0 0 E
Maine □ 148 45 20N 69 0W
Mainland, Orkney, U.K. 33 59 0N 3 10W
Mainland, Shet., U.K. 30 60 15N 1 22W
Mainpuri ..... 89 27 18N 79 4 E
Mainz ..... 42 50 0N 8 17 E
Maiquetía 184 10 36N 66 57W
Maisi, Pta. de 178 20 10N 74 10W
Maitland, N.S.W., Australia . 117 32 33S 151 36 E
Maitland, S. Austral., Australia 119 34 23S 137 40 E
Maiz, Islas del 179 12 15N 83 4W
Maizuru ..... 106 35 25N 135 22 E
Majorca, I. = Mallorca ..... 51 39 30N 3 0 E
Makarikari = Makgadikgadi
Salt Pans ..... 136 20 40S 25 45 E
Makasar = Ujung Pandang . 113 5 10S 119 20 E
Makasar, Selat ..... 113 1 0S 118 20 E
Makedhonía = Macedonia □ 55 41 39N 22 0 E
Makena 160 20 39N 156 27W
Makeyevka ..... 68 48 0N 38 0 E
Makgadikgadi Salt Pans ... 136 20 40S 25 45 E
Makhachkala ..... 70 43 0N 47 30 E
Makkah ..... 82 21 30N 39 54 E
Makó ..... 59 46 14N 20 33 E
Makran Coast Range ..... 88 25 40N 64 0 E
Makurazaki ..... 108 31 15N 130 20 E
Makurdi ..... 131 7 43N 8 35 E
Malabar Coast ..... 90 11 0N 75 0 E
Malacca, Str. of ..... 111 3 0N 101 0 E
Malad City ..... 162 42 10N 112 20 E
Málaga 50 36 43N 4 23W
Malakal ..... 129 9 33N 31 50 E
Malang ..... 111 7 59S 112 45 E
Mälaren ..... 60 59 30N 17 10 E
Malatya ..... 81 38 25N 38 20 E
Malawi ■ ..... 137 13 0S 34 0 E
Malawi, L. ..... 137 12 30S 34 30 E
Malay Pen. ..... 97 7 25N 100 0 E
Malāyer ..... 84 34 19N 48 51 E
Malaysia ■ ..... 111 5 0N 110 0 E
Malbaie, La 148 47 40N 70 10W
Malbork ..... 58 54 3N 19 1 E
Malcolm ..... 120 28 51S 121 25 E
Maldives ■ ..... 78 7 0N 73 0 E
Maldonado 191 35 0S 55 0W
Malebo, Pool ..... 134 4 17S 15 20 E
Malegaon ..... 91 20 30N 74 38 E
Mali ■ 130 15 0N 2 0W
Mali Kyun ..... 94 13 0N 98 20 E
Malin Hd. 34 55 18N 7 24W
Malindi ..... 133 3 12S 40 5 E
Malines = Mechelen ..... 42 51 2N 4 29 E
Mallaig 32 57 0N 5 50W
Mallorca ..... 51 39 30N 3 0 E
Mallow 35 52 8N 8 40W
Malmédy ..... 42 50 25N 6 2 E
Malmö ..... 61 55 36N 12 59 E
Malmöhus län □ ..... 61 55 45N 13 30 E
Malone 151 44 50N 74 19W
Malta ■ ..... 49 35 50N 14 30 E
Malton 29 54 9N 0 48W
Maluku ..... 113 1 0S 127 0 E
Malvern, U.K. 24 52 7N 2 19W
Malvern, U.S.A. 168 34 22N 92 50W
Malvern Hills 24 52 0N 2 19W
Malvinas, Is. = Falkland Is. . 192 51 30S 59 0W
Mamers ..... 39 48 21N 0 22 E
Mamoré → 187 10 23S 65 53W
Mamou 130 10 15N 12 0W
Man 130 7 30N 7 40W
Man, I. of 28 54 15N 4 30W
Mana, Fr. Guiana 185 5 45N 53 55W
Mana, U.S.A. 160 22 3N 159 45W
Manaar, Gulf of = Mannar, G.
of ..... 90 8 30N 79 0 E
Manacapuru 185 3 16S 60 37W
Manado ..... 113 1 29N 124 51 E
Managua 179 12 6N 86 20W
Manaos = Manaus 185 3 0S 60 0W
Manapouri ..... 123 45 34S 167 39 E
Manaung ..... 93 18 45N 93 40 E
Manaus 185 3 0S 60 0W
Mancha, La 50 39 10N 2 54W
Manchester, U.K. 28 53 30N 2 15W
Manchester, U.S.A. 164 42 58N 71 29W
Mandalay ..... 93 22 0N 96 4 E
Mandale = Mandalay ..... 93 22 0N 96 4 E
Mandurah ..... 120 32 36S 115 48 E
Manfredónia, G. di ..... 49 41 30N 16 10 E
Mangalore ..... 90 12 55N 74 47 E
Mangla Dam ..... 89 33 9N 73 44 E
Mangole ..... 113 1 50S 125 55 E
Mangonui ..... 122 35 1S 173 32 E
Mangyshlak P-ov. ..... 70 44 30N 52 30 E
Manhattan 158 39 10N 96 40W
Manicoré 185 5 48S 61 16W
Manicouagan → 148 49 30N 68 30W
Manila ..... 112 14 40N 121 3 E
Manilla ..... 116 30 45S 150 43 E
Manipur □ ..... 93 25 0N 94 0 E
Manisa ..... 80 38 38N 27 30 E
Manistee 167 44 15N 86 20W
Manistique 150 45 59N 86 18W
Manitoba □ 153 55 30N 97 0W
Manitoba, L. 153 51 0N 98 45W
Manitoulin I. 150 45 40N 82 30W
Manitowoc 167 44 8N 87 40W
Manizales 184 5 5N 75 32W
Manjil ..... 81 36 46N 49 30 E
Manjimup ..... 120 34 15S 116 6 E
Mankato 166 44 8N 93 59W
Manly ..... 117 33 48S 151 17 E
Mannar, G. of ..... 90 8 30N 79 0 E
Mannar I. ..... 90 9 5N 79 45 E
Mannheim ..... 42 49 28N 8 29 E
Mannum ..... 119 34 50S 139 20 E
Manosque ..... 37 43 49N 5 47 E
Manouane, L. 148 50 45N 70 45W
Mans, Le ..... 39 48 0N 0 10 E
Mansel I. 146 62 0N 80 0W
Mansfield, Australia ..... 117 37 4S 146 6 E
Mansfield, U.K. 29 53 8N 1 12W
Mansfield, U.S.A. 167 40 45N 82 30W
Manta 184 1 0S 80 40W
Mantes-la-Jolie ..... 39 49 0N 1 41 E
Mantiqueira, Serra da 188 22 0S 44 0W
Mántova ..... 46 45 20N 10 42 E
Mantua = Mántova ..... 46 45 20N 10 42 E
Manu 187 12 10S 70 51W
Manukau ..... 122 35 14S 173 13 E
Manyara, L. ..... 135 3 40S 35 50 E
Manzanillo, Cuba 178 20 20N 77 31W
Manzanillo, Mexico 175 19 3N 104 20W
Manzhouli ..... 98 49 35N 117 25 E
Mapimí 174 25 49N 103 51W
Maple 152 43 51N 79 31W
Maputo ..... 137 25 58S 32 32 E
Maquinchao 192 41 15S 68 50W
Mar, Serra do 191 25 30S 49 0W
Mar Chiquita, L. 190 30 40S 62 50W
Mar del Plata 191 38 0S 57 30W
Mar Menor, L. 51 37 40N 0 45W
Marabá 188 5 20S 49 5W
Maracaibo 184 10 40N 71 37W

Maracaibo, Lago de 184 9 40N 71 30W
Maracay 184 10 15N 67 28W
Marajó, Ilha de 188 1 0S 49 30W
Maranhão = São Luís 188 2 39S 44 15W
Maranhão □ 188 5 0S 46 0W
Marañón → 186 4 30S 73 35W
Maraş 80 37 37N 36 53 E
Marathón 55 38 11N 23 58 E
Marbella 50 36 30N 4 57W
Marble Bar 114 21 9S 119 44 E
March 25 52 33N 0 5 E
Marché 36 46 0N 1 20 E
Marche □ 47 43 22N 13 10 E
Marchena 50 37 18N 5 23W
Marches = Marche □ 47 43 22N 13 10 E
Mardan 89 34 20N 72 0 E
Mardin 81 37 20N 40 43 E
Mareeba 121 16 59S 145 28 E
Margarita 175 9 20N 79 55W
Margarita I. 185 11 0N 64 0W
Margate 25 51 23N 1 24 E
Mari El □ 68 56 30N 48 0 E
Maria van Diemen, C. 122 34 29S 172 40 E
Marianao 178 23 8N 82 24W
Marianna 169 30 45N 85 15W
Maribor 52 46 36N 15 40 E
Maricourt 146 61 30N 72 0W
Marie-Galante 180 15 56N 61 16W
Marienberg 41 52 30N 6 35 E
Marietta, Ga., U.S.A. 169 34 0N 84 30W
Marietta, Ohio, U.S.A. 164 39 27N 81 27W
Marília 188 22 13S 50 0W
Marín 50 42 23N 8 42W
Marinette 167 45 4N 87 40W
Maringá 191 23 26S 52 2W
Marion, Ill., U.S.A. 166 37 45N 88 55W
Marion, Ind., U.S.A. 167 40 35N 85 40W
Marion, Ohio, U.S.A. 167 40 38N 83 8W
Mariupol 68 47 5N 37 31 E
Marken 40 52 26N 5 12 E
Market Drayton 28 52 55N 2 30W
Market Harborough 25 52 29N 0 55W
Market Rasen 29 53 24N 0 20W
Markham, Mt. 15 83 0S 164 0 E
Marlborough 24 51 26N 1 44W
Marlborough □ 123 41 45S 173 33 E
Marlborough Downs 24 51 25N 1 55W
Marlin 168 31 25N 96 50W
Marmagao 91 15 25N 73 56 E
Marmara, Sea of = Marmara Denizi 80 40 45N 28 15 E
Marmara Denizi 80 40 45N 28 15 E
Marmaris 80 36 50N 28 14 E
Marne → 39 8 23N 18 36 E
Maroochydore 116 26 29S 153 5 E
Marquesas Is. 123 9 30S 140 0W
Marquette 150 46 30N 87 21W
Marrakech 126 31 9N 8 0W
Marree 118 29 39S 138 1 E
Marsabit 133 2 18N 38 0 E
Marseille 37 43 18N 5 23 E
Marseilles = Marseille 37 43 18N 5 23 E
Marshall, Minn., U.S.A. 166 44 25N 95 45W
Marshall, Mo., U.S.A. 166 39 8N 93 15W
Marshall, Tex., U.S.A. 168 32 29N 94 20W
Marshalltown 166 42 5N 92 56W
Marshfield 166 44 42N 90 10W
Martaban, G. of 93 16 5N 96 30 E
Martha's Vineyard 164 41 25N 70 35W
Martigues 37 43 24N 5 4 E
Martinique 180 14 40N 61 0W
Martinsburg 164 39 30N 77 57W
Martinsville, Ind., U.S.A. 167 39 29N 86 23W
Martinsville, Va., U.S.A. 165 36 41N 79 52W
Marton 122 40 4S 175 23 E
Marugame 109 34 15N 133 40 E
Maruoka 106 36 9N 136 16 E
Marwar 91 25 43N 73 45 E
Mary 70 37 40N 61 50 E
Maryborough = Port Laoise 35 53 2N 7 20W
Maryborough, Queens., Australia 116 25 31S 152 37 E
Maryborough, Vic., Australia 117 37 0S 143 44 E
Maryland □ 164 39 10N 76 40W
Maryport 28 54 43N 3 30W
Marysville 172 39 14N 121 40W
Maryville 165 35 50N 84 0W
Marzūq 127 25 53N 13 57 E
Masan 98 35 11N 128 32 E
Masaya 179 12 0N 86 7W
Masbate, I. 112 12 21N 123 36 E
Mascota 175 20 32N 104 49W
Maseru 137 29 18S 27 30 E
Mashhad 86 36 20N 59 35 E
Masisea 186 8 35S 74 22W
Masjed Soleyman 84 31 55N 49 18 E
Mask, L. 34 53 36N 9 24W
Mason City 166 43 9N 93 12W
Masqat 83 23 37N 58 36 E
Massachusetts □ 164 42 25N 72 0W
Massawa = Mitsiwa 132 15 35N 39 25 E
Massena 151 44 52N 74 55W
Massif Central 37 45 30N 2 21 E
Massillon 167 40 47N 81 30W
Mastanli = Momchilgrad 53 41 33N 25 23 E
Masterton 123 40 56S 175 39 E
Mastūrah 82 23 7N 38 52 E
Masuda 108 34 40N 131 51 E
Matachewan 151 47 56N 80 39W
Matadi 134 5 52S 13 31 E
Matagalpa 179 13 0N 85 58W
Matamoros, Coahuila, Mexico 174 25 32N 103 15W
Matamoros, Puebla, Mexico 177 18 2N 98 17W
Matane 148 48 50N 67 33W
Matanzas 178 23 0N 81 40W
Matapan, C. = Taínaron, Ákra 54 36 22N 22 27 E
Matarani 186 77 0S 72 10W
Matehuala 177 23 39N 100 39W
Mathura 89 27 30N 77 40 E
Matlock 28 53 8N 1 32W
Mato Grosso □ 188 14 0S 55 0W
Mato Grosso, Planalto do 188 15 0S 59 57W
Matopo Hills 137 20 36S 28 20 E
Matrah 83 23 37N 58 30 E
Matsubara 106 34 33N 135 34 E
Matsudo 107 35 47N 139 54 E
Matsue 109 35 25N 133 10 E
Matsumoto 107 36 15N 138 0 E
Matsusaka 106 34 34N 136 32 E
Matsutō 106 36 31N 136 34 E
Matsuura 108 33 20N 129 49 E
Matsuyama 109 33 45N 132 45 E
Mattancheri 90 9 50N 76 15 E
Mattawa 151 46 20N 78 45W
Matterhorn 44 45 58N 7 39 E
Matucana 186 11 55S 76 25W
Maturín 185 9 45N 63 11W
Mau Ranipur 91 25 16N 79 8 E
Maubeuge 38 50 17N 3 57 E
Maudin Sun 93 16 0N 94 30 E
Maui 160 20 45N 156 20 E
Maulamyaing 93 16 30N 97 40 E
Mauna Kea 160 19 50N 155 28W
Mauna Loa 160 21 8N 157 10W
Maungmagan Kyunzu 94 14 0N 97 48 E
Mauritania ■ 126 20 50N 10 0W
Mauritius ■ 9 20 0S 57 0 E
Mawlaik 93 23 40N 94 26 E
May Pen 180 17 58N 77 15W
Maya → 75 54 31N 134 41 E
Mayagüez 180 18 12N 67 9W
Mayerthorpe 155 53 57N 115 8W
Mayfield 169 36 45N 88 40W
Maykop 70 44 35N 40 25 E
Maynooth 34 53 22N 6 38W
Mayo 144 63 38N 135 57W
Mayo □ 34 53 47N 9 7W
Mayor I. 122 37 16S 176 17 E
Maysville 167 38 39N 83 46W
Mazagán = El Jadida 126 33 11N 8 17W
Mazán 186 3 30S 73 0W
Mazar-e Sharīf 87 36 41N 67 0 E
Mazarredo 192 47 10S 66 50W

Mazatenango	**177**	14 35N	91 30W
Mazatlán	**175**	23 13N	106 25W
Mbandaka	**134**	0 1N	18 18 E
Mdina	**49**	35 51N	14 25 E
Mead, L.	**173**	36 1N	114 44W
Meadville	**164**	41 39N	80 9W
Meander River	**145**	59 2N	117 42W
Meath □	**34**	53 32N	6 40W
Meaux	**39**	48 58N	2 50 E
Mecca = Makkah	**82**	21 30N	39 54 E
Mechelen	**42**	51 2N	4 29 E
Mecklenburger Bucht	**42**	54 20N	11 40 E
Medan	**111**	3 40N	98 38 E
Medellín	**184**	6 15N	75 35W
Medford	**171**	42 20N	122 52W
Mediaş	**57**	46 9N	24 22 E
Medicine Hat	**152**	50 0N	110 45W
Medina = Al Madīnah	**82**	24 35N	39 52 E
Medina	**167**	41 9N	81 50W
Medina del Campo	**50**	41 18N	4 55W
Mediterranean Sea	**124**	35 0N	15 0 E
Medley	**152**	54 25N	110 16W
Médoc	**36**	45 10N	0 56W
Medvezhi, Ostrava	**73**	71 0N	161 0 E
Medway →	**25**	51 28N	0 45 E
Meekatharra	**120**	26 32S	118 29 E
Meerut	**89**	29 1N	77 42 E
Mega	**133**	3 57N	38 19 E
Mégantic, L.	**148**	45 32N	70 53W
Mégara	**55**	37 58N	23 22 E
Meghalaya □	**93**	25 50N	91 0 E
Mei Xian	**99**	24 16N	116 6 E
Meknès	**126**	33 57N	5 33W
Mekong →	**95**	9 30N	106 15 E
Melaka	**96**	2 15N	102 15 E
Melaka □	**96**	2 15N	102 15 E
Melanesia	**122**	4 0S	155 0 E
Melbourne	**117**	37 50S	145 0 E
Melchor Muzquiz	**174**	27 53N	101 31W
Melfort	**152**	52 50N	104 37W
Melilla	**126**	35 21N	2 57W
Melitopol	**68**	46 50N	35 22 E
Melo	**191**	32 20S	54 10W
Melrose	**31**	53 35N	2 44W
Melton Mowbray	**29**	52 46N	0 52W
Melun	**39**	48 32N	2 39 E
Melville	**152**	50 55N	102 50W
Melville, L.	**147**	53 30N	60 0W
Melville I., Australia	**114**	11 30S	131 0 E
Melville I., Canada	**12**	75 30N	112 0W
Melville Pen.	**146**	68 0N	84 0W
Memel = Klaipeda	**68**	55 43N	21 10 E
Memphis	**169**	35 7N	90 0W
Menai Strait	**26**	53 14N	4 10W
Ménaka	**131**	15 59N	2 18 E
Menan = Chao Phraya →	**94**	13 32N	100 36 E
Menasha	**167**	44 13N	88 27W
Mende	**37**	44 31N	3 30 E
Mendip Hills	**27**	51 17N	2 40W
Mendocino	**172**	39 26N	123 50W
Mendoza	**190**	32 50S	68 52W
Menindee	**118**	32 20S	142 25 E
Menindee, L.	**118**	32 20S	142 25 E
Menominee	**150**	45 9N	87 39W
Menorca	**51**	40 0N	4 0 E
Mentawai, Kepulauan	**111**	2 0S	99 0 E
Menzies	**120**	29 40S	120 58 E
Meppel	**41**	52 42N	6 12 E
Merbein	**119**	34 10S	142 2 E
Merca	**133**	1 48N	44 50 E
Merced	**172**	37 18N	120 30W
Mercedes, Buenos Aires, Argentina	**190**	34 40S	59 30W
Mercedes, Corrientes, Argentina	**191**	29 10S	58 5W
Mercedes, San Luis, Argentina	**190**	33 40S	65 21W
Mercedes, Uruguay	**191**	33 12S	58 0W
Mere	**24**	51 5N	2 16W
Mergui Arch. = Myeik Kyunzu	**94**	11 30N	97 30 E
Mérida, Mexico	**177**	20 58N	89 37W
Mérida, Spain	**50**	38 55N	6 25W
Mérida, Venezuela	**184**	8 24N	71 8W
Mérida, Cord. de	**182**	9 0N	71 0W
Meriden	**164**	41 33N	72 47W
Meridian	**169**	32 20N	88 42W
Merowe	**129**	18 29N	31 46 E
Merredin	**120**	31 28S	118 18 E
Merrill	**156**	45 11N	89 41W
Merritt	**155**	50 10N	120 45W
Merriwa	**116**	32 6S	150 22 E
Mersey →	**28**	53 20N	2 56W
Merseyside □	**28**	53 25N	2 55W
Mersin	**80**	36 51N	34 36 E
Merthyr Tydfil	**27**	51 45N	3 23W
Méru	**39**	49 13N	2 8 E
Merville	**38**	50 38N	2 38 E
Mesa	**160**	33 20N	111 56W
Mesa, La	**173**	32 48N	117 5W
Meshed = Mashhad	**86**	36 20N	59 35 E
Mesolóngion	**54**	38 21N	21 28 E
Mesopotamia = Al Jazirah	**81**	33 30N	44 0 E
Mesquite	**173**	36 47N	114 6W
Messina, Italy	**49**	38 10N	15 32 E
Messina, S. Africa	**137**	22 20S	30 0 E
Messina, Str. di	**49**	38 5N	15 35 E
Messíni	**54**	37 4N	22 1 E
Meta →	**184**	6 12N	67 28W
Metairie	**169**	29 59N	90 9W
Metán	**190**	25 30S	65 0W
Metropolis	**169**	37 10N	88 47W
Metz	**37**	49 8N	6 10 E
Meuse →	**42**	50 45N	5 41 E
Mexia	**168**	31 38N	96 32W
Mexicali	**174**	32 40N	115 29W
México, Mexico	**177**	19 20N	99 10W
Mexico, U.S.A.	**166**	39 10N	91 55W
México □	**177**	19 20N	99 30W
Mexico ■	**174**	20 0N	100 0W
Mexico, G. of	**138**	25 0N	90 0W
Mezen →	**69**	66 11N	43 59 E
Mhow	**91**	22 33N	75 50 E
Miahuatlán	**177**	16 21N	96 36W
Miami	**170**	25 45N	80 15W
Miami Beach	**170**	25 49N	80 6W
Mīāneh	**81**	37 30N	47 40 E
Mianwali	**89**	32 38N	71 28 E
Miaoli	**99**	24 37N	120 49 E
Miass	**69**	54 59N	60 6 E
Michigan □	**167**	44 40N	85 40W
Michigan, L.	**150**	44 0N	87 0W
Michigan City	**167**	41 42N	86 56W
Michikamau L.	**147**	54 20N	63 10W
Michipicoten	**150**	47 55N	84 55W
Michoacán □	**175**	19 10N	101 50W
Michurinsk	**68**	52 58N	40 27 E
Micronesia	**122**	11 0N	160 0 E
Mid Glamorgan □	**27**	51 40N	3 25W
Middelburg	**40**	51 30N	3 36 E
Middle Andaman I.	**94**	12 30N	92 30 E
Middlesboro	**165**	36 36N	83 43W
Middlesbrough	**29**	54 35N	1 14W
Middleton	**148**	44 57N	65 4W
Middletown, Conn., U.S.A.	**164**	41 37N	72 40W
Middletown, N.Y., U.S.A.	**164**	41 28N	74 28W
Middletown, Ohio, U.S.A.	**167**	39 29N	84 25W
Midland, Canada	**151**	44 45N	79 50W
Midland, Mich., U.S.A.	**167**	43 37N	84 17W
Midland, Tex., U.S.A.	**161**	32 0N	102 3W
Międzyrzec Podlaski	**58**	51 58N	22 45 E
Miercurea Ciuc	**57**	46 21N	25 48 E
Mieres	**50**	43 18N	5 48W
Migennes	**39**	47 58N	3 31 E
Mihara	**109**	34 24N	133 5 E
Miki	**109**	34 48N	134 59 E
Míkonos	**55**	37 30N	25 25 E
Mikuni-Tōge	**107**	36 50N	138 50 E
Mikura-Jima	**107**	33 52N	139 36 E
Milagro	**184**	2 11S	79 36W
Milan = Milano	**46**	45 28N	9 10 E
Milano	**46**	45 28N	9 10 E
Milâs	**80**	37 20N	27 50 E

Mildura	**119**	34 13S	142 9 E
Miles	**116**	26 40S	150 9 E
Miles City	**163**	46 24N	105 50W
Milford	**164**	38 52N	75 27W
Milford Haven	**27**	51 43N	5 2W
Milk →	**163**	48 5N	106 15W
Millau	**37**	44 8N	3 4 E
Millicent	**119**	37 34S	140 21 E
Millinocket	**148**	45 45N	68 45W
Millmerran	**116**	27 53S	151 16 E
Millom	**28**	54 13N	3 16W
Millville	**164**	39 22N	75 0W
Milne Inlet	**146**	72 30N	80 0W
Mílos	**55**	36 44N	24 25 E
Milton Keynes	**25**	52 3N	0 42W
Milwaukee	**167**	43 9N	87 58W
Milwaukie	**171**	45 27N	122 39W
Minamata	**108**	32 10N	130 30 E
Minas	**191**	34 20S	55 10W
Minas Gerais □	**188**	18 50S	46 0W
Minatitlán	**177**	17 59N	94 31W
Mindanao	**112**	8 0N	125 0 E
Mindanao Sea = Bohol Sea	**112**	9 0N	124 0 E
Minden	**168**	32 40N	93 20W
Mindoro	**112**	13 0N	121 0 E
Mindoro Strait	**112**	12 30N	120 30 E
Mine	**108**	34 12N	131 7 E
Minehead	**27**	51 12N	3 29W
Mineral Wells	**161**	32 50N	98 5W
Mingan	**148**	50 20N	64 0W
Mingenew	**120**	29 12S	115 21 E
Minho □	**50**	41 25N	8 20W
Minneapolis	**166**	44 58N	93 20W
Minnedosa	**153**	50 14N	99 50W
Minnesota □	**156**	46 40N	94 0W
Mino	**106**	35 32N	136 55 E
Mino-Kamo	**106**	35 23N	137 2 E
Mino-Mikawa-Kōgen	**106**	35 10N	137 23 E
Minorca = Menorca	**51**	40 0N	4 0 E
Minot	**163**	48 10N	101 15W
Minsk	**68**	53 52N	27 30 E
Mintaka Pass	**89**	37 0N	74 58 E
Miquelon, I.	**149**	47 2N	56 20W
Miraj	**91**	16 50N	74 45 E
Miranda do Douro	**50**	41 30N	6 16W
Mirpur Khas	**88**	25 30N	69 0 E
Mirzapur	**92**	25 10N	82 34 E
Mirzapur-cum-Vindhyachal = Mirzapur	**92**	25 10N	82 34 E
Miscou I.	**148**	47 57N	64 31W
Mishawaka	**167**	41 40N	86 8W
Mishima	**107**	35 10N	138 52 E
Miskitos, Cayos	**179**	14 26N	82 50W
Miskolc	**59**	48 7N	20 50 E
Misool	**113**	1 52S	130 10 E
Misrātah	**127**	32 24N	15 3 E
Mission City	**154**	49 10N	122 15W
Mississippi □	**169**	33 0N	90 0W
Mississippi →	**169**	29 0N	89 15W
Mississippi, Delta of the	**169**	29 15N	90 30W
Missoula	**162**	46 52N	114 0W
Missouri □	**166**	38 25N	92 30W
Missouri →	**166**	38 50N	90 8W
Mistassini L.	**151**	51 0N	73 30W
Mitaka	**107**	35 40N	139 33 E
Mitchell, Australia	**116**	26 29S	147 58 E
Mitchell, U.S.A.	**163**	43 40N	98 0W
Mitchell →	**115**	15 12S	141 35 E
Mitilíni	**55**	39 6N	26 35 E
Mito	**107**	36 20N	140 30 E
Mitsiwa	**132**	15 35N	39 25 E
Mitsukaidō	**107**	36 1N	139 59 E
Mittagong	**117**	34 28S	150 29 E
Mitú	**184**	1 8N	70 3W
Miura	**107**	35 12N	139 40 E
Miyake-Jima	**107**	34 0N	139 30 E
Miyako	**103**	39 40N	141 59 E
Miyakonojō	**108**	31 40N	131 5 E
Miyanojō	**108**	31 54N	130 27 E
Miyazaki	**108**	31 56N	131 30 E
Miyazu	**106**	35 35N	135 10 E
Miyoshi	**109**	34 48N	132 51 E
Mizamis = Ozamis	**112**	8 15N	123 50 E
Mizen Hd.	**35**	51 27N	9 50W
Mizoram □	**93**	23 30N	92 40 E
Mizunami	**106**	35 22N	137 15 E
Mława	**58**	53 9N	20 25 E
Mobara	**107**	35 25N	140 18 E
Moberley	**166**	39 25N	92 25W
Mobile	**169**	30 41N	88 3W
Mobutu Sese Seko, L.	**132**	1 30N	31 0 E
Moçâmedes = Namibe	**134**	15 7S	12 11 E
Moctezuma, R. →	**177**	21 59N	98 34W
Módena	**46**	44 39N	10 55 E
Modesto	**172**	37 43N	121 0W
Moe	**117**	38 12S	146 19 E
Moei →	**94**	17 25N	98 10 E
Moengo	**185**	5 45N	54 20W
Moffat	**31**	55 20N	3 27W
Mogadishu = Muqdisho	**133**	2 2N	45 25 E
Mogador = Essaouira	**126**	31 32N	9 42W
Mogami →	**103**	38 45N	140 0 E
Mogi das Cruzes	**191**	23 31S	46 11W
Mogilev	**68**	53 55N	30 18 E
Mointy	**71**	47 10N	73 18 E
Moisie	**148**	50 12N	66 1W
Mojave Desert	**173**	35 0N	116 30W
Mold	**26**	53 10N	3 10W
Molde	**65**	62 45N	7 9 E
Moldova ■	**68**	47 0N	28 0 E
Molfetta	**49**	41 12N	16 35 E
Moline	**166**	41 30N	90 30W
Molise □	**49**	41 45N	14 30 E
Mollendo	**187**	17 0S	72 0W
Mölndal	**60**	57 40N	12 3 E
Molong	**117**	33 5S	148 54 E
Molopo →	**136**	28 30S	20 13 E
Molotov = Perm	**69**	58 0N	57 10 E
Molucca Sea	**113**	4 0S	124 0 E
Moluccas = Maluku	**113**	1 0S	127 0 E
Mombasa	**135**	4 2S	39 43 E
Mombetsu	**103**	42 27N	142 4 E
Momchilgrad	**53**	41 33N	25 23 E
Mompós	**184**	9 14N	74 26W
Møn	**61**	54 57N	12 15 E
Mona, Canal de la	**180**	18 30N	67 45W
Monach Is.	**32**	57 32N	7 40W
Monaco ■	**37**	43 46N	7 23 E
Monaghan	**34**	54 15N	6 58W
Monaghan □	**34**	54 10N	7 0W
Monastir = Bitola	**52**	41 5N	21 10 E
Mönchengladbach	**42**	51 12N	6 23 E
Monchique	**50**	37 19N	8 38W
Monclova	**174**	26 50N	101 30W
Moncton	**148**	46 7N	64 51W
Monessen	**164**	40 9N	79 50W
Monforte	**50**	39 6N	7 25W
Mongalla	**129**	5 8N	31 42 E
Monghyr = Munger	**92**	25 23N	86 30 E
Mongolia ■	**98**	47 0N	103 0 E
Monmouth, U.K.	**26**	51 48N	2 43W
Monmouth, U.S.A.	**166**	40 50N	90 40W
Monroe, La., U.S.A.	**168**	32 32N	92 4W
Monroe, Mich., U.S.A.	**167**	41 55N	83 26W
Monroe, N.C., U.S.A.	**165**	35 2N	80 37W
Monrovia, Liberia	**130**	6 18N	10 47W
Monrovia, U.S.A.	**173**	34 7N	118 1W
Mons	**42**	50 27N	3 58 E
Mont-de-Marsan	**36**	43 54N	0 31W
Mont Laurier	**151**	46 35N	75 30W
Montague	**172**	41 47N	122 30W
Montana □	**163**	47 0N	110 0W
Montargis	**39**	48 0N	2 43 E
Montauban	**36**	44 0N	1 21 E
Montbéliard	**37**	47 31N	6 48 E
Montceau-les-Mines	**37**	46 40N	4 23 E
Montdidier	**38**	49 38N	2 35 E
Monte-Carlo	**37**	43 46N	7 23 E
Monte Caseros	**191**	30 10S	57 50W
Montego Bay	**180**	18 30N	78 0W
Montélimar	**37**	44 33N	4 45 E
Montemorelos	**176**	25 11N	99 42W

Montenegro □	**52**	42 40N	19 20 E
Monterey	**173**	36 35N	121 57W
Montería	**184**	8 46N	75 53W
Monterrey	**176**	25 40N	100 30W
Montes Claros	**188**	16 30S	43 50W
Montevideo, Uruguay	**191**	34 50S	56 11W
Montevideo, U.S.A.	**166**	44 55N	95 40W
Montgomery = Sahiwal	**89**	30 45N	73 8 E
Montgomery, U.K.	**26**	52 34N	3 9W
Montgomery, U.S.A.	**169**	32 20N	86 20W
Montluçon	**37**	46 22N	2 36 E
Montmagny	**148**	46 58N	70 34W
Montmorency	**148**	46 53N	71 11W
Montpelier, Idaho, U.S.A.	**163**	42 15N	111 20W
Montpelier, Vt., U.S.A.	**151**	44 15N	72 38W
Montpellier	**37**	43 37N	3 52 E
Montréal	**151**	45 31N	73 34W
Montrose, U.K.	**33**	56 43N	2 28W
Montrose, U.S.A.	**163**	38 30N	107 52W
Montserrat	**180**	16 40N	62 10W
Monywa	**93**	22 7N	95 11 E
Monze, C.	**88**	24 47N	66 37 E
Mo'oka	**107**	36 26N	140 1 E
Moonta	**119**	34 6S	137 32 E
Moora	**120**	30 37S	115 58 E
Moorfoot Hills	**31**	55 44N	3 8W
Moorhead	**156**	46 51N	96 44W
Mooroopna	**117**	36 25S	145 22 E
Moose Jaw	**152**	50 24N	105 30W
Moosehead L.	**148**	45 34N	69 40W
Moosomin	**152**	50 9N	101 40W
Moosonee	**140**	51 17N	80 39W
Mopti	**130**	14 30N	4 0W
Moradabad	**89**	28 50N	78 50 E
Moranbah	**121**	22 1S	148 6 E
Moratuwa	**90**	6 45N	79 55 E
Morava →	**59**	48 10N	16 59 E
Moravian Hts. = Ceskomoravská Vrchovina	**59**	49 30N	15 40 E
Morawa	**120**	29 13S	116 0 E
Morawhanna	**185**	8 30N	59 40W
Moray Firth	**33**	57 50N	3 30W
Morden	**153**	49 15N	98 10W
Mordvinia □	**68**	54 20N	44 30 E
Møre og Romsdal fylke □	**65**	62 30N	8 0 E
Morecambe	**28**	54 5N	2 52W
Morecambe B.	**28**	54 7N	3 0W
Moree	**116**	29 28S	149 54 E
Morehead City	**165**	34 46N	76 44W
Morelia	**175**	19 42N	101 7W
Morelos □	**177**	18 45N	99 0W
Morena, Sierra	**50**	38 20N	4 0W
Moresby I.	**154**	52 30N	131 40W
Morgan City	**168**	29 40N	91 15W
Morganton	**165**	35 46N	81 48W
Morgantown	**164**	39 39N	79 58W
Moriguchi	**106**	34 44N	135 34 E
Morlaix	**36**	48 36N	3 52W
Mornington	**117**	38 15S	145 5 E
Moro G.	**112**	6 30N	123 0 E
Morocco ■	**126**	32 0N	5 50W
Moroleón	**177**	20 8N	101 12W
Morón	**178**	22 8N	78 39W
Morotai	**113**	2 10N	128 30 E
Morrilton	**168**	35 10N	92 45W
Morrinhos	**188**	17 45S	49 10W
Morris	**153**	49 25N	97 22W
Morristown	**165**	36 18N	83 20W
Mortes, R. das →	**188**	11 45S	50 44W
Mortlake	**119**	38 5S	142 50 E
Moruya	**117**	35 58S	150 3 E
Morvern	**30**	56 38N	5 44W
Morwell	**117**	38 10S	146 22 E
Moscos Is.	**94**	14 0N	97 30 E
Moscow = Moskva	**68**	55 45N	37 35 E
Moscow	**171**	46 45N	116 59W
Mosel →	**42**	50 22N	7 36 E
Moselle = Mosel →	**42**	50 22N	7 36 E
Mosgiel	**123**	45 53S	170 21 E
Mosjøen	**65**	65 51N	13 12 E
Moskva	**68**	55 45N	37 35 E
Mosquera	**184**	2 35N	78 24W
Mosquitos, Golfo de los	**179**	9 15N	81 10W
Moss Vale	**117**	34 32S	150 25 E
Mosselbaai	**136**	34 11S	22 8 E
Mossman	**121**	16 21S	145 15 E
Mossoró	**189**	5 10S	37 15W
Mostaganem	**127**	35 54N	0 5 E
Mostar	**52**	43 22N	17 50 E
Mosul = Al Mawşil	**81**	36 15N	43 5 E
Motala	**60**	58 32N	15 1 E
Motherwell	**31**	55 48N	4 0W
Motihari	**92**	26 30N	84 55 E
Motueka	**123**	41 7S	173 1 E
Motul	**177**	21 6N	89 17W
Moúdhros	**55**	39 50N	25 18 E
Moule	**180**	16 20N	61 22W
Moulins	**37**	46 35N	3 19 E
Moultrie	**170**	31 11N	83 47W
Moundsville	**164**	39 53N	80 43W
Mount Airy	**165**	36 31N	80 37W
Mount Barker, S. Austral., Australia	**119**	35 5S	138 52 E
Mount Barker, W. Austral., Australia	**120**	34 38S	117 40 E
Mount Carmel	**167**	38 20N	87 48W
Mount Forest	**151**	43 59N	80 43W
Mount Gambier	**119**	37 50S	140 46 E
Mount Isa	**115**	20 42S	139 26 E
Mount Lofty Ra.	**119**	34 35S	139 5 E
Mount Magnet	**120**	28 2S	117 47 E
Mount Maunganui	**122**	37 40S	176 14 E
Mount Morgan	**121**	23 40S	150 25 E
Mount Pearl	**149**	47 31N	52 47W
Mount Pleasant, Mich., U.S.A.	**167**	43 35N	84 47W
Mount Pleasant, Tex., U.S.A.	**168**	33 5N	95 0W
Mount Sterling	**165**	38 0N	84 0W
Mount Vernon, Ill., U.S.A.	**166**	38 17N	88 57W
Mount Vernon, N.Y., U.S.A.	**164**	40 57N	73 49W
Mount Vernon, Wash., U.S.A.	**171**	48 25N	122 20W
Mount Whaleback	**114**	23 18S	119 44 E
Mountain City	**172**	41 54N	116 0W
Mountain View	**172**	37 26N	122 5W
Moura, Australia	**121**	24 35S	149 58 E
Moura, Brazil	**185**	1 32S	61 38W
Mourne →	**34**	54 45N	7 39W
Mourne Mts.	**34**	54 10N	6 0W
Moyale	**133**	3 30N	39 0 E
Mozambique ■	**137**	19 0S	35 0 E
Mozambique Chan.	**137**	20 0S	39 0 E
Mu Us Shamo	**98**	39 0N	109 0 E
Muaná	**188**	1 25S	49 15W
Muang Chiang Rai	**94**	19 52N	99 50 E
Muck	**32**	56 50N	6 15W
Mucuri	**189**	18 0S	39 36W
Mudanjiang	**98**	44 38N	129 30 E
Mudgee	**117**	32 32S	149 31 E
Muğla	**80**	37 15N	28 22 E
Mukden = Shenyang	**98**	41 50N	123 25 E
Mukhtuya = Lensk	**74**	60 48N	114 55 E
Mukinbudin	**120**	30 55S	118 5 E
Muktsar	**89**	30 30N	74 30 E
Mulchén	**190**	37 45S	72 20W
Mulgrave	**149**	45 38N	61 31W
Mulhacén	**50**	37 4N	3 20W
Mülheim	**42**	51 26N	6 53 E
Mulhouse	**37**	47 40N	7 20 E
Mull	**30**	56 27N	6 0W
Muller, Pegunungan	**111**	0 30N	113 30 E
Mullet Pen.	**34**	54 10N	10 2W
Mullewa	**120**	28 29S	115 30 E
Mullingar	**34**	53 31N	7 20W
Mullumbimby	**116**	28 30S	153 30 E
Multan	**89**	30 15N	71 36 E
Muna	**113**	5 0S	122 30 E
München	**43**	48 8N	11 33 E
Munchen-Gladbach = Mönchengladbach	**42**	51 12N	6 23 E
Muncie	**167**	40 10N	85 20W
Mundo Novo	**189**	11 50S	40 29W
Mungana	**121**	17 8S	144 27 E
Munger	**92**	25 23N	86 30 E

Munich = München	**43**	48 8N	11 33 E
Munising	**150**	46 25N	86 39W
Munku-Sardyk	**74**	51 45N	100 20 E
Münster	**42**	51 58N	7 37 E
Munster □	**35**	52 20N	8 40W
Muqdisho	**133**	2 2N	45 25 E
Murallón, Cuerro	**192**	49 48S	73 30W
Murchison →	**120**	27 45S	114 0 E
Murchison Falls = Kabarega Falls	**132**	2 15N	31 30 E
Murcia	**51**	38 20N	1 10W
Murcia □	**51**	37 50N	1 30W
Mureş →	**56**	46 15N	20 13 E
Mureşul = Mureş →	**56**	46 15N	20 13 E
Murfreesboro	**169**	35 50N	86 21W
Murgon	**116**	26 15S	151 54 E
Müritz See	**43**	53 25N	12 40 E
Murmansk	**69**	68 57N	33 10 E
Muroran	**103**	42 25N	141 0 E
Muroto	**109**	33 18N	134 9 E
Muroto-Misaki	**109**	33 15N	134 10 E
Murphysboro	**166**	37 50N	89 20W
Murray	**169**	36 40N	88 20W
Murray →	**119**	35 20S	139 22 E
Murray Bridge	**119**	35 6S	139 14 E
Murrumbidgee →	**117**	34 43S	143 12 E
Murrurundi	**116**	31 42S	150 51 E
Murtoa	**119**	36 35S	142 28 E
Murupara	**122**	38 28S	176 42 E
Murwillumbah	**116**	28 18S	153 27 E
Muş	**81**	38 45N	41 30 E
Musashino	**107**	35 42N	139 34 E
Muscat = Masqat	**83**	23 37N	58 36 E
Muscat & Oman = Oman ■	**83**	23 0N	58 0 E
Muscatine	**166**	41 25N	91 5W
Musgrave Ras.	**114**	26 0S	132 0 E
Musi →	**111**	2 20S	104 56 E
Muskegon	**167**	43 15N	86 17W
Muskegon →	**167**	43 25N	86 0W
Muskegon Hts.	**167**	43 12N	86 17W
Muskogee	**168**	35 50N	95 25W
Musselburgh	**31**	55 57N	3 3W
Muswellbrook	**116**	32 16S	150 56 E
Mutare	**137**	18 58S	32 38 E
Mutsu	**103**	41 5N	140 55 E
Mutsu-Wan	**103**	41 5N	140 55 E
Muzaffargarh	**89**	30 5N	71 14 E
Muzaffarnagar	**89**	29 26N	77 40 E
Muzaffarpur	**92**	26 7N	85 23 E
Mwanza	**135**	2 30S	32 58 E
Mweru, L.	**135**	9 0S	28 40 E
My Tho	**95**	10 29N	106 23 E
Myanaung	**93**	18 18N	95 22 E
Myeik Kyunzu	**94**	11 30N	97 30 E
Myingyan	**93**	21 30N	95 20 E
Myitkyina	**93**	25 24N	97 26 E
Mýrdalsjökull	**64**	63 40N	19 6W
Myrtle Point	**171**	43 0N	124 4W
Mysore = Karnataka □	**90**	13 15N	77 0 E
Mysore	**90**	12 17N	76 41 E

N

Naaldwijk	**40**	51 59N	4 13 E
Nabari	**106**	34 37N	136 5 E
Naberezhnyye Chelny	**68**	55 42N	52 19 E
Nablus = Nābulus	**80**	32 14N	35 15 E
Nābulus	**80**	32 14N	35 15 E
Nacogdoches	**168**	31 33N	94 39W
Nacozari	**174**	30 24N	109 39W
Nadiad	**91**	22 41N	72 56 E
Nadym	**69**	65 35N	72 42 E
Nagahama	**106**	35 23N	136 16 E
Nagaland □	**93**	26 0N	94 30 E
Nagano	**107**	36 40N	138 10 E
Nagaoka	**105**	37 27N	138 51 E
Nagappattinam	**90**	10 46N	79 51 E
Nagasaki	**108**	32 47N	129 50 E
Nagato	**108**	34 19N	131 5 E
Nagercoil	**90**	8 12N	77 26 E
Nagornyy	**75**	55 58N	124 57 E
Nagoya	**106**	35 10N	136 50 E
Nagpur	**91**	21 8N	79 10 E
Nahanni Butte	**144**	61 2N	123 31W
Nahāvand	**84**	34 10N	48 22 E
Naicam	**152**	52 30N	104 30W
Nain	**147**	56 34N	61 40W
Nainpur	**91**	22 30N	80 10 E
Nairn	**33**	57 35N	3 54W
Nairobi	**132**	1 17S	36 48 E
Naivasha	**132**	0 40S	36 30 E
Najafābād	**85**	32 40N	51 15 E
Najibabad	**89**	29 40N	78 20 E
Naka →	**107**	36 20N	140 36 E
Naka-no-Shima	**104**	29 51N	129 46 E
Nakama	**108**	33 56N	130 43 E
Nakamura	**109**	33 0N	133 0 E
Nakano	**107**	36 45N	138 22 E
Nakanojō	**107**	36 35N	138 51 E
Nakatsu	**108**	33 34N	131 15 E
Nakatsugawa	**106**	35 29N	137 30 E
Nakhichevan □	**70**	39 25N	45 26 E
Nakhodka	**75**	42 53N	132 54 E
Nakhon Phanom	**95**	17 23N	104 43 E
Nakhon Ratchasima	**95**	14 59N	102 12 E
Nakhon Sawan	**94**	15 35N	100 10 E
Nakhon Si Thammarat	**96**	8 29N	100 0 E
Nakina	**140**	50 10N	86 40W
Nakskov	**61**	54 50N	11 8 E
Nakuru	**132**	0 15S	36 4 E
Nalchik	**70**	43 30N	43 33 E
Nalgonda	**91**	17 6N	79 15 E
Nam Co	**101**	30 30N	90 45 E
Nam Dinh	**95**	20 25N	106 5 E
Nam-Phan	**95**	10 30N	106 0 E
Nam Tha	**95**	20 58N	101 30 E
Nam Tok	**94**	14 21N	99 4 E
Namaland	**136**	24 30S	17 0 E
Namangan	**71**	41 0N	71 40 E
Namaqualand	**136**	30 0S	17 25 E
Nambour	**116**	26 32S	152 58 E
Nambucca Heads	**116**	30 37S	153 0 E
Namerikawa	**106**	36 46N	137 20 E
Namib Desert = Namib-Woestyn	**124**	22 30S	15 0 E
Namib-Woestyn	**124**	22 30S	15 0 E
Namibe	**134**	15 7S	12 11 E
Namibia ■	**136**	22 0S	18 9 E
Nampa	**171**	43 34N	116 34W
Namsos	**65**	64 29N	11 30 E
Namur	**42**	50 27N	4 52 E
Nanaimo	**154**	49 10N	124 0W
Nanango	**116**	26 40S	152 0 E
Nanao	**105**	37 0N	137 0 E
Nanchang	**99**	28 42N	115 55 E
Nanching = Nanjing	**99**	32 2N	118 47 E
Nanching	**99**	32 3N	118 47 E
Nancy	**37**	48 42N	6 12 E
Nanda Devi	**101**	30 23N	79 59 E
Nandan	**109**	34 10N	134 42 E
Nanded	**91**	19 10N	77 20 E
Nandurbar	**91**	21 20N	74 15 E
Nanga Parbat	**89**	35 10N	74 35 E
Nangarhár □	**87**	34 20N	70 0 E
Nanjing	**99**	32 2N	118 47 E
Nanking = Nanching	**99**	32 3N	118 47 E
Nanking = Nanjing	**99**	32 2N	118 47 E
Nankoku	**109**	33 39N	133 44 E
Nanning	**99**	22 48N	108 20 E
Nanping	**99**	26 38N	118 10 E
Nantes	**36**	47 12N	1 33W
Nanticoke	**164**	41 12N	76 1W
Nanton	**155**	50 21N	113 46W
Nanuque	**189**	17 50S	40 21W
Napa	**172**	38 18N	122 17W
Napier	**122**	39 30S	176 56 E
Naples = Nápoli	**49**	40 50N	14 17 E
Napo →	**186**	3 20S	72 40W
Nápoli	**49**	40 50N	14 17 E

Nara, Japan **106** 34 40N 135 49 E
Nara, Mali **130** 15 10N 7 20W
Naracoorte **119** 36 58S 140 45 E
Narasapur **92** 16 26N 81 40 E
Narayanganj **92** 23 40N 90 33 E
Narayanpet **91** 16 45N 77 30 E
Narbonne **37** 43 11N 3 0 E
Narita **107** 35 47N 140 19 E
Narmada → **91** 21 38N 72 36 E
Narooma **117** 36 14S 150 4 E
Narrabri **116** 30 19S 149 46 E
Narrandera **117** 34 42S 146 31 E
Narrogin **120** 32 58S 117 14 E
Narromine **116** 32 12S 148 12 E
Naruto **109** 34 11N 134 37 E
Narvik **64** 68 28N 17 26 E
Narym **71** 59 0N 81 30 E
Naser, Buheirat en **128** 23 0N 32 30 E
Nashua **164** 42 50N 71 25W
Nashville **169** 36 12N 86 46W
Nasik **91** 19 58N 73 50 E
Nasirabad **91** 26 15N 74 45 E
Nassau **178** 25 0N 77 20W
Nasser, L. = Naser, Buheirat en **128** 23 0N 32 30 E
Nässjö **60** 57 39N 14 42 E
Natal **189** 5 47S 35 13W
Natashquan **149** 50 14N 61 46W
Natchez **168** 31 35N 91 25W
Natchitoches **168** 31 47N 93 4W
Nathalia **117** 36 1S 145 13 E
National City **173** 32 39N 117 7W
Natuna Besar, Kepulauan **111** 4 0N 108 15 E
Natuna Selatan, Kepulauan **111** 2 45N 109 0 E
Nauru ■ **122** 1 0S 166 0 E
Nauta **186** 4 31S 73 35W
Nautanwa **92** 27 20N 83 25 E
Nautla **177** 20 20N 96 50W
Navarra □ **51** 42 40N 1 40W
Navojoa **174** 27 0N 109 30W
Navsari **91** 20 57N 72 59 E
Nawabshah **88** 26 15N 68 25 E
Nawalgarh **89** 27 50N 75 15 E
Náxos **55** 37 8N 25 25 E
Nāy Band **87** 27 20N 52 40 E
Nayakhan **73** 61 56N 159 0 E
Nayarit □ **175** 22 0N 105 0W
Ndélé **129** 8 25N 20 36 E
Ndjamena **131** 12 10N 14 59 E
Ndola **135** 13 0S 28 34 E
Neagh, Lough **34** 54 35N 6 25W
Near Is. **142** 53 0N 172 0 E
Neath **27** 51 39N 3 49W
Nebraska □ **163** 41 30N 100 0W
Nebraska City **166** 40 40N 95 52W
Nebrodi Mts. **49** 37 55N 14 45 E
Neches → **168** 29 55N 93 52W
Neckar → **42** 49 31N 8 26 E
Necochea **190** 38 30S 58 50W
Needles, The **24** 50 39N 1 35W
Neenah **167** 44 10N 88 30W
Neepawa **153** 50 15N 99 30W
Negapatam = Nagappattinam **90** 10 46N 79 51 E
Negeri Sembilan □ **96** 2 45N 102 10 E
Negotin **53** 44 16N 22 37 E
Negra, Pta. **186** 6 6S 81 10W
Negro →, Argentina **190** 41 2S 62 47W
Negro →, Brazil **185** 3 0S 60 0W
Negros **112** 9 30N 122 40 E
Nehbandān **85** 31 35N 60 5 E
Nei Monggol Zizhiqu □ **98** 42 0N 112 0 E
Neijiang **99** 29 35N 104 55 E
Neiva **184** 2 56N 75 18W
Nellore **90** 14 27N 79 59 E
Nelson, Canada **155** 49 30N 117 20W
Nelson, N.Z. **123** 41 18S 173 16 E
Nelson, U.K. **28** 53 50N 2 14W
Nelson → **153** 54 33N 98 2W
Néma **126** 16 40N 7 15W
Neman → **68** 55 25N 21 10 E
Nemours **39** 48 16N 2 40 E
Nemunas = Neman → **68** 55 25N 21 10 E
Nemuro **103** 43 20N 145 35 E
Nemuro-Kaikyō **103** 43 30N 145 30 E
Nenagh **35** 52 52N 8 11W
Nenana **142** 64 30N 149 20W
Nene → **29** 52 38N 0 13 E
Neosho **168** 36 56N 94 28W
Neosho → **168** 35 59N 95 10W
Nepal ■ **92** 28 0N 84 30 E
Nephi **162** 39 43N 111 52W
Ness, Loch **33** 57 15N 4 30W
Netanya **80** 32 20N 34 51 E
Netherlands ■ **41** 52 0N 5 30 E
Netherlands Antilles ■ **181** 12 15N 69 0W
Netherlands Guiana = Surinam ■ **185** 4 0N 56 0W
Nettilling L. **146** 66 30N 71 0W
Netzahualcoyotl, Presa **177** 17 10N 93 30W
Neuchâtel **44** 47 0N 6 55 E
Neuchâtel, Lac de **44** 46 53N 6 50 E
Neuquén **190** 38 55S 68 0 E
Neuse → **165** 35 5N 76 30W
Neusiedler See **45** 47 50N 16 47 E
Nevada **166** 37 51N 94 22W
Nevada □ **172** 39 20N 117 0W
Nevada, Sierra, Spain **50** 37 3N 3 15W
Nevada, Sierra, U.S.A. **172** 39 0N 120 30W
Nevada City **172** 39 20N 121 0W
Nevada de Sta. Marta, Sa. **184** 10 55N 73 50W
Nevers **37** 47 0N 3 9 E
New Albany **167** 38 20N 85 50W
New Amsterdam **185** 6 15N 57 36W
New Bedford **164** 41 40N 70 52W
New Bern **165** 35 8N 77 3W
New Braunfels **161** 29 43N 98 9W
New Brighton **123** 43 29S 172 43 E
New Britain, Papua N. G. **115** 5 50S 150 20 E
New Britain, U.S.A. **164** 41 41N 72 47W
New Brunswick **164** 40 30N 74 28W
New Brunswick □ **148** 46 50N 66 30W
New Caledonia = Nouvelle Calédonie **122** 21 0S 165 0 E
New Castile = Castilla La Nueva **50** 39 45N 3 20W
New Castle, Ind., U.S.A. **164** 39 55N 85 23W
New Castle, Pa., U.S.A. **164** 41 0N 80 20W
New England Ra. **116** 30 20S 151 45 E
New Forest **24** 50 53N 1 40W
New Glasgow **149** 45 35N 62 36W
New Hampshire □ **164** 43 40N 71 40W
New Haven **164** 41 20N 72 54W
New Hebrides = Vanuatu ■ **122** 15 0S 168 0 E
New Iberia **168** 30 2N 91 54W
New Ireland **115** 3 20S 151 50 E
New Jersey □ **164** 40 30N 74 10W
New Kensington **164** 40 36N 79 43W
New London **164** 41 23N 72 8W
New Mexico □ **161** 34 30N 106 0W
New Norfolk **119** 42 46S 147 2 E
New Orleans **169** 30 0N 90 5W
New Philadelphia **164** 40 29N 81 25W
New Plymouth **122** 39 4S 174 5 E
New Providence **178** 25 25N 78 35W
New Radnor **26** 52 15N 3 10W
New Siberian Is. = Novosibirskiye Ostrova **72** 75 0N 142 0 E
New South Wales □ **116** 33 0S 146 0 E
New Ulm **166** 44 15N 94 30W
New Waterford **149** 46 13N 60 4W
New Westminster **154** 49 13N 122 55W
New York □ **164** 42 40N 76 0W
New York City **164** 40 45N 74 0W
New Zealand ■ **122** 40 0S 176 0 E
Newark, N.J., U.S.A. **164** 40 41N 74 12W
Newark, N.Y., U.S.A. **164** 43 2N 77 10W
Newark, Ohio, U.S.A. **167** 40 5N 82 24W
Newark-on-Trent **29** 53 6N 0 48W
Newberry, Mich., U.S.A. **150** 46 20N 85 32W
Newberry, S.C., U.S.A. **165** 34 17N 81 37W
Newburgh **164** 41 30N 74 1W
Newburyport **164** 42 48N 70 50W

Newcastle, Australia	**117**	33 0S	151 46 E
Newcastle, Canada	**148**	47 1N	65 38W
Newcastle, U.K.	**34**	54 13N	5 54W
Newcastle Emlyn	**26**	52 2N	4 29W
Newcastle-under-Lyme	**28**	53 2N	2 15W
Newcastle-upon-Tyne	**28**	54 59N	1 37W
Newfoundland □	**149**	53 0N	58 0W
Newhaven	**25**	50 47N	0 4 E
Newmarket	**25**	52 15N	0 23 E
Newnan	**170**	33 22N	84 48W
Newport, Gwent, U.K.	**27**	51 35N	3 0W
Newport, I. of W., U.K.	**25**	50 42N	1 18W
Newport, Ark., U.S.A.	**168**	35 38N	91 15W
Newport, Ky., U.S.A.	**167**	39 5N	84 23W
Newport, Oreg., U.S.A.	**171**	44 41N	124 2W
Newport, R.I., U.S.A.	**164**	41 13N	71 19W
Newport, Vt., U.S.A.	**148**	44 57N	72 17W
Newport Beach	**173**	33 40N	117 58W
Newport News	**165**	37 2N	76 30W
Newquay	**27**	50 24N	5 6W
Newry	**34**	54 10N	6 20W
Newton, Iowa, U.S.A.	**166**	41 40N	93 3W
Newton, Mass., U.S.A.	**164**	42 21N	71 10W
Newton Abbot	**27**	50 32N	3 37W
Newton Stewart	**31**	54 57N	4 30W
Newtonmore	**33**	57 4N	4 7W
Newtown	**26**	52 31N	3 19W
Newtownards	**34**	54 37N	5 40W
Ngaoundéré	**131**	7 15N	13 35 E
Ngoring Hu	**101**	34 55N	97 5 E
Nguru	**131**	12 56N	10 29 E
Nha Trang	**95**	12 16N	109 10 E
Nhill	**119**	36 18S	141 40 E
Niagara Falls, Canada	**151**	43 7N	79 5W
Niagara Falls, U.S.A.	**164**	43 5N	79 0W
Niamey	**131**	13 27N	2 6 E
Nias	**111**	1 0N	97 30 E
Nicaragua ■	**179**	11 40N	85 30W
Nicaragua, Lago de	**179**	12 0N	85 30W
Nice	**37**	43 42N	7 14 E
Nichinan	**108**	31 38N	131 23 E
Nicobar Is.	**8**	9 0N	93 0 E
Nicosia	**80**	35 10N	33 25 E
Nicoya, Pen. de	**179**	9 45N	85 40W
Nidd →	**28**	54 1N	1 32W
Niederösterreich □	**45**	48 25N	15 40 E
Niedersachsen □	**42**	52 45N	9 0 E
Nieuw Nickerie	**185**	6 0N	56 59W
Niger ■	**131**	13 30N	10 0 E
Niger →	**131**	5 33N	6 33 E
Nigeria ■	**131**	8 30N	8 0 E
Nii-Jima	**107**	34 20N	139 15 E
Niigata	**103**	37 58N	139 0 E
Niihama	**109**	33 55N	133 16 E
Niimi	**109**	34 59N	133 28 E
Nijkerk	**41**	52 13N	5 30 E
Nijmegen	**41**	51 50N	5 52 E
Nikki	**131**	9 58N	3 12 E
Nikkō	**107**	36 45N	139 35 E
Nikolayev	**68**	46 58N	32 0 E
Nikolayevsk-na-Amur	**75**	53 8N	140 44 E
Nikolskoye	**73**	55 12N	166 0 E
Nikšić	**52**	42 50N	18 57 E
Nîl, Nahr en →	**128**	30 10N	31 6 E
Nîl el Abyad →	**129**	15 38N	32 31 E
Nîl el Azraq →	**129**	15 38N	32 31 E
Nile = Nîl, Nahr en →	**128**	30 10N	31 6 E
Niles	**164**	41 8N	80 40W
Nîmes	**37**	43 50N	4 23 E
Nimule	**129**	3 32N	32 3 E
Nīnawá	**81**	36 25N	43 10 E
Nineveh = Nīnawá	**81**	36 25N	43 10 E
Ningbo	**99**	29 51N	121 28 E
Ningde	**99**	26 38N	119 23 E
Ningpo = Ningbo	**99**	29 51N	121 28 E
Ningsia Hui A.R. = Ningxia Huizu Zizhiqu □	**98**	38 0N	106 0 E
Ningxia Huizu Zizhiqu □	**98**	38 0N	106 0 E
Niobrara →	**163**	42 45N	98 0W
Nioro du Sahel	**130**	15 15N	9 30W
Niort	**36**	46 19N	0 29W
Nipawin	**152**	53 20N	104 0W
Nipigon	**150**	49 0N	88 17W
Nipigon, L.	**150**	49 50N	88 30W
Niš	**53**	43 19N	21 58 E
Nişāb	**83**	14 25N	46 29 E
Nishinomiya	**106**	34 45N	135 20 E
Nishio	**106**	34 52N	137 3 E
Nishiwaki	**109**	34 59N	134 58 E
Niterói	**188**	22 52S	43 0W
Nith →	**31**	55 20N	3 5W
Nitra	**59**	48 19N	18 4 E
Nivernais	**37**	47 0N	3 40 E
Nizamabad	**91**	18 45N	78 7 E
Nizhne Kolymsk	**73**	68 34N	160 55 E
Nizhneudinsk	**74**	54 54N	99 3 E
Nizhnevartovsk	**69**	60 56N	76 38 E
Nizhniy Novgorod	**68**	56 20N	44 0 E
Nizhniy Tagil	**69**	57 55N	59 57 E
Nizhnyaya Tunguska →	**74**	64 20N	93 0 E
Nizké Tatry	**59**	48 55N	20 0 E
Nkongsamba	**131**	4 55N	9 55 E
Noatak	**142**	67 32N	162 59W
Nobeoka	**108**	32 36N	131 41 E
Noda	**107**	35 56N	139 52 E
Nogales	**174**	31 20N	110 56W
Nōgata	**108**	33 48N	130 44 E
Nogent-le-Rotrou	**39**	48 20N	0 50 E
Noi →	**94**	14 50N	100 15 E
Noirmoutier, Î. de	**36**	46 58N	2 10W
Nojima-Zaki	**107**	34 54N	139 53 E
Nok Kundi	**88**	28 50N	62 45 E
Nome	**142**	64 30N	165 24W
Nong Khae	**95**	14 29N	100 53 E
Nong Khai	**95**	17 50N	102 46 E
Nonoava	**174**	27 28N	106 44W
Noord Brabant □	**40**	51 40N	5 0 E
Noord Holland □	**40**	52 30N	4 45 E
Noordbeveland	**40**	51 35N	3 50 E
Noordoostpolder	**41**	52 45N	5 45 E
Noordwijk aan Zee	**40**	52 14N	4 26 E
Nootka I.	**154**	49 32N	126 42W
Nord-Trøndelag fylke □	**65**	64 20N	12 0 E
Nordaustlandet	**13**	79 14N	23 0 E
Nordegg	**155**	52 29N	116 5W
Nordkapp	**67**	71 10N	25 44 E
Nordkinn	**67**	71 8N	27 40 E
Nordland fylke □	**65**	65 40N	13 0 E
Nordrhein-Westfalen □	**42**	51 45N	7 30 E
Nordvik	**72**	74 2N	111 32 E
Nore →	**35**	52 40N	7 20W
Norfolk	**165**	36 40N	76 15W
Norfolk □	**29**	52 39N	1 0 E
Norfolk I.	**122**	28 58S	168 3 E
Norilsk	**72**	69 20N	88 6 E
Norman	**168**	35 12N	97 30W
Norman Wells	**144**	65 17N	126 51W
Normandie	**39**	48 45N	0 10 E
Normandin	**151**	48 49N	72 31W
Normandy = Normandie	**39**	48 45N	0 10 E
Normanton	**115**	17 40S	141 10 E
Norquinco	**192**	41 51S	70 55W
Norristown	**164**	40 9N	75 21W
Norrköping	**60**	58 37N	16 11 E
Norrland □	**66**	66 50N	18 0 E
Norseman	**114**	32 8S	121 43 E
Norsk	**75**	52 30N	130 0 E
North Andaman I.	**94**	13 15N	92 40 E
North Battleford	**152**	52 50N	108 17W
North Bay	**151**	46 20N	79 30W
North Bend	**171**	43 28N	124 14W
North Berwick	**31**	56 4N	2 44W
North C.	**122**	34 23S	173 4 E
North Carolina □	**165**	35 30N	80 0W
North Channel, Br. Is.	**30**	55 0N	5 30W
North Channel, Canada	**150**	46 0N	83 0W
North Dakota □	**163**	47 30N	100 0W
North Downs	**25**	51 17N	0 30 E
North European Plain	**17**	55 0N	20 0 E
North I.	**122**	38 0S	175 0 E
North Korea ■	**98**	40 0N	127 0 E
North Minch	**32**	58 5N	5 55W

North Ossetia □ **70** 43 30N 44 30 E
North Platte **163** 41 10N 100 50W
North Platte → **163** 41 15N 100 45W
North Pole **12** 90 0N 0 0 E
North Ronaldsay **33** 59 20N 2 30W
North Saskatchewan → **143** 53 15N 105 5W
North Sea **16** 56 0N 4 0 E
North Sentinel I. **94** 11 35N 92 15 E
North Sporades = Voríai Sporádhes **55** 39 15N 23 30 E
North Sydney **149** 46 12N 60 15W
North Tonawanda **164** 43 5N 78 50W
North Uist **32** 57 40N 7 15W
North Vancouver **154** 49 25N 123 3W
North Walsham **29** 52 49N 1 22 E
North West Frontier □ **89** 34 0N 71 0 E
North West Highlands **32** 57 35N 5 2W
North West River **147** 53 30N 60 10W
North West Territories □ **145** 67 0N 110 0W
North York Moors **29** 54 25N 0 50W
North Yorkshire □ **28** 54 15N 1 25W
Northallerton **28** 54 20N 1 26W
Northam **120** 31 35S 116 42 E
Northampton, Australia **120** 28 27S 114 33 E
Northampton, U.K. **25** 52 14N 0 54W
Northampton, U.S.A. **164** 42 22N 72 31W
Northampton □ **25** 52 16N 0 55W
Northcliffe **120** 34 39S 116 7 E
Northern Circars **92** 17 30N 82 30 E
Northern Ireland □ **34** 54 45N 7 0W
Northern Territory □ **114** 16 0S 133 0 E
Northfield **166** 44 30N 93 10W
Northumberland □ **28** 55 12N 2 0W
Northumberland Is. **121** 21 30S 149 50 E
Northumberland Str. **148** 46 20N 64 0W
Northwich **28** 53 16N 2 30W
Norton Sd. **142** 64 0N 164 0W
Norwalk **164** 41 9N 73 25W
Norway ■ **18** 63 0N 11 0 E
Norwegian Sea **16** 66 0N 1 0 E
Norwich **29** 52 38N 1 17 E
Nos Kaliakra **53** 43 21N 28 30 E
Noshiro **103** 40 12N 140 0 E
Noss Hd. **33** 58 29N 3 4W
Nossob → **136** 26 55S 20 37 E
Noteć → **58** 52 44N 15 26 E
Notre Dame de Koartac = Koartac **146** 60 55N 69 40W
Nottaway → **140** 51 22N 78 55W
Nottingham **29** 52 57N 1 10W
Nottingham □ **29** 53 10N 1 0W
Nouâdhibou **126** 20 54N 17 0W
Nouâdhibou, Ras **126** 20 50N 17 0W
Nouakchott **126** 18 9N 15 58W
Noumea **122** 22 17S 166 30 E
Nouveau Comptoir **140** 53 0N 78 49W
Nouvelle Calédonie **122** 21 0S 165 0 E
Nova Friburgo **188** 22 16S 42 30W
Nova Granada **188** 20 30S 49 20W
Nova Lisboa = Huambo **134** 12 42S 15 54 E
Nova Scotia □ **149** 45 10N 63 0W
Novara **46** 45 27N 8 36 E
Novaya Sibir, Ostrov **72** 75 10N 150 0 E
Novaya Zemlya **69** 75 0N 56 0 E
Novgorod **68** 58 30N 31 25 E
Novi Pazar **52** 43 12N 20 28 E
Novi Sad **52** 45 18N 19 52 E
Novocherkassk **68** 47 27N 40 5 E
Novokuznetsk **71** 53 45N 87 10 E
Novomoskovsk **68** 54 5N 38 15 E
Novorossiysk **68** 44 43N 37 46 E
Novosibirsk **71** 55 0N 83 5 E
Novosibirskiye Ostrova **72** 75 0N 142 0 E
Nowgong **93** 26 20N 92 50 E
Nowra **117** 34 53S 150 35 E
Nowy Sącz **59** 49 40N 20 41 E
Noyon **38** 49 34N 3 0 E
Nûbîya, Es Sahrâ En **129** 21 30N 33 30 E
Nueces → **161** 27 50N 97 30W
Nueltin L. **145** 60 30N 99 30W
Nueva Gerona **178** 21 53N 82 49W
Nueva Rosita **174** 27 57N 101 13W
Nuevitas **178** 21 30N 77 20W
Nuevo Laredo **176** 27 30N 99 30W
Nuevo Leon □ **176** 25 40N 100 0W
Nuhaka **122** 39 3S 177 45 E
Nukey Bluff, Mt. **118** 32 26S 135 29 E
Nukus **70** 42 20N 59 7 E
Nulato **142** 64 40N 158 10W
Nullarbor Plain **114** 30 45S 129 0 E
Numan **131** 9 29N 12 3 E
Numazu **107** 35 7N 138 51 E
Numurkah **117** 36 5S 145 26 E
Nuneaton **25** 52 32N 1 29W
Nunivak **142** 60 0N 166 0W
Nunspeet **41** 52 21N 5 45 E
Nuoro **48** 40 20N 9 20 E
Nuremburg = Nürnberg **43** 49 26N 11 5 E
Nuriootpa **119** 34 27S 139 0 E
Nürnberg **43** 49 26N 11 5 E
Nurran, L. = Terewah, L. **116** 29 52S 147 35 E
Nutak **147** 57 28N 61 59W
Nuweveldberge **136** 32 10S 21 45 E
Nuyts Arch. **118** 32 35S 133 20 E
Nyaake **130** 4 52N 7 37W
Nyainqentanglha Shan **101** 30 0N 90 0 E
Nyasa, L. = Malawi, L. **137** 12 30S 34 30 E
Nyíregyháza **59** 47 58N 21 47 E
Nyngan **116** 31 30S 147 8 E
Nysa **58** 50 30N 17 22 E

O

Oahe L. **163** 45 30N 100 25W
Oahu **160** 21 30N 158 0W
Oak Hill **165** 38 0N 81 7W
Oak Park **167** 41 55N 87 45W
Oak Ridge **169** 36 1N 84 12W
Oakengates **28** 52 42N 2 29W
Oakey **116** 27 25S 151 43 E
Oakham **29** 52 40N 0 43W
Oakland **172** 37 50N 122 18W
Oakridge **171** 43 47N 122 31W
Oamaru **123** 45 5S 170 59 E
Oaxaca **177** 17 2N 96 40W
Oaxaca □ **177** 17 0N 96 30W
Ob → **69** 66 45N 69 30 E
Oba **150** 49 4N 84 7W
Obama **106** 35 30N 135 45 E
Oban **30** 56 25N 5 30W
Obbia **133** 5 25N 48 30 E
Oberhausen **42** 51 28N 6 50 E
Oberon **117** 33 45S 149 52 E
Oberösterreich □ **45** 48 10N 14 0 E
Obi, Is. **113** 1 30S 127 30 E
Obihiro **103** 42 56N 143 12 E
Obskaya Guba **69** 69 0N 73 0 E
Ocala **170** 29 11N 82 5W
Ocampo **174** 28 11N 108 23W
Ocaña **184** 8 15N 73 20W
Occidental, Cordillera **184** 5 0N 76 0W
Ocean City **164** 39 18N 74 34W
Oceanside **173** 33 13N 117 26W
Ochil Hills **31** 56 14N 3 40W
Oconee → **170** 31 58N 82 32W
Oconto **167** 44 52N 87 53W
Ocotlán **175** 20 21N 102 46W
Ōda **109** 35 11N 132 30 E
Ódáðahraun **64** 65 5N 17 0W
Odate **103** 40 16N 140 34 E
Odawara **107** 35 20N 139 6 E
Ödemiş **80** 38 15N 28 0 E
Odense **61** 55 22N 10 23 E
Oder → **58** 53 33N 14 38 E
Odessa, Ukraine **68** 46 30N 30 45 E
Odessa, U.S.A. **161** 31 51N 102 23W
Odra → **58** 53 33N 14 38 E
Odžak **52** 45 3N 18 18 E
Offaly □ **35** 53 15N 7 30W

Offenbach	**42**	50 6N	8 46 E
Oga-Hantō	**103**	39 58N	139 47 E
Ogaden	**133**	7 30N	45 30 E
Ōgaki	**106**	35 21N	136 37 E
Ogbomosho	**131**	8 1N	4 11 E
Ogden	**163**	41 13N	112 1W
Ogdensburg	**151**	44 40N	75 27W
Ohio □	**167**	40 20N	14 10 E
Ohio →	**167**	38 0N	86 0W
Ohrid	**52**	41 8N	20 52 E
Ohridsko, Jezero	**52**	41 8N	20 52 E
Oil City	**164**	41 26N	79 40W
Oise →	**38**	49 0N	2 4 E
Oisterwijk	**40**	51 35N	5 12 E
Ōita	**108**	33 14N	131 36 E
Ojos del Salado, Cerro	**190**	27 0S	68 40W
Oka →	**68**	56 20N	43 59 E
Okawa	**108**	33 9N	130 21 E
Okaya	**107**	36 0N	138 10 E
Okayama	**109**	34 40N	133 54 E
Okazaki	**106**	34 57N	137 10 E
Okeechobee, L.	**170**	27 0N	80 50W
Okehampton	**27**	50 44N	4 1W
Okha	**75**	53 40N	143 0 E
Okhotsk	**75**	59 20N	143 10 E
Okhotsk, Sea of	**77**	55 0N	145 0 E
Okhotsko Kolymskoye	**73**	63 0N	157 0 E
Oki-no-Shima	**109**	32 44N	132 33 E
Oki-Shotō	**109**	36 5N	133 15 E
Okinawa-Jima	**99**	26 32N	128 0 E
Oklahoma □	**161**	35 20N	97 30W
Oklahoma City	**161**	35 25N	97 30W
Okmulgee	**168**	35 38N	96 0W
Oktabrsk	**70**	49 28N	57 25 E
Oktyabrskoy Revolyutsii, Os.	**72**	79 30N	97 0 E
Oktyabrskoye	**69**	62 28N	66 3 E
Ōkuchi	**108**	32 4N	130 37 E
Okuru	**123**	43 55S	168 55 E
Okushiri-Tō	**103**	42 15N	139 30 E
Olanchito	**179**	15 30N	86 30W
Öland	**61**	56 45N	16 38 E
Olary	**118**	32 18S	140 19 E
Olavarría	**190**	36 55S	60 20W
Old Castile = Castilla La Vieja	**50**	41 55N	4 0W
Old Town	**148**	45 0N	68 41W
Oldenburg	**42**	53 10N	8 10 E
Oldenzaal	**41**	52 19N	6 53 E
Oldham	**28**	53 33N	2 8W
Olds	**155**	51 50N	114 10W
Olekma →	**74**	60 22N	120 42 E
Olekminsk	**74**	60 25N	120 30 E
Olenek	**72**	68 28N	112 18 E
Olenek →	**72**	73 0N	120 10 E
Oléron, Île d'	**36**	45 55N	1 15W
Oleśnica	**58**	51 13N	17 22 E
Olifants →	**137**	24 5S	31 20 E
Ólimbos, Óros	**54**	40 6N	22 23 E
Oliveira	**188**	20 39S	44 50W
Oliver	**155**	49 13N	119 37W
Ollagüe	**187**	21 15S	68 10W
Olney	**167**	38 40N	88 0W
Olomouc	**59**	49 38N	17 12 E
Olsztyn	**58**	53 48N	20 29 E
Olt →	**57**	43 50N	24 40 E
Olympia, Greece	**54**	37 39N	21 39 E
Olympia, U.S.A.	**171**	47 0N	122 58W
Olympic Mts.	**171**	47 50N	123 45W
Olympus, Mt. = Ólimbos, Óros	**54**	40 6N	22 23 E
Olympus, Mt.	**171**	47 52N	123 40W
Ōmachi	**107**	36 30N	137 50 E
Omae-Zaki	**107**	34 36N	138 14 E
Omagh	**34**	54 36N	7 20W
Omaha	**166**	41 15N	96 0W
Omak	**171**	48 24N	119 31W
Oman ■	**83**	23 0N	58 0 E
Oman, G. of	**83**	24 30N	58 30 E
Omdurmân	**129**	15 40N	32 28 E
Ōme	**107**	35 47N	139 15 E
Omeo	**117**	37 6S	147 36 E
Omihachiman	**106**	35 7N	136 3 E
Ōmiya	**107**	35 54N	139 38 E
Omo →	**132**	6 25N	36 10 E
Omolon →	**73**	68 42N	158 36 E
Omono-Gawa →	**103**	39 46N	140 3 E
Omsk	**71**	55 0N	73 12 E
Ōmura	**108**	32 56N	130 0 E
Ōmuta	**108**	33 0N	130 26 E
Onega	**68**	64 0N	38 10 E
Onega, L. = Onezhskoye Ozero	**68**	62 0N	35 30 E
Onehunga	**122**	36 55S	174 48 E
Oneida	**164**	43 5N	75 40W
Onekotan, Ostrov	**75**	49 25N	154 45 E
Onezhskoye Ozero	**68**	62 0N	35 30 E
Ongerup	**120**	33 58S	118 28 E
Ongole	**90**	15 33N	80 2 E
Onguren	**74**	53 38N	107 36 E
Onitsha	**131**	6 6N	6 42 E
Ono, Fukui, Japan	**106**	35 59N	136 29 E
Ono, Hyōgo, Japan	**109**	34 51N	134 56 E
Onoda	**108**	34 2N	131 25 E
Onomichi	**109**	34 25N	133 12 E
Onslow	**114**	21 40S	115 12 E
Onslow B.	**165**	34 20N	77 20W
Ontake-San	**106**	35 53N	137 29 E
Ontario	**173**	34 2N	117 40W
Ontario □	**140**	52 0N	88 10W
Ontario, L.	**151**	43 40N	78 0W
Oodnadatta	**118**	27 33S	135 30 E
Ooldea	**114**	30 27S	131 50 E
Oostende	**42**	51 15N	2 50 E
Oosterhout	**40**	51 39N	4 47 E
Oosterschelde	**40**	51 33N	4 0 E
Opala	**73**	51 58N	156 30 E
Opava	**58**	49 57N	17 58 E
Opelousas	**168**	30 35N	92 7W
Ophir	**142**	63 10N	156 40W
Opole	**58**	50 42N	17 58 E
Oporto = Porto	**50**	41 8N	8 40W
Opp	**169**	31 19N	86 13W
Oppland fylke □	**60**	61 15N	9 40 E
Opua	**122**	35 19S	174 9 E
Oradea	**56**	47 2N	21 58 E
Öræfajökull	**64**	64 2N	16 39W
Orai	**91**	25 58N	79 30 E
Oran, Algeria	**127**	35 45N	0 39W
Oran, Argentina	**190**	23 10S	64 20W
Orange, Australia	**117**	33 15S	149 7 E
Orange, France	**37**	44 8N	4 47 E
Orange, U.S.A.	**168**	30 10N	93 50W
Orange → = Oranje →	**136**	28 41S	16 28 E
Orange, C.	**185**	4 20N	51 30W
Orangeburg	**170**	33 35N	80 53W
Oranje →	**136**	28 41S	16 28 E
Oraşul Stalin = Braşov	**57**	45 38N	25 35 E
Orbost	**117**	37 40S	148 29 E
Orchies	**38**	50 28N	3 14 E
Ordos = Mu Us Shamo	**98**	39 0N	109 0 E
Ordu	**81**	40 55N	37 53 E
Ordzhonikidze = Vladikavkaz	**70**	43 0N	44 35 E
Ore Mts. = Erzgebirge	**43**	50 25N	13 0 E
Örebro	**60**	59 20N	15 18 E
Oregon □	**171**	44 0N	121 0W
Oregon City	**171**	45 21N	122 35W
Orel	**68**	52 57N	36 3 E
Orenburg	**70**	51 45N	55 6 E
Orense	**50**	42 19N	7 55W
Orepuki	**123**	46 19S	167 46 E
Orford Ness	**24**	52 6N	1 31 E
Oriental, Cordillera	**184**	6 0N	73 0W
Orillia	**151**	44 40N	79 24W
Orinoco →	**185**	9 15N	61 30W
Orissa □	**92**	20 0N	84 0 E
Oristano	**48**	39 54N	8 35 E
Oristano, Golfo di	**48**	39 50N	8 22 E
Orizaba	**177**	18 51N	97 6W
Orkney Is.	**33**	59 0N	3 0W
Orland	**172**	39 46N	122 12W
Orlando	**170**	28 30N	81 25W
Orléanais	**39**	48 0N	2 0 E
Orléans	**39**	47 54N	1 52 E

Ormara	**88**	25 16N	64 33 E
Ormskirk	**28**	53 35N	2 53W
Örnsköldsvik	**66**	63 17N	18 40 E
Orocué	**184**	4 48N	71 20W
Oroville	**172**	39 31N	121 30W
Orsha	**68**	54 30N	30 25 E
Orsk	**70**	51 12N	58 34 E
Ortegal, C.	**50**	43 43N	7 52W
Orūmīyeh	**81**	37 40N	45 0 E
Orūmīyeh, Daryācheh-ye	**81**	37 50N	45 30 E
Oruro	**187**	18 0S	67 9W
Oruzgān □	**87**	33 30N	66 0 E
Oryakhovo	**53**	43 40N	23 57 E
Osage ⟶	**166**	38 35N	91 57W
Ōsaka	**106**	34 40N	135 30 E
Osceola	**169**	35 40N	90 0W
Ösel = Saaremaa	**68**	58 30N	22 30 E
Osh	**71**	40 37N	72 49 E
Oshawa	**151**	43 50N	78 50W
Oshima	**107**	33 55N	132 14 E
Oshkosh	**167**	44 3N	88 35W
Oshogbo	**131**	7 48N	4 37 E
Osijek	**52**	45 34N	18 41 E
Oskaloosa	**166**	41 18N	92 40W
Oslo	**60**	59 55N	10 45 E
Osmaniye	**80**	37 5N	36 10 E
Osnabrück	**42**	52 16N	8 2 E
Osorno	**190**	40 25S	73 0W
Oss	**41**	51 46N	5 32 E
Ossa, Mt.	**119**	41 52S	146 3 E
Ostend = Oostende	**42**	51 15N	2 50 E
Östergötlands län □	**60**	58 35N	15 45 E
Östersund	**66**	63 10N	14 38 E
Østfold fylke □	**60**	59 25N	11 25 E
Ostfriesische Inseln	**42**	53 45N	7 15 E
Ostia	**46**	41 40N	12 20 E
Ostrava	**59**	49 51N	18 18 E
Ostróda	**58**	53 42N	19 58 E
Ostrołeka	**58**	53 4N	21 32 E
Ostrów Mazowiecka	**58**	52 50N	21 51 E
Ostrów Wielkopolski	**58**	51 36N	17 44 E
Ōsumi-Kaikyō	**104**	30 55N	131 0 E
Ōsumi-Shotō	**104**	30 30N	130 0 E
Oswego	**164**	43 29N	76 30W
Oswestry	**28**	52 52N	3 3W
Ōta	**107**	36 18N	139 22 E
Otago □	**123**	44 44S	169 10 E
Ōtake	**109**	34 12N	132 13 E
Otaki	**122**	40 45S	175 10 E
Otaru	**103**	43 10N	141 0 E
Otaru-Wan = Ishikari-Wan	**103**	43 25N	141 1 E
Otira Gorge	**123**	42 53S	171 33 E
Otoineppu	**103**	44 44N	142 16 E
Otranto	**49**	40 9N	18 28 E
Otranto, C. d'	**49**	40 7N	18 30 E
Otranto, Str. of	**52**	40 15N	18 40 E
Ōtsu	**106**	35 0N	135 50 E
Ottawa, Canada	**151**	45 27N	75 42W
Ottawa, U.S.A.	**166**	38 40N	95 6W
Ottawa ⟶ = Outaouais ⟶	**140**	45 27N	74 8W
Ottawa Is.	**146**	59 35N	80 10W
Otter Rapids, Ont., Canada	**151**	50 11N	81 39W
Otter Rapids, Sask., Canada	**152**	55 38N	104 44W
Ottumwa	**166**	41 0N	92 25W
Otwock	**58**	52 5N	21 20 E
Ouachita ⟶	**168**	31 38N	91 49W
Ouachita Mts.	**168**	34 50N	94 30W
Ouagadougou	**130**	12 25N	1 30W
Ouahran = Oran	**127**	35 45N	0 39W
Ouargla	**127**	31 59N	5 16 E
Oubangi ⟶	**131**	1 0N	17 50 E
Oudenbosch	**40**	51 35N	4 32 E
Oudtshoorn	**136**	33 35S	22 14 E
Ouessant, Île d'	**36**	48 28N	5 6W
Oujda	**127**	34 41N	1 55W
Oulu	**67**	65 1N	25 29 E
Oulujärvi	**67**	64 25N	27 15 E
Oulujoki ⟶	**67**	65 1N	25 30 E
Ouse ⟶	**29**	54 3N	0 7 E
Outaouais ⟶	**140**	45 27N	74 8W
Outer Hebrides	**32**	57 30N	7 40W
Outlook	**152**	51 30N	107 0W
Outreau	**38**	50 40N	1 36 E
Ouyen	**119**	35 1S	142 22 E
Ovalle	**190**	30 33S	71 18W
Overflakkee	**40**	51 44N	4 10 E
Overijssel □	**41**	52 25N	6 35 E
Oviedo	**50**	43 25N	5 50W
Owaka	**123**	46 27S	169 40 E
Owase	**106**	34 7N	136 12 E
Owatonna	**166**	44 3N	93 10W
Owen Sound	**151**	44 35N	80 55W
Owen Stanley Range	**115**	8 30S	147 0 E
Owensboro	**167**	37 40N	87 5W
Owosso	**167**	43 0N	84 10W
Owyhee ⟶	**171**	43 46N	117 2W
Oxford, U.K.	**25**	51 45N	1 15W
Oxford, U.S.A.	**165**	36 19N	78 36W
Oxford □	**25**	51 45N	1 15W
Oxford L.	**153**	54 51N	95 37W
Oxnard	**173**	34 10N	119 14W
Oyabe	**106**	36 47N	136 56 E
Oyama	**107**	36 18N	139 48 E
Oyana	**108**	32 32N	130 30 E
Oyo	**131**	7 46N	3 56 E
Oyonnax	**37**	46 16N	5 40 E
Ozamis	**112**	8 15N	123 50 E
Ozark	**169**	31 29N	85 39W
Ozark Plateau	**168**	37 20N	91 40W
Ozarks, L. of	**166**	38 10N	92 40W
Ozu, Ehime, Japan	**109**	33 30N	132 33 E
Ozu, Kumamoto, Japan	**108**	32 52N	130 52 E

P

Paarl	**136**	33 45S	18 56 E
Pabna	**92**	24 1N	89 18 E
Pacaraima, Sierra	**185**	4 0N	62 30W
Pacasmayo	**186**	7 20S	79 35W
Pachuca	**177**	20 10N	98 40W
Padang	**111**	1 0S	100 20 E
Pádova	**47**	45 24N	11 52 E
Padstow	**27**	50 33N	4 57W
Padua = Pádova	**47**	45 24N	11 52 E
Paducah	**169**	37 0N	88 40W
Pag	**52**	44 30N	14 50 E
Pagalu = Annobón	**131**	1 25S	5 36 E
Pagastikós Kólpos	**54**	39 15N	23 0 E
Page	**160**	36 57N	111 27W
Pahala	**160**	19 12N	155 25W
Pahang □	**96**	3 30N	102 45 E
Pahiatua	**122**	40 27S	175 50 E
Paignton	**27**	50 26N	3 33W
Painesville	**167**	41 42N	81 18W
Paint Hills = Nouveau Comptoir	**140**	53 0N	78 49W
Painted Desert	**160**	36 0N	111 30W
Paisley	**31**	55 51N	4 27W
Paita	**186**	5 11S	81 9W
Pak Sane	**95**	18 22N	103 39 E
Pakistan ■	**78**	30 0N	70 0 E
Pakistan, East = Bangladesh ■	**92**	24 0N	90 0 E
Pakokku	**93**	21 20N	95 0 E
Pakse	**95**	15 5N	105 52 E
Paktīā □	**87**	33 0N	69 15 E
Palanpur	**91**	24 10N	72 25 E
Palatka	**170**	29 40N	81 40W
Palawan	**112**	9 30N	118 30 E
Palembang	**111**	3 0S	104 50 E
Palencia	**50**	42 1N	4 34W
Palermo	**48**	38 8N	13 20 E
Palestine	**168**	31 42N	95 35W
Palghat	**90**	10 46N	76 42 E
Pali	**91**	25 50N	73 20 E
Palizada	**177**	18 15N	92 5W
Palk Bay	**90**	9 30N	79 15 E
Palk Strait	**90**	10 0N	79 45 E
Palm Is.	**121**	18 40S	146 35 E
Palm Springs	**173**	33 51N	116 35W

Palma, La	**179**	8 15N	78 0W
Palma de Mallorca	**51**	39 35N	2 39 E
Palma Soriano	**178**	20 15N	76 0W
Palmas, C.	**130**	4 27N	7 46W
Palmer Land	**14**	73 0S	60 0W
Palmerston North	**122**	40 21S	175 39 E
Palmi	**49**	38 21N	15 51 E
Palmira	**184**	3 32N	76 16W
Palmyra = Tudmur	**80**	34 36N	38 15 E
Palo Alto	**172**	37 25N	122 8W
Pamirs	**71**	37 40N	73 0 E
Pamlico Sd.	**165**	35 20N	76 0W
Pampa	**161**	35 35N	100 58W
Pampas	**190**	35 0S	63 0W
Pamplona	**51**	42 48N	1 38W
Panaca	**173**	37 51N	114 23W
Panaji	**91**	15 25N	73 50 E
Panamá	**179**	9 0N	79 25W
Panama ■	**179**	8 48N	79 55W
Panamá, Golfo de	**179**	8 4N	79 20W
Panama Canal	**175**	9 10N	79 37W
Panama City	**169**	30 10N	85 41W
Panay	**112**	11 10N	122 30 E
Pančevo	**52**	44 52N	20 41 E
Pandharpur	**91**	17 41N	75 20 E
Pangfou = Bengbu	**99**	32 58N	117 20 E
Pangkalpinang	**111**	2 0S	106 0 E
Pangnirtung	**146**	66 8N	65 54W
Panjim = Panaji	**91**	15 25N	73 50 E
Panjinad Barrage	**89**	29 22N	71 15 E
Pantelleria	**48**	36 52N	12 0 E
Pánuco	**177**	22 3N	98 10W
Paoting = Baoding	**98**	38 50N	115 28 E
Paot'ou = Baotou	**98**	40 32N	110 2 E
Papien Chiang = Da →	**95**	21 15N	105 20 E
Papua, Gulf of	**115**	9 0S	144 50 E
Papua New Guinea ■	**115**	8 0S	145 0 E
Pará = Belém	**188**	1 20S	48 30W
Pará □	**188**	3 20S	52 0W
Paracatu	**188**	17 10S	46 50W
Paragua, La	**185**	6 50N	63 20W
Paraguay ■	**191**	23 0S	57 0W
Paraguay →	**191**	27 18S	58 38W
Paraíba = João Pessoa	**189**	7 10S	34 52W
Paraíba □	**189**	7 0S	36 0W
Parakou	**131**	9 25N	2 40 E
Paramaribo	**185**	5 50N	55 10W
Paraná	**190**	31 45S	60 30W
Paraná □	**191**	24 30S	51 0W
Paraná →	**190**	33 43S	59 15W
Paranaguá	**191**	25 30S	48 30W
Paranaíba →	**188**	20 6S	51 4W
Parbhani	**91**	19 8N	76 52 E
Parecis, Serra dos	**187**	13 0S	60 0W
Parent	**151**	47 55N	74 35W
Paria, Golfo de	**180**	10 20N	62 0W
Parika	**185**	6 50N	58 20W
Parintins	**185**	2 40S	56 50W
Pariparit Kyun	**94**	14 55S	93 45 E
Paris, France	**39**	48 50N	2 20 E
Paris, Tenn., U.S.A.	**169**	36 20N	88 20W
Paris, Tex., U.S.A.	**168**	33 40N	95 30W
Park Range	**163**	40 0N	106 30W
Parker	**173**	34 8N	114 16W
Parkersburg	**164**	39 18N	81 31W
Parkes	**117**	33 9S	148 11 E
Parma	**46**	44 50N	10 20 E
Parnaguá	**188**	10 10S	44 38W
Parnaíba	**189**	2 54S	41 47W
Parnaíba →	**188**	3 0S	41 50W
Parnassós	**54**	38 35N	22 30 E
Pärnu	**68**	58 28N	24 33 E
Páros	**55**	37 5N	25 12 E
Parral	**190**	36 10S	71 52W
Parramatta	**117**	33 48S	151 1 E
Parras	**174**	25 30N	102 20W
Parrett →	**27**	51 7N	2 58W
Parry Is.	**12**	77 0N	110 0W
Parry Sound	**151**	45 20N	80 0W
Parsons	**166**	37 20N	95 17W
Paruro	**187**	13 45S	71 50W
Parvān □	**87**	35 0N	69 0 E
Pasadena, Calif., U.S.A.	**173**	34 5N	118 9W
Pasadena, Tex., U.S.A.	**168**	29 45N	95 14W
Pasaje	**184**	3 23S	79 50W
Pascagoula	**169**	30 21N	88 30W
Pasco	**171**	46 10N	119 0W
Pasco, Cerro de	**186**	10 45S	76 10W
Paso Robles	**173**	35 40N	120 45W
Passero, C.	**49**	36 42N	15 8 E
Passo Fundo	**191**	28 10S	52 20W
Pasto	**184**	1 13N	77 17W
Patagonia	**192**	45 0S	69 0W
Patan	**91**	23 54N	72 14 E
Patchogue	**164**	40 46N	73 1W
Paterson	**164**	40 55N	74 10W
Pathankot	**89**	32 18N	75 45 E
Patiala	**89**	30 23N	76 26 E
Patkai Bum	**93**	27 0N	95 30 E
Pátmos	**55**	37 21N	26 36 E
Patna	**92**	25 35N	85 12 E
Patos, Lag. dos	**191**	31 20S	51 0 E
Patos de Minas	**188**	18 35S	46 32W
Pátrai	**54**	38 14N	21 47 E
Patuca →	**179**	15 50N	84 18W
Pátzcuaro	**175**	19 32N	101 36W
Pau	**36**	43 19N	0 25W
Paulistana	**189**	8 9S	41 9W
Paulo Afonso	**189**	9 21S	38 15W
Pavia	**46**	45 10N	9 10 E
Pavlodar	**71**	52 33N	77 0 E
Pavlovo	**74**	63 5N	115 25 E
Pawtucket	**164**	41 51N	71 22W
Payette	**171**	44 0N	117 0W
Payne Bay = Bellin	**146**	60 0N	70 0W
Payne L.	**146**	59 30N	74 30W
Paynes Find	**120**	29 15S	117 42 E
Paysandú	**191**	32 19S	58 8W
Paz, La, Argentina	**190**	30 50S	59 45W
Paz, La, Bolivia	**187**	16 20S	68 10W
Paz, La, Mexico	**174**	24 10N	110 18W
Pazardzhik	**53**	42 12N	24 20 E
Peace →	**145**	59 0N	111 25W
Peace River	**155**	56 15N	117 18W
Peak, The	**28**	53 24N	1 53W
Peak Hill	**116**	32 47S	148 11 E
Pearl City	**160**	21 24N	158 0W
Pearl Harbor	**160**	21 20N	158 0W
Peary Land	**13**	82 40N	33 0W
Pebas	**186**	3 10S	71 46W
Pechenga	**69**	69 30N	31 25 E
Pechora →	**69**	68 13N	54 15 E
Pechorskaya Guba	**69**	68 40N	54 0 E
Pecos	**161**	31 25N	103 35W
Pecos →	**161**	29 42N	102 30W
Pécs	**59**	46 5N	18 15 E
Pedro Afonso	**188**	9 0S	48 10W
Pedro Juan Caballero	**191**	22 30S	55 40W
Peebles	**31**	55 40N	3 12W
Peekskill	**164**	41 18N	73 57W
Peel	**28**	54 14N	4 40W
Peel →	**144**	67 0N	135 0W
Pegasus Bay	**123**	43 20S	173 10 E
Pegu	**93**	17 20N	96 29 E
Pegu Yoma	**93**	19 0N	96 0 E
Pehuajó	**190**	35 45S	62 0W
Peip'ing = Beijing	**98**	39 55N	116 20 E
Pekalongan	**111**	6 53S	109 40 E
Pekan	**96**	3 30N	103 25 E
Pekanbaru	**111**	0 30N	101 15 E
Pekin	**166**	40 35N	89 40W
Peking = Beijing	**98**	39 55N	116 20 E
Peleng	**113**	1 20S	123 30 E
Pelly →	**144**	62 47N	137 19W
Pelly Bay	**146**	68 38N	89 50W
Peloponnes = Pelopónnisos □	**54**	37 10N	22 0 E
Pelopónnisos □	**54**	37 10N	22 0 E
Peloro, C.	**49**	38 15N	15 40 E
Pelorus Sound	**123**	40 59S	173 59 E
Pelotas	**191**	31 42S	52 23W
Pelvoux, Massif de	**37**	44 52N	6 20 E
Pematangsiantar	**111**	2 57N	99 5 E
Pemba	**135**	5 0S	39 45 E

Pembroke, Canada	**151**	45 50N	77 7W
Pembroke, U.K.	**27**	51 41N	4 57W
Pen-y-Ghent	**28**	54 10N	2 15W
Penas, G. de	**192**	47 0S	75 0W
Pench'i = Benxi	**98**	41 20N	123 48 E
Pendembu	**130**	9 7N	12 14W
Pendleton	**171**	45 35N	118 50W
Penetanguishene	**151**	44 50N	79 55W
Penguin	**119**	41 8S	146 6 E
Penicuik	**31**	55 50N	3 14W
Peninsular Malaysia □	**96**	4 0N	102 0 E
Pennines	**28**	54 50N	2 20W
Pennsylvania □	**164**	40 50N	78 0W
Penola	**119**	37 25S	140 21 E
Penonomé	**179**	8 31N	80 21W
Penrith, Australia	**117**	33 43S	150 38 E
Penrith, U.K.	**28**	54 40N	2 45W
Pensacola	**169**	30 30N	87 10W
Pensacola Mts.	**14**	84 0S	40 0W
Penshurst	**119**	37 49S	142 20 E
Penticton	**155**	49 30N	119 38W
Pentland Firth	**33**	58 43N	3 10W
Pentland Hills	**31**	55 48N	3 25W
Penza	**68**	53 15N	45 5 E
Penzance	**27**	50 7N	5 32W
Penzhinskaya Guba	**73**	61 30N	163 0 E
Peoria	**166**	40 40N	89 40W
Perak □	**96**	5 0N	101 0 E
Perche	**36**	48 31N	1 1 E
Pereira	**184**	4 49N	75 43W
Perenjori	**120**	29 26S	116 16 E
Pergamino	**190**	33 52S	60 30W
Périgueux	**36**	45 10N	0 42 E
Perlis □	**96**	6 30N	100 15 E
Perm	**69**	58 0N	57 10 E
Pernambuco = Recife	**189**	8 0S	35 0W
Pernambuco □	**189**	8 0S	37 0W
Pernatty Lagoon	**118**	31 30S	137 12 E
Pernik	**53**	42 35N	23 2 E
Peron Pen.	**120**	26 0S	113 10 E
Péronne	**38**	49 55N	2 57 E
Perouse Str., La	**77**	45 40N	142 0 E
Perpignan	**37**	42 42N	2 53 E
Perry, Iowa, U.S.A.	**166**	41 48N	94 5W
Perry, Okla., U.S.A.	**168**	36 20N	97 20W
Persepolis	**85**	29 55N	52 50 E
Persia = Iran ■	**86**	33 0N	53 0 E
Persian Gulf = Gulf, The	**85**	27 0N	50 0 E
Perth, Australia	**120**	31 57S	115 52 E
Perth, Canada	**151**	44 55N	76 15W
Perth, U.K.	**31**	56 24N	3 27W
Perth Amboy	**164**	40 31N	74 16W
Peru	**167**	40 42N	86 0W
Peru ■	**186**	8 0S	75 0W
Perúgia	**46**	43 6N	12 24 E
Pervouralsk	**69**	56 55N	60 0 E
Pésaro	**47**	43 55N	12 53 E
Pescara	**47**	42 28N	14 13 E
Peshawar	**89**	34 2N	71 37 E
Pesqueria →	**176**	25 54N	99 11W
Petah Tiqwa	**80**	32 6N	34 53 E
Petaling Jaya	**96**	3 4N	101 42 E
Petaluma	**172**	38 13N	122 39W
Petatlán	**177**	17 31N	101 16W
Peterborough, Australia	**118**	32 58S	138 51 E
Peterborough, Canada	**151**	44 20N	78 20W
Peterborough, U.K.	**25**	52 35N	0 14W
Peterhead	**33**	57 30N	1 49W
Peterlee	**29**	54 45N	1 18W
Petersburg, Alaska, U.S.A.	**143**	56 50N	133 0W
Petersburg, Va., U.S.A.	**164**	37 17N	77 26W
Petit Goâve	**180**	18 27N	72 51W
Petitsikapau, L.	**147**	54 37N	66 25W
Petlad	**91**	22 30N	72 45 E
Petone	**123**	41 13S	174 53 E
Petoskey	**150**	45 22N	84 57W
Petrich	**53**	41 24N	23 13 E
Petrolia	**150**	42 54N	82 9W
Petrolina	**189**	9 24S	40 30W
Petropavlovsk	**71**	54 53N	69 13 E
Petropavlovsk-Kamchatskiy	**73**	53 3N	158 43 E
Petrópolis	**188**	22 33S	43 9W
Petrovaradin	**52**	45 16N	19 55 E
Petrozavodsk	**68**	61 41N	34 20 E
Pevek	**73**	69 41N	171 19 E
Pforzheim	**42**	48 53N	8 43 E
Phan Rang	**95**	11 34N	109 0 E
Phangan, Ko	**96**	9 45N	100 0 E
Phenix City	**169**	32 30N	85 0W
Philadelphia	**164**	40 0N	75 10W
Philippi	**55**	41 1N	24 16 E
Philippines ■	**112**	12 0N	123 0 E
Philippopolis = Plovdiv	**53**	42 8N	24 44 E
Phitsanulok	**94**	16 50N	100 12 E
Phnom Penh	**95**	11 33N	104 55 E
Phoenix	**160**	33 30N	112 10W
Phoenix Is.	**123**	3 30S	172 0W
Phra Chedi Sam Ong	**94**	15 16N	98 23 E
Phuket	**96**	7 52N	98 22 E
Piacenza	**46**	45 2N	9 42 E
Piauí □	**188**	7 0S	43 0W
Picardie	**38**	50 0N	2 15 E
Picardie, Plaine de	**37**	50 0N	2 0 E
Picardy = Picardie	**38**	50 0N	2 15 E
Picayune	**169**	30 31N	89 40W
Pickering	**29**	54 15N	0 46W
Picton, Australia	**117**	34 12S	150 34 E
Picton, N.Z.	**123**	41 18S	174 3 E
Pictou	**149**	45 41N	62 42W
Pidurutalagala	**90**	7 10N	80 50 E
Piedad, La	**175**	20 20N	102 1W
Piedmont = Piemonte □	**46**	45 0N	7 30 E
Piedmont Plat.	**165**	34 0N	81 30W
Piedras Negras	**174**	28 42N	100 31W
Piemonte □	**46**	45 0N	7 30 E
Pierre	**163**	44 23N	100 20W
Pietermaritzburg	**137**	29 35S	30 25 E
Pietrosul	**57**	47 35N	24 43 E
Pikeville	**165**	37 30N	82 30W
Pilcomayo →	**190**	25 21S	57 42W
Pilsen = Plzen	**43**	49 45N	13 22 E
Pimenta Bueno	**187**	11 35S	61 10W
Pinang □	**96**	5 20N	100 20 E
Pinar del Río	**178**	22 26N	83 40W
Pinaroo	**119**	35 17S	140 53 E
Pinawa	**153**	50 9N	95 50W
Pincher Creek	**155**	49 30N	113 57W
Pinczów	**58**	50 30N	20 35 E
Pindos Óros	**54**	40 0N	21 0 E
Pindus Mts. = Pindos Óros	**54**	40 0N	21 0 E
Pine Bluff	**168**	34 10N	92 0W
Pine Pass	**155**	55 25N	122 42W
Pineville	**168**	31 22N	92 30W
Ping →	**94**	15 42N	100 9 E
Pingdong	**99**	22 39N	120 30 E
Pingliang	**99**	35 35N	106 31 E
Pingxiang	**99**	22 6N	106 46 E
Piniós →	**54**	37 48N	21 20 E
Pinjarra	**120**	32 37S	115 52 E
Piombino	**46**	42 54N	10 30 E
Piotrków Trybunalski	**58**	51 23N	19 43 E
Piqua	**167**	40 10N	84 10W
Piracicaba	**188**	22 45S	47 40W
Piræus = Piraiévs	**55**	37 57N	23 42 E
Piraiévs	**55**	37 57N	23 42 E
Pirapora	**188**	17 20S	44 56W
Pírgos	**54**	37 40N	21 27 E
Pirin Planina	**53**	41 40N	23 30 E
Pirineos	**51**	42 40N	1 0 E
Pisa	**46**	43 43N	10 23 E
Pisagua	**187**	19 40S	70 15W
Pisco	**186**	13 50S	76 12W
Pistóia	**46**	43 57N	10 53 E
Pitcairn I.	**10**	25 5S	130 5W
Piteå	**67**	65 20N	21 25 E
Piteşti	**57**	44 52N	24 54 E
Pithiviers	**39**	48 10N	2 13 E
Pitlochry	**33**	56 43N	3 43W
Pitt I.	**154**	53 30N	129 50W
Pittsburg, Kans., U.S.A.	**166**	37 21N	94 43W
Pittsburg, Tex., U.S.A.	**168**	32 59N	94 58W
Pittsburgh	**164**	40 25N	79 55W
Pittsfield	**164**	42 28N	73 17W
Pittsworth	**116**	27 41S	151 37 E

Piura	**186**	5 15S	80 38W
Placentia	**149**	47 20N	54 0W
Placerville	**172**	38 47N	120 51W
Placetas	**178**	22 15N	79 44W
Plainfield	**164**	40 37N	74 28W
Plainview	**161**	34 10N	101 40W
Plaster Rock	**148**	46 53N	67 22W
Plata, La	**191**	35 0S	57 55W
Plata, Río de la	**191**	34 45S	57 30W
Platte →	**163**	39 16N	94 50W
Plattsburg	**151**	44 41N	73 30W
Plauen	**43**	50 29N	12 9 E
Pleasantville	**164**	39 25N	74 30W
Plenty, Bay of	**122**	37 45S	177 0 E
Plessisville	**148**	46 14N	71 47W
Pleven	**53**	43 26N	24 37 E
Płock	**58**	52 32N	19 40 E
Ploieşti	**57**	44 57N	26 5 E
Plovdiv	**53**	42 8N	24 44 E
Plymouth	**27**	50 23N	4 9W
Plzen	**43**	49 45N	13 22 E
Po →	**47**	44 57N	12 4 E
Po Hai = Bo Hai	**98**	39 0N	120 0 E
Pobeda	**73**	65 12N	146 12 E
Pobedy Pik	**71**	40 45N	79 58 E
Pocatello	**163**	42 50N	112 25W
Pochutla	**177**	15 50N	96 31W
Poços de Caldas	**188**	21 50S	46 33W
Podgorica	**52**	42 30N	19 19 E
Podkamennaya Tunguska →	**74**	61 50N	90 13 E
Point Edward	**150**	43 0N	82 30W
Pointe-à-Pitre	**180**	16 10N	61 30W
Pointe Noire	**134**	4 48S	11 53 E
Poissy	**39**	48 55N	2 0 E
Poitiers	**36**	46 35N	0 20 E
Poitou, Plaines et Seuil du	**36**	46 30N	0 1W
Pokaran	**91**	27 0N	71 50 E
Pokrovsk = Engels	**68**	51 28N	46 6 E
Pola = Pula	**52**	44 54N	13 57 E
Poland ■	**58**	52 0N	20 0 E
Polden Hills	**27**	51 7N	2 50W
Polesye	**17**	52 0N	28 10 E
Polillo Is.	**112**	14 56N	122 0 E
Políyiros	**55**	40 23N	23 25 E
Pollachi	**90**	10 35N	77 0 E
Polotsk	**68**	55 30N	28 50 E
Poltava	**68**	49 35N	34 35 E
Polynesia	**123**	10 0S	162 0W
Pomona	**173**	34 2N	117 49W
Pompano Beach	**170**	26 12N	80 6W
Ponca City	**168**	36 40N	97 5W
Ponce	**180**	18 1N	66 37W
Pond Inlet	**146**	72 40N	77 0W
Pondicherry	**90**	11 59N	79 50 E
Ponnyadaung	**93**	22 0N	94 10 E
Ponoka	**155**	52 42N	113 40W
Pont-Audemer	**39**	49 21N	0 30 E
Ponta Grossa	**191**	25 7S	50 10W
Ponta Pora	**188**	22 20S	55 35W
Pontchartrain, L.	**169**	30 12N	90 0W
Pontefract	**29**	53 42N	1 19W
Pontevedra	**50**	42 26N	8 40W
Pontiac	**167**	42 40N	83 20W
Pontianak	**111**	0 3S	109 15 E
Pontine Is. = Ponziane, Isole	**48**	40 55N	13 0 E
Pontoise	**39**	49 3N	2 5 E
Pontypool	**27**	51 42N	3 1W
Pontypridd	**27**	51 36N	3 21W
Ponziane, Isole	**48**	40 55N	13 0 E
Poochera	**118**	32 43S	134 51 E
Poole	**24**	50 42N	1 58W
Pooley I.	**154**	52 45N	128 15W
Poona = Pune	**91**	18 29N	73 57 E
Poopó, Lago de	**187**	18 30S	67 35W
Popayán	**184**	2 27N	76 36W
Poplar Bluff	**169**	36 45N	90 22W
Popocatépetl, Volcán	**177**	19 2N	98 38W
Porcher I.	**154**	53 50N	130 30W
Porcupine →	**142**	66 35N	145 15W
Pori	**67**	61 29N	21 48 E
Porkkala	**67**	59 59N	24 26 E
Port Adelaide	**119**	34 46S	138 30 E
Port Alberni	**154**	49 40N	124 50W
Port Albert	**115**	38 42S	146 42 E
Port Alfred	**148**	48 18N	70 53W
Port Angeles	**171**	48 7N	123 30W
Port Antonio	**180**	18 10N	76 30W
Port Arthur	**168**	30 0N	94 0W
Port-au-Prince	**180**	18 40N	72 20W
Port Augusta	**118**	32 30S	137 50 E
Port Blair	**94**	11 40N	92 30 E
Port-Cartier	**148**	50 2N	66 50W
Port Chalmers	**123**	45 49S	170 30 E
Port Colborne	**151**	42 50N	79 10W
Port Coquitlam	**154**	49 15N	122 45W
Port Darwin	**192**	51 50S	59 0W
Port-de-Paix	**180**	19 50N	72 50W
Port Elgin	**150**	44 25N	81 25W
Port Elizabeth	**136**	33 58S	25 40 E
Port Erin	**28**	54 5N	4 45W
Port Etienne = Nouâdhibou	**126**	20 54N	17 0W
Port Fairy	**119**	38 22S	142 12 E
Port Glasgow	**30**	55 57N	4 40W
Port Harcourt	**131**	4 40N	7 10 E
Port Harrison = Inoucdjouac	**146**	58 25N	78 15W
Port Hawkesbury	**149**	45 36N	61 22W
Port Hope	**151**	43 56N	78 20W
Port Huron	**167**	43 0N	82 28W
Port Kembla	**117**	34 52S	150 49 E
Port Laoise	**35**	53 2N	7 20W
Port Lavaca	**158**	28 38N	96 38W
Port Lincoln	**119**	34 42S	135 52 E
Port Lyautey = Kenitra	**126**	34 15N	6 40W
Port Macquarie	**116**	31 25S	152 25 E
Port Morant	**180**	17 54N	76 19W
Port Moresby	**115**	9 24S	147 8 E
Port Nelson	**143**	57 3N	92 36W
Port Nolloth	**136**	29 17S	16 52 E
Port Nouveau-Québec	**146**	58 30N	65 59W
Port of Spain	**180**	10 40N	61 31W
Port Phillip B.	**117**	38 10S	144 50 E
Port Pirie	**118**	33 10S	138 1 E
Port Said = Bûr Sa'îd	**128**	31 16N	32 18 E
Port Simpson	**154**	54 30N	130 20W
Port Stanley	**150**	42 40N	81 10W
Port Sudan = Bûr Sûdân	**129**	19 32N	37 9 E
Port Talbot	**27**	51 35N	3 48W
Port Townsend	**171**	48 7N	122 50W
Portadown	**34**	54 27N	6 26W
Portage La Prairie	**153**	49 58N	98 18W
Portarlington	**35**	53 10N	7 10W
Porte, La	**167**	41 36N	86 43W
Porterville	**173**	36 5N	119 0W
Porthcawl	**27**	51 28N	3 42W
Porthmadog	**26**	52 55N	4 13W
Portile de Fier	**56**	44 42N	22 30 E
Portland, Australia	**119**	38 20S	141 35 E
Portland, Maine, U.S.A.	**148**	43 40N	70 15W
Portland, Oreg., U.S.A.	**171**	45 35N	122 40W
Portland, Bill of	**24**	50 31N	2 27W
Portland Prom.	**146**	58 40N	78 33W
Porto	**50**	41 8N	8 40W
Pôrto Alegre	**191**	30 5S	51 10W
Porto Empédocle	**48**	37 18N	13 30 E
Porto Mendes	**191**	24 30S	54 15W
Porto Novo	**131**	6 23N	2 42 E
Pôrto Seguro	**189**	16 26S	39 5W
Pôrto Velho	**187**	8 46S	63 54W
Portoferráio	**46**	42 50N	10 20 E
Portoscuso	**48**	39 12N	8 22 E
Portovíejo	**184**	1 7S	80 28W
Portpatrick	**30**	54 50N	5 7W
Portree	**32**	57 25N	6 11W
Portrush	**34**	55 13N	6 40W
Portsmouth, Domin.	**180**	15 34N	61 27W
Portsmouth, U.K.	**25**	50 48N	1 6W
Portsmouth, N.H., U.S.A.	**164**	43 5N	70 45W
Portsmouth, Ohio, U.S.A.	**167**	38 45N	83 0W
Portsmouth, Va., U.S.A.	**165**	36 50N	76 20W
Porttipahta	**67**	68 5N	26 40 E
Portugal ■	**50**	40 0N	7 0W
Portuguese-Guinea = Guinea-Bissau ■	**130**	12 0N	15 0W

Portuguese Timor ■ = Timor	**113**	9 0S	125 0 E
Portumna	**35**	53 5N	8 12W
Porvenir	**192**	53 10S	70 16W
Posadas	**191**	27 30S	55 50W
Poshan = Boshan	**98**	36 28N	117 49 E
Poste-de-la-Baleine	**140**	55 17N	77 45W
Potchefstroom	**137**	26 41S	27 7 E
Potenza	**49**	40 40N	15 50 E
Potomac →	**165**	38 0N	76 23W
Potosí	**187**	19 38S	65 50W
Potsdam, Germany	**43**	52 23N	13 4 E
Potsdam, U.S.A.	**151**	44 40N	74 59W
Pottsville	**164**	40 39N	76 12W
Pouce Coupé	**155**	55 40N	120 10W
Poughkeepsie	**164**	41 40N	73 57W
Poulaphouca Res.	**35**	53 8N	6 30W
Póvoa de Varzim	**50**	41 25N	8 46W
Powell, L.	**163**	37 25N	110 45W
Powell River	**154**	49 50N	124 35W
Powys □	**26**	52 20N	3 20W
Poyang Hu	**99**	29 10N	116 10 E
Poyarkovo	**75**	49 36N	128 41 E
Poznań	**58**	52 25N	16 55 E
Prachuap Khiri Khan	**94**	11 49N	99 48 E
Prague = Praha	**58**	50 5N	14 22 E
Praha	**58**	50 5N	14 22 E
Prainha, Amazonas, Brazil	**187**	7 10S	60 30W
Prainha, Pará, Brazil	**185**	1 45S	53 30W
Prairie du Chien	**166**	43 1N	91 9W
Prato	**46**	43 53N	11 5 E
Pratt	**161**	37 40N	98 45W
Prepansko Jezero	**52**	40 55N	21 0 E
Preparis North Channel	**94**	15 12N	93 40 E
Preparis South Channel	**94**	14 36N	93 40 E
Prescott	**160**	34 35N	112 30W
Preservation Inlet	**123**	46 8S	166 35 E
Presidencia Roque Saenz Peña	**190**	26 45S	60 30W
Presidente Prudente	**188**	22 5S	51 25W
Presidio	**161**	29 30N	104 20W
Prespa, L. = Prepansko Jezero	**52**	40 55N	21 0 E
Presque Isle	**148**	46 40N	68 0W
Preston, Borders, U.K.	**28**	55 48N	2 18W
Preston, Lancs., U.K.	**21**	53 46N	2 42W
Prestonpans	**31**	55 58N	3 0W
Prestwick	**31**	55 30N	4 38W
Pretoria	**137**	25 44S	28 12 E
Préveza	**55**	38 57N	20 47 E
Prichard	**169**	30 47N	88 5W
Prilep	**52**	41 21N	21 37 E
Prince Albert	**152**	53 15N	105 50W
Prince Albert Pen.	**145**	72 30N	116 0W
Prince Albert Sd.	**145**	70 25N	115 0W
Prince Charles I.	**146**	67 47N	76 12W
Prince Edward I. □	**148**	46 20N	63 20W
Prince George	**154**	53 55N	122 50W
Prince of Wales I., Canada	**145**	73 0N	99 0W
Prince of Wales I., U.S.A.	**143**	55 30N	133 0W
Prince Patrick I.	**12**	77 0N	120 0W
Prince Rupert	**154**	54 20N	130 20W
Princess Royal I.	**154**	53 0N	128 40W
Princeton	**155**	49 27N	120 30W
Principe, I. de	**131**	1 37N	7 27 E
Principe da Beira	**187**	12 20S	64 30W
Pripet = Pripyat →	**68**	51 20N	30 9 E
Pripet Marshes = Polesye	**17**	52 0N	28 10 E
Pripyat →	**68**	51 20N	30 9 E
Pripyat Marshes = Polesye	**17**	52 0N	28 10 E
Priština	**52**	42 40N	21 13 E
Privolzhskaya Vozvyshennost	**17**	51 0N	46 0 E
Prizren	**52**	42 13N	20 45 E
Proddatur	**90**	14 45N	78 30 E
Progreso	**177**	21 17N	89 40W
Prokopyevsk	**71**	54 0N	86 45 E
Proserpine	**121**	20 21S	148 36 E
Provence	**37**	43 40N	5 46 E
Providence	**164**	41 50N	71 28W
Provo	**163**	40 16N	111 37W
Prudhoe Bay	**142**	70 20N	148 20W
Pruszków	**58**	52 9N	20 49 E
Prut →	**57**	46 3N	28 10 E
Przemyśl	**58**	49 50N	22 45 E
Przeworsk	**58**	50 6N	22 32 E
Pskov	**68**	57 50N	28 25 E
Pucallpa	**186**	8 25S	74 30W
Puebla	**177**	19 3N	98 12W
Puebla □	**177**	18 50N	98 0W
Pueblo	**163**	38 20N	104 40W
Puelches	**190**	38 5S	65 51W
Puente Alto	**190**	33 32S	70 35W
Puerto Armuelles	**179**	8 20N	82 51W
Puerto Ayacucho	**184**	5 40N	67 35W
Puerto Barrios	**177**	15 40N	88 32W
Puerto Cabello	**184**	10 28N	68 1W
Puerto Cabezas	**179**	14 0N	83 30W
Puerto Castilla	**179**	16 0N	86 0W
Puerto Cortes, Costa Rica	**179**	8 55N	84 0W
Puerto Cortés, Honduras	**177**	15 51N	88 0W
Puerto Heath	**187**	12 34S	68 39W
Puerto La Cruz	**185**	10 13N	64 38W
Puerto Libertad	**174**	29 55N	112 41W
Puerto Lobos	**192**	42 0S	65 3W
Puerto Maldonado	**187**	12 30S	69 10W
Puerto Montt	**190**	41 28S	73 0W
Puerto Padre	**178**	21 13N	76 35W
Puerto Pinasco	**191**	22 36S	57 50W
Puerto Plata	**180**	19 48N	70 45W
Puerto Quepos	**179**	9 29N	84 6W
Puerto Rico ■	**180**	18 15N	66 45W
Puerto Vallarta	**175**	20 37N	105 15W
Puertollano	**50**	38 43N	4 7W
Puget Sd.	**171**	47 15N	122 30W
Púglia □	**49**	41 0N	16 30 E
Pula	**52**	44 54N	13 57 E
Pulaski, Tenn., U.S.A.	**169**	35 10N	87 0W
Pulaski, Va., U.S.A.	**165**	37 4N	80 49W
Pulicat, L.	**90**	13 40N	80 15 E
Pullman	**171**	46 49N	117 10W
Punakha	**92**	27 42N	89 52 E
Punata	**187**	17 32S	65 50W
Pune	**91**	18 29N	73 57 E
Punjab □, India	**89**	31 0N	76 0 E
Punjab □, Pakistan	**89**	30 0N	72 0 E
Puno	**187**	15 55S	70 3W
Punta Alta	**190**	38 53S	62 4W
Punta Arenas	**192**	53 10S	71 0W
Punta Gorda	**177**	16 10N	88 45W
Puntabie	**118**	32 12S	134 13 E
Puntarenas	**179**	10 0N	84 50W
Punto Fijo	**184**	11 50N	70 13W
Puquio	**186**	14 45S	74 10W
Pur →	**69**	67 31N	77 55 E
Purbeck, Isle of	**24**	50 40N	2 5W
Purmerend	**40**	52 30N	4 58 E
Purnia	**92**	25 45N	87 31 E
Pursat	**95**	12 34N	103 50 E
Purus →	**185**	3 42S	61 28W
Pusan	**98**	35 5N	129 0 E
Putao	**93**	27 28N	97 30 E
Putorana, Gory	**72**	69 0N	95 0 E
Putumayo →	**184**	3 7S	67 58W
Puy, Le	**37**	45 2N	3 53 E
Puy-de-Dôme	**37**	45 46N	2 57 E
Puyallup	**171**	47 10N	122 22W
Pwllheli	**26**	52 54N	4 26W
Pyasina →	**72**	73 30N	87 0 E
Pyatigorsk	**70**	44 2N	43 6 E
Pyinmana	**93**	19 45N	96 12 E
Pyŏngyang	**98**	39 0N	125 30 E
Pyramid L.	**172**	40 0N	119 30W
Pyrénées	**124**	42 45N	0 18 E

Q

Qā'emshahr	**86**	36 30N	52 55 E
Qahremānshahr = Bākhtarān	**84**	34 23N	47 0 E
Qaidam Pendi	**100**	37 0N	95 0 E
Qal'at al Akhḍar	**82**	28 0N	37 10 E
Qamar, Ghubbat al	**83**	16 20N	52 30 E
Qamdo	**101**	31 15N	97 6 E

Qandahār . . . **87** 31 32N 65 30 E
Qaşr-e Qand . . . **85** 26 15N 60 45 E
Qatar ■ . . . **85** 25 30N 51 15 E
Qāyen . . . **86** 33 40N 59 10 E
Qazvin . . . **81** 36 15N 50 0 E
Qena . . . **128** 26 10N 32 43 E
Qeshm . . . **85** 26 55N 56 10 E
Qilian Shan . . . **100** 38 30N 96 0 E
Qingdao . . . **98** 36 5N 120 20 E
Qinghai □ . . . **101** 36 0N 98 0 E
Qinghai Hu . . . **100** 36 40N 100 10 E
Qinhuangdao . . . **98** 39 56N 119 30 E
Qiqihar . . . **98** 47 26N 124 0 E
Qom . . . **86** 34 40N 51 0 E
Qomsheh . . . **85** 32 0N 51 55 E
Qondūz □ . . . **87** 36 50N 68 50 E
Qu Xian . . . **99** 30 48N 106 58 E
Quang Ngai . . . **95** 15 13N 108 58 E
Quantock Hills . . . **27** 51 8N 3 10W
Quanzhou . . . **99** 24 55N 118 34 E
Quatsino . . . **154** 50 30N 127 40W
Queanbeyan . . . **117** 35 17S 149 14 E
Québec . . . **148** 46 52N 71 13W
Québec □ . . . **140** 50 0N 70 0W
Queen Alexandra Ra. . . . **15** 85 0S 170 0 E
Queen Charlotte . . . **154** 53 15N 132 2W
Queen Charlotte Is. . . . **154** 53 20N 132 10W
Queen Charlotte Str. . . . **154** 51 0N 128 0W
Queen Elizabeth Is. . . . **138** 76 0N 95 0W
Queen Mary Land . . . **15** 70 0S 95 0 E
Queen Maud G. . . . **145** 68 15N 102 30W
Queen Maud Mts. . . . **15** 86 0S 160 0W
Queenscliff . . . **117** 38 16S 144 39 E
Queensland □ . . . **115** 22 0S 142 0 E
Queenstown, Australia . . . **119** 42 4S 145 35 E
Queenstown, N.Z. . . . **123** 45 1S 168 40 E
Quelimane . . . **137** 17 53S 36 58 E
Quelpart = Cheju Do . . . **99** 33 29N 126 34 E
Querétaro . . . **177** 20 36N 100 23W
Querétaro □ . . . **177** 21 0N 99 55W
Quesnel . . . **154** 53 0N 122 30W
Quetta . . . **88** 30 15N 66 55 E
Quezaltenango . . . **177** 14 50N 91 30W
Quezon City . . . **112** 14 38N 121 0 E
Qui Nhon . . . **95** 13 40N 109 13 E
Quibdo . . . **184** 5 42N 76 40W
Quillabamba . . . **186** 12 50S 72 50W
Quilon . . . **90** 8 50N 76 38 E
Quilpie . . . **116** 26 35S 144 11 E
Quimper . . . **36** 48 0N 4 9W
Quincy, Calif., U.S.A. . . . **172** 39 56N 121 0W
Quincy, Fla., U.S.A. . . . **170** 30 34N 84 34W
Quincy, Ill., U.S.A. . . . **166** 39 55N 91 20W
Quincy, Mass., U.S.A. . . . **164** 42 14N 71 0W
Quintana Roo □ . . . **177** 19 40N 88 30W
Quirindi . . . **116** 31 28S 150 40 E
Quitman . . . **170** 30 49N 83 35W
Quito . . . **184** 0 15S 78 35W
Quixadá . . . **189** 4 55S 39 0W
Quorn . . . **118** 32 25S 138 0 E
Quseir . . . **128** 26 7N 34 16 E

R

Raahe . . . **67** 64 40N 24 28 E
Raasay . . . **32** 57 25N 6 4W
Rabat . . . **126** 34 2N 6 48W
Rabaul . . . **115** 4 24S 152 18 E
Rābigh . . . **82** 22 50N 39 5 E
Race, C. . . . **149** 46 40N 53 5W
Rach Gia . . . **95** 10 5N 105 5 E
Racibórz . . . **58** 50 7N 18 18 E
Racine . . . **167** 42 41N 87 51W
Radium Hot Springs . . . **155** 50 35N 116 2W
Radnor Forest . . . **26** 52 17N 3 10W
Radom . . . **58** 51 23N 21 12 E
Radomir . . . **53** 42 37N 23 4 E
Radstock . . . **27** 51 17N 2 25W
Radville . . . **152** 49 30N 104 15W
Rae . . . **145** 62 50N 116 3W
Rae Bareli . . . **92** 26 18N 81 20 E
Raetihi . . . **122** 39 25S 175 17 E
Rafaela . . . **190** 31 10S 61 30W
Rafḥā . . . **82** 29 35N 43 35 E
Rafsanjān . . . **85** 30 30N 56 5 E
Ragama . . . **90** 7 0N 79 50 E
Raglan . . . **122** 37 55S 174 55 E
Ragusa . . . **49** 36 56N 14 42 E
Rahaeng = Tak . . . **94** 16 52N 99 8 E
Raichur . . . **91** 16 10N 77 20 E
Rainier, Mt. . . . **171** 46 50N 121 50W
Rainy L. . . . **153** 48 42N 93 10W
Rainy River . . . **153** 48 43N 94 29W
Raipur . . . **92** 21 17N 81 45 E
Rajahmundry . . . **92** 17 1N 81 48 E
Rajapalaiyam . . . **90** 9 25N 77 35 E
Rajasthan □ . . . **91** 26 45N 73 30 E
Rajasthan Canal . . . **89** 28 0N 72 0 E
Rajkot . . . **91** 22 15N 70 56 E
Rajshahi □ . . . **92** 25 0N 89 0 E
Raleigh . . . **165** 35 47N 78 39W
Raleigh B. . . . **165** 34 50N 76 15W
Rambouillet . . . **39** 48 40N 1 48 E
Rampur . . . **89** 28 50N 79 5 E
Ramsey . . . **28** 54 20N 4 21W
Rancagua . . . **190** 34 10S 70 50W
Ranchi . . . **92** 23 19N 85 27 E
Rangiora . . . **123** 43 19S 172 36 E
Rangoon . . . **93** 16 45N 96 20 E
Rangpur . . . **92** 25 42N 89 22 E
Raniwara . . . **91** 24 50N 72 10 E
Rankin Inlet . . . **145** 62 30N 93 0W
Rankins Springs . . . **117** 33 49S 146 14 E
Rannoch, L. . . . **33** 56 41N 4 20W
Rannoch Moor . . . **30** 56 38N 4 48W
Rapid City . . . **163** 44 0N 103 0W
Ras Dashen . . . **132** 13 8N 38 26 E
Rasa, Punta . . . **192** 40 50S 62 15W
Rasht . . . **81** 37 20N 49 40 E
Rat Is. . . . **142** 51 50N 178 15 E
Ratangarh . . . **89** 28 5N 74 35 E
Rath Luirc . . . **35** 52 21N 8 40W
Rathlin I. . . . **34** 55 18N 6 14W
Ratibor = Racibórz . . . **58** 50 7N 18 18 E
Ratlam . . . **91** 23 20N 75 0 E
Ratnagiri . . . **91** 16 57N 73 18 E
Rattray Hd. . . . **33** 57 38N 1 50W
Raub . . . **96** 3 47N 101 52 E
Raukumara Ra. . . . **122** 38 5S 177 55 E
Ravenna . . . **47** 44 28N 12 15 E
Ravenshoe . . . **121** 17 37S 145 29 E
Ravensthorpe . . . **120** 33 35S 120 2 E
Rawalpindi . . . **89** 33 38N 73 8 E
Rawlins . . . **163** 41 50N 107 20W
Ray, C. . . . **149** 47 33N 59 15W
Raymond . . . **155** 49 30N 112 35W
Razgrad . . . **53** 43 33N 26 34 E
Ré, Île de . . . **36** 46 12N 1 30W
Reading, U.K. . . . **25** 51 27N 0 57W
Reading, U.S.A. . . . **164** 40 20N 75 53W
Reay Forest . . . **32** 58 20N 4 55W
Rebun-Tō . . . **103** 45 23N 141 2 E
Recife . . . **189** 8 0S 35 0W
Reconquista . . . **190** 29 10S 59 45W
Recreo . . . **190** 29 25S 65 10W
Red ⟶ . . . **168** 31 0N 91 40W
Red Bluff . . . **172** 40 11N 122 11W
Red Cliffs . . . **119** 34 19S 142 11 E
Red Deer . . . **155** 52 20N 113 50W
Red Lake . . . **153** 51 3N 93 49W
Red Oak . . . **166** 41 0N 95 10W
Red Sea . . . **128** 25 0N 36 0 E
Red Tower Pass = Turnu Rosu Pasul . . . **57** 45 33N 24 17 E
Red Wing . . . **166** 44 32N 92 35W
Redcar . . . **29** 54 37N 1 4W
Redcliff . . . **152** 50 10N 110 50W
Redcliffe . . . **116** 27 12S 153 0 E
Redding . . . **172** 40 30N 122 25W
Redditch . . . **24** 52 18N 1 57W
Redlands . . . **173** 34 0N 117 11W

Redruth	**27**	50 14N	5 14W
Redwater	**155**	53 55N	113 6W
Redwood City	**172**	37 30N	122 15W
Ree, L.	**34**	53 35N	8 0W
Reedley	**173**	36 36N	119 27W
Regensburg	**43**	49 1N	12 7 E
Réggio di Calábria	**49**	38 7N	15 38 E
Réggio nell' Emilia	**46**	44 42N	10 38 E
Regina	**152**	50 27N	104 35W
Rehovot	**80**	31 54N	34 48 E
Reichenbach	**43**	50 36N	12 19 E
Reidsville	**165**	36 21N	79 40W
Reims	**39**	49 15N	4 0 E
Reina Adelaida, Arch.	**192**	52 20S	74 0W
Reindeer L.	**143**	57 15N	102 15W
Reliance	**145**	63 0N	109 20W
Remanso	**189**	9 41S	42 4W
Remarkable, Mt.	**118**	32 48S	138 10 E
Remscheid	**42**	51 11N	7 12 E
Rendsburg	**42**	54 18N	9 41 E
Renfrew, Canada	**151**	45 30N	76 40W
Renfrew, U.K.	**31**	55 52N	4 24W
Renkum	**41**	51 58N	5 43 E
Renmark	**119**	34 11S	140 43 E
Rennes	**36**	48 7N	1 41W
Reno	**172**	39 30N	119 50W
Republic	**150**	46 25N	87 59W
Republican →	**163**	39 3N	96 48W
Repulse Bay	**146**	66 30N	86 30W
Requena	**186**	5 5S	73 52W
Resht = Rasht	**81**	37 20N	49 40 E
Resistencia	**190**	27 30S	59 0W
Resolution I., Canada	**146**	61 30N	65 0W
Resolution I., N.Z.	**123**	45 40S	166 40 E
Retalhuleu	**177**	14 33N	91 46W
Réthimnon	**55**	35 18N	24 30 E
Réunion	**9**	22 0S	56 0 E
Reval = Tallinn	**68**	59 22N	24 48 E
Revelstoke	**155**	51 0N	118 10W
Revilla Gigedo, Is.	**139**	18 40N	112 0W
Rewa	**92**	24 33N	81 25 E
Rewari	**89**	28 15N	76 40 E
Rexburg	**163**	43 55N	111 50W
Rey Malabo	**131**	3 45N	8 50 E
Reykjavík	**64**	64 10N	21 57 E
Reynosa	**176**	26 5N	98 18W
Rhayader	**26**	52 19N	3 30W
Rhein →	**42**	51 52N	6 20 E
Rheinland-Pfalz □	**42**	50 0N	7 0 E
Rhin = Rhein →	**42**	51 52N	6 20 E
Rhine = Rhein →	**42**	51 52N	6 20 E
Rhineland-Palatinate = Rheinland-Pfalz □	**42**	50 0N	7 0 E
Rhinelander	**150**	45 38N	89 29W
Rhode Island □	**164**	41 38N	71 37W
Rhodes = Ródhos	**55**	36 15N	28 10 E
Rhodesia = Zimbabwe ■	**137**	20 0S	30 0 E
Rhodope Mts. = Rhodopi Planina	**53**	41 40N	24 20 E
Rhodopi Planina	**53**	41 40N	24 20 E
Rhön	**42**	50 24N	9 58 E
Rhondda	**27**	51 39N	3 30W
Rhône →	**37**	43 28N	4 42 E
Rhum	**32**	57 0N	6 20W
Rhyl	**26**	53 19N	3 29W
Rhymney	**27**	51 45N	3 17W
Riachão	**188**	7 20S	46 37W
Riau, Kepulauan	**111**	0 30N	104 20 E
Ribatejo □	**50**	39 15N	8 30W
Ribble →	**28**	54 13N	2 20W
Ribeirão Prêto	**188**	21 10S	47 50W
Riberalta	**187**	11 0S	66 0W
Riccarton	**123**	43 32S	172 37 E
Richland	**171**	46 15N	119 15W
Richmond, Australia	**116**	20 43S	143 8 E
Richmond, N.Z.	**123**	41 20S	173 12 E
Richmond, N. Yorks., U.K.	**28**	54 24N	1 43W
Richmond, Surrey, U.K.	**25**	51 28N	0 18W
Richmond, Calif., U.S.A.	**172**	37 58N	122 21W
Richmond, Ind., U.S.A.	**167**	39 50N	84 50W
Richmond, Ky., U.S.A.	**165**	37 40N	84 20W
Richmond, Va., U.S.A.	**165**	37 33N	77 27W
Richwood	**165**	38 17N	80 32W
Ridgeway	**164**	42 56S	147 16 E
Riga	**68**	56 53N	24 8 E
Rīgestān □	**87**	30 15N	65 0 E
Rigolet	**147**	54 10N	58 23W
Rijeka	**52**	45 20N	14 21 E
Rijssen	**41**	52 19N	6 30 E
Rijswijk	**40**	52 4N	4 22 E
Rímini	**47**	44 3N	12 33 E
Rîmnicu Vîlcea	**57**	45 9N	24 21 E
Rimouski	**148**	48 27N	68 30W
Rinía	**55**	37 23N	25 13 E
Rio Branco	**187**	9 58S	67 49W
Rio Claro	**180**	10 20N	61 25W
Río Cuarto	**190**	33 10S	64 25W
Rio de Janeiro	**188**	23 0S	43 12W
Rio de Janeiro □	**188**	22 50S	43 0W
Río Gallegos	**192**	51 35S	69 15W
Rio Grande	**191**	32 0S	52 20W
Rio Grande →	**161**	25 57N	97 9W
Rio Grande do Norte □	**189**	5 40S	36 0W
Rio Grande do Sul □	**191**	30 0S	53 0W
Río Mulatos	**187**	19 40S	66 50W
Rio Negro	**191**	26 0S	50 0W
Rio Verde	**188**	17 50S	51 0W
Ríobamba	**184**	1 50S	78 45W
Ríohacha	**184**	11 33N	72 55W
Rioja, La	**190**	29 20S	67 0W
Rioja, La □	**50**	42 20N	2 20W
Ríosucio	**184**	7 27N	77 7W
Ripon	**28**	54 8N	1 31W
Rishiri-Tō	**103**	45 11N	141 15 E
Ritchies Archipelago	**94**	12 5N	94 0 E
Rivas	**179**	11 30N	85 50W
Riverhead	**164**	40 53N	72 40W
Riverside	**173**	34 0N	117 22W
Riverton	**153**	51 1N	97 0W
Riviera di Levante	**46**	44 23N	9 15 E
Riviera di Ponente	**46**	43 50N	7 58 E
Rivière-du-Loup	**148**	47 50N	69 30W
Riyadh = Ar Riyāḑ	**83**	24 41N	46 42 E
Roanne	**37**	46 3N	4 4 E
Roanoke, Ala., U.S.A.	**169**	33 9N	85 23W
Roanoke, Va., U.S.A.	**165**	37 19N	79 55W
Roanoke →	**165**	35 56N	76 43W
Roanoke Rapids	**165**	36 28N	77 42W
Robinvale	**119**	34 40S	142 45 E
Roblin	**152**	51 14N	101 21W
Roboré	**187**	18 10S	59 45W
Robson, Mt.	**155**	53 10N	119 10W
Roca, C. da	**50**	38 40N	9 31W
Rocha	**191**	34 30S	54 25W
Rochdale	**28**	53 36N	2 10W
Roche-sur-Yon, La	**36**	46 40N	1 25W
Rochefort	**36**	45 56N	0 57W
Rochelle, La	**36**	46 10N	1 9W
Rochester, Minn., U.S.A.	**166**	44 1N	92 28W
Rochester, N.H., U.S.A.	**164**	43 19N	70 57W
Rochester, N.Y., U.S.A.	**164**	43 10N	77 40W
Rock Hill	**165**	34 55N	81 2W
Rock Island	**166**	41 30N	90 35W
Rock Sprs.	**163**	41 40N	109 10W
Rockall	**16**	57 37N	13 42W
Rockford	**166**	42 20N	89 0W
Rockglen	**152**	49 11N	105 57W
Rockhampton	**119**	23 22S	150 32 E
Rockingham	**120**	32 15S	115 38 E
Rockland	**148**	44 6N	69 6W
Rocky Mount	**165**	35 55N	77 48W
Rocky Mountain House	**155**	52 22N	114 55W
Rocky Mts.	**138**	55 0N	121 0W
Ródhos	**55**	36 15N	28 10 E
Roebourne	**114**	20 44S	117 9 E
Roermond	**41**	51 12N	6 0 E
Roes Welcome Sd.	**146**	65 0N	87 0W
Rogaland fylke □	**60**	59 12N	6 20 E
Rogers	**168**	36 20N	94 5W
Rohri	**88**	27 45N	68 51 E
Rohtak	**89**	28 55N	76 43 E
Rojo, C.	**177**	21 33N	97 20W
Rolla	**166**	37 56N	91 42W
Roma, Australia	**116**	26 32S	148 49 E

Roma, Italy	**46**	41 54N	12 30 E
Romaine →	**141**	50 18N	63 47W
Roman	**57**	46 57N	26 55 E
Romana, La	**180**	18 27N	68 57W
Romania ■	**57**	46 0N	25 0 E
Romans	**37**	45 3N	5 3 E
Romanzof, C.	**142**	62 0N	165 50W
Rome = Roma	**46**	41 54N	12 30 E
Rome, Ga., U.S.A.	**169**	34 20N	85 0W
Rome, N.Y., U.S.A.	**164**	43 14N	75 29W
Romilly	**39**	48 31N	3 44 E
Romney Marsh	**25**	51 0N	1 0 E
Rona	**32**	57 33N	6 0W
Rondônia □	**187**	11 0S	63 0W
Rong, Koh	**95**	10 45N	103 15 E
Ronge, L. la	**152**	55 6N	105 17W
Roosendaal	**40**	51 32N	4 29 E
Roraima □	**185**	2 0N	61 30W
Roraima, Mt.	**185**	5 10N	60 40W
Rosario, Argentina	**190**	33 0S	60 40W
Rosário, Brazil	**188**	3 0S	44 15W
Rosario, Mexico	**175**	22 58N	105 53W
Rosario, Paraguay	**191**	24 30S	57 35W
Rosário do Sul	**191**	30 15S	54 55W
Roscommon	**34**	53 38N	8 11W
Roscommon □	**34**	53 40N	8 15W
Roscrea	**35**	52 58N	7 50W
Roseau	**180**	15 20N	61 24W
Roseburg	**171**	43 10N	123 20W
Rosenberg	**168**	29 30N	95 48W
Rosendaël	**38**	51 3N	2 24 E
Rosetown	**152**	51 35N	107 59W
Roseville	**172**	38 46N	121 17W
Rosewood	**116**	27 38S	152 36 E
Roskilde	**61**	55 38N	12 3 E
Ross on Wye	**24**	51 55N	2 34W
Ross Sea	**15**	74 0S	178 0 E
Rossan Pt.	**34**	54 42N	8 47W
Rossland	**155**	49 6N	117 50W
Rosslare	**35**	52 17N	6 23W
Røssvatnet	**65**	65 45N	14 5 E
Rosthern	**152**	52 40N	106 20W
Rostock	**43**	54 4N	12 9 E
Rostov	**68**	47 15N	39 45 E
Roswell	**161**	33 26N	104 32W
Rosyth	**31**	56 2N	3 26W
Rother →	**25**	50 59N	0 40 E
Rotherham	**29**	53 26N	1 21W
Rothesay	**30**	55 50N	5 3W
Roto	**117**	33 0S	145 30 E
Rotorua	**122**	38 9S	176 16 E
Rotorua, L.	**122**	38 5S	176 18 E
Rotterdam	**40**	51 55N	4 30 E
Rotuma	**122**	12 25S	177 5 E
Roubaix	**37**	50 40N	3 10 E
Rouen	**38**	49 27N	1 4 E
Round Mt.	**116**	30 26S	152 16 E
Roussillon	**37**	42 30N	2 35 E
Rouyn	**151**	48 20N	79 0W
Rovaniemi	**67**	66 29N	25 41 E
Rovno	**68**	50 40N	26 10 E
Ruahine Ra.	**122**	39 55S	176 2 E
Ruapehu	**122**	39 17S	175 35 E
Rub' al Khali	**83**	18 0N	48 0 E
Rubh a' Mhail	**30**	55 55N	6 10W
Rubio	**184**	7 43N	72 22W
Rubtsovsk	**71**	51 30N	81 10 E
Rudnyy	**71**	52 57N	63 7 E
Rudolf, Ostrov	**69**	81 45N	58 30 E
Rufiji →	**135**	7 50S	39 15 E
Rufino	**190**	34 20S	62 50W
Rugby	**25**	52 23N	1 16W
Rügen	**43**	54 22N	13 25 E
Ruhr →	**42**	51 25N	6 44 E
Rukwa L.	**135**	8 0S	32 20 E
Rumania = Romania ■	**57**	46 0N	25 0 E
Rumford	**148**	44 30N	70 30W
Rumoi	**103**	43 56N	141 39W
Runcorn	**28**	53 20N	2 44W
Rupat	**111**	1 45N	101 40 E
Rupert →	**140**	51 29N	78 45W
Rupert House = Fort Rupert	**140**	51 30N	78 40W
Ruschuk = Ruse	**53**	43 48N	25 59 E
Ruse	**53**	43 48N	25 59 E
Russell	**152**	50 50N	101 20W
Russellville, Ala., U.S.A.	**169**	34 30N	87 44W
Russellville, Ark., U.S.A.	**168**	35 15N	93 8W
Russia ■	**78**	60 0N	100 0 E
Ruston	**168**	32 30N	92 58W
Rutherglen	**31**	55 50N	4 11W
Rutland I.	**94**	11 25N	92 40 E
Ruwenzori	**132**	0 30N	29 55 E
Rwanda ■	**135**	2 0S	30 0 E
Ryan, L.	**30**	55 0N	5 2W
Ryazan	**68**	54 40N	39 40 E
Rybache	**71**	46 40N	81 20 E
Rybinsk	**68**	58 5N	38 50 E
Ryde	**25**	50 44N	1 9W
Rye	**25**	50 57N	0 46 E
Rylstone	**117**	32 46S	149 58 E
Ryōhaku-Sanchi	**106**	36 9N	136 49 E
Ryūgasaki	**107**	35 54N	140 11 E
Rzeszów	**58**	50 5N	21 58 E

S

Sa Dec	**95**	10 20N	105 46 E
Saar →	**42**	49 41N	6 32 E
Saarbrücken	**42**	49 15N	6 58 E
Saaremaa	**68**	58 30N	22 30 E
Saarland □	**42**	49 15N	7 0 E
Sabadell	**51**	41 28N	2 7 E
Sabae	**106**	35 57N	136 11 E
Sabah □	**112**	6 0N	117 0 E
Sábana de la Mar	**180**	19 7N	69 24W
Sabhah	**127**	27 9N	14 29 E
Sabi →	**137**	18 50S	31 40 E
Sabinas	**174**	27 51N	101 7W
Sabinas Hidalgo, R. →	**176**	26 50N	99 35W
Sabine →	**158**	30 0N	93 35W
Sable, C., Canada	**148**	43 29N	65 38W
Sable, C., U.S.A.	**159**	25 13N	81 0W
Sable I.	**149**	44 0N	60 0W
Sabrina Coast	**15**	68 0S	120 0 E
Sabzevār	**86**	36 15N	57 40 E
Saco	**148**	43 30N	70 27W
Sacramento	**172**	38 33N	121 30 E
Sacramento →	**172**	38 3N	121 56W
Sacramento Mts.	**161**	32 30N	105 30W
Sado, Shima	**103**	38 15N	138 30 E
Safed Koh	**87**	34 0N	70 0 E
Saffron Walden	**25**	52 2N	0 15 E
Safi	**126**	32 18N	9 20W
Saga	**108**	33 15N	130 16 E
Sagami-Nada	**107**	34 58N	139 30 E
Sagami-Wan	**107**	35 15N	139 25 E
Sagamihara	**107**	35 33N	139 25 E
Sagar	**91**	14 14N	75 6 E
Sagara	**107**	34 41N	138 12 E
Saginaw	**167**	43 26N	83 55W
Saginaw B.	**167**	43 50N	83 40W
Saglouc	**146**	62 14N	75 38W
Sagres	**50**	37 0N	8 58W
Sagua la Grande	**178**	22 50N	80 10W
Saguenay →	**148**	48 22N	71 0W
Sahara	**126**	23 0N	5 0 E
Saharanpur	**89**	29 58N	77 33 E
Saharien, Atlas	**127**	33 30N	1 0 E
Sahiwal	**89**	30 45N	73 8 E
Sahuaripa	**174**	29 3N	109 14W
Saigō	**109**	36 12N	133 20 E
Saigon = Thanh Pho Ho Chi Minh	**95**	10 58N	106 40 E
Saijō, Ehime, Japan	**109**	33 55N	133 11 E
Saijō, Hiroshima, Japan	**109**	34 25N	132 45 E
Saikhoa Ghat	**93**	27 50N	95 40 E
Saiki	**108**	32 58N	131 51 E
Saimaa	**67**	61 15N	28 15 E
Şa'in Dezh	**81**	36 40N	46 25 E
St. Abb's Head	**31**	55 55N	2 10W
St. Albans, U.K.	**25**	51 44N	0 19W

Place	Map	Lat.	Long.
St. Albans, U.S.A.	**151**	44 49N	73 7W
St. Alban's Head	**24**	50 34N	2 3W
St. Albert	**155**	53 37N	113 32W
St. Andrews	**31**	56 20N	2 48W
St. Arnaud	**119**	36 40S	143 16 E
St. Asaph	**26**	53 15N	3 27W
St-Augustin-Saguenay	**141**	51 13N	58 38W
St. Augustine	**170**	29 52N	81 20W
St. Austell	**27**	50 20N	4 48W
St. Bee's Hd.	**28**	54 30N	3 38 E
St. Boniface	**153**	49 53N	97 5W
St. Bride's B.	**26**	51 48N	5 15W
St-Brieuc	**36**	48 30N	2 46W
St. Catharines	**151**	43 10N	79 15W
St. Charles	**166**	38 46N	90 30W
St. Christopher-Nevis ■	**180**	17 20N	62 40W
St. Cloud	**156**	45 30N	94 11W
St. Croix	**180**	17 45N	64 45W
St. David's	**26**	51 54N	5 16W
St. David's Head	**26**	51 55N	5 16W
St-Denis	**39**	48 56N	2 22 E
St-Dizier	**37**	48 40N	5 0 E
St. Elias, Mt.	**144**	60 14N	140 50W
St. Elias Mts.	**144**	60 33N	139 28W
St-Étienne	**37**	45 27N	4 22 E
St-Félicien	**151**	48 40N	72 25W
St. Gallen	**44**	47 25N	9 20 E
St. George, Australia	**116**	28 1S	148 30 E
St. George, Bermuda	**180**	32 24N	64 42W
St. Georges, Fr. Guiana	**185**	4 0N	52 0W
St. George's, Grenada	**180**	12 5N	61 43W
St. George's Channel	**20**	52 0N	6 0W
St. Gotthard P. = San Gottardo, Paso del	**44**	46 33N	8 33 E
St. Helena	**125**	15 55S	5 44W
St. Helena B.	**136**	32 40S	18 10 E
St. Helens, Australia	**119**	41 20S	148 15 E
St. Helens, U.K.	**28**	53 28N	2 44W
St. Helens, U.S.A.	**171**	45 55N	122 50W
St. Helier	**36**	49 11N	2 6W
St-Hyacinthe	**151**	45 40N	72 58W
St. Ives, Cambs., U.K.	**25**	52 20N	0 5W
St. Ives, Corn., U.K.	**27**	50 13N	5 29W
St-Jean	**151**	45 20N	73 20W
St-Jérôme	**151**	45 47N	74 0W
St. John	**148**	45 20N	66 8W
St. John's	**149**	47 35N	52 40W
St. John's →	**170**	30 20N	81 30W
St. Johnsbury	**148**	44 25N	72 1W
St. Joseph, Mich., U.S.A.	**167**	42 5N	86 30W
St. Joseph, Mo., U.S.A.	**166**	39 46N	94 50W
St. Kilda, N.Z.	**123**	45 53S	170 31 E
St. Kilda, U.K.	**22**	57 9N	8 34W
St. Lawrence	**149**	46 54N	55 23W
St. Lawrence →	**148**	49 30N	66 0W
St. Lawrence, Gulf of	**149**	48 25N	62 0W
St. Lawrence I.	**142**	63 0N	170 0W
St. Leonard	**148**	47 12N	67 58W
St-Louis	**130**	16 8N	16 27W
St. Louis	**166**	38 40N	90 12W
St. Lucia ■	**180**	14 0N	60 50W
St. Maarten	**180**	18 0N	63 5W
St-Malo	**36**	48 39N	2 1W
St-Marc	**180**	19 10N	72 41W
St-Martin, I.	**180**	18 0N	63 0W
St. Mary Pk.	**118**	31 32S	138 34 E
St. Marys	**164**	41 27N	78 33W
St. Matthews, I. = Zadetkyi Kyun	**94**	10 0N	98 25 E
St. Michael's Mt.	**27**	50 7N	5 30W
St. Moritz	**44**	46 30N	9 51 E
St-Nazaire	**36**	47 17N	2 12W
St. Neots	**25**	52 14N	0 16W
St-Omer	**38**	50 45N	2 15 E
St. Pascal	**148**	47 32N	69 48W
St. Paul	**166**	44 54N	93 5W
St. Paul, I.	**149**	47 12N	60 9W
St-Petersburg = Sankt-Peterburg	**68**	59 55N	30 20 E
St. Petersburg	**170**	27 45N	82 40W
St-Pierre et Miquelon □	**149**	46 55N	56 10W
St-Quentin	**38**	49 50N	3 16 E
St-Raphaël	**37**	43 25N	6 46 E
St-Servan-sur-Mer	**36**	48 38N	2 0W
St. Thomas, Canada	**151**	42 45N	81 10W
St. Thomas, W. Indies	**180**	18 21N	64 55W
St-Tropez	**37**	43 17N	6 38 E
St. Vincent and the Grenadines ■	**180**	13 0N	61 10W
Ste-Adresse	**38**	49 31N	0 5 E
Ste. Anne de Beaupré	**148**	47 2N	70 58W
Ste. Marie	**180**	14 48N	61 1W
Ste-Rose	**180**	16 20N	61 45W
Ste. Rose du lac	**153**	51 4N	99 30W
Saintes	**36**	45 45N	0 37W
Saintonge	**36**	45 40N	0 50W
Sajama	**187**	18 7S	69 0W
Sakai	**106**	34 30N	135 30 E
Sakaide	**109**	34 15N	133 50 E
Sakaiminato	**109**	35 38N	133 11 E
Sakakawea, L.	**163**	47 30N	102 0W
Sakata	**103**	38 55N	139 50 E
Sakha □	**72**	62 0N	130 0 E
Sakhalin	**79**	51 0N	143 0 E
Sakhalinskiy Zaliv	**75**	54 0N	141 0 E
Saku	**107**	36 17N	138 31 E
Sakura	**107**	35 43N	140 14 E
Sakurai	**106**	34 30N	135 51 E
Salaberry-de-Valleyfield	**151**	45 15N	74 8W
Salado →	**190**	31 40S	60 41W
Salado, R. →	**176**	26 52N	99 19W
Salamanca, Spain	**50**	40 58N	5 39W
Salamanca, U.S.A.	**164**	42 10N	78 42W
Salamis	**55**	37 56N	23 30 E
Salcombe	**27**	50 14N	3 47W
Sale	**117**	38 6S	147 6 E
Salem, India	**90**	11 40N	78 11 E
Salem, Mass., U.S.A.	**164**	42 29N	70 53W
Salem, Oreg., U.S.A.	**171**	45 0N	123 0W
Salem, Va., U.S.A.	**165**	37 19N	80 8W
Salerno	**49**	40 40N	14 44 E
Salford	**28**	53 30N	2 17W
Salida	**163**	38 35N	106 0W
Salina, Italy	**49**	38 35N	14 50 E
Salina, U.S.A.	**161**	38 50N	97 40W
Salina Cruz	**177**	16 10N	95 12W
Salinas, Ecuador	**184**	2 10S	80 58W
Salinas, U.S.A.	**173**	36 40N	121 41W
Salinas →	**173**	36 45N	121 48W
Salinas Grandes	**190**	30 0S	65 0W
Salisbury = Harare	**137**	17 43S	31 2 E
Salisbury, U.K.	**24**	51 4N	1 48W
Salisbury, Md., U.S.A.	**165**	38 20N	75 38W
Salisbury, N.C., U.S.A.	**165**	35 20N	80 29W
Salisbury Plain	**24**	51 13N	1 50W
Salle, La	**166**	41 20N	89 6W
Salmon	**162**	45 12N	113 56W
Salmon →	**171**	45 51N	116 46W
Salmon Arm	**155**	50 40N	119 15W
Salmon River Mts.	**162**	45 0N	114 30W
Salon-de-Provence	**37**	43 39N	5 6 E
Salonica = Thessaloníki	**54**	40 38N	22 58 E
Salop = Shropshire □	**24**	52 36N	2 45W
Salt Fork →	**161**	36 37N	97 7W
Salt Lake City	**163**	40 45N	111 58W
Salta	**190**	24 57S	65 25W
Saltcoats	**30**	55 38N	4 47W
Saltillo	**174**	25 25N	101 0W
Salto	**191**	31 27S	57 50W
Salton Sea	**173**	33 20N	115 50W
Salûm	**128**	31 31N	25 7 E
Salvador	**189**	13 0S	38 30W
Salween →	**93**	16 31N	97 37 E
Salzburg	**45**	47 48N	13 2 E
Salzburg □	**45**	47 15N	13 0 E
Salzgitter	**43**	52 13N	10 22 E
Sam Neua	**95**	20 29N	104 0 E
Sama	**69**	60 12N	60 22 E
Samangán □	**87**	36 15N	68 3 E
Samar	**112**	12 0N	125 0 E
Samara	**68**	53 8N	50 6 E
Samarkand	**70**	39 40N	66 55 E
Sāmarrā	**81**	34 12N	43 52 E
Sambalpur	**92**	21 28N	84 4 E

Sambhal **89** 28 35N 78 37 E
Sámos **55** 37 45N 26 50 E
Samothráki **55** 40 28N 25 28 E
Samsun **80** 41 15N 36 22 E
Samut Prakan **95** 13 32N 100 40 E
Samut Sakhon **94** 13 31N 100 13 E
Samut Songkhram → **94** 13 24N 100 1 E
San Andreas **172** 38 0N 120 39W
San Andres Mts. **161** 33 0N 106 45W
San Andrés Tuxtla **177** 18 27N 95 13W
San Angelo **161** 31 30N 100 30W
San Antonio, Chile **190** 33 40S 71 40W
San Antonio, U.S.A. **161** 29 30N 98 30W
San Antonio, C., Argentina **191** 36 15S 56 40W
San Antonio, C., Cuba **178** 21 50N 84 57W
San Antonio de los Baños **178** 22 54N 82 31W
San Antônio Falls **182** 9 30S 65 0W
San Antonio Oeste **192** 40 40S 65 0W
San Bernardino **173** 34 7N 117 18W
San Bernardino Str. **112** 13 0N 125 0 E
San Bernardo **190** 33 40S 70 50W
San Blas, C. **169** 29 40N 85 12W
San Carlos, Chile **190** 36 10S 72 0W
San Carlos, Mexico **174** 29 1N 100 51W
San Carlos, Nic. **179** 11 12N 84 50W
San Carlos de Bariloche **192** 41 10S 71 25W
San Clemente I. **173** 32 53N 118 30W
San Cristóbal, Argentina **190** 30 20S 61 10W
San Cristóbal, Dom. Rep. **180** 18 25N 70 6W
San Cristóbal, Venezuela **184** 16 50N 92 40W
San Cristóbal de las Casas **177** 16 45N 92 38W
San Diego **173** 32 43N 117 10W
San Felipe, Chile **190** 32 43S 70 42W
San Felipe, Colombia **184** 1 55N 67 6W
San Fernando, Chile **190** 34 30S 71 0W
San Fernando, Mexico **174** 30 0N 115 10W
San Fernando, Trin. & Tob. **180** 10 20N 61 30W
San Fernando, U.S.A. **173** 34 15N 118 29W
San Fernando de Apure **184** 7 54N 67 15W
San Francisco **172** 37 47N 122 30W
San Francisco de Macorîs **180** 19 19N 70 15W
San Francisco del Oro **174** 26 52N 105 51W
San Gabriel **191** 0 36N 77 49W
San Gottardo, Paso del **44** 46 33N 8 33 E
San Ignacio **187** 16 20S 60 55W
San Joaquin → **172** 37 4N 121 51W
San Jorge, Golfo **192** 46 0S 66 0W
San Jorge, G. de **51** 40 50N 0 55W
San José, Bolivia **187** 17 53S 60 50W
San José, Costa Rica **179** 10 0N 84 2W
San Jose, U.S.A. **172** 37 20N 121 53W
San José de Mayo **191** 34 27S 56 40W
San José del Cabo **175** 23 3N 109 41W
San José del Guaviare **184** 2 35N 72 38W
San Juan, Argentina **190** 31 30S 68 30W
San Juan, Dom. Rep. **180** 18 49N 71 12W
San Juan, Puerto Rico **180** 18 28N 66 8W
San Juan → **179** 10 56N 83 42W
San Juan de los Morros **184** 9 55N 67 21W
San Juan Mts. **163** 38 30N 108 30W
San Julián **192** 49 15S 67 45W
San Leandro **172** 37 40N 122 6W
San Lorenzo **184** 1 15N 78 50W
San Lucas, C. de **175** 22 50N 110 0W
San Luis **190** 33 20S 66 20W
San Luis de la Paz **177** 21 18N 100 31W
San Luis Obispo **173** 35 21N 120 38W
San Luis Potosí **177** 22 9N 100 59W
San Luis Potosí □ **177** 22 30N 100 30W
San Marcos **177** 14 59N 91 52W
San Marino ■ **47** 43 56N 12 25 E
San Mateo **172** 37 32N 122 19W
San Matías **187** 16 25S 58 20W
San Matías, Golfo **192** 41 30S 64 0W
San Miguel **177** 13 30N 88 12W
San Miguel de Tucumán **190** 26 50S 65 20W
San Pedro → **175** 21 45N 105 30W
San Pedro de las Colonias **174** 25 45N 102 59W
San Pedro de Macorís **180** 18 30N 69 18W
San Pedro Sula **177** 15 30N 88 0W
San Rafael, Argentina **190** 34 40S 68 21W
San Rafael, U.S.A. **172** 37 59N 122 32W
San Roque **190** 28 25S 58 45W
San Salvador, Bahamas **178** 24 0N 74 40W
San Salvador, El Salv. **177** 13 40N 89 10W
San Salvador de Jujuy **190** 24 10S 64 48W
San Sebastián **51** 43 17N 1 58W
San Valentin, Mte. **192** 46 30S 73 30W
Sana' **82** 15 27N 44 12 E
Sanandaj **81** 35 18N 47 1 E
Sancti-Spíritus **178** 21 52N 79 33W
Sanda **106** 34 53N 135 14 E
Sandgate **116** 27 18S 153 3 E
Sandomierz **58** 50 40N 21 43 E
Sandpoint **171** 48 20N 116 34W
Sandringham **29** 52 50N 0 30 E
Sandstone **120** 27 59S 119 16 E
Sandusky **167** 41 25N 82 40W
Sandwip Chan. **93** 22 35N 91 35 E
Sandy C. **119** 41 25S 144 45 E
Sandy Lake **153** 53 0N 93 15W
Sanford, Fla., U.S.A. **170** 28 45N 81 20W
Sanford, Maine, U.S.A. **148** 43 28N 70 47W
Sanford, N.C., U.S.A. **165** 35 30N 79 10W
Sangay **184** 2 0S 78 20W
Sangihe, P. **113** 3 45N 125 30 E
Sangli **91** 16 55N 74 33 E
Sangre de Cristo Mts. **161** 37 0N 105 0W
Sankt-Peterburg **68** 59 55N 30 20 E
Sankuru → **134** 4 17S 20 25 E
Sanliurfa **81** 37 12N 38 50 E
Sano **107** 36 19N 139 35 E
Sanok **59** 49 35N 22 10 E
Sanquhar **31** 55 21N 3 56W
Sanshui **99** 23 10N 112 56 E
Santa Ana, Bolivia **187** 13 50S 65 40W
Santa Ana, Mexico **174** 30 33N 111 7W
Santa Ana, U.S.A. **173** 33 48N 117 55W
Santa Bárbara, Mexico **174** 26 48N 105 49W
Santa Barbara, U.S.A. **173** 34 25N 119 40W
Santa Barbara I. **160** 33 29N 119 2W
Santa Catarina □ **191** 27 25S 48 30W
Santa Clara, Cuba **178** 22 20N 80 0W
Santa Clara, U.S.A. **162** 37 21N 122 0W
Santa Clotilde **186** 2 33S 73 45W
Santa Cruz, Bolivia **187** 17 43S 63 10W
Santa Cruz, U.S.A. **172** 36 55N 122 1W
Santa Cruz, Is. **122** 10 30S 166 0 E
Santa Cruz de Tenerife **126** 28 28N 16 15W
Santa Cruz del Sur **178** 20 44N 78 0W
Santa Cruz do Sul **191** 29 42S 52 25W
Santa Fe, Argentina **190** 31 35S 60 41W
Santa Fe, U.S.A. **161** 35 40N 106 0W
Santa Inés, I. **192** 54 0S 73 0W
Santa Isabel = Rey Malabo **131** 3 45N 8 50 E
Santa Lucia Range **173** 36 0N 121 20W
Santa Maria, Brazil **191** 29 40S 53 48W
Santa Maria, U.S.A. **173** 34 58N 120 29W
Santa Maria da Vitória **188** 13 24S 44 12W
Santa Maria di Leuca, C. **49** 39 48N 18 20 E
Santa Marta **184** 11 15N 74 13W
Santa Maura = Levkás **54** 38 40N 20 43 E
Santa Monica **173** 34 0N 118 30W
Santa Rosa, Argentina **190** 36 40S 64 17W
Santa Rosa, U.S.A. **172** 38 26N 122 43W
Santa Rosa I., Calif., U.S.A. **173** 34 0N 120 6W
Santa Rosa I., Fla., U.S.A. **169** 30 23N 87 0W
Santa Rosalía **174** 27 19N 112 17W
Santana do Livramento **191** 30 55S 55 30W
Santander **50** 43 27N 3 51W
Santander Jiménez **176** 24 13N 98 28W
Santarém, Brazil **185** 2 25S 54 42W
Santarém, Portugal **50** 39 12N 8 42W
Santiago, Brazil **191** 29 11S 54 52W
Santiago, Chile **190** 33 24S 70 40W
Santiago, Panama **179** 8 0N 81 0W
Santiago de Compostela **50** 42 52N 8 37W
Santiago de Cuba **178** 20 0N 75 49W
Santiago de los Cabelleros **180** 19 30N 70 40W
Santiago del Estero **190** 27 50S 64 15W
Santiago Ixcuintla **175** 21 50N 105 11W
Santo Amaro **189** 12 30S 38 43W
Santo Ângelo **191** 28 15S 54 15W
Santo Domingo **180** 18 30N 64 54W

Place	Page	Lat.	Long.
Santo Tomé	**191**	28 40S	56 5W
Santoña	**50**	43 29N	3 27W
Santos	**191**	24 0S	46 20W
São Borja	**191**	28 39S	56 0W
São Carlos	**188**	22 0S	47 50W
São Francisco →	**189**	10 30S	36 24W
São Francisco do Sul	**191**	26 15S	48 36W
São João del Rei	**188**	21 8S	44 15W
São José do Rio Prêto	**188**	20 50S	49 20W
São Leopoldo	**191**	29 50S	51 10W
São Lourenço	**188**	22 7S	45 3W
São Luís	**188**	2 39S	44 15W
São Paulo	**191**	23 32S	46 37W
São Paulo □	**188**	22 0S	49 0W
São Paulo de Olivença	**184**	3 27S	68 48W
São Roque, C. de	**189**	5 30S	35 16W
São Tomé	**131**	0 10N	6 39 E
São Tomé & Principe ■	**131**	0 12N	6 39 E
São Vicente, Cabo de	**50**	37 0N	9 0W
Saône →	**37**	45 44N	4 50 E
Sapporo	**103**	43 0N	141 21 E
Sapulpa	**168**	36 0N	96 0W
Saqqez	**81**	36 15N	46 20 E
Sar Planina	**52**	42 10N	21 0 E
Saragossa = Zaragoza	**51**	41 39N	0 53W
Sarajevo	**52**	43 52N	18 26 E
Saranac Lake	**151**	44 20N	74 10W
Sarangani B.	**112**	6 0N	125 13 E
Saransk	**68**	54 10N	45 10 E
Sarapul	**69**	56 28N	53 48 E
Sarasota	**165**	27 20N	82 30W
Saratoga Springs	**164**	43 5N	73 47W
Saratov	**68**	51 30N	46 2 E
Sarawak □	**111**	2 0N	113 0 E
Sardegna	**48**	39 57N	9 0 E
Sardinia = Sardegna	**48**	39 57N	9 0 E
Sargodha	**89**	32 10N	72 40 E
Sarh	**131**	9 5N	18 23 E
Sārī	**86**	36 30N	53 4 E
Sarina	**121**	21 22S	149 13 E
Sarmiento	**192**	45 35S	69 5W
Sarnia	**150**	42 58N	82 23W
Saronikós Kólpos	**55**	37 45N	23 45 E
Sarre = Saar →	**42**	49 41N	6 32 E
Sarre, La	**151**	48 45N	79 15W
Sarthe →	**36**	47 33N	0 31W
Sasaram	**92**	24 57N	84 5 E
Sasebo	**108**	33 10N	129 43 E
Saskatchewan □	**152**	54 40N	106 0W
Saskatchewan →	**152**	53 37N	100 40W
Saskatoon	**152**	52 10N	106 38W
Sassandra	**130**	5 0N	6 8W
Sássari	**48**	40 44N	8 33 E
Sata-Misaki	**108**	30 59N	130 40 E
Satara	**91**	17 44N	73 58 E
Satmala Hills	**91**	20 15N	74 40 E
Satna	**92**	24 35N	80 50 E
Satpura Ra.	**91**	21 25N	76 10 E
Sattahip	**95**	12 41N	100 54 E
Satu Mare	**56**	47 46N	22 55 E
Sauðarkrókur	**64**	65 45N	19 40W
Saudi Arabia ■	**82**	26 0N	44 0 E
Sault Ste. Marie, Canada	**150**	46 30N	84 20W
Sault Ste. Marie, U.S.A.	**150**	46 27N	84 22W
Saumur	**36**	47 15N	0 5W
Sava →	**52**	44 50N	20 26 E
Savanna la Mar	**180**	18 10N	78 10W
Savannah	**170**	32 4N	81 4W
Savannah →	**170**	32 2N	80 53W
Savannakhet	**95**	16 30N	104 49 E
Savoie □	**37**	45 26N	6 35 E
Savona	**46**	44 19N	8 29 E
Sawankhalok	**94**	17 19N	99 50 E
Sawara	**107**	35 55N	140 30 E
Sawatch Mts.	**163**	38 30N	106 30W
Sawu, I.	**113**	10 35S	121 50 E
Sawu Sea	**113**	9 30S	121 50 E
Saxony, Lower = Niedersachsen □	**42**	52 45N	9 0 E
Sayan, Zapadnyy	**77**	52 30N	94 0 E
Saydā	**80**	33 35N	35 25 E
Sayḩut	**83**	15 12N	51 10 E
Sayula	**175**	19 52N	103 36W
Sazan	**52**	40 30N	19 20 E
Scafell Pikes	**28**	54 26N	3 14W
Scalloway	**30**	60 9N	1 16W
Scandinavia	**16**	64 0N	12 0 E
Scapa Flow	**33**	58 52N	3 6W
Scarborough	**29**	54 17N	0 24W
Schaffhausen	**44**	47 42N	8 39 E
Schefferville	**146**	54 48N	66 50W
Schelde →	**42**	51 15N	4 16 E
Schenectady	**164**	42 50N	73 58W
Scheveningen	**40**	52 6N	4 16 E
Schiedam	**40**	51 55N	4 25 E
Schiermonnikoog	**41**	53 30N	6 15 E
Schleswig-Holstein □	**42**	54 10N	9 40 E
Schouten I.	**119**	42 20S	148 20 E
Schouten Is.	**113**	1 0S	136 0 E
Schouwen	**40**	51 43N	3 45 E
Schreiber	**150**	48 45N	87 20W
Schwäbische Alb	**42**	48 30N	9 30 E
Schwarzwald	**42**	48 0N	8 0 E
Schwerin	**43**	53 37N	11 22 E
Schwyz	**44**	47 2N	8 39 E
Scilly, Isles of	**20**	49 55N	6 15W
Scone, Australia	**116**	32 5S	150 52 E
Scone, U.K.	**31**	56 25N	3 26W
Scoresbysund	**13**	70 20N	23 0W
Scotia Sea	**14**	56 5S	56 0W
Scotland □	**23**	57 0N	4 0W
Scottsbluff	**163**	41 55N	103 35W
Scottsdale	**119**	41 9S	147 31 E
Scranton	**164**	41 22N	75 41W
Scunthorpe	**29**	53 35N	0 38W
Scutari = Üsküdar	**80**	41 0N	29 5 E
Seaforth	**150**	43 35N	81 25W
Searcy	**168**	35 15N	91 45W
Seascale	**28**	54 24N	3 29W
Seattle	**171**	47 41N	122 15W
Sebastián Vizcaíno, B.	**174**	28 0N	114 30W
Sebastopol = Sevastopol	**68**	44 35N	33 30 E
Sebring	**170**	27 30N	81 26W
Sebta = Ceuta	**126**	35 52N	5 18W
Sebuku, Teluk	**111**	4 0N	118 10 E
Sechura, Desierto de	**186**	6 0S	80 30W
Seclin	**38**	50 33N	3 2 E
Sedalia	**166**	38 40N	93 18W
Segamat	**96**	2 30N	102 50 E
Ségou	**130**	13 30N	6 16W
Segovia = Coco →	**179**	15 0N	83 8W
Segovia	**50**	40 57N	4 10W
Séguéla	**130**	7 55N	6 40W
Segura →	**51**	38 6N	0 54W
Seine →	**38**	49 26N	0 26 E
Seistan	**85**	30 50N	61 0 E
Seki	**106**	35 29N	136 55 E
Sekondi-Takoradi	**130**	4 58N	1 45W
Selangor □	**96**	3 10N	101 30 E
Selby	**29**	53 47N	1 5W
Sélibabi	**130**	15 10N	12 15W
Selkirk, Canada	**153**	50 10N	96 55W
Selkirk, U.K.	**31**	55 33N	2 50W
Selkirk Mts.	**155**	51 15N	117 40W
Selma, Ala., U.S.A.	**169**	32 30N	87 0W
Selma, Calif., U.S.A.	**173**	36 39N	119 39W
Selsey Bill	**24**	50 44N	0 47W
Selvas	**187**	6 30S	67 0W
Semarang	**111**	7 0S	110 26 E
Semey	**71**	50 30N	80 10 E
Semipalatinsk = Semey	**71**	50 30N	80 10 E
Semnān	**86**	35 55N	53 25 E
Semnān □	**86**	36 0N	54 0 E
Sendai, Kagoshima, Japan	**108**	31 50N	130 20 E
Sendai, Miyagi, Japan	**103**	38 15N	140 53 E
Senegal ■	**130**	14 30N	14 30W
Senegal →	**126**	15 48N	16 32W
Senge Khambab = Indus →	**88**	24 20N	67 47 E
Senhor-do-Bonfim	**189**	10 30S	40 10W
Senja I.	**64**	69 15N	17 30 E
Senlis	**39**	49 13N	2 35 E
Sennâr	**129**	13 30N	33 35 E
Senneterre	**151**	48 25N	77 15W

Sens	**39**	48 11N	3 15 E
Senta	**52**	45 55N	20 3 E
Seoul = Sŏul	**98**	37 31N	126 58 E
Sept-Îles	**148**	50 13N	66 22W
Seram	**113**	3 10S	129 0 E
Seram Sea	**113**	2 30S	128 30 E
Seremban	**96**	2 43N	101 53 E
Serena, La	**190**	29 55S	71 10W
Sereth = Siret →	**57**	47 58N	26 5 E
Sergipe □	**189**	10 30S	37 30W
Sérifos	**55**	37 9N	24 30 E
Serny Zavod	**70**	39 59N	58 50 E
Serov	**69**	59 29N	60 35 E
Serowe	**137**	22 25S	26 43 E
Serpukhov	**68**	54 55N	37 28 E
Serra do Navio	**185**	0 59N	52 3W
Sérrai	**55**	41 5N	23 31 E
Sesheke	**134**	17 29S	24 13 E
Setana	**103**	42 26N	139 51 E
Sète	**37**	43 25N	3 42 E
Sétif	**127**	36 9N	5 26 E
Seto	**106**	35 14N	137 6 E
Setonaikai	**109**	34 20N	133 30 E
Settle	**28**	54 5N	2 18W
Setúbal	**50**	38 30N	8 58W
Sevastopol	**68**	44 35N	33 30 E
Seven Sisters	**154**	54 56N	128 10W
Severn →, Canada	**140**	56 2N	87 36W
Severn →, U.K.	**24**	51 35N	2 38W
Severnaya Zemlya	**72**	79 0N	100 0 E
Severodinsk	**69**	64 27N	39 58 E
Sevilla	**50**	37 23N	6 0W
Seville = Sevilla	**50**	37 23N	6 0W
Seward	**142**	60 6N	149 26W
Seward Pen.	**142**	65 0N	164 0W
Seychelles ■	**78**	5 0S	56 0 E
Seyðisfjörður	**64**	65 16N	14 0W
Seymour	**117**	37 0S	145 10 E
Seyne-sur-Mer, La	**37**	43 7N	5 52 E
Sézanne	**39**	48 40N	3 40 E
Sfax	**127**	34 49N	10 48 E
Sfîntu Gheorghe	**57**	45 52N	25 48 E
Shaanxi □	**99**	35 0N	109 0 E
Shaba □	**135**	8 0S	25 0 E
Shache	**100**	38 20N	77 10 E
Shaftesbury	**24**	51 0N	2 12W
Shahdād	**85**	30 30N	57 40 E
Shakhty	**68**	47 40N	40 16 E
Shamanovo	**73**	69 45N	147 20 E
Shamo = Gobi	**98**	44 0N	111 0 E
Shamokin	**164**	40 47N	76 33W
Shan □	**93**	21 30N	98 30 E
Shandong □	**99**	36 0N	118 0 E
Shanghai	**99**	31 15N	121 26 E
Shangqiu	**99**	34 26N	115 36 E
Shangrao	**99**	28 25N	117 59 E
Shannon →	**35**	52 35N	9 30W
Shansi = Shanxi □	**98**	37 0N	112 0 E
Shantou	**99**	23 18N	116 40 E
Shantung = Shandong □	**99**	36 0N	118 0 E
Shanxi □	**98**	37 0N	112 0 E
Shaoguan	**99**	24 48N	113 35 E
Shaoxing	**99**	30 0N	120 35 E
Shaoyang	**99**	27 14N	111 25 E
Shap	**28**	54 32N	2 40W
Sharjah = Ash Shāriqah	**85**	25 23N	55 26 E
Shark B.	**120**	25 55S	113 32 E
Sharon	**164**	41 18N	80 30W
Shashi	**99**	30 25N	112 14 E
Shasta, Mt.	**172**	41 30N	122 12W
Shasta L.	**172**	40 50N	122 15W
Shaunavon	**152**	49 35N	108 25W
Shawano	**167**	44 45N	88 38W
Shawinigan	**151**	46 35N	72 50W
Shawnee	**168**	35 15N	97 0W
Shcherbakov = Andropov	**68**	58 5N	38 50 E
Shebele, Wabi →	**133**	2 0N	44 0 E
Sheboygan	**167**	43 46N	87 45W
Sheerness	**24**	51 26N	0 47 E
Sheffield	**28**	53 23N	1 28W
Shekhupura	**89**	31 42N	73 58 E
Shelburne	**148**	43 47N	65 20W
Shelby, Mont., U.S.A.	**163**	48 30N	111 52W
Shelby, N.C., U.S.A.	**165**	35 18N	81 34W
Shelbyville, Ind., U.S.A.	**167**	39 30N	85 42W
Shelbyville, Tenn., U.S.A.	**169**	35 30N	86 25W
Shelikhova, Zaliv	**73**	59 30N	157 0 E
Shellharbour	**117**	34 31S	150 51 E
Shelton	**171**	47 15N	123 6W
Shenandoah	**166**	40 50N	95 25W
Shensi = Shaanxi □	**99**	35 0N	109 0 E
Shenyang	**98**	41 50N	123 25 E
Shepparton	**117**	36 23S	145 26 E
Sheppey, I. of	**24**	51 23N	0 50 E
Sherborne	**27**	50 56N	2 31W
Sherbrooke	**148**	45 28N	71 57W
Sheridan	**163**	44 50N	107 0W
Sherman	**168**	33 40N	96 35W
Sherridon	**152**	55 8N	101 5W
Sherwood Forest	**29**	53 5N	1 5W
Shetland Is.	**30**	60 30N	1 30W
Shibām	**83**	16 0N	48 36 E
Shibata	**103**	37 57N	139 20 E
Shibetsu	**103**	44 10N	142 23 E
Shibukawa	**107**	36 29N	139 0 E
Shibushi-Wan	**108**	31 24N	131 8 E
Shiel, L.	**32**	56 48N	5 32W
Shihchiachuangi = Shijiazhuang	**98**	38 2N	114 28 E
Shijiazhuang	**98**	38 2N	114 28 E
Shikarpur	**88**	27 57N	68 39 E
Shikine-Jima	**107**	34 19N	139 13 E
Shikoku	**109**	33 30N	133 30 E
Shikoku □	**109**	33 30N	133 30 E
Shikoku-Sanchi	**109**	33 30N	133 30 E
Shillong	**93**	25 35N	91 53 E
Shimabara	**108**	32 48N	130 20 E
Shimada	**107**	34 49N	138 10 E
Shimizu	**107**	35 0N	138 30 E
Shimo-Jima	**108**	32 15N	130 7 E
Shimo-Koshiki-Jima	**108**	31 40N	129 43 E
Shimoda	**107**	34 40N	138 57 E
Shimodate	**107**	36 20N	139 55 E
Shimoga	**90**	13 57N	75 32 E
Shimonoseki	**108**	33 58N	131 0 E
Shin, L.	**33**	58 7N	4 30W
Shin-Tone →	**107**	35 44N	140 51 E
Shinano →	**105**	36 50N	138 30 E
Shingū	**106**	33 40N	135 55 E
Shinji Ko	**109**	35 26N	132 57 E
Shinjō	**103**	38 46N	140 18 E
Shinminato	**106**	36 47N	137 4 E
Shinshiro	**106**	34 54N	137 30 E
Shio-no-Misaki	**106**	33 25N	135 45 E
Shiogama	**103**	38 19N	141 1 E
Shiojiri	**107**	36 6N	137 58 E
Shipka	**53**	42 46N	25 33 E
Shirane-San, Gumma, Japan	**107**	36 48N	139 22 E
Shirane-San, Yamanashi, Japan	**107**	35 42N	138 9 E
Shīrāz	**85**	29 42N	52 30 E
Shire →	**137**	17 42S	35 19 E
Shiriya-Zaki	**103**	41 25N	141 30 E
Shivpuri	**91**	25 26N	77 42 E
Shizuoka	**107**	35 0N	138 24 E
Shkoder = Shkodra	**52**	42 6N	19 20 E
Shkodra	**52**	42 6N	19 20 E
Shkumbini →	**52**	41 5N	19 50 E
Shō-Gawa →	**106**	36 47N	137 4 E
Shōbara	**109**	34 51N	133 1 E
Shoeburyness	**24**	51 31N	0 49 E
Sholapur = Solapur	**91**	17 43N	75 56 E
Shoshone	**172**	43 0N	114 27W
Shreveport	**168**	32 30N	93 50W
Shrewsbury	**28**	52 42N	2 45W
Shrirampur	**92**	22 44N	88 21 E
Shropshire □	**24**	52 36N	2 45W
Shuangyashan	**98**	46 37N	131 22 E
Siahan Range	**88**	27 30N	64 40 E
Sialkot	**89**	32 32N	74 30 E
Siam = Thailand ■	**95**	16 0N	102 0 E
Sian = Xi'an	**99**	34 15N	109 0 E

Siberia 77 60 0N 100 0 E
Siberut 111 1 30S 99 0 E
Sibi 88 29 30N 67 54 E
Sibiu 57 45 45N 24 9 E
Sichuan □ 99 31 0N 104 0 E
Sicilia 49 37 30N 14 30 E
Sicily = Sicilia 49 37 30N 14 30 E
Sicuani 187 14 21S 71 10W
Sidi-bel-Abbès 127 35 13N 0 39W
Sidlaw Hills 31 56 32N 3 10W
Sidley, Mt. 15 77 2S 126 2W
Sidmouth 27 50 40N 3 13W
Sidney 154 48 39N 123 24W
Sidon = Saydā 80 33 35N 35 25 E
Sidra, G. of = Surt, Khalīj 127 31 40N 18 30 E
Siedlce 58 52 10N 22 20 E
Siena 46 43 20N 11 20 E
Sierra Blanca Pk. 161 33 20N 105 54W
Sierra Leone ■ 130 9 0N 12 0W
Sífnos 55 37 0N 24 45 E
Siglufjörður 64 66 12N 18 55W
Sihanoukville = Kompong Som 95 10 38N 103 30 E
Siirt 81 37 57N 41 55 E
Sikar 89 27 33N 75 10 E
Sikeston 169 36 52N 89 35W
Sikhote Alin, Khrebet 75 46 0N 136 0 E
Síkinos 55 36 40N 25 8 E
Sikkim □ 92 27 50N 88 30 E
Silchar 93 24 49N 92 48 E
Silesia = Slask 58 51 0N 16 30 E
Siling Co 101 31 50N 89 20 E
Silloth 28 54 53N 3 25W
Simbirsk 68 54 20N 48 25 E
Simcoe 151 42 50N 80 20W
Simenga 74 62 42N 108 25 E
Simeulue 111 2 45N 95 45 E
Simferopol 68 44 55N 34 3 E
Simi Valley 173 34 16N 118 47W
Simla 89 31 2N 77 9 E
Simplon Pass 44 46 15N 8 0 E
Simushir, Ostrov 75 46 50N 152 30 E
Sinai = Es Sînâ' 128 29 0N 34 0 E
Sinaloa 174 25 50N 108 20W
Sinaloa □ 174 25 0N 107 30W
Sincelejo 184 9 18N 75 24W
Sinclair Mills 155 54 5N 121 40W
Sind □ 88 26 0N 69 0 E
Sind Sagar Doab 89 32 0N 71 30 E
Singa 129 13 10N 33 57 E
Singapore ■ 96 1 17N 103 51 E
Singapore, Straits of 96 1 15N 104 0 E
Singkaling Hkamti 92 26 0N 95 39 E
Singleton 117 32 33S 151 0 E
Singora = Songkhla 97 7 13N 100 37 E
Sinkiang Uighur = Xinjiang Uygur Zizhiqu □ 100 42 0N 86 0 E
Sioux City 166 42 32N 96 25W
Sioux Falls 166 43 35N 96 40W
Sioux Lookout 153 50 10N 91 50W
Siping 98 43 8N 124 21 E
Sipora 111 2 18S 99 40 E
Siracusa 49 37 4N 15 17 E
Sirajganj 92 24 25N 89 47 E
Siret → 57 47 58N 26 5 E
Síros 55 37 28N 24 57 E
Sitapur 92 27 38N 80 45 E
Sitka 143 57 9N 135 20W
Sittard 41 51 0N 5 52 E
Sivas 80 39 43N 36 58 E
Siverek 81 37 50N 39 19 E
Sivrihisar 80 39 30N 31 35 E
Sîwa 128 29 11N 25 31 E
Siwalik Range 92 28 0N 83 0 E
Sizewell 24 52 13N 1 38 E
Sjumen = Kolarovgrad 53 43 18N 26 55 E
Skadarsko Jezero 52 42 10N 19 20 E
Skagerrak 60 57 30N 9 0 E
Skagway 143 59 23N 135 20W
Skaraborgs län □ 60 58 20N 13 30 E
Skeena → 154 54 9N 130 5W
Skegness 29 53 9N 0 20 E
Skellefte → 66 65 30N 18 30 E
Skellefteå 67 64 45N 20 58 E
Skerries, The 26 53 27N 4 40W
Skiddaw 28 54 39N 3 9W
Skien 60 59 12N 9 35 E
Skierniewice 58 51 58N 20 10 E
Skikda 127 36 50N 6 58 E
Skipton 28 53 57N 2 1W
Skíros 55 38 55N 24 34 E
Skopje 52 42 1N 21 32 E
Skowhegan 148 44 49N 69 40W
Skull 35 51 32N 9 40W
Skye 32 57 15N 6 10W
Skyros = Skíros 55 38 55N 24 34 E
Slaney → 35 52 52N 6 45W
Slask 58 51 0N 16 30 E
Slave → 145 61 18N 113 39W
Slave Coast 124 6 0N 2 30 E
Sleaford 29 53 0N 0 22W
Sliedrecht 40 51 50N 4 45 E
Slieve Aughty 35 53 4N 8 30W
Slieve Bloom 35 53 4N 7 40W
Slieve Donard 34 54 10N 5 57W
Slieve Mish 35 52 12N 9 50W
Slievenamon 35 52 25N 7 37W
Sligo 34 54 17N 8 28W
Sligo □ 34 54 10N 8 35W
Slovak Republic ■ 59 48 30N 20 0 E
Slovakian Ore Mts. = Slovenské Rudohorie 59 48 45N 20 0 E
Slovenia ■ 52 45 58N 14 30 E
Slovenské Rudohorie 59 48 45N 20 0 E
Słupsk 58 54 30N 17 3 E
Slyne Hd. 34 53 25N 10 10W
Smara 126 32 9N 8 16W
Smithers 154 54 45N 127 10W
Smithfield 165 35 31N 78 16W
Smiths Falls 151 44 55N 76 0W
Smithton 119 40 53S 145 6 E
Smolensk 68 54 45N 32 0 E
Smolikas, Óros 54 40 9N 20 58 E
Smyrna = İzmir 80 38 25N 27 8 E
Snæfell, Iceland 64 64 48N 15 34W
Snaefell, U.K. 28 54 18N 4 26W
Snæfellsjökull 64 64 49N 23 46W
Snake → 171 46 12N 119 2W
Sneek 41 53 2N 5 40 E
Snowdon 26 53 4N 4 8W
Snowdrift 145 62 24N 110 44W
Snowy Mts. 117 36 30S 148 20 E
Sobat → 129 8 32N 32 40 E
Sobral 177 3 50S 40 20W
Soch'e = Shache 100 38 20N 77 10 E
Sochi 70 43 35N 39 40 E
Société, Is. de la 123 17 0S 151 0W
Society Is. = Société, Is. de la 123 17 0S 151 0W
Socorro 161 34 4N 106 54W
Socotra 78 12 30N 54 0 E
Söderhamn 60 61 18N 17 10 E
Södermanlands län □ 60 59 10N 16 30 E
Södertälje 60 59 12N 17 39 E
Sodo 132 7 0N 37 41 E
Sofala 137 33 4S 149 43 E
Sofia = Sofiya 53 42 45N 23 20 E
Sofiya 53 42 45N 23 20 E
Sogn og Fjordane fylke □ 60 61 40N 6 0 E
Soissons 39 49 25N 3 19 E
Sōja 109 34 40N 133 45 E
Söke 80 37 48N 27 28 E
Sol Iletsk 70 51 10N 55 0 E
Solapur 91 17 43N 75 56 E
Soledad, Colombia 184 10 55N 74 46W
Soledad, Venezuela 185 8 10N 63 34W
Solent, The 24 50 45N 1 25W
Solesmes 38 50 10N 3 30 E
Solikamsk 69 59 38N 56 50 E
Solimões = Amazonas → 185 0 5S 50 0W
Sóller 51 39 46N 2 43 E
Sololá 177 14 49N 91 10 E

Solomon Is. ■	**122**	6 0S	155 0 E
Solṭānābād	**86**	36 29N	58 5 E
Solway Firth	**31**	54 45N	3 38W
Somali Rep. ■	**133**	7 0N	47 0 E
Sombor	**52**	45 46N	19 9 E
Sombrerete	**175**	23 38N	103 39W
Somerset, Bermuda	**180**	32 16N	64 55W
Somerset, U.S.A.	**169**	37 5N	84 40W
Somerset □	**27**	51 9N	3 0W
Somerset I.	**145**	73 30N	93 0W
Somme □	**36**	50 0N	2 20 E
Somport, Puerto de	**51**	42 48N	0 31W
Søndre Strømfjord	**147**	66 59N	50 40W
Songkhla	**97**	7 13N	100 37 E
Sonora □	**174**	29 20N	110 40W
Soochow = Suzhou	**99**	31 19N	120 38 E
Sop's Arm	**149**	49 46N	56 56W
Sør-Rondane	**14**	72 0S	25 0 E
Sør-Trøndelag fylke □	**65**	63 0N	10 0 E
Sorata	**187**	15 50S	68 40W
Sorel	**151**	46 0N	73 10W
Soria	**51**	41 43N	2 32W
Sorocaba	**191**	23 31S	47 27W
Sørøya	**67**	70 40N	22 30 E
Sorsogon	**112**	13 0N	124 0 E
Sosnowiec	**58**	50 20N	19 10 E
Sotteville-lès-Rouen	**38**	49 24N	1 5 E
Sŏul	**98**	37 31N	126 58 E
Souris, Man., Canada	**153**	49 40N	100 20W
Souris, P.E.I., Canada	**149**	46 21N	62 15W
South Africa, Rep. of ■	**136**	32 0S	17 0 E
South Australia □	**118**	32 0S	139 0 E
South Bend	**167**	41 38N	86 20W
South Carolina □	**165**	33 45N	81 0W
South Charleston	**165**	38 20N	81 40W
South China Sea	**77**	10 0N	113 0 E
South Dakota □	**163**	45 0N	100 0W
South Downs	**25**	50 53N	0 10W
South Georgia	**183**	54 30S	37 0W
South Glamorgan □	**27**	51 30N	3 20W
South Haven	**167**	42 22N	86 20W
South Island	**123**	44 0S	170 0 E
South Korea ■	**98**	36 0N	128 0 E
South Orkney Is.	**14**	63 0S	45 0W
South Platte →	**163**	41 7N	100 42W
South Pole	**14**	90 0S	0 0 E
South Porcupine	**151**	48 30N	81 12W
South Ronaldsay	**33**	58 46N	2 58W
South Sandwich Is.	**14**	57 0S	27 0W
South Sentinel I.	**94**	11 1N	92 16 E
South Shetland Is.	**14**	62 0S	59 0W
South Shields	**28**	54 59N	1 26W
South Taranaki Bight	**122**	39 40S	174 5 E
South Uist	**32**	57 20N	7 15W
South West Africa = Namibia ■	**136**	22 0S	18 9 E
South West Cape	**123**	47 16S	167 31 E
South Yorkshire □	**29**	53 30N	1 20W
Southampton	**25**	50 54N	1 23W
Southampton I.	**146**	64 30N	84 0W
Southend-on-Sea	**25**	51 32N	0 42 E
Southern Alps	**123**	43 41S	170 11 E
Southern Cross	**120**	31 12S	119 15 E
Southern Indian L.	**143**	57 10N	98 30W
Southern Uplands	**31**	55 30N	3 3W
Southland □	**123**	45 51S	168 13 E
Southport, Australia	**116**	27 58S	153 25 E
Southport, U.K.	**28**	53 38N	3 1W
Southwold	**25**	52 19N	1 41 E
Sovetskaya Gavan	**75**	48 50N	140 0 E
Sōya-Kaikyō = Perouse Str., La	**77**	45 40N	142 0 E
Spain ■	**50**	40 0N	5 0W
Spalding	**29**	52 47N	0 9W
Spandau	**43**	52 35N	13 7 E
Spanish Fork	**163**	40 10N	111 37W
Spanish Town	**180**	18 0N	76 57W
Sparks	**172**	39 30N	119 45W
Sparta = Spárti	**54**	37 5N	22 25 E
Sparta	**166**	43 55N	90 47W
Spartanburg	**165**	35 0N	82 0W
Spárti	**54**	37 5N	22 25 E
Spartivento, C., Calabria, Italy	**49**	37 56N	16 4 E
Spartivento, C., Sard., Italy	**48**	38 52N	8 50 E
Spassk-Dalniy	**75**	44 40N	132 48 E
Speightstown	**180**	13 15N	59 39W
Spence Bay	**145**	69 32N	93 32W
Spencer	**166**	43 5N	95 19W
Spencer G.	**119**	34 0S	137 20 E
Spenser Mts.	**123**	42 15S	172 45 E
Sperrin Mts.	**34**	54 50N	7 0W
Spessart	**42**	50 10N	9 20 E
Spey →	**33**	57 26N	3 25W
Spézia, La	**46**	44 8N	9 50 E
Spinazzola	**49**	40 58N	16 5 E
Spithead	**25**	50 43N	1 5W
Spitzbergen = Svalbard	**13**	78 0N	17 0 E
Split	**52**	43 31N	16 26 E
Splügenpass	**44**	46 30N	9 20 E
Spokane	**171**	47 45N	117 25W
Sporyy Navolok, Mys	**69**	75 50N	68 40 E
Spratly, I.	**112**	8 20N	112 0 E
Spring Mts.	**173**	36 20N	115 43W
Springfield, Ill., U.S.A.	**166**	39 48N	89 40W
Springfield, Mass., U.S.A.	**164**	42 8N	72 37W
Springfield, Mo., U.S.A.	**168**	37 15N	93 20W
Springfield, Ohio, U.S.A.	**167**	39 58N	83 48W
Springfield, Oreg., U.S.A.	**171**	44 2N	123 0W
Springfield, Tenn., U.S.A.	**169**	36 35N	86 55W
Springfield, Vt., U.S.A.	**164**	43 20N	72 30W
Springhill	**148**	45 40N	64 4W
Springs	**137**	26 13S	28 25 E
Springwood	**117**	33 41S	150 33 E
Spurn Hd.	**29**	53 34N	0 8 E
Squamish	**154**	49 45N	123 10W
Sredinnyy Khrebet	**73**	57 0N	160 0 E
Srednekolymsk	**73**	67 27N	153 40 E
Sremska Mitrovica	**52**	44 59N	19 33 E
Srepok →	**95**	13 33N	106 16 E
Sretensk	**74**	52 10N	117 40 E
Sri Lanka ■	**90**	7 30N	80 50 E
Srinagar	**89**	34 5N	74 50 E
Stadskanaal	**41**	53 4N	6 55 E
Staffa	**30**	56 26N	6 21W
Stafford	**28**	52 49N	2 9W
Stafford □	**28**	52 53N	2 10W
Staines	**25**	51 26N	0 30W
Stalingrad = Volgograd	**68**	48 40N	44 25 E
Stalino = Donetsk	**68**	48 0N	37 45 E
Stalinogorsk = Novomoskovsk	**68**	54 5N	38 15 E
Stalybridge	**28**	53 29N	2 4W
Stamford, U.K.	**25**	52 39N	0 29W
Stamford, U.S.A.	**164**	41 5N	73 30W
Stanislav = Ivano-Frankovsk	**68**	48 40N	24 40 E
Stanley, Canada	**152**	55 24N	104 22W
Stanley, Falk. Is.	**192**	51 40S	59 51W
Stanovoy Khrebet	**75**	55 0N	130 0 E
Stanthorpe	**116**	28 36S	151 59 E
Stara Planina	**53**	43 15N	23 0 E
Stara Zagora	**53**	42 26N	25 39 E
Starkville	**169**	33 26N	88 48W
Start Pt.	**27**	50 13N	3 38W
State College	**164**	40 47N	77 49W
Staten, I. = Estados, I. de los	**192**	54 40S	64 30W
Statesboro	**170**	32 26N	81 46W
Statesville	**165**	35 48N	80 51W
Staunton	**165**	38 7N	79 4W
Stavanger	**60**	58 57N	5 40 E
Staveren	**40**	52 53N	5 22 E
Stavropol	**70**	45 5N	42 0 E
Stawell	**119**	37 5S	142 47 E
Steenwijk	**41**	52 47N	6 7 E
Stefanie L. = Chew Bahir	**132**	4 40N	36 50 E
Steiermark □	**45**	47 26N	15 0 E
Steinbach	**153**	49 32N	96 40W
Steinkjer	**65**	63 59N	11 31 E
Stellarton	**149**	45 32N	62 30W
Stephenville	**149**	48 31N	58 35W
Stereá Ellas □	**54**	38 50N	22 0 E
Sterling, Colo., U.S.A.	**163**	40 40N	103 15W
Sterling, Ill., U.S.A.	**166**	41 45N	89 45W

Sterlitamak	**71**	53 40N	56 0 E
Stettin = Szczecin	**58**	53 27N	14 27 E
Stettler	**155**	52 19N	112 40W
Steubenville	**164**	40 21N	80 39W
Stevens Port	**166**	44 32N	89 34W
Stewart	**144**	63 19N	139 26W
Stewart I.	**123**	46 58S	167 54 E
Stikine →	**144**	56 40N	132 30W
Stillwater, Minn., U.S.A.	**166**	45 3N	92 47W
Stillwater, Okla., U.S.A.	**168**	36 5N	97 3W
Stillwater Ra.	**172**	39 45N	118 6W
Štip	**53**	41 42N	22 10 E
Stirling	**31**	56 7N	3 57W
Stirling Ra.	**120**	34 23S	118 0 E
Stockholm	**60**	59 20N	18 3 E
Stockholms län □	**60**	59 30N	18 20 E
Stockport	**28**	53 25N	2 11W
Stockton	**172**	38 0N	121 20W
Stockton-on-Tees	**29**	54 34N	1 20W
Stoke-on-Trent	**28**	53 1N	2 11W
Stonehaven	**33**	56 58N	2 11W
Stonehenge	**24**	51 9N	1 45W
Stonewall	**153**	50 10N	97 19W
Stora Lulevatten	**66**	67 10N	19 30 E
Storavan	**66**	65 45N	18 10 E
Store Bælt	**61**	55 20N	11 0 E
Storm B.	**119**	43 10S	147 30 E
Storm Lake	**166**	42 35N	95 11W
Stornoway	**32**	58 12N	6 23W
Storsjön	**66**	63 12N	14 18 E
Storuman	**66**	65 5N	17 10 E
Stour →, Here. & Worcs., U.K.	**24**	52 25N	2 13W
Stour →, Kent, U.K.	**25**	51 15N	1 20 E
Stour →, Suffolk, U.K.	**25**	51 55N	1 5 E
Stourbridge	**24**	52 28N	2 8W
Stowmarket	**25**	52 11N	1 0 E
Strabane	**34**	54 50N	7 28W
Stralsund	**43**	54 17N	13 5 E
Strangford, L.	**34**	54 30N	5 37W
Stranraer	**30**	54 54N	5 0W
Strasbourg	**37**	48 35N	7 42 E
Stratford, Canada	**151**	43 23N	81 0W
Stratford, N.Z.	**122**	39 20S	174 19 E
Stratford-on-Avon	**24**	52 12N	1 42W
Strath Spey	**33**	57 15N	3 40W
Strathalbyn	**119**	35 13S	138 53 E
Strathclyde □	**30**	56 0N	4 50W
Strathmore	**33**	56 40N	3 4W
Strathy Pt.	**33**	58 35N	4 0W
Streaky B.	**118**	32 51S	134 18 E
Streator	**167**	41 9N	88 52W
Strómboli	**49**	38 48N	15 12 E
Stromeferry	**32**	57 20N	5 33W
Stromness	**33**	58 58N	3 18W
Stronsay	**33**	59 8N	2 38W
Stroud	**24**	51 44N	2 12W
Strumica	**53**	41 28N	22 41 E
Stuart L.	**154**	54 30N	124 30W
Stung Treng	**95**	13 31N	105 58 E
Sturgeon Bay	**167**	44 52N	87 20W
Sturgeon Falls	**151**	46 25N	79 57W
Stuttgart, Germany	**42**	48 46N	9 10 E
Stuttgart, U.S.A.	**168**	34 30N	91 33W
Styria = Steiermark □	**45**	47 26N	15 0 E
Suakin	**129**	19 8N	37 20 E
Subotica	**52**	46 6N	19 49 E
Suchitoto	**177**	13 56N	89 0W
Suchou = Suzhou	**99**	31 19N	120 38 E
Süchow = Xuzhou	**99**	34 18N	117 10 E
Sucre	**187**	19 0S	65 15W
Sudan ■	**129**	15 0N	30 0 E
Sudbury, Canada	**151**	46 30N	81 0W
Sudbury, U.K.	**25**	52 2N	0 44 E
Sudetan Mts. = Sudety	**58**	50 20N	16 45 E
Sudety	**58**	50 20N	16 45 E
Suez = El Suweis	**128**	29 58N	32 31 E
Suez Canal = Suweis, Qanâl es	**128**	31 0N	32 20 E
Suffolk	**165**	36 47N	76 33W
Suffolk □	**25**	52 16N	1 0 E
Sugluk = Saglouc	**146**	62 14N	75 38W
Suhbaatar	**98**	50 17N	106 10 E
Suir →	**35**	52 15N	7 10W
Suita	**106**	34 45N	135 32 E
Sukhona →	**68**	60 30N	45 0 E
Sukhumi	**70**	43 0N	41 0 E
Sukkertoppen	**147**	65 26N	52 55W
Sukkur	**88**	27 42N	68 54 E
Sukkur Barrage	**88**	27 40N	68 50 E
Sukumo	**109**	32 56N	132 44 E
Sulaiman Range	**89**	30 30N	69 50 E
Sulawesi □	**113**	2 0S	120 0 E
Sulina	**57**	45 10N	29 40 E
Sulitjelma	**66**	67 9N	16 3 E
Sullana	**186**	4 52S	80 39W
Sullivan	**167**	39 5N	87 26W
Sullivan I. = Lambi Kyun	**96**	10 50N	98 20 E
Sulphur Springs	**168**	33 5N	95 36W
Sulu Arch.	**112**	6 0N	121 0 E
Sulu Sea	**112**	8 0N	120 0 E
Suluq	**128**	31 44N	20 14 E
Sumatera □	**111**	0 40N	100 20 E
Sumatra = Sumatera □	**111**	0 40N	100 20 E
Sumba	**113**	9 45S	119 35 E
Sumbawa	**113**	8 26S	117 30 E
Sumburgh Hd.	**30**	59 52N	1 17W
Summerland	**155**	49 32N	119 41W
Summerside	**148**	46 24N	63 47W
Sumoto	**109**	34 21N	134 54 E
Sumter	**165**	33 55N	80 22W
Sumy	**68**	50 57N	34 50 E
Sunbury, Australia	**117**	37 35S	144 44 E
Sunbury, U.S.A.	**164**	40 50N	76 46W
Sunda, Selat	**111**	6 20S	105 30 E
Sundarbans, The	**92**	22 0N	89 0 E
Sunderland	**28**	54 54N	1 22W
Sundsvall	**66**	62 23N	17 17 E
Sungei Patani	**96**	5 38N	100 29 E
Sungei Siput	**96**	4 51N	101 6 E
Sungurlu	**80**	40 12N	34 21 E
Sunnyside	**171**	46 24N	120 2W
Sunnyvale	**172**	37 23N	122 2W
Suntar	**74**	62 15N	117 30 E
Suō-Nada	**108**	33 50N	131 30 E
Superior	**150**	46 45N	92 5W
Superior, L.	**150**	47 40N	87 0W
Suphan Dağı	**81**	38 54N	42 48 E
Sūr	**80**	22 34N	59 32 E
Surabaja = Surabaya	**111**	7 17S	112 45 E
Surabaya	**111**	7 17S	112 45 E
Surakarta	**111**	7 35S	110 48 E
Surat	**91**	21 12N	72 55 E
Surat Thani	**96**	9 6N	99 20 E
Suratgarh	**89**	29 18N	73 55 E
Surgut	**69**	61 14N	73 20 E
Surin	**95**	14 50N	103 34 E
Surinam ■	**185**	4 0N	56 0W
Surrey □	**25**	51 16N	0 30W
Surt	**127**	31 11N	16 39 E
Surt, Khalīj	**127**	31 40N	18 30 E
Suruga-Wan	**107**	34 45N	138 30 E
Susaki	**109**	33 22N	133 17 E
Susanville	**172**	40 28N	120 40W
Susquehanna →	**164**	39 33N	76 5W
Sutherland Falls	**123**	44 48S	167 46 E
Sutlej →	**89**	29 23N	71 3 E
Sutton-in-Ashfield	**29**	53 7N	1 20W
Suva	**122**	18 6S	178 30 E
Suwa	**107**	36 2N	138 8 E
Suwa-Ko	**107**	36 3N	138 5 E
Suwannee →	**170**	29 18N	83 9W
Suwanose-Jima	**104**	29 38N	129 43 E
Suweis, Qanâl es	**128**	31 0N	32 20 E
Suzaka	**107**	36 39N	138 19 E
Suzhou	**99**	31 19N	120 38 E
Suzu-Misaki	**105**	37 31N	137 21 E
Svalbard	**13**	78 0N	17 0 E
Svartenhuk Halvø	**146**	71 50N	54 30W
Svendborg	**61**	55 4N	10 35 E
Sverdlovsk = Yekaterinburg	**69**	56 50N	60 30 E
Sverdrup Is.	**12**	79 0N	97 0W

Svishtov 53 43 36N 25 23 E
Svobodnyy 75 51 20N 128 0 E
Swabian Alps = Schwäbische Alb 42 48 30N 9 30 E
Swakopmund 136 22 37S 14 30 E
Swale → 28 54 5N 1 20W
Swan Hill 117 35 20S 143 33 E
Swan Hills 155 54 42N 115 24W
Swan Islands 178 17 22N 83 57W
Swan River 152 52 10N 101 16W
Swanage 24 50 36N 1 59W
Swansea 27 51 37N 3 57W
Swartberge 136 33 20S 22 0 E
Swatow = Shantou 99 23 18N 116 40 E
Swaziland ■ 137 26 30S 31 30 E
Sweden ■ 66 57 0N 15 0 E
Sweetwater 161 32 30N 100 28W
Swift Current 152 50 20N 107 45W
Swindon 24 51 33N 1 47W
Switzerland ■ 44 46 30N 8 0 E
Swords 34 53 27N 6 15W
Sydney, Australia 117 33 53S 151 10 E
Sydney, Canada 149 46 7N 60 7W
Sydney Mines 149 46 18N 60 15W
Sydprøven 147 60 30N 45 35W
Sydra G. of = Surt, Khalīj 127 31 40N 18 30 E
Syktyvkar 69 61 45N 50 40 E
Sylacauga 169 33 10N 86 15W
Sylhet 92 24 54N 91 52 E
Sylvan Lake 155 52 20N 114 3W
Syracuse 164 43 4N 76 11W
Syrdarya → 71 46 3N 61 0 E
Syria ■ 80 35 0N 38 0 E
Syrian Desert 76 31 0N 40 0 E
Syzran 68 53 12N 48 30 E
Szczecin 58 53 27N 14 27 E
Szechwan = Sichuan □ 99 31 0N 104 0 E
Szeged 59 46 16N 20 10 E
Székesfehérvár 59 47 15N 18 25 E
Szolnok 59 47 10N 20 15 E
Szombathely 59 47 14N 16 38 E

T

Tabacal 190 23 15S 64 15W
Ţābah 82 26 55N 42 38 E
Tabasco □ 177 18 0N 92 40W
Taber 155 49 47N 112 8W
Tablas 112 12 25N 122 2 E
Table Mt. 136 34 0S 18 22 E
Table Top, Mt. 121 23 24S 147 11 E
Tabora 135 5 2S 32 50 E
Tabrīz 81 38 7N 46 20 E
Tabūk 82 28 23N 36 36 E
Tachibana-Wan 108 32 45N 130 7 E
Tachikawa 107 35 42N 139 25 E
Tacna 187 18 0S 70 20W
Tacoma 171 47 15N 122 30W
Tacuarembó 191 31 45S 56 0W
Tademaït, Plateau du 127 28 30N 2 30 E
Tadoussac 148 48 11N 69 42W
Taegu 98 35 50N 128 37 E
Taejŏn 98 36 20N 127 28 E
Taganrog 68 47 12N 38 50 E
Tagish 144 60 19N 134 16W
Tagua, La 184 0 3N 74 40W
Tagus = Tajo → 50 38 40N 9 24W
Tahiti 123 17 37S 149 27W
Tahoua 131 14 57N 5 16 E
Taibei 99 25 4N 121 29 E
T'aichung = Taizhong 99 24 12N 120 35 E
Taidong 99 22 43N 121 9 E
Taihape 122 39 41S 175 48 E
Tailem Bend 119 35 12S 139 29 E
Taimyr = Taymyr, Poluostrov 72 75 0N 100 0 E
Tain 33 57 49N 4 4W
Tainan 99 23 17N 120 18 E
Taínaron, Ákra 54 36 22N 22 27 E
T'aipei = Taibei 99 25 4N 121 29 E
Taiping 96 4 51N 100 44 E
Taisha 109 35 24N 132 40 E
Taitao, Pen. de 192 46 30S 75 0W
Taiwan ■ 99 23 30N 121 0 E
Taiyuan 98 37 52N 112 33 E
Taizhong 99 24 12N 120 35 E
Ta'izz 83 13 35N 44 2 E
Tajikistan ■ 71 35 30N 70 0 E
Tajimi 106 35 19N 137 8 E
Tajo → 50 38 40N 9 24W
Tak 94 16 52N 99 8 E
Takachiho 108 32 42N 131 18 E
Takada 105 37 7N 138 15 E
Takahashi 109 34 51N 133 39 E
Takamatsu 109 34 20N 134 5 E
Takaoka 106 36 47N 137 0 E
Takapuna 122 36 47S 174 47 E
Takasago 109 34 45N 134 48 E
Takasaki 107 36 20N 139 0 E
Takatsuki 106 34 51N 135 37 E
Takawa 108 33 38N 130 51 E
Takayama 106 36 18N 137 11 E
Takayama-Bonchi 106 36 0N 137 18 E
Takefu 106 35 50N 136 10 E
Takehara 109 34 21N 132 55 E
Taketa 108 32 58N 131 24 E
Takhār □ 87 36 40N 70 0 E
Takla Landing 154 55 30N 125 50W
Takla Makan 76 39 0N 83 0 E
Taku 108 33 18N 130 3 E
Talara 186 4 38S 81 18 E
Talaud, Kepulauan 113 4 30N 127 10 E
Talca 190 35 28S 71 40W
Talcahuano 190 36 40S 73 10W
Ţalesh, Kūhhā-ye 81 39 0N 48 30 E
Talguppa 90 14 10N 74 45 E
Taliabu 113 1 45S 125 0 E
Talkeetna 142 62 20N 150 9W
Tall 'Afar 81 36 22N 42 27 E
Talladega 169 33 28N 86 2W
Tallahassee 170 30 25N 84 15W
Tallangatta 117 36 15S 147 19 E
Tallinn 68 59 22N 24 48 E
Tallulah 168 32 25N 91 12W
Tamale 130 9 22N 0 50W
Tamana 108 32 58N 130 32 E
Tamano 109 34 29N 133 59 E
Tamanrasset 127 22 50N 5 30 E
Tamar → 27 50 33N 4 15W
Tamaulipas □ 176 24 0N 98 45W
Tambellup 120 34 4S 117 37 E
Tambov 68 52 45N 41 28 E
Tamgak, Mts. 127 19 12N 8 35 E
Tamil Nadu □ 90 11 0N 77 0 E
Tammerfors = Tampere 67 61 30N 23 50 E
Tamo Abu, Pegunungan 111 3 10N 115 0 E
Tampa 170 27 57N 82 38W
Tampa B. 170 27 40N 82 40W
Tampere 67 61 30N 23 50 E
Tampico 177 22 20N 97 50W
Tamrah 83 20 24N 45 25 E
Tamsagbulag 98 47 14N 117 21 E
Tamworth, Australia 116 31 7S 150 58 E
Tamworth, U.K. 24 52 38N 1 41W
Tana →, Kenya 133 2 32S 40 31 E
Tana →, Norway 67 70 30N 28 23 E
Tana, L. 132 13 5N 37 30 E
Tanabe 106 33 44N 135 22 E
Tanana 142 65 10N 152 15W
Tananarive = Antananarivo 137 18 55S 47 31 E
Tanba-Sanchi 106 35 7N 135 48 E
Tandil 190 37 15S 59 6W
Tando Adam 88 25 45N 68 40 E
Tane-ga-Shima 104 30 30N 131 0 E
Tanen Tong Dan 93 16 30N 98 30 E
Tanezrouft 127 23 9N 0 11 E
Tanga 135 5 5S 39 2 E
Tanganyika, L. 135 6 40S 30 0 E
Tanger 126 35 50N 5 49W
Tanggula Shan 101 32 40N 92 10 E

Tangier = Tanger 126 35 50N 5 49W
Tangshan 98 39 38N 118 10 E
Tanimbar, Kepulauan 113 7 30S 131 30 E
Taniyama 108 31 31N 130 31 E
Tanjore = Thanjavur 90 10 48N 79 12 E
Tannu Ola 74 51 0N 94 0 E
Tanout 131 14 50N 8 55 E
Tanta 128 30 45N 30 57 E
Tantung = Dandong 98 40 10N 124 20 E
Tanunda 119 34 30S 139 0 E
Tanzania ■ 135 6 40S 34 0 E
Tapa Shan = Daba Shan 99 32 0N 109 0 E
Tapachula 177 14 54N 92 17W
Tapajós → 185 2 24S 54 41W
Tapanui 123 45 56S 169 18 E
Tapi → 91 21 8N 72 41 E
Tara → 71 56 42N 74 36 E
Tarabagatay, Khrebet 71 48 0N 83 0 E
Tarābulus, Lebanon 80 34 31N 35 50 E
Tarābulus, Libya 127 32 49N 13 7 E
Taranaki □ 122 39 5S 174 51 E
Táranto 49 40 30N 17 11 E
Táranto, G. di 49 40 0N 17 15 E
Tarapoto 186 6 30S 76 20W
Tarare 37 45 54N 4 26 E
Tararua Range 123 40 45S 175 25 E
Tarauacá 187 8 6S 70 48W
Tarbela Dam 89 34 8N 72 52 E
Tarbert 32 57 54N 6 49W
Tarbes 36 43 15N 0 3 E
Tarcoola 118 30 44S 134 36 E
Taree 116 31 50S 152 30 E
Tarfaya 126 27 55N 12 55W
Tarifa 50 36 1N 5 36W
Tarija 187 21 30S 64 40W
Tarim → 100 41 5N 86 40 E
Tarim Pendi 100 40 0N 84 0 E
Tarko Sale 69 64 55N 77 50 E
Tarn → 36 44 5N 1 6 E
Tarnobrzeg 58 50 35N 21 41 E
Tarnów 58 50 3N 21 0 E
Tarragona 51 41 5N 1 17 E
Tarrasa 51 41 34N 2 1 E
Tarsus 80 36 58N 34 55 E
Tartagal 190 22 30S 63 50W
Tarṭūs 80 34 55N 35 55 E
Tarumizu 108 31 29N 130 42 E
Tarutao, Ko 96 6 33N 99 40 E
Taschereau 151 48 40N 78 40W
Tashi Chho Dzong = Thimphu 92 27 31N 89 45 E
Tashkent 71 41 20N 69 10 E
Tasman B. 123 40 59S 173 25 E
Tasman Mts. 123 41 3S 172 25 E
Tasman Sea 122 36 0S 160 0 E
Tasmania □ 119 42 0S 146 30 E
Tatabánya 59 47 32N 18 25 E
Tatarsk 71 55 14N 76 0 E
Tatarstan □ 70 55 30N 51 30 E
Tateyama 107 35 0N 139 50 E
Tatra = Tatry 59 49 20N 20 0 E
Tatry 59 49 20N 20 0 E
Tatsuno 109 34 52N 134 33 E
Tat'ung = Datong 98 40 6N 113 18 E
Taubaté 191 23 0S 45 36W
Tauern 45 47 15N 12 40 E
Taumarunui 122 38 53S 175 15 E
Taunggyi 93 20 50N 97 0 E
Taungup Taunggya 93 18 20N 93 40 E
Taunton, U.K. 27 51 1N 3 7W
Taunton, U.S.A. 164 41 54N 71 6W
Taunus 42 50 15N 8 20 E
Taupo 122 38 41S 176 7 E
Taupo, L. 122 38 46S 175 55 E
Tauranga 122 37 42S 176 11 E
Taurus Mts. = Toros Daglari 80 37 0N 35 0 E
Taverny 39 49 2N 2 13 E
Tavistock 27 50 33N 4 9W
Tavoy 94 14 2N 98 12 E
Tawas City 167 44 16N 83 31W
Tay → 33 56 37N 3 38W
Tayabamba 186 8 15S 77 16W
Taylor Mt. 161 35 16N 107 36W
Taymā 82 27 35N 38 45 E
Taymyr, Poluostrov 72 75 0N 100 0 E
Tayshet 74 55 58N 98 1 E
Tayside □ 31 56 25N 3 30W
Taz → 69 67 32N 78 40 E
Tbilisi 70 41 43N 44 50 E
Tchad = Chad ■ 131 15 0N 17 15 E
Tchad, L. 131 13 30N 14 30 E
Tch'eng-tou = Chengdu 99 30 38N 104 2 E
Tch'ong-k'ing = Chongqing 99 29 35N 106 25 E
Te Anau, L. 123 45 15S 167 45 E
Te Kuiti 122 38 20S 175 11 E
Tecuala 175 22 23N 105 27W
Tefé 185 3 25S 64 50W
Tegal 111 6 52S 109 8 E
Tegucigalpa 179 14 5N 87 14W
Tehachapi Mts. 173 35 0N 118 40W
Tehrān 86 35 44N 51 30 E
Tehuacán 177 18 27N 97 23W
Tehuantepec 177 16 21N 95 13W
Tehuantepec, G. de 177 16 0N 94 50W
Tehuantepec, Istmo de 177 17 0N 94 30W
Teifi → 26 52 4N 4 14W
Teignmouth 27 50 33N 3 30W
Tejo → 50 38 40N 9 24W
Tekax 177 20 12N 89 17W
Tekeli 71 44 50N 79 0 E
Tekirdağ 80 40 58N 27 30 E
Tel Aviv-Yafo 80 32 4N 34 48 E
Tela 179 15 40N 87 28W
Telanaipura = Jambi 111 1 38S 103 30 E
Telegraph Cr. → 144 58 0N 131 10W
Telemark fylke □ 60 59 25N 8 30 E
Teles Pires → 187 7 21S 58 3W
Telford 28 52 42N 2 31W
Tell City 167 38 0N 86 44W
Teme → 24 52 23N 2 15W
Temerloh 96 3 27N 102 25 E
Temirtau 71 50 5N 72 56 E
Temora 117 34 30S 147 30 E
Temosachic 174 28 57N 107 51W
Temple 158 31 5N 97 22W
Temuco 190 38 45S 72 40W
Temuka 123 44 14S 171 17 E
Tenali 91 16 15N 80 35 E
Tenancingo 177 19 0N 99 33W
Tenango 177 19 7N 99 33W
Tenby 27 51 40N 4 42W
Tenerife 126 28 15N 16 35W
Teng Xian 99 35 5N 117 10 E
Tennessee □ 169 36 0N 86 30W
Tennessee → 169 37 4N 88 34W
Tenri 106 34 39N 135 49 E
Tenryū 107 34 52N 137 49 E
Tenryū-Gawa → 107 35 39N 137 48 E
Tenterfield 116 29 0S 152 0 E
Teófilo Otoni 189 17 50S 41 30W
Tepic 175 21 30N 104 54W
Terang 119 38 15S 142 55 E
Terek → 70 44 0N 47 30 E
Terengganu □ 96 4 55N 103 0 E
Teresina 188 5 9S 42 45W
Terewah, L. 116 29 52S 147 35 E
Termez 70 37 15N 67 15 E
Términos, L. de 177 18 37N 91 33W
Terneuzen 40 51 20N 3 50 E
Terni 46 42 34N 12 38 E
Terrace 154 54 30N 128 35W
Terre Haute 167 39 28N 87 24W
Terrell 168 32 44N 96 19W
Terschelling 40 53 25N 5 20 E
Teruel 51 40 22N 1 8W
Teshio 103 44 53N 141 44 E
Teslin 144 60 10N 132 43W
Test → 24 51 7N 1 30W
Tete 137 16 13S 33 33 E
Teteven 53 42 58N 24 17 E
Tétouan 126 35 35N 5 21W
Tetuán = Tétouan 126 35 35N 5 21W

Teuco →	**190**	25 35S	60 11W
Teutoburger Wald	**42**	52 5N	8 20 E
Tevere →	**46**	41 44N	12 14 E
Tewkesbury	**24**	51 59N	2 8W
Texarkana, Ark., U.S.A.	**168**	33 25N	94 0W
Texarkana, Tex., U.S.A.	**168**	33 25N	94 3W
Texas □	**161**	31 40N	98 30W
Texel	**40**	53 5N	4 50 E
Teziutlán	**177**	19 49N	97 21W
Tezpur	**93**	26 40N	92 45 E
Thabana Ntlenyana	**137**	29 30S	29 16 E
Thailand ■	**95**	16 0N	102 0 E
Thailand, G. of	**95**	11 30N	101 0 E
Thal Desert	**89**	31 10N	71 30 E
Thame →	**24**	51 35N	1 8W
Thames	**122**	37 7S	175 34 E
Thames →	**25**	51 30N	0 35 E
Thane	**91**	19 12N	72 59 E
Thanh Hoa	**95**	19 48N	105 46 E
Thanh Pho Ho Chi Minh	**95**	10 58N	106 40 E
Thanjavur	**90**	10 48N	79 12 E
Thar Desert	**89**	28 0N	72 0 E
Thásos	**55**	40 40N	24 40 E
Thaungdut	**93**	24 30N	94 40 E
Thazi	**93**	21 0N	96 5 E
The Dalles	**171**	45 40N	121 11W
The Grenadines, Is.	**180**	12 40N	61 20W
The Hague = 's-Gravenhage	**40**	52 7N	4 17 E
The Macumba →	**118**	27 52S	137 12 E
The Neales →	**118**	28 8S	136 47 E
The Pas	**152**	53 45N	101 15W
The Rock	**117**	35 15S	147 2 E
The Warburton →	**118**	28 4S	137 28 E
Thebes = Thívai	**55**	38 19N	23 19 E
Thermaïkos Kólpos	**54**	40 15N	22 45 E
Thermopolis	**163**	43 35N	108 10W
Thessalía □	**54**	39 30N	22 0 E
Thessalon	**150**	46 20N	83 30W
Thessaloníki	**54**	40 38N	22 58 E
Thessaly = Thessalía □	**54**	39 30N	22 0 E
Thetford Mines	**148**	46 8N	71 18W
Thicket Portage	**153**	55 19N	97 42W
Thies	**130**	14 50N	16 51W
Thimphu	**92**	27 31N	89 45 E
Thionville	**37**	49 20N	6 10 E
Thíra	**55**	36 23N	25 27 E
Thirsk	**29**	54 15N	1 20W
Thisted	**61**	56 58N	8 40 E
Thívai	**55**	38 19N	23 19 E
Thomaston	**170**	32 54N	84 20W
Thomasville, Ga., U.S.A.	**170**	30 50N	84 0W
Thomasville, N.C., U.S.A.	**165**	35 55N	80 4W
Thon Buri	**94**	13 43N	100 29 E
Thornaby on Tees	**29**	54 36N	1 19W
Thrace = Thráki □	**55**	41 9N	25 30 E
Thráki □	**55**	41 9N	25 30 E
Three Hills	**155**	51 43N	113 15W
Three Hummock I.	**119**	40 25S	144 55 E
Thule	**13**	77 40N	69 0W
Thundelarra	**120**	28 53S	117 7 E
Thunder B.	**150**	45 0N	83 20W
Thunder Bay	**150**	48 20N	89 15W
Thüringer Wald	**43**	50 35N	11 0 E
Thurles	**35**	52 40N	7 53W
Thursday I.	**115**	10 30S	142 3 E
Thurso	**33**	58 34N	3 31W
Tian Shan	**100**	43 0N	84 0 E
Tianjin	**98**	39 8N	117 10 E
Tianshui	**99**	34 32N	105 40 E
Tiber = Tevere →	**46**	41 44N	12 14 E
Tibesti	**127**	21 0N	17 30 E
Tibet = Xizang □	**101**	32 0N	88 0 E
Tibooburra	**118**	29 26S	142 1 E
Ticul	**177**	20 24N	89 32W
Tiel	**40**	51 53N	5 26 E
Tien Shan	**76**	42 0N	80 0 E
Tien-tsin = Tianjin	**98**	39 8N	117 10 E
T'ienching = Tianjin	**98**	39 8N	117 10 E
Tientsin = Tianjin	**98**	39 8N	117 10 E
Tierra de Campos	**50**	42 10N	4 50W
Tierra del Fuego □	**192**	54 0S	67 45W
Tiffin	**167**	41 8N	83 10W
Tiflis = Tbilisi	**70**	41 43N	44 50 E
Tifton	**170**	31 28N	83 32W
Tignish	**148**	46 58N	64 2W
Tigris = Dijlah, Nahr →	**81**	31 0N	47 25 E
Tijuana	**174**	32 32N	117 1W
Tiksi	**72**	71 40N	128 45 E
Tilburg	**40**	51 31N	5 6 E
Tilbury	**25**	51 27N	0 24 E
Tillsonburg	**151**	42 53N	80 44W
Tílos	**55**	36 27N	27 27 E
Timaru	**123**	44 23S	171 14 E
Timbuktu = Tombouctou	**130**	16 50N	3 0W
Timişoara	**56**	45 43N	21 15 E
Timmins	**151**	48 28N	81 25W
Timor	**113**	9 0S	125 0 E
Timor Sea	**113**	10 0S	127 0 E
Tinaca Pt.	**112**	5 30N	125 25 E
Tindouf	**126**	27 42N	8 10W
Tinnevelly = Tirunelveli	**90**	8 45N	77 45 E
Tinogasta	**190**	28 5S	67 32W
Tínos	**55**	37 33N	25 8 E
Tioman, Pulau	**96**	2 50N	104 10 E
Tipperary	**35**	52 28N	8 10W
Tipperary □	**35**	52 37N	7 55W
Tipton	**24**	52 32N	2 4W
Tirana	**52**	41 18N	19 49 E
Tiraspol	**68**	46 55N	29 35 E
Tire	**80**	38 5N	27 50 E
Tirebolu	**81**	40 58N	38 45 E
Tiree	**30**	56 31N	6 55W
Tîrgu Mureş	**57**	46 31N	24 38 E
Tirol □	**45**	47 3N	10 43 E
Tiruchchirappalli	**90**	10 45N	78 45 E
Tirunelveli	**90**	8 45N	77 45 E
Tisa →	**59**	45 15N	20 17 E
Tisdale	**152**	52 50N	104 0W
Titicaca, L.	**187**	15 30S	69 30W
Titograd = Podgorica	**52**	42 30N	19 19 E
Titov Veles	**53**	41 46N	21 47 E
Titovo Užice	**52**	43 55N	19 50 E
Tiverton	**27**	50 54N	3 30W
Tívoli	**46**	41 58N	12 45 E
Tizimín	**177**	21 9N	88 9W
Tjirebon = Cirebon	**111**	6 45S	108 32 E
Tlaxcala □	**177**	19 25N	98 10W
Tlaxiaco	**177**	17 18N	97 40W
Tlemcen	**127**	34 52N	1 21W
To-Shima	**107**	34 31N	139 17 E
Toamasina	**137**	18 10S	49 25 E
Toba Kakar	**88**	31 30N	69 0 E
Tobago	**180**	11 10N	60 30W
Tobermory	**30**	56 37N	6 4W
Tobolsk	**69**	58 15N	68 10 E
Tobruk = Tubruq	**128**	32 7N	23 55 E
Tocantins →	**188**	1 45S	49 10W
Toccoa	**165**	34 32N	83 17W
Tochigi	**107**	36 25N	139 45 E
Tocopilla	**190**	22 5S	70 10W
Todos Santos	**175**	23 27N	110 13W
Tōgane	**107**	35 33N	140 22 E
Togliatti	**68**	53 32N	49 24 E
Togo ■	**130**	6 15N	1 35 E
Tōhoku □	**103**	39 50N	141 45 E
Tōjō	**109**	34 53N	133 16 E
Tokai	**106**	35 2N	136 55 E
Tokaj	**58**	48 8N	21 27 E
Tokara Kaikyō	**104**	30 0N	130 0 E
Tokat	**80**	40 22N	36 35 E
Tokelau Is.	**123**	9 0S	171 45W
Toki	**106**	35 18N	137 8 E
Tokoname	**106**	34 53N	136 51 E
Tokorozawa	**107**	35 47N	139 28 E
Tokushima	**109**	34 4N	134 34 E
Tokuyama	**108**	34 3N	131 50 E
Tōkyō	**107**	35 45N	139 45 E
Tōkyō-Wan	**107**	35 25N	139 47 E
Tolbukhin = Dobrich	**53**	43 37N	27 49 E
Toledo, Spain	**50**	39 50N	4 2W
Toledo, U.S.A.	**167**	41 37N	83 33W
Tolga	**127**	34 40N	5 22 E

Tolima, Vol.	**184**	4 40N	75 19W
Toluca	**177**	19 20N	99 40W
Tomakomai	**103**	42 38N	141 36 E
Tombigbee →	**169**	31 4N	87 58W
Tombouctou	**130**	16 50N	3 0W
Tomini, Teluk	**113**	0 10S	122 0 E
Tomsk	**71**	56 30N	85 5 E
Tonalá	**177**	16 4N	93 45W
Tonantins	**184**	2 45S	67 45W
Tonbridge	**25**	51 12N	0 18 E
Tong Xian	**98**	39 55N	116 35 E
Tonga ■	**123**	19 50S	174 30W
Tongchuan	**99**	35 6N	109 3 E
Tonghua	**98**	41 42N	125 58 E
Tongking, G. of	**95**	20 0N	108 0 E
Tongue	**33**	58 29N	4 25W
Tonk	**91**	26 6N	75 54 E
Tonkin = Bac Phan	**95**	22 0N	105 0 E
Tonlé Sap	**95**	13 0N	104 0 E
Tonopah	**172**	38 4N	117 12W
Tonoshō	**109**	34 29N	134 11 E
Tooele	**162**	40 30N	112 20W
Toowoomba	**116**	27 32S	151 56 E
Topeka	**166**	39 3N	95 40W
Toppenish	**171**	46 27N	120 16W
Torbay	**27**	50 26N	3 31W
Torino	**46**	45 4N	7 40 E
Tormes →	**50**	41 18N	6 29W
Torne älv →	**67**	65 50N	24 12 E
Torneå = Tornio	**67**	65 50N	24 12 E
Torneträsk	**66**	68 24N	19 15 E
Tornio	**67**	65 50N	24 12 E
Toro, Cerro del	**190**	29 10S	69 50W
Toronto, Australia	**117**	33 0S	151 30 E
Toronto, Canada	**151**	43 39N	79 20W
Toros Daglari	**80**	37 0N	35 0 E
Torquay	**27**	50 27N	3 31W
Torre Annunziata	**49**	40 45N	14 26 E
Tôrre de Moncorvo	**50**	41 12N	7 8W
Torremolinos	**50**	36 38N	4 30W
Torrens, L.	**119**	31 0S	137 50 E
Torreón	**174**	25 33N	103 26W
Torres Vedras	**50**	39 5N	9 15W
Torridge →	**27**	50 51N	4 10W
Torrington	**164**	41 50N	73 9W
Tortosa	**51**	40 49N	0 31 E
Tortosa, C.	**51**	40 41N	0 52 E
Toruń	**58**	53 0N	18 39 E
Tory I.	**34**	55 17N	8 12W
Tosa-Shimizu	**109**	32 52N	132 58 E
Tosa-Wan	**109**	33 15N	133 30 E
Toscana	**46**	43 30N	11 5 E
Tostado	**190**	29 15S	61 50W
Tosu	**109**	33 22N	130 31 E
Totnes	**27**	50 26N	3 41W
Totonicapán	**177**	14 58N	91 12W
Tottori	**109**	35 30N	134 15 E
Toubkal, Djebel	**126**	31 0N	8 0W
Touggourt	**127**	33 6N	6 4 E
Toulon	**37**	43 10N	5 55 E
Toulouse	**36**	43 37N	1 27 E
Toungoo	**93**	19 0N	96 30 E
Touraine	**36**	47 20N	0 30 E
Tourane = Da Nang	**95**	16 4N	108 13 E
Tourcoing	**38**	50 42N	3 10 E
Tournai	**42**	50 35N	3 25 E
Tours	**36**	47 22N	0 40 E
Townsville	**121**	19 15S	146 45 E
Towson	**164**	39 26N	76 34W
Toyama	**106**	36 40N	137 15 E
Toyama-Wan	**105**	37 0N	137 30 E
Toyohashi	**106**	34 45N	137 25 E
Toyokawa	**106**	34 48N	137 27 E
Toyonaka	**106**	34 50N	135 28 E
Toyooka	**109**	35 35N	134 48 E
Toyota	**106**	35 3N	137 7 E
Tozeur	**127**	33 56N	8 8 E
Trabzon	**81**	41 0N	39 45 E
Tracy	**172**	37 46N	121 27W
Trafalgar, C.	**50**	36 10N	6 2W
Trail	**155**	49 5N	117 40W
Tralee	**35**	52 16N	9 42W
Tralee B.	**35**	52 17N	9 55W
Tran Ninh, Cao Nguyen	**95**	19 30N	103 10 E
Trangan	**113**	6 40S	134 20 E
Trangie	**116**	32 4S	148 0 E
Transantarctic Mts.	**15**	85 0S	170 0W
Transcona	**153**	49 55N	97 0W
Transilvania	**57**	46 19N	25 0 E
Transylvania = Transilvania	**57**	46 19N	25 0 E
Transylvanian Alps	**17**	45 30N	25 0 E
Trápani	**48**	38 1N	12 30 E
Traralgon	**117**	38 12S	146 34 E
Trasimeno, L.	**46**	43 10N	12 5 E
Travers, Mt.	**123**	42 1S	172 45 E
Traverse City	**167**	44 45N	85 39W
Travnik	**52**	44 17N	17 39 E
Tredegar	**27**	51 47N	3 16W
Tregaron	**26**	52 14N	3 56W
Treinta y Tres	**191**	33 16S	54 17W
Trelew	**192**	43 10S	65 20W
Trenque Lauquen	**190**	36 5S	62 45W
Trent →	**29**	53 33N	0 44W
Trentino-Alto Adige □	**47**	46 30N	11 0 E
Trento	**47**	46 5N	11 8 E
Trenton, Canada	**151**	44 10N	77 34W
Trenton, Mo., U.S.A.	**166**	40 5N	93 37W
Trenton, N.J., U.S.A.	**164**	40 15N	74 41W
Tréport, Le	**38**	50 3N	1 20 E
Tres Arroyos	**190**	38 26S	60 20W
Três Lagoas	**188**	20 50S	51 43W
Tres Montes, C.	**192**	46 50S	75 30W
Tres Puntas, C.	**192**	47 0S	66 0W
Treviso	**47**	45 40N	12 15 E
Trichinopoly = Tiruchchirappalli	**90**	10 45N	78 45 E
Trichur	**90**	10 30N	76 18 E
Trier	**42**	49 45N	6 37 E
Trieste	**47**	45 39N	13 45 E
Tríkkala	**54**	39 34N	21 47 E
Trincomalee	**90**	8 38N	81 15 E
Trinidad, Bolivia	**187**	14 46S	64 50W
Trinidad, Colombia	**184**	5 25N	71 40W
Trinidad, Cuba	**178**	21 48N	80 0W
Trinidad, Uruguay	**191**	33 30S	56 50W
Trinidad, U.S.A.	**163**	37 15N	104 30W
Trinidad & Tobago ■	**180**	10 30N	61 20W
Trinity →	**168**	30 30N	95 0W
Trinity Mts.	**172**	40 20N	118 50W
Tripoli = Tarābulus, Lebanon	**80**	34 31N	35 50 E
Tripoli = Tarābulus, Libya	**127**	32 49N	13 7 E
Trípolis	**54**	37 31N	22 25 E
Tripura □	**93**	24 0N	92 0 E
Trivandrum	**90**	8 41N	77 0 E
Trois-Riviéres	**151**	46 25N	72 34W
Troitsk	**71**	54 10N	61 35 E
Trollhättan	**60**	58 17N	12 20 E
Tromsø	**66**	69 40N	18 56 E
Trondheim	**65**	63 36N	10 25 E
Trossachs, The	**31**	56 14N	4 24W
Trotternish	**32**	57 32N	6 15W
Trouville	**38**	49 21N	0 5 E
Trowbridge	**24**	51 18N	2 12W
Troy, Ala., U.S.A.	**169**	31 50N	85 58W
Troy, N.Y., U.S.A.	**164**	42 45N	73 39W
Troyes	**39**	48 19N	4 3 E
Trucial States = United Arab Emirates ■	**85**	23 50N	54 0 E
Trujillo, Honduras	**179**	16 0N	86 0W
Trujillo, Peru	**186**	8 6S	79 0W
Trujillo, Venezuela	**184**	9 22N	70 38W
Trundle	**117**	32 53S	147 35 E
Trung-Phan	**95**	16 0N	108 0 E
Truro, Canada	**149**	45 21N	63 14W
Truro, U.K.	**27**	50 17N	5 2W
Tselinograd	**71**	51 10N	71 30 E
Tsinan = Jinan	**98**	36 38N	117 1 E
Tsinghai = Qinghai □	**101**	36 0N	98 0 E
Tsingtao = Qingdao	**98**	36 5N	120 20 E
Tsu	**106**	34 45N	136 25 E

Tsuchiura	**107**	36 5N	140 15 E
Tsugaru-Kaikyō	**103**	41 35N	141 0 E
Tsukumi	**108**	33 4N	131 52 E
Tsukushi-Sanchi	**108**	33 25N	130 30 E
Tsuruga	**106**	35 45N	136 2 E
Tsurugi-San	**109**	33 51N	134 6 E
Tsuruoka	**103**	38 44N	139 50 E
Tsushima, Gifu, Japan	**106**	35 10N	136 43 E
Tsushima, Nagasaki, Japan	**104**	34 20N	129 20 E
Tuamotu Arch.	**123**	17 0S	144 0W
Tubarão	**191**	28 30S	49 0W
Tubruq	**128**	32 7N	23 55 E
Tubuai Is.	**123**	25 0S	150 0W
Tucacas	**184**	10 48N	68 19W
Tucson	**160**	32 14N	110 59W
Tucumcari	**161**	35 12N	103 45W
Tucupita	**185**	9 2N	62 3W
Tucuruí	**188**	3 42S	49 44W
Tudmur	**80**	34 36N	38 15 E
Tuktoyaktuk	**144**	69 27N	133 2W
Tula, Mexico	**177**	23 0N	99 43W
Tula, Russia	**68**	54 13N	37 38 E
Tulare	**173**	36 15N	119 26W
Tulcán	**184**	0 48N	77 43W
Tullahoma	**169**	35 23N	86 12W
Tullamore	**35**	53 17N	7 30W
Tully	**121**	17 56S	145 55 E
Tulsa	**168**	36 10N	96 0W
Tulua	**184**	4 6N	76 11W
Tuma →	**179**	13 6N	84 35W
Tumaco	**184**	1 50N	78 45W
Tumatumari	**185**	5 20N	58 55W
Tumbarumba	**117**	35 44S	148 0 E
Túmbes	**186**	3 37S	80 27W
Tumkur	**90**	13 18N	77 6 E
Tummel, L.	**33**	56 43N	3 55W
Tummo	**127**	22 45N	14 8 E
Tump	**88**	26 7N	62 16 E
Tumucumaque, Serra	**188**	2 0N	55 0W
Tumut	**117**	35 16S	148 13 E
Tunbridge Wells	**25**	51 7N	0 16 E
Tundzha →	**53**	41 40N	26 35 E
Tunis	**127**	36 50N	10 11 E
Tunisia ■	**127**	33 30N	9 10 E
Tunja	**184**	5 33N	73 25W
Tunxi	**99**	29 42N	118 25 E
Tupelo	**169**	34 15N	88 42W
Tupiza	**187**	21 30S	65 40W
Tupper L.	**151**	44 18N	74 30W
Tuque, La	**151**	47 30N	72 50W
Túquerres	**184**	1 5N	77 37W
Tura	**92**	25 30N	90 16 E
Turayf	**82**	31 41N	38 39 E
Turfan = Turpan	**100**	43 58N	89 10 E
Turfan Depression = Turpan Hami	**100**	42 40N	89 25 E
Tŭrgovishte	**53**	43 17N	26 38 E
Turgutlu	**80**	38 30N	27 48 E
Turin = Torino	**46**	45 4N	7 40 E
Turkana, L.	**132**	3 30N	36 5 E
Turkestan	**71**	43 17N	68 16 E
Turkey ■	**80**	39 0N	36 0 E
Turkmenistan ■	**70**	39 0N	59 0 E
Turks Is.	**180**	21 20N	71 20W
Turku	**67**	60 30N	22 19 E
Turlock	**172**	37 30N	120 55W
Turnagain, C.	**122**	40 28S	176 38 E
Turnhout	**42**	51 19N	4 57 E
Tŭrnovo	**53**	43 5N	25 41 E
Turnu Rosu Pasul	**57**	45 33N	24 17 E
Turnu-Severin	**56**	44 39N	22 41 E
Turpan	**100**	43 58N	89 10 E
Turpan Hami	**100**	42 40N	89 25 E
Turukhansk	**74**	65 21N	88 5 E
Tuscaloosa	**169**	33 13N	87 31W
Tuscany = Toscana	**46**	43 30N	11 5 E
Tuskegee	**169**	32 24N	85 39W
Tutrakan	**53**	44 2N	26 40 E
Tuvalu ■	**122**	8 0S	178 0 E
Tuxpan	**177**	20 57N	97 24W
Tuxtla Gutiérrez	**177**	16 45N	93 7W
Tuy Hoa	**95**	13 5N	109 10 E
Tuyen Hoa	**95**	17 50N	106 10 E
Tuz Gölü	**80**	38 45N	33 30 E
Ţūz Khurmātū	**81**	34 56N	44 38 E
Tuzla	**52**	44 34N	18 41 E
Tver	**68**	56 55N	35 55 E
Tweed →	**31**	55 42N	2 10W
Tweed Heads	**116**	28 10S	153 31 E
Twin Falls	**172**	42 30N	114 30W
Two Harbors	**156**	47 1N	91 40W
Tyler	**168**	32 18N	95 18W
Tyne →	**28**	54 58N	1 28W
Tyne & Wear □	**28**	54 55N	1 35W
Tynemouth	**28**	55 1N	1 27W
Tyrol = Tirol □	**45**	47 3N	10 43 E
Tyrrhenian Sea	**48**	40 0N	12 30 E
Tyumen	**69**	57 11N	65 29 E
Tzukong = Zigong	**99**	29 15N	104 48 E

U

Uaupés	**184**	0 8S	67 5W
Ubangi = Oubangi →	**131**	1 0N	17 50 E
Ube	**108**	33 56N	131 15 E
Uberaba	**188**	19 50S	47 55W
Uberlândia	**188**	19 0S	48 20W
Ubon Ratchathani	**95**	15 15N	104 50 E
Ucayali →	**186**	4 30S	73 30W
Uchi Lake	**153**	51 5N	92 35W
Uchiura-Wan	**103**	42 25N	140 40 E
Uchur →	**75**	58 48N	130 35 E
Udaipur	**91**	24 36N	73 44 E
Uddevalla	**60**	58 21N	11 55 E
Údine	**47**	46 5N	13 10 E
Udmurtia □	**69**	57 30N	52 30 E
Udon Thani	**95**	17 29N	102 46 E
Ueda	**107**	36 24N	138 16 E
Uelen	**73**	66 10N	170 0W
Uelzen	**43**	53 0N	10 33 E
Ueno	**106**	34 45N	136 8 E
Ufa	**69**	54 45N	55 55 E
Uganda ■	**132**	2 0N	32 0 E
Uinta Mts.	**162**	40 45N	110 30W
Uithuizen	**41**	53 24N	6 41 E
Uji	**106**	34 53N	135 48 E
Ujjain	**91**	23 9N	75 43 E
Újpest	**59**	47 32N	19 6 E
Ujung Pandang	**113**	5 10S	119 20 E
Ukiah	**172**	39 10N	123 9W
Ukraine ■	**68**	49 0N	32 0 E
Ulaanbaatar	**98**	47 55N	106 53 E
Ulan Bator = Ulaanbaatar	**98**	47 55N	106 53 E
Ulan Ude	**74**	51 45N	107 40 E
Ulcinj	**52**	41 58N	19 10 E
Ulhasnagar	**91**	19 15N	73 10 E
Ulladulla	**117**	35 21S	150 29 E
Ullapool	**32**	57 54N	5 10W
Ullswater	**28**	54 35N	2 52W
Ulm	**42**	48 23N	10 0 E
Ulster □	**34**	54 35N	6 30W
Ulverston	**28**	54 13N	3 7W
Ulverstone	**119**	41 11S	146 11 E
Ulyanovsk = Simbirsk	**68**	54 20N	48 25 E
Ulyasutay	**100**	47 56N	97 28 E
Umbrella Mts.	**123**	45 35S	169 5 E
Umbria □	**46**	42 53N	12 30 E
Ume älv →	**66**	63 45N	20 20 E
Umeå	**66**	63 45N	20 20 E
Umm al Qaywayn	**85**	25 30N	55 35 E
Umm Lajj	**82**	25 0N	37 23 E
Umnak	**142**	53 20N	168 20W
Umpang	**94**	16 3N	98 54 E
Umtata	**137**	31 36S	28 49 E
Unalaska	**142**	53 40N	166 40W
Ungava B.	**146**	59 30N	67 30W
Ungava Pen.	**146**	60 0N	74 0W
União da Vitória	**191**	26 13S	51 5W
Unimak	**142**	55 0N	164 0W

Union City	**169**	36 25N	89 0W
Uniontown	**164**	39 54N	79 45W
United Arab Emirates ■	**85**	23 50N	54 0 E
United Kingdom ■	**18**	55 0N	3 0W
United States of America ■	**139**	37 0N	96 0W
Unity	**152**	52 30N	109 5W
Unnao	**92**	26 35N	80 30 E
Unst	**30**	60 50N	0 55W
Uozu	**106**	36 48N	137 24 E
Upata	**185**	8 1N	62 24W
Upper Austria = Oberösterreich □	**45**	48 10N	14 0 E
Upper Hutt	**123**	41 8S	175 5 E
Upper Taimyr →	**72**	74 15N	99 48 E
Upper Volta = Burkina Faso ■	**130**	12 0N	1 0W
Uppsala	**60**	59 53N	17 38 E
Uppsala län □	**60**	60 0N	17 30 E
Ur	**84**	30 55N	46 25 E
Uracara	**185**	2 20S	57 50W
Urakawa	**103**	42 9N	142 47 E
Ural →	**70**	47 0N	51 48 E
Ural Mts. = Uralskie Gory	**69**	60 0N	59 0 E
Uralsk	**70**	51 20N	51 20 E
Uralskie Gory	**69**	60 0N	59 0 E
Uranium City	**145**	59 34N	108 37W
Urawa	**107**	35 50N	139 40 E
Urbana, Ill., U.S.A.	**167**	40 7N	88 12W
Urbana, Ohio, U.S.A.	**167**	40 9N	83 44W
Urbana, La	**184**	7 8N	66 56W
Urcos	**187**	13 40S	71 38W
Ures	**174**	29 26N	110 24W
Urfa = Sanliurfa	**81**	37 12N	38 50 E
Urgench	**70**	41 40N	60 41 E
Uribia	**184**	11 43N	72 16W
Urk	**41**	52 39N	5 36 E
Urmia = Orūmīyeh	**81**	37 40N	45 0 E
Urmia, L. = Orūmīyeh, Daryācheh-ye	**81**	37 50N	45 30 E
Uruapan	**175**	19 30N	102 0W
Uruçuí	**188**	7 20S	44 28W
Uruguaiana	**191**	29 50S	57 0W
Uruguay ■	**191**	32 30S	56 30W
Uruguay →	**191**	34 12S	58 18W
Urumchi = Ürümqi	**100**	43 45N	87 45 E
Ürümqi	**100**	43 45N	87 45 E
Urup, Os.	**75**	46 0N	151 0 E
Usa	**108**	33 31N	131 21 E
Uşak	**80**	38 43N	29 28 E
Usfan	**82**	21 58N	39 27 E
Ushant = Ouessant, Île d'	**36**	48 28N	5 6W
Ushibuka	**108**	32 11N	130 1 E
Ushuaia	**192**	54 50S	68 23W
Usk →	**26**	51 37N	2 56W
Üsküdar	**80**	41 0N	29 5 E
Usolye Sibirskoye	**74**	52 48N	103 40 E
Uspenskiy	**71**	48 41N	72 43 E
Ussuriysk	**75**	43 48N	131 59 E
Ust-Aldan = Batamay	**74**	63 30N	129 15 E
Ust-Ilimsk	**74**	58 3N	102 39 E
Ust-Kamchatsk	**73**	56 10N	162 28 E
Ust-Kamenogorsk	**71**	50 0N	82 36 E
Ust Maya	**75**	60 30N	134 28 E
Ust Olenek	**72**	73 0N	119 48 E
Ust Port	**69**	69 40N	84 26 E
Ust Urt = Ustyurt, Plato	**70**	44 0N	55 0 E
Ust Vorkuta	**69**	67 24N	64 0 E
Ústí nad Labem	**58**	50 41N	14 3 E
Ustica	**48**	38 42N	13 10 E
Ustinov	**69**	56 51N	53 14 E
Ustyurt, Plato	**70**	44 0N	55 0 E
Usu	**100**	44 27N	84 40 E
Usuki	**108**	33 8N	131 49 E
Usumbura = Bujumbura	**135**	3 16S	29 18 E
Utah □	**163**	39 30N	111 30W
Utah, L.	**163**	40 10N	111 58W
Uthai Thani	**94**	15 22N	100 3 E
Utica	**164**	43 5N	75 18W
Uto	**108**	32 41N	130 40 E
Utrecht	**40**	52 5N	5 8 E
Utrecht □	**40**	52 6N	5 7 E
Utrera	**50**	37 12N	5 48W
Utsunomiya	**107**	36 30N	139 50 E
Uttar Pradesh □	**92**	27 0N	80 0 E
Uttoxeter	**28**	52 53N	1 50W
Uusikaupunki	**66**	60 47N	21 25 E
Uvalde	**161**	29 15N	99 48W
Uvs Nuur	**74**	50 20N	92 30 E
Uwajima	**109**	33 10N	132 35 E
Uzbekistan ■	**70**	41 30N	65 0 E

V

Vaal →	**137**	29 4S	23 38 E
Vaals	**41**	50 46N	6 1 E
Vaasa	**67**	63 6N	21 38 E
Vác	**58**	47 49N	19 10 E
Vach →	**69**	60 45N	76 45 E
Vadodara	**91**	22 20N	73 10 E
Vadsø	**67**	70 3N	29 50 E
Váh →	**59**	47 55N	18 0 E
Vaigach	**69**	70 10N	59 0 E
Val d'Or	**151**	48 7N	77 47W
Valahia	**57**	44 35N	25 0 E
Valcheta	**192**	40 40S	66 8W
Valdés, Pen.	**192**	42 30S	63 45W
Valdez	**142**	61 14N	146 17W
Valdivia	**190**	39 50S	73 14W
Valdosta	**170**	30 50N	83 20W
Valence	**37**	44 57N	4 54 E
Valencia, Spain	**51**	39 27N	0 23W
Valencia, Venezuela	**184**	10 11N	68 0W
Valencia □	**51**	39 20N	0 40W
Valencia, Albufera de	**51**	39 20N	0 27W
Valencia, G. de	**51**	39 30N	0 20 E
Valencia de Alcántara	**50**	39 25N	7 14W
Valenciennes	**38**	50 20N	3 34 E
Valentia I.	**35**	51 54N	10 22W
Valera	**184**	9 19N	70 37W
Valkenswaard	**41**	51 21N	5 29 E
Valladolid, Mexico	**177**	20 41N	88 12W
Valladolid, Spain	**50**	41 38N	4 43W
Valle d'Aosta □	**46**	45 45N	7 22 E
Valle de la Pascua	**184**	9 13N	66 0W
Valle de Santiago	**177**	20 23N	101 12W
Vallecas	**50**	40 23N	3 41W
Vallejo	**172**	38 12N	122 15W
Valletta	**49**	35 54N	14 30 E
Valley City	**163**	46 57N	98 0W
Valley View	**155**	40 39N	76 33W
Valona = Vlóra	**52**	40 32N	19 28 E
Valparaíso, Chile	**190**	33 2S	71 40W
Valparaíso, Mexico	**175**	22 46N	103 34W
Valsad	**91**	20 40N	72 58 E
Van	**81**	38 30N	43 20 E
Van, L. = Van Gölü	**81**	38 30N	43 0 E
Van Buren, Canada	**148**	47 10N	67 55W
Van Buren, U.S.A.	**168**	35 28N	94 18W
Van Gölü	**81**	38 30N	43 0 E
Van Wert	**167**	40 52N	84 31W
Vancouver, Canada	**154**	49 15N	123 10W
Vancouver, U.S.A.	**171**	45 44N	122 41W
Vancouver I.	**154**	49 50N	126 0W
Vandalia	**166**	38 57N	89 4W
Vanderhoof	**154**	54 0N	124 0W
Vänern	**60**	58 47N	13 30 E
Vanier	**151**	45 27N	75 40W
Vankarem	**73**	67 51N	175 50 E
Vännäs	**66**	63 58N	19 48 E
Vannes	**36**	47 40N	2 47W
Vanua Levu	**122**	16 33S	179 15 E
Vanuatu ■	**122**	15 0S	168 0 E
Varanasi	**92**	25 22N	83 0 E
Varangerfjorden	**67**	70 3N	29 25 E
Varaždin	**52**	46 20N	16 20 E
Vardak □	**87**	34 0N	68 0 E
Vardø	**67**	70 23N	31 5 E
Värmland	**60**	60 0N	13 30 E
Varna	**53**	43 13N	27 56 E

Vascongadas	**50**	42 50N	2 45W
Västerås	**60**	59 37N	16 38 E
Västmanlands län □	**60**	59 45N	16 20 E
Vatnajökull	**64**	64 30N	16 48W
Vatra-Dornei	**57**	47 22N	25 22 E
Vättern	**60**	58 25N	14 30 E
Vaygach, Ostrov	**69**	70 0N	60 0 E
Veendam	**41**	53 5N	6 52 E
Vega, La	**180**	19 20N	70 30W
Veghel	**41**	51 37N	5 32 E
Vegreville	**155**	53 30N	112 5W
Vela, La	**184**	11 27N	69 34W
Vellore	**90**	12 57N	79 10 E
Venado Tuerto	**190**	33 50S	62 0W
Vendôme	**39**	47 47N	1 3 E
Véneto □	**47**	45 40N	12 0 E
Venézia	**47**	45 27N	12 20 E
Venézia, Golfo di	**47**	45 20N	13 0 E
Venezuela ■	**184**	8 0N	65 0W
Venezuela, Golfo de	**184**	11 30N	71 0W
Vengurla	**91**	15 53N	73 45 E
Venice = Venézia	**47**	45 27N	12 20 E
Venlo	**41**	51 22N	6 11 E
Venraij	**41**	51 31N	6 0 E
Ventnor	**24**	50 35N	1 12W
Ventoux	**37**	44 10N	5 17 E
Ventura	**173**	34 16N	119 18W
Veracruz	**177**	19 10N	96 10W
Veracruz □	**177**	19 20N	96 40W
Verde, R. →	**175**	15 59N	97 50W
Verdun	**37**	49 12N	5 24 E
Vereeniging	**137**	26 38S	27 57 E
Verkhoyansk	**72**	67 35N	133 25 E
Verkhoyanskiy Khrebet	**72**	66 0N	129 0 E
Vermilion	**152**	53 20N	110 50W
Vermont □	**164**	43 40N	72 50W
Verneuil-sur-Avre	**39**	48 45N	0 55 E
Vernon, Canada	**155**	50 20N	119 15W
Vernon, France	**39**	49 5N	1 30 E
Vernon, U.S.A.	**161**	34 10N	99 20W
Verona	**46**	45 27N	11 0 E
Versailles	**39**	48 48N	2 8 E
Vert, C.	**130**	14 45N	17 30W
Verviers	**42**	50 37N	5 52 E
Vest-Agder fylke □	**60**	58 30N	7 15 E
Vesterålen	**64**	68 45N	15 0 E
Vestfjorden	**64**	67 55N	14 0 E
Vestfold fylke □	**60**	59 15N	10 0 E
Vestspitsbergen	**13**	78 40N	17 0 E
Vesuvio	**49**	40 50N	14 22 E
Vesuvius, Mt. = Vesuvio	**49**	40 50N	14 22 E
Viacha	**187**	16 39S	68 18W
Viborg	**61**	56 27N	9 23 E
Vicenza	**47**	45 32N	11 31 E
Vichy	**37**	46 9N	3 26 E
Vicksburg	**169**	32 22N	90 56W
Victor Harbor	**119**	35 30S	138 37 E
Victoria, Canada	**154**	48 30N	123 25W
Victoria, Chile	**190**	38 13S	72 20W
Victoria, U.S.A.	**158**	28 50N	97 0W
Victoria □	**117**	37 0S	144 0 E
Victoria, L.	**132**	1 0S	33 0 E
Victoria de las Tunas	**178**	20 58N	76 59W
Victoria Falls	**137**	17 58S	25 52 E
Victoria I.	**145**	71 0N	111 0W
Victoria Ld.	**15**	75 0S	160 0 E
Victoriaville	**148**	46 4N	71 56W
Vidalia	**170**	32 13N	82 25W
Vidin	**53**	43 59N	22 50 E
Viedma	**192**	40 50S	63 0W
Vienna = Wien	**45**	48 12N	16 22 E
Vienne	**37**	45 31N	4 53 E
Vienne →	**36**	47 13N	0 5 E
Vientiane	**95**	17 58N	102 36 E
Vientos, Paso de los	**180**	20 0N	74 0W
Vietnam ■	**95**	19 0N	106 0 E
Vigo	**50**	42 12N	8 41W
Vijayawada	**92**	16 31N	80 39 E
Vila Real de Santo António	**50**	37 10N	7 28W
Vilhelmina	**66**	64 35N	16 39 E
Vilhena	**187**	12 40S	60 5W
Villa Bella	**187**	10 25S	65 22W
Villa Bens = Tarfaya	**126**	27 55N	12 55W
Villa Cisneros = Dakhla	**126**	23 50N	15 53W
Villa Dolores	**190**	31 58S	65 15W
Villa María	**190**	32 20S	63 10W
Villa Montes	**187**	21 10S	63 30W
Villaguay	**190**	32 0S	59 0W
Villahermosa	**177**	17 59N	92 55W
Villanueva de la Serena	**50**	38 59N	5 50W
Villarreal	**51**	39 55N	0 3W
Villarrica	**191**	39 15S	72 15W
Villazón	**187**	22 0S	65 35W
Ville Platte	**168**	30 45N	92 17W
Villefranche-sur-Saône	**37**	45 59N	4 43 E
Villers-Cotterêts	**39**	49 15N	3 4 E
Vilnius	**68**	54 38N	25 19 E
Vilskutskogo, Proliv	**72**	78 0N	103 0 E
Vilyuy →	**74**	64 24N	126 26 E
Vilyuysk	**74**	63 40N	121 35 E
Viña del Mar	**190**	33 0S	71 30W
Vincennes	**167**	38 42N	87 29W
Vindhya Ra.	**91**	22 50N	77 0 E
Vinh	**95**	18 45N	105 38 E
Vinita	**168**	36 40N	95 12W
Vinkovci	**52**	45 19N	18 48 E
Vinnitsa	**68**	49 15N	28 30 E
Viramgam	**91**	23 5N	72 0 E
Virden	**153**	49 50N	100 56W
Vire	**36**	48 50N	0 53W
Vírgenes, C.	**192**	52 19S	68 21W
Virgin →	**173**	36 50N	114 10W
Virgin Is.	**180**	18 40N	64 30W
Virginia	**156**	47 30N	92 32W
Virginia □	**165**	37 45N	78 0W
Virginia Beach	**165**	36 54N	75 58W
Visalia	**173**	36 25N	119 18W
Visby	**60**	57 37N	18 18 E
Viscount Melville Sd.	**145**	74 10N	108 0W
Višegrad	**52**	43 47N	19 17 E
Vishakhapatnam	**92**	17 45N	83 20 E
Vistula = Wisła →	**58**	54 22N	18 55 E
Vitebsk	**68**	55 10N	30 15 E
Viti Levu	**122**	17 30S	177 30 E
Vitim →	**74**	59 26N	112 34 E
Vitória, Brazil	**189**	20 20S	40 22W
Vitoria, Spain	**50**	42 50N	2 41W
Vitória da Conquista	**189**	14 51S	40 51W
Vizianagaram	**92**	18 6N	83 30 E
Vlaardingen	**40**	51 55N	4 21 E
Vladikavkaz	**70**	43 0N	44 35 E
Vladimir	**68**	56 15N	40 30 E
Vladivostok	**75**	43 10N	131 53 E
Vlieland	**40**	53 16N	4 55 E
Vlissingen	**40**	51 26N	3 34 E
Vlóra	**52**	40 32N	19 28 E
Vltava →	**59**	50 21N	14 30 E
Vogelkop	**113**	1 25S	133 0 E
Vogels Berg	**42**	50 37N	9 30 E
Vohimena, Tanjon' i	**137**	25 36S	45 8 E
Voi	**133**	3 25S	38 32 E
Volendam	**40**	52 30N	5 4 E
Volga →	**68**	48 30N	46 0 E
Volga Hts. = Privolzhskaya Vozvyshennost	**17**	51 0N	46 0 E
Volgograd	**68**	48 40N	44 25 E
Vollenhove	**41**	52 40N	5 58 E
Vologda	**68**	59 10N	40 0 E
Vólos	**54**	39 24N	22 59 E
Volsk	**68**	52 5N	47 22 E
Volta →	**130**	5 46N	0 41 E
Volta, L.	**130**	7 30N	0 15 E
Volta Redonda	**188**	22 31S	44 5W
Voorburg	**40**	52 5N	4 24 E
Vopnafjörður	**64**	65 45N	14 40W
Voríai Sporádhes	**55**	39 15N	23 30 E
Voronezh	**68**	51 40N	39 10 E
Voroshilovgrad = Lugansk	**68**	48 38N	39 15 E
Vosges	**37**	48 20N	7 10 E
Vostochnyy Sayan	**74**	54 0N	96 0 E
Vrangelya, Ostrov	**73**	71 0N	180 0 E
Vranje	**53**	42 34N	21 54 E
Vratsa	**53**	43 13N	23 30 E

Vršac 52 45 8N 21 18 E
Vught 40 51 38N 5 20 E
Vulcan 155 50 25N 113 15W
Vyatka = Kirov 69 58 35N 49 40 E
Vyborg 68 60 43N 28 47 E
Vychegda → 69 61 18N 46 36 E
Vychodné Beskydy 59 49 30N 22 0 E

W

Wa 130 10 7N 2 25W
Waal → 41 51 59N 4 30 E
Waalwijk 40 51 42N 5 4 E
Wabash 167 40 48N 85 46W
Wabash → 167 37 46N 88 2W
Wąbrzeźno 58 53 16N 18 57 E
Waco 168 31 33N 97 5W
Wâd Medanî 129 14 28N 33 30 E
Waddenzee 40 53 6N 5 10 E
Waddington, Mt. 154 51 23N 125 15W
Waddinxveen 40 52 2N 4 40 E
Wadena 152 51 57N 103 47W
Wadi Halfa 129 21 53N 31 19 E
Wageningen 41 51 58N 5 40 E
Wager Bay 146 65 56N 90 49W
Wagga Wagga 117 35 7S 147 24 E
Wagin 120 33 17S 117 25 E
Waigeo 113 0 20S 130 40 E
Waihi 122 37 23S 175 52 E
Waikerie 119 34 9S 140 0 E
Waikokopu 122 39 3S 177 52 E
Waimate 123 44 45S 171 3 E
Wainwright, Canada 152 52 50N 110 50W
Wainwright, U.S.A. 142 70 39N 160 1W
Waipara 123 43 3S 172 46 E
Waipu 122 35 59S 174 29 E
Waipukurau 122 40 1S 176 33 E
Wairoa 122 39 3S 177 25 E
Waitara 122 38 59S 174 15 E
Wajima 105 37 30N 137 0 E
Wajir 133 1 42N 40 5 E
Wakasa-Wan 106 35 40N 135 30 E
Wakatipu, L. 123 45 5S 168 33 E
Wakayama 106 34 15N 135 15 E
Wakefield, N.Z. 123 41 24S 173 5 E
Wakefield, U.K. 28 53 41N 1 31W
Wakkanai 103 45 28N 141 35 E
Wałbrzych 58 50 45N 16 18 E
Walcha 116 30 55S 151 31 E
Walcheren 40 51 30N 3 35 E
Wales □ 26 52 30N 3 30W
Walgett 116 30 0S 148 5 E
Walkerton 151 44 10N 81 10W
Walla Walla 171 46 3N 118 25W
Wallaceburg 150 42 34N 82 23W
Wallachia = Valahia 57 44 35N 25 0 E
Wallangarra 116 28 56S 151 58 E
Wallaroo 119 33 56S 137 39 E
Wallasey 28 53 26N 3 2W
Wallerawang 117 33 25S 150 4 E
Wallis & Futuna 122 13 18S 176 10W
Wallowa, Mts. 171 45 20N 117 30W
Wallsend, Australia 117 32 55S 151 40 E
Wallsend, U.K. 28 54 59N 1 30W
Walney, Isle of 28 54 5N 3 15W
Walpole 120 34 58S 116 44 E
Walsall 24 52 36N 1 59W
Walvis Bay 136 23 0S 14 28 E
Wana 88 32 20N 69 32 E
Wanaka L. 123 44 33S 169 7 E
Wang Saphung 95 17 18N 101 46 E
Wanganui 122 39 56S 175 3 E
Wangaratta 117 36 21S 146 19 E
Wanxian 99 30 42N 108 20 E
Warabi 107 35 49N 139 41 E
Warangal 91 17 58N 79 35 E
Warburton 117 37 47S 145 42 E
Wardha 91 20 45N 78 39 E
Wardha → 91 19 57N 79 11 E
Warialda 116 29 29S 150 33 E
Warley 24 52 30N 2 0W
Warner Mts. 172 41 30N 120 20W
Waroona 120 32 50S 115 58 E
Warracknabeal 119 36 9S 142 26 E
Warragul 117 38 10S 145 58 E
Warrego → 116 30 24S 145 21 E
Warrego Ra. 121 24 58S 146 0 E
Warren, Australia 116 31 42S 147 51 E
Warren, Ark., U.S.A. 168 33 35N 92 3W
Warren, Mich., U.S.A. 167 42 31N 83 2W
Warren, Ohio, U.S.A. 164 41 18N 80 52W
Warren, Pa., U.S.A. 164 41 52N 79 10W
Warrenpoint 34 54 7N 6 15W
Warrensburg 166 38 45N 93 45W
Warrington, U.K. 28 53 25N 2 38W
Warrington, U.S.A. 169 30 22N 87 16W
Warrnambool 119 38 25S 142 30 E
Warsaw = Warszawa 58 52 13N 21 0 E
Warszawa 58 52 13N 21 0 E
Warta → 58 52 35N 14 39 E
Warthe = Warta → 58 52 35N 14 39 E
Warwick, Australia 116 28 10S 152 1 E
Warwick, U.K. 24 52 17N 1 36W
Warwick, U.S.A. 164 41 43N 71 25W
Warwick □ 24 52 20N 1 30W
Wasatch Ra. 163 40 30N 111 15W
Wasco 173 35 37N 119 16W
Wash, The 29 52 58N 0 20 E
Washim 91 20 3N 77 0 E
Washington, D.C., U.S.A. 165 38 52N 77 0W
Washington, Ind., U.S.A. 167 38 40N 87 8W
Washington, Mo., U.S.A. 166 38 35N 91 1W
Washington, Pa., U.S.A. 164 40 10N 80 20W
Washington □ 171 47 45N 120 30W
Wassenaar 40 52 8N 4 24 E
Waterbury 164 41 32N 73 0W
Waterford 35 52 16N 7 8W
Waterford □ 35 52 10N 7 40W
Waterloo, Canada 151 43 30N 80 32W
Waterloo, U.S.A. 166 42 27N 92 20W
Watertown, N.Y., U.S.A. 151 43 58N 75 57W
Watertown, Wis., U.S.A. 167 43 15N 88 45W
Waterville 148 44 35N 69 40W
Watling I. = San Salvador 178 24 0N 74 40W
Watrous 152 51 40N 105 25W
Watson Lake 144 60 6N 128 49W
Watsonville 173 36 55N 121 49W
Watubela, Kepulauan 113 4 28S 131 35 E
Wauchope 116 31 28S 152 45 E
Waukegan 167 42 22N 87 54W
Waukesha 167 43 0N 88 15W
Wausau 166 44 57N 89 40W
Wauwatosa 167 43 6N 87 59W
Waveney → 25 52 24N 1 20 E
Wâw 129 7 45N 28 1 E
Waxahachie 168 32 22N 96 53W
Waycross 170 31 12N 82 25W
Waynesboro, Pa., U.S.A. 164 39 46N 77 32W
Waynesboro, Va., U.S.A. 165 38 4N 78 57W
Waynesville 165 35 31N 83 0W
Wazirabad 89 32 30N 74 8 E
Weald, The 25 51 7N 0 9 E
Webo = Nyaake 130 4 52N 7 37W
Weddell Sea 14 72 30S 40 0W
Wedderburn 117 36 26S 143 33 E
Wee Waa 116 30 11S 149 26 E
Weert 41 51 15N 5 43 E
Weesp 40 52 18N 5 2 E
Weifang 98 36 47N 119 10 E
Weiser 171 44 10N 117 0W
Welbourn Hill 118 27 21S 134 6 E
Welch 165 37 29N 81 36W
Welland 151 43 0N 79 15W
Welland → 29 52 43N 0 10W
Wellingborough 25 52 18N 0 41W
Wellington, Australia 116 32 35S 148 59 E
Wellington, N.Z. 123 41 19S 174 46 E
Wellington, Shrops., U.K. 28 52 42N 2 31W
Wellington, Somst., U.K. 27 50 58N 3 13W
Wellington □ 123 40 8S 175 36 E
Wellington, I. 192 49 30S 75 0W

Wells, Norfolk, U.K. 29 52 57N 0 51 E
Wells, Somst., U.K. 27 51 12N 2 39W
Wells, U.S.A. 172 41 8N 115 0W
Wellsville, N.Y., U.S.A. 164 42 9N 77 53W
Wellsville, Ohio, U.S.A. 164 40 36N 80 40W
Welshpool 26 52 40N 3 9W
Wem 28 52 52N 2 45W
Wenatchee 171 47 30N 120 17W
Wenchow = Wenzhou 99 28 0N 120 38 E
Wensleydale 28 54 18N 2 0W
Wentworth 119 34 2S 141 54 E
Wenzhou 99 28 0N 120 38 E
Werribee 117 37 54S 144 40 E
Werris Creek 116 31 18S 150 38 E
Weser → 42 53 33N 8 30 E
West Bengal □ 92 23 0N 88 0 E
West Bromwich 24 52 32N 2 1W
West Falkland 192 51 40S 60 0W
West Frankfort 166 37 56N 89 0W
West Glamorgan □ 27 51 40N 3 55W
West Memphis 169 35 5N 90 11W
West Midlands □ 24 52 30N 1 55W
West Palm Beach 170 26 44N 80 3W
West Schelde = Westerschelde → 40 51 25N 3 25 E
West Siberian Plain 76 62 0N 75 0 E
West Sussex □ 25 50 55N 0 30W
West Virginia □ 165 39 0N 81 0W
West Yorkshire □ 28 53 45N 1 40W
Western Australia □ 114 25 0S 118 0 E
Western Ghats 90 14 0N 75 0 E
Western Isles □ 32 57 30N 7 10W
Western Sahara ■ 126 25 0N 13 0W
Western Samoa ■ 123 14 0S 172 0W
Westerschelde → 40 51 25N 3 25 E
Westerwald 42 50 39N 8 0 E
Westfriesche Eilanden 40 53 20N 5 10 E
Westland □ 123 43 33S 169 59 E
Westland Bight 123 42 55S 170 5 E
Westlock 155 54 9N 113 55W
Westmeath □ 34 53 30N 7 30W
Westminster 164 39 34N 77 1W
Weston 165 39 3N 80 29W
Weston-super-Mare 27 51 20N 2 59W
Westport 123 41 46S 171 37 E
Westray 33 59 18N 3 0W
Wetar 113 7 30S 126 30 E
Wetaskiwin 155 52 55N 113 24W
Wewaka 168 35 10N 96 35W
Wexford 35 52 20N 6 28W
Wexford □ 35 52 20N 6 25W
Weyburn 152 49 40N 103 50W
Weymouth 27 50 36N 2 28W
Whakatane 122 37 57S 177 1 E
Whale Cove 145 62 11N 92 36W
Whalsay 30 60 22N 1 0W
Whangamomona 122 39 8S 174 44 E
Whangarei 122 35 43S 174 21 E
Wharfe → 29 53 55N 1 30W
Wheeler Pk. 172 38 57N 114 15W
Wheeling 164 40 2N 80 41W
Whernside 28 54 14N 2 24W
Whitby 29 54 29N 0 37W
Whitchurch 28 52 58N 2 42W
White →, Ark., U.S.A. 168 33 53N 91 3W
White →, Ind., U.S.A. 167 38 25N 87 45W
White →, S. Dak., U.S.A. 163 43 45N 99 30W
White Cliffs 118 30 50S 143 10 E
White Mts. 157 44 15N 71 15W
White Nile = Nîl el Abyad → 129 15 38N 32 31 E
White Russia = Belorussia ■ 68 53 30N 27 0 E
White Sea = Beloye More 69 66 30N 38 0 E
Whitecliffs 123 43 26S 171 55 E
Whitehaven 28 54 33N 3 35W
Whitehorse 144 60 43N 135 3W
Whitney, Mt. 173 36 35N 118 14W
Whitstable 25 51 21N 1 2 E
Whitsunday I. 121 20 15S 149 4 E
Whittier 142 60 46N 148 48W
Whyalla 118 33 2S 137 30 E
Wichita 158 37 40N 97 20W
Wichita Falls 161 33 57N 98 30W
Wick 33 58 26N 3 5W
Wickepin 120 32 50S 117 30 E
Wicklow 35 53 0N 6 2W
Wicklow □ 35 52 59N 6 25W
Wicklow Mts. 35 53 0N 6 30W
Widnes 28 53 22N 2 44W
Wieluń 58 51 15N 18 34 E
Wien 45 48 12N 16 22 E
Wiesbaden 42 50 7N 8 17 E
Wigan 28 53 33N 2 38W
Wight, I. of 25 50 40N 1 20W
Wigtown 31 54 52N 4 27W
Wigtown B. 31 54 46N 4 15W
Wilcannia 118 31 30S 143 26 E
Wildwood 164 38 59N 74 46W
Wilhelmshaven 42 53 30N 8 9 E
Wilkes Barre 164 41 15N 75 52W
Wilkes Sub-Glacial Basin 15 75 0S 130 0 E
Wilkie 152 52 27N 108 42W
Willamina 171 45 9N 123 32W
Willemstad 181 12 5N 69 0W
Williams L. 154 51 48N 90 45W
Williamsburg 165 37 17N 76 44W
Williamson 165 37 46N 82 17W
Williamsport 164 41 18N 77 1W
Williamstown 117 37 51S 144 52 E
Williston 163 48 10N 103 35W
Willits 172 39 28N 123 17W
Willmar 156 45 5N 95 0W
Wilmette 167 42 6N 87 44W
Wilmington, Del., U.S.A. 164 39 45N 75 32W
Wilmington, N.C., U.S.A. 165 34 14N 77 54W
Wilson 165 35 44N 77 54W
Wilsons Promontory 117 38 55S 146 25 E
Wilton 24 51 5N 1 52W
Wiltshire □ 24 51 20N 2 0W
Wiluna 120 26 36S 120 14 E
Wimereux 38 50 45N 1 37 E
Winchester, U.K. 25 51 4N 1 19W
Winchester, Ind., U.S.A. 167 40 10N 84 56W
Winchester, Ky., U.S.A. 165 38 0N 84 8W
Winchester, Va., U.S.A. 164 39 14N 78 8W
Wind River Range 163 43 0N 109 30W
Windermere 28 54 24N 2 56W
Windermere, L. 28 54 20N 2 57W
Windhoek 136 22 35S 17 4 E
Windsor, Australia 117 33 37S 150 50 E
Windsor, Nfld., Canada 149 48 57N 55 40W
Windsor, Ont., Canada 150 42 18N 83 0W
Windsor, U.K. 25 51 28N 0 36W
Windward Is. 181 13 0N 63 0W
Windward Passage = Vientos, Paso de los 180 20 0N 74 0W
Winisk → 140 55 17N 85 5W
Winkler 153 49 10N 97 56W
Winnemucca 172 41 0N 117 45W
Winnfield 168 31 57N 92 38W
Winnipeg 153 49 54N 97 9W
Winnipeg, L. 153 52 0N 97 0W
Winnipegosis L. 153 52 30N 100 0W
Winona 166 44 2N 91 39W
Winooski 151 44 31N 73 11W
Winschoten 41 53 9N 7 3 E
Winslow 161 35 2N 110 41W
Winston-Salem 165 36 7N 80 15W
Winter Haven 170 28 0N 81 42W
Winter Park 170 28 34N 81 19W
Winterswijk 41 51 58N 6 43 E
Winterthur 44 47 30N 8 44 E
Wirral 28 53 25N 3 0W
Wisbech 29 52 39N 0 10 E
Wisconsin □ 166 44 30N 90 0W
Wisconsin → 166 43 0N 91 15W
Wisconsin Rapids 166 44 25N 89 50W
Wishaw 31 55 46N 3 55W
Wisła → 58 54 22N 18 55 E
Witham → 29 53 3N 0 8W
Withernsea 29 53 43N 0 2 E
Witney 24 51 47N 1 29W
Włocławek 58 52 40N 19 3 E
Wodonga 117 36 5S 146 50 E

Wokam	**113**	5 45S	134 28 E
Woking	**25**	51 18N	0 33W
Wolin	**58**	53 50N	14 37 E
Wollaston L.	**145**	58 7N	103 10W
Wollaston Pen.	**145**	69 30N	115 0W
Wollongong	**117**	34 25S	150 54 E
Wolverhampton	**24**	52 35N	2 6W
Wondai	**116**	26 20S	151 49 E
Wŏnsan	**98**	39 11N	127 27 E
Wonthaggi	**117**	38 37S	145 37 E
Woodburn	**116**	29 6S	153 23 E
Woodenbong	**116**	28 24S	152 39 E
Woodend	**117**	37 20S	144 33 E
Woodland	**172**	38 40N	121 50W
Woods, L. of the	**153**	49 15N	94 45W
Woodstock, N.B., Canada	**148**	46 11N	67 37W
Woodstock, Ont., Canada	**151**	43 10N	80 45W
Woolgoolga	**116**	30 6S	153 11 E
Woomera	**118**	31 30S	137 10 E
Woonsocket	**164**	42 0N	71 30W
Wooroloo	**120**	31 48S	116 18 E
Worcester, U.K.	**24**	52 12N	2 12W
Worcester, U.S.A.	**164**	42 14N	71 49W
Workington	**28**	54 39N	3 34W
Worksop	**29**	53 19N	1 9W
Wormerveer	**40**	52 30N	4 46 E
Worms	**42**	49 37N	8 21 E
Worthing	**25**	50 49N	0 21W
Worthington	**166**	43 35N	95 36W
Wou-han = Wuhan	**99**	30 31N	114 18 E
Woy Woy	**117**	33 30S	151 19 E
Wrangel I.	**138**	71 0N	180 0 E
Wrangell	**143**	56 30N	132 25W
Wrangell Mts.	**142**	61 40N	143 30W
Wrath, C.	**32**	58 38N	5 0W
Wrekin, The	**28**	52 41N	2 35W
Wrexham	**26**	53 5N	3 0W
Wrigley	**144**	63 16N	123 37W
Wrocław	**58**	51 5N	17 5 E
Września	**58**	52 21N	17 36 E
Wu Jiang →	**99**	29 40N	107 20 E
Wubin	**120**	30 6S	116 37 E
Wuhan	**99**	30 31N	114 18 E
Wuhsi = Wuxi	**99**	31 33N	120 18 E
Wuhu	**99**	31 22N	118 21 E
Wulumuchi = Ürümqi	**100**	43 45N	87 45 E
Wuppertal	**42**	51 15N	7 8 E
Würzburg	**42**	49 46N	9 55 E
Wutongqiao	**99**	29 22N	103 50 E
Wuxi	**99**	31 33N	120 18 E
Wuzhong	**98**	38 2N	106 12 E
Wuzhou	**99**	23 30N	111 18 E
Wyalkatchem	**120**	31 8S	117 22 E
Wyandotte	**167**	42 14N	83 13W
Wycheproof	**119**	36 0S	143 17 E
Wye →	**27**	51 36N	2 40W
Wyndham	**114**	15 33S	128 3 E
Wynnum	**116**	27 27S	153 9 E
Wynyard	**152**	51 45N	104 10W
Wyoming □	**163**	42 48N	109 0W
Wytheville	**165**	37 0N	81 3W

X

Xánthi	**55**	41 10N	24 58 E
Xapuri	**187**	10 35S	68 35W
Xenia	**167**	39 42N	83 57W
Xiamen	**99**	24 25N	118 4 E
Xi'an	**99**	34 15N	109 0 E
Xiangfan	**99**	32 2N	112 8 E
Xiangtan	**99**	27 51N	112 54 E
Xiao Hinggan Ling	**98**	49 0N	127 0 E
Xigazê	**101**	29 5N	88 45 E
Xingtai	**98**	37 3N	114 32 E
Xingu →	**188**	1 30S	51 53W
Xining	**98**	36 34N	101 40 E
Xinjiang Uygur Zizhiqu □	**100**	42 0N	86 0 E
Xinxiang	**99**	35 18N	113 50 E
Xinyang	**99**	32 6N	114 3 E
Xinzhu	**99**	24 49N	120 57 E
Xique-Xique	**188**	10 50S	42 40W
Xizang □	**101**	32 0N	88 0 E
Xuanhua	**98**	40 40N	115 2 E
Xuchang	**99**	34 2N	113 48 E
Xuzhou	**99**	34 18N	117 10 E

Y

Ya'an	**99**	29 58N	103 5 E
Yablonovy Khrebet	**74**	53 0N	114 0 E
Yablonovy Ra. = Yablonovy Khrebet	**74**	53 0N	114 0 E
Yacuiba	**187**	22 0S	63 43W
Yaizu	**107**	34 52N	138 20 E
Yakima	**171**	46 42N	120 30W
Yaku-Jima	**104**	30 20N	130 30 E
Yakutat	**143**	59 29N	139 44W
Yakutsk	**75**	62 5N	129 50 E
Yalgoo	**120**	28 16S	116 39 E
Yalinga	**129**	6 33N	23 10 E
Yamaga	**108**	33 1N	130 41 E
Yamagata	**103**	38 15N	140 15 E
Yamaguchi	**108**	34 10N	131 32 E
Yamal, Poluostrov	**69**	71 0N	70 0 E
Yamato	**107**	35 27N	139 25 E
Yamatotakada	**106**	34 31N	135 45 E
Yamazaki	**109**	35 0N	134 32 E
Yamba	**116**	29 26S	153 23 E
Yambol	**53**	42 30N	26 36 E
Yamdena	**113**	7 45S	131 20 E
Yame	**108**	33 13N	130 35 E
Yamma-Yamma, L.	**118**	26 16S	141 20 E
Yampa →	**163**	40 37N	108 59W
Yamuna →	**92**	25 30N	81 53 E
Yamzho Yumco	**101**	28 48N	90 35 E
Yana →	**72**	71 30N	136 0 E
Yanagawa	**108**	33 10N	130 24 E
Yanai	**109**	33 58N	132 7 E
Yanco	**117**	34 38S	146 27 E
Yangch'ü = Taiyuan	**98**	37 52N	112 33 E
Yangquan	**98**	37 58N	113 31 E
Yangtze Kiang = Chang Jiang →	**99**	31 48N	121 10 E
Yanji	**98**	42 59N	129 30 E
Yantai	**98**	37 34N	121 22 E
Yao	**106**	34 32N	135 36 E
Yaoundé	**131**	3 50N	11 35 E
Yaqui →	**174**	27 37N	110 39W
Yare →	**25**	52 36N	1 28 E
Yarensk	**69**	61 10N	49 8 E
Yarkand = Shache	**100**	38 20N	77 10 E
Yarmouth	**148**	43 50N	66 7W
Yaroslavl	**68**	57 35N	39 55 E
Yarram	**117**	38 29S	146 9 E
Yashiro-Jima	**109**	33 55N	132 15 E
Yass	**117**	34 49S	148 54 E
Yasugi	**109**	35 26N	133 15 E
Yatsushiro	**108**	32 30N	130 40 E
Yavari →	**186**	4 21S	70 2W
Yavatmal	**91**	20 20N	78 15 E
Yawatahama	**109**	33 27N	132 24 E
Yazd	**85**	31 55N	54 27 E
Yazoo →	**169**	32 35N	90 50W
Yazoo City	**169**	32 48N	90 28W
Ye Xian	**98**	37 8N	119 57 E
Yegros	**191**	26 20S	56 25W
Yekaterinburg	**69**	56 50N	60 30 E
Yelizavetgrad = Kirovograd	**68**	48 35N	32 20 E
Yell	**30**	60 35N	1 5W
Yellow Sea	**99**	35 0N	123 0 E
Yellowhead P.	**155**	52 53N	118 25W
Yellowknife	**145**	62 27N	114 29W
Yellowstone →	**163**	47 58N	103 59W
Yellowstone National Park	**163**	44 35N	110 0W
Yemen ■	**82**	15 0N	44 0 E
Yenisey →	**69**	71 50N	82 40 E
Yeniseyskiy Zaliv	**69**	72 20N	81 0 E

Yeo →	**27**	51 10N	3 0W
Yeola	**91**	20 0N	74 30 E
Yeovil	**27**	50 57N	2 38W
Yeppoon	**121**	23 5S	150 47 E
Yerevan	**70**	40 10N	44 31 E
Yes Tor	**27**	50 41N	3 59W
Yetman	**116**	28 56S	150 48 E
Yezd = Yazd	**85**	31 55N	54 27 E
Yiannitsa	**54**	40 46N	22 24 E
Yibin	**99**	28 45N	104 32 E
Yichang	**99**	30 40N	111 20 E
Yichun	**98**	47 44N	128 52 E
Yilan	**99**	24 51N	121 44 E
Yinchuan	**98**	38 30N	106 15 E
Yingkou	**98**	40 37N	122 18 E
Yingtan	**99**	28 12N	117 0 E
Yining	**100**	43 58N	81 10 E
Yíthion	**54**	36 46N	22 34 E
Yiyang	**99**	28 45N	112 16 E
Yogyakarta	**111**	7 49S	110 22 E
Yōkaichiba	**107**	35 42N	140 33 E
Yokkaichi	**106**	35 0N	136 38 E
Yokohama	**107**	35 27N	139 28 E
Yokosuka	**107**	35 20N	139 40 E
Yokote	**103**	39 20N	140 30 E
Yonago	**109**	35 25N	133 19 E
Yoneshiro →	**103**	40 15N	140 15 E
Yonezawa	**103**	37 57N	140 4 E
Yongji	**99**	34 52N	110 28 E
Yonkers	**164**	40 57N	73 51W
York, Australia	**120**	31 52S	116 47 E
York, U.K.	**29**	53 58N	1 7W
York, U.S.A.	**164**	39 57N	76 43W
Yorke Pen.	**119**	34 50S	137 40 E
Yorkshire Wolds	**29**	54 0N	0 30W
Yorkton	**152**	51 11N	102 28W
Yosemite National Park	**172**	38 0N	119 30W
Youghal	**35**	51 58N	7 51W
Young	**117**	34 19S	148 18 E
Younghusband Pen.	**119**	36 0S	139 25 E
Youngstown	**164**	41 7N	80 41W
Yuba City	**172**	39 12N	121 37W
Yūbari	**103**	43 4N	141 59 E
Yūbetsu	**103**	43 13N	144 5 E
Yucatán □	**177**	20 50N	89 0W
Yucatán, Canal de	**178**	22 0N	86 30W
Yucatan Str. = Yucatán, Canal de	**178**	22 0N	86 30W
Yuci	**98**	37 42N	112 46 E
Yugoslavia ■	**52**	44 0N	21 0 E
Yukon →	**142**	65 30N	150 0W
Yukon Territory □	**144**	63 0N	135 0W
Yuma	**173**	32 45N	114 37W
Yunnan □	**101**	25 0N	102 30 E
Yuribei	**69**	71 8N	76 58 E
Yurimaguas	**186**	5 55S	76 7W
Yushu	**101**	33 5N	96 55 E
Yuzhno-Sakhalinsk	**75**	46 58N	142 45 E
Yvetot	**38**	49 37N	0 44 E

Z

Zaandam	**40**	52 26N	4 49 E
Zabaykalskiy	**74**	49 40N	117 25 E
Zabid	**82**	14 0N	43 10 E
Zābol	**85**	31 0N	61 32 E
Zābol □	**87**	32 0N	67 0 E
Zabrze	**58**	50 18N	18 50 E
Zacapa	**177**	14 59N	89 31W
Zacatecas	**175**	22 47N	102 35W
Zacatecas □	**175**	23 0N	103 0W
Zacatecoluca	**177**	13 29N	88 51W
Zadar	**52**	44 8N	15 14 E
Zadetkyi Kyun	**94**	10 0N	98 25 E
Zagreb	**52**	45 50N	16 0 E
Zāhedān	**86**	29 30N	60 50 E
Zahlah	**80**	33 52N	35 50 E
Zaïre ■	**134**	3 0S	23 0 E
Zaïre →	**134**	6 4S	12 24 E
Zákinthos	**54**	37 47N	20 57 E
Zambeze →	**135**	18 55S	36 4 E
Zambezi = Zambeze →	**135**	18 55S	36 4 E
Zambia ■	**135**	15 0S	28 0 E
Zamboanga	**112**	6 59N	122 3 E
Zamora, Mexico	**175**	20 0N	102 21W
Zamora, Spain	**50**	41 30N	5 45W
Zandvoort	**40**	52 22N	4 32 E
Zanesville	**167**	39 56N	82 2W
Zanjan	**81**	36 40N	48 35 E
Zante = Zákinthos	**54**	37 47N	20 57 E
Zanzibar	**135**	6 12S	39 12 E
Zaouiet El-Kala = Bordj Omar Driss	**127**	28 10N	6 40 E
Zaouiet Reggane	**127**	26 32N	0 3 E
Zapadnaya Dvina →	**68**	57 4N	24 3 E
Západné Beskydy	**59**	49 30N	19 0 E
Zapala	**190**	39 0S	70 5W
Zaporozhye	**68**	47 50N	35 10 E
Zaragoza, Mexico	**174**	28 29N	100 55W
Zaragoza, Spain	**51**	41 39N	0 53W
Zaranj	**87**	30 55N	61 55 E
Zaria	**131**	11 0N	7 40 E
Zaruma	**184**	3 40S	79 38W
Zaskar Mountains	**89**	33 15N	77 30 E
Zavitinsk	**75**	50 10N	129 20 E
Zaysan, Oz.	**71**	48 0N	83 0 E
Zayü	**101**	28 48N	97 27 E
Zduńska Wola	**58**	51 37N	18 59 E
Zeebrugge	**42**	51 19N	3 12 E
Zeeland □	**40**	51 30N	3 50 E
Zeila	**133**	11 21N	43 30 E
Zeist	**40**	52 5N	5 15 E
Zemlya Frantsa Iosifa	**13**	81 0N	55 0 E
Zentsūji	**109**	34 14N	133 47 E
Zeya	**75**	53 48N	127 14 E
Zêzere →	**50**	39 28N	8 20W
Zhanghua	**99**	24 6N	120 29 E
Zhangjiakou	**98**	40 48N	114 55 E
Zhangzhou	**99**	24 30N	117 35 E
Zhanjiang	**99**	21 15N	110 20 E
Zhdanov = Mariupol	**68**	47 5N	37 31 E
Zhejiang □	**99**	29 0N	120 0 E
Zhengzhou	**99**	34 45N	113 34 E
Zhenjiang	**99**	32 11N	119 26 E
Zhenyuan	**99**	27 4N	108 21 E
Zhijiang	**99**	27 27N	109 42 E
Zhitomir	**68**	50 20N	28 40 E
Zhumadian	**99**	32 59N	114 2 E
Zhupanovo	**73**	53 40N	159 52 E
Zhuzhou	**99**	27 49N	113 12 E
Zibo	**98**	36 47N	118 3 E
Zielona Góra	**58**	51 57N	15 31 E
Zierikzee	**40**	51 40N	3 55 E
Zigong	**99**	29 15N	104 48 E
Zile	**80**	40 15N	35 52 E
Žilina	**59**	49 12N	18 42 E
Zimbabwe	**137**	20 16S	30 54 E
Zimbabwe ■	**137**	20 0S	30 0 E
Zinder	**131**	13 48N	9 0 E
Zipaquirá	**184**	5 0N	74 0W
Zitácuaro	**175**	19 24N	100 22W
Zlatograd	**53**	41 22N	25 7 E
Zlatoust	**69**	55 10N	59 40 E
Zlin	**59**	49 14N	17 40 E
Zomba	**137**	15 22S	35 19 E
Zonguldak	**80**	41 28N	31 50 E
Zorritos	**186**	3 43S	80 40W
Zoutkamp	**41**	53 20N	6 18 E
Zrenjanin	**52**	45 22N	20 23 E
Zufar	**83**	17 40N	54 0 E
Zug	**44**	47 10N	8 31 E
Zuid-Holland □	**40**	52 0N	4 35 E
Zuidhorn	**41**	53 15N	6 23 E
Zungeru	**131**	9 48N	6 8 E
Zunyi	**99**	27 42N	106 53 E
Zürich	**44**	47 22N	8 32 E
Zutphen	**41**	52 9N	6 12 E
Zuwārah	**127**	32 58N	12 1 E
Zvolen	**59**	48 33N	19 10 E
Zwickau	**43**	50 43N	12 30 E
Zwolle	**41**	52 31N	6 6 E
Zyryanovsk	**71**	49 43N	84 20 E